The Phonology of Polish

THE
PHONOLOGY
OF
POLISH

—

Edmund Gussmann

OXFORD
UNIVERSITY PRESS

OXFORD

UNIVERSITY PRESS

Great Clarendon Street, Oxford OX2 6DP

Oxford University Press is a department of the University of Oxford.
It furthers the University's objective of excellence in research, scholarship,
and education by publishing worldwide in

Oxford New York

Auckland Cape Town Dar es Salaam Hong Kong Karachi
Kuala Lumpur Madrid Melbourne Mexico City Nairobi
New Delhi Shanghai Taipei Toronto

With offices in

Argentina Austria Brazil Chile Czech Republic France Greece
Guatemala Hungary Italy Japan Poland Portugal Singapore
South Korea Switzerland Thailand Turkey Ukraine Vietnam

Oxford is a registered trade mark of Oxford University Press
in the UK and in certain other countries

Published in the United States
by Oxford University Press Inc., New York

British Library Cataloguing in Publication Data
Data available

Library of Congress Cataloging in Publication Data
Data available

Typeset by SPI Publisher Services, Pondicherry, India
Printed in Great Britain
on acid-free paper by
Biddles Ltd, www.biddles.co.uk

ISBN 978-0-19-926747-7

1 3 5 7 9 10 8 6 4 2

Do A-P,
le buíochas
agus mórchion

CONTENTS

PREFACE

Polish has been present in phonological studies from the second half of the nineteenth century, starting with the early works of Jan Ignacy Niecisław Baudouin de Courtenay, a Frenchman by ancestry who considered himself Polish not only on account of his first names. One of the founders of European structuralism in linguistics, he has indelibly influenced both the course of modern phonology and the study of Polish (see Jakobson 1960, Stankiewicz 1972). In more recent times the language has figured prominently in theoretical debates on both sides of the Atlantic. This book represents the results of my own involvement in the area extending well over 30 years. It is an attempt to cover the main areas of the phonology of the modern language and to enrich them by an investigation of large chunks of its morphophonology.

A phonological description does not exist outside a theoretical framework: whether a certain set of facts will be viewed as phonological, morphophonological, or purely phonetic with little structural relevance is something that makes sense within a specific model or theory only. As is well known, the second part of the twentieth century was dominated in phonology by the derivational–generative paradigm, which, among other things, tried to eliminate the phonology–morpho(pho)nology distinction that was at the centre of the structuralist view of the organization of the sound structure of language. This line of research seems to have reached a dead end and a return to non-derivational frameworks is the order of the day. This book joins the non-derivational tradition in developing a Government Phonology account of Polish. It is primarily, however, a description of a language and not a study of a particular theoretical framework; the model is subordinated to description and basically serves the aim of organizing the data. It is hoped that the description will serve as a source of data long after the framework—as of necessity any framework—will lose its intellectual attractiveness. For this reason we avoid theoretical speculations which a purely theoretical study would encourage, although a certain amount of general discussion is unavoidable. One point which we develop at some length concerns the distinction between phonology and morphophonology, a distinction that we believe was overlooked for too long to the detriment of the discipline at large. We hope to make a convincing case not only for the distinction itself but to explore consequences of such a distinction for the mechanisms of sound organization.

The variety described in the book normally goes by the name of educated standard Polish. It shows remarkably little dialectal variation; it is the language of the media and education. This is not to say that it is completely homogeneous or variation-free; indeed, the existing normative dictionaries fulminate against excesses, departures, and what they view as corruptions. We will sometimes use that evidence in our discussion.

In writing the book I have been lucky to receive assistance and comments from a number of friends and colleagues. Here I would like to mention just those who took their time to read a preliminary version of the manuscript and offer their suggestions and advice. First of all I would like to thank the series editor, Jacques Durand, for inviting me to contribute the Polish volume to the series, for his constant interest in the progress of the work, and for commenting on the pre-final version of the manuscript. My gratitude goes to Przemysław Czarnecki (Poznań), Kazimierz Polański (Katowice), and Bogdan Szymanek (Lublin). I am grateful to John Harris (London) for the numerous suggestions and most of all to Eugeniusz Cyran (Lublin) for his gentle savaging of the first version; both John and Eugeniusz tried to convince me of the need to engage in extensive theoretical discussions and I am sure they will be disappointed to see that, for reasons outlined above, I have been very reluctant to follow their ideas. No doubt I will have reasons to regret my obduracy. Finally, there is John Davey of Oxford University Press whose angelic patience and helpful advice have weathered many a crisis. The book is dedicated to A-P, with gratitude and great affection.

ABBREVIATIONS

acc.	accusative
adj.	adjective
dat.	dative
der.	derived
dim.	diminutive
emph.	emphatic
expr.	expressive
fem.	feminine
gen.	genitive
imper.	imperative
imperf.	imperfective
inf.	infinitive
instr.	instrumental
iterat.	iterative
loc.	locative
masc.	masculine
n.	noun
neut.	neuter
nom.	nominative
part.	participle
perf.	perfective
pl.	plural
pres.	present
sg.	singular
vb.	verb
voc.	vocative

1

SOUNDS, LETTERS, AND THEORIES

Phonological analysis traditionally depends on the adequacy of the phonetic transcriptions it employs. In the present study we supply a phonetic transcription of all forms used, in addition to conventional spelling and glosses. In this way readers not familiar with Polish should get a reasonable approximation of how the individual forms sound. Obviously transcription is, to a certain extent, a matter of convention but it avoids some of the pitfalls of the traditional spelling, such as making distinctions in symbols where there is none in sounds and, conversely, using the same orthographic form for distinct phonetic events. Phonetic transcription prides itself on being consistent in its use of symbols. The choice of the symbols varies with traditions, though. In this book we make an attempt to adhere consistently to the system developed by the International Phonetic Association (IPA) and codified for example in the *Handbook of the International Phonetic Association* (1999), with minimal adjustments. This system was used effectively in Karaś and Madejowa's (1977) *Dictionary of Polish Pronunciation* even though in some points it departs from the IPA system. The IPA-based systems of transcription differ in certain ways from those traditionally employed by Slavic and Polish works in phonetics and phonology but the systems are mutually translatable and no problems should arise in going from one to the others: whether we use [ʃ], as in this book, or [š], as in most Slavic works, changes nothing. Another point which should be mentioned is that the IPA symbols are consistent within an individual language but do not necessarily correspond to exactly the same physical reality across languages; a case in point is the Polish vowel [ɨ] in *ty* [tɨ] 'you, sg.'. Karaś and Madejowa (1977) and Jassem (1983) use this symbol to denote a vowel which is described as almost half close, retracted to (almost) central position. The same symbol is used by Jassem (1983: 99) to denote the Russian vowel which is both higher and distinctly central (or perhaps even back advanced to the central position); in addition, the Polish vowel, in terms of its positioning on the vowel diagram, is very close to the English vowel of *bit*, which is transcribed [i] by Jassem and [ɪ] by other authors—in fact, the English *bit* and the Polish *byt* [bɨt] 'existence' sound remarkably similar. Evidently the IPA system allows for a good deal of latitude and must be taken in the context of description. As a means of introduction we will now survey the basic phonetic segments of Polish. It should be kept in mind that since our objective is the phonological interpretation of the sound structure we provide no detailed phonetic description of the individual segments and also overlook various sound details conditioned by the phonetic environment.

1.1 VOWELS

Standard phonetic descriptions normally identify six oral vowels and two nasal nuclei.

(1)   [i] front, high
       igła [igwa] 'needle', miłość [mʲiwɔɕtɕ] 'love, n.', sini [ɕiɲi] 'pale, nom. pl.'
       [ɨ] front, half-close, retracted
       myły [mɨwɨ] 'they (fem.) washed', wydry [vɨdrɨ] 'otter, nom. pl'
       [ɛ] front, half-open
       teraz [tɛras] 'now', wesele [vɛsɛlɛ] 'wedding', etap [ɛtap] 'stage'
       [a] front, open
       lata [lata] 'summer, nom. pl.', miała [mʲawa] 'she had', czas [tʃas] 'time'
       [u] back, high, round
       stół [stuw] 'table', pióro [pʲurɔ] 'pen', ul [ul] 'beehive'
       [ɔ] back, half-open, round
       most [mɔst] 'bridge', siodło [ɕɔdwɔ] 'saddle', ono [ɔnɔ] 'it'

With reference to orthography we would like to make two comments. The vowel [u] has two historically justified spelling reflexes: <u> and <ó>; synchronically their choice is largely arbitrary (and obviously a headache for learners) since *kura* [kura] 'hen' and *góra* [gura] 'mountain' differ in the voicing of the initial plosive only.

The letter <i> has a double function: primarily it denotes the front high vowel [i] as in the first examples in (1) above. It also has a purely orthographic role of marking the palatal(ized) nature of the preceding consonant when a vowel follows, e.g. *sień* [ɕɛɲ] 'porch'. In the nominative plural of the noun for 'porch', *sieni-e* [ɕɛɲɛ], the letter <i> has no independent vocalic value after either of the two consonants.

The vexed question of the Polish nasal vowels will be taken up in a few places in the body of the book. Here we would like to note that nasal vowels as found in, say, French are not attested in Polish; what we do find are mid vowels [ɛ, ɔ] followed by a nasalized labio-velar glide [w̃], in some cases the nasalized palatal glide [ʲ̃], hence the nasal nuclei are better regarded as diphthongs (Biedrzycki 1963, 1978; Wierzchowska 1971: 135). Examples are provided in (2a); note that the orthographic nasal vowels <ę, ą> in some other forms correspond to sequences of an oral vowel and a nasal consonant homorganic with the following stop (2b).

(2) (a) tężec [tɛᵂʒɛts] 'tetanus', gęsty [gɛᵂstɨ] 'thick', męski [mɛᵂsci] 'manly'; wąs [vɔᵂs] 'moustache', idą [idɔᵂ] 'they go', kąsać [kɔᵂsatɕ] 'bite, vb.', gęś [gɛʲɕ] 'goose', pięść [pʲɛʲɕtɕ] 'fist';

(b) wędka [vɛntka] 'fishing rod', sędzia [sɛɲdʑa] 'judge, n.', tępy [tɛmpɨ] 'blunt'; bąk [bɔŋk] 'bumble bee', pstrąg [pstrɔŋk] 'trout', wątroba [vɔntrɔba] 'liver'

Phonetic descriptions, for example, Dukiewicz (1995: 32–3), record the existence of other nasal nuclei (diphthongs) as well but these are found in loan words only and always admit a variant with an oral vowel and a nasal consonant:

(3) instynkt [iᵂstɨŋkt] or [instɨŋkt] 'instinct'
tramwaj [traᵂvaj] or [tramvaj] 'tram'
kunszt [kuᵂʃt] or [kunʃt] 'artistry'
symfonia [sɨᵂfɔɲja] or [sɨmfɔɲja] 'symphony'

The nasal diphthongs basically exhaust the scope for nuclear complexity in Polish—there are no oral diphthongs in the language, just as there is no quantity distinction. Obviously, oral vowels can be followed by the semivowels [j, w] but—contrary to some descriptions (Biedrzycki 1978)—these are concatenations of segments where the vowel and the semi-vowel are independent units; some examples:

(4) daj [daj] 'give, imper.'   daje [dajɛ] '(s)he gives'
dał [daw] 'he gave'   dała [dawa] 'she gave'

The semivowels form onsets of the second syllable, a point that is uncontroversial with the right-hand words. The final consonant in the left-hand words would traditionally be analyzed as occupying the coda position, hence it does *not* constitute a unit with the preceding vowel and thus is not an off-glide of a diphthong. In the framework adopted in this book, the final consonant is followed by an empty nucleus and, consequently, must be regarded as syllable onset, a point that will recur on a number of occasions in the following chapters.

1.2 CONSONANTS

The relative segmental paucity in the vowel system is compensated by the complex consonantal inventory, to say nothing of consonant combinations which will be discussed in Chapter 5. In the sonorant section, apart from the two semivowels illustrated in [4], we find nasal consonants, a lateral, and a trill. Here are examples of the main segments in each group.

(5) (a) nasals
[m] bilabial
mowa [mɔva] 'speech', samotność [samɔtnɔɕtɕ] 'loneliness', dom [dɔm] 'house'

[mʲ] bilabial palatalized

miły [mʲiwɨ] 'pleasant', miód [mʲut] 'honey', mieszać [mʲɛʃatɕ] 'mix, vb.'

It should be noted that a pure palatalized bilabial occurs before the high vowel [i] in all varieties of standard Polish. Before other vowels there is a growing tendency to render the labial as a labial-palatal glide sequence. Thus the last words in (5) could be transcribed as *miód* [mʲjut] 'honey', *mieszać* [mʲjɛʃatɕ] 'mix, vb.' The phonological relevance of these facts will be discussed at length in Chapter 3.

[n] dental

nawet [navɛt] 'even', ona [ɔna] 'she', plon [plɔn] 'harvest'

[ɲ] palatal

niania [ɲaɲa] 'nanny', śnieg [ɕɲɛk] 'snow', państwo [paɲstfɔ] 'state', koń [kɔɲ] 'horse'

The palatal nasal can be realized as a nasal glide [j̃] before a fricative and in word-final position, hence the two last examples could be more narrowly transcribed as [paj̃stfɔ] and [kɔj̃].

[ŋ] velar

sęk [sɛŋk] 'knot', pręga [prɛŋga] 'stripe', wstęga [fstɛŋga] 'ribbon'

(b) lateral

[l] alveolar

las [las] 'wood', kolec [kɔlɛts] 'thorn', stal [stal] 'steel'

(c) trill

[r] alveolar

rura [rura] 'pipe', krowa [krɔva] 'cow', ser [sɛr] 'cheese'

The lateral and the trill display a measure of palatalization in combination with a following [i, j], although with the trill the situation emerges in loan words exclusively:

(6)   lis [lʲis] 'fox', batalia [batalʲja] 'struggle', Walia [valʲja] 'Wales'
        riposta [rʲipɔsta] 'repartee', awaria [avarʲja] 'breakdown', Maria [marʲja] 'Mary'

The palatalized quality of the lateral is negligible, that is to say, it is [lʲ] rather than [ʎ], and we will normally disregard it in our transcriptions.

Sonorants tend to be devoiced word-finally after a voiceless obstruent, as in *wiatr* [vʲatr̥] 'wind', *pasm* [pasm̥] 'band, gen. pl.', *pieśń* [pʲɛɕɲ̥] 'song', *myśl* [mɨɕl̥] 'thought, n.', or when flanked by voiceless consonants: *trwać* [tr̥fatɕ] 'last, vb.', *plwać* [pl̥fatɕ] 'spit, vb.'. Additional contextually conditioned variants will be mentioned as they appear in the course of the discussion.

Among obstruents we have plosives, fricatives and affricates; apart from the unremarkable division along the voiced parameter, there is the important factor of palatalization which plays a crucial role in Polish and which will figure prominently in the main part of this book. Here we present a list of segments to the extent that these can be or have been traditionally identified out of context.

Thus the list represents an inventory of segments recognized by past phonetic and phonological descriptions. Consider examples of plosives first.

(7) (a) [p, b] bilabial

pułapka [puwapka] 'trap, n.', potem [pɔtɛm] 'afterwards', potop [pɔtɔp] 'deluge'

brak [brak] 'shortage', rabarbar [rabarbar] 'rhubarb', obok [ɔbɔk] 'nearby'

(b) [pʲ, bʲ] bilabial palatalized

piła [pʲiwa] 'saw, n.', sapie [sapʲɛ] '(s)he pants', piasek [pʲasɛk] 'sand' biały [bʲawɨ] 'white', obibok [ɔbʲibɔk] 'lazybones', biuro [bʲurɔ] 'office'

As with the palatalized bilabial nasal, above, these stops are commonly rendered with a following palatal glide before a vowel other than [i], as in biały [bʲjawɨ] 'white', biuro [bʲjurɔ] 'office', sapie [sapʲjɛ] '(s)he pants', piasek [pʲjasɛk] 'sand'

(c) [t, d] dental

otwór [ɔtfur] 'opening', talerz [talɛʃ] 'plate', matka [matka] 'mother' dywan [dɨvan] 'carpet', wada [vada] 'flaw', mądry [mɔndrɨ] 'wise'

(d) [tʲ, dʲ] dental palatalized

tik [tʲik] 'twitch', sympatia [sɨmpatʲja] 'liking', plastik [plastʲik] 'plastic, n.' diwa [dʲiva] 'diva', adiustacja [adʲjustatsja] 'adjustment', melodia [mɛlɔdʲja] 'melody'

Word-internally, these consonants appear in foreign vocabulary only, even if some of them are fully assimilated and frequently used.

(e) [c, ɟ] palato-velar

kiwać [civatɕ] 'nod, vb.', okien [ɔcɛn] 'window, gen. pl.', wielki [vʲɛlci] 'large'

ginąć [ɟinɔɲtɕ] 'perish', ogier [ɔɟɛr] 'stallion', srogi [srɔɟi] 'severe'

(f) [k, g] velar

kołdra [kɔwdra] 'quilt', walizka [valiska] 'suitcase', potok [pɔtɔk] 'stream, n.'

gniew [gɲɛf] 'anger', ogrom [ɔgrɔm] 'vastness', bagaż [bagaʃ] 'luggage'

(8) fricatives

(a) [f, v] labio-dental

fala [fala] 'wave', fruwać [fruvatɕ] 'fly, vb.', oferma [ɔfɛrma] 'wimp' walka [valka] 'struggle', zabawa [zabava] 'play, n.', wrona [vrɔna] 'crow'

(b) [fʲ, vʲ] palatalized labio-dental

film [fʲilm] 'film', ofiara [ɔfʲara] 'sacrifice, n.', fiut [fʲut] 'dick' bawić [bavʲitɕ] 'play, vb.', wiara [vʲara] 'faith', wiór [vʲur] 'chip'

As with other labials, the fricatives before non-[i] can be realized with the palatal glide, i.e. *ofiara* [ɔfʲjara] 'sacrifice, n.', *fiut* [fʲjut] 'dick', *wiara* [vʲjara] 'faith', *wiór* [vʲjur] 'chip'

(c) [s, z] dental

kosa [kɔsa] 'scythe', sprawa [sprava] 'issue', los [lɔs] 'fate'
koza [kɔza] 'goat', złom [zwɔm] 'junk', baza [baza] 'base'

(d) [sʲ, zʲ] palatalized dental

sinus [sʲinus] 'sine', sinologia [sʲinɔlɔjja] 'sinology', Helsinki [xɛlsʲinci] zirytować [zʲirɨtɔvatɕ] 'irritate', Azja [azʲja] 'Asia', wizja [vʲizʲja] 'vision'

These consonants appear either in loanwords or involve prefix bound-aries (the latter in *z-irytować*).

(e) [ɕ, ʑ] alveolo-palatal

siano [ɕano] 'hay', oś [ɔɕ] 'axis', kwaśny [kfaɕnɨ] 'sour'
zioło [ʑɔwɔ] 'herb', kozioł [kɔʑɔw] 'he-goat', wyraźny [vɨraʑnɨ] 'distinct'

(e) [ʃ, ʒ] alveolar

szał [ʃaw] 'rage', pasza [paʃa] 'fodder', szron [ʃrɔn] 'hoar-frost'
rzeka [ʒɛka] 'river', marzenie [maʒɛɲɛ] 'dream, n.', żałoba [ʒawɔba] 'mourning'

(f) [ʃʲ, ʒʲ] palatalized alveolar

suszi [suʃʲi] 'sushi', szintoizm [ʃʲintɔism] 'Shintoism'
żigolak [ʒʲigɔlak] 'gigolo', żiguli [ʒʲiguli] 'make of a car'

These sounds are normally found in loanwords only.

(g) [ç] palato-velar

histeria [çistɛrʲja] 'hysteria', hierarchia [çjɛrarcja] 'hierarchy', zakochiwać [zakɔçivatɕ] 'fall in love'

(h) [x] velar

chochoł [xɔxɔw] 'straw covering', machać [maxatɕ] 'wave, vb.', dach [dax] 'roof', chrabąszcz [xrabɔʷʃtʃ] 'bug'

As mentioned above, palatalized non-labials appear primarily in loanwords. They also occur as a juncture phenomenon, as in *los i fortuna* [lɔsʲ‿i‿fɔrtuna] 'fate and fortune'. We will discuss it in somewhat greater detail in Chapter 3.

Finally, we need to look at a few groups of affricates which are illustrated in (9).

(9) (a) [ts, dz] dental

cały [tsawɨ] 'whole', macka [matska] 'tentacle', noc [nɔts] 'night'
władza [vwadza] 'authority', dzban [dzban] 'pitcher', rodzynek [rɔdzɨnek] 'raisin'

(b) [tɕ, dʑ] alveolo-palatal

ciało [tɕawɔ] 'body', karcić [kartɕitɕ] 'punish', pięć [pʲɛɲtɕ] 'five'
dziumdzia [dʑumdʑa] 'sluggard', gardzić [gardʑitɕ] 'despise', dźwig [dʑvʲik] 'crane'

(c) [tʃ, dʒ] alveolar

czas [tʃas] 'time', czwartek [tʃfartɛk] 'Thursday', mecz [mɛtʃ] 'match'
dżdżysty [dʒdʒɨstɨ] 'rainy', móżdżek [muʒdʒɛk] 'brain, dim.', gwiżdże
[gvʲiʒdʒɛ] '(s)he whistles'

(d) [tsʲ, dzʲ, tʃʲ, dʒʲ] palatalized dentals and alveolars

Citroen [tsʲitrɔɛn] 'make of car', cis [tsʲis] 'C sharp'
Chile [tʃʲilɛ] 'Chile', chipsy [tʃʲipsɨ] 'potato crisps'
dżihad [dʒʲixat] 'jihad', dżinsy [dʒʲinsɨ] 'jeans'

The last class of affricates is again found in loanwords; [dzʲ] seems a potential
segment.

In our transcriptions throughout we do away with the tie bar, so instead of [t͡s, t͡ʃ,
d͡z, d͡ʒ] we use [ts, tʃ dz, dʒ] for close transitions; at the same time we introduce the
symbols [t-ʃ, d-ʒ] for open transitions or consonant sequences which are not affricates.
Thus the distinction *czysta* 'clean, fem.' ∼ *trzysta* 'three hundred' we represent as
[tʃɨsta] and [t-ʃɨsta], respectively; the initial consonant in the first word is an affricate
(IPA [t͡ʃ]) while [t-ʃ] is a consonant sequence where a plosive is followed by a fricative.

Before concluding the survey of the principal consonantal segments of the
language we need to make a brief comment about two loaded terms: *palatal* and
palatalized. The terms suggest primary and secondary articulation but, obviously,
what counts as primary and what as secondary cannot be determined independently of the phonological interpretation. If we were to follow the transcriptional
conventions we would conclude that [ɕ, ʑ, tɕ, ʑ, ɲ, c, ɟ, ç] are palatal consonants
while those with the raised subscript [pʲ, mʲ, tʲ, tsʲ] would qualify as palatalized.
Phonologically and morphophonologically, however, the palatal group patterns
with palatalized labials; therefore both are referred to as 'palatalized'. Even worse,
some of the non-palatalized and non-palatal consonants, such as [ts, tʃ] have been
referred to as *functionally* palatal or palatalized, thus adding to the general confu-
sion. In our discussion in subsequent chapters we will fundamentally leave out
palatalized coronals ([tʲ, sʲ, tsʲ, tʃʲ]) and other sounds illustrated in (6, 7d, 8d, 8f, 9d)
and concentrate on the remaining palatal and palatalized segments. It is hoped that
the context and the accompanying transcriptions will remove any ambiguities.

A few points worth noting about the spelling of the consonants:

- The sound [ʒ] is rendered orthographically either as <ż>, e.g. *może* [mɔʒɛ]
  '(s)he can' or as <rz>, e.g. *morze* [mɔʒɛ] 'sea'.
- The sound [x] is rendered orthographically either as <ch>, e.g. *chata* [xata]
  'cottage', or as <h>, e.g. *hałas* [xawas] 'noise'.
- The affricates [ts, dz, tʃ, dʒ] are spelled <c, dz, cz, dż>, e.g. *noc* [nɔts] 'night',
  wodza [vɔdza] 'leader, gen. sg.', *czyn* [tʃɨn] 'deed', *dżungla* [dʒuŋgla] 'jungle',
  respectively, while the open transitions [t-ʃ, d-ʒ] are recorded as <trz> and
  <drz>, e.g: *trzeba* [t-ʃɛba] 'it is necessary', *drzewo* [d-ʒɛvɔ] 'tree'.
- The palatals [ɕ, ʑ, tɕ, dʑ, ɲ] are spelled <ś, ź, ć, dź, ń> pre-consonantally and
  word-finally, e.g.:

coś [tsɔɕ] 'something'   myśl [mɨɕl̥] 'thought, n.'
paź [paɕ] 'page boy'   koźlę [kɔʑlɛ] 'kid'
być [bɨtɕ] 'be'   paćka [patɕka] 'gunge'
żołądź [ʒɔwɔɲtɕ] 'acorn'   dźgnąć [dʑgnɔɲtɕ] 'stab'
koń [kɔɲ] 'horse'   bańka [baɲka] 'bubble'

and as <si, zi, ci, dzi, ni> before a vowel, as in the following examples.:

dzisiaj [dʑiɕaj] 'today'   pazia [paʑa] 'page boy, gen. sg.'
babcia [baptɕa] 'grandma'   żołędzia [ʒɔwɛɲdʑa] 'acron, gen. sg.'
konia [kɔɲa] 'horse, gen. sg.'

As noted above, the letter <i> marks the palatalized quality of the preceding consonant and denotes the vowel [i] only if no other vowel letter follows; if it does, then <i> has a purely graphic function and corresponds to no vocalic segment. In the forms we supply with relevant morphological division throughout the book, the letter <i> in its diacritic function is put together with the consonant whose palatal quality it denotes; thus the forms *babcia* [baptɕa] 'grandma', *konia* [kɔɲa] 'horse, gen. sg.', *pazia* [paʑa] 'page boy, gen. sg.', *żołędzia* [ʒɔwɛɲdʑa] 'acorn, gen. sg.' are broken up as *babci-a, koni-a, pazi-a,* and *żołędzi-a*, where *-a* is the inflectional morpheme while <i> is here a way of representing the palatality of the stem-final consonant.

1.3 REMARKS ON STRESS AND INTONATION

Against the background of the segmental phonology and morphophonology of Polish, word stress is a singularly unremarkable property. This is not to say that it is not without its problems but the predominant pattern is straightforward enough: the focus of primary word stress is the penultimate nucleus.[1] The addition of inflectional and derivational suffixes means that stress can shift, but it remains firmly associated with the last-but-one vowel, as in (10):

(10)   człowiek ['tʃwɔvʲɛk] 'human being'
        człowiek-a [tʃwɔ'vʲɛka] 'gen. sg.'
        człowiek-owi [tʃwɔvʲɛ'kɔvʲi] 'dat. sg.'
        człowiecz-y [tʃwɔ'vʲɛtʃɨ] 'human'

Because of its total predictability we do not include stress in our transcriptions, which are cumbersome enough as it is. The only exception to this convention are a few points where stress is explicitly mentioned as relevant to the argument. Here we would like to outline some of the complications besetting the superficially simple regularity. They introduce variety into the Polish stress pattern in that they bring cases of both antepenultimate and final stress.

---

[1] The existence of secondary stress is generally recognized: it is found in alternating syllables preceding the main stress. See Rubach and Booij (1985) for some discussion.

Antepenultimate stress is found in some loans, such as those in (11), although it should be added that the tendency towards unification is quite strong and penultimate stress can frequently be heard in them, despite the normative censure.

(11) fizyka ['fʲizɨka] physics   matematyka [matɛ'matɨka]
                                          'mathematics'
     logika ['lɔɟika] 'logic'   uniwersytet [uɲi'vɛrsitɛt] 'university'
     papryka ['paprɨka] 'paprika'   dynamika [dɨ'namʲika] 'dynamics'
     republika [rɛ'publika] 'republic'   fonetyka [fɔ'nɛtɨka] 'phonetics'

What is also striking is that some of these words obligatorily move to the penultimate pattern when endings—inflectional or derivational—are attached (12a) while others stay antepenultimate (12b) in some cases but move the stress in others.

(12) (a) uniwersytet [uɲi'vɛrsitɛt]   uniwerystet-u [uɲivɛrsi'tɛtu] 'gen. sg.'
         'university'   (never *[uɲivɛr'sitɛtu])
                                  uniwersytet-ami [uɲivɛrsitɛ'tamʲi] 'instr. pl.'
                                  uniwersyte-cki [uɲivɛrsi'tɛtsci] 'adj.'

     (b) republik-a [rɛ'publika]   republik [rɛ'publik] 'gen. pl.'
         'republic'   republik-om [rɛ'publikɔm] 'dat. pl.'
                                  republik-anin [rɛpubli'kaɲin] 'republican, n.'
         fonetyk-a [fɔ'nɛtɨka]   fonetyc-e [fɔ'nɛtitsɛ] 'dat. sg.'
         'phonetics' or   fonetyk-om [fɔ'nɛtikɔm] 'dat. pl.'
         'phonetician, gen. sg.'   fonetyk-ami [fɔnɛti'kamʲi] 'instr. pl.'

The last word is particularly interesting since *fonetyk* [fɔ'nɛtik] on the reading 'phonetician' has penultimate stress but some of its oblique forms acquire the antepenultimate one: *fonetyk-a* [fɔ'nɛtika], *fonetyki-em* [fɔ'nɛticɛm] 'instr. sg.', *fonetyk-u* [fɔ'nɛtiku] 'loc., voc. sg.', *fonetyk-ów* [fɔ'nɛtikuf] 'gen. pl.', but *fonetyk-ami* [fɔnɛti'kamʲi] 'instr. pl.'. For some discussion of the theoretical issues connected with this sort of stress variation, see Franks (1985), Halle and Vergnaud (1987: 57–8), and Hammond (1989). As noted above, the variation tends to disappear and the penultimate model becomes widespread—many speakers would have penultimate stress in all words in (12).

Another case where stress departs from the penultimate syllable—or, more accurately, may depart—involves grammatical conditioning. When the endings of the first- and second-person plural of the preterite are attached, stress can go to the antepenultimate nucleus.

(13) czytal-i [tʃɨ'tali] 'they read, past'   czytal-i-ś-my [tʃɨ'talicmɨ] 'we read, past'
                                       czytal-i-ś-cie [tʃɨ'talictɕɛ] 'you (pl.) read, past'

Furthermore, in the conditional involving the suffix *-by-*, the stress can be antepenultimate or even\asterisk pre-antepenultimate. Consider the conditional paradigm of the verb *pis-a-ć* [pʲisatɕ] 'write':

(14) pisał-by-m ['pʲisawbɨm] 'I (masc.) would write'

pisał-by-ś ['pʲisawbɨɕ] 'you (masc.) would write'
pisał-by ['pʲisawbɨ] 'he would write'
pisał-a-by [pʲi'sawabɨ] 'she would write'
pisał-o-by [pʲi'sawɔbɨ] 'it would write'
pisal-i-by-ś-my [pʲi'salibɨɕmɨ] 'we (masc.) would write'
pisal-i-by-ś-cie [pʲi'salibɨɕtɕɛ] 'you (masc.) would write'
pisal-i-by [pʲi'salibɨ] 'they (masc.) would write'

Stress is antepenultimate if the ending of the conditional contains just one vowel (the singular, 3rd pers. pl.); when the ending of the conditional is followed by a personal ending containing a vowel, stress goes to the pre-antepenultimate nucleus (1st and 2nd pers. pl.). It seems that both the *-my, -cie* endings of the preterite plural and the *-by-* suffix are clitics that do not affect stress placement. In fact they can be detached from the verb and either placed separately or attached to some other word in the sentence (usually initial):

(15)   wiele pisal-i-ś-my 'we wrote a lot' = wiele-ś-my pisali
       chętnie pisal-i-by-ś-my 'we would gladly write' = chętnie byśmy pisali

Note that the combination of the adverb *wiele* 'much' with the clitic yet again produces antepenultimate stress: ['vʲɛlɛɕmɨ].

Finally, it may be noted that, at the other extreme, word-final stress is occasionally found in borrowings, as in *bardak* [bar'dak] 'mess, chaos', *barachło* [bara'xwɔ] 'junk'. Final stress may also occur in oblique forms containing native Polish endings, as is the case of the second of the examples: *barachł-a* [bara'xwa] 'gen. sg.', *barachł-e* [bara'xlɛ] 'loc. sg.'; curiously enough, the first word adopts native or penultimate stress with the same endings: *bardak-u* [bar'daku] 'gen., loc. sg.', *bardaki-em* [bar'dacɛm] 'instr. sg.'—the decision seems to rest with individual lexical items. Final stress is regularly found in acronyms where names of letters are given a syllabic shape, as in PZU [pɛzɛt'u], RP [ɛr'pɛ], PZWS [pɛzɛtvu'ɛs], H_2O [hadva'ɔ].

Intonation remains the least adequately described aspect of spoken Polish. Steffen-Batogowa (1966) and Dukiewicz (1978) offer descriptions with a heavy phonetic bias but little attention is paid to systematizing the intonational contours from the point of view of their linguistic relevance. Some very preliminary attempts in that direction can be found in Biedrzycki (1974: 135–42), Puppel *et al.* (1977: 234–42) and Fisiak *et al.* (1978: 244–50).

1.4 STRUCTURALIST ANALYSES: CONCERNS, ASSUMPTIONS, RESULTS

Polish is quite lucky in having had a long tradition of structuralist descriptions of the sound structure, starting in the second half of the nineteenth century with the works of Baudouin de Courtenay. His influence on the study of Polish and the development of phonology at large has been expertly described by Jakobson (1960) and Stankiewicz (1972: 3–48). In developing his numerous definitions of the phoneme, Baudouin often relied on Polish (and Russian) for his data. The works where he directly addresses the phonology of Modern Polish include Baudouin de Courtenay (1898, 1915, 1922). His contribution continues to be felt and some of his interpretations, abandoned for a while, are being resurrected (Gussmann 2004*a*). It is also worth pointing out that Baudouin's work on and typology of sound alternations is regarded by some contemporary phonologists as comprehensive and of lasting value (Anderson 1985: 73–9). The classical structuralist tradition that Baudouin launched is developed most fully in the works of Stieber (1948, 1958, 1966, 1973) and its most recent statement is Sawicka (1995); important other contributions include Trager (1939), Zwoliński (1958), and Biedrzycki (1963, 1978).

The structuralist approach to phonology in most of its variants is predominantly paradigmatic. It sets as its objective the identification of the contrastive units of the language (phonemes), where contrastiveness is determined by the phonetic context alone. Sounds which can appear in the same phonetic context are regarded as representing different phonemes irrespectively of other properties of the words they appear in, such as the grammatical category or lexical stratification (e.g. native vs. non-native). Hence, for example, the Polish 'minimal pairs':

(16)   kon-a [kɔna] '(s)he is at the point of death'   koni-a [kɔɲa] 'horse, gen. sg.'
       pan [pan] 'gentleman'   pań [paɲ] 'lady, gen. pl.'

would suffice to demonstrate the distinctiveness of the sounds [n] and [ɲ]. Furthermore, although views would not be so unanimous here, a contrast established in one place would be regarded as valid for the language as a whole (hence the slogan *Once a phoneme, always a phoneme*); some varieties of European structuralist phonology envisaged the possibility of suspending contrasts in some phonologically defined conditions, a procedure which resulted in the notion of *neutralization*. Thus the presence of the palatal nasal [ɲ] before another palatalized stop in words such as *pędzi* [pɛɲdʑi] '(s)he rushes', *pięć* [pʲɛɲtɕ] 'five' could be treated as realizing the nasal archiphoneme /N/ rather than the palatal nasal phoneme itself. In this way the same sound [ɲ] could be traced back to different phonological sources. However, the initial purpose of the analysis was the establishment of an inventory of contrasting units (with or without neutralization) and these could then be studied with reference to their combinatorial (phonotactic) potential.

The application of the structural method to the Polish data yielded an inventory of phonemes where the majority of segments discussed in the first part of this introduction would be regarded as phonemic. There is no dearth of examples showing that voiced and voiceless consonants can contrast:

(17)   wata [vata] 'cotton-wool'   wada [vada] 'flaw'
       kosa [kɔsa] 'scythe'   koza [kɔza] 'goat'

The same could be done for various pairs of plain and palatal(ized) consonants:

(18) byt [bɨt] 'existence'   być [bɨtɕ] 'be'
      sadło [sadwɔ] 'fat, n.'   siadło [ɕadwɔ] 'it sat down'

and for different places and manners of articulation:

(19) cało [tsawɔ] 'in one piece'   ciało [tɕawɔ] 'body'
      chleb [xlɛp] 'bread'   klep [klɛp] 'pat, imper. sg.'

Although very simple in outline, the procedure for establishing a comprehensive list of contrasts is not always straightforward when applied, leading to the emergence of partially different results and conflicting accounts. The list of such problem areas embraces at least the following three issues.

1. The status of the velar nasal [ŋ]
The velar nasal has a highly restricted distribution in Polish since it appears only before a following velar plosive. It is not the case, however, that the dental [n] is barred from that position and thus minimal pairs can be found such as

(20) łąka [wɔŋka] 'meadow'   łonka [wɔnka] 'bosom, dim. nom. pl.'

Admittedly, the second member of the pair is morphologically complex and involves a diminutive suffix, but morphology is traditionally viewed as independent of phonology and having no influence on it. In such a case the ineluctable conclusion is that both [n] and [ŋ] belong to or represent separate phonemes; the highly restricted distribution of the velar nasal remains nothing more than an accidental gap in the distribution of phonemes.

2. The status of the palato-velars [c, ɟ, ç]
These consonants are also highly restricted in their occurrence (they never appear word-finally or preconsonantally). They are found predominantly, though not exclusively, before front vowels; however, since the plain velars, too, can be found before front vowels, they have to be regarded as being phonemically distinct from each other. Thus, partial or near-minimal pairs such as

(21) kędy [kɛndɨ] 'which way'   kieł [cɛw] 'tusk'
      gęsty [gɛʷstɨ] 'thick'   giętki [ɟɛntci] 'pliable'
      herbata [xɛrbata] 'tea'   hieroglif [çɛrɔglif] 'hieroglyph'

can be found; they are partial in the sense that the vowel following the initial velar cannot be held responsible for the emergence of the specific variant, as both of them—palatal and non-palatal—are possible in that context. There would be an additional problem with the spirant [ç]: depending on the phonetic transcription of the word *hieroglif* as [çɛrɔglif] or [çjɛrɔglif], one could argue for the phonemic or allophonic status of the consonant.[2] As with the velar nasal, the distributional

---

[2] The case neatly illustrated the role played by what Chao (1934) described as *under-analysis* or *over-analysis* of phonetic systems.

restrictions in the occurrence of the specific phonemes must be swept aside since factors such as morphological complexity and synchronic foreignness of a word are not taken into account in establishing the phonemes of the language. We will discuss the issue of the palato-velars in great detail in Chapter 3, where different conclusions will be drawn.

3. The status of the vowels [i, ɨ] and of palatalized consonants
The position of the two vowels has been dogging Polish phonological studies from the word go. Baudouin de Courtenay regarded them as a single phoneme, a view that dominated the Polish phonological studies till about the middle of the twentieth century. From that time on, the predominant position has been that the two vowels belong to separate phonemes. We will again study this issue closely in Chapter 2; here we will merely announce the issue: depending on whether we take these two sounds to be one or two phonemes we may arrive at a different interpretation of several other consonants, specifically, the palatalized ones. To take just one example here: we mentioned in section 1.2 above that the sounds [tʲ, rʲ] appear before a following [i]. Now consider the following pairs of words.

(22)   tryk [trɨk] 'ram'   trik [trʲik] 'trick'
       plastyk [plastɨk] 'plastic artist'   plastik [plastʲik] 'plastic, n.'

If the two vowels [i, ɨ] are non-contrastive, we have to view the palatalized consonants [rʲ, tʲ] as realizing phonemes distinct from those realized by the non-palatalized [r, t], a conclusion that most scholars would baulk at, if only because the palatalized consonants appear in just a few loans.

1.5 MORPHOLOGY AND MORPHOPHONOLOGY

The identification of contrasting units (phonemes) and an analysis of their combinatorial possibilities (phonotactics) did not exhaust the structuralist study of sounds. It was realized quite early that some legitimate issues go beyond the domain of phonology understood as a combination of phonemics and phonotactics; these concerns called for the establishment of an additional level which came to be named morpho(pho)nology (or morphophonemics).

The justification for this level was the recognition of regularities in the phonemic shape of morphemes which are not conditioned by the phonetic context alone. Consider a simple Polish example, the noun *żab-a* [ʒaba] 'frog' and its diminutive *żab-k-a* [ʒapka]. The root morpheme appears in two phonetic shapes—[ʒab] and [ʒap]—which must also be two distinct phonemic shapes /ʒab/ and /ʒap/ since [b] and [p] are realizations of two different phonemes as shown by numerous minimal pairs, for example *był* [bɨw] 'he was' ~ *pył* [pɨw] 'dust, n.', *snoby* [snɔbɨ] 'snob, nom. pl.' ~ *snopy* [snɔpɨ] 'sheaf, nom. pl.'. To capture the fact that the two phonemic representations /ʒab/ and /ʒap/ realize the same morpheme, the morphophonemic level was set up. The nature of this level and the way it is converted into the phonemic level depended on specific theoretical models that need not concern us here (see Fischer-Jørgensen 1975; Anderson 1985; Gussmann 2003 for more detailed presentations).

The example just given is maximally simple and would not constitute sufficient justification for morphophonology within every theoretical framework—note that a phonological approach which embraces the concept of neutralization would handle the same facts in a different way. It would be claimed that the opposition of voicing is suspended before a following obstruent in Polish, hence the voiceless [p] of [ʒapka] could realize the archiphoneme /P/, which is a distinct entity from the phonemes /p/ and /b/. The same procedure could not be extended to most instances of alternating segments, however: when different phonemes appear in the same environment within a morpheme, no neutralization could be evoked. Consider the following examples:

(23)   kos [kɔs] 'scythe, gen. pl.'   koś [kɔɕ] 'reap, imper.'
        los-em [lɔsɛm] 'fate, instr. sg.'   losi-e [lɔɕɛ] 'loc. sg.'

Here both [s] and [ɕ] appear either word-finally or before the vowel [ɛ]; their selection is not determined by phonetic or phonological but, rather, by grammatical and lexical factors. The study of such non-phonologically conditioned alternations constitutes a major concern of morphophonology, while the phonemes involved in alternations are said to make up morphophonemes. It was the Polish scholar, Henryk Ułaszyn, who was instrumental in the launching of morphophonology and who is credited with coining the term *Morphonema* 'morphoneme' in 1931. With or without haplology, morpho(pho)nology was recognized as a legitimate field of study which led to data-rich descriptive accounts starting with Trubetzkoy's (1934) study of Russian, and taking a new impetus with Jakobson's (1948) seminal paper devoted to Russian conjugation. Aspects of Polish were described in a series of papers by Stankiewicz (1954, 1955, 1960, 1966, 1967) and Schenker (1954); a book-length description of the morphophonology of Bulgarian inflection by Aronson (1968) also deserves mention. (More recently, an extensive survey of Polish is Kowalik's (1997) monograph which will be discussed in greater detail in Ch. 4). Further development of this approach was halted by the generative conflation of phonology and morphophonology (see below) and despite an occasional maverick (Andersen 1969a), little progress was made in mainstream linguistics either in refining the means and ends of morphophonology or in using it for descriptive purposes. A noteworthy exception is Dressler, who works within the framework of natural linguistics—his 1985 monograph remains the single most comprehensive and detailed proposal addressing both the place of morphophonology in linguistics and the shape of its statements. Maiden (1991) and Harasowska (1999) remain relatively isolated examples of using morphophonology to approach descriptive issues. The early history of the discipline is summarized in Kilbury (1976), while Hockett (1958: 269–300) surveys the field from the point of view of American structuralism.

Polish morphology has been described in detail in traditional terms in numerous works addressing both the totality of inflection (Schenker 1964; Tokarski 1973) and derivation (Grzegorczykowa 1979; Grzegorczykowa and Puzynina 1979) as well as numerous specific issues, one example of which is Westfal's (1956) book-length description of the distribution of the -*a* and -*u* endings in the genitive singular masculine. Grzegorczykowa, Laskowski, and Wróbel (1998) offer an informed and user-friendly survey of the field. While comprehensive and at times excruciatingly exhaustive when it comes to data, the traditional accounts pay little or no attention to theoretical issues, either phonological or morphological; nominal and verbal paradigms are listed with no attempt to understand their structure, derivatives are classified and described on semantic basis, no attention is paid to the formal side of derivational morphology and numerous questions remain unanswered and even unasked. The descriptions in most cases make an effort to eschew any theoretical considerations of a formal nature. For this reason we will frequently have to rely on ad hoc or intuitive judgements with reference to morphology in our phonological analyses and morphophonological forays. An account of Polish morphology, informed of the major theoretical innovations, remains a pressing challenge for the future.

1.6 DERIVATIONAL–GENERATIVE ANALYSES: CONCERNS, ASSUMPTIONS, RESULTS

The advent of derivational-generative phonology marked a dramatic change in the objectives and methods of analyzing the sound structure of language. Rather than chop up the phonetic string into sequences of contrastive units as structuralist phonology would have it, the generative approach consisted in an attempt to discover the phonological regularities of the language as revealed in morphophonological alternations and distributional restrictions. This was precipitated by arguments (Halle 1959) showing not only the detrimental aspects of the structuralist phoneme and the phonemic level of representation but their downright linguistic irrelevance. The arguments, fully developed in Chomsky (1964) and Postal (1968), resulted in the abandonment of the 'taxonomic' phoneme and of the phonemic level of representation. Once this happened, what was left was the morphophonological level (also called 'systematic phonological') and the phonetic level; the two were connected by an intricate set of phonological generalizations (rules) which made up the major part of the phonological system of the language. Much research in the second part of the twentieth century went into exploring ways of formulating phonological generalizations, discovering their properties and interactions, as well as defining the nature of underlying (morpho)phonological representations and the segments which go into their construction. In various ways, all these concerns have been reflected in the generative studies of Polish (see Gladney 1971); in the chapters which follow we will have occasion to address specific issues and take exception to individual solutions.

Here it needs to be stressed that the derivational-generative approach regarded morphophonological alternations as a direct reflection of the phonological regularities of the language. In effect, the separation of morphophonology and phonology ceased to exist and the two traditional components were conflated into a single module. This is seen most clearly in the programme of Lexical Phonology (Booij and Rubach 2003), where a distinction is made between lexical and post-lexical rules; although the former often correspond to traditional morphophonological regularities, they are both analyzed and expressed in the same derivational terms. Attempts to recast morphophonological rules within frameworks such as Optimality Theory reintroduce a measure of derivationalism into an allegedly non-derivational model (Rubach and Booij 2001).

Large chunks of Polish were described in changing generative terms in four major monographs (Laskowski 1975a; Gussmann 1980a; Rubach 1984; Bethin 1992) and a number of studies of individual problems. The centre of Polish phonology was seen as formed by the so-called rules of palatalization and phenomena directly dependent on them. The controversial problem areas within the broadly understood generative paradigm include the following four issues.

1. The predictability of palatalizations

The degree to which segments involved in palatalization alternations can be claimed to be predictable translates into the predictability of palatalization as a phonological process. While few generativists would question the fact that the [t ~ tɕ] alternation may be regarded as phonologically controlled before some front vowels, as in *lot* [lɔt] 'flight' ~ *loci-e* [lɔtɕɛ] 'loc. sg.', questions arose whether the consonant [tɕ] should also be derived from a plain plosive:

(a) before non-front vowels, e.g. *ciał-o* [tɕawɔ] 'body', where alternations with a front vowel are available, e.g. *ciel-e* [tɕɛlɛ] 'loc. sg.';

(b) before a non-front vowel, e.g. *cioci-a* [tɕɔtɕa] 'aunt', where no alternations with a front vowel are available;

(c) at the end of the word, with or without alternations, e.g. *chęć* [xɛntɕ] 'willingness' ~ *chęt-n-y* [xɛntnɨ] 'willing' vs. -*ć* [tɕ] [ending of the infinitive], which occurs in literally hundreds if not thousands of forms;

(d) before a consonant, e.g. *ćma* [tɕma] 'moth'.

Answers to such questions produced descriptions of varying degree of abstractness, hence of different derivational depth and rule interaction. While the earlier descriptions tended to reduce the underlying inventory of segments and, consequently, the representations of linguistic forms to a very simple set of consonants, later research favoured only partial predictability of so-called palatalization reflexes and refrained from deriving them when alternations with plain consonants were not available. This went hand in hand with the changing view of the vowel system: while earlier a rich inventory of vocalic segments was recognized, including contrasts eliminated in every position (absolute neutralization), later studies favoured a more concrete system, adhering closely to the phonetic data.

2. The phonological status of vowel alternations

Partly connected with the problems of palatalization are vowel alternations, such as [ɛ ~ ɔ], e.g. *zieleń* [ʑɛlɛɲ] 'greenness' ~ *zielon-y* [ʑɛlɔnɨ] 'green', [ɛ ~ a], e.g. *ciast-o* [tɕastɔ] 'cake' ~ *cieści-e* [tɕɛɕtɕɛ] 'loc. sg.', and alternations of so-called nasal vowels—phonetically sequences of an oral vowel and a nasal segment, e.g. *pięć* [pʲɛɲtɕ] 'five'~ *piąt-k-a* [pʲɔntka] 'fiver'. Totally unconnected with palatalization are the alternations of back vowels [ɔ–u], as in *wod-a* [vɔda] 'water' ~ *wód-k-a* [vutka] 'vodka'. They have all been described as phonological regularities although in certain cases the contexts were grammatically and lexically circumscribed. As with palatalization alternations there is the problem of how to handle non-alternating vowels which appear in the 'wrong' or opaque environment, for example, back vowels after palatalized consonants, as in *ciark-i* [tɕarci] 'creeps, nom. pl.'.

3. The status of the vowel-zero alternation

Alternations between the vowel [ɛ] and zero, e.g. *bez* [bɛs] 'lilac' ~ *bz-u* [bzu] 'gen. sg.', have been described in a variety of ways at the different stages of the development of generative phonology, thus using partially different mechanisms. They have all viewed the alternations as lying within the purview of phonology and reflecting its mechanism. What has been challenged in various ways is the nature of the melodic element(s) underlying the alternation, but not its phonological status.

4. Non-phonological alternations

The express objective of derivational descriptions was to provide most morphemes with a single phonological form. The qualification 'most' was meant to exclude from the single underlying requirement instances of suppletion such as *id-ę* [idɛ] 'I go' ~ *szed-l-em* [ʃedwɛm] 'I went' and *dobr-y* [dɔbrɨ] 'good' ~ *lep-sz-y* [lɛpʃɨ] 'better' (in Polish and English, incidentally). It soon turned out that almost any detailed account of a language will readily yield a sizable number of alternations which, while not strictly suppletive, cannot be accommodated by means of rules of any generality. Here belong, for instance, remnants of the ancient apophonic alternations such as *nieś-ć* [ɲɛɕtɕ] 'carry' ~ *nos-i-ć* [nɔɕitɕ] 'carry, iterat.' but also assorted detritus of historical development, dialect borrowings, etc. A case in point might be the palatalization alternations of [k] and [x]: in appropriate contexts these emerge as [tʃ] and [ʃ] respectively; the alternations have massive lexical support and are almost exceptionless. Almost but not quite: the very common words *ptak* [ptak] 'bird' and *druh* [drux] 'scout' alternate their final obstruents with [ʃ] and [ʒ] in *ptaszek* [ptaʃɛk] 'bird, dim.' and *druż-yn-a* [druʒɨna] 'team, pack' (rather than the theoretically expected and perfectly well-formed **ptaczek* [ptatʃɛk] and **drusz-yn-a* [druʃɨna]). Synchronically, the regular rules of palatalization have to be pre-empted in some way and the unexpected forms allowed to appear on the surface. Devising an appropriate mechanism to achieve the required objective is not an issue, nor is it a particularly disturbing sign since partial (ir)regularities are a fact that any model has to come to terms with. Depending on the adopted theoretical mechanisms, the number of such irregular formations can vary enormously and, as we shall see, can undermine large chunks of the description and the model it is based on. The existence of such forms also raises the question of whether some sort of morphophonology should not be revived and recognized as a legitimate language component with properties of its own.

1.7 GOVERNMENT PHONOLOGY: CONCERNS, ASSUMPTIONS, AMBITIONS

In many ways Government Phonology (GP) can be seen as a reaction against the theoretical and descriptive excesses that derivational generativism spawned. It is also a return to some of the more traditional concerns that generative phonology gave short shrift to. A return to earlier concerns is not a return of the phonemic prodigal son who, recognizing the sinfulness of his ways, embraces again complementary distributions and juncture phonemes, among other things. Quite conversely, in many ways GP moves further away from traditional structuralism than did classical generative phonology. Halle's (1959) well-known arguments against the distributional or taxonomic phoneme (reviewed in Anderson 1974: 34–6) show that it must be abandoned since it makes impossible the statement of generalizations: what is a single regularity (Russian voice assimilation in Halle's example) has to be split into an allophonic statement (for alternating non-contrastive segments) and a morphophonemic rule (for alternating phonemes). The unity of the regularity not only remains unexpressed but, given the constraints of the framework, is inexpressible. Although a model of phonology working with neutralization would not be open to such straightforward censure, there can be no doubt that the argument is cogent. It seems, however, that by blaming the phonemic level, Halle did not go far enough, as the alleged culprit—the phoneme—is itself a fruit of a far more basic failing of (most of) structuralist phonology, namely, its preoccupation with paradigmatic relations. GP is a non-derivational framework, and in this it parts ways with its immediate generative predecessor, but it is fundamentally a syntagmatically oriented framework and as such it could not be further away from the classical structuralist tradition. It is legitimate to view it as a return to the way of thinking and concerns that dominated Firthian prosodic analysis (as exemplified in Palmer 1970). Derivational-generative phonology, although it did away with the phoneme, still continued to recognize the central role of the segment and the establishment of underlying segments figures prominently in most studies. For GP, segments and paradigmatically identifiable units are either secondary or of little relevance. Thus, although it would be absurd to doubt that *nasz* [naʃ] 'our' differs from *masz* [maʃ] 'you have' in the (place of articulation of the) initial nasal, this does not allow us to identify the nasals with those in *sąd* [sɔnt] 'court, n.' and *dąb* [dɔmp] 'oak' because syntagmatically the nasals in the last two words are strictly connected with the following plosive and as such are viewed as phonologically different units from the initial nasals. The syntagmatic bias of GP means that concern with inventories of segments—contrastive, underlying, derived or what have you—is viewed as both misguided and misleading. This does not mean that the segment is entirely absent from this approach to phonology, not only because most of the phonological tradition relies on the notion of the segment and one cannot break away with past analyses and results; as a means of arriving at an understanding of a regularity it is frequently practicable, or unavoidable, to talk in terms of chunks, but only as a means rather than an aim. Fundamentally, however, the segment is de-emphasized so that the properties spanning skeletal slots can be brought into sharper relief. If no such properties or relations can be established, what is left may be regarded as a segment sequence. In this, GP harks back to the distinction between prosodies and phonematic units within the Firthian approach.

Government Phonology attempts to provide a highly constrained, universal, framework which separates phonological from non-phonological phenomena. Unlike its immediate generative predecessor

1. GP describes all phonological phenomena with reference to a single level of representation;
2. it constructs a restrictive theory of syllabic constituents;
3. it defines phonological phenomena by reference to the phonological context;
4. it operates with a small number of primes, called elements;
5. it recognizes the need for a separate morphophonology component.

A more comprehensive presentation of some of these and related points illustrating the workings of GP follows in Chapter 2, but detailed discussions are widely available in print (Kaye, Lowenstamm, and Vergnaud 1985, 1989, 1990; Charette 1991; Brockhaus 1995a, b; Cyran 1997, 1998, 2003; Harris 1990, 1994, 1997; Harris and Lindsey 1995; Kaye 1990, 1991/2, 1995; Scheer 1997, 1998a, b, 2004; Gussmann 2002).

It should be stressed that, in the body of the book, we will not be attempting to concentrate on model-internal theoretical issues and, in fact, we will openly be taking theoretical shortcuts, leaving some questions unsolved or indicating solutions whose validity must await more research. In other words, since ours is an attempt to provide a comprehensive descriptive account of Modern Polish, we will maximally refrain from engaging in superfluous theoretical polemic, a position which some readers may find disappointing. The framework adopted in this book is, naturally enough, the one we identify with most closely without following blindly all its consequences or even without agreeing with all its major pronouncements, which, par for the course, evolve as research progresses. Any phonological system can only be described in terms of some theoretical model but in a work concentrating on data, the model, its subtleties, its merits and

demerits, its strong and weak points must be subordinated to descriptive objectives. Readers looking for current theoretical debate will find little here to whet
their appetite or satisfy theoretical thirst but we hope that the rich data we present
will make up for this and will prove more intriguing in the long run than partisan
theoretical statements. The only significant departure from the non-theoretical
stance adopted in this book is the attempt to explore the nature of morphophonological regularities on the basis of Polish. We will not only provide ample
evidence for the distinction between phonology and morphophonology but will
also argue that phonology and morphophonology each display properties of
their own and use fundamentally different mechanisms for the statement of
their regularities. By shedding light on these issues we hope to contribute to an
understanding of the ways in which sounds can function in language.

2

SOME THEORETICAL HURDLES

The present chapter is not an introduction to or even a survey of Government Phonology; listed in the Introduction are numerous sources available in the literature which can adequately serve the purpose of introducing or surveying the model. Here we would like to single out a few issues where clarification seems particularly significant in view of the use that will be made of them in the following chapters. Additionally, some ideas, while well entrenched with GP thinking, need not necessarily be obvious to followers of other frameworks, hence spelling out some details may remove misunderstandings. It should also make it possible for us to apply the model in the course of the analysis without interrupting the discussion by constant references to theoretical issues. Below we concentrate on three groups of problems which, needless to say, are interconnected.

2.1 SYLLABIC CONSTITUENTS AND EMPTY CATEGORIES

The syllable in phonological theory is an issue larger than life. The literature, even if we restrict ourselves to the structuralist and post-structuralist tradition is vast.[1] GP makes its own contribution to the existing abundance of views by stressing (1) the restricted nature of constituent structure and (2) the independence of the syllabic constituent level from the melodic level. We shall look briefly at the two conditions and consider their implications.

The constituents GP recognizes are those of most theories: there is the onset and the rhyme, where the latter in turn is conventionally divided into the nucleus and the coda. Both the onset and the rhyme can be binary in the sense that they can dominate two skeletal points, in which case we talk about branching onsets and rhymes, or non-binary or non-branching when they dominate a single point. No other structures are allowed, and in particular no ternary (or larger) constituents are possible—for the technicalities behind this reasoning see Kaye, Lowenstamm, and

---

[1] A highly personal selection of the most important surveys and contributions includes Kuryłowicz (1948), Haugen (1956), Fudge 1969, Lass (1984: 248–70), Selkirk 1982, Clements and Keyser (1983), Giegerich (1992: ch. 6), Kenstowicz (1994: ch. 6), Blevins (1995), Rennison and Kühnhammer (1999), Ewen and van der Hulst (2001: ch. 3), Gussmann (2002: chs. 4–5), Féry and van de Vijver (2003), and Steriade (2003). Van der Hulst and Ritter (1999) occupy a special place in this list as a collection of both theoretical and descriptive studies.

Vergnaud (1990)) so that the full array of possibilities can be depicted as (1) where (a) exhausts the onset arrangements while (b) those of the rhyme:

(1)   (a) non-branching   branching

(b) non-branching   branching   branching

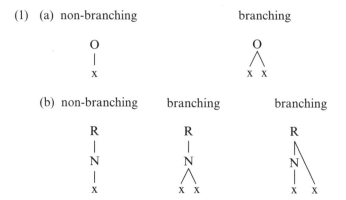

Non-branching onset and rhyme each dominates a single skeletal position, e.g. *ma* [ma] '(s)he has'; a branching onset dominates two skeletal positions, e.g.: [kr] in *krew* [krɛf] 'blood', *mokry* [mɔkrɨ] 'wet'. A rhyme which dominates a branching nucleus covers complex nuclei (long vowels and diphthongs), a possibility which does not exist for Polish. The second type of a branching rhyme where a simplex nucleus is followed by a complement (a coda) is commonplace, as [ar] in *warty* [vartɨ] 'worthy' or [ɛŋ] in *ręka* [rɛŋka] 'hand'. The representations in (1) basically exhaust the structural possibilities for syllabic constituents. A few comments are called for. The segments which qualify for a branching onset have to conform to complexity requirements reminiscent of the sonority cline of classical phonology in that the left-hand or governing member of the onset must be more complex, or stronger, in order to govern the right-hand member; for details see Charette (1991) and Harris (1990, 1994).

Most characteristically, GP does not recognize the syllable as a separate unit of representation (see Brockhaus 1999); in other words, while the existence of constituents such as the onset and the rhyme appears incontrovertible, there is little if any evidence in favour of the two of them together. There are regularities which take the onset, the rhyme, or the nucleus as their domain but those which take the onset and the rhyme at the same time appear lacking.[2] Thus the level above the skeletal one, normally referred to as the syllabic level, consists of sequences of onsets and rhymes. If evidence in favour of the syllabic constituent were to be found, the model could easily be amended to accommodate it. Below, the term 'syllable', when used, should be understood as an informal abbreviation for 'syllabic constituents'.

Another break with tradition is the absence of the coda as a separate constituent; what is usually referred to as the coda is treated as a rhymal complement in

---

[2] Similarly, the syllable as a constituent is rejected by Dziubalska-Kołaczyk (2002), within a somewhat different framework of Beats-and-Binding.

GP. Were it to be a constituent, it should admit both branching and non-branching variants, hence the rhyme could dominate as many as four skeletal positions. The current doctrine allows only two, so it is either a branching nucleus (a long vowel, a diphthong) or a non-branching nucleus and a rhymal complement.[3] We will be using the term 'coda' as an informal shortcut for rhymal complement.

A position where GP makes a drastic break with the past (but cf. Vennemann 1988) concerns the claim that the coda consonant must be licensed by a following onset (Kaye 1990). Codas unlicensed by onsets simply do not exist. This claim, extensively discussed in the literature (Harris 1994: 66–83; Harris and Gussmann 1998, 2002; Gussmann 2002: ch. 6) implies that word-final consonants are *never* codas; since consonants can only be either onsets or codas this means that word-final consonants are always onsets. The conclusion is not just a logical inference from a specific assumption but has been supported by a good deal of empirical evidence discussed in the literature mentioned above. A final implication of the word-final onset claim is that such onsets must be followed, that is, licensed, by a nucleus which dominates no melody, in other words, an empty nucleus. Given this background, consider representations of the word *ręka* [rɛŋka] 'hand', mentioned earlier, and its genitive plural form *rąk* [rɔŋk].

```
(2)  O     R     O     R      O     R     O     R
     |    /\     |     |      |    /\     |     |
     |   N  \    |     N      |   N  \    |     N
     |   |   \   |     |      |   |   \   |     |
     x   x   x   x     x      x   x   x   x     x
     |   |   |   |     |      |   |   |   |     |
     r   ɛ   ŋ   k     a      r   ɔ   ŋ   k
```

Note that syllabically, that is to say, as far as onsets and rhymes are concerned, the two forms are identical: the nasal is a rhymal complement (traditionally, a coda) in both cases, as it is licensed by the following velar plosive in the onset. The final onset in the left-hand representation is uncontroversial presumably under any theory since it is followed by the vowel [a]; GP maintains that the right-hand representation differs from it only in that there is no melody attached to the final nucleus. This provides an instance of what is extensively used in GP, namely, empty categories (onsets and nuclei).

Empty categories are no novelty in contemporary linguistics since one can hardly imagine any work in generative syntax without them. They have also been used in phonology, starting perhaps with Anderson (1982) and Clements and Keyser (1983) and extended to prosodic morphology (see Broselow 1995: 182–5). Conceptually they are completely unsurprising in a tradition which recognizes

---

[3] Provisions have been made for so-called super-heavy rhymes comprising two skeletal positions (Harris 1994: 77–81; Cyran 1994). It remains an open question whether, in a language such as Polish, with no branching nuclei, the coda itself could dominate two positions.

any form of underspecification since an empty onset or an empty nucleus is melodic underspecification taken further a step or two. In this book we shall make extensive use of empty nuclei; it should be noted, however, that empty onsets are also found in Polish although their role in the phonology of the language is limited. As a case in point, consider words which orthographically—and in conventional broad transcription—begin with a vowel. The expression *on i ona* 'he and she' is normally transcribed [ɔn i ɔna] while in actual fact it should be either [ʔɔn ʔi ʔɔna], if a pause is made after every word, or [ʔɔn i ɔna] in connected speech, without pauses. The glottal stop seems to be the regular filler of empty onsets in Polish. However, empty categories in Polish find their fullest confirmation with reference to nuclei; in Chapter 5 we will explore the wide use of empty nuclei and their far-reaching consequences for the vocalic and consonantal phonology of the language.

The view of syllabic organization adumbrated above is based on the independence of the syllabic constituent level from the melodic level. In other words, the syllabic tier consists of sequences of onsets and rhymes of the type listed in (1) and is associated through the skeletal level with melodic units. Crucially, however, the syllabic tier is independent in the sense that it is not a projection of the melodic tier: the syllabic tier combines onsets and rhymes in the same way as the melodic tier combines vowels and consonants. The two tiers are linked but the linkage has to respect the properties of each of them, for instance a branching onset cannot dominate segments where a weaker (less complex) consonant precedes a stronger (more complex one). The claim frequently encountered that a consonantal cluster found word-initially is necessarily a well-formed onset cannot be upheld as mechanically true within this view. Consider a Polish word like *rdza* [rdza] 'rust', with an initial sequence of a sonorant (a trill) followed by an obstruent (an affricate); the complexity/strength requirements would be grossly violated if the word were to begin with a branching onset. Melodically the word starts with a sonorant–obstruent sequence but this does not make the sequence a syllabic unit, i.e. an onset; syllabically the word, as any word, starts with an onset–rhyme sequence but this does not mean that the onset must be attached to whatever is found melodically at the beginning of the word. As we will see in many places in the body of the book, syllabification is not the application of a mechanical algorithm which projects consonants as onsets, failing that as codas, and vowels as nuclei. Were this to be the case, the syllable would arguably be a superfluous device since whatever were to be expressed by it could just as well be expressed by reference to vowel and consonant sequences (a procedure successfully adopted in Chomsky and Halle 1968). Syllabification within GP contributes information which cannot be deduced from or reduced to that coming from linear sequences of vowels and consonants.

A by-product of the mutual independence of syllabic and melodic units is the absence of any notion of resyllabification within GP and the unavailability of such a mechanism in accounting for phonological regularities. Resyllabification is possible within a framework that 'derives' the syllabic level from the melodic one;

given the assumption that a morpheme can have just one phonological representation (inclusive of its syllabic structure), different phonetic forms of that morpheme suggest that resyllabification must have taken place. GP rejects both the
projective nature of syllabification and the single 'underlying' hypothesis; once this
is done, no need for resyllabification arises and the mechanism itself, as, indeed, its
absence, must be seen as resulting from a specific theoretical bias.

Finally, it should be added that the model of syllabic units in (1) is what might
be called the standard or traditional approach. Starting with Lowenstamm
(1996), a view has been developing that recognizes no constituents at all and
where representations consist of CV sequences only. For a specific defence and
application of this model see also Lowenstamm (1999), Rowicka (1999), Szigetvári (1999), Ségéral and Scheer (2001a, b), Cyran (2003), Scheer (2004), and
Scheer and Szigetvári (2005), with numerous other references therein.

2.2 THE IRRELEVANCE OF PHONETICS

It must be stated at the outset that the title of this section is deliberately
provocative and exaggerated. It is intended to underline that the phonetic categories as supplied by the conventional analysis need not be and in many cases
cannot be taken as the proper building blocks of phonological representations
and need not or cannot be reflected in the statement of phonological regularities.
We will adopt the position that whatever is relevant in phonetics is phonological
or that it is phonology that homes in on phonetic relevance (Gussmann 2004b).
The phonetic issue arises in connection with the substance of representations.

Unlike generative phonology, which relies on binary distinctive features, GP,
along with other models (Dependency Phonology, see Durand 1986, Anderson
and Ewen 1987, and Particle Phonology, see Schane 1995, 2005; see also Durand
2005) resorts to monovalent primes called *elements*. Their full list is still a matter
of debate and reduction in the number can be expected; for our purposes we
adopt the following primes in (3):

(3)   {I}   denotes frontness in vowels and palatality in consonants;
       {A} denotes openness of vowels and coronality in consonants;
       {U} denotes rounding of vowels and labiality of consonants;
       {ʔ} denotes occlusion in consonants;
       {h} denotes noise in consonants;
       {N} denotes nasality in vowels and consonants;
       {H} denotes high tone and voicelessness in consonants;
       {L} denotes low tone and voicedness in consonants.

Elements can be combined to form more complex expressions with the salient
element occupying the head position and the remaining ones appearing as
operators. The head position can be empty, in which case the corresponding
non-nuclear expression is a velar consonant and the nuclear one is a lax vowel.

This view of phonological representation invites a question of detailed phonetic interpretability, a question which GP shares with practically all other approaches to phonology. Briefly, phonological descriptions concentrate on the main structural characteristics of the sound system of a given language as seen in distributional restrictions, productive phonological processes and, partly, sound alternations. Within generative phonology the segments, and consequently also the rules, were built round binary distinctive features while in GP both expressions and generalizations are cast in terms of monovalent elements expressing the presence of a certain property. An exposure to elementary phonetics shows that the distinctions which can be heard and produced are much more finely grained than the mere presence (or absence) of, say, voicing, nasality, rounding, or what have you. Structuralist phonology produced several different views with regard to the issue at hand; defining the phoneme as a bundle of distinctive features, it was forced into supplying non-distinctive or redundant features in such a way as to bring the distinctive bundle into conformity with the phonetic requirements; defining the phoneme as a class of sounds it avoided the problems of phonetic characterization of allophones but was forced into the unenviable position of claiming that a word is made up of classes of sounds, for instance. Generative phonology tried to cope with this difficulty by admitting not only binary but also n-ary feature values, which meant that a consonant could be [3voice] or a vowel could be [4nasal]. This programme was consistently applied only with reference to English word stress in Chomsky and Halle (1968) and very early recognized as misguided; while n-ary feature values were still floating around, this was nothing more than lip service paid to a problem for which no cogent or comprehensive account could be offered. GP goes one step further and dismisses the phonetic detail altogether by adopting the position that what counts linguistically is the elemental phonological characterization while the rest is phonetic 'packaging' which plays no role in the functioning of the system (Harris 1996; Harris and Lindsey 2000). Although possibly too curt and rash, the position defines clearly what constitutes the domain of phonological structuring.

The view of phonology that GP promotes is at odds with much of the phonological tradition also because it does not recognize a strict division between phonetics and phonology as commonly understood. This means that the phonological representation is not a subpart of the phonetic one, its filtered-out or depleted version in some sense or that the phonetic representation is a more redundant or enriched version of the phonological representation. Rather, there is just one relevant level (cf. Harris and Lindsey's 1995:46 ff. terse statement: *There is no level of "systematic phonetic" representation*') which contains all the linguistically significant information both with reference to the melody and to phonological relations. Melodically this information consists in a combination of elements whose structural organization contributes to their interpretation (see Ritter 1997, Cyran and Nilsson 1998). What needs to be stressed from our point of view is that the actual elemental composition and structure of an expression is seen as a compromise between the phonological behaviour and the phonetic substance with priority given to the former. In other words, unless we have reason to think otherwise, the phonetic melody will reflect the elements which we posit for the phonological representation. If there are clashes between what the phonic matter and the phonological behaviour prompt, the latter is given the upper hand. Obviously, one would like to reduce both the number of such clashes and the distance between the two sources of evidence, but their existence cannot be ruled out—nor is it anything to be surprised by.

As a case in point consider the Polish alveolar trill [r], as in *rura* [rura] 'tube, pipe'. Phonologically, the consonant seems to be a mono-elemental expression {A}, leaving aside its further structure. Phonetically, the most frequent exponent of this element is the alveolar trill [r], as just mentioned. However, the consonant is subject to tremendous variation, mostly of an idiolectal nature, where side by side with the alveolar trill one also encounters speakers realizing it as the uvular trill [ʀ], the uvular fricative [ʁ], and, on occasion, as a dental approximant [ɹ]. Needless to say, the different phonetic shapes of the consonant have absolutely no bearing on its phonological properties, on its distribution or ability to combine with other segments, or on the morphophonological alternations it is involved in. Thus, where the dominant dialect combines the trill with an obstruent in a branching onset, e.g. [tr, gr], one also finds idiolects with combinations of the obstruent with the uvular trill [tʀ, gʀ], the uvular fricative [tʁ, gʁ], etc.; where the trill can be followed by the central vowel [ɨ] to the exclusion of the front one [i], [rɨ] vs. *[ri], so will the uvular fricative, [ʁɨ] vs. *[ʁi]; where [r] alternates with [ʒ] or [ʃ], so does [ʁ]; as in (4), for example.

(4) gr-a [gra] or [gʁa] 'game'   grz-e [gʒɛ] 'dat. sg.'
     tr-ę [trɛ] or [tʁɛ] 'I rub'   trz-e [tʃɛ] '(s)he rubs'[4]

In other words, being an alveolar trill or a uvular fricative is phonologically insignificant, it is a packaging or a phonetic effect. What matters is the presence of the element {A} and its interaction with the phonological environment. Thus our conventional transcriptions containing the trill [r] should be understood as a short cut for the phonological or linguistically significant representations containing the element {A} attached to a skeletal point which itself is syllabically connected to a non-nuclear position, that is, an onset or a coda.[5] The elements, then, are primarily cognitive units that are only indirectly reflected in the phonetic substance (Harris 1994; Ploch 1999).

---

[4] Throughout the book, Polish examples supplied in conventional spelling are transcribed phonetically and translated. In most cases the conventional spelling is enriched by morphemic divisions indicated by hyphens.

[5] This short discussion disguises—or bypasses—a number of theoretically significant issues. Briefly, it suggests that in acquisition, speakers work out the elemental structure of [r] correctly as {A} but give it distinct articulatory executions. This, in turn, would mean that [r] and, say, [ʁ] have similar acoustic signatures and consequently that pure articulatory categories are incorrect as units of the descriptive phonological alphabet. Another implication should be kept open, namely the possibility of inherent ambiguity in the representation of segments, an ambiguity which creates the space for change. For some technical discussion see Ingleby and Brockhaus (2002).

Another striking illustration of a case where the phonetic packaging must be seen as hiding a phonological structure—a structure which cannot be read off directly from the surface data—concerns the bilabial semivowel [w] of *skała* [skawa] 'rock', *łapa* [wapa] 'paw'. Phonetically, there is little more that can be said about this sound: it is a bilabial semivowel which does not differ from what is found initially in the English *water*. There are some speakers, however, who consistently use the velarized lateral [ł] in words where the absolute majority have [w], i.e. [skała, łapa]. This latter type of pronunciation is used by speakers—mostly of the older generation—from the former Polish eastern territories; elsewhere, and to the extent that it is used at all, [ł] is regarded as an affectation. Generally, the velarized lateral is not found in either standard or regional Polish and Polish learners of, say, Russian have a hard time mastering the sound—normally they replace it by [w].

Historical evidence reveals that the labial glide is a relatively recent arrival in Polish and it seems to have replaced a velarized lateral. We would like to argue that the fully glide-like representation of the former velarized lateral is too radical a step to take with reference to the Polish [w], where by 'a fully glide-like representation' we mean the association of the element {U} to a non-nuclear position.

Our first argument comes from phonotactics. It is generally assumed that branching onsets cannot contain homorganic consonants, a ban that excludes sequences such as [pm, tl]. As our transcriptions above indicate, we find in a dominant (or glide) variety of Polish combinations of labials and the labial glide. More examples follow in (5).

(5) płac-i-ć [pwatɕitɕ] 'pay, vb.'   płot [pwɔt] 'fence'
     pług [pwuk] 'plough, n.'   pływ-a-ć [pwɨvatɕ] 'swim, vb.'
     błąd [bwɔnt] 'mistake'   błękit [bwɛŋcit] 'blueness'
     błag-a-ć [bwagatɕ] 'beg'   błysk [bwɨsk] 'flash, n.'
     własn-ość [vwasnɔɕtɕ] 'property'   władz-a [vwadza] 'power'
     włókn-o [vwuknɔ] 'fibre'   wło-sk-i [vwɔsci] 'Italian'

The evidence is ample and unambiguous: phonetic sequences violating the homorganicity ban are richly attested in the language. Note that in the older/regional variety which maintains the velarized lateral among its sounds, words like those in (5) are totally unremarkable. They all begin with a labial obstruent and a dental lateral [pł, bł, vł], hence no violation of homorganicity is incurred. To avoid the violation in the standard language we have to assume that what is pronounced as [w] is representationally a lateral. One way of thinking of such double identity is to maintain that the elements making up a lateral are present in the structure but are not licensed and hence remain inaudible phonetically. If we were to assume that the lateral is the combination {A•U}, then the standard dialect might be seen as one that has severed the association of {A} with the head element. Graphically, such a lateral masquerading as a semivowel might be represented as

(6)   x
      |
      <u>U</u>

      A

or in some alternative way. The crucial point is that the coronality element remains in the structure and is available for phonotactic purposes.

Another relevant phonotactic observation concerning [w] is that it cannot be followed by the vowel [i] but may be followed by [ɨ]. This restriction holds for the native vocabulary, e.g. *lys-y* [wɨsɨ] 'bald', *zl-y* [zwɨ] 'bad', but it also extends to recent loans; thus *weekend*, originally pronounced [wʲikɛnt] with the strongly non-Polish combination [wʲi], is heard more and more often now as [wɨkɛnt]. On the other hand, the lateral [l] cannot be followed by [ɨ] but readily combines with [i], e.g.: *liść* [liɕtɕ] 'leaf', *dol-i* [dɔli] 'fate, gen. sg.'. In the next chapter, where we analyze the palatalization complex and its connection with vowels, it will be argued that this distribution can be explained if [w] and [l] are seen as related by morphophonological palatalization. It should be added that the Polish lateral [l], while functioning as a palatalized consonant, is phonetically hard in most contexts. Possibly before the vowel [i], it may be pronounced as [lʲ], e.g. *list* [lʲist] (but hardly [ʎist]) 'letter' but generally it is the non-palatalized coronal lateral [l]. This we take to be a phonetic effect, or simply a way a language chooses to realize a certain representational combination phonetically. It hardly needs stressing that arguments for the melodic make-up come primarily from syntagmatic relations. In view of what has been said so far we could represent the lateral [l] as containing the palatality component {I}, which appears together with the coronality element {A} and the delinked labio-velarity {U}, as illustrated in (7).

(7)   x
      |
      A
      |
      I

      U

In terms of the representations (6) and (7), the two segments, while maintaining the element {A}, replace {U} and {I}. To conclude, representationally, Polish has two laterals, a palatalized and a velarized one. The slight paradox is that the palatalized lateral is phonetically non-palatalized while the velarized lateral is phonetically a labial semivowel.

The above examples show that the linguistically significant composition or identity of a segment may depart markedly from the way it is produced and perceived. The linguistic significance can be seen in the way the segment interacts with other segments in the language, in its place in the sound pattern of the language. The phonological patterning overrides considerations of the phonetic substance which at times may disguise the elemental composition, a position which recapitulates Sapir's (1925) view of the relation between phonetics and phonology. In general, the elemental composition of segments must be studied through their involvement in syntagmatic relations. We will find ample evidence for this view in our survey of palatalization-related phenomena.

2.3 MORPHOPHONOLOGY

Phonological regularities within GP are constrained by the possibilities of the model. A requirement is that phonological regularities establish a direct link with the context in which they occur (Kaye, Lowenstamm, and Vergnaud's 1990: 14 non-arbitrariness condition). The context is specifically restricted to phonological information and domain boundaries (Kaye 1995); it should be kept in mind that phonological information should not be equated with traditional phonetic labels as it can also include empty categories and skeletal and syllabic organization. Furthermore, as argued in the preceding section, the phonological specification of segments and properties of their combinations also need to be teased out and disentangled from the raw data: it is not the case that the primary data are given and the analyst's job is to interpret them. Quite conversely, the analyst's job consists largely in identifying the data. In any event, phonological operations within GP are local in that they spread or delink elements of the melodic level as conditioned by the phonological contexts.

Phonology circumscribed along such lines does not exhaust the domain of sound structure. For this reason a return to morphophonology is postulated; large chunks of this book will be devoted to the description of non-phonological alternations. Such alternations range from robust and productive to individual and idiosyncratic: an adequate description must reflect them in some way. Since segment alternations have played a major role in the development of derivational–generative phonology and have been studied for Polish in great detail, we believe that while not part of phonology proper as GP sees it, they should also be presented in this book. Stating that non-phonological alternations belong to morphophonology does not in itself solve anything, apart from coming close to circularity. Morphophonological alternations are defined negatively as those for which no non-arbitrary phonological description is available. It is crucial that they cannot be handled phonologically in a non-arbitrary fashion although, as the history of phonology shows, theoretical ingenuity has often served as a replacement for insightfulness.

As an illustration of the need for non-arbitrariness, we shall look briefly at the denominal suffix -arz [aʃ] which is used to derive agentive nouns. This suffix and others will be discussed at length in the body of the book; here we will merely indicate what is meant by non-phonological alternations. The suffix can be added to noun stems ending in a consonant; this effects no changes in the shape of the base, in other words, no alternations emerge.

(8) karczm-a [kartʃma] 'inn'   karczm-arz [kartʃmaʃ] 'inn-keeper'
     młyn [mwɨn] 'mill'   młyn-arz [mwɨnaʃ] 'miller'
     piłk-a [pʲiwka] 'ball'   piłk-arz [pʲiwkaʃ] 'ball-player'

However, in a number of other cases involving the same suffix, the stem-final consonant is modified, as shown by the following examples:

(9) reklam-a [rɛklama] 'advertisement'   reklami-arz [rɛklamʲaʃ] 'advertiser'
     komin [kɔmʲin] 'chimney'   komini-arz [kɔmʲiɲaʃ] 'chimney-sweep'
     mlek-o [mlɛkɔ] 'milk'   mlecz-arz [mlɛtʃaʃ] 'milkman'

The significance of such examples cannot be overstated: in an identical morphological context a consonant either is or is not replaced by its palatal(ized) counterpart. One can easily devise ad hoc means of handling the data; for instance, the vowel of the palatalizing suffix in (9) can be represented as [æ] and assigned the palatalizing role and converted to [a] after doing its job. Alternatively, the suffix in (9) can be supplied with two vowels, [ia], of which the first is deleted after evincing palatalization. There is little point in pursuing this line of thinking. What is crucial is that we are dealing with the same morphological unit which appears to produce different effects on the final consonant of the base. There is nothing in the base or in the suffix that could justify a phonological interpretation of the alternations in (9) as against the absence of any such alternations in (8). Short of marking individual lexical items for their susceptibility to palatalization, in effect abandoning any claim to the phonological nature of the process, we have no way of ensuring where palatalization will take place. This means quite simply that alternations normally subsumed under the palatalization heading are not of a phonological nature and cannot be described within phonology. Their place is within morphophonology. This line of reasoning will be pursued in subsequent chapters.

The preceding discussion has outlined problem areas in a general and deliberately inconclusive way. A description of the phonology of a single language is not the place for excessive theoretical speculation, but theoretical issues cannot be avoided if a description is to go beyond whimsically garnered lists of examples. The central ideas of GP that we identified in this chapter will be put to use in this study of Polish and it is there that their role and strength will be tested.

PALATALIZATIONS AND THE VOWEL SYSTEM

3.1 OVERVIEW

The chapter presents the phonology of palatals and palatalized consonants. The discussion is placed against the background of the earlier descriptions within the structuralist and the generative traditions which viewed the palatalization complex in largely divergent ways. What is common to all traditions is the mutual dependence of consonantal and vocalic units (phonemes, segments) and relations (rules). This insight is adopted here and consonantal palatalization phenomena are studied in close connection with vocalic variability (vowel alternations).

Contrary to the structuralist tradition, which viewed palatalizations as historical relics and, contrary to the generative paradigm, which interpreted most palatals as resulting from live synchronic processes, it is shown that palatalized consonants are due to live phonological regularities in restricted cases only (labials and velars). The massive alternations involving palatals and palatalized segments must be described as morphophonological relations.

The elemental representations of vowels and consonants viewed as syntagmatic units and involved in the phonological palatalization are investigated. The approach allows us to explain a number of striking distributional gaps (the absence of certain vowels word initially, for example) and the restricted combinability of certain vowels and consonants. A few constraints are put forward which control the observed phonological behaviour.

3.2 PALATALIZED LABIALS AND PROBLEMS OF THE VOWEL SYSTEM

Polish palatalized labial consonants constitute a long-standing issue in the phonology of the language. Phonetically, five such consonants must be identified, [pʲ, bʲ, mʲ, fʲ, vʲ], as in the following examples:

(1) pi-ć [pʲitɕ] 'drink,vb.'   pięść [pʲɛ̃ɕtɕ] 'fist'
     bi-ł [bʲiw] 'he beat'   biał-y [bʲawɨ] 'white'
     mił-y [mʲiwɨ] 'nice'   miód [mʲut] 'honey'
     fik-a-ć [fʲikatɕ] 'frolic' fiolet [fʲɔlɛt] 'violet'
     widok [vʲidɔk] 'sight'   wiar-a [vʲara] 'faith'

A tradition that goes back to Baudouin de Courtenay and classical structuralism maintains that palatalized labials are just labials with the added component of palatality. This leads to the view that palatalization is a distinctive marker contrasting palatalized and non-palatalized consonants. Instances of contrast can easily be supplied:

(2) pasek [pasɛk] 'strap'   piasek [pʲasɛk] 'sand'
     bał-y [bawɨ] 'they (fem.) feared' biał-y [bʲawɨ] 'white'
     mał-y [mawɨ] 'small'   mia-ł-y [mʲawɨ] 'they (fem.) had'
     fok [fɔk] 'seal, gen. pl.'   fiok [fʲɔk] 'hair lock'
     wara [vara] 'beware'   wiar-a [vʲara] 'faith'

The recognition of distinctive units such as [b–bʲ] has a direct bearing on the contrastive vowel system of the language. As mentioned in Chapter 1, it is generally agreed that the basic phonetic inventory of oral vowels embraces the following units: [i, ɨ, ɛ, u, ɔ, a]. All these vowels except [ɨ] can appear after palatalized labials, whereas [i] is never found after non-palatalized consonants, as shown in (1) and (2). This restriction is traditionally accounted for by an analysis in which labials allow for the structural conflation of the two phonetic segments [i] and [ɨ] into one phonological unit, with a straightforward distribution: [ɨ] appears after non-palatalized consonants, while [i] occurs elsewhere. This means that pairs of words such as

(3) pi-ł [pʲiw] 'he drank'   pył [pɨw] 'dust'
     mił-y [mʲiwɨ] 'nice'   my-ł-y [mɨwɨ] 'they (fem.) washed'

differ phonologically in the nature of the labial, which can be either palatalized or non-palatalized. The nature of the following vowel—either [i] or [ɨ]—is determined by the preceding consonant. Thus a phoneme-based representation of the words would not distinguish them vocalically but consonantally as /pʲiw/–/piw/, /mʲiwi/–/miwi/, etc. The analysis predicts, correctly, that combinations of a palatalized consonant and a retracted vowel, i.e. *[pʲɨ], or of a non-palatalized consonant and a front vowel, i.e. *[pi], never emerge and, in fact, are totally impossible phonetically.

The conflation of the two vowels [i] and [ɨ] into one contrastive unit was hailed as a major result of the structuralist analysis, primarily because it allows us to lower the overall number of vocalic contrastive units. Furthermore, the analysis appears to supply an elegant account for allophonic variation: the front or palatal vowel appears after a palatalized or front consonant and the retracted or non-palatalized vowel manifests itself after a non-palatalized consonant. The impossible combinations noted above, *[pʲɨ] *[pi], are exactly what can be expected if the quality of the vowels in question is determined by the palatal quality of the preceding consonant.

The same reasoning has been used to account for a puzzling gap in the distribution of the vowel [ɨ], namely, its total absence word-initially. While there is no shortage of words, both native and foreign, beginning with [i], such as *igla* [igwa] 'needle', *iść* [içtç] 'go', *idea* [idɛa] 'idea', *Itaka* [itaka] 'Ithaca', no word can begin with [ɨ]. This is hardly surprising, a structuralist analysis would reply, since the result is exactly what complementary distribution predicts. It should be added, however, that while the post-consonantal distribution of vowels can be viewed as phonetic—or assimilatory—in nature, nothing of this sort can readily be claimed for the word-initial situation: there is no conceivable phonetic argument which would require initial [i] rather than [ɨ]. Note that the neat or elegant statement of the distribution—[ɨ] after non-palatalized consonants and [i] elsewhere—could easily be replaced by a different but equally neat or elegant claim: [i] after palatalized consonants and [ɨ] elsewhere. The revised version preserves the original insight about the close connection of vowel and consonant frontness, while it is factually incorrect about the vowel quality appearing word-initially. In other words, the relation between vowel quality and the initial position remains arbitrary, in no way disguised by what complementary distribution succeeds in capturing. Unless the complementary distribution statement connects the variant with the context in an explanatory fashion, as it does in the consonant–vowel combination, it is nothing more than a re-statement of facts. If the facts were completely different, a statement covering them in an observationally adequate way would remain equally non-explanatory. Thus the total exclusion of [ɨ] word-initially continues to be a mystery for which an adequate explanation must be sought.

Another striking property of the palatalized labials needs to be mentioned here, namely, the fact that their distribution is restricted to the position before a vowel. No palatalized labials appear either pre-consonantally or word-finally. If such consonants are forced by the morphology into word-final or pre-consonantal position, they emerge non-palatalized. Consider the following examples (disregard final obstruent devoicing):

(4) ziemi-a [ʑɛmʲa]   ziem [ʑɛm]   ziem-n-y [ʑɛmnɨ]
     'earth'   'gen. pl.'   'adj.'

     ziem-sk-i [ʑɛmsci]   ziem-ni-ak [ʑɛmɲak]
     'adj.'   'potato'

     gołębi-a [gɔwɛmbʲa]   gołąb [gɔwɔmp]   gołęb-n-y [gɔwɛmbnɨ]
     'pigeon, gen. sg.'   'nom. sg.'   'adj.'

     gołęb-nik [gɔwɛmbɲik]
     'dovecote'

     żółwi-a [ʒuwvʲa]   żółw [ʒuwf]
     'turtle, gen. sg.'   'nom. sg.'

The regularity here is quite straightforward and exceptionless: no palatalized labials are found before a consonant or at the end of the word. At least two options for describing this situation are at hand. For one thing, one could resort to the notion of defective distribution and claim that palatalized labials do not appear word-finally and pre-consonantally. Alternatively, in terms of a model which recognises the non-arbitrary nature of such restricted distribution we might say that palatalization is neutralized for labials word-finally and pre-consonantally. It is perhaps noteworthy that the neutralization also embraces the suppression of palatalization before what is itself a palatalized consonant: *ziem-ni-ak* [ʑɛmɲak] 'potato', *gołęb-nik* [gɔwɛmbɲik] 'dovecote', thus the suppression becomes a case of dissimilation. Stating that a certain property is neutralized in some context basically amounts to making an observation about the distribution of segments without supplying any rationale for that distribution. In this sense, whether we speak of defective distribution or neutralization makes little difference. Put simply, why should palatal labials get depalatalized before another consonant, including another palatal(ized) consonant? Thus, within the classical analysis, palatalized labials must be followed by a vowel. Additionally, within the defective distribution approach, the alternations of palatalized and non-palatalized labials as in (4) would have to be handled by a morphophonological statement since the consonants involved must be treated as realizing separate phonemes (see (2)).

The above interpretation is not the only structural effort attempting to come to grips with the palatalized labial complex. It has been noted that an increasing tendency with palatalized labials is to pronounce them *asynchronously*, that is, in such way that the palatalization gesture is retarded with respect to the labial gesture. As briefly described in Chapter 1 the result is that the palatalized labials come to be followed by the glide [j]. The asynchronous pronunciation seems to be the norm before back vowels, apparently less dominant before the front [ɛ] and not found at all before the front high vowel [i] (see Karaś and Madejowa 1977: LV and the body of the dictionary). Hence, the left-hand-column words in (1) maintain the synchronous pronunciation while those in the right-hand column are more adequately transcribed with a glide following the palatalized labial. The revised transcriptions are given in (5).

(5) pi-ć [pʲitɕ] 'drink,vb.'   pięść [pʲjɛ̃ɕtɕ] 'fist'
     bi-ł [bʲiw] 'he beat'   biał-y [bʲjawɨ] 'white'
     mił-y [mʲiwɨ] 'nice'   miód [mʲjut] 'honey'
     fik-a-ć [fʲikatɕ] 'frolick' fiolet [fʲjɔlɛt] 'violet'
     widok [vʲidɔk] 'sight'   wiar-a [vʲjara] 'faith'

Since the glide is an independent phonological unit (cf. *da-m* [dam] 'I'll give'~ *da-sz* [daʃ] 'you'll give'~*da* [da] '(s)he'll give'~*daj* [daj] 'imper. sg.'), the pairs of words in (2) which were used to argue for the phonemic status of palatalized labials now lead to different conclusions. A word like *biał-y* is now transcribed [bʲjawɨ], differing from a word like *ba-l-y* [bawɨ] not only in the palatalization of the initial consonant but also in the presence of the palatal glide.

Adopting a transcription which mirrors more closely the current pronunciation we discover that palatalized labials appear in two contexts, namely, before the front high vowel [i] and before the palatal glide [j]. The appearance of a palatalized consonant before a prototypically palatalizing vowel and the palatal glide points to an alternative interpretation of the facts, where palatalized labials are contextual variants of labials before /i/ and /j/. This allows us to reduce the inventory of contrastive segments by five since none of the palatalized labial consonants appears in it any longer; the palatal glide, as we just noted, needs to be recognized as a contrastive segment in any analysis, so the only addition to the list of phonological segments is the vocalic contrast /i~ɨ/. In this way the net gain of four contrastive segments can be effected.

This analysis has enjoyed considerable popularity (Zwoliński 1958; Jassem 1966; Biedrzycki 1963, 1978) and it is not without its strong points. It has often been noted that speakers of Polish very strongly feel that the vowels [i] and [ɨ] are different and separate units, unlike the palatalized and non-palatalized labials. Regrettably, the strength of this argument cannot be evaluated in any but most superficially impressionistic terms. We will disregard it in the overall evaluation of the proposal.

We will also leave aside the argument concerned with the numerical reduction of contrastive segments, since this may be regarded as only a limited achievement. It must be stressed that the analysis, as it stands, provides a simple and natural account of the appearance of palatalized labials. These are possible before two most strongly palatalizing segments, namely the vowel [i] and the semivowel [j]. Palatalized labials are contextually limited allophones of labial consonant in a palatalizing environment, a phenomenon which is completely unremarkable. There is no need to invoke any defective distribution or palatalized labial neutralization with its peculiar claim that disallows the consonants in a disjoint set of contexts (word-finally and pre-consonantally), and surreptitiously introduces a dissimilatory sub-clause. The strong points of this interpretation must be juxtaposed with its weaker sides.

The first major weakness of the reinterpretation is, in fact, the perfect inverse of its strength: while we seem to understand the limited distribution of palatalized labials, we have absolutely nothing to say about other restrictions involving the new inventory of phonemes. For one thing, there is absolutely no reason why the now contrastive vowels /i/ and /ɨ/ cannot appear in the same context, and thus, for example, word-initially. While earlier on, this restriction was blamed on the complementary distribution of the two vowels, we have now deprived ourselves of this glib excuse and may only fall back again on the notion of defective distribution of phonemes. This is nothing but a gesture of phonological despair which admits that it does not understand why things are the way they are. Note, however, that in this the interpretation is not really different from the earlier one where we found no justification for the peculiar distribution of allophones, either—there is no reason why [ɨ] is barred from the word-initial position. Thus, in one case we speak of the defective distribution of the phonemes /i/ and /ɨ/, in the other, of the arbitrary allophonic variation of [i] and [ɨ]. When all is said and done, the two solutions are equally arbitrary with reference to this specific set of data.

Moving into the non-labial region for a moment we find there areas where the second solution fares less impressively than the first one. Note that after palatalized non-labial consonants we find the front vowel [i], while after non-palatalized ones we find [ɨ]:

(6) (a) sił-a [ɕiwa] 'strength'   zim-a [ʑima] 'winter'
       nigdy [ɲigdɨ] 'never'   dzik-i [dʑici] 'savage'
       cisz-a [tɕiʃa] 'silence'   wrog-i [vrɔɟi] 'hostile'
       chichot [ɕixot] 'giggle, n.'

    (b) sygnał [sɨgnaw] 'signal, n.'   łz-y [wzɨ] 'tear, nom. pl.'
       ryb-a [rɨba] 'fish, n.'   nygus [nɨgus] 'brat'
       dyni-a [dɨɲa] 'pumpkin'   tygiel [tɨɟɛl] 'crucible'
       cynk [tsɨŋk] 'zink'   rdz-y [rdzɨ] 'rust, gen. sg.'
       czyn [tʃɨn] 'deed'   drożdż-y [drɔʒdʒɨ] 'yeast, gen. pl.'
       szyb-k-o [ʃɨpkɔ] 'quickly'   żyt-o [ʒɨtɔ] 'rye'
       chytr-y [xɨtrɨ] 'cunning'

In (6a) we have examples where the front (palatal) vowel [i] follows a palatalized consonant, whereas in (6b) the retracted vowel [ɨ] appears after a non-palatalized consonant. The distribution makes phonetic sense and conforms to what is found in the appropriate contexts involving labials. The intuitive, two-vowel solution is pretty helpless in the face of these facts; if /i/ and /ɨ/ are independent units—just as, say, /a/ and /ɔ/—then they should be able to combine freely with other segments, be they palatalized or non-palatalized. It is no doubt unreasonable to expect lexical support for every segment combining with every other segment. It is equally unreasonable to tolerate a reverse situation, however. The fact that the allegedly independent phoneme /i/ can never follow non-palatalized phonemes while an equally independent phoneme /ɨ/ can never come after a palatalized phoneme is an unmistakable sign that the analysis is seriously flawed. The distributional vagaries are not the only indicator of this conclusion.

Another relevant piece of evidence concerns the numerous alternations between the vowel [ɛ] and zero (described in detail in Ch. 5). Some examples are presented in (7).

(7) wini-en [vʲiɲɛn] 'guilty'   win-n-a [vʲinna] 'fem.'
    godzi-en [gɔdʑɛn] 'worthy'   god-n-a [gɔdna] 'fem.'
    len [lɛn] 'linen'   ln-u [lnu] 'gen. sg.'
    bodzi-ec [bɔdʑɛts] 'stimulus'   bodź-c-a [bɔtɕtsa] 'gen. sg.'
    chrzest [xʃɛst] 'baptism'   chrzt-u [xʃtu] 'gen. sg.'
    wyżeł [vɨʒɛw] 'pointer'   wyżł-y [vɨʒwɨ] 'nom. pl.'

Leaving aside the phonological or morphophonological nature of the alternation, one thing is beyond dispute, namely, that the alternation involves the vowel [ɛ] and zero. Against this background consider the forms in (8):

(8)   pewien [pɛvʲjɛn] 'certain'   pewn-a [pɛvna] 'fem.'
      pies [pʲjɛs] 'dog'   ps-a [psa] 'gen. sg.'
      wy-bier-a-ć [vɨbʲjɛratɕ] 'choose'   wy-br-a-ć [vɨbratɕ] 'id. perf.'
      samiec [samʲjɛts] 'male'   samc-a [samtsa] 'gen. sg.'

The significance of these examples cannot be overstated: if taken seriously they point to the existence of two different types of alternation involving zero. On the one hand we have the vowel [ɛ], as in the examples in (7). The examples in (8) would have to mean that the alternation of [jɛ] with zero also exists in Polish. Strangely enough, the latter type of alternation would be restricted to the context after a labial consonant. In any event, the unity of the alternation would be destroyed even though in other ways—(morpho)phonologically, grammatically, and even lexically, the two groups behave identically. The need to recognize these two distinct types of alternation could only be a by-product of a faulty interpretation.

We have seen that the traditional formulation conflating [i] and [ɨ] into one phoneme fares much better in *not* creating massive and unaccountable gaps in the distribution and combinability of phonological segments. In some cases the two interpretations are equally weak or flawed. The only area where the more recent analysis treating /i/ and /ɨ/ as distinctive units scores better is in the number of phonemes that need to be recognized. It is doubtful whether the economy of four such segments comes anywhere near compensating for the linguistic complications and artificialities the economy introduces into a complete description.[1]

The above survey, in addition to focussing on the respective advantages and disadvantages of the two solutions, has taken them as a starting point for identifying the phonological issues that the palatalized labial consonants confront us with. The following areas will be regarded as worthy of an insightful discussion:

(9)   1. the relation between the vowels [i∼ɨ] and the preceding consonants;
      2. the absence of [ɨ] word-initially;
      3. the impossibility of palatalized labials pre-consonantally and word-finally;
      4. the almost general phonetic realization of palatalized labials as sequences with the palatal glide before a vowel, unless the vowel happens to be [i].

We shall try to study these questions in a framework where individual segments play a far less important role than was the case in either classical structuralism or classical generativism.

Let us start by considering some representational possibilities as far as palatalized labials are concerned. The most obvious way might perhaps be to regard

---

[1] With respect to the derivational analyses, which will be discussed in detail below, it can be noted here that palatalized labials were viewed as predominantly derived from plain ones in the context of a following front vowel; the vowel would often be deleted or turned into a back (non-palatalizing) segment. For a survey of the generative views see Gussmann (1992a).

palatalized labials proper, [mʲ, pʲ] etc., as dominated by a single skeletal position, while the decomposed or asynchronous ones, i.e. [mʲj, pʲj], as representing two such positions. In the latter case we would then be dealing with a branching onset with the glide appearing in the governed position. The simplified representations might take the following forms:

(10)

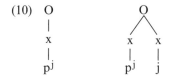

In Government Phonology terms, the melodic complex represented as [pʲ] would be a shorthand for the element combination {ʔ•U•H•h•I}, that is, stopness, labiality, tonality (voicelessness), noise, and palatality. Even if the number of elements making up the expression could be reduced, it would still remain a very complex segment. Hence it is not surprising that a fissure into two segments could take place and thus a branching onset could be formed. The palatal glide in it is nothing but the element {I} associated with a non-nuclear position, such as the governed or right-hand member of a branching onset. The branching onset in (10) would presumably contain a single instance of the palatality element doubly attached to both skeletal positions; hence the elemental representation could have the following shape:

(10′)

Representations along the lines of (10′) might be claimed to reflect fairly closely the phonetic facts. Polish seems to be in the process of change from a mono-segmental pronunciation of palatalized labials to a bi-segmental one. In phonological terms this would appear to be quite a drastic change. It would involve in the first place a melody fissure with the palatality now being copied onto a separate skeletal position; concomitantly, however, the onset would change from a non-branching into a branching one.[2]

Obviously, these are possible and plausible steps if the constituent structure change is merely a mechanical consequence of the melody fissure. The mechanical change of constituent structure is a complication since in the framework adopted here, constituent structure is not a mere projection of segmental sequencing but enjoys a large degree of independence. The fact that a very minor change in

---

[2] Since we are entertaining a theoretical possibility we do not need to explore how the loss of palatality would work if it were to be a phonological regularity and what it would mean if it were a morphophonological modification.

articulation should automatically bring about a syllabic restructuring seems far-fetched. What would be even more complicated are the alternations of the vowel [ɛ] and zero—in fact, of the sequence [jɛ] with zero, as illustrated in (8). We would need not only to simplify the melody by suppressing [j] but also to remove its skeletal position and consequently change the branching onset into a non-branching one. Given these complications, it is worth considering an alternative interpretation. It is quite close to the representations in (10′) but exploits the phonological mechanism for representing complex melodies such as short diph-thongs and affricates.

We wish to propose that a melody complex attached to a single skeletal position, as in the left-hand structure in (10′), best represents the single complex palatalized labial. The fissured representation, on the other hand, continues to be dominated by a single position though the element for palatality is detached from elements characterizing labial plosives. Thus, rather than (10′), we propose (11) as an adequate specification of the consonants.

(11)

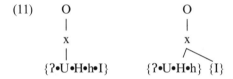

The difference is not only notational. The bi-segmental representation is such on the melodic level only, while the skeletal and the syllabic structures are identical in both cases. The fissured structure is just like that for an affricate where a changing melody behaves as a single segment. This representation avoids the pitfalls of the traditional two-segment interpretation. First of all, the alter-nation between the vowel [ɛ] and zero need not be complicated since the glide is not part of the nucleus or of the preceding branching onset but part of the mono-segmental non-branching onset. The pre-consonantal and word-final depalatali-zation involves a melodic simplification without any concomitant change in the higher levels of representation, skeletal or syllabic. Finally, and perhaps least importantly, it treats the diachronic change together with its synchronic dialectal variation [pʲ] > [pʲj] as a minor phonetic modification which has little phono-logical significance.

The monosegmental interpretation of palatalized labials has an interesting side-effect: it seems to hold good for native or assimilated vocabulary. In weakly assimilated loanwords the pronunciation without the glide does not seem possible in the varieties or dialects which normally favour glide-less palatalized labials. Thus, in the examples in (12) the glide is obligatory in all varieties of Polish.

(12)   biografi-a [bʲjɔgrafʲja] 'biography'
       fobi-a [fɔbʲja] 'phobia'

mafi-a [mafʲja] 'mafia'
rewi-a [rɛvʲja] 'variety show'
infami-a [infamʲja] 'infamy'

The palatal glide in these forms can be interpreted as a separate melody *cum* skeletal position, that is, as the right-hand representation in (10) and (10′). There may also be morphophonological reasons to think that the glide does not form a branching onset with the preceding labial but belongs to a separate onset: *mafi-a* yields an adjective *mafij-n-y* [mafʲijnɨ] 'of the mafia' where the palatalized [fʲ] and the glide [j] are separated by a nucleus and of necessity appear in two distinct onsets. This brings us to the unexpected conclusion that the palatalized labial in a sequence such as [fʲja] emerges as a phonetic result of the glide following a plain consonant (*mafi-a* [mafʲja]); however, the [fʲ] in *mafij-n-y* [mafʲijnɨ] (*[mafɨjnɨ]) is a single segment with inherent palatality, as in the left-hand representations of (10, 10′, 11). On reflection, the conclusion is in fact quite welcome: an adjective like *mafij-n-y* is very much a native formation albeit with a foreign base, hence it displays native properties such as the existence of palatalized labials. The base *mafi-a* is felt to be entirely foreign and this has its phonological consequences. In subsequent sections we will see other cases where a word with a foreign base and a native inflectional or derivational suffix exhibits partly native behaviour and partly non-native.

An additional remark concerning the traditional process of depalatalization is called for. The depalatalization is, in our terms, nothing more far-reaching than a suppression of the element {I} in the melody. This takes place before a consonant or at the end of a word. Interpreted syllabically, word-final position is the onset licensed by an empty nucleus. Similarly, what is a pre-consonantal position is, in effect, a position before a silent nucleus, an obvious conclusion in view of the vowel–zero alternations, e.g. *pies* [pʲɛs] 'dog'~*ps-y* [psɨ] 'nom. pl.'. Labial depalatalization can thus be regarded as the loss of the element {I} before an empty nucleus; this, however, fails to cover the absence of palatalized labials in branching onsets, in other words, the non-existence and impossibility of onsets like *[pʲl, bʲr, fʲl] and the like. The non-existence of such forms is not inconsistent with {I}-loss before an empty nucleus but, presumably, would need to be stated separately as a ban on palatalized labials in branching onsets. Rather than doing that, we can reformulate the labial depalatalization regularity as a licensing constraint which connects positively the appearance of the consonants with phonetically realized nuclei.[3] A preliminary version of the constraint is given in (13).

(13) *Depalatalization constraint I*
The element {I} in a labial consonant must be directly licensed by a melodically filled nucleus.

---

[3] For a discussion of the role of licensing constraints in GP, see Kaye (2001).

The formulation of the constraint will be refined as we proceed, so at this stage we need to note only that it accounts for the absence of palatalized labials in any but the prevocalic position. Vocalic is understood here to denote a nucleus dominating a melody. It is perhaps not necessary to indicate that the depalatalization constraint does no depalatalizing in the traditional or the derivational generative sense of the word in that it does not convert a palatalized consonant into its non-palatalized congener. Rather, it amounts to a statement that the only place where palatalized labials can make their appearance is before a vowel. Obviously, by extension, the constraint also defines contexts where a palatalized labial cannot appear. This covers both the position of the head in a branching onset, in a coda position and in a word-final non-branching onset.

It seems that the constraint and the accompanying discussion provide a partial answer to question 3 in (9)—the impossibility of palatalized labials pre-consonantally and word-finally. What is more, the constraint is reflected in the morphology of the language in a way which merits some discussion now. The problem is found within nominal flection where some stem-final labials emerge palatalized before a vocalic desinence (14a) and others remain intact (14b). The desinence we use is -a [a], representing the genitive singular.

(14) (a) Wrocław [vrɔtswaf] 'place name'   Wrocławi-a [vrɔtswavʲa]
         Radom [radɔm] 'place name'   Radomi-a [radɔmʲa]
         karp [karp] 'carp'   karpi-a [karpʲa]
         jastrząb [jast-ʃɔmp] 'hawk'   jastrzębi-a [jast-ʃɛmbʲa]

      (b) Kraków [krakuf] 'place name'   Krakow-a [krakova]
         Chełm [xɛwm] 'place name'   Chełm-a [xɛwma]
         sęp [sɛmp] 'vulture'   sęp-a [sɛmpa]
         ząb [zɔmp] 'tooth'   zęb-a [zɛmba]

Given the depalatalization constraint (13) we can account for the apparently aberrant behaviour of final labials before a suffixal vowel. All we need to assume is that the stems illustrated in (14a) end in a palatalized labial while those in (14b) in a plain labial. Constraint (13) ensures that the {I} element associated with some occurrences of the labial is not licensed, hence labials are not pronounced/heard as palatalized. This means, of course, that what appears to be one segment may, in fact, be two (or more) when interpreted as a unit of the phonological organization. In a way which is hardly questionable, phonological units cannot be read off from the phonetic.

The complex segmental nature of palatalized labials as in (11) coupled with the depalatalization constraint (13) jointly provide a straightforward answer to the question of why the glide is heard before all vowels except for a following [i]. Obviously, a following vowel licenses the {I} element in the preceding onset which can thus be realized phonetically. When the licensing vowel is [i], in other words, when the nucleus contains just the {I} element itself, the same element would appear in two successive phonological expressions. The well-known mechanism of the Obligatory Contour Principle (OCP) ensures that the two instances of the same element are conflated, as in the diagram in (15) for the pronoun *mi* [mʲi] 'me, dat.'.

(15)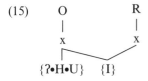

The double attachment of the element {I} is responsible for the perception of labial palatality followed by the vowel [i]; if the rhyme were to contain other elements, then {I} would be heard as a separate glide after a palatalized labial, as in the word *pies* [pʲɛs] 'dog'.

(16)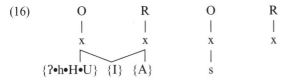

Within GP, the association of both {I} and {A} with the same skeletal position specifies the phonetic vowel [ɛ].

    We are now ready to face the question of the relation between the vowels [i] and [ɨ], that is, their mutual exclusiveness. Note that after palatalized labials and—more generally—all palatalized consonants the retracted vowel [ɨ] is not possible and, conversely, [i] cannot follow a plain (non-palatalized) consonant: *[mʲɨ], *[mi]. The only attested combinations are [i] after a palatalized consonant and [ɨ] after a plain one: *mi* [mʲi] 'me', *my* [mɨ] 'we'. Both vowels contain the element {I} and the representational difference between them reduces to whether this element is in the head or the operator position. The front and tenser [i] is normally regarded as headed while the retracted and laxer [ɨ] contains the element in the operator position and is empty headed. If the two nuclei were to appear in isolation, their presumed representational shape would be as in (17), where, by convention, the head element is underlined:

(17)

The left-hand expression contains just the element {I} in the head position and represents the vowel [i], while the empty-headed expression with {I} as operator represents [ɨ]. We now need to connect the appearance of the two vowels with the character of the preceding consonant.

It is generally accepted that palatalized consonants contain the active palatality element {I} as their salient property. This means that not only our labials but also coronals and velars, all listed in (18), comprise in their melodic make-up this particular element.

(18)   pʲ   bʲ   mʲ
       fʲ   vʲ

       ɕ   ʑ   ɲ
       tɕ   dʑ
       c   ɟ   ç

The element {I} appears not only in these expressions since the palatal consonants [tʃ, dʒ, ʃ, ʒ] are assumed to contain it as well. What distinguishes these consonants from those in (18) is the position of the element in the structure of the expression. In what follows we will assume that in truly palatalized consonants the element {I} occupies the salient head position, while in the palatal ones it is one of the operators. What thus turns the palatalized consonants in (18)—and also the non-nuclear {I} itself, i.e. [j]—into one group, a natural class, is the fact that they are all headed by {I}.

Returning now to the distribution of the vowels [i, ɨ] after consonants, it is easy to observe that the I-headedness of the consonant goes hand in hand with the I-headedness of the following vocalic expression. The gist of this relationship, which can be formalized in a few ways, is that the element {I} must occupy either the head or the operator position *both* in the onset *and* in the nucleus simultaneously. No misalignment is possible here. We will refer to this restriction as the *I-alignment* and formulate it tentatively as follows:

(19)   *I-alignment*
       {I} occupies the same intrasegmental position in onset-nucleus pairs.

The formulation requires some discussion. At face value, I-alignment maintains that there is total agreement in the positioning of the {I} element between the onset and the nucleus: either it is head or operator in both constituents. As an example consider the words in (20).

(20)   (a) mich-a [mʲixa] 'big basin'
       (b) cich-a [tɕixa] 'silent, fem.'
       (c) czyh-a [tʃɨxa] '(s)he lurks'
       (d) kich-a [cixa] '(s)he sneezes'

The word-initial onsets in (20a, b, d) are described as palatalized consonants. In our terms this means that they are I-headed and the following vowel containing the element {I} may place it only in the head position. In (20c), on the other hand, the initial onset [tʃ] also contains the element {I} in its composition which must agree in its placement with that of the following nucleus; in this instance they are both operators. As above, however, (see (15)) there is only one instance of the element, which is shared by the onset-nucleus domain, due to the OCP. In other words, the element is shared or doubly attached to the onset and the nuclear position. In the case of palatalized onsets the element is head of both expressions, just as it is operator in both with non-palatalized onsets:

(21)

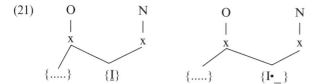

The above interpretation may be viewed as onset-driven, in other words, it seems to be the case that the headedness of the nucleus is determined by the onset. This would be strongly reminiscent of the traditional Slavic view of the sounds [i] and [ɨ] constituting a single phoneme whose contextual realization depends on the segment (if any) that precedes. Such a perspective, although it is possible in some cases, is an oversimplification if taken as generally valid. Note that representations like those in (21) are not the result of turning an underlying segment into some surface realization or the selection of an allophone in a context but simply a static representation capturing the relevant generalizations. Within the framework of this book the distinction between underlying and surface, or phonemic and allophonic, loses its significance; as discussed in Chapter 2, there are no hidden structures from which concrete, phonetic forms are derived—recall again the apt formulation of Harris and Lindsey (1995: 46): '*there is no level of "systematic phonetic" representation* distinct from some *systematic phonemic* or *underlying* any more than there is a *systematic phonemic* level distinct from anything else.' In brief, there is just one level of representation, whether it be called phonetic or phonemic is totally irrelevant. This is a single level of *interpreted representations* which reflects all the linguistically relevant properties of the sound structure of the language. The question of whether some segments constitute one or more phonemes, in other words, whether they are in some sense derived, is an outgrowth of the typical preoccupation with paradigmatic relations, and the concomitant goal of reducing the number of contrastive units, a preoccupation that characterises much of the phonological tradition, past and present. These concerns and goals are a consequence of a specific view of language structure rather than a necessary property of language itself. To ask whether the [i] of *mi* [mʲi] 'me' is the same phoneme (underlying segment) as the [ɨ] of *czy* [tʃɨ] 'if' is to disregard the close—in fact, inseparable—connection between the vowel and the preceding consonant in favour of lumping some vowels together. Within the monostratal, non-derivational, model assumed in this book, what matters phonologically are the mutual relations between successive melodic and syllabic units. Segmental inventories, if relevant at all, are secondary or derivative of the syntagmatic relations found and defined over melodies and constituents. Chopping across the relations in an attempt to determine a number of units is bound to artificially distort the picture. With reference to the two Polish vowels, what is significant is not whether they are one or two phonemes but the fact that one of them invariably accompanies palatalized and the other non-palatalized consonants. This is adequately reflected in representations like (21) and formalized in generalizations like I-alignment (19). Such generalizations hold true for representations and are read off them. They are not, at least not primarily, instructions to change one set of properties into another one.

This syntagmatically biased approach may be too strong if it were to be decided that individual morphemes need to be supplied with phonological representations. In Polish, a number of different inflectional morphemes, for example the nominative masculine plural, appear as either [i] or [ɨ] in conformity with I-alignment. Thus the hard-stemmed *kwiat* [kfʲat] 'flower' has its plural as *kwiat-y* [kfʲatɨ], whereas the soft-stemmed *kość* [kɔɕtɕ] 'bone' appears in the nominative plural as *kość-i* [kɔɕtɕi]; it is clear that the shape of the plural desinence depends on the nature of the final consonant of the stem. If there were to be a single phonological shape of the desinence, we would presumably have to decide between a headed and a non-headed {I} expression, that is, between [i] and [ɨ]. The need for such a unified representation is a question which morphology and possibly the lexicon must decide. It is not obvious what would be lost if both variants were included in the morphological/lexical representation; also it is perfectly possible to imagine representations where headedness is not specified and I-alignment ensures phonological well-formedness in any case.

The interaction between phonology and morphology hinted at above is much more broadly based. We will look at a few other instances now.

3.3 MORPHOLOGICAL INTERLUDE I

In the course of this book we will frequently refer to morphological implications and consequences of specific phonological solutions. Morphology will also be used as a source of additional evidence supporting or disfavouring a given solution. In the present context there is morphological support for the existence of word-final palatalized labials, hence, indirectly, for the reality of the depalatalization constraint. Let us consider it in brief.

It is a generally recognized fact about Polish declensions that they are determined not only by the gender of nouns but also by whether the stems end in a palatalized or non-palatalized (plain) consonant. In a nutshell, the way the stem ends has a significant influence on the choice of the inflectional ending. Thus, for example, most masculine nouns ending in a palatalized consonant take -*e* [ɛ] as the marker of the nominative and accusative plural (22a), while those terminating in a plain consonant take -*y* [ɨ], (22b), including labials (22c).

(22) (a) liść [liɕtɕ] 'leaf'   liści-e [liɕtɕɛ]
         gwóźdź [gvuɕtɕ] 'nail'   gwoździ-e [gvɔʑdʑɛ]
         łoś [wɔɕ] 'elk'   łosi-e [wɔɕɛ]
         gałąź [gawɔ̃ʷɕ] 'branch'   gałęzi-e [gawɛ̃ʲʑɛ]
         koń [kɔɲ] 'horse'   koni-e [kɔɲɛ]
         kraj [kraj] 'country'   kraj-e [krajɛ]

     (b) las [las] 'wood'   las-y [lasɨ]
         głaz [gwas] 'boulder'   głaz-y [gwazɨ]
         płot [pwɔt] 'fence'   płot-y [pwɔtɨ]
         gród [grut] 'fortress'   grod-y [grɔdɨ]
         stół [stuw] 'table'   stoł-y [stɔwɨ]⁴
         wór [vur] 'sack'   wor-y [vɔrɨ]

     (c) dom [dɔm] 'house'   dom-y [dɔmɨ]
         rów [ruf] 'ditch'   row-y [rɔvɨ]
         chleb [xlɛp] 'bread'   chleb-y [xlɛbɨ]
         snop [snɔp] 'sheaf'   snop-y [snɔpɨ]

Against this background it comes as no surprise that stems ending in a palatalized labial behave like other palatalized consonants. This happens irrespectively of whether the labial appears before a vowel (mostly in feminine nouns) where it is not subject to the depalatalization constraint, or whether it is phonetically plain due to the working of the constraint. The two groups are exemplified in (23).

(23) (a) ziemi-a [ʑɛmʲa] 'earth'   ziemi-e [ʑɛmʲɛ]
         głębi-a [gwɛmbʲa] 'depth'   głębi-e [gwɛmbʲɛ]
         utopi-a [utɔpʲa] 'utopia'   utopi-e [utɔpʲɛ]
         mafi-a [mafʲa] 'mafia'   mafi-e [mafʲɛ]

     (b) żuraw [ʒuraf] 'crane'   żurawi-e [ʒuravʲɛ]
         jastrząb [jast-ʃɔmp] 'hawk'   jastrzębi-e [jast-ʃɛmbʲɛ]
         karp [karp] 'carp'   karpi-e [karpʲɛ]

It is quite clear that morphology makes no distinction between the two groups in (23). It treats them in the same fashion as it treats other stems ending in a palatalized consonant, illustrated in (22a), and selects the desinences accordingly. This is significant for words like those in (23b), which end phonetically in a plain consonant but are analyzed by the morphology in the same way as those which end in a palatalized segment. The conclusion comes as no surprise in view of the depalatalization constraint which holds for (23b). Crucially, the representations of the forms do contain the element responsible for palatalization, {I}, and in this way the morphology can see the difference between, say, *paw* [paf] 'peacock'~*pawi-e* [pavʲɛ] and *traf* [traf] 'hit, chance'~*traf-y* [trafɨ]: the {I} element is part of

---

⁴ Recall that [w] is in reality a velarized lateral, see Ch. 1.

the former but not of the latter word. Thus the phonetic inaudibility of some property does not indicate its absence; or the phonetic identity of two forms does not necessarily imply their linguistic identity.

The discrepancy between the phonetic and the linguistic representation can be further appreciated in another case of phonologically driven morphological desinence selection. Apart from the class of palatalized consonants, there is another group which behaves in the same way although its members cannot be characterized as palatalized. This latter group comprises the following consonants: [ʃ, ʒ, tʃ, dʒ, ts, dz, l]. The Polish linguistic tradition labels them *functionally soft* (or *functionally palatalized*) since they select the same desinence as those ending in a phonetically palatalized class. Consider nouns ending in these consonants and their plurals in (24).

(24)   kosz [kɔʃ] 'basket'   kosz-e [kɔʃɛ]
       wąż [vɔʷʃ] 'snake'   węż-e [vɛʷʒɛ]
       klacz [klatʃ] 'filly'   klacz-e [klatʃɛ]
       noc [nɔts] 'night'   noc-e [nɔtsɛ]
       pieniądz [pʲɛɲɔnts] 'money'   pieniądz-e [pʲɛɲɔndzɛ]
       fal-a [fala] 'wave'   fal-e [falɛ]

This non-palatalized class does not differ morphologically from the palatalized one, hence the concept of functionally palatalized consonants serves the purpose rather well. It is very clearly an attempt not to allow 'surface phonetics' to override considerations of linguistic (morphological) patterning. Nonetheless, the label is nothing but a label or a diacritic; phonetically speaking, the Polish [s] is as 'soft' or palatalized as the Polish [ʃ] but it is only the latter that is included in the group of functionally soft consonants. Within the classical derivational model, the theoretical machinery would have to be even more complex, since most, if not all, of the functionally soft consonants would be claimed to be derived from an underlying plain consonant. In such a case in selecting a desinence one would have to take into account not only the consonant but also its immediate environment which is responsible for the palatalization. Alternatively, and even less persuasively, one could argue that the morphological rule needs to refer to a stage in the derivation at which the consonants are palatalized before subsequent rules deprive them of this palatality. This view of interlacing phonology and morphology seems unnecessarily complex and will not be pursued here.

Our model prompts a different solution, one which requires less theoretical machinery to cover the facts. We argued above that palatalized consonants are I-headed while palatals contain the same element as an operator—morphology now suggests that the same element appears in a class called *functionally soft*. If this is the case, then it is precisely the {I} element that unites the palatalized and the functionally palatalized group: the morphology refers to the presence of this element in the make-up of the relevant segment without paying attention to its head–operator status within an expression. And, indeed, without paying attention to whether it is licensed, as the case of the depalatalization constraint documents. The morphological regularity can directly access the element {I}, present in the linguistic representation of forms. The fact that in some cases the {I} element is a head, in others an operator, and in still others it is not licensed, hence inaudible phonetically, is irrelevant to the working of the morphological regularity.

3.4 PALATALIZED AND PLAIN VELARS

In phonetic terms the following obstruents in the velar and palato-velar region are normally identified: [k, c, g, ɟ, x, ç]. Furthermore, the palato-velars are regarded as the palatalized congeners of the plain velars. Phonologically, the situation is different and more complex. For one thing, the fricatives [x, ç] show a markedly different pattern as compared to the plosives and for this reason we will look at them later. Let us concentrate on the plosives first.

Starting with the phonetics of the palatalized velar or palato-velar plosives it should be noted that these consonants can be regarded either as single units [c, ɟ] or as combinations involving the palatal glide, that is, [cj, ɟj], before all vowels other than [i]. In this the velars do not differ from labials: the glide may be present or not in (25a) but its segmental status is questionable; very much like the palatalized labials (see (12)) the glide is required in relatively unassimilated or rarely used loans (25b). The following examples illustrate the consonants.

(25) (a) kiedy [cɛdɨ]/[cjɛdɨ] 'when'
           kiosk [cɔsk]/[cjɔsk] 'kiosk'
           roki-em [rɔcɛm]/[rɔcjɛm] 'year, instr. sg.'
           giętk-i [ɟɛntci]/[ɟjɛntci] 'pliable'
           gią-ć [ɟɔɲtɕ]/[ɟjɔɲtɕ] 'fold'

      (b) autarki-a [autarcja] 'autarchy'
           fonologi-a [fɔnɔlɔɟja] 'phonology'
           energi-a [ɛnɛrɟja] 'energy'

No glide is allowed before the front vowel [i] in a way which again parallels closely the impossibility of the [ji] sequence after palatalized labials:

(26) kit [cit] 'putty'
      mak-i [maci] 'poppy, nom. pl.'
      gina-ć [ɟinɔɲtɕ] 'perish'
      drog-i [drɔɟi] 'dear'

The fact that the glide is more easily perceived before a following back vowel merely strengthens the case for its status as a phonetic effect. If we follow the interpretation adopted for palatalized labials, we can represent palato-velars either as single or as fissured melodies dominated by a single skeletal position. Thus [ɟ] can be represented in either of the two ways:

(27)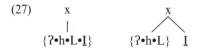

The status of palato-velars as dominated by single phonological positions can be confirmed in the same way as the status of palatalized labials. Note that when the vowel following a palato-velar is removed (it alternates with the phonetic zero), the glide accompanying the preceding consonant also disappears. Consider the following examples where the palato-velars are transcribed as two segments:

(28)   kier [cjɛr] 'ice float, gen. pl.'   kr-a [kra] 'nom. sg.'
       gier [ɟjɛr] 'game, gen. pl.'   gr-a [gra] 'nom. sg.'
       gią-ć [ɟjɔɲtɕ] 'fold'   gn-ę [gnɛ] 'I fold'
       za-gię-t-y [zaɟjɛntɨ] 'folded'   za-gn-ę [zagnɛ] 'I'll fold'

Unless we are ready to break up the vowel deletion generalization into two distinct regularities: the deletion of the vowel on the one hand and the deletion of a glide and a vowel on the other, the glide must be part of the palato-alveolar rather than a separate segment (where by a separate segment we understand a melody attached to a skeletal position different from the skeletal position associated with the melody of the velar plosive).

Another point of similarity between palatalized labials and velars is their non-appearance word-finally or before consonants. In positive terms they can appear only before a phonetically realized nucleus, hence the depalatalization constraint must be broadened to include the two classes of consonants.

(29) *Depalatalization constraint II*
     The element {I} in velars and labials must be directly licensed by a melod-
     ically filled nucleus.

The same OCP mechanism which disfavours the palatal glide before the vowel [i] in words like *piw-o* [pʲivɔ] (*[pʲjivɔ]) 'beer' is at work with palato-velars, hence no glide is possible in words like *kit-a* [cita] '(fox's) tail', not *[cjita], or *gitar-a* [ɟitara] 'guitar', not *[ɟjitara]. Although the similarities between palatalized labials and velars are significant and due more to the working of the system than to chance, there are also equally striking differences to which we now turn.

While combinations of [c, ɟ] with other segments—or rather the extremely limited presence of such combinations—can be accounted for by invoking the depalatalization constraint, we would expect, following the labial pattern, to find non-palatalized consonants followed by the retracted vowel [ɨ]. This does not happen and combinations like [kɨ, gɨ] are practically non-existent in the language. Evidence is amply available to show that the absence is not an accidental gap but is due to systematic phonological reasons.

Let us start by recalling that the plural ending of hard stem nouns regularly appears as [ɨ] (see (21b, c) for examples). Since the velar plosives [k, g] are obviously hard rather than palatalized, we would expect nouns ending in them to follow the same pattern. Consider the examples below which go against the predictions.

(30) *Singular*   *Plural*
    stok [stɔk] 'hillside'   stok-i [stɔci]
    walk-a [valka] 'fight'   walk-i [valci]
    drog-a [drɔga] 'road'   drog-i [drɔɟi]
    czołg [tʃɔwk] 'tank'   czołg-i [tʃɔwɟi]

Similarly, the adjectival ending of the masculine singular appears either as [ɨ] or as [i]. Consider the examples in (31), where words in the left-hand column ending in -*a* [a] represent the nominative feminine singular, while those in the right-hand column are the same adjectives in the masculine singular.

(31) *Feminine*   *Masculine*
    (a) dobr-a [dɔbra] 'good'   dobr-y [dɔbrɨ]
        prost-a [prɔsta] 'straight'   prost-y [prɔstɨ]
        zdrow-a [zdrɔva] 'healthy'   zdrowy [zdrɔvɨ]
        jesien-n-a [jɛɕɛnna] 'autumnal'   jesien-n-y [jɛɕɛnnɨ]

    (b) wilcz-a [vʲiltʃa] 'lupine'   wilcz-y [vʲiltʃɨ]
        boż-a [bɔʒa] 'divine'   boż-y [bɔʒɨ]
        kobiec-a [kɔbʲɛtsa] 'feminine'   kobiec-y [kɔbʲɛtsɨ]
        cudz-a [tsudza] 'alien'   cudz-y [tsudzɨ]

    (c) psi-a [pɕa] 'canine'   ps-i [pɕi]
        głupi-a [gwupʲa] 'stupid'   głup-i [gwupʲi]
        letni-a [lɛtɲa] 'of the summer'   let-n-i [lɛtɲi]
        niedźwiedzi-a [ɲɛdʑvʲɛdʑa] 'ursine' niedźwiedz-i [ɲɛdʑvʲɛdʑi]

    (d) ubog-a [ubɔga] 'poor'   ubog-i [ubɔɟi]
        srog-a [srɔga] 'severe'   srog-i [srɔɟi]
        wiel-k-a [vʲɛlka] 'great'   wiel-k-i [vʲɛlci]
        cien-k-a [tɕɛnka] 'thin'   cien-k-i [tɕɛnci]

We are primarily interested in the masculine ending—the words in left-hand column are given for comparison only as they have nothing directly of relevance to offer here. Note first of all that, where applicable, all examples conform to I-alignment (19) in that the element {I} occupies either the operator position in both the onset and the final nucleus (31b), or it is head in both segments (31c). The examples in (31a) are different in that the stem-final consonant does not contain the element {I} in its make-up but still they take [ɨ] as the desinence. This means that the headless {I•_} must be regarded as the basic or morphophonological form.[5] In (31b, c) the stem-final consonant is, in traditional terms,

---

[5] This is one of the possibilities and depends on the view of the relationship between morphology, morphophonology, and phonology. As mentioned above, it is possible to imagine the lexical representation of the morpheme in question as containing the element {I}, without further structure.

morphophonologically palatalized. The adjectives can be related to derivation-ally more basic nouns whose stem-final consonants are plain (non-palatal or non-palatalized): *wilcz-a* in (31b) is morphologically derived from *wilk* [vʲilk] 'wolf' and *psi-a* in (31c) from *pies* [pʲɛs] 'dog'. If the morphological derivation yields a stem-final non-palatalized consonant, the vowel of the ending remains unmodified as [ɨ] in (31b); if the consonant is palatalized, the vowel is I-aligned as per the I-alignment constraint (18). The data in (31d) show that the constraint in its current formulation does not cover all relevant modifications since the stem-final plain velars emerge as palato-velars while the masculine ending is I-aligned.

The feminine forms indicate the relevant stems end in a velar plosive which is not palatalized. I-alignment should not be applicable here since the onset con-tains no {I} element, hence the final onset–nucleus sequence should be [kɨ, gɨ]. This does not happen and, what is more, such sequences are generally absent in the language. The obvious question is what prevents this configuration from arising or what turns the velar plosives seen in the feminine adjectives into palato-velars in the masculine ones. A possible area to look for an answer is the nature of the expressions which come to stand in a nucleus–onset relation.

In terms of the element theory, velar consonants are held to be headless or empty headed, hence [k] corresponds to the element combination {ʔ•h•H•_}. The vowel [ɨ], as we saw above, differs from the vowel [i] in headedness, namely [i] is {I̲} while [ɨ] is {I•_ }. If a velar were to be an onset licensed by a following empty-headed nucleus, the emerging configuration would have an empty-headed onset licensed by an empty-headed nucleus. The facts of standard Polish (but not necessarily all regional dialects) appear to indicate that this situation is eschewed. We can formalise it in a constraint which disfavours such sequences of empty-headed expressions.

(32) *Empty Heads*
An empty-headed nucleus cannot license an empty-headed onset.

The Empty Heads constraint rules out the retracted vowel after a velar plosive. To make such a potential sequence pronounceable, the disfavoured configuration needs to be modified. The nucleus as the licensor can be expected to take the initiative: the only thing that can be done to rectify the structure in conformity with the constraint is to promote its one and only operator—{I}—to the head position. However, the element {I} cannot be associated just to the nuclear head since I-alignment requires that it should be attached to the onset head as well. This is particularly easy with velars since their heads are empty. The attachment of the {I} element to the onset comes about due to I-alignment, which in its essence is a description of palatalization. In (33) we offer a revised version of I-alignment which brings out more clearly the scope of the constraint.

(33) *I-alignment* (revised)
A nucleus shares I-head with the onset it licenses.

The constraint, interpreted exhaustively, means that an I-headed nucleus licenses an I-headed onset and also that an I-headed onset cannot be licensed by a nucleus with {I} as operator.

Given the generalizations (32)–(33), it follows that sequences such as [kɨ, gɨ] are not well formed in Polish since they would require an empty-headed onset to be licensed by an empty-headed nucleus:

(34)

The licensing which the nucleus has to discharge requires, as per Empty Heads (32), that its head should be filled, and the only element which can be promoted to the head position is {I}. I-alignment on the other hand requires that the element {I} as head must license another head, which translates into the double attachment of that element. Hence -ki of kita [cita] '(fox's) tail' and -g-i of drog-i [drɔɟi] 'dear' have the following representational shapes, where {I} is the head of both expressions simultaneously:

(35)

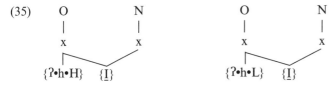

The constraint that {I} can only be the head of both the nucleus and the preceding onset (I-alignment) is one of the constraints that define the language specific properties of elements. We will have other opportunities to encounter similar constrains which delimit or otherwise define the peculiarities of individual elements.

At this point we may show that the analysis developed so far explains one of the puzzles of the Polish vowel system, namely, the non-existence of word-initial [ɨ]. Note that syllabically, a word-initial vowel constitutes a nucleus which licenses a preceding empty onset. An empty onset is, of course, an empty-headed expression which, in accordance with (32), must be licensed by a headed one. For this reason the representation of, say, the conjunction i [i] 'and' can only assume the following shape:

(36)

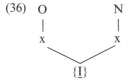

The Empty Heads constraint prevents the empty-headed {I•_} from appearing after an empty onset while the I-alignment ensures that the {I} element is attached, as head, to both skeletal positions. In this way the impossibility of initial [ɨ] follows from the same factors which make ungrammatical a combination of this vowel with a preceding velar plosive: a sequence of two empty-headed expressions is inadmissible (even if one of them, apart from being empty-headed, contains no operators either). There is no need for any separate account of the impossibility of the word-initial [ɨ], as it is already present in our description. As we will see directly below, the account has a much wider scope. Before developing the account we need to concentrate briefly on the fact that a configuration like (36) is normally pronounced as [i] and not as [ji], a possibility implied by the double attachment of the element.

We noted that palatalized labials are normally pronounced with a glide before a full nucleus, with the exception of [i]. Similarly, the palato-velars admit a variant pronunciation with a glide, but again not before a following [i]. The glide is impossible before [i] in word-initial position, a fact which can hardly be a coincidence.[6] In fact, whether Polish tolerates the sequence [ji] in the first place is something of a question. The Karaś and Madejowa (1977) normative dictionary makes a point of supplying every single item starting with the orthographic *i* with a ban against the pronunciation [ji], so *iść* [iɕtɕ] 'go' and *izolacja* [izɔlatsja] 'isolation' are not to be pronounced *[jiɕtɕ] and *[jizɔlatsja] (where the fact that a normative dictionary fulminates against some forms clearly suggests that they do occur). On the other hand, it admits a variant with this sequence in two cases; after another vowel (37a) and when the vowel [i] is an I-aligned inflectional marker added to a stem ending in [j], as in (37b). In fact, the last example of (37a) represents a combination of both factors.

(37) (a) dwo-i-ć [dvɔitɕ] or [dvɔjitɕ] 'double, vb.'
          ma-i-ć [maitɕ] or [majitɕ] 'emblazon'
          ro-i-ć [rɔitɕ] or [rɔjitɕ] 'swarm, vb.'
          mo-i-m [mɔim] or [mɔjim] 'my, loc. sg. masc.'
          szu-i [ʃui] or [ʃuji] 'swindler, gen. sg.' (cf. szu-a [ʃuja] 'nom. sg.')

      (b) parti-i [partʲi] or [partʲji] 'party, gen. sg.' (cf. parti-a [partʲja] 'nom. sg.')
          parodi-i [parɔdʲi] or [parɔdʲji] 'parody, gen. sg.' (cf. parodi-a [parɔdʲja] 'nom. sg.')
          misj-i [mʲisʲi] or [mʲisʲji] 'mission, gen. sg.' (cf. misj-a [mʲisʲja] 'nom. sg.')
          poezj-i [pɔɛzʲi] or [pɔɛzʲji] 'poetry, gen. sg.' (cf. poezj-a [pɔɛzʲja] 'nom. sg.')
          lekcj-i [lɛktsʲi] or [lɛktsʲji] 'lesson, gen. sg.' (cf. lekcj-a [lɛktsʲja] 'nom. sg.')

It seems that the distinctions introduced by the *Dictionary* do correspond to some linguistic reality. Speakers of the standard dialect very strongly object to initial [ji] in *iść*, etc. Such variants are regarded as uneducated, presumably because

---

[6] The only exception seems to be the loan *jidysz* [jidɨʃ] 'Yiddish' but even here one occasionally hears the pronunciation [idɨʃ].

they occur in regional dialects. The two possibilities illustrated in (37) arouse no strong feelings. In fact most speakers, when questioned, are uncertain as to which variant they prefer. For (37a) this may be connected with the fact that vowel sequences in Polish are generally very infrequent and generally associated either with foreign words such as *teatr* [tɛatr̥] 'theatre' or involve prefix boundaries, as in *za-okrągl-i-ć* [zaɔkrɔŋglitɕ] 'round, vb.'. For (37b) this also seems to correlate with the foreign nature of domain-internal combinations of a palatalized consonant followed by the palatal glide (cf. also (12)). Keeping in mind these glitches we will assume that the standard language has a constraint we formulate as (38).

(38) *Operators required*
      Doubly attached {I} must license operators.

This is another of the set of constraints specifying phonological properties of elements in Polish. On the one hand it admits onset–nucleus sequences such as in *piwo* [pʲivɔ] 'beer' and *kita* [cita] 'fox's tail' since the element {I} licenses other elements responsible for the stops of the onset. On the other hand, it disfavours configurations like (36) and results in the failure of the initial onset to be melodically realized.

Before moving on to other issues, let us summarize the main observations and the phonological basis shaping them.

1. Palatalized labials differ from plain labials in their infrasegmental composition. The palatalized consonants are bifurcated melodies, or consonantal diphthongs, with the {I} element acting as head and being separate from the remaining elements. It is perceived as the glide [j].
2. The combination of a palatalized labial with a following glide is structurally totally equivalent to a palatalized labial without any glide, i.e. [pʲj]=[pʲ].
3. Palatalized labials occur before front and back vowels. If the licensing nucleus is front, that is, if it contains the {I} element in its make-up, then the {I} element is shared as head between the nucleus and the onset. The glide of the onset is not heard when the nucleus contains nothing apart from {I}. This follows from the Obligatory Contour Principle.
4. The retracted vowel [ɨ] is not possible after a palatalized labial due to the operation of the I-alignment constraint.
5. Palatalized labials are only possible before a phonetically pronounced nucleus, which follows from the depalatalization constraint (13).
6. Palato-velars are only possible before a melodically filled nucleus, as per the depalatalization constraint II (28).
7. Palato-velars may be followed by the glide [j] before a following vowel other than [i].
8. [i] differs from [ɨ] in being headed.
9. Velars cannot be followed by either of the two high vowels; the impossibility of the [i] (*[ki]) follows from I-alignment (33) and the impossibility of [ɨ] (*[kɨ]) follows from the Empty Heads constraint (32).

To conclude:

- {I} when headed is heard as [i] and when empty-headed it is perceived as [ɨ].
- The headed {I} in the nucleus is doubly attached and also occupies the head position in the preceding or licensed onset. When the onset contains other elements, it is perceived as palatalized (e.g. *mil-y* [mʲiwɨ] 'nice', *sag-i* [saɟi] 'saga, pl.'). The {I} onset head is not perceived if the licensing nucleus contains no operators. This means that when the onset is empty, the double attachment is not realized phonetically and what is heard is the vowel [i] at the beginning of a word.
- When {I} is an operator, the nucleus may license an {I} operator in the onset (e.g. *czyt-a* [tʃɨta] '(s)he reads') but does not have to (e.g. *syt-y* [sɨtɨ] 'full up').
- Unheaded {I} does not appear after an empty onset due to the Empty Heads constraint, hence no word begins with [ɨ].

3.5 PALATALS AND THE FRONT MID VOWEL(S)

A problem which is closely related to the emergence of [ci, ɟi], where [kɨ, gɨ] might be expected, is the shape of the velars before the other front vowel, that is, before the vowel [ɛ]. Consider alternations of plain velars with palato-velars where the latter occur before the ending *-em* [ɛm] of the instrumental singular masculine and neuter (39a) and also before the adjectival *-e* [ɛ] of the nominative plural (non-masculine personal) (39b).

(39) (a) rak [rak] 'crab'   raki-em [racɛm]
           ok-o [ɔkɔ] 'eye'   oki-em [ɔcɛm]
           drąg-u [drɔŋgu] 'pole, gen. sg.'   drągi-em [drɔŋɟɛm]
           tang-o [taŋgɔ] 'tango'   tangi-em [taŋɟɛm]
      (b) dalek-a [dalɛka] 'distant, fem.'   daleki-e [dalɛcɛ]
           szyb-k-a [ʃɨpka] 'swift, fem.'   szyb-ki-e [ʃɨpcɛ]
           wrog-a [vrɔga] 'hostile, fem.'   wrogi-e [vrɔɟɛ]
           drug-a [druga] 'second, fem.'   drugi-e [druɟɛ]

The alternations follow closely the pattern found when the ending begins with the high front vowel (see (30) and (31d)). As can be seen, a stem-final velar, when followed by the front vowel, is realized as a palato-velar. This is further confirmed by instances of a vowel alternating with zero: while non-velars can be either palatalized or not before such a vowel, (non-palatalized) velars are impossible before it. Compare the two groups of examples:

(40) (a) wieś [vʲɛɕ] 'village'   ws-i [fɕi] 'gen. pl.'
           wesz [vɛʃ] 'louse'   wsz-y [fʃɨ] 'gen. pl.'
           dzień [dʑɛɲ] 'day'   dni-a [dɲa] 'gen. sg.'
           den [dɛn] 'bottom, gen. pl.'   dn-o [dnɔ] 'nom. sg.'

(b) kieł [cɛw] 'tusk'   kł-y [kwɨ] 'nom. pl.'
    okien [ɔcɛn] 'window, gen. pl.'   okn-o [ɔknɔ] 'nom. sg.'
    giez [ɟɛs] 'gadfly'   gz-a [gza] 'gen. sg.'
    ogień [ɔɟɛɲ] 'fire'   ogni-a [ɔgɲa] 'gen. sg.'

The conclusion is clear: the alternating vowel cannot appear after a velar—
alternations like [gɛw]–[gwa] are not on record. Additionally, cases where the
velar can precede the vowel, in other words, sequences [kɛ, gɛ], are rare and
restricted to well-defined classes; we will look at those a bit later on. For the
moment we will assume that a combination of a velar with the vowel [ɛ] is
impossible.

Comparing the behaviour of [ɛ] with that of the [i ~ ɨ] tandem, we have to
conclude that the vowel [ɛ] of the inflectional endings is empty-headed. This
vowel would then consist of two elements, both of which are operators, that is,
{I•A•_}. When morphologically placed after an empty-headed consonant (a
velar) it has to comply with the Empty Heads constraint (32) and promote
the element {I} to the head position, thereby yielding an expression {A•I}.
I-alignment in its turn ensures that the head element is shared, that is to say
that it is attached to both the nucleus and the preceding onset. The structure in
(41) is a representation of [cɛ].

(41)

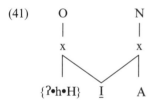

The discussion so far indicates that we have two expressions corresponding to
the phonetic vowel [ɛ], namely, the empty-headed {I•A•_} and the I-headed
{A•I}. We have just seen examples where the latter object is found after palato-
velars; we expect this to appear also after other palatalized consonants. This is
amply confirmed by combinations of the vowel [ɛ] with a preceding palatalized
consonant, as illustrated in (42).

(42) cień [tɕɛɲ] 'shadow'   siedzi-e-ć [ɕɛdʑɛtɕ] 'sit'
      ziew-a-ć [ʑɛvatɕ] 'yawn'   nieb-o [ɲɛbɔ] 'heaven'
      piekł-o [pʲɛkwɔ] 'hell'   dzieł-o [dʑɛwɔ] 'deed'
      wieni-ec [vʲɛɲɛts] 'wreath'   mieści-e [mʲɛɕtɕɛ] 'town, loc. sg.'

In terms of elements and their arrangements, a combination of a palatalized
consonant and the vowel [ɛ] captures a situation where the element {I} is in the
head position of both the consonant and the licensing nucleus, an instance of
which is presented in (41). This sharing relation might be said to correspond to
the traditional concept of a palatalizing [ɛ] in the same way as a doubly attached
headed {I} was argued earlier to correspond to palatalization in general.

After non-palatalized consonants, where I-alignment is inapplicable, the empty-headed expression can be expected. In simple terms, the appearance of a non-palatalized consonant before the vowel [ɛ] means that the vowel is empty headed, i.e. {I•A•_}. Taking again the ending -em of the instrumental singular masculine and neuter and the adjectival -e [ɛ] of the nominative plural (non-masculine personal) (cf. (39)) we see that when attached to a stem-final hard consonant no sharing relation emerges.

(43)　(a)　płot [pwɔt] 'fence'　　　płot-em [pwɔtɛm]
　　　　　chleb [xlɛp] 'bread'　　　chleb-em [xlɛbɛm]
　　　　　las [las] 'wood'　　　　　las-em [lasɛm]
　　　　　ud-o [udɔ] 'thigh'　　　　ud-em [udɛm]
　　　　　słow-o [swɔvɔ] 'word'　　słow-em [swɔvɛm]

　　　(b)　prost-y [prɔstɨ] 'straight'　prost-e [prɔstɛ]
　　　　　krzyw-y [kʃɨvɨ] 'crooked'　krzyw-e [kʃɨvɛ]
　　　　　młod-y [mwɔdɨ] 'young'　　młod-e [mwɔdɛ]
　　　　　bos-y [bɔsɨ] 'barefoot'　　bos-e [bɔsɛ]

A sequence such as [bɛ] reflects the absence of a sharing relation, in other words, an empty-headed nucleus licensing a consonantal melody without the element {I}. In such as case no I-alignment is possible. The sequence [bɛ] is shown in (44).

(44)

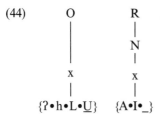

The situation depicted in [44] corresponds to the derivational notion of a non-palatalizing e, a situation we will consider in greater detail in the next section. Here we merely note that an analysis of velars and their combinations with front vowels leads to the recognition of two different phonological objects involving the elements {A} and {I}: empty headed {A•I•_} and headed {A•I}. We will have ample opportunity to return to them below. For the moment we need to consider another implication of the proposed structure of expressions.

The behaviour of velars before what is heard as [ɛ] is exactly parallel to what happens when morphologically [ɨ] is made to follow the consonants. Note that also word-internally the behaviour is the same: just as [kɨ] is ungrammatical in most cases, so is [kɛ] (with the exception of a handful of words to be discussed presently). We noted, as a striking property of the vowel [ɨ], its inability to appear word-initially. If our parallel between the two vowels were to hold, we would expect similar restrictions to be found with word-initial [ɛ], that is to say that it should be banned from that position.

At first glance the prediction seems obviously mistaken since there is no dearth of words beginning just with [ɛ] in Polish; see (45) for just a few examples.

(45) enigm-a [ɛɲigma] 'enigma'
      eukaliptus [ɛwkaliptus] 'eucalyptus'
      energi-a [ɛnɛrɟja] 'energy'
      Europ-a [ɛwrɔpa] 'Europe'
      Edmund [ɛdmunt] 'personal name'

What is immediately obvious is that all these words are borrowings, some of them quite recent. In fact, the glosses to words like those in (45) are entirely superfluous to any English speaker. There are no native words beginning with [ɛ]. Is this an accident?

We may assume for the moment that [ɛ] as an empty-headed expression cannot appear after an empty onset in native words but is allowed in loans, possibly as a marker of their foreignness. In the native vocabulary, on the other hand, the strategy developed above for the initial high vowel should find applicability as well. The Empty Heads constraint would promote the element {I} to the head position and I-alignment would attach it as head to the onset–nucleus configuration. Thus an attempt to place the vowel in word-initial position yields the following structure:

(46) O   N
      | |
      x   x
       _____ /|
            I   A

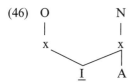

This structure represents the phonetic [jɛ]. Unsurprisingly, there is no shortage of native words beginning with this combination, almost all of them being native:

(47) jest [jɛst] 'is'   jeleń [jɛlɛɲ] 'deer'
      jedwab [jɛdwap] 'silk'   jechać [jɛxatɕ] 'go'
      je-m [jɛm] 'I eat'   jeśli [jɛɕli] 'if'
      Jerzy [jɛʒɨ] 'personal name'   Jelitkowo [jɛlitkɔvɔ] 'place name'

This means then that the borrowings in (45) fail to conform to the Empty Heads constraint, a failure which can be regarded as a phonological exponent of the borrowed status. But an alternative phonological interpretation is also available, since an expression which appears to fail to conform to a constraint may simply not qualify for it. In other words, to be able to conform to a constraint such as Empty Heads, an expression has to be empty-headed to begin with. We have seen two possible combinations of the two elements {A} and {I}: I-headed and empty headed. The theory of elements admits yet another possible fusion of the two elements, namely, one where the element {A} is dominant: {I•A̲}. This A-headed expression does not qualify either for the Empty Heads or the I-alignment constraint—it is a non-sharing (non-palatalizing) mid front vowel. Its existence will be further justified below.

The analysis above brings us to the conclusion that [ci] and [cɛ] are representationally similar in that both have doubly attached {I} in the head position. Furthermore, the initial [i] is representationally equivalent to [jɛ], and they differ because the nucleus of [jɛ] contains an additional element as compared to [i], and partly due to the application of constraint (38), which bars the element {I} on its own to be associated to two positions. Dialects which do not have that particular constraint bring out the similarity even better as they admit initially both [ji] and [jɛ] (iś-ć (standard) [içtç], (regional) [jiçtç] 'go (on foot)'; jech-a-ć (both standard and regional) [jɛxatç] 'go, travel').

In the high front vowel region, Polish isolates two objects, headed {I̱} and headless {I•_}; in the mid front region it likewise identifies three objects, headed {A•I̱} and {I•A̱} as well as headless {A•I•_}. Although we speak of separate vocalic objects it hardly needs to be stressed that they are strictly connected with preceding onsets: we have the I-headed [ɛ] in raki-em [racɛm] (39a), jest [jɛst] (47) and kiel [cɛw] (40b), the headless one in plot-em [pwɔtɛm] (43a), prost-e [prɔstɛ] (43b) and the A-headed in enigm-a [ɛɲigma] (45). The important point to note is that the three mid expressions are pronounced in the same way, as [ɛ]. The idea that two or more different phonological expressions can be given the same phonetic shape is in no way particularly new and we will have much opportunity to see it in action below. A classical example of this situation is the neutralization of voice distinction in some positions: in Polish the two words grat [grat] 'piece of junk' and grad [grat] 'hail' are homophonous although in one case the final obstruent is not specified for voicelessness, while in the other its voicedness, {L}, is not licensed (see Ch. 6 for a full discussion). While representationally different, the two forms are pronounced in the same way. Similarly, Polish does not package differently the three phonological expressions {A•I̱}, {I•A̱} and {A•I•_}, whose phonological distinction is revealed through the different patterns of behaviour. The most important aspect of this behaviour is the fact that palatalization, or I-sharing in our terms, is not a mechanical consequence of placing a front vowel after a consonant but rather reflects a relationship between the vowel and the preceding consonant. A front, or I-containing vowel can be called palatalizing if it shares this element in the head position with the preceding onset. If the sharing is not present, no palatalization effects can be observed even if the vowel itself is phonetically front. Thus [ɨ] is front (contains {I}) but is not a sharing expression; in the same way all [ɛ]s contain {I} but only some of them share it with the preceding consonant. The existence of non-sharing mid vowel is a major source of opacity of the traditional palatalization regularity in Polish. This problem deserves closer scrutiny of the context of historical phonological debates.

In the preceding pages we have found evidence justifying the recognition of three phonological expressions corresponding to the phonetic object [ɛ], two of them headed and one empty-headed. We showed how palato-velars can only be followed by the headed vowel [ɛ] (i.e. {A•I̱}), in the same way as they can only be followed by the headed {I̲}). The impossibility of initial [i̵] follows from the same factors which ban an unheaded [ε] initially. In this sense, somewhat unexpectedly, the necessary presence of a palato-velar before a high front vowel is just another aspect of the presence of initial [jε].

The question might be asked at this stage why it is the case that word-initially only headless front vowels {I•_} and {A•I•_} are found and why they are made to conform to the constraints which result in the phonetic [i] and [jε], respectively. The answer must be that there is no evidence that this is indeed the situation. Given the phonetic *ile* [ilε] 'how many', *jezior-o* [jɛʑɔrɔ] 'lake', *kis-ną-ć* [cisnɔɲtɕ] 'sour, vb.', and *kiedy* [cɛdɨ] 'when', we cannot decide whether the initial nucleus is underlyingly headed or headless if only because the notion of any underlying representation distinct from the surface is incoherent within our model. There are no phonological structures from which phonetic shapes are in any sense derived: what we have is a single level of representation which contains all linguistically important information. Whether a specific word 'starts with' an empty-headed nucleus which is 'turned into' a headed one or whether it 'starts with' a headed vowel are non-questions; a well-formed representation can begin only with a headed-front vowel (leaving aside borrowings). This is because of the existence of the constraints we have identified (Empty Heads, I-alignment, etc.) which disallow other shapes. The existing forms must conform to the constraints of the language and this is the main property that a phonological description brings out; indeterminate or non-unique representations are a by-product of specific phonological models, namely, those which tilt towards segments and segmentation, in other words, those with a paradigmatic bias. All paradigmatic conclusions which we occasionally draw, such as the existence of three objects corresponding to [ε], are invariably derivative of syntagmatic constraints and of little theoretical significance. Similarly, the use of morphophonological alternations in the course of an analysis is merely one of the methods of arriving at generalizations rather than a view that different shapes of the same morpheme must have a single representation. Allomorphs are units of morphology, and while they may be a useful tool in the search for and identification of phonological generalizations, they do not define the data for analysis.

3.6 THE SO-CALLED NON-PALATALIZING *E*s

A major point in Polish phonology, one which has attracted a lot of attention and theoretical discussion in the past, is the existence of what was traditionally called non-palatalizing *es* and what we call non-sharing *es*. Traditionally, front vowels were viewed as palatalization triggers, so there was a problem what to do with those front nuclei which fail to palatalize or which appear after a non-palatalized consonants. With the high vowel [i̵] the solution was commonly adopted which viewed it as underlyingly non-front. There was some plausibility behind this step, since phonetically the vowel [i̵] is retracted or even close to central, hence assuming it is phonologically back and gets advanced is not essentially different from assuming that it is phonologically front which gets centralized. The same procedure could not be taken with respect to the front mid vowel.

The vowel [ɛ] appearing after a palatalized consonant means in our terms that the element {I} is the doubly attached head in accordance with I-alignment (33). If the onset were to be empty-headed, this constraint, together with the Empty Heads constraint (32), ensures that double attachment is established. This yields two effects: velars are banned at the expense of palato-velars and empty onsets acquire the palatal glide. The mid vowel appearing after palatalized consonants—or the palatalizing e of some models—is an I-headed expression, {A•I}. In word-initial position it takes the shape of [jɛ]. The vowel that appears word-initially in borrowings is, we have suggested, an A-headed expression, {I•A̲}, hence none of our constraints is involved. We have also argued that the non-sharing vowel in the endings -em, -e is empty-headed, {A•I•_}, and is subject to no modification since the preceding consonant does not contain the element {I}, hence no need for I-alignment, and the consonant's head is filled, hence no need for Empty Heads to operate. The question arises as to whether this last interpretation can be extended to other instances of the non-palatalizing e.

That part of past research that viewed the existence of opaque sequences such as Ce, that is, a non-palatalized consonant preceding the vowel [ɛ], as an issue did so because of the assumed general regularity in the language whereby a front vowel necessarily palatalizes a preceding consonant. The opaque forms with a non-palatalized consonant before that vowel constituted a challenge to the assumption and needed to be dealt with in some way. First of all, let us consider some more examples of such opaque combinations.

(48) (a) sen [sɛn] 'sleep'   mech [mɛx] 'moss'
          wiader-k-o [vʲadɛrkɔ] 'pail, dim.'   kot-ek [kɔtɛk] 'kitten'

      (b) mew-a [mɛva] 'seagull'   mebel [mɛbɛl] 'furniture'
          diabeł [dʲjabɛw] 'devil'   inwestycj-a [invɛstɨtsja] 'investment'

      (c) teraz [tɛras] 'now'   serc-e [sɛrtsɛ] 'heart'
          merd-a-ć [mɛrdatɕ] 'wag the tail'   paster-sk-i [pastɛrsci] 'shepherd, adj.'

      (d) m-ego [m-ɛgɔ] 'my, gen. sg. masc.'   dobr-ego [dɔbrɛgɔ] 'good, gen. sg.
                                                     masc.'
          tw-ej [tfɛj] 'your, dat. sg. fem.'   ostr-ej [ɔstrɛj] 'sharp, dat. sg. fem.'

      (e) lot-em [lɔtɛm] 'flight, instr. sg.'   powod-em [pɔvɔdɛm] 'cause, instr.
                                                     sg.'
          bor-em [bɔrɛm] 'forest, instr. sg.'   las-em [lasɛm] 'wood, instr. sg.'

      (f) ładn-e [wadnɛ] 'pretty, nom. pl.'   strom-e [strɔmɛ] 'steep, nom. pl.'
          szar-e [ʃarɛ] 'grey, nom. pl.'   łys-e [wɨsɛ] 'bald, nom. pl.'

      (g) kret [krɛt] 'mole'   kres [krɛs] 'end'
          sejm [sɛjm] 'parliament'   deszcz [dɛʃtʃ] 'rain'
          wesel-e [vɛsɛlɛ] 'wedding'   nawet [navɛt] 'even'

The words have been divided into seven groups roughly corresponding to the subregularities that have been posited in the literature in response to the failure of palatalization. The nonpalatalizing *es* in words like those in (48a) were claimed to derive from an underlying back lax vowel which was turned into [ɛ] after the palatalization regularity has played its part. In generative terms, the rule deriving the front vowel was ordered after palatalization.

The words in (48b) with non-palatalizing *es* were dismissed as counter-examples on the grounds of their synchronic foreignness. While the category of foreignness is not objectionable in principle, it proved an irksome asset in that certain words would need to be marked as foreign for the purpose of some rules and native for others. As a case in point, consider the words *mebel* [mɛbɛl] 'furniture' and *diabeł* [dʲjabɛw] 'devil', both obvious loans, and therefore argu-ably resistant to native palatalization. At the same time, however, both words undergo the unquestionable native regularity whereby the second vowel is sup-pressed before an inflectional ending, as in *mebl-e* [mɛblɛ], *diabł-y* [dʲjabwɨ] 'nom. pl.'. No non-arbitrary solution has been devised which would bypass the charge of diacritic juggling.

The non-palatalizing *es* in (48c) were claimed to be derived from the back unrounded high vowel, that is to say that the following [r] was seen as exerting a lowering and fronting effect on the high vowel, a regularity ordered again after palatalization.

The forms in (48d) were derived in an even more intricate fashion. It has been observed that possessive pronouns in the singular display a longer and a shorter form, as in *twoj-ego* [tfɔjɛgɔ] 'your, gen. sg. masc.', side by side with *tw-ego* [tfɛgɔ], *swo-jej* [sfɔjɛj] 'one's, gen. dat. sg. fem.', alternating with *sw-ej* [sfɛj]. Of course the longer variants are well behaved phonologically in that the vowel [ɛ] follows the palatal glide, an unremarkable situation. The shortened version contains the offending combination of a non-palatalized consonant and the vowel [ɛ], a situation which can be handled neatly by deriving the shorter version from the longer one. If the truncation process were to apply after palatalization, nothing more would need to be said about the particular case of opacity here. While the derivation of the pronominal forms looked persuasive because of the existence of the alternative shapes (*moj-ego* [mɔjɛgɔ]∼*m-ego* [mɛgɔ] 'my, gen. sg. masc.'), many researchers baulked at the idea of extending the analysis to the endings of adjectives, none of which show similar variation. This step would amount to restructuring all adjectival forms on the basis of several pronominal cases.

The inflectional ending *-em* of the instrumental singular of nouns (48e) and the ending *-e* of the nominative plural of adjectives (48f) were problematic in the same way as the adjectival endings above: they followed a non-palatalized consonant. Since the *-e* ending of the locative singular was well behaved in that it evinced palatalization (e.g. *lot* [lɔt] 'flight'∼*loci-e* [lɔtcɛ] 'loc. sg.', *ród* [rut] 'family, clan'∼*rodzi-e* [rɔdʑɛ] 'loc. sg.', etc.) no straightforward way of connecting the phonological irregularity with morphology suggested itself. For this reason a more radical step was taken (Rubach 1984): the palatalizing vowel in the *-e* of the locative singular was said to be underlying a front mid vowel, roughly what it is on the surface. In the case of the non-palatalizing vowel in *-em* and *-e* it was suggested that underlyingly it cannot be a front vowel (since it does not palatalize) but may be assumed to be mid back differing in rounding from /ɔ/. The underlying mid back unrounded /ɣ/ was subject to absolute neutralization and merged with /ɛ/, obviously after the application of palatalization.

The repertoire of possibilities reviewed above should be sufficient to handle any case of palatalization opacity. In particular, the recognition of a vowel which never emerges on the surface—the back mid unrounded /ɣ/—should be enough to cover all outstanding cases. For reasons never made clear this step was not taken and forms such as those in (48g) came to be regarded as genuine exceptions requiring a diacritic which prevented them from being palatalized.

Discussing the relation between the initial vowel of the endings *-em*, *-e* (see (39) and (43)), we proposed that the vowel is empty-headed: {A•I•_}. Whenever it is combined with a stem-final consonant which itself does not contain the element {I}, the consonant and the vowel do not contract any relationship. In particular, no I-sharing can be envisaged for the simple reason that the consonant does not itself contain it and, being headed, it cannot, unlike the velar stops, receive the {I} element by Empty Heads. It seems that this solution can be extended to all instances of non-sharing [ɛ] in (48). The proposal obviates all these individual solutions made within the derivational approach and obviously it avoids their difficulties and arbitrariness. In accordance with general assumptions of the element theory, it assumes that a mid front vowel is a combination of two elements, namely, {I} and {A}, a combination which may be headed or headless. If there is no sharing of the element {I} by a consonant and the following {A•I•_}, the phonetic effect is a non-palatalized consonant followed by the vowel [ɛ]. Recall that in the case of palatalization we have the element {I} doubly attached to the head of the consonant and the vowel. What needs to be stressed is that there are no adjustments or changes going on between the vowels and the consonants. Quite conversely, either consonants and vowels are I-aligned, which we interpret as palatalization, or they are not. The identification of two vocalic objects is derivative of the syntagmatic relations established between vowels and consonants. In actual fact, the two vocalic expressions are nothing but a simplifying metaphor; at least the I-headed vowel is not really an independent unit since it always needs an onset with which it shares the element {I}. If attached to an empty onset, it is perceived as [jɛ]. The empty-headed expression may be seen as displaying a degree of independence of the environment.

Summing up the vocalic expressions as described so far, we discern in the structure of Polish the element {I} on its own, either as headed {Į} or headless {I•_}, and in combination with the element {A}; the palatality element can either be head, yielding {A•I}, or operator, resulting in {I•A̲}, or both elements can be operators with the head position empty, {A•I•_}. Note that the three combinations exhaust the logically available possibilities supplied by the structure of expressions where zero or one element can appear in the head and two function as operators.

3.7 ELEMENT COMBINATIONS IN LOANS
AND IN NASAL VOWELS

In our discussion of the element combinations yielding the vowel [ɛ] we devoted relatively little attention to the A-headed expression. It was suggested in connection with this vowel appearing word-initially in loan words (see (45)) that {I•A} was its possible representation, most in keeping with what has been determined about Polish vowels so far. We would like to return to this expression now and see whether it is found more generally in Polish.

A good diagnostic context for the expression {I•A} should be the position after velar plosives, in other words, after empty-headed consonants. If an A-headed vowel were to follow a velar plosive, the Empty Heads constraint would be inoperative (the licensing nucleus would be headed). As a result, I-alignment would not be active either ({I} would not be in the head). The phonetic result should be a combination of velar plosive and the mid vowel, i.e. [kɛ, gɛ]. Such combinations are found in borrowings, (49a), and in words where the vowel is part of the nasal nucleus, (49b).

(49)　(a)　kelner [kɛlnɛr] 'waiter'　　　　　genez-a [gɛnɛza] 'origin'
　　　　　　kemping [kɛmpʲiŋk] 'camping'　　germań-sk-i [gɛrmaɲsci] 'Germanic'
　　　　　　keks [kɛks] 'fruit cake'　　　　　generał [gɛnɛraw] 'general'
　　　　　　Keni-a [kɛɲja] 'Kenya'　　　　　Genew-a [gɛnɛva] 'Geneva'
　　　　　　sake [sakɛ] 'sake (a drink)'　　　ewangeli-a [ɛvaŋgɛlja] 'gospel'

　　　(b)　kędy [kɛndɨ] 'which way'　　　　　gęś [gɛʲɕ] 'goose'
　　　　　　kędzior [kɛɲdʑɔr] 'lock of hair'　　gęb-a [gɛmba] 'gob'
　　　　　　kęs [kɛʷs] 'bite, n.'　　　　　　　gęst-y [gɛʷstɨ] 'thick'
　　　　　　wlok-ę [vlɔkɛ⁽ʷ⁾] 'I drag'　　　　mog-ę [mɔgɛ⁽ʷ⁾] 'I can'
　　　　　　mąk-ę [mɔŋkɛ⁽ʷ⁾] 'flour, acc. sg.'　obelg-ę [ɔbɛlgɛ⁽ʷ⁾] 'insult, acc. sg.'

The borrowings in (49a) seem quite straightforward: the sequences [kɛ, gɛ] are empty-headed onsets followed by A-headed nuclei. Nothing happens there because nothing can happen. The fact that the combination of the elements {A} and {I} with the former as head appears in loans, both word-initially (45) and internally (49a) might signify that this particular structure of the expression is marked or in some sense costly and hence used in relatively unassimilated vocabulary. What happens in the process of nativization is that the marked A-headed expression is replaced by the common I-headed one yielding a sequence of a palato-velar and the mid vowel [cɛ, ɟɛ] (see (41)), which conforms to the regular constraints.[7] A number of words have already followed this path.

(50)　kielich [cɛlix] 'chalice'　　　gfield-a [ɟɛwda] 'stock exchange'
　　　etykiet-a [ɛticɛta] 'etiquette'　szlagier [ʃlaɟɛr] 'hit'

---

[7] Note again that in a synchronic description it does not matter whether the vowel is the I-headed {A•I} or the empty-headed {I•A•_} since in both cases the phonetic form conforms to the Empty Heads and I-alignment constraints.

while others have fluctuating forms: side by side with *ewangelia* [ɛvaŋgɛlja] 'gospel' we also encounter [ɛvaɲɟɛlja].

The presence of velars rather than palato-velars before the front nasal nucleus (49b) indicates again that the vowel is headed and that the head is an element different from {I}. This is a plausible conclusion in view of the existence of forms, admittedly very few, where the nasal nucleus is preceded by a palato-velar, hence I-sharing must be observed:

(51)   gięt-k-i [ɟentci] 'pliable'
gięci-e [ɟɛɲtɕɛ] 'bending'
z-gięt-y [zɟɛntɨ] 'bent, crooked'

Our suggested representations for the phonetic mid vowels should have a bearing on the vexed question of nasal nuclei. Following the pattern of loan words, we initially conclude that the front nasal nucleus is an A-headed vowel. We will take an initial look at the vowels now leaving their alternations for a later occasion (Ch. 6); here we will follow those interpretations—both traditional and generative—which regard nasal nuclei as different from and irreducible to sequences of oral vowels and nasal consonants. Although we consistently adopt a fully phonetic transcription where an oral vowel plus a nasal consonant (including a nasal glide) should be taken to denote a nasal nucleus, occasionally we will resort to the short cut [ɛN] and [ɔN]. The proper phonological structure of these nuclei will be discussed in detail later on and in Chapter 6.

Nasal nuclei are mid vowels, hence in terms of elements we operate with, they are made up of the same two elements which define oral vowels, that is, {I, A}, {U, A}. Additionally, an element is necessary to cover the nasal resonance; bypassing the well-known discussion of whether nasality calls for a separate element or whether {L} (low tone) will suffice (Nasukawa 1998, 2005; Ploch 1999 and references therein), we will assume without further discussion that the element responsible for nasality in both vowels and consonants is {N}. Thus the front nasal vowel is a composite of {A•I•N} in the same way as the back nasal vowel is a composite of {A•U•N}. What remains to be determined is the internal structure of the expression, in particular the head element, if any, and the consequence of the structure for the syntagmatics of the language. Restrictions on the distribution are a good place to start the analysis.

A striking fact about the Polish nasal vowels is the total absence of these nuclei in absolute initial position of the word. Briefly, no word can start with *ę* [ɛN] or *ą* [ɔN]. After an onset, on the other hand, both the front (52a) and the back nasal (52b) are possible. This striking discrepancy has been noted on occasion but no systematic account has been offered.

(52)   (a)   między [mʲɛndzɨ] 'between'   mędrzec [mɛnd-ʒɛts] 'sage'
sięg-a [ɕɛŋga] '(s)he reaches'   sęp [sɛmp] 'vulture'
ciężar [tɕɛʷʒar] 'burden'   tęcz-a [tɛntʃa] 'rainbow'
cętk-a [tsɛntka] 'speckle'   często [tʃɛʷstɔ] 'often'
z-gięt-y [zɟɛntɨ] 'bent'   gęst-y [gɛʷstɨ] 'thick'
prosi-ę [prɔɕɛ⁽ʷ⁾] 'piglet'   prosz-ę [prɔʃɛ⁽ʷ⁾] 'I request'

(b) piąt-k-a [pʲɔntka] 'fiver'   pąk [pɔŋk] 'bud'

ziąb [ʑɔmp] 'chill'   ząb [zɔmp] 'tooth'

dziąsł-o [dʑɔᵂswɔ] 'alveolus'   dąs-a-ć [dɔᵂsatɕ] 'sulk'

cążk-i [tsɔᵂʃci] 'pliers'   czǎst-k-a [tʃɔᵂstka] 'part, dim.'

gią-ć [ɟɔɲtɕ] 'bend'   gąs-k-a [gɔᵂska] 'goose, dim.'

łodzi-ą [wɔdʑɔᵂ] 'boat, instr. sg.' błądz-ą [bwɔndzɔᵂ] 'they err'

We will be taking a closer look at the various combinations of nasal nuclei with their onsets later on—the point here is to document the relative freedom that nasal vowels appear to enjoy in combining with consonants. Against this background the total absence of an initial nasal without a preceding onset is singularly remarkable. However, our discussion above has already revealed two similar cases: we noted the total absence of initial [ɨ] ({I•_}) and also initial [ɛ] ({A•I•_}). In relation to the former case we discovered that the regularities of the language force the phonetic implementation [i], while in the second case they force [jɛ]. Could something similar be the case with the nasal nuclei?

If in place of the expected initial [ɛ] we found [jɛ], in place of the expected [ɛN] we should find [jɛN]. This is confirmed by the native lexical stock. In (53a) we offer more examples for the initial oral sequence and these should be contrasted with the nasal one in (53b).

(53)   (a) jezior-o [jɛʑɔrɔ] 'lake'   jeleń [jɛlɛɲ] 'deer'

          jemioł-a [jɛmʲɔwa] 'mistletoe' jedwab [jɛdvap] 'silk'

          jesiotr [jɛɕɔtr̩] 'sturgeon'   jeniec [jɛɲɛts] 'captive'

     (b) język [jɛᵂzɨk] 'tongue'   jęcz-e-ć [jɛntʃɛtɕ] 'groan'

          jędz-a [jɛndza] 'termagant'   jęczmień [jɛntʃmʲɛɲ] 'barley'

          jędr-n-y [jɛndrnɨ] 'pithy'   jętk-a [jɛntka] 'May-fly'

Recall that the initial [jɛ] was interpreted as a case of double attachment: the I-head was associated with the onset and with {A} in the nucleus. The representation in (43) is reproduced in (54).

(54)

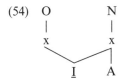

With the front nasal nucleus we need to enrich its representation by the addition of the nasal component. The resulting structure is straightfoward; see (55).

(55)

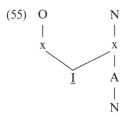

The representation in (55) conforms to the two relevant constraints we formulated in connection with the I-headed mid front vowel, namely, I-alignment and Operators Required. Recall that in such a case the sharing relation between the consonant and the nucleus is traditionally referred to as palatalization and the vowel is said to be palatalizing. The same is true of the front nasal nucleus, which can contract a sharing relation with its onset. In addition to some of the examples in (52a), the following words document this observation.

(56)   księg-a [kɕɛŋga] 'book'   więc-ej [vʲɛntsɛj] 'more'
          piękn-y [pʲɛŋknɨ] 'beautiful' dźwięk [dʑvʲɛŋk] 'sound'
          ścięgn-o [ɕtɕɛŋgnɔ] 'sinew' śnię-t-y [ɕɲɛntɨ] 'dead'

In our terms, the data in (56) are governed by the same constraints which can be seen in combinations of a palatalized consonant and the mid vowel in (57).

(57)   ksieni [kɕɛɲi] 'abbess'   wiedz-a [vʲɛdza] 'knowledge'
          piesz-y [pʲɛʃɨ] 'pedestrian'   niedźwiedź [ɲɛdʑvʲɛtɕ] 'bear, n.'
          ścier-k-a [ɕtɕɛrka] 'rag'   śnieg [ɕɲɛk] 'snow'

Thus both with the nasal nucleus (56) and the oral one (57) the onset and the following nucleus share their I-head, while the onset contains also other melodic elements. The same was true when the onset contained no additional elements and the palatal glide appeared in it, as shown in (53). This allows us to conclude that the nasal vowel appearing after a palatalized consonant is {N•A•I}—in other words, it is an I-headed mid vowel with the nasal component.

For the completeness of the picture we should look at the {N•A•I} combinations after palato-velars. While there is no dearth of examples involving the oral vowel after a palato-velar stop (58a), those involving the nasal ones are less frequent. Nonetheless, they are to be found as (58b) shows.

(58)   (a) kier-ow-a-ć [cɛrɔvatɕ] 'manage'   ogier [ɔɟɛr] 'stallion'
             okiełzn-a-ć [ɔcɛwznatɕ] 'bridle, vb.'   mgieł [mɟɛw] 'mist, gen. pl.'
             kieszeń [cɛʃɛɲ] 'pocket'   bagien-n-y [baɟɛnnɨ] 'of the bog'
      (b) religi-ę [reliɟjɛ⁽ʷ⁾] 'religion,   fonologi-ę [fɔnɔlɔɟjɛ⁽ʷ⁾]
             acc. sg.'   'phonology, acc.'
             autarki-ę [awtarcjɛ⁽ʷ⁾] 'auratchy, acc.' z-gię-t-y [zɟɛntɨ] 'crooked'

Admittedly, the number of forms with a nasal nucleus after a palato-velar is small in the extreme and perhaps there is just one clear case, namely, z-gię-t-y [zɟɛntɨ]. In the loans the palato-velar plosive is followed by the palatal glide.[8] What is relevant is that the few words that do exist conform completely to the expected patterns while they do not have to. As we saw in (49b), a point to which we return presently, the front nasal may also follow a non-palatalized velar plosive, hence if a sequence [cɛN] or [ɟɛN] were to be impossible, forms like those in (58b) could easily contain a velar

---

[8] Note that in some cases the glide re-appears in a different combination, e.g. religij-n-y [rɛliɟijnɨ] 'religious'. Such forms will be discussed in a later chapter.

plosive (z-gię-t-y *[zgɛntɨ]). They do not, hence their infrequency notwithstanding, we can legitimately claim that the expression {N•A•I} can be doubly attached through its head with the preceding onset. It should be added that the word-final nasal glide in (58b) is optional or present in very careful styles only; in colloquial, unmonitored, speech the final vowel are oral [ɛ]s. Below, such nuclei will be transcribed without the glide or with the nasal glide in brackets: religi-ę [reliɟjɛ⁽ʷ⁾] 'religion, acc. sg.'; fonologi-ę [fɔnɔlɔɟjɛ⁽ʷ⁾] 'phonology, acc.'

The last remark brings us to the problem of the nasal nucleus following a non-palatalized onset, alluded to above. The examples in (49b), reproduced as (59a) below, show very clearly that velar plosives can be followed by a nasal nucleus. The additional examples in (59b) document that the front nasal vowel can follow any non-palatalized consonant.

(59) (a) kędy [kɛndɨ] 'which way'   gęś [gɛʲɕ] 'goose'
       kędzior [kɛɲdʑɔr] 'lock of hair'   gęb-a [gɛmba] 'gob'
       kęs [kɛʷs] 'bite, n.'   gęst-y [gɛʷstɨ] 'thick'
       wlok-ę [vlɔkɛ⁽ʷ⁾] 'I drag'   mog-ę [mɔgɛ⁽ʷ⁾] 'I can'
       mąk-ę [mɔŋkɛ⁽ʷ⁾] 'flour, acc. sg.' obelg-ę [ɔbɛlgɛ⁽ʷ⁾] 'insult, acc. sg.'

   (b) pędz-i-ć [pɛɲdʑitɕ] 'rush, vb.'   będzi-e [bɛɲdʑɛ] '(s)he will be'
       wędz-i-ć [vɛɲdʑitɕ] 'smoke, vb.'   męt-n-y [mɛntnɨ] 'opaque'
       sęk [sɛŋk] 'knot'   zęb-y [zɛmbɨ] 'teeth'
       rękaw [rɛŋkaf] 'sleeve'   nęc-i-ć [nɛɲtɕitɕ] 'lure, vb.'
       częst-y [tʃɛʷstɨ] 'frequent'   ob-cęg-i [ɔptsɛɲɟi] 'pincers'
       chęt-n-y [xɛntnɨ] 'willing'   rzęs-a [ʒɛʷsa] 'eyelash'

It is clear that there is no necessary connection between a nasal nucleus and a preceding non-palatalized onset consonant. This is yet another parallel with the oral vowels. Recall that, as shown in (49a) and partly reproduced below, the front vowel [ɛ] can follow a (non-palatalized) velar plosive, even though this seems restricted to relatively unassimilated loans.

(60) kelner [kɛlnɛr] 'waiter'   genez-a [gɛnɛza] 'origin'
      kemping [kɛmpʲiŋk] 'camping'   germań-sk-i [gɛrmaɲsci] 'Germanic'
      keks [kɛks] 'fruit cake'   generał [gɛnɛraw] 'general'

These examples were interpreted as containing an A-headed nucleus, hence no I-sharing was possible. Since the nasal nuclei in (59a) exhibit no sharing effects, either, this must mean that the nuclei are not I-headed; they cannot be empty-headed since then the Empty Heads and I-alignment constraints would have to be involved and the result would be a palato-velar followed by a mid vowel, [cɛ, ɟɛ]. We are left with the only option: just like the oral vowels licensing velars in (60), they have to be A-headed; they differ from the oral expressions in containing the additional element responsible for nasality, in other words, they are {N•I•A}. Thus the parallelism between the oral and nasal front nuclei is complete and hence our decision to supply them with identical internal structure and sharing relations, apart from the nasal element itself, of course.

Let us tabulate and exemplify the structures identified so far; the representations are schematic, therefore no full element specification for consonants is supplied—consonantal melodies are replaced by [..].

(61) (a)

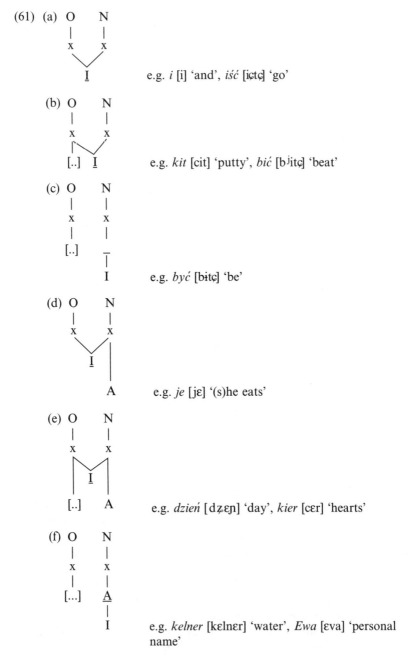

e.g. *i* [i] 'and', *iść* [ictɕ] 'go'

(b)

e.g. *kit* [cit] 'putty', *bić* [bʲitɕ] 'beat'

(c)

e.g. *być* [bɨtɕ] 'be'

(d)

e.g. *je* [jɛ] '(s)he eats'

(e)

e.g. *dzień* [dʑɛɲ] 'day', *kier* [cɛr] 'hearts'

(f)

e.g. *kelner* [kɛlnɛr] 'water', *Ewa* [ɛva] 'personal name'

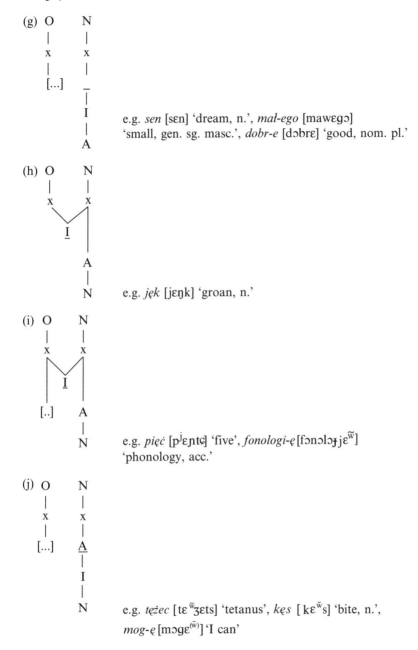

(g) e.g. *sen* [sɛn] 'dream, n.', *mał-ego* [mawɛgɔ] 'small, gen. sg. masc.', *dobr-e* [dɔbrɛ] 'good, nom. pl.'

(h) e.g. *jęk* [jɛŋk] 'groan, n.'

(i) e.g. *pięć* [pʲɛɲtɕ] 'five', *fonologi-ę* [fɔnɔlɔɟjɛ̃ʷ] 'phonology, acc.'

(j) e.g. *tężec* [tɛ̃ʷʒets] 'tetanus', *kęs* [kɛ̃ʷs] 'bite, n.', *mog-ę* [mɔgɛ̃ʷ] 'I can'

If a paradigmatic list were to be made—and keeping in mind the dubious significance of such a list—the above structures could be reduced to the expressions in (62) involving different combinations of the elements {I}, {A}, and {N}.

(62)   for the element {I} alone: {<u>I</u>}, {I•_}
     for the elements {I} and {A}: {A•<u>I</u>}, {I•<u>A</u>}, {I•A•_}
     for the elements {I], {A} and {N}: {N•A•<u>I</u>}, {N•I•<u>A</u>}

This gives us a total of seven expressions. There seem to be no empty-headed vowels containing the three elements functioning as operators, an exclusion for which some general theoretical justification should be provided.

3.8 BACK VOWELS: THE BACK NASAL VOWEL

So far we have been concerned with front vowels since the remaining expressions are not particularly problematic. We have [u] which can hardly be anything else but {<u>U</u>}, [ɔ] which is a combination of two elements {A•<u>U</u>}, and [a] which is simply {<u>A</u>}. They are involved in various morphophonological alternations which will be discussed in Chapter 6. At this stage we would like to consider the question of the back nasal vowel [ɔN], since it is reasonable to assume that its structure is similar in relevant respects to the front nasal nucleus.

The mid back vowel [ɔ] being a combination of {A} and {U}, the back nasal might be headed by the high element, in other words, it would take the shape {N•A•<u>U</u>}. Being U-headed it can follow either palatalized or non-palatalized consonants, since of course there is no I-sharing characteristic of palatalized consonants in combination with front vowels. This is indeed the case as shown by the examples.

(63)   (a) siąś-ć [ɕɔ^{w}ɕtɕ] 'sit down'   wzią-ć [vʑɔɲtɕ] 'take, vb.'
         miąższ [mʲɔ^{w}ʃ] 'pulp'   pią-ć [pʲɔɲtɕ] 'climb, vb.'
         lubi-ą [lubʲɔ^w] 'they like'   dziąsł-o [dʑɔ^{w}swɔ] 'alveolus'
         ciąg [tɕɔŋk] 'sequence'   gią-ć [ɟɔɲtɕ] 'bend, vb.'
         anarchi-ą [anarɕɔ^w] 'anarchy, instr. sg.'

     (b) sądz-i-ć [sɔɲdʑitɕ] 'judge, vb.'   żąd-a-ć [ʒɔndatɕ] 'demand, vb.'
         chrząszcz [xʃɔ^{w}ʃtʃ] 'bug, n.'   władz-ą [vwadzɔ^w] 'power, instr. sg.'
         błąd [bwɔnt] 'mistake, n.'   mąc-i-ć [mɔntɕitɕ] 'confuse'
         płon-ą-ć [pwɔnɔɲtɕ] 'burn'   kąt [kɔnt] 'corner'
         gąszcz [gɔ^{w}ʃtʃ] 'thicket'   kruch-ą [kruxɔ^w] 'brittle, fem. instr. sg.'

It can be concluded that the back nasal displays little or no interaction with the preceding onset. One aspect of the vowel remains puzzling, though: like the front nasal, it is barred from word initial position. This we recorded above by noting that no Polish word begins, or could begin, with a nasal nucleus. For the front vowel we invoked I-alignment (33) and Operators Required (38), as shown by the representation in (55). It is not obvious whether this interpretation can be extended in its entirety to the back nasal but there are some promising indications.

As the nasality element in the front nasal nucleus is invariably an operator (see (61 h–j)), we may expect the back nasal nucleus to be structured similarly and represent it as {N•A•U̱}. If this melody were to be preceded by an empty onset we could assume that some mechanism is at work that spreads the head of the nucleus to the onset; in such a case, the head could be doubly attached, yielding the structure in (64).

(64)

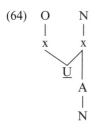

The predicted phonetic realization of a structure such as the one in (64) is [wɔN]. Polish does supply instances of such a sequence. It also supplies an intriguing twist to the proposal. Let us start with illustrating the initial sequences.

(65) łąk-a [wɔŋka] 'meadow'   łącz-y-ć [wɔntʃʲitɕ] 'connect'
       łącz-nik [wɔntʃɲik] 'hyphen' łątk-a [wɔntka] 'puppet'

These examples provide an interpretation which is almost too pat: just like the front nasal is preceded initially by a front glide, the back nasal is in similar circumstances preceded by a back glide. The patness of the proposal can be appreciated by considering the twist which we discussed at some length in Chapter 2. The fact is that the back glide in (65)—and in all other instances of the orthographic *l*—is of a relatively recent provenance, so recent that it co-exists with the earlier phonetic shape. The earlier variant is the velarized lateral [ɫ]. It appears in the speech of the older generation of speakers coming from the former eastern territories of Poland; it also appears in studied stage Polish. Although a rapidly disappearing dialectal or individual feature in the present day language, it is still part of the Polish phonological system *sensu largo*. The words in (65) can also be heard in the form given in (66) and speakers of Polish have no problem in establishing an identity relation between them.

(66) łąk-a [ɫɔŋka] 'meadow'   łącz-y-ć [ɫɔntʃʲitɕ] 'connect'
       łącz-nik [ɫɔntʃɲik] 'hyphen' łątk-a [ɫɔntka] 'puppet'

As argued in Chapter 2, the back glide must be seen as an interpretation—or a packaging—of a lateral (presumably a velarized lateral). The lateral apart from the element {U} responsible for velarization must contain other elements, possibly the place element {A} and the occlusion element {ʔ}. The representational properties coupled with the close morphophonological link of [w] with the lateral [l] make it an unlikely realization of an empty onset before a back nasal. An alternative has to be sought.

A possibility was briefly mentioned in Chapter 2 that the voiced labio-dental fricative [v] has some glide properties which can be seen in the progressive voice assimilation. Since this segment also contains the prime {U}, it is not unreasonable to suggest that this consonant is linked with the following back nasal nucleus. Apart from the labiality element {U}, the fricative [v] must also contain {h} responsible for noise and {L} accounting for voicing. That is why we cannot view the possible double attachment of {U} as a live phonological mechanism. Rather, it must be a static formulation which attempts to answer the question of why the back nasal does not appear word-initially. Appropriate examples would comprise the following cases:

(67)   wąs-k-i [vɔ^{w}sci] 'narrow'   wawóz [vɔ^{w}vus] 'gorge'
      wątrob-a [vɔntrɔba] 'liver'   wąż [vɔ^{w}ʃ] 'snake'
      wąs [vɔ^{w}s] 'moustache'   wątp-i-ć [vɔntp^{j}itɕ] 'doubt, vb.'

The significance of this attempt to account for the absence of the nasal vowel initially should be seen in a proper perspective. As stated above, this is not a live phonological regularity by any stretch of the imagination; the status of the initial spirant [v] as a glide is not available in synchronic terms—in fact, there is convincing evidence to show that the initial spirant is an obstruent because of its involvement in the progressive voice assimilation (see Ch. 7). Thus the fricative can only be taken as structurally analogous to the palatal glide preceding the front non-nasal and nasal vowel (see examples in (53b)). Although there is evidence for morphophonological relatedness of the palatal glide [j] and the labio-dental fricative [v],[9] no phonologically plausible account of the relationship can be formulated (and, indeed, none should be attempted).

In view of the above, we can represent the initial sequences [vɔN] as an onset–nucleus where the consonantal onset shares the element {U} with the nucleus.

(68)

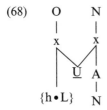

[9] In Gussmann (1981) the alternation [j~v], referred to as the glide shift, is discussed in abstract derivational terms. Examples involve primarily morphologically conditioned cases in the category of derived imperfectives (der. imperf.), e.g. prze-żyj-ą [pʃɛʒɨjɔ^{w}] 'they will experience'~prze-żyw-aj-ą [pʃɛʒɨvajɔ^{w}] 'der. imperf.', form-uj-ę [fɔrmujɛ$^{(w)}$] 'I form'~form-ow-a-ć [fɔrmɔvatɕ] 'inf.'; there are also lexically related words which instantiate the alternation, e.g. żyj-ą [ʒɨjɔ^{w}] 'they live'~żyw-y [ʒɨvɨ] 'alive', pij-ę [p^{j}ijɛ$^{(w)}$] 'I drink'~piw-o [p^{j}ivɔ] 'beer', kuj-e [kujɛ] '(s)he forges'~kow-al [kɔval] 'smith'.

3.9 PALATALIZATION AS A PHONOLOGICAL REGULARITY?

We have had a sufficient look at various palatalization-related phenomena in Modern Polish to take a break and ask a more basic question, namely: How broad are palatalizations as live synchronic phonological regularities in the contemporary language? The answer is best placed in the context of the different phonological traditions that have developed in the Slavic literature. In what follows we shall be talking about the modern language leaving aside the vast and equally, if not more, challenging problem of the history of Polish and Slavic palatalizations.

Traditional and structural descriptions of Polish left no doubt as to the status of palatalized consonants: apart from a few controversial cases, they are all separate phonemes. The questionable cases involved the palatalized labials we have discussed above and the status of palato-velars (palatalized velars), a problem to which we will return below. In this part of our discussion we will concentrate on the palatalized coronals [ɕ, ʑ, tɕ, dʑ, ɲ] and also on consonants which are not palatalized phonetically but which, for historical and morphophonological reasons, have been included into the palatalization complex. These non-palatalized segments include the dental affricates [ts, dz], the post-alveolars [ʃ, ʒ, tʃ, dʒ], and the lateral [l]. The existence of numerous pairs and triplets of the type exemplified in (69) precluded any doubt as to the phonemic status of the segments involved: they must all be regarded as separate phonemes.

(69) prac [prats]   pr-a-ć [pratɕ]   pracz [pratʃ]
      'job, gen. pl.'   'laundry, vb.'   'laundryman'

      rad-ę [radɛ⁽ʷ⁾]   radz-ę [radzɛ⁽ʷ⁾]   radzi-e [radʑɛ]
      'advice, acc. sg.'   'I advise'   'advice, dat. sg.'

      kas-a [kasa]   kasz-a [kaʃa]   Kasi-a [kaɕa]
      'paydesk'   'gruel'   'personal name'

      pan [pan]   pań [paɲ]
      'gentleman'   'lady, gen. pl.'

      sta-ł [stał/staw]   stal [stal]
      'he stood'   'steel'

In structuralist terms, the ability of two or more segments to appear in the same context amounted to the proof of their distinctiveness. Since there are minimal pairs galore, the possibilities of a phonological analysis are basically exhausted with the establishment of all existing contrasts.

The advent of the generative model in phonology in the early 1960s marked a dramatic change in most props on the phonological scene. Surface contrasts were rejected out of hand, hence the classical phoneme went down the drain as did most of the notions associated with it. In their place, the concept of the underlying representations was recognized together with derivational statements mediating between them and the more concrete, systematic phonetic representations. The underlying or systematic phonemic level came remarkably close to the structural morphophonological level and in the early works these terms were used interchangeably. Since surface contrasts were of no relevance and the morphophonological or deep level became all important, it is not surprising that the generative analysis took morphophonological alternations as providing direct evidence for the existing phonological regularities, or 'rules' as they were called.

One of the crucial differences between a structuralist morphophonological analysis and a generative systematic phonemic (or phonological) one was the latter's claim to exclusiveness: the only linguistically significant level of representation is the abstract underlying level. The phonetic representation was viewed as entirely derivative of the underlying representation, given the existence of phonological rules. The morphophonological bias meant in effect that any morphological alternation could be used as evidence in phonological analysis.

In terms of Polish, this view of phonology meant, among other things, that all alternations between palatalized and non-palatalized consonants, and between dental affricates and palatals alternating with other consonants as well, should be described as rule-governed. The simple non-palatalized consonants were regarded as basic or appearing in underlying representations. Consider a few examples of alternations involving coronals and velars.

(70) [d ~ dʑ ~ dz]
      wid-a-ć [vʲidatɕ]   widzi-e-ć [vʲidʑɛtɕ]   widz-ę [vʲidzɛ⁽ʷ⁾]
      'to be seen'   'see'   'I see'

      [t ~ tɕ ~ ts]
      sierot-a [ɕɛrɔta]   sieroci-e [ɕɛrɔtɕɛ]   sieroc-a [ɕɛrɔtsa]
      'orphan'   'dat. sg.'   'adj. fem.'

      [s ~ ɕ ~ ʃ]
      wy-nos [vɨnɔs]   wy-nos-i [vɨnɔɕi]'   wy-nosz-ąc [vɨnɔʃɔnts]
      'takeaway'   '(s)he carries out'   'carrying'

      [z ~ ʑ ~ ʒ]
      wyraz-u [vɨrazu]   wyraz-i-ć [vɨraʑitɕ]   wyraż-ę [vɨraʒɛ⁽ʷ⁾]
      'word, gen. sg.'   'express'   'I'll express'

      [r ~ ʒ ~ ʃ]
      bior-ę [bʲɔrɛ⁽ʷ⁾]   bierz-e-sz [bʲɛʒɛʃ]   bierz [bʲɛʃ]
      'I take'   'you take'   'imper.'

      [n ~ ɲ]
      ran-a [rana]   rani-ę [raɲɛ⁽ʷ⁾]
      'wound, n.'   'I wound'

      [w ~ l]
      sta-ł-y [stawɨ]   stal-i [stali]
      'they (fem.) stood'   'they (masc.) stood'

[k ∼ tɕ ∼ tʃ]

prorok [prɔrɔk]	proroc-k-i [prɔrɔtsci]	prorocz-y [prɔrɔtʃɨ]
'prophet'	'of the prophet'	'prophetic'

[g ∼ dz ∼ ʒ]

wag-a [vaga]	wadz-e [vadzɛ]	waż-y-ć [vaʒɨtɕ]
'scales'	'loc. sg.'	'weigh'

[x ∼ ʃ ∼ ɕ]

Włoch [vwɔx]	Włosz-k-a [vwɔʃka]	Włoś-i [vwɔɕi]
'an Italian'	'fem.'	'nom. pl.'

The morphophonological richness of Slavic in general and Polish in particular proved both seductive and persuasive: the possibility of deriving most—perhaps all—alternations by means of rules applying to abstract representations became the official generative programme. It was attempted in its most ambitious version only once when Lightner (1963) set out to eliminate as much allomorphy as possible:

> We suggest that the sharping [= palatalization, EG] of consonants and nasalization of vowels in Polish is always predictable (and hence nonphonemic). Moreover, the occurrence of the palatals *cz ż sz* [= tʃ, ʒ, ʃ, EG] and of the glides *j w* is shown to be predictable. Furthermore, we want to indicate that at least some of the rather complex consonant and vowel alternations that occur in Polish inflection may be accounted for by a simple set of rules, all of which are of general application.

Since the palatalization of consonants and the appearance of (non-palatalized) palatals are to be invariably predictable, appropriately abstract rules and representations have to be posited. Of course, once the objective is set this way, the very existence of surface segments often becomes the immediate justification for individual rules and their interactions. In other words, morphological alternations are the starting point of the analysis, which is subsequently extended to non-aternating forms, that is to say, to forms which regularly appear in just one shape. This produces a strategy which might be called the generalization transferral: a generalization (rule) established on the basis of alternations is transferred onto non-alternating words.

Lightner's solutions, which reflect in the majority the chain of events familiar from Common Slavic and the history of Polish, eliminate underlying allomorphy but provide practically no evidence for the reality of either the rules or the representations. As a result, all work in the generative phonology of Polish which came after Lightner tried in various ways to justify the need for specific rules and, in the process, to bridle the abstractness of representations. The most important of these studies, including Laskowski (1975a), Gussmann (1978, 1980a), Rubach (1984), Bethin (1992), and Szpyra (1989, 1995), in various ways attempt to come to grips with this issue. None of them, however, attempts to undermine the basic tenet of the generative model, namely, the conviction that morphophonological alternations emerge as the result of phonological rules or, alternatively, that allomorphy is the best source of information about phonological regularities (see, however, Gussmann 1992a, 1997a). But it is almost obvious that unless this assumption or tenet can be upheld, the rest is mere window dressing: whether the rules are cyclic or not; whether there are ordered rules or violable constraints; whether rules operate on binary on monovalent elements; whether there is feature geometry or not—all these and a host of other questions fade into insignificance unless we know what can constitute a phonological generalization and what must be assigned to other components of the language. It is the contention of this book that only a tiny portion of morphophonological alternations can legitimately be used as evidence of phonological regularities. In other words, phonological regularities exist independently of any alternations although, on occasion, they may lead to such alternations. We will argue that morphophonological alternations belong to morphophonology and/or morphology, as has been traditionally maintained (see also Darden 1989). Rather than review even the major proposals made in the literature to account for alternations by phonological means, a task not only very difficult but primarily futile, we will take a close look at a few suffixes and the effects they have. Attention will be focussed on the evidence that morphological alternations can have for identifying phonological generalizations.

To make our discussion maximally constrained we will consider the vowel taken to be truly palatalizing, that is, the front high /i/. All generative analyses of Polish assume, in contradistinction to the predominant structuralist view, that there are two phonological high unrounded segments: the front /i/ and the back /ɨ/. The former invariably palatalizes a preceding consonant, whereas the latter never does so. This does not mean that there is a one-to-one correspondence between underlying and surface segments: since rules can modify segments in various ways, it often happens that what is phonologically /i/ emerges as [ɨ], and, conversely, the phonological /ɨ/ manifests itself on the surface as [i]. The elimination of allomorphy means that, barring cases of suppletion, every morpheme should have one phonological representation. Keeping these assumptions in mind, let us look at a few suffixes.

3.10 THE SUFFIXES -*IZM*/-*YZM*, -*IST-A*/-*YST-A*, -*IZACJ-A*/-*YZACJ-A* AND THEIR IMPLICATIONS

An argument most frequently marshalled by proponents of derivational phonological descriptions in support of the claim that broadly based palatalizations constitute a synchronic regularity of Modern Polish comes from loan words. Briefly, an obvious borrowing like *fiat* [fʲjat] 'make of car' can take the native diminutive suffix -*ik* and when it does so, the final consonant is converted into a palatalized affricate, yielding *fiac-ik* [fʲjatɕik] 'a small Fiat'; similarly, a borrowing in the computer language *czat* [tʃat] 'chat' appears as *czaci-e* [tʃatɕɛ] in the locative singular. Cases such as these are claimed to testify to the reality of a regularity deriving palatalized consonants. Similarly, an older loan such as *teatr* [tɛatr̥] 'theatre' with the same suffix deriving the diminutive *teatrz-yk* [tɛat-ʃɨk] documents the reality of palatalization turning underlying /r/ into an intermediate (unattested) /rʲ/ which is subsequently converted by a context-free rule into a hard or non-palatalized [ʒ]; this segment undergoes progressive devoicing to [ʃ] while the front vowel of the suffix is backed to [ɨ] after a non-palatalized consonant. Thus, although the final product is not a palatalized consonant phonetically, the process involved is believed to be the same, namely, palatalization of a consonant before a front vowel. This line of reasoning establishes both rules and the ordering relations: palatalization (r > rʲ), depalatalization or hardening (rʲ > ʒ), devoicing (ʒ > ʃ), vowel backing (i > ɨ). Since they apply to loans, the rules must be productive. A similar view is broadly adopted within the Optimality Theory framework as well (see Rubach and Booij 2001). It is a contention of this book, and especially of the immediately following section, that the argument is hasty and unwarranted. To see why this is so, we will take a detailed look at three nominalizing suffixes, all of which appear at the surface either with the front or the retracted vowel. These are: *-izm* [ism̥]/*-yzm* [ɨsm̥], *-ist-a* [ista]/*-yst-a* [ɨsta], and *-izacj-a* [izatsja]/*-yzacj-a* [ɨzatsja]. These are very frequent suffixes, with numbers of derivatives going into the hundreds. As is often the case with morphological regularities, properties of derivational bases, individual truncations or extensions, and of the semantics of the derivatives tend to be idiosyncratic. The morphology behind the distribution and the semantics of the suffixes is not our concern here (for an exhaustive study see Waszakowa 1994)—we will concentrate on the the initial vowel of the suffixes and on the ways the final consonant of the base is affected by the addition of the suffixes.

The two vowels [i] and [ɨ] that begin the suffixes have been analyzed as realizations of a single phoneme within the traditional structuralist interpretation. In such a case, whatever happens to be the final consonant of the base lies outside the purview of phonology since all palatalized consonants are treated as phonemes separate from their non-palatalized congeners. The more recent, two-phoneme, approach treats the vowels as realization of two contrastive units and partly predicts the appearance of palatalized consonants. It claims that the labial consonant before /i/ must be palatalized but has nothing to say about the distribution of the two vocalic phonemes /i/ and /ɨ/. The derivational generative model would aim to say that while two vowels have to be recognized as contrastive underlying segments, the shape of the base-final consonant can always be predicted, irrespective of whether it is phonetically palatalized or not. One point of agreement that may be noted between the more recent structuralist and the generative phonological approach is that both of them recognize two contrastive vocalic units /i/ and /ɨ/ and both agree in viewing palatalized labials as derived. The generative approach goes further and views all consonantal effects before underlying /i/ as derived while the structuralist tradition has nothing to say about the connection between the vowel and the preceding non-labial consonant.

Taking first the suffix *-izm/-yzm*, let us consider derivatives from nominal bases. The variant *-izm* appears after a palatalized consonant, as in the following examples.

(71)   snob-a [snɔba] 'snob, gen. sg.'   snob-izm [snɔbʲism̩] 'snobbery'
        utopi-a [utɔpʲja] 'utopia'   utop-izm [utɔpʲism̩] 'utopian theory'
        islam [islam] 'Islam'   islam-izm [islamʲism̩] 'Islamic theory'
        biografi-a [bʲjɔgrafʲja]   biograf-izm [bʲjɔgrafʲism̩]
        'biography'   'biographic approach'
        pasyw-n-y [pasɨvnɨ] 'passive'   pasyw-izm [pasɨvʲism̩] 'passivity'
        nazi [nazʲi] 'Nazi'   naz-izm [naʑism̩] 'Nazism'
        Lenin [lɛɲin]   lenin-izm [lɛɲiɲism̩] 'Leninism'
        Marks [marks]   marks-izm [markɕism̩] 'Marxism'
        liberał [libɛraw] 'liberal, n.'   liberal-izm [libɛralism̩] 'liberalism'
        Franco [frankɔ]   frank-izm [francism̩] 'Francoism'
        biologi-a [bʲjɔlɔɟja] 'biology'   biolog-izm [bʲjɔlɔɟism̩] 'biological
        approach'

        Czech-y [tʃɛxɨ] ' the   czech-izm [tʃɛçism̩] 'a Czech borrowing'
        Czech Republic'

It is not relevant from our point of view whether the base or the motivating noun does or does not contain a palatalized consonant. In fact, in some cases the decision as to what constitutes the motivating base is not obvious, hence *radykal-izm* [radɨkalism̩] 'radicalism' could be argued to be derived either from the noun *radykał* [radɨkaw] 'radical, n.' or from the adjective *radykal-n-y* [radɨkalnɨ] 'radical, adj.', with truncation of the adjectival suffix *-n*. The ultimate decision has to be morphologically grounded. What is directly relevant here is that on either interpretation we end up with the variant [ism̩] of the suffix while the preceding lateral [l] is a palatalized congener of [w] (i.e. of [ɫ]). Within a structuralist analysis the alternation of the consonants cannot be phonologically conditioned by the following vowel since the two consonant are independently contrastive, for example *lask-a* [laska] 'stick, n.' vs. *łask-a* [waska] 'grace', and *skal-a* [skala] 'scale' vs. *skał-a* [skawa] 'rock, n.'. It could thus be concluded that the suffix begins with /i/ after base-final labials and these labials, as elsewhere in the language, take their palatalized allophones before this vowel. The appearance of the front vowel in the suffix after palatalized non-labials (e.g. *lenin-izm*, *marks-izm*) has to be regarded as an accident; similarly fortuitous is the appearance of the variant *-yzm* with [ɨ] after non-palatalized consonants (as exemplified below). The structuralist two-phoneme analysis is so obviously flawed that it is hardly worth pursuing its consequences any further.

The generative position would be that the suffix begins with the front vowel and evinces palatalization of the base-final consonant in all cases in (71); this leads us to the conclusion that palatalization is a phonological regularity affecting recent loans, foreign names, etc. as well. The consonants affected include labials, velars, the lateral and nasal coronal, and the coronal fricatives. The situation is different, however, if we turn to the remaining coronals. Consider examples of the same type of derivatives ending in these consonants.

(72) dyletant [dɨlɛtant] 'dilettante'   dyletant-yzm [dɨlɛtantɨsm̥] 'dilettantism'
      dogmat [dɔgmat] 'dogma'   dogmat-yzm [dɔgmatɨsm̥] 'dogmatism'
      Budd-a [budda] 'Buddha'   budd-yzm [buddɨsm̥] 'Buddhism'
      awangard-a [avangarda]   awangard-yzm [avangardɨsm̥]
      'vanguard'   'avant-gardism'
      Hitler [çitlɛr]   hitler-yzm [çitlɛrɨsm̥] 'Hitlerism'
      rygor [rɨgɔr] 'rigour'   rygor-yzm [rɨgɔrɨsm̥] 'austerity'
      fetysz [fɛtɨʃ] 'fetish'   fetysz-yzm [fɛtɨʃɨsm̥] 'fetishism'
      rewanż-u [rɛvanʒu]   rewanż-yzm [rɛvanʒɨsm̥] 'revengefulness'
      'revenge, gen. sg.'

As the examples show, with bases ending in [t, d, r, ʃ, ʒ] no palatalization takes place. There are further complications connected with the velars, which, as shown in (71), emerge as [c, ɟ, ç] before the suffix -ism. Instances can be found, however, where the voiceless velar plosive alternates with the dental affricate [ts] as shown in (73).

(73) mistyk [mʲistɨk] 'mistic, n.'   mistyc-yzm [mʲistɨtsɨsm̥] 'misticism'
      krytyk [krɨtɨk] 'critic, n.'   krytyc-yzm [krɨtɨtsɨsm̥] 'criticism'

The alternations in (73) would have to be regarded as purely lexical, hence as non-Polish or borrowed alternations. With regard to the hundreds of examples like those in (71)–(72), the generative tradition would probably want to say that there is only one underlying representation of the suffix, say /izm/. In the course of derivation, but prior to phonology proper, the representation of the suffix is adjusted by some allomorphy rule in such a way that the front /i/ is backed to /ɨ/ when the base ends in one of /t, d, r, ʃ, ʒ/. In this way the rule of palatalization could be claimed to apply across the board, that is, before any front vowel. The gimmicky nature of this solution hardly needs stressing: a class of consonants is removed from the domain of a rule which can then be claimed to be of general applicability. There are more complications to which we return below.

Consider now the second of our borrowed suffixes, which also appears either with initial [i] or [ɨ]. It is the personal suffix -ist-a [ista]/-yst-a [ɨsta] (obviously related to the English -ist, e.g. Marxist). The morphology of the suffix(es?) has been described in Waszakowa (1994: 197–208); as above we are interested here in the distribution of the two variants and the effect they have on the preceding consonant. As with the previous suffix, this one can also claim a lot of lexical support and is productively extended to recent or novel formations, for example, and-yst-a [andɨsta] 'mountain climber in the Andes' and panel-ist-a [panɛlista] 'member of a panel'.

In (74) we present cases exemplifying the suffix -ist-a, hence the necessary presence of a preceding palatalized consonant. This may mean that alternations with a non-palatalized consonant are to be expected:

(74) WOP [vɔp] 'Border Defence Army'   wop-ist-a [vɔpʲista] 'a soldier of WOP'

służ-b-a [swuʒba] 'service'   służ-b-ist-a [swuʒbʲista] 'martinet'

program [prɔgram]   program-ist-a [prɔgramʲista]
'programme'   'programmer'

harf-a [harfa] 'harp'   harf-ist-a [harfʲista] 'harpist'

rezerw-a [rɛzɛrva] 'reserve, n.'   rezerw-ist-a [rɛzɛrvʲista] 'reservist'

tenis [tɛɲis] 'tennis'   tenis-ist-a [tɛɲiɕista] 'tennis-player'

bas [bas] 'bass'   bas-ist-a [baɕista] 'bass-player'

kraj-obraz-u [krajɔbrazu]   kraj-obraz-ist-a [krajɔbraʑista]
'landscape, gen. sg.'   'landscape painter'

flet [flɛt] 'flute'   fleci-st-a [flɛtɕista] 'flautist'

ballad-a [ballada] 'ballad'   balladz-ist-a [balladʑista]
    'ballad writer'

finał [fʲinaw] 'end'   final-ist-a [fʲinalista] 'finalist'

afer-a [afɛra] 'scandal'   aferz-yst-a [afɛʒɨsta] 'schemer'

Franco [frankɔ]   frank-ist-a [francista] 'Frankoist'

czołg-u [tʃɔwgu] 'tank, gen. sg.'   czołg-ist-a [tʃɔwɟista] 'tank-driver'

szach-y [ʃaxɨ] 'chess'   szach-ist-a [ʃaçista] 'chess-player'

As the examples show, all plain consonants emerge as palatalized before our suffix. This also holds for the consonant [r], which is turned into the (non-palatalized) alveolar fricative [ʒ], as elsewhere in the language and after which, as after all non-palatalized consonants, the vowel must be the retracted [ɨ]. The variant -yst-a appears additionally after the remaining non-palatalized dental and alveolar affricates [ts, dz, tʃ, dʒ] and the alveolar voiceless spirant [ʃ]. Examples follow.

(75) klasyc-yzm [klasɨtsɨsm̥] 'classicism'   klasyc-yst-a [klasɨtsɨsta] 'classicist'

brydż-a [brɨdʒa] 'bridge, gen. sg.'   brydż-yst-a [brɨdʒɨsta] 'bridge player'

szantaż-u [ʃantaʒu] 'blackmail,   szantaż-yst-a [ʃantaʒɨsta]
gen. sg.'   'blackmailer'

fetysz [fɛtɨʃ] 'fetish'   fetysz-yst-a [fɛtɨʃɨsta] 'fetishist'

The basic difference that strikes the eye is the fact that the dentals [t, d, r] which resisted palatalization before the suffix -ism (see examples in (72)) appear susceptible to it before the suffix -ist-a. This creates the rare but remarkable case where the same base undergoes palatalization before one but not the other suffix.

(76) awangard-a [avangarda]   awangard-yzm [avangardɨsm̥]
awangardz-ist-a [avangardʑista]

We noted above that a generative account of the failure of palatalization before selected consonants would require an adjustment rule specifying that the vowel of the morpheme /izm/ is retracted after a specific group of consonants. Although in keeping with the nature of readjustment rules, which are supposed to capture idiosyncratic properties of stems and affixes, this solution supplies no particular evidence for the phonological reality of palatalization; the latter works once we decide to remove all possible obstacles from its path. The suffix *-ist-a/-yst-a* strengthens this feeling of unease: this time the class of consonants that must be removed from the possible sphere of palatalizing activity includes a partially different group of consonants; the consonants that appear to be subject to the process are the dentals /t, d, r/. Since this is a different suffix, it might be seen as unsurprising that the readjustment rule affecting it singles out different consonants for special treatment. However, the story does not end here.

Although examples like those in (74) strongly support the susceptibility of /t, d, r/ to palatalization, there are others which equally strongly argue against it. Consider just a few out of many such cases:

(77) Bonapart-e [bɔnapartɛ]   bonapart-yst-a [bɔnapartɨsta]
                                      'supporter of Bonaparte'
      esperanto [ɛspɛrantɔ]   esperant-yst-a [ɛspɛrantɨsta]
      'Esperanto'   'specialist in Esperanto'
      Conrad-a [kɔnrada]   konrad-yst-a [kɔnradɨsta]
      'Conrad, gen.'   'specialist in the works of J. Conrad'
      stypendium [stɨpɛndʲjum]   stypend-yst-a [stɨpɛndɨsta]
      'stipend'   'stipend holder'
      parodi-a [parɔdʲja] 'parody'   parod-yst-a [parɔdɨsta] 'parodist'
      humor [xumɔr] 'humour'   humor-yst-a [xumɔrɨsta] 'humorist'
      rygor [rɨgɔr] 'rigour'   rygor-yst-a [rɨgɔrɨsta] 'rigorist'

Furthermore, there are certain words where a variant with the palatalized consonant co-exists with one without it. The choice of the form may on occasion carry certain connotations, but in others it seems to be left entirely up to the speaker, in other words, it remains in morphological free variation.

(78) propagand-yst-a [prɔpagandɨsta] or propagandz-ist-a [prɔpagaɲdʑista]
      'propagandist'
      ballad-yst-a [balladɨsta]   balladz-ist-a [balladʑista]
      'ballad writer'
      alt-yst-a [altɨsta]   alc-ist-a [altɕista]
      'alto singer'
      dyszkant-yst-a [dɨʃkantɨsta]   dyszkanc-ist-a [dɨʃkaɲtɕista]
      'treble singer'
      manier-yst-a [maɲɛrɨsta]   manierz-yst-a [maɲɛʒɨsta]
      'follower of mannerism'
      humor-yst-a [xumɔrɨsta]   humorz-yst-a [xumɔʒɨsta]
      'humorist'

The conclusion that must be drawn from such facts is that the putative vowel adjustment is not suffix-driven, as the term 'readjustment rule' appears to indicate, but rather that it is the lexical property of individual derivatives. Although certain tendencies can be observed, they are nothing more than tendencies.

It is impossible to decide in advance where the adjustment will take place—witness the pair *aferz-yst-a~rygor-yst-a*—hence it is impossible to predict whether palatalization will be found or not. This means that palatalization is not even an affix-specific property but rather belongs to the lexical idiosyncrasies of specific derivatives.

The same conclusion emerges from the third of the suffixes in focus, namely, *-izacj-a* [izatsja]/*-yzacj-a* [ɨzatsja], obviously a borrowing related to the English *-ization*. The variant with a preceding palatalized consonant is selected almost invariably in the same cases as does the suffix *-ist-a* (see (74)), that is to say, after all plain consonants except for [t, d, r]. Even though not every possibility is confirmed lexically, the general pattern is overwhelming.

(79) etap [ɛtap] 'stage'   etap-izacj-a [ɛtapʲizatsja]
                                              'division into stages'
      sylab-a [sɨlaba] 'syllable'   sylab-izacj-a [sɨlabʲizatsja]
                                              'syllabification'
      kolektyw-u [kɔlɛktɨvu]   kolektyw-izacj-a
      'collective, n., gen.'   [kɔlɛktɨvʲizatsja] 'collectivization'
      atom [atɔm] 'atom'   atom-izacj-a [atɔmʲizatsja]
                                              'atomization'
      ekran [ɛkran] 'screen'   ekran-izacj-a [ɛkraɲizatsja]
                                              'turning into a film'
      kanał [kanaw] 'channel, sewer'   kanal-izacj-a [kanalizatsja]
                                              'sewerage'
      dyftong-u [dɨftɔŋgu]   dyftong-izacj-a [dɨftɔŋɟizatsja]
      'diphthong, gen. sg.'   'diphthongization'
      Czech-y [tʃɛxɨ] 'the Czech Republic'   czechiz-acj-a [tʃɛçizatsja]
                                              'making something Czech-like'

With the consonants [t, d, r] and the non-palatalized [ʃ, ts], the suffix invariably selects the variant *-yzacj-a*.

(80) klimat [klimat] 'climate'   klimat-yzacj-a [klimatɨzatsja] 'air conditioning'
      bastard-a [bastarda]   bastard-yzacj-a [bastardɨzatsja] 'bastardization'
      'bastard, gen. sg.'
      kategori-a [katɛgɔrʲja]   kategor-yzacj-a [katɛgɔrɨzatsja] 'categorization'
      'category'
      walor [valɔr] 'asset'   walor-yzacj-a [valɔrɨzatsja] 'raising the value'
      fetysz [fɛtɨʃ] 'fetish'   fetysz-yzacj-a [fɛtɨʃɨzatsja]
                                       'turning sth in a fetish'
      Grecj-a [grɛtsja] 'Greece'   grec-yzacj-a [grɛtsɨzatsja] 'making
                                       something Greek-like'

In comparison to the suffix *-ist-a*, what is striking here is the total resistance of the consonants [t, d, r] to palatal modifications. Recall that with *-ist-a* we found variation. As documented by Kreja (1989: 69), there are over 30 derivatives involving [r] which show no palatalized alternants and over 40 that do. For [t] the numbers are: over 30 without and over 20 with alternations, and likewise for [d], 18 without and 16 with an alternation. In some cases we recorded the possibility of (free) variation between the two situations (*ballad-yst-a/balladz-ist-a*) while nothing of the sort seems to occur with the suffix *-izacj-a/-yzacj-a*. Fundamentally, however, the question remains why, say, *hazard-u* [xazardu] 'gambling, gen.', *poker* [pɔkɛr] 'game of poker', and the like should result with palatalization before *-ist-a*, that is, *hazardz-ist-a* [xazardʑista] 'gambler', *pokerz-yst-a* [pɔkɛʑista] 'poker player', while *motor* [mɔtɔr] 'motor' and *spirant* [spʲirant] 'spirant' remain unaffected before *-izacj-a*: *motor-yzacj-a* [mɔtɔrɨzatsja] 'motor-ization' and *spirant-yzacj-a* [spʲrantɨzatsja] 'spirantization'. This question, we submit, lies outside the domain of phonology proper. Factors determining the selection of the palatalized variant have nothing to do with the phonological context; phonologically, both [tɨ] and [tɕi] are well-formed and the selection of one or the other variant is the matter for the lexicon. Preferences or suffix-specific idiosyncrasies are captured by the morphophonology of the language. The mor-phophonological regularities are not divorced from the phonology of the lan-guage but do not possess the necessary force that characterizes phonological properties. We will consider some of the morphophonological regularities affect-ing alternations of palatalized and non-palatalized consonant in the following chapter. Here we conclude that the behaviour of the specific class of productive suffixes argues against the generative view of palatalization as a phonological regularity. We will see many more cases supporting this conclusion below. First, we need to look at velar and palato-velar spirants.

3.11 THE VELAR AND THE PALATO-VELAR SPIRANTS: [x] AND [ç]

In the section devoted to palatalized and plain velars we pointed out that the fricatives [x, ç] differ from velar plosives and call for special treatment. Let us start by looking at the plain spirant.

Unlike the plosives [k, g], the voiceless velar spirant [x] has a voiced counter-part limited in occurrence to the position before another voiced obstruent, including the sandhi position, see (81).

(81)   klechda [klɛɣda] 'folk tale'   Bohdan [bɔɣdan] 'personal name'
        tychże [tɨɣʒɛ] 'of these, emph.'   dach był [daɣbɨw] 'the roof was'

In classical structural terms this is a case of allophonic variation (the phoneme /x/ has the allophone [ɣ] before a voiced obstruent) while in generative terms this is a case of voice assimilation with the feature [α voice] of the last obstruent in a cluster spreading to all preceding members. In non-derivational terms, on the other hand, examples like those in (81) would be interpreted as an instance of voice uniformity in obstruent clusters or as voice sharing (see Ch. 7). All the approaches agree in viewing the voiced velar spirant as dependent on or resulting from the immediately following consonantal context. Standard Polish has no [ɣ] initially or intervocalically. In what follows we shall concentrate on the voiceless spirant only.

Just like the velar plosives, the spirant can appear as the head of branching onsets (81a) and it can be followed by most vowels (82b).

(82) (a) chleb [xlɛp] 'bread'   po-chlebi-a-ć [pɔxlɛbʲatɕ] 'flatter'
         chłod-n-y [xwɔdnɨ] 'cool'   rychł-o [rɨxwɔ] 'soon'
         chrabąszcz [xrabɔʷʃtʃ] 'bug, n.'   czochr-a-ć [tʃɔxratɕ] 'tousle'

      (b) herbat-a [xɛrbata] 'tea'   cich-e [tɕixɛ] 'silent, nom. pl.'
         chyb-i-ć [xɨbʲitɕ] 'miss, vb.'   duch-y [duxɨ] 'ghost, nom. pl.'
         hałas [xawas] 'noise'   mach-a [maxa] '(s)he waves'
         chuć [xutɕ] 'lust'   tch-u [txu] 'breath, gen. sg.'
         chorob-a [xɔrɔba] 'illness'   uch-o [uxɔ] 'ear'
         chęć [xɛɲtɕ] 'willingness'   troch-ę [trɔxɛ⁽ʷ⁾] 'a little'
         Chąśn-o [xɔʲɕnɔ] 'place name'   ropuch-ą [rɔpuxɔʷ] 'toad, instr. sg.'

In contrast to the velar plosives, the possibility of the spirant to combine with [ɨ] is the most remarkable difference: unlike [k] or [g], which can be followed by the vowel in exceptional cases, the sequence [xɨ] is commonplace in both native and borrowed vocabulary:

(83) chyba [xɨba] 'perhaps'   po-chyl-a-ć [pɔxɨlatɕ] 'tilt, vb.'
      chyż-y [xɨʒɨ] 'swift'   chymus [xɨmus] 'chyme'
      hydrant [xɨdrant] 'hydrant'   hymn [xɨmn] 'hymn'

Recall that with velar plosives the Empty Heads and I-alignment constraints combined to ensure that sequences like [kɨ, gɨ] do not emerge and, where expected on morphological grounds (see (30)–(31)), they are replaced by their palato-velar congeners and followed by the vowel [i]. With the velar spirant the constraints appear inactive as both in the nominative plural of nouns (84a) (cf. (30)) and the masculine nominative singular of adjectives (84b) (cf. (31d)) we encounter the velar rather than the palato-velar spirant.

(84) (a) duch [dux] 'ghost'   duch-y [duxɨ]
         ropuch-a [rɔpuxa] 'toad'   ropuch-y [rɔpuxɨ]
         szprych-a [ʃprɨx-a] 'spoke, n.'   szprych-y [ʃprɨxɨ]

      (b) głuch-a [gwuxa] 'deaf, fem.'   głuch-y [gwuxɨ]
         błah-a [bwaxa] 'insignificant, fem.' błah-y [bwaxɨ]
         kruch-a [kruxa] 'fragile, fem.'   kruch-y [kruxɨ]

Unlike in the case of the velar plosives, then, it would appear that the empty-headed velar spirant can be followed by the empty-headed vowel [ɨ]. This is not to say that the palato-velar spirant [ç] does not exist or cannot appear before the headed vowel [i]:

(85) chichot [çixɔt] 'giggle, n.'   machin-a [maçina] 'machinery'
      histeri-a [çistɛrʲja] 'hysteria'   chiń-sk-i [çiɲsci] 'Chinese'
      chirurg-a [çirurga] 'surgeon, gen. sg.' chinin-a [çiɲina] 'quinine'

Admittedly, most of the words containing [çi] are borrowings, and *chichot* 'giggle' with its derivatives could be argued to be onomatopeic. We will see below, however, that the sequence is found elsewhere in fully native vocabulary, while here we just note that [çi] is not required in borrowed words since numerous of these admit the sequence [xɨ]:

(86) chymozyn-a [xɨmɔzɨna] 'rennet'   hybrid-a [xɨbrɨda] 'hybrid'
      hymn [xɨmn] 'hymn'   hydroliz-a [xɨdrɔliza] 'hydrolysis'

Thus, in foreign words we find both [xɨ] and [çi] and in some cases both variants seem possible, as in *hyzop* [xɨzɔp] or *hizop* [çizɔp] 'hyssop', the choice being left up to the individual speaker. In borrowings we therefore have the palato-velar spirant which appears to parallel the palato-velar plosives, and we also find the velar spirant which, unlike the plosives, can be followed by an empty-headed nucleus.

The velar plosives before the vowel [ɛ] appearing in the nominal ending *-em* of the instrumental singular masculine and neuter and the adjectival *-e* of the nominative plural behave in the same way as before the empty-headed vowel [ɨ] (see (39)): the stem-final consonant is replaced by its palato-velar congeners and the vowel becomes headed. The same is true about the velars before the vowel [ɛ] alternating with zero, see (40b). When the stem ends in the velar spirant, nothing happens, as in the examples in (87).

(87) (a) duch [dux] 'ghost'   duch-em [duxɛm] 'instr. sg.'
         mech [mɛx] 'moss'   mch-em [mxɛm] 'instr. sg.'
         błah-a [bwaxa] 'insignificant, fem.'   błah-e [bwaxɛ] 'nom. pl.'
         głuch-a [gwuxa] 'deaf, fem.'   głuch-e [gwuxɛ] 'nom. pl.'

      (b) pchł-a [pxwa] 'flea'   pcheł [pxɛw] 'gen. pl.'
         pochw-a [pɔxfa] 'sheath'   pochew [pɔxɛf] 'gen. pl.'

Examples like those in (84) and (87) lead to the ineluctable conclusion that the voiceless velar spirant does not behave like a velar: if it is true that an empty-headed onset cannot be licensed by an empty-headed nucleus, then an object that fails to conform to this condition must straightforwardly be described as being different from what it appears to be. Cases of this sort are not rare or untypical: word-final voiceless obstruents may result from terminal devoicing, different phonological expressions may correspond to the phonetic [ɛ], the back semivowel [w] must be treated phonologically as a velarized lateral, etc. (Gussmann 2001). We could say something similar in the case of the phonetic velar spirant: contrary to its phonetic nature, the velar spirant is not velar, but, say, glottal. This supposition might be strengthened by the absence of an independent voiced equivalent of the spirant, a situation to be expected with the glottal consonant. Additionally, we might also add the phonetic observation going back to Jassem (1954: 98), who noted that the initial spirants in words like *chata* [xata] 'hut' and *hymn* [xɨmn] 'hymn' are increasingly more often pronounced with the glottal [h] as [hata] and [hɨmn]. This is a surprising development since the standard inventory of spirants in Polish does not include the glottal spirant at all, one of the distinctive features of the Polish accent in English and German being the pronunciation of *have* and *haben* as [xɛf] and [xabɛn], respectively. The occasional emergence of the phonetic [h] noted by Jassem might be argued to give credence to the claim that this unit is part of the abstract system of the language's phonology. In terms of the element theory, what is a velar spirant in Polish could be regarded as a glottal spirant, in other words, as a headed expression consisting solely of the element {h} and containing no operators, that is, as {h̲}. The distance from the phonetic [x] would be seen as even smaller than that in the case of the velarized lateral, leading to {?•U} pronounced as [w]. The (phonologically) glottal spirant, being obviously non-velar, behaves as other non-velar consonants in Polish and, in particular, it does not require the licensing nucleus to be headed; {h̲}, itself headed, tolerates an empty-headed licensing nucleus. If this were to exhaust the case, we would merely be dealing with another instance of a familiar situation, namely, the possibility that a certain phonological expression is misleadingly packaged phonetically. However, this is not the whole story.

The question suggests itself at this stage as to whether Polish possesses a velar spirant as a phonological object at all or whether all instances of the phonetic [x] are merely the packaging for the phonological headed {h̲}. In (85) we supplied examples of the palato-velar [ç]. Since the following nucleus is—predictably enough—headed, we might extend to it the interpretation of the velar stops alternating with palato-alveolars; we can view the sequence [çi] as conforming to the Empty Heads and the I-alignment constraints. A somewhat different situation prevails in combinations of the palato-velar spirant with the vowel [ɛ] since the glide is obligatory there. Consider:

(88)   hierarchi-a [çjɛrarçja] 'hierarchy'   hien-a [çjɛna] 'hyena'
        hierologlif [çjɛrɔglif] 'hieroglyph'   Hieronim [çjɛrɔɲim] 'personal name'

The presence of the glide means that the conditioning factor for I-alignment is found not in the licensing nucleus but in the following onset. We return to this issue presently.

In (85) and (88) we illustrated the existence of the palato-velar spirant [ç] in Polish but the question of its relatedness to [x] looms large, no matter how the latter is understood as a phonological object. The examples in (85) and (88) are not very telling since they cover domain-internal combinations and could be viewed as unrelated to the velar spirant problem. In other words, the initial onset–nucleus sequences in examples like *chimer-a* [çimɛra] 'chimera' (and *chimer-ycz-n-y* [çimɛrɨtʃnɨ] 'whimsical') and *hierarchi-a* [çjɛrarçja] 'hierarchy' (and *hierar-chicz-n-y* [çjɛrarçitʃnɨ] 'hierarchical') could be regarded as a simple instantiation of I-alignment where, as in other cases, no question of derivation needs to arise. The obvious difficulty would be of a diachronic nature since we seem unable to offer phonologically cogent reasons why we have [çi] in *histori-a* [çistɔrʲja] 'history' but [xɨ] in *hymn* [xɨmn] 'hymn'. This is, however, a diachronic question which need nor preoccupy us in a synchronic description: synchronically, neither of the forms violates I-alignment. The crucial issue is that apart from [ç] appearing domain-internally we also have cases of alternations involving [x–ç]. To these we now turn.

In a number of derivationally related words, the velar spirant of the base corresponds to the palato-velar in the derivative where the first segment of the suffixes is the vowel [i]. Consider several such examples.

(89) monarch-a [mɔnarxa] 'monarch'   monarch-in-i [mɔnarçiɲi] 'id. fem.'
      Czech [tʃɛx] 'Czech, n.'   czech-izm [tʃɛçism̩] 'a Czech borrowing'
      szach-y [ʃaxɨ] 'check'   szach-ist-a [ʃaçista] 'chess player'
      katech-ez-a [katɛxɛza]   katech-izacj-a [katɛçizatsja]
      'catechesis'   'catechization'
      psych-o- [psɨxɔ] 'psycho-'   psych-ik-a [psɨçika] 'psyche'
      Lech [lɛx] 'personal name'   Lech-it-a [lɛçita] 'one of the Lekh tribe'
      roz-dmuch-a-ć [rɔzdmuxatɕ]   rozd-much-iw-a-ć [rozdmuçivatɕ]
      'blow out'   'der. imper.'
      pod-słuch-a-ć [pot-swuxatɕ]   pod-słuch-iw-a-ć [pɔt-swuçivatɕ]
      'eavesdrop'   'der. imper.'

The majority of the suffixes are obviously foreign (-izm, -ist-a, -izacj-a, -ik(-a), -it-a) but two are native, -in-i and -iw-, so there is little prospect of connecting the surprising phonological effects with the foreignness of the affix. Furthermore, since [çi], as we saw in (85), is perfectly possible in foreign words, it is precisely the native suffixes that constitute a challenge.

The suffix forming derived imperfectives (der. imper.) appears in two shapes, either as -yw- [ɨv] as in (90a) or as -iw- [iv] as in (90b–c).

(90) (a) za-grzeb-a-ć [zagʒɛbatɕ] 'bury'   za-grzeb-yw-a-ć [zagʒɛbɨvatɕ]
          wy-łap-a-ć [vɨwapatɕ] 'catch out'   wy-łap-yw-a-ć [vɨwapɨvatɕ]
          wy-śpiew-a-ć [vɨɕpʲevatɕ] 'sing'   wy-śpiew-ywa-ć [vɨɕpʲevɨvatɕ]
          za-łam-a-ć [zawamatɕ] 'break'   za-łam-yw-a-ć [zawamɨvatɕ]
          ob-gad-a-ć [ɔbgadatɕ] 'gossip'   ob-gad-yw-a-ć [ɔbgadɨvatɕ]
          czyt-a-ć [tʃɨtatɕ] 'read'   czyt-yw-a-ć [tʃɨtɨvatɕ]
          w-skaz-a-ć [fskazatɕ] 'indicate'   w-skaz-yw-a-ć [fskazɨvatɕ]
          pis-a-ć [pʲisatɕ] 'write'   pis-yw-a-ć [pʲisɨvatɕ]
          przy-woł-a-ć [pʃɨvɔwatɕ] 'summon'   przy-woł-yw-a-ć [pʃɨvɔwɨvatɕ]
          z-jedn-a-ć [zjɛdnatɕ] 'win over'   z-jedn-yw-a-ć [zjɛdnɨvatɕ]
          obiec-a-ć [ɔbʲɛtsatɕ] 'promise'   obiec-yw-a-ć [ɔbʲɛtsɨvatɕ]

      (b) wy-kp-i-ć [vɨkpʲitɕ] 'ridicule'   wy-kp-i-wa-ć [vɨkpʲivatɕ]
          wy-drw-i-ć [vɨdrvʲitɕ] 'jest'   wy-drw-iw-a-ć [vɨdrvʲivatɕ]
          prze-gn-i-ć [pʃɛgɲitɕ] 'rot through' prze-gn-iw-a-ć [pʃɛgɲivatɕ]
          roz-strzel-a-ć [rɔsst-ʃɛlatɕ] 'execute' roz-strzel-iw-a-ć [rɔsst-ʃɛlivatɕ]

      (c) o-płak-a-ć [ɔpwakatɕ] 'mourn'   o-płak-iw-a-ć [ɔpwacivatɕ]
          w-czołg-a-ć [ftʃɔwgatɕ] 'crawl in'   w-czołg-iw-a-ć [ftʃɔwɟivatɕ]
          za-koch-a-ć [zakɔxatɕ] 'fall in love' za-koch-iw-a-ć [zakɔçivatɕ]

The largest group of examples embraces bases ending in a plain (non-palatalized) consonant; they remain unaffected before the suffix [ɨv]. Similarly unaffected are the bases in (b) which end in a palatalized consonant and their derived imperfectives display the variant [iv], as per I-alignment. Finally, group (c) contains bases ending in velars and these, too, have their derived imperfectives ending in a palato-velar and the suffix beginning with the front vowel. The behaviour of velar plosives is not novel: recall the examples of nominative plurals like *stok* [stɔk] 'hillside'~*stok-i* [stɔci] (see (30)) or the nominative singular of masculine adjectives like *ubog-a* [ubɔga] 'poor, fem. sg.'~*ubog-i* [ubɔɟi] (see (31d)). In those cases, as well as in the case of bases ending in a velar plosive in (90c), we are dealing with the same regularity. Since a velar is empty-headed, it cannot be licensed by an empty-headed nucleus, the result of which is the operation of Empty Heads and I-alignment constraints. It is crucial that with the alleged velar spirant nothing of this sort happens, so that we have *duch-y* [duxɨ] 'ghost, nom. pl.' and *gluch-y* [gwuxɨ] 'deaf, masc. sg.' Since both inflectional endings and the derived imperfective suffix are unambiguously native, we would expect the same pattern in all cases. As the last example of (90) and last two examples of (89) show, this is not the case: in the derived imperfectives, rather than finding the same [xɨ] we have in plurals of nouns and in masculine singular adjectives, we actually encounter the palato-velar and a headed vowel, [çi]. Thus, the unquestionably native suffixes *-in-* of (89) and *-iw-* of (90) behave in the same way as the unquestionably foreign suffixes (*-izm*, *-ist-a*, *-izacj-a*) in (89), that is to say, there is no phonological ground for separating the native suffixes from the foreign ones. The reason for the distinct behaviour of the velar spirant cannot be associated with the foreignness of either suffixes or bases.

Let us repeat just three examples involving the velar spirant.

(91)   Czech [tʃɛx] 'Czech, n.'   czech-izm [tʃɛçism̥] 'a Czech borrowing'
       szach [ʃax] 'check'   szach-ist-a [ʃaçista] 'chess player'
       pod-słuch-a-ć [pɔt-swuxatɕ]   pod-słuch-iw-a-ć [pɔt-swuçivatɕ] 'der. imper.'
       'eavesdrop'

Recall also that we have been led to argue that the phonetic [x] should be understood as a headed, (possibly) glottal expression containing the element {h} and the velarity of the segment is merely the way it is pronounced, or its packaging. The existence of words exemplified in (91) might be taken to indicate that, apart from the headed expression, Polish also has an empty-headed one, namely, {h•_}. This is a true velar spirant which consequently displays the phonological behaviour of a velar; it conforms to Empty Heads and I-alignment. The glottal spirant, while packaged in the same way, is a different expression, hence it refuses to conform to either of the two constraints. We could thus conclude that morphemes displaying the alternation [x~ç] contain a velar spirant, while those which maintain [x] contain a glottal one. Unfortunately, this simple account fails and the conclusion is untenable as it stands.

Where our reasoning holds is in the claim that the words in the right-hand column in (91) contain a velar spirant corresponding to the phonetic [ç] since, as a velar, it must conform to the two constraints, which it does. It does not neces-sarily follow that the base morpheme must contain this phonological expression in all contexts. In fact, there is direct evidence that it does not do so in the words in the left-hand column of (91). Consider our diagnostic contexts for velars, the endings of the nominative plural and also that of the instrumental singular.

(92) Czech [tʃɛx] 'Czech, n.'   Czech-em [tʃɛxɛm] 'instr. sg'
      Czech-y [tʃɛxɨ] 'the Czech Republic'
      szach [ʃax] 'check, n.'   szach-em [ʃaxɛm] 'instr. sg.'
      szach-y [ʃaxɨ] 'game of chess'
      słuch [swux] 'hearing'   słuch-em [swuxɛm] 'instr. sg.'
      słuch-y [swuxɨ] 'rumours'
      pod-słuch [pot-swux] 'eavesdropping' pod-słuch-em [pɔt-swuxɛm]
                                            'instr.sg.'
      pod-słuch-y [pɔt-swuxɨ] 'nom. pl.'

In other words, while the right-hand words in (91) contain a velar spirant, the left-hand ones must be seen as having non-velars. In both cases the phonological behaviour attests to the different status of the segments. This means, of course, that the same morpheme may have different phonological structures depending on the neighbouring morphemes. In our case, the morpheme *słuch* 'hearing', for instance, ends in a velar spirant only before the suffix of the derived imperfective, elsewhere it seems to end in a non-velar or glottal fricative. The positioning of an appropriate phonological expression in a given word that is in combination with other morphemes is the task of morphophonology. Phonology merely ensures that all phonological constraints are conformed to. The nature of the morphophonological regularities and their Polish forms will occupy us in the next part of this book.

3.12 PALATALIZATION EFFECTS IN LOANWORDS

One of the points we made earlier concerns the presence of palato-velars in loanwords, particularly relatively unassimilated ones: these consonants appear either before the vowel [i] or before the glide [j] followed by some other vowel. We find palato-velars followed by the glide ([cj, ɟj, çj]) where considerations of etymology, orthography or the evidence of alternations might point to plain, non-palatalized velars. This is found in words like those in (93).

(93) kiosk [cjɔsk] 'kiosk'   giaur [ɟjaur] 'infidel'
      Toki-o [tɔcjɔ] 'Tokyo'   kolegium [kɔlɛɟjum] 'college'
      autarki-a [awtarcja] 'autarchy'   Norwegi-a [nɔrvɛɟja] 'Norway'
      kiur [cjur] 'curium'   religi-a [rɛliɟja] 'religion'
      chiazm [çjasm̥] 'chasm'   monarchi-a [mɔnarçja] 'monarchy'
      Hyundai [çjundaj] 'car make'   Monachi-um [mɔnaçjum] 'Munich'
      hiob-ow-y [çjɔbɔvɨ] 'Job, adj.'   hiacynt [çjatsɨnt] 'hyacinth'

A few comments are called for. We have included the palato-velar spirant among the examples in (93) despite the fact that it does not have to be related to the velar spirant, as argued in the preceding section.

The connection between the degree of nativization and the phonology can best be appreciated in the very common word *kiosk*, where the pronunciation with the glide, [cjɔsk], and one without it, [cɔsk], are equally acceptable. The same cannot be said about the remaining words in (93), presumably because of their less common character.

The brunt of our argument concerning palato-alveolars, and especially the palato-alveolar plosives, is that they are in effect linked structures where the element {I} is doubly attached under specific conditions. The appearance of palato-velars is then strictly determined phonologically. Translating this into more established terminology we can claim that palato-velars are derived and predictable. This explains their limited distribution, including the total absence in consonantal clusters and word-finally. However, since ours is not a contrast-oriented framework, the (un)predictability of a segment is of secondary import-ance. We are simply not interested in establishing contrasts, be they taxonomic or derivational–generative. The fact that certain segments of our representations do, on occasion, correspond directly to generative or structural contrastive units is accidental and derivative. Our aim is to determine to what extent and through what mechanisms syntagmatic relations between consecutive melodies are established. Thus we have seen that Polish has two constraints (Empty Heads, I-alignment) which account for the co-occurrence of palato-velars and front vowels. It would be worth investigating what such an analysis holds for borrowings like those in (93); in particular, since these loans all contain the palatal glide, it seems natural to ask whether the analysis can be extended to them as well. This possibility needs to be explored not just because of the presence of the glide—the element {I} associated with a non-nuclear position—but also for other phonological and morphological reasons. Consider adjectival derivatives of three of the forms given earlier.

(94)   Toki-o [tɔcjɔ] 'Tokyo'   tokij-sk-i [tɔcijsci] 'of Tokyo'
       religi-a [rɛliɉja] 'religion'   religij-n-y [rɛliɉijnɨ] 'religious'
       Monachi-um [mɔnaçjum] 'Munich'   monachij-sk-i [mɔnaçijsci] 'of Munich'

With the suffix -*sk-i* [sci], -*n-y* [nɨ] attached to the base noun, the palatal glide is preceded by the vowel [i]—one might say that [j] is replaced by [ij]. It should be added that the -*o* of *Tokio*, like -*a* and -*um* of the two other words, are regarded by the Polish inflectional system as exponents of the nominative-singular ending (feminine in the case of -*a* and neuter with -*o*, -*um*). The adjectival suffixes are appended to the nominal stem bases without the inflectional ending. If the bases were to end with a palato-alveolar, the inevitable consequence would be loss of palatalization, as is typically the case before an empty nucleus (or a consonant). This, as we see, does not happen and the front vowel appears before the glide; rather than entertain the possibility of the vowel being inserted by fiat, we would like to see whether it could not be found in the structure.

Assuming that the loans in (93) do, in fact, contain the glide [j] as part of the representations, we need to consider the relevant syntagmatic relations between the glide and the preceding velar. Below a representation of the name *Tokio* is depicted with elemental structure provided for the relevant segments only.

(95)

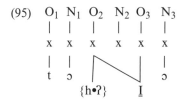

In terms of elements, the glide [j] is the resonance element {I} attached to a non-nuclear position. In (95) the glide is separated from the velar by an empty nuclear position which does not prevent it from being attached to the velar's empty head. The result is a palato-velar plosive with the glide itself following it. The double attachment of {I} is controlled by the same mechanism of Empty Heads and I-alignment which ensures that it is found in combinations of a velar in the onset and a front vowel in the following nucleus. In the case at hand, the element {I} is not in the following nucleus (N_2) but in the directly adjacent melody of the following onset (O_3), a fact which seems irrelevant from the point of view of palatalization. Consider now the representation of the denominal adjective *tokij-sk-i* [tɔcijsci] 'of Tokyo' in (96).

(96)

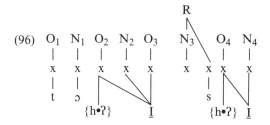

In the representation we place the spirant [s] in the rhyme dominating N_3 although other configurations could also be entertained (and will be discussed in Ch. 5). The final onset–nucleus pair (O_4–N_4) displays the regular effects of the two constraints we have evoked to account for the existence of palato-velars, Empty Heads and I-alignment. The novel situation is the configuration O_2–N_2–O_3: although this string looks exactly like the corresponding string in (95), there is an interpretational difference in that unlike (95) the middle nucleus N_2 is here filled by a melody. The difference seems attributable to the fact that the nucleus following the glide, N_3, is melodically filled in (95) but remains empty in (96). Leaving aside for the moment the technicalities of the mechanism and its implication, we will say that N_3, when melodically empty, makes it impossible for N_2 to remain empty as well. Spreading from O_3 therefore ensures that the preceding nucleus acquires a melody. It is not an arbitrary melody that 'gets inserted' but the result of the presence in the direct neighbourhood of the vocalic element {I} which I-aligns to the preceding available empty heads both in the nucleus N₂ and the empty-headed onset O₂. The phonetic effect is the sequence [cij] in the case of *tokijski* and [ɟij] or [çij] for the two other adjectival derivatives in (94). In this way the palato-velars in words of foreign origin illustrated in (93) can be regarded as controlled by mechanisms fully exploited in the native vocabulary.

It was noted above that some of the fully assimilated or common loans do not necessarily display the glide, hence the word *kiosk* has alternative pronunciations, [çjɔsk] or [çɔsk]. Such words indicate the existence or co-existence of two somewhat different representations, one with the glide in the second onset (97a), and one where the element responsible for the glide is integrated with the first onset (97b). The latter situation realizes presumably the more radical or innovative shape of the word with the foreign configuration eliminated in favour of a single expression.

(97) (a)

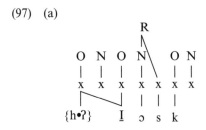

(b)

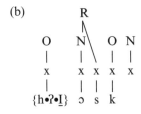

In the discussion above we have restricted our attention to loanwords involving velars and palato-velars in the relevant position. There are numerous examples in Polish of words ending in a palatalized consonant other than the palato-velar followed by the palatal glide; they all appear to be borrowings or derived from borrowings. While often enough the sequence is a suffix, there are also others where the case for its suffixhood could not readily be made. What is important is that, phonologically, the presence or absence of a morpheme boundary has no phonological consequences; the behaviour of the segments is not affected by morphology. For this reason, in the list in (98) we concentrate on the phonological rather than grammatical contexts. The palato-velars are omitted since examples of these have been provided above.

(98)   (a) atrofi-a [atrɔfʲja] 'atrophy'   terapi-a [tɛrapʲja] 'therapy'
           fobi-a [fɔbʲja] 'phobia'   hrabi-a [xrabʲja] 'count'
           chemi-a [xɛmʲja] 'chemistry'   bigami-a [bʲigamʲja] 'bigamy'
           alomorfi-a [alɔmɔrfʲja] 'allomorphy'   filozofi-a [fʲilɔzɔfʲja] 'philosophy'
           rewi-a [rɛvʲja] 'review'   endywi-a [ɛndɨvʲja] 'endive'
           anomali-a [anɔmalʲja] 'anomaly'   archiwali-a [arɕivalʲja] 'archives'
           mani-a [maɲja] 'mania'   Brytani-a [brɨtaɲja] 'Britain'

    (b) parti-a [partʲja] 'party'   besti-a [bɛstʲja] 'beast'
           komedi-a [kɔmɛdʲja] 'comedy'   melodi-a [mɛlɔdʲja] 'melody'
           dygresj-a [dɨgrɛsʲja] 'digression'   koncesj-a [kɔntsɛsʲja] 'concession'
           okazj-a [ɔkazʲja] 'opportunity'   inwazj-a [invazʲja] 'invasion'
           reżyseri-a [rɛʒisɛrʲja] 'directing'   seri-a [sɛrʲja] 'series'
           demokracj-a [dɛmɔkratsʲja]   asymilacj-a [asɨmʲilatsʲja]
           'democracy'   'assimilation'

Let us start with a comment on the phonetics of the palatalized consonants. In (98a) we transcribe palatalized labials with the palatal glide, unlike earlier on in the book when we insisted that the glide, in the forms or dialects of Polish where is does appear, is mechanically predictable and need not overburden the transcription. With the loans above, the situation is different; this follows from our observation that in loanwords the glide is obligatory in all varieties of Polish. Likewise the glide follows the lateral and the palatal nasal.

(99)   (a) lila [lila] 'lilac, adj.'   lili-a [lilʲja] 'lily'
           bal-a [bala] 'log, gen. sg.'   bali-a [balʲja] 'tub'

    (b) dani-a [daɲa] 'dish, nom. pl.'   Dani-a [daɲja] 'Denmark'
           Mani-a [maɲa] 'personal name'   mani-a [maɲja] 'mania'

Here the native words in the left-hand column do not show the glide which is manifestly present in the loans in the right-hand column.

The examples in (98) have been divided into two groups on the basis of the palatalization reflexes of the stem-final consonants. In (98a) the palatalized consonants are exactly the same as in native vocabulary, as discussed in the first part of this chapter. This gives us the palatalized labials [pʲ, bʲ, mʲ, fʲ, vʲ], the palatal nasal [ɲ], and the lateral with minimal traces of palatalization [l]. The coronal obstruents and the sonorant [r], on the other hand, display palatalization effects not found in the native vocabulary, that is, the sounds [tʲ, dʲ, sʲ, zʲ, rʲ, tsʲ]. With some of these sounds the palatalization is hardly audible or distinguishible from the following glide, as is the case with the affricate [ts]. What is beyond doubt is that if there is any softening of affricates like [ts], it is only found with loan words. It is uncontroversial that the group comprising the coronal obstruents and [r] (coronal, for short) does not display the effects characteristic of palatalization as revealed in alternations in native words. What we find with that group of consonants are phonetic effects due to the mere juxtaposition of sounds, not different in kind from, say, the rounding that a consonant will display before a rounded vowel. Thus, loans when processed by Polish phonology constitute valid data for the identification of the relevant phonological regularity.

If we compare the palatal and palatalized consonants found in loans with those found in native words or the fully assimilated loans, we have to conclude that the group of consonants consisting of labials and [n, l] (labial, for short) has identical palatalized reflexes in native and non-native vocabulary; in other words, the [mʲ] in *miar-a* [mʲara] 'measurement' does not differ from the [mʲ] in *chemi-a* [xɛmʲja] 'chemistry'; similarly, the [ɲ, l] of *nic* [ɲits] 'nothing' and *liść* [lictc] 'leaf' are identical to the sonorants in *lini-a* [liɲja] 'line'. In the same context (as exemplified in (98b)) the coronal group displays merely effects due to the phonetic neighbourhood, and thus the [sʲ] of *misj-a* [mʲisʲja] 'mission' is markedly different from [c] of *misi-a* [mʲica] 'bear, gen. sg.'. We find no identification of [sʲ, zʲ, tʲ, dʲ] with the [c, ʑ, tc, dʑ] of the native vocabulary—*misj-a* [mʲisʲja] 'mission' does not even approach *[mʲicja]. In this way the palatal (or prepalatal) coronals [c, ʑ, tc, dʑ] must be viewed as phonologically unrelated to the plain obstruents [s, z, t, d]. The classical palatalized consonants such as [c, dʑ] etc. are not phonologically related to the plain [t, d] any more than [k] is related to [ts] or [r] to [ʒ]. In this they fundamentally differ from our labial group whose palatalization reflexes are the same both in native and foreign vocabulary.

Differences between the two groups of consonants are brought into sharp relief once they are subject to further morphological and phonological processing. Further derivatives from the nominal bases in (98) can be expected to reveal the way the palatalized consonants are handled. Consider adjectival derivatives with the fully native suffixes -*n-y* [nɨ], -*sk-i* [sci].

(100)   (a) utopi-a [utɔpʲja] 'utopia'   utopij-n-y [utɔpʲijnɨ] 'utopian'
            mafi-a [mafʲja] 'mafia'   mafij-n-y [mafʲijnɨ] 'adj.'
            antynomi-a [antɨnɔmʲja]   antynomij-n-y [antɨnɔmʲijnɨ] 'adj.'
            'antynomy'
            Bibli-a [bʲiblja] 'Bible'   biblijny [bʲiblijnɨ] 'biblical'
            Kaliforni-a [kalifɔrɲja]   kalifornij-sk-i [kalifɔrɲijsci] 'adj.'
            'California'

        (b) parti-a [partʲja] 'party'   partyj-n-y [partɨjnɨ] 'partisan'
            melodi-a [mɛlɔdʲja] 'melody'   melodyj-n-y [mɛlɔdɨjnɨ] 'melodious'
            dygresj-a [dɨgrɛsʲja] 'digression' dygresyj-n-y [dɨgrɛsɨjnɨ] 'digressive'
            okazj-a [ɔkazʲja] 'opportunity'   okazyj-n-y [ɔkazɨjnɨ] 'occasional'
            seri-a [sɛrʲja] 'series'   seryj-n-y [sɛrɨjnɨ] 'serial'
            asymilacj-a [asɨmʲilatsʲja]   asymilacyj-n-y [asɨmʲilatsɨjnɨ]
            'assimilation'   'assimilatory'

Not every consonant is attested in the required context but the pattern is completely clear: the palatals of the labial group (i.e. [p, b, f, v, m, n, l]) are followed by [ij], whereas those of the coronal set (i.e. [t, d, s, z, r, ts,]) are non-palatalized and are followed by [ɨj]. The question is what is behind this difference and how it fits into our account of palatalization in Polish.

The suffixes *-n-y* [nɨ], *-sk-i* [sci] can be argued to start with an empty nucleus. We assumed this representation in (96) for the latter suffix in the word *tokij-sk-i* [tɔcijsci] and we will adopt it here as well. Likewise we will assume that the suffix *-n-y* starts with an empty nucleus (both suffixes will be discussed in detail in Ch. 4). Let us first consider examples based on the nouns *utopi-a* [utɔpʲja] and *parti-a* [partʲja].

(101) (a)

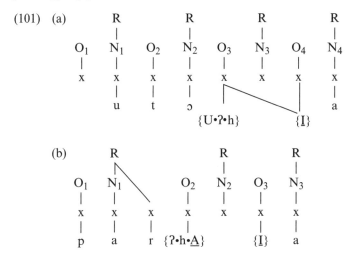

    (b)

The two representations above are intended to reflect the difference between what we call phonological palatalization and the surface palatalizing effects due to the presence of the palatal glide in the neighbourhood of a consonant. In both cases we have an empty nucleus separating a consonant from the onset glide (I-headed non-nuclear position). The intervening nucleus is phonetically silent since it contains no melody attached or floating (see Ch. 5 for a full discussion). The effect is that N₃ in (101a) and N₂ in (101b) are not supplied with any melodic matter. True palatalization is evinced in what we have called the labial group, which also comprises the coronal lateral and nasal. This is the case illustrated by *utopi-a* [utɔpʲja] in (101a): the {I} element is attached as onset head to both O₃ and O₄ in exactly the same way as when an I-headed nucleus follows a labial in the onset, as in *pi-ć* [pʲitɕ] 'drink, vb.', *bie-c* [bʲɛts] 'run, vb.'. When the onset is filled by a coronal, no palatalization or double attachment of {I} takes place and we end up with the neighbourhood or surface palatalization of coronals. The question that immediately suggests itself and to which we only have a tenuous answer at the moment concerns the reason for this bifurcation; put simply, why is the labial group susceptible to palatalization while the coronal one is not?

There can hardly be an a priori answer to this question and we will turn the tables in our attempt to find a plausible line of investigation. We will suggest that the facts as given reflect a genuine phonological pattern which needs to be identified. We have assumed throughout that a consonant which is palatal(ized) must be I-headed, either on its own or when linked with the following I-headed nucleus. The latter situation has been captured by a constraint we have called I-alignment (33). Furthermore, we have seen that the labial group is, roughly speaking, susceptible to palatalization while the coronal one is not. Since labials can be assumed to be U-headed while coronals are A-headed, the palatalization of the former denotes the demoting of the element {U} to the operator status under the influence of a following I-head. This we have in (101a). When a coronal or A-headed consonant finds itself before a following I-head, it refuses to—is strong enough to?—resist demotion to the operator position. The result of the failure of {I} to get doubly attached is the surface or contact-type of palatalization (101b) which we render in transcription as [tʲ, rʲ], etc. It might as well be called a phonetic effect with some phonological basis; in other words it is evoked by the presence of a neighbouring expression containing the element {I}. Why {U} succumbs and demotes to the operator position and {A} does not must for the moment remain a stipulation about the strength of these two elements.

This conclusion forces us to claim that the lateral (i.e. [ł]) realized as [w] and the coronal nasal [n] are not A-headed despite the fact that they are classified as coronals. The fact is unsurprising with the lateral: as we argued above, it is a U-headed lateral, a fact which is partly responsible for its present-day phonetic realization as [w]. Additionally, the bases for the -i-a derivatives hardly ever end in a velarized lateral, a purely native phonological object. When found in loan-words, the non-velarized, or morphophonologically palatalized, lateral may be simply I-headed, as in *archiwal-n-y* [arçivalnɨ] 'archival'~*archwa-l-ia* [arçivalja] 'archives'. If this is the case, then the lateral as an I-headed object blends with the following glide in accordance with the OCP. Thus we are left with the nasal as failing to conform in an obvious way to the U-headedness of palatalization undergoing expressions. The evidence of palatalization, involving alternations like *tyran* [tɨran] 'tyrant'~*tyran-i-a* [tɨraɲja] 'tyranny', suggests unequivocally that the {I} element can be attached to the onset's head position, in other words, that position cannot be taken by {A}. One could speculatively claim that just like the lateral, the nasal is also phonologically velarized or U-headed, but the evidence for this claim is not overabundant; one possible argument is the realization of the nasal vowels [ɛ̃, ɔ̃] as back diphthongs [ɛʷ, ɔʷ], to which we will return at a later stage. Keeping in mind that the point has not been fully made, we will tentatively adopt the position that palatalization in present-day Polish as a phonological regularity affects U-headed consonantal expressions which, under the influence of a following I-headed onset, are forced to accept {I} as head and demote {U} to the operator position. The surface palatalization of coronals or A-headed objects is a phonetic effect arising when the coronals are followed by an I-headed onset (and, as we will see later, exceptionally also by an I-nucleus). This establishes the second case for phonological palatalization, the first one being the regularities involved in the representations of palato-velars as discussed in the preceding sections.

It should be remarked in passing that our conclusion is directly opposed to parts of the structuralist interpretation of palatalized labials. It will be recalled that within this interpretation, the palatalization of labials is invariably due to the following palatal glide or the front high vowel /i/. We have argued at length in the first part of this chapter that this is a faulty analysis; we have claimed, in agreement with the more distant tradition, that palatalized labials are either linked structures or form independent segments. The relevant cases are words like *min-a* [mʲina] 'mien, face', *mie-ć* [mʲɛtɕ] 'have' for linked structures, and *miód* [mʲut] 'honey' for an independent segment. Palatalization in such cases can be, at most, a static statement describing the properties of the element {I} and specifically the I-alignment constraint. In terms of an alternative derivational framework it could be said to be lexical, unpredictable, underlying, or the like. Where we can talk about what looks like a measure of phonological derivation is the palatalization regularity involving longer stretches, not just onset–nuclei sequences. But on closer inspection it turns out that we are dealing with the same mechanisms: palatalization as I-headedness due to I-sharing between consecutive syllabic and melodic positions. To see this clearly let us now turn to the adjectives *utopij-n-y* [utɔpʲijnɨ] 'utopian' and *partyj-n-y* [partɨjnɨ] 'partisan', which are *-n-y* adjectival derivatives from the bases *utopi-a* [utɔpʲja] 'utopia' and *parti-a* [partʲja] 'party'. The final *-a* is a marker of the nominative singular of feminine nouns. Here are the possible representations of the adjectives:

(102) (a)

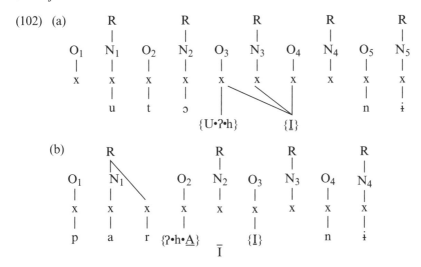

(b)

The derivatives contain the suffix *-n-y* [nɨ], which starts with an empty nucleus; what is more, the final nucleus of the base noun (N₃ in (102a) and N₂ in (102b)) would also be empty if not filled by the melody spread from the following onset. As we argue in Chapter 6, Polish does not tolerate sequences of empty nuclei, a situation which is here pre-empted by spreading. The melody, then, is not created by fiat but is due to the propagation of the element {I} from the non-nuclear position, O_4(in 102a) and O_3 (in 102b). In (102a) the element {I} occupies the head of the labial onset demoting its {U} to the operator position; I-alignment requires that it must also occupy the head position in the licensing nucleus N_3, which results in the phonetic [i]. In (102b), on the other hand, the {I} element cannot unseat the element {A} from the onset and since there is no {I} in the onset the same I-alignment lodges it in the operator position of the nucleus, which is a phonological structure of the phonetic [ɨ]. Thus both the base nouns and the derived adjectives are controlled by the same mechanisms referring directly to palatalization or I-sharing. The nouns differ from the related adjectives in that they have just one empty nucleus, a situation well tolerated in Polish. From the point of view of palatalization we can say that we get the back vowel in *partyj-n-y* [partɨjni], for instance, because we do *not* get I-alignment in *partia* [partʲja]. The phonetic [tʲ] here, and other palatalized coronals, are due to surface adjacency rather than an instantiation of the phonological I-alignment which truly reflects palataliation as a phonological regularity.

The above analysis of palatalization restricts it to a group of U-headed segments in a specific phonological configuration. The same segments ('palatalized reflexes'), encountered elsewhere, must also have the element {I} in their head positions but this I-head may but need not be linked to the following nucleus. The specific configuration which is distinctly palatalizing involves distant spreading of the {I} element. Directly adjacent segments must share the head element {I} as per I-alignment.

The analysis of palatalization along the lines presented here founders in an interesting way. There are a number of words, all of them loans and some quite recent, where word-internally we find sequences of coronals followed by the vowel [i]. The coronal displays the same effects as before [j] in the examples above—what we have called neighbourhood or adjacency surface palatalization. Here are some examples:

(103)   butik [butʲik] 'boutique'
        plastik [plastʲik] 'plastic, n.'
        diwa [dʲiva] 'diva'
        sinus [sʲinus] 'sine'
        maksimum [maksʲimum] 'maximum'
        Zinowiew [zʲinɔvʲɛf] 'proper name'
        ozi [ɔzʲi] '(an acronym for) secret agent'
        riposta [rʲipɔsta] 'repartee'

These words differ from the cases discussed above in that the I-head in the nucleus is directly adjacent to the onset. In such a case we would expect the I-head of the nucleus to be attached to the head position in the onset, as required by I-alignment. Clearly this does not happen, since as we argued above, [tʲ] etc. are not the result of I-alignment; rather, they emerge in defiance of it. In the case at hand it seems that the failure to conform to I-alignment is a marker of foreignness in Polish phonology. Words such as those in (103) contain an {I} head which *does not* license another {I} head. The existence of violations of constraints is simply another way of saying that there is exceptionality in phonology: the most general regularities do on occasion fail to be confirmed. We have seen one such case above in connection with the constraint we called Empty Heads in (32): *An empty-headed nucleus cannot license an empty-headed onset*. This constraint was justified by the virtually total absence in Polish of sequences such as [kɨ, gɨ] and the presence of [ci, ɟi] in places where they could be expected. The absence is virtually total but not absolute as individual words can be found where such offending combinations appear in strongly felt borrowings such as *kynolog* [kɨnɔlɔk] 'dog doctor', *gyros* [gɨrɔs] 'gyros', *gytia* [gɨtʲja] 'gyttja', or proper names such as *Kydryńsk-i* [kɨdrɨɲsci]. The existence of a handful of words which fail to conform to some regularity, especially when the offending vocabulary is otherwise marked, in no way undermines the reality of regularity itself. If anything, it strengthens it by making the exceptions stand out in relief against the overridingly systematic pattern. Furthermore, one may expect a tendency for the offending forms to start conforming to the prevailing patterns and this is indeed what in some cases can be found. Side by side with *maksimum* [maksʲi-mum] we find a derivative with a native suffix *maksym-al-n-y* [maksɨmalnɨ] 'maximal'; the noun *plastik* [plastʲik] denoting the substance 'plastic' exists side by side with the noun *plastyk* [plastɨk] 'visual artist' and the name *Kydryński* can be heard as pronounced with initial [ci] rather than [kɨ]. In other words, some of the loans behave in accordance with the native Polish regularity in demoting {I} from the head to the operator position after an A-headed expression or by observing I-alignment and Empty Heads. This process can be expected to continue.

3.13 PALATALIZATIONS: PHONOLOGY, MORPHOPHONOLOGY, OR BOTH?

We argued above that there can be no general, phonologically based palatalization regularity in Modern Polish that could cover the appearance of the palatalized consonants in (18). This is not due to the existence of 'minimal pairs' like *kon-a* [kɔna] '(s)he is on the point of death' ~*koni-a* [kɔɲa] 'horse, gen. sg.', frequent as these are. Fundamentally, the notion of a minimal pair is a statement about the non-identity or (morphological or lexical) distinctiveness of two forms associated with some sound difference. The minimal pair test says nothing of significance about the phonological nature of this sound difference and, apart from the crudely simplistic approaches, cannot connect the phonological distinctiveness with a phonetic property which an individual observer decides to single out. To make this more concrete, consider a straightforward case of a minimal pair in English, namely the words *pair, pare, pear*, all pronounced [pʰeə] and *bear, bare* pronounced [b̥eə]. Nobody is likely to doubt that *pair–bear* are distinct linguistic forms; on the other hand, prior to a phonological analysis, it is impossible to say what the relevant sound distinction is involved here: is it the presence or absence of aspiration? is it the presence or absence of partial voicing? or is it a combination of the two? or perhaps something still different? Similarly, in the case of the Polish *kon-a* [kɔna]~*koni-a* [kɔɲa] pair, one cannot say in advance that palatalization is the distinctive property since one could say, and it has been said in the past, that what is phonetically a palatal nasal is phonologically a sequence of a non-palatalized (or dental) nasal followed by a palatalizing vowel or glide. In the latter case, [kona] could consist of four contrastive units (/kɔna/) while [kɔɲa] could contain one more unit, a 'palatalizer' in the form of a front vowel or the palatal glide, namely, /konia/ with palatalization and vowel deletion deriving the phonetically attested form. Alternatively, one could talk of palatalization as a separate phoneme or of palatalization as a prosody of the syllable (for a survey of some of the proposed interpretations, see Sawicka and Grzybowski 1999). Basically, then, the minimal-pair test merely states that two forms are different—hardly a significant achievement. Palatalization must be dismissed as a phonological regularity for reasons other than the existence of pairs of words with plain and palatalized consonants.

Palatalization is not a live phonological regularity because there is no systematic connection between the appearance of palatalized consonants and the environment. It should be stressed that the environment need not be equated with the immediately adjacent segments. In other words, we would not rule out on principle the possibility of 'deriving' a palatalized consonant from a sequence of a non-palatalized one followed by a palatalizer. If it could be done in a non-arbitrary and non-ad hoc way, the road would be open for a phonological description of palatalization. As it happens, this is not the case. Earlier, we studied the case of a few suffixes (*-izm/-yzm*, *-ist-a/-yst-a*, *-izacj-a/-yzacj-a*) which behave erratically in that they can be preceded in some cases by a palatalized consonant while in others by a plain one; in still others both forms appear to co-exist. Thus, it is not the case that a specific suffix is or is not responsible for palatalization; palatalization reflexes emerge irrespective of whether the suffix begins with a front or a back vowel. Were it to begin with a back vowel and invariably require a preceding palatalized consonant, one could claim that its first segment is not the back vowel but a palatalizer deleted after causing palatalization or merged with the preceding consonant into a palatalized one. In the examples that follow we illustrate the case where the same suffix *-arz* [aʃ], added to a stem with a non-palatalized consonant, leaves that consonant intact in some cases and 'palatalizes' it in others.

(104) (a) karczm-a [kartʃma] 'tavern'   karczm-arz [kartʃmaʃ] 'tavern keeper'
           reklam-a [rɛklama]   reklami-arz [rɛklamʲaʃ] 'advertiser'
           'advertisement'

       (b) gospod-a [gɔspɔda] 'inn'   gospod-arz [gɔspɔdaʃ] 'inn keeper'
           lod-y [lɔdɨ] 'ice cream'   lodzi-arz [lɔdʑaʃ] 'ice-cream vendor'

(c) moc [mɔts] 'might' moc-arz [mɔtsaʃ] 'mighty ruler'
    owc-a [ɔftsa] 'sheep' owcz-arz [ɔftʃaʃ] 'sheep farmer'

(d) druk [druk] 'printing' druk-arz [drukaʃ] 'printer'
    mlek-o [mlɛkɔ] 'milk' mlecz-arz [mlɛtʃaʃ] 'milkman'

(e) legend-a [lɛgɛnda] 'legend' legend-arz [lɛgɛndaʃ] 'legend collector'
    or legendzi-arz [lɛgɛɲdʑaʃ]

The significance of such examples cannot be overstated: bases ending in a labial (a), a dental (b, c), or a velar (d), when combined with the suffix in question, either remain intact or display a consonant which could be called its palatalized congener.[10] In the case of (e) both forms seem equally acceptable and their choice is not governed by linguistic principles. Note additionally that the resistance of a word like *druk* [druk] 'printing' (d) to palatalization cannot be associated with the word's foreign origin: before a different suffix the final consonant is affected, as in *drucz-ek* [drutʃɛk] 'a printed form'. Thus the presence of a given consonant in the bases is determined not by the phonology of the language but rather has to be seen as an idiosyncratic property of specific morphological derivatives.

In sum, then, palatalization can be regarded as a sharing relation involving the presence of the element {I} simultaneously in a consonantal onset and the nucleus. We have argued that this relationship can be established with the element {I} in the head position which corresponds to the traditional combination of a palatalized consonant and a front vowel (in loans also the palatal glide). Of the phonetically palatalized consonants it is only palato-velars and some palatalized labials that can be viewed as conditioned by the phonological contexts, in other words, as predictable. Alternations between such palatalized consonants and their plain (non-palatalized) congeners result from the workings of the phonology. The presence of a palatalized consonant in other contexts (before back vowel, before a consonant, or word-finally) cannot be viewed as reflecting a palatalization relation in the phonological sense of the word. Alternations involving such palatalized consonants with non-palatalized ones belong to morphophonology—these will be discussed at length below and in particular in the next chapter.

3.14 EXCURSUS ON JUNCTURE PALATALIZATION

We hinted earlier at a variety of palatalization effects which can be found at word junctures. By 'word junctures' we mean both boundaries of lexical words and certain prefix–stem boundaries, although with prefixes a limited number of

[10] This is an oversimplification: the suffix-*arz* can modify the preceding, stem-final consonant. In certain cases the results of the modifications are palatalized consonants, as in (a–b) and partly in (d), but in others the modified consonants can in no way be called palatalized (c–d). At most we can say that the suffix can modify the preceding consonant and sometimes the modification results in a palatalized segment. Strictly speaking, then, the modifications are found in selected derivatives only; furthermore, the modifications are palatalized consonants with certain groups of consonants only.

consonants is attested in the required position. The facts we briefly survey below confirm the conclusion that palatalization phenomena in Modern Polish do not constitute a single or uniform phonological generalization but are split between regular phonology, morphophonology, and phonetic effects.

When a word or prefix ending in a coronal consonant precedes a word beginning with the vowel [i] or the consonant [j], neighbourhood palatalization takes place. Obviously the vowel and the semivowel represent the same element {I} so what we have here is not different in kind from the surface palatalization of coronals found word-internally. In (105a) we offer examples of prefixes and in (105b) some lexical combinations.

(105)   (a) od-jech-a-ć [ɔdʲjɛxatɕ] = od+jechać 'depart'
            pod-jeś-ć [pɔdʲjɛɕtɕ] = pod+jeść 'eat a little'
            roz-iskrz-y-ć [rozʲiskʃɨtɕ] = roz+iskrzyć 'flare up'
            z-ignor-ow-a-ć [zʲignɔrɔvatɕ] = z+ignorować 'ignore'
            bez-imien-n-y [bɛzʲimʲɛnnɨ] = bez+imienny 'nameless'

        (b) brat i siostra [bratʲ i ɕɔstra] 'brother and sister'
            las iglasty [lasʲ iglastɨ] 'coniferous wood'
            dar imienny [darʲ imʲɛnnɨ] 'personal gift'

The coronals provide no new information or evidence and thus basically confirm what we know on other grounds. The situation is the same with true labials, that is, excluding the lateral and the nasal which we thought could be U-headed. Thus the effect of labial palatalization across junctures is the same as in all other cases. Differences emerge with the two sonorants: the velarized lateral (the labial glide) remains unaffected in a perceptible way by the following {I} head, while the nasal is palatalized rather than palatal, as elsewhere. The examples are grouped below but they include very few prefixes.

(106)   (a) ob-jech-a-ć [ɔbʲjɛxatɕ] = ob+jechać 'drive around'
            chleb i masło [xlɛpʲ i maswɔ] 'bread and butter'
            sam idę [samʲ idɛ] 'I go on my own'
            staw jest [stafʲ jɛst] 'the pond is'

        (b) stół jadalny [stuw jadalnɨ] 'dining table'
            kochał inną [kɔxaw innɔʷ] 'he loved another'

        (c) stal i węgiel [stalʲ i vɛŋɟɛl] 'steel and coal'

        (d) pan i pani [panʲ i paɲi] 'a gentleman and a lady'
            ran innych [ranʲ innɨx] 'other wound, gen. pl.'

The examples in (106a) are unremarkable: true labials are palatalized in the same way in every context. The velarized lateral (106b) is really fully resistant to palatalization and as such confirms yet again our suspicion that it must be grouped together with the coronals. The lateral [l] is palatalized only before the following vowel [i] as a result of neighbourhood palatalization (106c), while elsewhere it is a neutral coronal lateral. Loans with input [l] are always identified

3.15 MORPHOLOGICAL INTERLUDE II

with the Polish [l] and never with the Polish [w]. For this reason the labial glide [w] shows no or negligible traces of palatalization across the juncture.

The most interesting and novel situation arises with the nasal [n] in (106d). As we have seen, word-internally it is invariably palatalized to [ɲ] in the relevant contexts by I-alignment. This is also found in loans, foreign proper names, etc., as in *nirwana* [ɲirvana] 'Nirvana', *Nixon* [ɲiksɔn], and *Titanic* [tʲitaɲik]. However, no such palatalization is found across junctures or, more precisely, what is found there are adjacency effects. Hence Polish makes a difference between *pan i pan-i* [panʲ i paɲi] 'a gentleman and a lady' and *pan-i pan-i* [paɲi paɲi] in e.g. *Pani pani pomoże* 'This lady will help you'. Similarly *ran innych* [ranʲ innɨx] 'other wound, gen. pl.' is different from *rań innych* [raɲ innɨx] 'wound others, imper.'. The behaviour of the nasal indicates that the juncture palatalization is distinct from what is found word-internally despite the fact that in most cases their effects coincide.

3.15 MORPHOLOGICAL INTERLUDE II: ALLOMORPHY, MORPHOPHONOLOGY, PALATALIZATIONS

In *Morphological interlude I* we pointed out that Polish inflectional morphology takes heed of whether a stem ends in a soft (palatalized) consonant or a hard (non-palatalized) one. The preliminary discussion showed that different desi-nences are selected depending upon the way a stem terminates. Thus the mascu-line non-personal inanimate nouns *kamień* [kamʲɛɲ] 'stone' and *dzwon* [dzvɔn] 'bell' select, respectively, *-e* [ɛ] and *-y* [ɨ] as their nominative plural markers: *kamieni-e* [kamʲɛɲɛ], *dzwon-y* [dzvɔnɨ]. We also indicated that the term *palatal-ized* in this context has a non-phonetic or structural meaning in that it denotes the presence of the element {I} in the representation; phonetically, no consonant can be described as phonetically palatalized unless it contains the element {I} in the head position. In what follows we shall take a closer look at the relation between the selection of the desinence and the shape of the stem-final consonant. Before we proceed it must be pointed out that Polish inflectional morphology is notori-ously complex and we intend to offer no phonological master key to its mysteries and intricacies. Rather, we will concentrate on the phonological and morpho-phonological aspects as they bear on the issues relevant to this book; as is well known, the selection of desinences is determined not only by these consid-erations but also by gender, specific semantic subcategorizations and finally lexical idiosyncrasies which, on occasion, override the morphological and semantic regularities. They are dealt with in morphological descriptions and entered in dictionaries.[11] Additionally, since markers of certain cases can be identical for specific classes of nouns, in what follows we will refer to just one

---

[11] Westfal (1956) is indicative of the scale and complexity of the problem: 400 pages are devoted to determining the distribution of the two endings, *-a* and *-u*, markers of the inanimate genitive singular masculine case.

of them: thus, rather than characterize specific desinences as implementing the nominative, the accusative, and the vocative plural, we will just talk about the nominative plural.

As another illustration of the role of the palatalized–non-palatalized distinction with the stem-final consonant, consider the nominative singular of neuter nouns. This takes either the -o [ɔ] or the -e [ɛ] endings:

(107)   (a) lat-o [latɔ] 'summer'   gniazd-o [gɲazdɔ] 'nest'
            światł-o [ɕfʲatwɔ] 'light'   ok-o [ɔkɔ] 'eye'
        (b) dani-e [daɲɛ] 'dish'   przejści-e [pʃɛjɕtɕɛ] 'passage'
            narzędzi-e [naʒɛɲdʑɛ] 'tool'   pogotowi-e [pɔgɔtɔvʲɛ] 'ambulance'
            serc-e [sɛrtsɛ] 'heart'   naręcz-e [narɛntʃɛ] 'armful'
            ziel-e [ʑɛlɛ] 'plant'   morz-e [mɔʒɛ] 'sea'

The distribution of the allomorphs is straightforward on the assumption that consonants such as [ts, tʃ, l, ʒ] are taken to belong to the palatalized class despite their phonetics. In this distribution of allomorphs does not differ from what we noted with the two desinences characterizing the nominative plural of masculine non-personal nouns (the *kamienie-dzwony* case, see (22), above). There, too, palatals, the lateral and dental affricates patterned with the palatalized group, for example, *rycerz* [rɨtsɛʃ] 'knight'~*rycerz-e* [rɨtsɛʒɛ], *przyjaciel* [pʃɨjatɕɛl] 'friend'~*przyjaciel-e* [pʃɨjatɕɛlɛ], *koc* [kɔts] 'blanket'~*koc-e* [kɔtsɛ]. In this sense then, the nominative singular neuter allomorphs in (107) introduce no novel developments. The non-palatalized consonants which belong with the palatalized ones constitute the group [l, ts, dz, ʃ, ʒ, tʃ, dʒ]. We shall refer to them as the 'I-operator palatals' in contrast to the truly palatalized consonants which we refer to as 'I-head palatals'. When a short cut will be required we will talk of palatalized consonants but it should be kept in mind that this is a phonological and morpho(phono)logical rather than a phonetic statement.

A more interesting case can be found in the dative (and locative) of feminine nouns. Textbook accounts make the situation attractively simple: -e [ɛ] is attached to stems ending in a non-palatalized, -i/-y [i ɨ] to stems ending in a palatalized consonant. Consider some examples:

(108)   (a) łap-a [wapa] 'paw'   łapi-e [wapʲɛ]
            ryb-a [rɨba] 'fish'   rybi-e [rɨbʲɛ]
            raf-a [rafa] 'reef'   rafi-e [rafʲɛ]
            traw-a [trava] 'grass'   trawi-e [travʲɛ]
            ram-a [rama] 'frame'   rami-e [ramʲɛ]
            ros-a [rɔsa] 'dew'   rosi-e [rɔɕɛ]
            skaz-a [skaza] 'blemish'   skazi-e [skaʑɛ]
            psot-a [psɔta] 'prank'   psoci-e [psɔtɕɛ]
            wod-a [vɔda] 'water'   wodzi-e [vɔdʑɛ]
            stron-a [strɔna] 'side'   stroni-e [strɔɲɛ]
            kar-a [kara] 'punishment'   karz-e [kaʒɛ]

łąk-a [wɔŋka] 'meadow'   łąc-e [wɔntsɛ]
wstęg-a [fstɛŋga] 'ribbon'   wstędz-e [fstɛndzɛ]
much-a [muxa] 'fly'   musz-e [muʃɛ]

(b) utopi-a [utɔpʲja] 'utopia'   utopi-i [utɔpʲi]
    fobi-a [fɔbʲja] 'phobia'   fobi-i [fɔbʲi]
    krwi-ą [kr̥fʲɔ̃ʷ] 'blood, instr.'   krw-i [kr̥fʲi]
    ziemi-a [ʑɛmʲa] 'earth'   ziem-i [ʑɛmʲi]
    gałąź [gawɔ̃ʷɕ] 'branch'   gałęz-i [gawɛʲʑi]
    kość [kɔɕtɕ] 'bone'   kośc-i [kɔɕtɕi]
    łódź [wutɕ] 'boat'   łodz-i [wɔdʑi]
    sień [ɕɛɲ] 'porch'   sien-i [ɕɛɲi]
    sól [sul] 'salt'   sol-i [sɔli]
    noc [nɔts] 'night'   noc-y [nɔtsɨ]
    władz-a [vwadza] 'power'   władz-y [vwadzɨ]
    mysz [mɨʃ] 'mouse'   mysz-y [mɨʃɨ]
    podróż [pɔdruʃ] 'journey'   podróż-y [pɔdruʒɨ]
    dzicz [dʑitʃ] 'savagery'   dzicz-y [dʑitʃɨ]

A comment is called for concerning the distinction between soft-stemmed and hard-stemmed nouns. The traditional notion of a soft-stemmed noun translates in our framework into a noun whose stem-final consonant is either an I-head or an I-operator palatal. In this sense the selection of the {I} allomorph of the dative desinence is determined by the presence of {I} in the final consonant of the stem (108b). When no {I} is available (108a), the allomorph assumes the shape {A•I}. What this account conceals is the fact that in the dative singular of feminine nouns, the stem is invariably palatal(ized): as the examples in (108a) document, the addition of the {A•I} allomorph is accompanied by the replacement of the final, hard, consonant of the stem by its palatal(ized) congener. The congener is again either an I-head or an I-operator palatal; the phonology ensures that the vowel of the desinence is {A•I} after an I-head palatal in *łapi-e* [wapʲɛ] 'paw', for instance, and {I•A̲} after an I-operator palatal in *musz-e* [muʃɛ] 'fly'. The crucial point is that it is misleading or inaccurate to connect directly the appearance of a specific allomorph with the consonantal shape of the stem since after [ʃ], for example, we find both variants: contrast the locative *musz-e* [muʃɛ] 'fly' with the locative *mysz-y* [mɨʃɨ] 'mouse'. What happens is the much more interesting situation where the selection of an allomorph goes hand in hand with the morphophonological modification of the consonantal shape of the stem. We are then dealing here with a case of phonologically conditioned allomorphy, a relatively unremarkable event. The allomorph, once selected, requires a palatalized consonant to precede it. It thus seems inevitable that a precedence or ordering relation should be introduced between allomorphy selection and morphophonological adjustment. The mechanism and nature of the adjustment needs to be worked out formally but we clearly need a morphological base form which is crucial in the selection of the desinence and a morphophonological modification. For the moment we shall adopt a very simple format which, with reference to the modifications in question, can be presented as in (109).

(109) *Morphophonology of palatalization before the dative -e*
Before the {A•I} of the dative replace the stem final
consonants in accordance with the table as follows:

p	b	f	v	m	n	w	r	t	d
p^j	b^j	f^j	v^j	m^j	ɲ	l	3	tɕ	dʑ

s	z	k	g	x
ɕ	ʑ	ts	dz	ʃ

The formulation in (109) is deliberately not restricted to feminine nouns since the regularities it lists are occasionally also found in masculine nouns ending in the nominative singular in *-a*, as in (110).

(110)   idiot-a [id^{j}jɔta] 'idiot'   idioci-e [id^{j}jɔtɕɛ]
włóczęg-a [vwutʃɛŋga] 'loiterer'   włóczędz-e [vwutʃɛndzɛ]

The statement in (109) must contain the reference to the melody of the desinence since masculine and neuter nouns can also take other allomorphs which do not evince the morphophonological palatalization, examples are *-owi* in the masculine *człowiek* [tʃwɔv^{j}ɛk] 'man'~*człowiek-owi* [tʃwɔv^{j}ɛkɔv^{j}i], and *-u* in the neuter *ok-o* [ɔkɔ] 'eye'~ndash;*ok-u* [ɔku]. We will return to the structure of the changes listed in (109) in the next chapter, after we have looked at other morphophonological modifications.

The information required by a morphophonological statement like (109) may be considerably more complex. One relatively simple case is the category of masculine personal nouns and adjectives. Polish morphology sets up this category and supplies it with distinctive case, verbal, and adjective agreement marking. We are concerned with the form of the nominative plural; the ending has the same shapes as that of the dative singular feminine of soft-stemmed nouns, in other words, it is either [i] or [ɨ]. The stem-final consonant undergoes modifications which are almost identical to those found as a result of the dative palatalization (109). Consider examples of nominative singular and nominative plural of some nouns and adjectives.

(111)   (a) chłop [xwɔp] 'peasant'   chłop-i [xwɔp^{j}i]
             ślep-y [ɕlɛpɨ] 'blind'   ślep-i [ɕlɛp^{j}i]
             student [studɛnt] 'student'   studenc-i [studɛɲtɕi]
             złot-y [zwɔtɨ] 'golden'   złoc-i [zwɔtɕi]
             Szwed [ʃfɛt] 'Swede'   Szwedz-i [ʃfɛdʑi]
             młod-y [mwɔdɨ] 'young'   młodz-i [mwɔdʑi]
             aktor [aktɔr] 'actor'   aktorz-y [aktɔʒɨ]

Francuz [frantsus] 'Frenchman'   Francuz-i [frantsuʑi]
technik [tɛxɲik] 'technician'   technic-y [tɛxɲitsɨ]
wiel-k-i [vʲɛlci] 'great'   wiel-c-y [vʲɛltsɨ]
Norweg [nɔrvɛk] 'a Norwegian'   Norwedz-y [nɔrvɛdzɨ]
ubog-i [ubɔɟi] 'poor'   ubodz-y [ubɔdzɨ]

(b) Włoch [vwɔx] 'an Italian'   Włos-i [vwɔɕi]
    mnich [mɲix] 'monk'   mnis-i [mɲiɕi]
    głuch-y [gwuxɨ] 'deaf'   głus-i [gwuɕi]
    cich-y [tɕixɨ] 'silent'   cis-i [tɕiɕi]

The examples in (111a) conform to the morphophonological regularity established above and their phonology is also regular. The latter includes the adjustment of the velar plosive plus the headless high front vowel of adjectives, e.g. [kɨ],
to a palato-velar and a headed high front vowel [ci]. This follows from the
phonological regularities of Empty Heads and I-alignment discussed in the earlier
part of this chapter. The consonantal alternations are, as we noted, almost
identical to those found before the -e ending, the qualification *almost* being
required by the facts of (111b).

The velar spirant alternates not with the palatal [ʃ] as predicted by (109) but
rather with the palatal spirant [ɕ]. Additionally, unlike the velar plosives, the
spirant does not seem to observe the Empty Heads constraint since it is followed
by the empty-headed high vowel {I•_}. Recall that in our discussion of the velar
and palatal spirants we concluded that what is packaged as a velar spirant is often
a non-velar consonant, presumably a glottal spirant. If we do not want to
complicate the morphophonological relatedness, we need to include yet another
pair into the list. With the glottal spirant represented as {h}, the morphophonology of palatalization can be recast as (112).

(112) *Morphophonology of palatalization I*
       Before the {A•I} of the dative and the {I} of the nominative plural
       masculine personal, replace the stem final consonants in accordance with
       the following table:

p	b	f	v	m	n	w	r	t	d
|	|	|	|	|	|	|	|	|	|
pʲ	bʲ	fʲ	vʲ	mʲ	ɲ	l	ʒ	tɕ	dʑ

s	z	k	g	x	h
|	|	|	|	|	|
ɕ	ʑ	ts	dz	ʃ	ɕ

The formulation requires a comment. The contexts where the replacements take
place includes now the -e of the dative singular and the -i/y of the nominative plural
masculine personal. The information we include makes reference, then, both to
the phonological and the grammatical contexts. The phonological context on its
own is not enough since we argued that the phonetic distinction between [ɨ] and [i]

is the function of I-alignment on the one hand while [ɛ] may correspond to different phonological expressions. Thus what we have morphophonologically is just the presence of high and mid front vowels, their heads determined by I-alignment within the phonology. Possibly this position needs to be revised and we may have to nail our flag to the mast by affirming that the palatalizing vowels are lexically— and morphophonologically—I-headed, and as such induce alignment. We will have ample opportunity to assess the advantages and disadvantages of such a step. If we do not take it, then the inclusion of the grammatical information into (112) is unavoidable. Note additionally that there is another (competing) ending of the nominative plural masculine, namely, -owie [ɔvʲɛ], which does not modify the final consonant of the stem in any way. In individual cases both suffixes are recognized as grammatical with the palatalization reflexes as predicted by (112):

(113) Norweg [nɔrvɛk] 'a Norwegian'   Norwedz-y [nɔrvɛdzɨ]
                                         Norweg-owie [nɔrvɛgɔvʲɛ]

       geolog [gɛɔlɔk] 'geologian'   geolodz-y [gɛɔlɔdzɨ]
                                         geolog-owie [gɛɔlɔgɔvʲɛ]

       doktor [dɔktɔr] 'doctor'   doktorz-y [dɔktɔʒɨ]
                                         doktor-owie [dɔktɔrɔvʲɛ]

The choice between a purely phonological and a phonologico-grammatical formulation of morphophonological contexts must be suspended until we have had an occasion to consider more data in detail.

The domain of inflectional morphology supplies us with another instance of allomorphy, which this time requires a somewhat puzzling context. The case in focus is the locative singular of the masculine and neuter and the vocative masculine singular. The desinences are -e and -i/-y. The -e ending attaches to hard-stemmed nouns except for velars and, just as in the case of the -e of the dative singular feminine discussed above it brings about the emergence of the palatal(ized) reflex in accordance with (112). Soft-stemmed nouns—those ending in an I-head or an I-operator consonant—and those ending in a velar attach the desinence -u. The examples in (114) illustrate both classes.

(114) (a) chłop [xwɔp] 'peasant'   chłopi-e [xwɔpʲɛ]
            Arab [arap] 'Arab'   Arabi-e [arabʲɛ]
            olbrzym [ɔlbʒɨm] 'giant'   olbrzymi-e [ɔlbʒɨmʲɛ]
            las [las] 'wood'   lesi-e [lɛɕɛ]
            wóz [vus] 'cart'   wozi-e [vɔʑɛ]
            lot [lɔt] 'flight'   loci-e [lɔtɕɛ]
            obiad [ɔbʲat] 'lunch'   obiedzi-e [ɔbʲɛdʑɛ]
            tron [trɔn] 'throne'   troni-e [trɔɲɛ]
            rosół [rɔsuw] 'broth'   rosole [rɔsɔlɛ]
            doktor [dɔktɔr] 'doctor'   doktorz-e [dɔktɔʒɛ]

       (b) słoń [swɔɲ] 'elephant'   słoni-u [swɔɲu]
            liść [liɕtɕ] 'leaf'   liści-u [liɕtɕu]

narzędzi-e [naʒɛɲdʑɛ] 'tool'   narzędzi-u [naʒɛɲdʑu]
serc-e [sɛrtsɛ] 'heart'   serc-u [sɛrtsu]
paź [paɕ] 'page boy'   pazi-u [paʑu]
król [krul] 'king'   król-u [krulu]
stol-arz [stɔlaʃ] 'joiner'   stol-arz-u [stɔlaʒu]

(c) człowiek [tʃwɔvʲɛk] 'man'   człowiek-u [tʃwɔvʲɛku]
jabł-k-o [japkɔ] 'apple'   jabł-k-u [japku]
próg [pruk] 'threshold'   prog-u [prɔgu]
wróg [vruk] 'enemy'   wrog-u [vrɔgu]
śmiech [ɕmʲɛx] 'laughter'   śmiech-u [ɕmʲɛxu]
duch [dux] 'spirit'   duch-u [duxu]

Group (b), comprising the palatal(ized) stems, is unsurprising, if only because we have had to use it in a few other instances; the hard-stemmed group (a) would be equally unsurprising if it also comprised the velar consonants [k, g, x], which, however, pattern with the soft-stems this time. The conditioning of the allomorphy becomes more complex and arbitrary. The factor which we used above in identifying the soft-stemmed group (the presence of the element {I} in the melody) can no longer be regarded as sufficient; if anything, we need a disjunction to capture the -u group by claiming, for example, that it is selected after an empty-headed expression (a velar consonant) or one containing the element {I}. Alternatively, the disjunction can be stated with reference to the -e allomorph, which is selected after a headed expression as long as it does not contain the element {I}. On neither interpretation is there any obvious connection between the specific allomorph selected and the context. Hence, despite a degree of regularity which we tried to establish by formulating the distribution in terms of some sort of natural classes, allomorphy is contextually irregular. In the case at hand, this is further confirmed by the exceptional cases when the -u variant is selected, in defiance of the prevailing pattern, after a hard-stemmed consonant. Thus *dom* [dɔm] 'house', *syn* [sɨn] 'son', and *pan* [pan] 'gentleman'—all obviously hard-stemmed—rather than yielding the locatives **domi-e* [dɔmʲɛ], **syni-e* [sɨɲɛ], and **pani-e* [paɲɛ], display the forms *dom-u* [dɔmu], *syn-u* [sɨnu], and *pan-u* [panu]. Characteristically for allomorphy, the vocative masculine which normally coincides with the locative does so only with the first two of the three nouns (i.e. *dom-u*, *syn-u*). The last item which is irregular in the locative behaves 'regularly' in the vocative: being hard-stemmed it selects -e with concomitant morphophonological palatalization (*pani-e* [paɲɛ]). The desinence allomorphy to a small extent involves lexical idiosyncrasy despite the fact that, generally, it can be captured by rules whose conditioning may be arbitrary. Furthermore, the (morpho)phonological shape of the allomorphs may reveal little or no common ground: what, say, [ɛ] and [u] as exponents of the locative case have in common is the fact that they are all vowels, hardly an impressive generalization. Thus the allomorphic variation and its contexts may be arbitrary and idiosyncratic.

Morphophonological replacements may be conditioned by phonological and non-phonological factors. The segments involved in an alternation need not necessarily be relatable phonologically, but they remain stable. The alternating segments listed in (112) are on occasion quite distant phonetically, as in [r] and [ʒ], but they are invariable whenever the morphophonological alternation is required. In the following chapter we shall explore the totality of palatalization alternations in Polish. These will be seen to be predominantly of morphophonological nature but will be supplemented by phonological generalizations.

4

THE MORPHOPHONOLOGY OF POLISH
PALATALIZATIONS

4.1 OVERVIEW

Based on the results arrived at in the preceding chapter we argue for a full-fledged morphophonological description of alternations involving palatals and palatalized consonants on the one hand and plain segments on the other. Morphophonological regularities, in contradistinction to phonological ones, are partly conditioned by grammatical (morphological) and lexical factors. This does not mean that they are necessarily erratic or irregular. Some of the alternations are regular and productive with both inflectional and derivational suffixes. The non-phonological conditioning is also seen in the absence of any non-arbitrary connection between the phonological environment and the nature of the changes the alternations reflect. We formulate several replacement statements which account for the alternations. A number of derivational suffixes are surveyed with a view to determining their palatalizational properties. Special attention is paid to conversion (paradigmatic derivation) accompanied by palatalization alternations while the traditional concept of soft stems is provided with a morphophonological interpretation. Another morphological category reviewed morphophonologically is the imperative, which forms part of the complex verbal system. As palatals are morphophonological segments, we consider the possibility of encoding their alternations by means of the replacement statements. The existence of morpheme-internal alternations supports this idea and also leads to the concept of depalatalization in a specified morphophonological environment.

4.2 THEORETICAL PRELIMINARIES

Our discussion of the phonology of the Polish palatalizations brought us to the conclusion that, contrary to the generative tradition, the absolute majority of alternations involving plain and complex consonants (which need not be phonetically palatalized) is not a going phonological concern. While the alternations are massively supported by the lexicon and some of them are undoubtedly productive and synchronically live in some sense, no purely phonological account is capable of capturing them. Let us recapitulate the main reasons for rejecting a purely phonological approach to palatalizations.

In the preceding chapter we argued at length that the distribution of the vowels [i] and [ɨ] is conditioned by the context. This view runs against the classical derivational-generative stand where the two vowels are regarded as separate segments, with the front one palatalizing the preceding consonant while the retracted one being in fact phonologically back. Our position is quite close to the structural phonemic tradition which views these two phonetic vowels as a single (phonemic) unit. If correct, this means that the prototypical palatalizer, the front high vowel, is simply not there to do the job of palatalizing a preceding consonant. We also argued against the physically phonetic view of palatalization in general, where the presence of a front vowel constitutes a necessary condition for the change (process, modification) to take place. We have noted numerous cases where the presence of a front vowel causes no palatalizing or any other effect, as in the contrast of the ending -em 'instr. sg.' and the ending -e 'loc. sg.'. Recall cases such as those in (1).

(1)   lot [lɔt] 'flight'   lot-em [lɔtɛm]   loci-e [lɔtɕɛ]

Here the vowel [ɛ] found in the desinence -em leaves the preceding consonant intact, while an identical vowel in the desinence -e appears to palatalize it. Unless we are prepared to uphold the patently absurd statement that it is the presence of the final nasal that inhibits the palatalization of the stem-final consonant, or something equally implausible, we must conclude that the frontness of the vowel and the palatalization of the consonant are separate issues. This is further evidenced by the fact that palatalized consonants freely occur before non-front vowels, before consonants and at the end of the word; even if within the framework adopted in this book some of the preconsonantal positions and all word-final positions are in fact prevocalic (before a following empty nucleus), these nuclei are not palatalizing in the sense in which front vowels are claimed to be palatalizing, that is to say that they do not contain any melodic unit corresponding to vowel frontness since they contain no melodic unit in the first place. As described in Chapter 3, palatalization as a live phonological regularity in Polish comprises fundamentally the mechanism responsible for the alternations of velars and palato-velars[1] and the distribution of the vowels [i] and [ɨ], that is, I-head alignment. The presence, the distribution, and the alternations of the phonetically and functionally palatalized consonants fall under the scope of morphophonology and the lexicon. In the present chapter we shall look at the morphophonological network involving such consonants and propose ways of describing them, thereby elaborating some of the tentative proposals introduced earlier. There are two groups of interrelated issues associated with morphophonology; they concern its syntagmatic and its paradigmatic aspects. The syntagmatics of morphophonology denotes the nature of the representations while its

---

[1] Marginally also labials, the coronal nasal, and lateral (see the discussion of the examples in (98a)).

paradigmatics refers to the mechanisms of segment alternations. We shall look at both of these in turn.

The nature of the morphophonological base must be seen in the context of the relationship between phonological complexity and morphological motivation (foundation). A basic question, which has received different answers in the history of the discipline, is whether a given morpheme possesses something which could be called a single morphophonological base or whether it co-occurs in different shapes which are somehow connected. Assuming for the moment the correctness—or at least the feasibility—of the single base model, we must handle a number of difficulties the model spawns. It is obviously not the case that one can mechanically take the entries—citation forms—in an ordinary dictionary, such as the nominative singular of nouns, the nominative singular masculine of adjectives, or the infinitive of verbs, and derive or in some other way predict their alternants. Taking Polish nouns as an example, it is easy to show that the nominative singular is not always the desirable base for the establishment of the morphophonemic syntagmatics. We will start, however, by considering a simple phonological example and then move over to purely morphophonological ones.

(2) (a) paw [paf] 'peacock'   pawi-a [pav^{j}a] 'gen. sg.'
     (b) przy-słowi-e [pʃiswɔv^{j}ɛ] 'proverb'   przy-słów [pʃiswuf] 'gen. pl.'
     (c) staw [staf] 'pond'   staw-u [stavu] 'gen. sg.'

If we abstract away the effects of final devoicing, the alternations in (2a–b) involve the two consonants [v ∼ v^j]; if the morphophonological base were to be identified with the nominative case, we would have to say that in (2a) we are dealing with palatalization before the desinential [a], while in (2b) there is depalatalization in word-final position. The untenability of the former claim is shown by (2c), where no palatalization takes place before the desinential vowel. The phonological regularity can be viewed either as labial depalatalization word-finally and preconsonantally or as palatalized labial licensing by a following full vowel. Crucially, the regularity is totally independent of the specific morphological category where it is found.

As typically morphophonemic alternations consider the examples in (3).

(3) (a) rów [ruf] 'ditch'   row-u [rɔvu] 'gen. sg.'
     (b) sow-a [sɔva] 'owl'   sów [suf] 'gen. pl.'
     (c) sen [sɛn] 'dream'   sn-y [snɨ] 'nom. pl.
     (d) dn-o [dnɔ] 'bottom'   den [dɛn] 'gen. pl.'

The appearance of the alternations [u ∼ ɔ] and [ɛ ∼ ø] has nothing to do with the particular grammatical case: it so happens that a feminine noun like *sow-a* or a neuter noun like *dn-o* ends in a vowel in the nominative singular and this fact alone—the presence of a full vowel in the final nucleus—is responsible for the particular vocalic melody which appears in the stem. Similarly, the final empty nucleus requires a melody to be present in the preceding stem nucleus, irrespective of the morphological shape of the noun. The selection of the morphophonological base form reflects the conviction of the directionality of the morphophonemic change: is it palatalization or depalatalization? is it vowel raising or lowering? is it insertion or deletion? In many individual cases, as we will see below, the answer is not always straightforward, but it is incontrovertible that the choice has to be guided by formal, morphophonemic rather than morphological and semantic considerations.

A more basic question might be asked at this stage, namely, whether a single morphophonemic base form is needed in the first place. We would like to review here an argument from morpholexical allomorphy, a type that was amply illustrated for different purposes in the preceding chapter. Certain inflectional endings appear in a few shapes where the choice of a specific desinence may depend on the morphophonemic shape of the base. To take just one example, consider briefly the argument discussed in *Morphological interlude II* (section 3.15) namely the ending of the locative singular of masculine and neuter nouns: it is either *-e* or *-u*. In (4) we find two nouns in the nominative singular and the locative singular.

(4)   okn-o [ɔknɔ] 'window'   okni-e [ɔkɲɛ] (cf. okien [ɔcɛn] 'gen. pl.')
       ogień [ɔɟɛɲ] 'fire'   ogni-u [ɔgɲu]

The genitive plural form of the first word—*okien* [ɔcɛn]—clearly shows that its two consonants are separated by an empty nucleus, which is realized as [ɛ] before the final empty nucleus in exactly the same way as the second word. The basic question that a morphological—or morpholexical—description of the language must face here is how to specify what decides the selection of the ending *-e* or *-u*. The answer seems to be that it is the palatalized or non-palatalized nature of the nasal that provides the required context for the endings. Note additionally that in the locative case itself the nasal preceding the desinence is palatalized in both cases; in one instance the palatalized nasal is part of the base to which the desinence is attached and in the other it emerges as a result of a morphophonological operation. In any case, it is the base form where the distinction between the palatalized and non-palatalized nasal, a distinction crucial to the selection of the allomorph, is maintained, and where it plays its role. This shows that in order to select the correct ending we need to be able to refer to a specific variant of the morpheme, which we call here the morphophonemic base form. Examples where the base plays a role in the selection of the ending are legion in Polish—any comprehensive description of its morphology will supply an adequate listing (Kreja 1989; Grzegorczykowa, Laskowski, and Wróbel 1998). Obviously, the base form is just one way of encoding the required information and alternative ways can easily be devised; for example, out of the existing alternants of a morpheme, one variant could be diacritically marked as constituting the reference form for desinence attachment. Such a mechanism would not in any way disguise the fact that the particular form is unpredictable and does not differ from the procedure for setting up a morphophonological base form. The choice of a specific marking mechanism is not something that will concern us here. The view that morpholexical selection can be phonologically conditioned is amply illustrated in Kiparsky (1996: 19).

The other moot question affecting morphophonology which is strictly connected with the existence, or not, of base forms concerns ways of representing alternations. Briefly, should the alternants be in some sense derived by phonologically or morphophonologically transforming the base or should they be selected from among the listed possibilities? The standard generative view had a straightforward answer: whatever can be cast in a phonological format, should be done so. As is well known, this postulate resulted in single representations for most morphemes and ordered rules deriving surface forms. What remained outside the scope of phonology in this approach were suppletive and fully irregular alternations. Such phonologically driven morphophonology led to highly abstract underlying representations, including absolutely neutralized segments, and complex rules subject to phonological, morphological and lexical conditioning. As numerous generative accounts show, morphophonological alternations can be described by phonological means, but the price this entails is very high.

Much of the research in Polish phonology following in the wake of Laskowski's (1975a) seminal monograph tried to reduce that price by curtailing abstract representations and arbitrary devices, even though this sometimes led to other, new and costly, mechanisms (see Gussmann 2006). It is not necessary for us here to trace the details of the different proposals; suffice it to say that two main trends may be distinguished in the ensuing tradition—one continues to view morphophonological alternations as the source of information about phonological regularities and continues to describe such alternations by phonological means. The other line of research attempts to revert to the traditional structural positions by teasing out phonological regularities from morphophonological replacements; in effect, this line concedes that the derivational-generative view of the nature of phonology was in error and that a return to the more traditional perspective is in order.

In an attempt to constrain what was regarded as the excessive abstractness of classical generative analyses, a separation of phonological processes was suggested into lexical and post-lexical rules. The theory of Lexical Phonology (see e.g. Rubach 1984; Mohanan 1986; Hargus and Kaisse 1993; see also Gussmann 1985, 1988) in effect re-introduced morphophonological regularities but continued to insist that they are controlled by phonological rules. This is openly admitted in Kiparsky (1996: 17): 'Morphophonemic alternations, on the other hand, are accounted for by phonological rules, applying subject to constraints on the lexical module.' These 'lexical' rules are claimed to display properties of their own but they crucially manipulate phonological matter, as shown by the analysis of German umlaut or English trisyllabic laxing (Kiparsky 1996: 26–30). For this reason, Lexical Phonology does not depart from the classical generative model as it continues to view morphophonological alternations as resulting from the operation of phonologically grounded mechanisms. It hardly requires stressing that we are not particularly concerned about the appellation used to describe a given mechanism—be it morphophonological, lexical, or some other term—what is of overriding importance is the nature of the processes. Both classical generative phonology and its subsequent transformations describe them in exactly the same way as fully-fledged phonological regularities, where features undergo all sorts of changes in contexts which involve not just phonological but also morphological or morpho-lexical conditioning.

The same method of treating morphophonological alternations is found within Optimality Theory. Although some regularities are openly called morphophonological or allomorphic, they are regarded as resulting from ranked constraints in much the same way as they were regarded as resulting from ordered rules within the classical paradigm. No matter how different ordered rules may appear to be from ranked constraints to true-blue Optimality Theory followers, outside spectators must be excused if for them the two are very much just notational variants. This is reinforced by the fact that both derivational-generative phonology and the allegedly non-derivational Optimality Theory take morphophonological alternations as the primary object of study which they break up into their ordered rules and ranked constraints respectively. Works such as Rubach and Booij (2001) or Ito and Mester (2003) are typical of this approach. Whether some alternations are purely phonological or purely morphophonological seems a totally arbitrary decision, unconnected to anything else in the framework, and certainly not derived from any general or independent principles.

The alternative or the more traditional approach views morphophonological alternations as fundamentally different from phonological regularities. Unlike phonological processes, morphophonological regularities are in essence segment replacements in specified contexts. The contexts may be partially phonological but most typically involve morphological and/or lexical information. This approach has been applied to the description of Polish morphophonology by Kowalik (1997), a description which is very different in spirit from Laskowski's monograph since it refuses to break up the alternating segments into atomic, phonetically based, operations. In this sense Kowalik's approach to morphophonology defines itself as diametrically opposed to the generative views, both in the *SPE* tradition and its later lexical garb. The question that suggests itself is whether the rejection of phonologically driven morphophonology is a retrograde step, or whether the generative model was misguided, in which case the recent reversal of positions is on the right track. This brings us again to the moot issue of whether morphophonology, as separate from phonology, is at all necessary.

Although never really discussed at length in the literature, non-phonological alternations—outside of suppletive or fully irregular forms—have always been recognized within generative phonology. As a case in point consider the alternation between [ɪə] and [æ] in the English pair *clear ~ clarity*. The morphological and semantic closeness of the two words seems indisputable, but none of the existing models of vowel alternations is capable of capturing the alternation between the diphthong and the vowel: the diphthong [ɪə] typically alternates with [e], as in *sincere ~ sincerity*, while the vowel [æ] alternates with the diphthong [eɪ], as in *vanity ~ vain*. Thus what we find in the pair *clear ~ clarity* falls outside the scope of phonology proper. On the other hand, even the otherwise expected or regular alternation [æ ~ eɪ] found in the name of the river and the city it flows through, *Cam* ~ *Cambridge*, would not qualify as meriting a phonological account because of the absence of contextual factors controlling it. Such isolated instances would probably not worry anybody and would be relegated to the lexicon as unpredictable and irregular. The situation becomes more complex when the examples, rather than being isolated, look quasi-regular or at least sub-regular. Consider the following case from Polish. The dental plosives [t, d] alternate with dental and alveolo-palatal affricates; restricting ourselves to the voiceless plosive, typical examples are:

(5) lot [lɔt] 'flight'   lec-ę [lɛtsɛ] 'I fly'   leć [lɛtɕ] 'imper.'
     kot [kɔt] 'cat'   koc-ur [kɔtsur] 'tomcat'   koc-i [kɔtɕi] 'feline'
     święt-y [ɕfʲɛntɨ]   święc-on-y [ɕfʲɛntsɔnɨ]   święc-i [ɕfʲɛɲtɕi] 'saint,
     'holy'   'hallowed'   nom.pl.'
     błot-o [bwɔtɔ] 'mud'   błoc-k-o [bwɔtskɔ] 'expr.'   błoc-isk-o [bwɔtɕiskɔ]
                                                           'expr.'

The alternations [t ~ ts ~ tɕ] are massively supported by the Polish lexicon and all past generative descriptions have attempted to provide an account of them in phonological terms, a point whose validity will be discussed later on. At this stage we may note that the voiceless velar plosive [k] regularly alternates with the post-alveolar affricate [tʃ], as in the following examples.

(6) skok [skɔk] 'jump, n.'   skocz-ek [skɔtʃɛk]   skocz [skɔtʃ] 'vb.,
                               'jumper'   imper.'
     człowiek [tʃwɔvʲɛk]   człowiecz-e [tʃwɔvʲɛtʃɛ]   człowiecz-y [tʃwɔvʲɛtʃɨ]
     'man'   'voc. sg.'   'human'
     smak [smak] 'taste, n.'   smacz-ek [smatʃɛk]   smacz-n-y [smatʃnɨ]
                               'dim.'   'tasty'

Again there is massive lexical support for this alternation. In principle there should be no alternation between [t] and [tʃ], in the same way as the alternations between the two English nuclei in *clear* ~ *clarity* are not supported by the system; in fact Kowalik (1997: 105–6) mentions the alternation only marginally in the context before a preceding [s]; see (7).

(7) post [pɔst] 'fast, n.'   poszcz-ę [pɔʃtʃɛ] 'I fast'
     zemst-a [zɛmsta] 'revenge'   zemszcz-ę [zɛmʃtʃɛ] 'I'll take revenge'
     tłust-y [twustɨ] 'fat, adj.'   tłuszcz [twuʃtʃ] 'grease'

Since the specific change of [t] into [tʃ] rather than the expected [ts] or [ɕ] takes place after [s]—which itself has to assimilate to the alveolar affricate, hence [ʃtʃ] rather than *[stʃ]—one might view it as a contextually determined subregularity. A formulation of the subregularity is a complex matter, assuming it is at all possible. For one thing, the presence of a preceding [s] is in itself insufficient to ensure the emergence of a following [tʃ]: in some other forms of the verbs for 'fast' and 'take revenge' the plosive alternates with the expected alveolo-palatal: *pościć* [pɔɕtɕitɕ] 'inf.', *pość* [pɔɕtɕ] 'imper.', etc. Basically, in the verbal contexts where [t] alternates with [ts], a [st] sequence alternates with [ʃtʃ]. Furthermore, the class of derivates involving nouns like *tłuszcz* [twuʃtʃ] 'grease' is quite restricted and morphologically unpredictable, so these derivatives would need to be entered in the lexicon. The lexically restricted nature of the alternation might bring us to the conclusion that it is not different from the English examples discussed above. However, a closer inspection of the data reveals that the scope of the unexpected alternation between [t] and [tʃ] is much broader even if past descriptions unaccountably fail to record them, let alone provide an insightful analysis.

Apart from the position involving the spirant [s] there are isolated but completely uncontroversial instances of adjectives derived from nouns:

(8)   robot-a [rɔbɔta] 'work, n.'   robocz-y [rɔbɔtʃɨ] 'working'
       ochot-a [ɔxɔta] 'willingness'   ochocz-y [ɔxɔtʃɨ] 'willing'

In synchronic morphological terms—that is, forgetting about the probable East Slavic origin of the adjectives—the above noun–adjective pairs are as related as the ones involving the alternation [t ∼ ts] in (9a) or those involving the alternation [t ∼ tɕ] in (9b):

(9)   (a) kobiet-a [kɔbʲɛta] 'woman'   kobiec-y [kɔbʲɛtsɨ] 'feminine'
           sierot-a [ɕɛrɔta] 'orphan'   sieroc-y [ɕɛrɔtsɨ] 'adj.'
       (b) kogut [kɔgut] 'rooster'   koguc-i [kɔgutɕi] 'adj.'
           czart [tʃart] 'devil'   czarc-i [tʃartɕi] 'adj.'

While the groups in (9) might be distinguished by means of some (morpho)phonological marker, which could be supported by evidence from elsewhere in the system—say /j/ in one case and /i/ in the other with subsequent deletion of both markers—the two words in (8) would have to be approached in some totally arbitrary or diacritic manner. Yet there is no escaping from the data: to speakers of Polish the adjective of *robot-a* [rɔbɔta] 'work' is *robocz-y* [rɔbɔtʃɨ] 'working', just as the adjective derived from *kogut* [kɔgut] 'rooster' is *koguc-i* [kɔgutɕi] 'adj.'. An adequate description should be able to capture these facts in some way. Of course it is possible to claim that in one group of words there is the marker /j/, in another the marker /i/, and in yet another there is a laryngeal; after doing their job, they are all deleted. The gimmicky nature of such 'interpretations' is hardly worth dwelling on.

A more complex case involving the [t ∼ tʃ] alternation is to be found in a group of verbs, traditionally regarded as a class requiring [a] as the verbalizing suffix. Throughout the present-tense paradigm the stem-final consonant [t] appears either as the expected [ts] or as the unexpected [tʃ]. Here are some examples of the infinitive and the first-person singular present tense (see Grzegorczykowa, Laskowski, and Wróbel 1998: 254).

(10)   szept-a-ć [ʃɛptatɕ] 'whisper'   szepc-ę [ʃɛptsɛ] or szepcz-ę [ʃɛptʃɛ]
        dygot-a-ć [dɨgɔtatɕ] 'tremble'   dygoc-ę [dɨgɔtsɛ] or dygocz-ę [dɨgɔtʃɛ]

łaskot-a-ć [waskɔtatɕ] 'tickle'	łaskoc-ę [waskɔtsɛ] or łaskocz-ę [waskɔtʃɛ]
chichot-a-ć [ɕixɔtatɕ] 'giggle'	chichoc-ę [ɕixɔtsɛ] or chichocz-ę [ɕixɔtʃɛ]
drept-a-ć [drɛptatɕ] 'mince about'	drepc-ę [drɛptsɛ] or drepcz-ę [drɛptʃɛ]
kłopot-a-ć [kwɔpɔtatɕ] 'worry'	kłopoc-ę [kwɔpɔtsɛ] or kłopocz-ę [kwɔpɔtʃɛ]
mamrot-a-ć [mamrɔtatɕ] 'mumble'	mamroc-ę [mamrɔtsɛ] or mamrocz-ę [mamrɔtʃɛ]

The selection of the variant appears to be predominantly a matter of free choice, and the most one can say is that there are individual preferences; the forms with [tʃ] seem more common and characteristic of the younger generation while those with [ts] appear overstudied or downright obsolete (see also Łoś 1922: 149). There is one verb I know where the variant with [tʃ] is the only one possible, namely:

(10′) pląt-a-ć [plɔntatɕ] 'confuse' plącz-ę [plɔntʃɛ] and never *plą[ts]ę.

If we assume, in line with the rest of the system, that the regular mor-phophonological change turns [t] into [ts] (cf. *lot* [lɔt] 'flight' ∼ *lec-ę* [lɛtsɛ] 'I fly'), then the forms with [tʃ] would require special marking in the present tense to allow for the existing optionality. Not only that, but the verb *plątać* requires marking that would obligatorily evince the regular alternation in the present tense.

The need for marking the optional alternation in the present tense contrasts with its obligatory nature in two other verbal categories, namely, in the impera-tive (imper.) and before the present participle (pres. part.) ending in -*ąc,* where only one variant is grammatical, and, what is worse, it is the unexpected one. Consider these forms of the verbs above:

(11) szept-a-ć [ʃɛptatɕ] 'whisper'	szepcz [ʃɛptʃ] 'imper.', *szepc [ʃɛpts]; szepcz-ąc [ʃɛptʃɔnts] 'pr. part.' *szepc-ąc [ʃɛptsɔnts]
dygot-a-ć [dɨgɔtatɕ] 'tremble'	dygocz [dɨgɔtʃ], *dygoc [dɨgɔts]; dygocz-ąc [dɨgɔtʃɔnts], *dygoc-ąc [dɨgɔtsɔnts]
łaskot-a-ć [waskɔtatɕ] 'tickle'	łaskocz [waskɔtʃ] *łaskoc [waskɔts]; łaskocz-ąc [waskɔtʃɔnts], *łaskoc-ąc [waskɔtsɔnts]
chichot-a-ć [ɕixɔtatɕ] 'giggle'	chichocz [ɕixɔtʃ], *chichoc [ɕixɔts]; chichocz-ąc [ɕixɔtʃɔnts], *chichoc-ąc [ɕixɔtsɔnts]
drept-a-ć [drɛptatɕ] 'mince about'	drepcz [drɛptʃ], *drepc [drɛpts]; drepcz-ąc [drɛptʃɔnts], *drepc-ąc [drɛptsɔnts]

kłopot-a-ć [kwɔpɔtatɕ] 'worry'   kłopocz [kwɔpɔtʃ], *kłopoc [kwɔpɔts]
kłopocz-ąc [kwɔpɔtʃɔnts],
*kłopoc-ąc [kwɔpɔtsɔnts]

mamrot-a-ć [mamrɔtatɕ]   mamrocz [mamrɔtʃ], *mamroc
'mumble'   [mamrɔts]
mamrocz-ąc [mamrɔtʃɔnts],
*mamroc-ąc [mamrɔtsɔnts]

pląt-a-ć [plɔntatɕ] 'confuse'   plącz [plɔntʃ], *pląc [plɔnts]
plącz-ąc [plɔntʃɔnts], *pląc-ąc
[plɔntsɔnts].

The need to list grammatical contexts and individual lexical items is characteristic of non-phonological alternations, even despite the fact that the changes themselves are often easily describable in phonological terms. Thus, *pace* Kiparsky (1996: 16), we believe that morphological and/or lexical conditioning crucially marks a regularity as unambiguously morphophonological. The possibility that there are morphophonological regularities that are purely phonologically conditioned is not germane here since one can always doctor representations in ways that will create a semblance of phonological conditioning (recall our earlier 'proposal' that a laryngeal conditions the change of [t] into [tʃ] in Polish, with subsequent deletion of the laryngeal, of course). We take it as a rule of thumb that non-phonological conditioning is a clear sign of a morphophonological process: purely phonological conditioning is strongly indicative of a phonological regularity as long as the purely phonological conditioning has a non-arbitrary basis. As outlined in Chapter 2, we adopt the position that phonological regularities are conditioned by the phonological environment, in agreement with the requirement of non-arbitrariness as formulated by Kaye, Lowenstamm, and Vergnaud (1990: 194): 'There is a direct relation between a phonological process and the context in which it occurs.' It should be added, however, that the nature of the context should be subjected to critical scrutiny in every instance if we want to avoid absurd phonological conditionings on the one hand, and if we do not want to reduce the whole of phonology to generalizations statable in purely and exclusively surface phonetic terms, on the other. As far as morphophonology goes, we reject the view that both the target and the structural change of a morphophonological regularity should be defined in purely phonological terms—quite conversely, we believe that while part or perhaps most of morphophonological alternations can be described as results of phonologically plausible processes in historical terms, no such requirement can be placed on them in a synchronic system. We adopt the view that morphophonological operations constitute replacements of segments, and whatever semblance to phonology they may have is nothing but synchronic accident.

With reference to the alternations of [t], as illustrated above, it goes without saying that we are dealing with a morphophonological regularity when the consonant's congener is [tʃ], as shown by the contexts where the alternation is made manifest. We will also assume that the alternation [t ∼ ts] is morphophonological because it is restricted to specific verbal categories and isolated lexical items (see also Rubach and Booij 2001). What remains to be considered is whether alternations between [t] and the 'truly palatalized' or alveolo-palatal [tɕ] are phonological or morphophonological; obviously whatever answer we supply for the voiceless dental plosive would also hold true for all other consonants involved in similar alterna- tions. In the preceding chapter we argued that palatalization as a phonological phenomenon is highly restricted and holds primarily for velars. Here we will look at the same problem from the point of view of alternations and we will take into account the phonological tradition. The simple question is then whether palataliza- tion is a phonological process in Modern Polish and, more generally, at what point a regularity ceases to be phonological. The classical position, as fully developed in Laskowski (1975*a*), affirms that palatalization takes place before front vowels; this was originally taken to mean not only that consonants were palatalized before phonologically front vowels, but also that whatever palatal(ized) consonants are found phonetically, have to be due to the working of the palatalization regularities. While the former claim would appear to be unexceptionable in principle, its reverse proved impossible to uphold and was soon abandoned (for an early instance of this, see Gussmann 1977). In brief, to claim that every palatal and palatalized consonant, and also some neither obviously palatal or palatalized ones like the dental affricates [ts, dz], are derived by means of palatalization rule(s) applying before a front vowel (or the front glide), would force massive restructuring of representations and require a number of ad hoc rules adjusting the representations, deleting the 'pala- talizers' after they had done their job, etc. In effect, the phonological derivation would become arbitrary and unmotivated.

We argued above for the necessity of recognizing a single base form in order to ensure the proper distribution of inflectional desinences. If this position is correct, then a variety of the derivational model seems the preferred option: if all the variants were to be listed, one of them would have to be additionally marked as the base, a step that would further increase the complexity of the description.

Let us go back to the [t ∼ tʃ] alternation in Modern Polish and trace its diachronic origin. Historically speaking the alternation [t ∼ tʃ] in Polish, unlike Russian, is marginal. In Polish the result of the historical process of iotation (palatalization by the palatal glide) results in the alternation [t ∼ ts], while the later, front-vowel palatalization yields the alternation [t ∼ tɕ]. The only instance where the [t ∼ tʃ] alternation is historically justified in Polish is after a preceding [s]; Stieber (1979: 78), talking of the development of the consonantal groups *stj, zdj* in Slavic languages, notes that their development is irregular and 'in Polish for example they did not turn into *sts zdz as could be expected but into ʃtʃ, ʒdʒ' (for a somewhat longer if equally non-conclusive account, see Shevelov 1964: 213–15). There is no obvious phonetic motivation for this change—note that in Modern Polish the sequence [sts] is perfectly well formed and regularly encountered; examples are *scalić* [stsalitɕ] 'merge', *scałować* [stsawɔvatɕ] 'kiss, vb.', *masce* [mastsɛ] 'mask, dat. sg.'. Since the early Slavic sequences *stj, zdj* show quirky developments in other Slavic languages, we may assume that the irregular development was in some way conditioned phonologically, even if we are unable to pin down the reasons convincingly. Whatever the causes, then, the appearance of [tʃ] for the expected [ts] after [s] may be assumed to have a historical phonological basis. This would account for the alternants in (7) like *post* [pɔst] 'fast, n.' ~ *poszcz-ę* [pɔʃtʃɛ] 'I fast'; in this way, side by side with the predominant pattern where [t] alternates with [ts] and [tɕ], we also find the subregularity of the plosive alternating with [tʃ]. The words *robocz-y*, *ochocz-y* in (8), borrowings from East Slavic, supply two additional cases of the [t ~ tʃ] alternation. Such loanwords increase its lexical support but at the same time they show that the alternation has no connection with the phonological context: it is found not only after [s] but also in the intervocalic position.

If it is correct to assume that the highly restricted, historically justified, alternation broadens its scope, then it must be the case that the alternation no longer has any phonological motivation: it is now found not only after [s] but also after a vowel in selected items. Thus the extension of the scope of the morphophonological regularity (see Andersen 1969*a*: 824 ff.) is divorced from the motivation of its phonological origin. The alternating segments continue to reflect the original phonological alternation, but by now their phonological relationship is synchronically arbitrary. Living a life of its own, with no phonological conditioning, the alternation continues to extend its scope. The remaining cases involving verbs are even more puzzling: while optionally admissible in the present tense, the alternation is obligatory in the imperative and the present participle. The scope of the alternation is in the process of spreading since the historically expected [t ~ ts] alternation variant in the present tense is being pushed out by the innovative, historically unexpected, one. The existence of the isolated verb *plątać*, where the alternation is obligatory also in the present tense, reinforces this conclusion. We have a case here of a morphophonological alternation whose historical origin can be traced back to phonology (basically the cluster *stj*) but which is, in most instances today, an independent morphophonological development. If non-phonological alternations are allowed to develop and spread, then their phonological texture plays no role in the process. In sum, we have identified a morphophonological alternation which must be described without reference to its phonological content. It is simply a replacement of the segment [t] by the segment [tʃ] in specified contexts.

We are now ready to consider the existing alternations between plain and palatal and palatalized consonants as morphophonological phenomena. These are cases where the alternating segments need not be phonologically relatable and where the context of the alternation may but does not have to include phonological categories; the context is normally morphological—involving specific affixes and grammatical categories—and lexical, hence in essence diacritic. The content of the alternation is expressed as a replacement process where one segment is replaced by another segment. Morphophonology, unlike phonology with its syntagmatic bias, is far more segment-oriented. Traditional Polish palatalizations as morphophonological regularities reveal the nature of such mechanisms.

4.3 REPLACEMENT PATTERNS OF POLISH PALATALIZATIONS

As argued above and also in Chapter 3, the majority of alternations of consonants termed 'palatalizations' are morphophonological replacements of segments.
We will continue to refer to them as 'palatalizations' since they are a detritus of
ancient phonological innovations, and because the generative literature handles
most of them as reflexes of live phonological processes dubbed 'palatalizations'.
No particular attention should be attached to the terminology.

Consonant replacements subsumed under the general notion of palatalization
are evinced in specific morphological contexts and may entail specific phonological conditioning. Classes of consonants can be affected in different ways and
these will be surveyed now with a view to establishing their number and structure.
Starting with a group embracing sonorants and labial obstruents we note that
these consonants exhibit just one alternant each. In Polish, then, sonorants and
labial obstruents alternate with just one palatalized reflex. Thus if a context
induces some variety of palatalization, a given sonorant or labial obstruent will
be replaced by one and the same consonant.[2] The first set of palatalization
replacements (PR) produces the following alternations, where the prime ′ indicates that the formulation will be revised presently:

PR1′ $\quad$ p $\quad$ b $\quad$ f $\quad$ v $\quad$ m $\quad$ r $\quad$ w $\quad$ n
$\qquad$ | $\quad$ | $\quad$ | $\quad$ | $\quad$ | $\quad$ | $\quad$ | $\quad$ |
$\qquad$ pʲ $\quad$ bʲ $\quad$ fʲ $\quad$ vʲ $\quad$ mʲ $\quad$ ӡ $\quad$ l $\quad$ ɲ

The replacements can be illustrated by changes found when the dative locative
singular -e is appended to a noun. Examples:

(12) $\quad$ małp-a [mawpa] 'monkey' $\qquad$ małpi-e [mawpʲɛ]
$\qquad$ bab-a [baba] 'crone' $\qquad$ babi-e [babʲɛ]
$\qquad$ raf-a [rafa] 'reef' $\qquad$ rafi-e [rafʲɛ]
$\qquad$ staw-u [stavu] 'pond, gen. sg.' $\qquad$ stawi-e [stavʲɛ]
$\qquad$ tam-a [tama] 'dam' $\qquad$ tami-e [tamʲɛ]
$\qquad$ por-a [pɔra] 'time' $\qquad$ porz- e [pɔӡɛ]
$\qquad$ dół [duw] 'hole' $\qquad$ dol-e [dɔlɛ]
$\qquad$ stan [stan] 'state' $\qquad$ stani-e [staɲɛ]

Dental and velar obstruents produce a more complex pattern since, depending
on the context, these consonants enter into one–many replacements. Thus in the
context of the dative locative -e desinence the two groups alternate as follows:

---

[2] As repeatedly argued in the text, the expression which behaves phonologically as the velarized
lateral [ɫ] is packaged phonetically as the bilabial semivowel [w] in most varieties of Polish. This should
be borne in mind whenever the segment [w] is evoked.

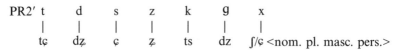

```
PR2'  t     d     s     z     k     g     x
      |     |     |     |     |     |     |
      tɕ    dʑ    ɕ     ʑ     ts    dz    ʃ/ɕ <nom. pl. masc. pers.>
```

as exemplified by (13).

(13) wat-a [vata] 'cotton wool'   waci-e [vatɕɛ]
      mod-a [mɔda] 'fashion'   modzi-e [mɔdʑɛ]
      los [lɔs] 'fate'   losi-e [lɔɕɛ]
      skaz-a [skaza] 'blemish'   skazi-e [skaʑɛ]
      ręk-a [rɛŋka] 'hand'   ręc-e [rɛntsɛ]
      wag-a [vaga] 'scales'   wadz-e [vadzɛ]
      much-a [muxa] 'fly'   musz-e [muʃɛ]

A word of comment is called for with reference to the velar fricative, which alternates either with [ʃ], as just illustrated, or with [ɕ]; the latter case appears in a strictly defined morphological environment of the nominative singular masculine virile nouns where in place of the expected [ʃ] we find [ɕ]. Thus side by side with the regular PR2' alternations in (14a) we find the [x] alternating with [ɕ] in (14b) before the -i ending denoting the specific grammatical category.

(14) (a) adwokat [advɔkat] 'lawyer'   adwokac-i [advɔkatɕi]
          sąsiad [sɔ‿ʷɕat] 'neighbour'   sąsiedz-i [sɔ‿ʷɕedʑi]
          Hindus [ɕindus] 'Hindu'   Hindus-i [ɕinduɕi]
          Francuz-a [frantsuza] 'Frenchman, gen. sg.' Francuz-i [frantsuʑi]
          Norweg-a [nɔrvɛga] 'Norwegian, gen. sg.'   Norwedz-y [nɔrvɛdzɨ]

      (b) Włoch [vwɔx] 'Italian'   Włos-i [vwɔɕi]
          mnich [mɲix] 'monk'   mnis-i [mɲiɕi]

This particular subregularity is strictly morphologically conditioned and needs to be stated as such.

The same obstruents in various derivationally related forms alternate with different consonants:

```
PR3'  t     d     s     z     k     g     zg      x
      |     |     |     |     |     |     |       |
      ts    dz    ʃ     ʒ     tʃ    ʒ     ʒdʒ     ʃ
```

Examples follow:

(15) lot [lɔt] 'flight'   lec-ę [lɛtsɛ] 'I fly'
      rad-a [rada] 'advice'   radz-ę [radzɛ] 'I advise'
      kos-a [kɔsa] 'scythe'   kosz-ę [kɔʃɛ] 'I mow'
      woz-u [vɔzu] 'cart, gen. sg.'   woż-ę [vɔʒɛ] 'I cart'
      skok [skɔk] 'jump, n.'   skocz-y-ć [skɔtʃɨtɕ] 'vb.'
      wag-a [vaga] 'scales'   waż-y-ć [vaʒɨtɕ] 'weigh'

mózg-u [muzgu] 'brain, gen. sg.'   od-móźdż-y-ć [ɔdmuʒdʑitɕ] 'excerebrate'
grzech [gʒɛx] 'sin, n.'   grzesz-y-ć [gʒɛʃitɕ] 'vb.'

The alternations listed as PR2′ and PR3′ can be partially combined and modified in specific morphological and lexical contexts. It is not the case, then, that the alternation series are immutable or constant. The full gamut of the alternation possibilities includes a few subcases that we will consider now.

In a number of contexts dental spirants alternate as in PR2′, velars display the pattern of PR3′ while dental plosives do not alternate at all. Additionally, the lateral alternates as in PR1. The result is PR4′ (again to be modified).

PR4′ w   s   z   k   g   x
     | | | | | |
     l   ɕ   ʑ   tʃ   ʒ   ʃ

Typical examples can be found in adjectives derived by means of the suffix *-n-y*:

(16) skał-a [skawa] 'rock'   skal-n-y [skalni] 'adj.'
      głos [gwɔs] 'voice'   głoś-n-y [gwɔɕni] 'loud'
      groz-a [grɔza] 'awe'   groź-n-y [grɔʑni] 'threatening'
      rok [rɔk] 'year'   rocz-n-y [rɔtʃni] 'annual'
      śnieg-u [ɕɲɛgu] 'snow, gen. sg.'   śnież-n-y [ɕɲɛʒni] 'snowy'
      strach [strax] 'fear'   strasz-n-y [straʃni] 'awful'

There is nothing new in terms of alternating segments—what is noteworthy is the limited number of segments involved in the series and also the fact that PR4′ is a combination of the general palatalization represented by the lateral and two different palatalizations of selected obstruents.

A different variety of the same pattern can be found in certain morphological contexts where all dental obstruents alternate as in PR2′, the velars as in P3′— labials and sonorants need not concern us here since they all follow the pattern set in PR1′. Thus we have a modification of the patterns formulated above which we shall call PR5′ for the moment:

PR5′ t   d   s   z   k   g   x
     | | | | | | |
     tɕ   dʑ   ɕ   ʑ   tʃ   ʒ   ʃ

This can be illustrated by the following cases involving the suffix *-in-a/-yn-a*:

(17) kot [kɔt] 'cat'   koc-in-a [kɔtɕina] 'expr.'
      rod-u [rɔdu] 'tribe'   rodz-in-a [rɔdʑina] 'family'
      pies [pʲɛs] 'dog'   ps-in-a [pɕina] 'expr.'
      brzoz-a [bʒɔza] 'birch'   brzez-in-a [bʒɛʑina] 'birch copse'
      ręk-a [rɛŋka] 'hand'   rącz-yn-a [rɔntʃina] 'expr.'
      drog-a [drɔga] 'road'   droż-yn-a [drɔʒina] 'expr.'
      okruch [ɔkrux] 'crumble'   okrusz-yn-a [ɔkruʃina] 'expr.'

Restrictions on the susceptibility of segments to alternate can be seen most clearly when it is only the velars that display any effects in a given context while all remaining consonants are unaffected. The velars alternate in the same way as in PR3′, PR4′, and PR5′

```
PR6′  k      g      zg      x
      |      |      |       |
      tʃ     ʒ      ʒdʒ     ʃ
```

A good example of this situation is the suffix -(e)k.

(18) krok [krɔk] 'step'   krocz-ek [krɔtʃɛk] 'dim.'
      wstęg-a [fstɛŋga] 'ribbon'   wstąż-ek [fstɔ\u02b73ɛk] 'dim. gcn. pl.'
      rózg-a [ruzga] 'rod'   różdż-ek [ruʒdʒɛk] 'wand, gen. pl.'
      uch-o [uxɔ] 'ear'   usz-k-o [uʃkɔ] 'dim.'

Since the velar obstruents alternate in the same way in PR3′, PR4′, PR5′, and PR6′ we can tease them out as a separate class and keep as the alternation series PR6′ while PR3′, PR4′ and PR5′ will be simplified by the elimination of the velars and their alternants. Furthermore, once the alternations involving velars have been removed from PR5′, we can transfer the four coronal obstruents to PR1′ and do away with it altogether. The same group of coronals can thus be removed from PR2′. The revised version of the alternating series can be summarized as follows:

```
PR1  p    b    f    v    m    r    w    n    t    d    s    z
     |    |    |    |    |    |    |    |    |    |    |    |
     pʲ   bʲ   fʲ   vʲ   mʲ   ʒ    1    ɲ    tɕ   dʑ   ɕ    ʑ
```

```
PR2  k      g      x
     |      |      |
     ts     dz     ʃ/ɕ <nom. pl. masc. pers.>
```

```
PR3  t      d      s      z
     |      |      |      |
     ts     dz     ʃ      ʒ
```

```
PR4  w      s      z
     |      |      |
     1      ɕ      ʑ
```

```
PR5  k      g      zg      x
     |      |      |       |
     tʃ     ʒ      ʒdʒ     ʃ
```

There are a few additional alternations that need to be handled here. One involves the alternations between alveolar and alveolo-palatal fricatives:

PR6 ʃ   ʒ
     | |
     ɕ   ʑ

as found, among other contexts, in the nominative plural masculine virile adjectives, for example, *piesz-y* [pʲɛʃi] 'pedestrian' ~ *pies-i* [pʲɛɕi], *duż-y* [duʒi] 'big' ~ *duz-i* [duʑi].

Yet another restricted set of replacements involves the dental affricates [ts] and [dz], whose place can be taken by the alveolar affricate [tʃ] and the alveolar fricative [ʒ], respectively, and also the dental voiceless plosive, which is replaced by the affricate, as discussed above. There is also the alveolar [ʃ]~alveolo-palatal [ɕ] alternation just illustrated for inflectional morphology (PR6) but found in a few derivational contexts. Because of the restricted nature of these alternations we place them jointly in one formula.

PR7 ts   dz   t   ʃ
     | | | |
     tʃ   ʒ   tʃ   ɕ

The alternations can be illustrated by *tajemn-ic-a* [tajɛmɲitsa] 'mystery' ~ *tajemn-icz-y* [tajɛmɲitʃi] 'mysterious', *mosiądz-u* [mɔɕɔndzu] 'brass, gen. sg.' ~ *mosięż-n-y* [mɔɕɛʷʒni] 'adj.', *kapelusz* [kapɛluʃ] 'hat' ~ *kapelus-ik* [kapɛluɕik] 'dim.' and the examples in the discussion of the irregular [t ~ tʃ] alternation above: *pląt-a-ć* [plɔntatɕ] 'confuse' ~ *plącz-ę* [plɔntʃɛ] 'I confuse'.

In our survey here we assumed that the plain consonants, appearing in the upper row, were replaced by their more complex reflexes in the lower row. Thus our view of morphophonological alternations entails the directionality of replacement from the plain to the palatal(ized) consonants. This approach is justified by the fact that the plain consonants are more freely distributed and less conditioned by contextual factors. Their palatal(ized) congeners are normally restricted to specific phonological and morphological positions, hence they may be said to come from the basic ones by our replacement operations. The derivational view of replacements seems intuitively justified when, for example, different forms of the same morphological paradigm are involved, as is frequently the case in Polish, or when the direction of morphological motivation is unambiguous: diminutives of nouns are formed by the addition of a suffix, for instance, *-ek* to a simple morphological base. In many cases, however, a given palatal(ized) reflex appears throughout a morphological paradigm and the consonant in its simpler shape can only be found in derivationally related forms, some of which may be quite distant. The question that arises with words preserving a given shape throughout a paradigm is what evidence there is for any derivation of the segments and what possible purpose such a direct derivational relationship could serve. The answer to the first part must be 'very little' and to the second part 'none at all'. Let us look at a couple of detailed examples.

The noun-stem *śmierć* [ɕmʲɛrtɕ] 'death', with an initial and a final alveolo-palatal consonant, displays the same shape in all cases of the paradigm. The initial consonant never alternates with a non-palatalized one, so the only reason to consider deriving it from a plain fricative is the presence of a following palatalized labial, in other words, some mechanism of palatal assimilation. The final alveolo-palatal in the noun alternates with the plosive [t] in the adjective *śmiert-el-n-y* [ɕmʲɛrtɛlnɨ] 'mortal', hence one could suggest that the voiceless dental plosive belongs to the basic ('underlying') shape of the noun and is replaced by [tɕ] in accordance with PR1. As argued elsewhere in this book (see *Morphological Interlude I* and *II* in Ch. 3), the division into soft and hard stems is crucial to the selection of desinences in a number of cases, so turning a palatalized (soft) consonant into a non-palatalized one would obscure a distinction important morphologically. The problem remains, however, since we would like to see expressed the morphophonological relatedness of the consonants in the two words. A model deriving one consonant from the other serves this function rather well, but is unserviceable otherwise, since it blurs or obliterates important morphological distinctions. An alternative that suggests itself takes our replacement regularities and uses them in a purely interpretative function: thus PR1 would not only replace [t] by [tɕ] in specified contexts, as in *kot* [kɔt] 'cat' ~ *koci-e* [kɔtɕɛ] 'loc. sg.', but it could also relate the [tɕ] of *śmierć* [ɕmʲɛrtɕ] 'death' with [t] found in *śmiert-el-n-y* [ɕmʲɛrtɛlnɨ] 'mortal'. In our alternation schema the downward movement from the plain to the palatalized consonant would amount to replacement, while the upward movement would denote relatedness.

The replace/relate approach to morphophonological alternations means that non-alternating segments will appear in one shape and will not be subjected to changes captured by series such as our PR1–PR5. Involvement in alternations is invariably the result of segment marking and it does not matter here whether the marking will be contained in a segment undergoing the alternation or in the segment (morpheme) inducing it. The marking is part of the lexical shape of morphemes (or perhaps words) and its very existence does not prejudge the directionality of the alternation, in other words, whether we are dealing with replacement or relatedness. This will depend on the morphological relationships between words: if the base word contains a (lower row) palatal(ized) segment and the more complex derivative contains a plain consonant, then we can talk about expressing relatedness; otherwise it is likely to be replacement. This leads ineluctably to indeterminacy of representations, a result which must be welcomed as desirable since morphological derivational relatedness of words is a matter of degree and, often enough, of individual decisions. In other words, speakers often differ in their evaluations of word relatedness. Consider the following relatively simple set of examples:

(19)   piek-ę [pʲɛkɛ] 'I bake'
       piecz [pʲɛtʃ] 'bake, imper.'
       piec [pʲɛts] 'stove, furnace'
       piek-arz [pʲɛkaʃ] 'baker'
       piecz-eń [pʲɛtʃɛɲ] 'roast, joint, n.'
       piecz-eni-arz [pʲɛtʃɛɲaʃ] 'sponger'
       piecz-yw-o [pʲɛtʃɨvɔ] 'bread products'

There can be no doubt that the verbal forms of 'bake' are morphophonologically related, with the [k] of the base being replaced by PR5 for [tʃ] and PR2 for
[ts]. (The bare base appears also in the agentive derivative *piek-arz* [pʲɛkaʃ]
'baker' of which nothing more needs to be said.) The noun *piec* [pʲɛts] 'stove'
presents something of a complication: there can be little doubt as to its semantic
relatedness to the verbal base but assuming that it contains a velar which is
replaced by PR2 is less than certain. The noun contains the dental affricate
throughout its paradigm and consequently some of the desinences are determined
by this particular morphophonological shape—specifically the ending of the
locative singular is -*u* (*piec-u* [pʲɛtsu]) while with non-palatal(ized) bases it is -*e*
(*stół* [stuw] ~ *stol-e* [stɔlɛ] 'table'). If that is the case, we have to assume that the
noun contains a final [ts] which is related to [k] by PR2. The words *piecz-eń*
[pʲɛtʃɛɲ] 'roast' and *piecz-yw-o* [pʲɛtʃɨvɔ] 'bread products' present a different type
of question: although we could easily suggest a morphophonemic [k] which is
replaced by [tʃ] due to PR5, the real question is whether any evidence we have
compels us to do so and further whether we gain anything by doing so. While the
semantic relation between baking and a roast or bread products is not paticularly
questionable, this can be captured in our model by applying PR5 in its relatedness
role. For speakers who fail to perceive this relatedness, the morphophonological
[tʃ] of these words will remain stable in the same way it is stable in numerous
other words. The word *piecz-eni-arz* [pʲɛtʃɛɲaʃ] with its highly lexicalized semantics ('sponger, cadger, loafer') brings the problem into focus: in today's usage its
link to *piecz-eń* [pʲɛtʃɛɲ] 'roast' is tenuous and to the noun *piec* [pʲɛts] 'stove',
practically non-existent. Apart from the mechanical possibility of obtaining the
desired effect, a dubious achievement in itself, there is nothing in the language
that requires or even prompts this course of action. If an individual speaker
happens to make the connection, then his/her private lexicon might contain the
information about PR5 being attached to the segment in either its derivational or
relational function. The well-known fact about speakers making or failing to
make various connections finds its natural expression in this method of capturing
morphophonological relations.

    The recognition of the dual function of the morphophonological alternating
series may have an unforeseen side effect. Traditional descriptions recognize not
only palatalization (either as processes or alternations) but also its converse,
namely depalatalization. We will outline some problems and a possible interpretation here but will revise the conclusions later on in this chapter. Consider a few

examples below, involving nouns and adjectives derived from them by the attachment of the suffix *-n-y* [nɨ]. The palatal(ized) consonant of the noun emerges as plain or non-palatal(ized) when the adjectival suffix is appended.

(20)   chęć [xɛɲtɕ] 'willingness'   chęt-n-y [xɛntnɨ] 'willing'
       żołędzi-a [ʒɔwɛɲdʑa] 'acorn, gen. sg.'   żołęd-n-y [ʒɔwɛndnɨ] 'adj.'
       władz-a [vwadza] 'authority'   wład-n-y [vwadnɨ] 'having authority'
       ambicj-a [ambʲitsʲja] 'ambition'   ambit-n-y [ambʲitnɨ] 'ambitious'
       cmentarz-a [tsmɛntaʒa] 'cemetery,   cmentar-n-y [tsmɛntarnɨ] 'adj.'
       gen. sg.'

Alternations such as these have been viewed as instances of depalatalization for significant morphological reasons. The nouns motivate the adjectives, in other words, the adjectives are derived from the nouns by means of the suffix, hence the shape of the motivating noun cannot be predicted—in our case the final consonant of the stem must be morphophonologically palatal(ized). This is further confirmed by the fact that the palatal(ized) consonant in the left-hand column words appears unmodified throughout the inflectional paradigm, and thus influences the selection of desinences, as we have seen. What alternations such as these show, then, is the existence of depalatalization, in other words, rather than change [t] into [tɕ], etc. we have to change [tɕ] into [t]. A descriptive account of such alternations is a complex matter because of cases where identical consonants fail to depalatalize in the same environment:

(21)   nędz-a [nɛndza] 'misery'   nędz-n-y [nɛndznɨ] 'miserable'
       noc [nɔts] 'night'   noc-n-y [nɔtsnɨ] 'nightly'
       męż-a [mɛʷʒa] 'man, gen. sg.'   męż-n-y [mɛʷʒnɨ] 'manly, valiant'

Here, in the same context, no depalatalization is found which would yield consonant alternations. This difficulty disappears on the interpretation that morphophonological alternations are always the result of lexical marking. Both nouns and adjectives in (21) contain the same consonants [dz, ts, ʒ] and no instruction to relate them to anything else. This does not exhaust the matter since we need to determine what the difference between the nouns and adjectives in (20) consists in.

Since we argue that an alternation can manifest either derivational or relational morphophonology, what is referred to as 'depalatalizations' can be seen as nothing more than the palatalization regularity in its relational function. To be concrete: the alternation [tɕ ~ t] found in *chęć* [xɛɲtɕ] 'willingness' ~ *chęt-n-y* [xɛntnɨ] 'willing' is an instance of PR1 where the lower row segment [tɕ] is related to the upper one [t]. All we need to do is direct the final consonant of the noun, [tɕ], to PR1, thereby capturing its relatedness to the plain plosive as it appears in other words, not just in the derived adjectives but in other related words such as *chęt-ni-e* [xɛntɲɛ] 'willingly', *chęt-k-a* [xɛntka] 'itch, urge, n'. On this view depalatalization is not an independent regularity—rather it is palatalization with its directionality reversed. This interpretation forces us to supply the nouns in (20) with a palatal(ized) consonant and the diacritic <PR1>, while the derived adjectives have plain consonants.

Depalatalization as a reversal of palatalization follows from the double function of our Palatalization Replacement statements (PRs), while its irregularity is a consequence of lexical marking. The idiosyncratic nature of marking is indirectly supported by the partial irregularity of the morphological process itself. In some cases the adjectival suffix is arbitrarily and unpredictably preceded by an intermorph which (morpho)phonologically is not necessary there: the noun *struktur-a* [struktura] 'structure' yields the adjective *struktur-al-n-y* [strukturalnɨ] even though *struktur-n-y*, without the intermorph *-al-*, would be perfectly well formed both morphologically and (morpho)phonologically. Second, the semantics of the adjectives is often non-compositional, that is to say that it is not the case that the *-n-y* [nɨ] adjective can be glossed 'id. adj.' since very often the semantic relatedness is quite distant and the actual reading results from lexicalization; while *glos* [gwɔs] 'voice' undoubtedly serves as the morphological base for *głoś-n-y* [gwɔɕnɨ], the latter means 'loud' rather than 'of the voice'.

This completes our initial survey of palatalization alternations in Polish and of possible ways of describing them in a comprehensive account. We will now look at them in greater detail in an attempt to clarify what specific phonological and morphological factors determine the individual alternation series.

4.4 PALATALIZATIONAL PROPERTIES OF MORPHOLOGICAL UNITS

4.4.1 *Inflectional morphology*

As our discussion above reveals, the alternations traditionally viewed as resulting from palatalization phenomena are morphophonological in nature. This means that a segment of the base is replaced by its congener in specified morphological and lexical contexts or that a segment in one word is related to a segment in another word. The morphological contexts comprise both morphological categories such as the imperative and specific inflectional and derivational suffixes such as *-e* of the dative singular or *-n-y* deriving adjectives from nouns. We would now like to review the alternations by looking at selected inflectional endings; we will then look more closely at the alternations PR1–5 by reviewing several derivational suffixes. The suffixal perspective will enable us to see whether and to what extent individual suffixes can depart from the general pattern.

Let us first consider a number of endings realized as *-e* [ɛ]. This vowel can mark:

dat. sg. masc.:
drużb-a [druʒba] 'best man'~ drużbi-e [druʒbʲɛ]
inwalid-a [invalida] 'invalid' ~ inwalidzi-e [invalidʑɛ]

dat. sg. fem.:
sow-a [sɔva] 'owl' ~ sowi-e [sɔvʲɛ]
much-a [muxa] 'fly' ~ musz-e [muʃɛ]
nog-a [nɔga] 'leg' ~ nodz-e [nɔdzɛ]

loc. sg. masc.:
ciamajd-a [tɕamajda] 'bungler' ~ ciamajdzi-e [tɕamajdʑɛ]
świat [ɕfʲat] 'world' ~ świeci-e [ɕfʲɛtɕɛ]
kos [kɔs] 'thrush' ~ kosi-e [kɔɕɛ]

loc. sg. fem.:
skał-a [skawa] 'rock' ~ skal-e [skalɛ]
uwag-a [uvaga] 'remark' ~ uwadz-e [uvadzɛ]
zim-a [ʑima] 'winter' ~ zimi-e [ʑinʲɛ]

loc. sg. neut.:
ciast-o [tɕastɔ] 'cake' ~ cieśc-ie [tɕɛɕtɕɛ]
siodł-o [ɕɔdwɔ] 'saddle' ~ siodl-e [ɕɔdlɛ]

voc. sg. masc.:
chłop [xwɔp] 'bloke' ~ chłopi-e [xwɔpʲɛ]
kot [kɔt] 'cat' ~ koci-e [kɔtɕɛ]

It must be stressed that these are independent inflectional categories and that their phonetic identity is a matter of chance. In most cases they compete with other endings that can be found for a given category so, for instance, the dative singular of masculine nouns apart from -e also uses -owi (człowiek [tʃwɔvʲɛk] 'man' ~ człowiek-owi [tʃwɔvʲɛkɔvʲi]), -u (Bóg [buk] 'God' ~ Bog-u [bɔgu]) and -i (sędzi-a [sɛndʑa] 'judge' ~ sędz-i [sɛndʑi]). The different categories above, represented by the vowel -e [ɛ], all evince the same morphophonological behaviour, in other words, the morphemes -e require the replacements we formulated as PR1 and PR2 earlier. In our discussion we adopt the convention that such requirements are part of the morpheme's individual properties and are placed in angled brackets, for example -e <PR1, PR2>. The convention is to be interpreted as follows: consonants of the upper row in PR1 and PR2 are replaced by their lower row congeners when the desinence follows. The information about the specific replacements which a given morpheme induces constitutes part of its morphophonological load. It follows from the above that this load is unpredictable and as such belongs to the lexical specification of a morpheme.[3]

The phonological consequences of the morphophonological replacement are straightforward and in agreement with what we determined about the nature of the vowel–consonant interaction in Chapter 3. When the replaced consonant is I-headed, the vowel is also I-headed (it is {A •I̲}), when the consonant contains {I} as an operator, the vowel must also place that element in the operator

[3] This is only one of the possible approaches to the representation of inflectional morphology. The proposal could easily be translated into other models, such as word-and-paradigm where the focus of interest is the word rather than the morpheme (Matthews 1972, 1991).

position either as the sole occupant of that position or accompanying {A}, that is, as an empty-headed expression. We thus expect to find that the vowel -e [ɛ] also corresponds to {A•I•_}; in surface terms this would mean that the stem final consonant is unaffected in any way by th addition of the vowel ending. At the risk of overkill we wish to stress that a number of desinences implemented as such neutral -e [ɛ] do exist. Consider the examples:

nom. pl. fem.:
szans-a [ʃansa] 'chance' ∼ szans-e [ʃansɛ]

acc. pl. fem.:
jędz-a [jɛndza] 'hag' ∼ jędz-e [jɛndzɛ]

voc. pl. fem.:
noc [nɔts] 'night' ∼ noc-e [nɔtsɛ]

nom. pl. masc.:
niuans [ɲuans] 'minutiae' ∼ niuans-e [ɲuansɛ]

acc. pl. masc.:
koc [kɔts] 'blanket' ∼ koc-e [kɔtsɛ]

voc. pl. masc.:
konwenans [kɔnvɛnans] 'convention' ∼ konwenans-e [kɔnvɛnansɛ]

nom. sg. neut.:
serc-e 'heart' [sɛrtsɛ]

acc. sg. neut.:
serc-e 'heart' [sɛrtsɛ]

voc. sg. neut.
serc-e 'heart' [sɛrtsɛ]

In our terms this means simply that no information about segment replacement is attached to the lexical representations of the endings which themselves are not I-headed.

The various -e morphemes above combine the replacement patterns PR1 and PR2 in that whenever the appropriate context contains a velar, PR2 works and otherwise it is PR1 that is called to act. An almost identical pattern can be found with the vowel -i/-y representing the category of the nominative plural of masculine personal nouns and adjectives; the difference is that the velar spirant alternates with [ɕ] rather than [ʃ] as above. Consider some examples:

(22) Sas [sas] 'Saxon'   Sas-i [saɕi]
      młod-y [mwɔdɨ] 'young'   młodz-i [mwɔdʑi]
      zdrow-y [zdrɔvɨ] 'healthy'   zdrow-i [zdrɔvʲi]
      grub-y [grubɨ] 'thick'   grub-i [grubʲi]
      mał-y [mawɨ] 'small'   mal-i [mali]
      Polak [pɔlak] 'Pole'   Polac-y [pɔlatsɨ]
      nag-i [naɟi] 'naked'   nadz-y [nadzɨ]

but:

Włoch [vwɔx] 'Italian'	Włos-i [vwɔɕi]
głuch-y [gwuxɨ] 'deaf'	głus-i [gwuɕi]
mnich [mɲix] 'monk'	mnis-i [mɲiɕi]

Since the two alternations required by the desinence in focus differ only in their treatment of the velar spirant, it was suggested earlier that this particular bit of information should be included in the replacement statement itself. Alternatively, we might extract the velar spirant both from PR2 and PR5 and subject it to two separate replacement procedures, of which one would turn it into [ʃ] and the other into [ɕ]—at the moment we see no compelling argument in favour of either solution so we will stick to the one which encodes the grammatical information directly into the replacement formula. Hence the ending -i/-y of the nominative plural masculine personal, just like the various -e endings, is associated with the morphophonological load <PR1, PR2>.

A verbal corollary to the nominal distinction just discussed appears in the plural ending of the past tense: the vowel in question is -i/-y (which in the first and second person is followed by the clitic -my, -ście respectively; our examples come from the third-person plural, which has no clitic). When the verb is in agreement with a masculine personal subject, its past-tense ending [w] is replaced by PR1 into [l], as in the following examples:

(23)   czyt-a-ł-y [tʃɨtawɨ] 'they (fem.) read' ~ czyt-a-l-i [tʃɨtali] 'they (masc.) read'
pros-i-ł-y [prɔɕiwɨ] 'they (fem.) asked' ~ pros-i-l-i [prɔɕili] 'they (masc.) asked'

We see, then, that the masculine personal ending is specified as <PR1>, while elsewhere the ending bears no such specification.

A case which clearly shows that PR1 does not have to go in tandem with PR2 involves the vowel -e as part of the present tense stem of verbs; when part of the second-person-singular-esz, third-person singular -e, first-person-plural-emy, and second-person-plural-ecie the vowel affects the anterior consonants according to PR1 and the velar ones according to PR5. Consider the examples where we contrast the first-person singular which displays no palatalization with the second-person singular:

(24)
rw-ę [rvɛ] 'tear'	rwi-e-sz [rvʲɛʃ]
dm-ę [dmɛ] 'blow'	dmi- e-sz [dmʲɛʃ]
jad-ę [jadɛ] 'I go'	jedzi-e-sz [jɛdʑɛʃ]
plot-ę [plɔtɛ] 'plait'	pleci-e-sz [plɛtɕɛʃ]
kradn-ę [kradnɛ] 'steal'	kradni-e-sz [kradɲɛʃ]
bior-ę [bʲɔrɛ] 'take'	bierz-e-sz [bʲɛʒɛʃ]
pas-ę [pasɛ] 'graze'	pasi-e-sz [paɕɛʃ]
gryz-ę [grɨzɛ] 'bite'	gryzi-e-sz [grɨʑɛʃ]
piek-ę [pʲɛkɛ] 'bake'	piecz-e-sz [pʲɛtʃɛʃ]
mog-ę [mɔgɛ] 'can, be able'	moż-e-sz [mɔʒɛʃ]

There appear to be no examples with the velar spirant but otherwise the pattern is quite clear: the endings call for the joint operation of PR1 and PR5. Thus the present-tense stem vowel -e is accompanied by the <PR1, PR5> morphophonological increment.[4]

The above discussion shows that inflectional endings in Polish enforce a constant and uniform set of changes on preceding consonants. The morphophonological aspect of inflectional morphology is almost completely regular, which is not to say that it is very simple or predictable. The crucial point is, however, that a given ending affects the preceding consonant in one way and does so whenever the right context appears. It is not the case, for instance, that the dative singular -e induces <PR1> in some nouns and <PR3> in others or that it affects some nouns and leaves others unaffected. The uniformity and regularity of inflectional morphophonology can be appreciated more fully when we consider superficially very similar alternations within derivationally related forms. It is to derivational morphology that we now turn our attention.

4.4.2 Derivational morphology: Suffixes

Words related by derivational morphological mechanisms are bound less closely together than different inflectional forms of the same lexeme. This statement verges on the banal but its relevance to phonological and morphophonological description of a language is anything but obvious. In the past, phonological descriptions assumed that there is a uniform set of rules (constraints or what have you) which manifests itself through morphophonological alternations; this is of course the case with classical generative phonology and its subsequent transformations such as Optimality Theory. No provision was made for separate rules (constraints) operating within inflectional paradigms and excluded from derivational relations or, conversely, no regularities were found to be operational within derivation but barred within inflection where an identical phonological configuration prevailed. Polish provides evidence that the distinction between inflection and derivation is not only a morphological headache, with criteria for separating the two types at times blurred, but also a morphophonological one.

Alternations of velars, as captured by PR2 and PR5, reveal characteristic restrictions. Thus PR2 is found exclusively within nominal paradigms; it is not encountered within verbal conjugations. PR5, on the other hand, is only marginally found within nominal paradigms while it is widespread within verbal forms.[5]

---

[4] We might as well point out at this stage that the extremely complex verbal structure of Polish requires an in-depth description which, as part of pure morphology, goes well beyond the scope of this book. Apart from verb classes (conjugational types) which display morphophonological effects of the sort just illustrated, there are others where the effects are seen throughout the present-tense paradigm and alternations with non-palatalized congeners are to be sought in the preterite. Another inflectional context where PR1 and PR5 jointly affect consonants is in the imperative; this is taken up in the final section of this chapter.

[5] The marginal forms within the nominal paradigm include the vocative singular of a few nouns: Bóż-e [bɔʒɛ] 'God', człowiecz-e [tʃwɔvʲɛtʃɛ] 'man' (the form is literary and exists side by side with the

In view of the fact that inflectional endings are enforced by the syntax and thus their presence, unlike that of derivational processes, is mandatory, this restriction can hardly be viewed as an accident. A further indication of the different status of our replacement formulae is the fact that alternations captured by PR2 are never found within derivation while their presence in inflection is both general and fully productive (see Gussmann 1977). Facts of this kind lead us to question the assumption that inflectional and derivational alternations enjoy an equal status within grammar as far as its morphophonology is concerned.

The factor which seems most important from our current perspective is the degree of the regularity of the replacements. In inflectional categories a given suffix invariably evinces a replacement—it is not the case that with some nouns the dative -e does and with others it does not change the final [k] into [ts]. In this sense, inflectional morphophonology is exceptionless. Words related derivationally present a very different situation as shown by the examples below. A number of derivatives and their bases (their motivating words) are listed in (25); as far as can be determined we are dealing with the same suffix and the same type of morphological derivation but the (a) examples show the application of a morphophonological replacement whereas those in (b) reveal the failure to do so. The significance of the evidence is straightforward: it is not true that individual suffixes uniformly evoke the same alternations.

(25) (a) krew-n-y [krɛvnɨ] 'relative'   krew-ni-ak [krɛvɲak] 'id.'
      (b) jedyn-y [jɛdɨnɨ] 'only'   jedyn-ak [jɛdɨnak] 'only child'

      (a) rower [rɔvɛr] 'bicycle'   rowerz-yst-a [rɔvɛʒista] 'bicycle rider'
      (b) terror [tɛrrɔr] 'terror'   terror-yst-a [tɛrrɔrɨsta] 'terrorist'

      (a) skrzydł-o [skʃɨdwɔ] 'wing'   skrzydl-at-y [skʃɨdlatɨ] 'winged'
      (b) kudł-y [kudwɨ] 'mop of hair'   kudł-at-y [kudwatɨ] 'shaggy'

      (a) ram-a [rama] 'frame'   rami-arz [ramʲaʃ] 'frame maker'
      (b) kram [kram] 'stall'   kram-arz [kramaʃ] 'stall keeper'

      (a) mał-y [mawɨ] 'small'   mal-eńk-i [malɛɲci] 'expr.'
      (b) star-y [starɨ] 'old'   star-eńk-i [starɛɲci] 'expr.'

      (a) komin [kɔmʲin] 'chimney'   komini-arz [kɔmʲiɲaʃ] 'chimney-sweep'
      (b) młyn [mwɨn] 'mill'   młyn-arz [mwɨnaʃ] 'miller'

      (a) mlek-o [mlɛkɔ] 'milk'   mlecz-arz [mlɛtʃaʃ] 'milkman'
      (b) aptek-a [aptɛka] 'chemist's'   aptek-arz [aptɛkaʃ] 'chemist'

      (a) kop-a [kɔpa] 'heap'   kopi-at-y [kɔpʲatɨ] 'heaping'
      (b) garb-u [garbu] 'hump, gen. sg.'   garb-at-y [garbatɨ] 'humpbacked'

      (a) masł-o [maswɔ] 'butter'   maśl-ank-a [maɕlanka] 'butter milk'
      (b) poseł [pɔsɛw] 'deputy'   posł-ank-a [pɔswanka] 'fem.'

common and morphophonologically uninteresting *człowiek-u* [tʃwɔvʲɛku]), *Kozacz-e* [kɔzatʃɛ] 'Cossack'. Additionally it is found as *ocz-* [ɔtʃ] throughout the plural of one noun, originally in its dual number, *ok-o* [ɔkɔ] 'eye'.

(a) futr-o [futrɔ] 'fur'   futrz-ak [fut-ʃak] 'fur rug'
(b) ponur-y [pɔnurɨ] 'morose'   ponur-ak [pɔnurak] 'sourpuss'

(a) groz-a [grɔza] 'dread, n.'   groź-n-y [grɔʐnɨ] 'threatening'
(b) żelaz-o [ʒɛlazɔ] 'iron'   żelaz-n-y [ʒɛlaznɨ] 'adj.'

(a) kwas [kfas] 'acid'   kwaś-n-y [kfaɕnɨ] 'sour'
(b) mięs-o [mʲɛ̃ʷsɔ] 'meat'   mięs-n-y [mʲɛ̃ʷsnɨ] 'meaty'

(a) szmat-a [ʃmata] 'rag'   szmaci-ak [ʃmatɕak] 'canvas shoe'
(b) prost-y [prɔstɨ] 'simple'   prost-ak [prɔstak] 'simpleton'

(a) skorup-a [skɔrupa] 'shell'   skorupi-ak [skɔrupʲak] 'crustacean'
(b) tęp-y [tɛmpɨ] 'dull'   tęp-ak [tɛmpak] 'dimwit'

(a) szarad-a [ʃarada] 'charade'   szaradz-ist-a [ʃaradʑista] 'charade
                                            enthusiast'

(b) metod-a [mɛtɔda] 'method'   metod-yst-a [mɛtɔdɨsta] 'methodist'

(a) grosz [grɔʃ] 'small coin'   gros-ik [grɔɕik] 'dim.'
(b) kosz [kɔʃ] 'basket'   kosz-yk [kɔʃɨk] 'dim.'

(a) ulic-a [ulitsa] 'street'   ulicz-k-a [ulitʃka] 'dim.'
(b) noc [nɔts] 'night'   noc-k-a [nɔtska] 'dim.'

(a) okolic-a [ɔkɔlitsa] 'vicinity'   okolicz-n-y [ɔkɔlitʃnɨ] 'neighbouring'
(b) płuc-o [pwutsɔ] 'lung'   płuc-n-y [pwutsnɨ] 'adj.'

(a) walc [valts] 'walse'   walcz-yk [valtʃɨk] 'dim.'
(b) koc [kɔts] 'blanket'   koc-yk [kɔtsɨk] 'dim.'

This lengthy list, which could easily be extended (see also Górska 1985), aims to show that the replacement operations are not controlled by individual suffixes. This remains true even if, statistically speaking, one can point to tendencies or clear dominance of one pattern over the other with a given affix. We see again here that alternations involving palatalized and functionally palatalized consonants cannot be regarded as controlled by the phonology because one and the same suffix sometimes would have to induce it in some cases and in other cases would fail to do so. Hence the alternations are undoubtedly morphophonological not so much in terms of the changes but rather in terms of the contexts they appear in. In other words, contrary to what is often assumed, individual suffixes propose but do not dispose: the decision whether a particular replacement will take place or not is associated not with a given suffix as a morphological unit but rather with a given suffix as part of a lexical entry. There is no conceivable reason why the final adjectival nasal in *krewn-* should be replaced by its palatal congener before the nominalizing suffix *-ak* in *krewni-ak* [krɛvɲak] 'relative' while no such replacement should take place in *jedyn-* yielding *jedyn-ak* [jɛdɨnak] 'only child' rather than the phonologically equally well-formed **jedyni-ak* [jɛdɨɲak]. The only place where instruction of this sort can be idiosyncratically entered is the lexicon. Thus the information concerning morphophonological replacements must be encoded in the lexical representation of words.

This conclusion may appear disheartening at first glance since it amounts to conceding defeat in that morphophonological effects must be viewed as unpredictable. There are a few mitigating circumstances which prompt a different assessment of the situation, the most predominant of which is the partial or predominant unpredictability of the morphological process itself. It is seldom the case that a derivational regularity, unlike inflectional, is fully and completely regular. The derivational base can be constrained in various ways, unpredictable truncations or its converse, so-called intermorphs may be effected; derivatives may be completely transparent formally and semantically but either isolated (English *laugh* ~ *laugh-ter*) or very rare (*constrain-t, complain-t, thef-t*). Most characteristically, however, the semantics of derivatives is often unpredictable to a greater or lesser extent. An inspection of the forms in (25) reveals all too clearly that the derivatives have to be entered in the lexicon: the suffix *-ank-a* attached to the stem *maśl-* 'butter' yields *maśl-ank-a* with its totally unpredictable reading 'buttermilk', while attached to the stem *poseł* 'deputy' it yields *posl-ank-a* with its equally unpredictable semantics 'female deputy'. To make the point even clearer, consider several additional derivatives with the suffix *-ank-a* from the point of view of their semantics.

(26) przed-szkol-e [pʃɛt-ʃkɔlɛ]   przed-szkol-ank-a [pʃɛt-ʃkɔlanka]
      'kindergarten'   'kindergarten teacher'
      owies [ɔvʲɛs] 'oats'   owsi-ank-a [ɔfɕanka] 'porridge'
      wod-a [vɔda] 'water'   wodzi-ank-a [vɔdʑanka] 'watery soup'
      sioł-o [ɕɔwɔ] 'village'   siel-ank-a [ɕɛlanka] 'idyll'
      glin-a [glina] 'clay'   glini-ank-a [gliɲanka] 'mud hut'
      słom-a [swɔma] 'straw'   słom-iank-a [swɔmʲanka] 'straw doormat'
      tk-a-ć [tkatɕ] 'weave'   tk-ank-a [tkanka] 'tissue'
      grz-a-ć [gʒatɕ] 'heat up'   grz-ank-a [gʒanka] '(piece of) toast'
      za-chc-ie-ć [zaxtɕɛtɕ] 'develop   za-chci-ank-a [zaxtɕanka] 'whim'
      a whim'
      skak-a-ć [skakatɕ] 'jump, vb.'   skak-ank-a [skakanka] 'skipping rope'
      skrob-a-ć [skrɔbatɕ] 'scratch, vb.' skrob-ank-a [skrɔbanka] 'abortion'

While formally quite transparent in most cases, these *-ank-a* derivatives offer a variety of semantic readings which in no way can be brought to anything like a common denominator, or even several common denominators. The forms have to be entered in the lexicon and their semantics specified for each entry individually. Against this semantic richness the morphophonological load (idiosyncrasy) in the form of PR1, PR5, or nothing, attached to a given *-ank-a*, does not significantly increase the burden of the lexical entry.

There are about three dozen derivational suffixes in Polish which influence the preceding consonant in accordance with our replacement patterns. Little point would be served in supplying extensive lists of the suffixes and examples of derivatives they appear in. Keeping in mind the fact that individual lexical items specify the type of replacement that takes place in a given derivative it should be noted that some suffixes are remarkably systematic in evincing a specific type of change. The replacements found in derivational morphology comprise PR1, PR5, and to some extent, also PR3 and PR7. We will now exemplify these replacements by a number of suffixes, aiming to be illustrative rather than comprehensive. In our presentation we follow earlier morphological and morphophonological descriptions of Grzegorczykowa and Puzynina (1979) and Kowalik (1997, 1998) and reverse dictionaries (Grzegorczykowa and Puzynina 1973, Tokarski 1993, Bańko et al. 2003). Let us stress again that the lists are not and are not meant to be exhaustive; they are subjugated to the purpose of illustrating the scope of the phenomena. Following this presentation we will comment in detail on a few suffixes (marked by an asterisk in (27)) that seem particularly interesting or offer additional evidence about the nature of the replacements. A special subsection follows where replacements in cases of conversion are attested and discussed.

(27) -ec <PR1, PR5>

skąp-y [skɔmpi] 'stingy'   skąpi-ec [skɔmpʲɛts] 'miser'
mądr-y [mɔndri] 'wise'   mędrz-ec [mɛnd-ʒɛts] 'sage'
wzór [vzur] 'pattern'   wzorz-ec [vzɔʒɛts] 'model'
kruch-y [kruxi] 'brittle'   krusz-ec [kruʃɛts] 'ore'
głuch-y [gwuxi] 'deaf'   głusz-ec [gwuʃɛts] 'grouse'
ud-o [udɔ] 'thigh'   udzi-ec [udʑɛts] 'haunch'

   -ik <PR1, PR5, PR7>

sklep [sklɛp] 'shop'   sklep-ik [sklɛpʲik] 'dim.'
łotr [wɔtr̥] 'villain'   łotrz-yk [wɔt-ʃik] 'dim.'
hak [xak] 'hook'   hacz-yk [xatʃik] 'dim.'
chłopi-ec [xwɔpʲɛts] 'boy'   chłopcz-yk [xwɔptʃik] 'dim.
arkusz [arkuʃ] 'sheet'   arkus-ik [arkuɕik] 'dim.'

   -ek <PR5, PR7>*

krok [krɔk] 'step'   krocz-ek [krɔtʃɛk] 'dim.'
nog-a [nɔga] 'leg'   nóż-ek [nuʒɛk] 'dim. gen. pl.'
duch [dux] 'spirit'   dusz-ek [duʃɛk] 'sprite'
zając [zajɔnts] 'hare'   zając-ek [zajɔntʃɛk] 'dim.'
pieniądz-e [pʲɛɲɔndzɛ] 'money'   pieniąż-ek [pʲɛɲɔʷʒɛk] 'coin'
ulic-a [ulitsa] 'street'   ulicz-k-a [ulitʃka] 'dim.'
lic-o [litsɔ] 'face'   licz-k-o [litʃkɔ] 'dim.'

   -ist-a/-yst-a <PR1>*

Marks [marks]   marks-ist-a [markɕista] 'Marxist'
hazard-u [xazardu] 'gambling,   hazardz-ist-a [xazardʑista] 'gambler'
gen. sg.'
gitar-a [ɟitara] 'guitar'   gitarz-yst-a [ɟitaʒista] 'guitar player'
flet [flɛt] 'flute'   flec-ist-a [flɛtɕista] 'flautist'

   -ist-y <PR1, PR5, PR7>

mgł-a [mgwa] 'mist'   mgl-ist-y [mglisti] 'misty'
złot-o [zwɔtɔ] 'gold, n.'   złoc-ist-y [zwɔtɕisti] 'golden'

srebr-o [srɛbrɔ] 'silver, n.'   srebrz-yst-y [srɛbʒɨstɨ] 'silvery'
wiek [vʲɛk] 'age, century'   wiecz-yst-y [vʲɛtʃɨstɨ] 'eternal'
ojciec [ɔjtɕɛts] 'father'   ojcz-yst-y [ɔjtʃɨstɨ] 'paternal'

-och <PR1>
tłust-y [twustɨ] 'fat'   tłuści-och [twuɕtɕɔx] 'fatso'
sp-a-ć [spatɕ] 'sleep, vb.'   śpi-och [ɕpʲɔx] 'sleepyhead'

-an-y <PR1, PR5>
słom-a [swɔma] 'straw'   słomi-an-y [swɔmʲanɨ] 'adj.'
wełn-a [vɛwna] 'wool'   wełni-an-y [vɛwɲanɨ] 'woolen'
burak [burak] 'beetroot'   buracz-an-y [buratʃanɨ] 'adj.'
blach-a [blaxa] 'metal sheet'   blasz-an-y [blaʃanɨ] 'metal, adj.'

-at-y <PR1, PR5>
łat-a [wata] 'patch'   łaci-at-y [watɕatɨ] 'patchy'
uch-o [uxɔ] 'ear'   usz-at-y [uʃatɨ] 'long-eared'

-ast-y <PR1, PR5, PR7>
kwiat [kfʲat] 'flower'   kwiaci-ast-y [kfʲatɕastɨ] 'floral'
bułk-a [buwka] 'roll, n.'   bułcz-ast-y [buwtʃastɨ] 'roll-like'
pal-ec [palɛts] 'finger'   pal-cz-ast-y [paltʃastɨ] 'fingerlike'

-n-y <PR4, PR5, PR7>*
głos [gwɔs] 'voice'   głoś-n-y [gwɔɕnɨ] 'loud'
wiatr [vʲatr] 'wind'   wietrz-n-y [vʲɛt-ʃnɨ] 'windy'
piekł-o [pʲɛkwɔ] 'hell'   piekiel-n-y [pʲɛcɛlnɨ] 'hellish'
nog-a [nɔga] 'leg'   noż-n-y [nɔʒnɨ] 'adj.'
granic-a [graɲitsa] 'boundary'   granicz-n-y [graɲitʃnɨ] 'adj.'

-nik <PR1, PR5, PR7>
głos [gwɔs] 'voice'   głoś-nik [gwɔɕɲik] 'loudspeaker'
sił-a [ɕiwa] 'strength'   sil-nik [ɕilɲik] 'engine'
rok [rɔk] 'year'   rocz-nik [rɔtʃɲik] 'yearbook'
miesiąc [mʲɛɕɔnts] 'month'   miesięcz-nik [mʲɛɕɛntʃɲik]
                                         'a monthly'

-an <PR1, PR5>
młod-y [mwɔdɨ] 'young'   młodzi-an [mwɔdʑan] 'youth'
siark-a [ɕarka] 'suphur'   siarcz-an [ɕartʃan] 'sulphate'

-arz <PR1, PR5, PR7>
lod-y [lɔdɨ] 'ice cream'   lodzi-arz [lɔdʑaʃ] 'ice-cream
                                         vendor'
mlek-o [mlɛkɔ] 'milk'   mlecz-arz [mlɛtʃaʃ] 'milkman'
owc-a [ɔftsa] 'sheep'   owcz-arz [ɔftʃaʃ] 'shepherd'

-ski <P1 >*
Londyn [lɔndɨn] 'London'   londyń-sk-i [lɔndɨɲsci] 'adj.'
generał [gɛnɛraw] 'general'   general-sk-i [gɛnɛralsci] 'adj.'

4.4.2.1 Four suffixes, their idiosyncrasies, and theoretical implications

We will look more closely at four of the suffixes illustrated above since their behaviour leads to interesting questions of a general nature. These are the diminutive nominal suffix -*ek*, two adjectival ones, -*n-y* and -*sk-i*, and the nominalizing -*ist-a/-yst-a*.

4.4.2.1.1 The suffix -*ek*

The suffix -*ek* is normally regarded as one of the most productive derivational affixes in the language; it has a variety of functions of which that of diminutivization seems to be most common (Grzegorczykowa and Puzynina 1979). Morphophonologically, the attachment of the suffix is accompanied by the change of velars into palatals and likewise of some dental affricates into palatals, by the replacements PR5 and PR7. Examples are provided above. The same suffix, when attached to plain anterior consonants, produces no changes, so that the final consonant of the base remains unchanged:

(28) słup-a [swupa] 'pole, gen. sg.'   słup-ek [swupɛk] 'dim.'
      grzyb-a [gʒɨba] 'mushroom, gen. sg.'   grzyb-ek [gʒɨbɛk] 'dim.'
      syf-u [sɨfu] 'syphilis, gen. sg.'   syf-ek [sɨfɛk] 'zit, pimple'
      pies [pʲɛs] 'dog'   pies-ek [pʲɛsɛk] 'dim.'
      obraz-u [ɔbrazu] 'picture, gen. sg.'   obraz-ek [ɔbrazɛk] 'dim.'
      świat [ɕfʲat] 'world'   świat-ek [ɕfʲatɛk] 'dim.'
      spod-u [spɔdu] 'bottom, gen. sg.'   spod-ek [spɔdɛk] 'saucer'

Concentrating for the moment on the contrast between velars and plain front consonants, we note the striking asymmetry in their susceptibility to replacements: velars obligatorily display effects of PR5 while front consonants resist any changes at all. Thus it is not the case, as seen by generative descriptions, that the suffix -*ek* contains an underlying front vowel which evinces palatalization of the preceding consonant. If that were the case, the total absence of palatalization in the case of non-velars would be incomprehensible as a phonological phenomenon or would require additional clarifications.[6] It must therefore be stated emphatically that the presence or absence of palatalization effects has nothing to do with the phonological make-up of the suffix: it is the specific suffix that enforces the replacement of the preceding velar consonant in accordance with the pattern we formulated as PR5. In other words, the replacements are required due to an idiosyncratic property of the suffix, here, it being marked as <PR5>.

---

[6] Gussmann (1980*a*: 60–4) puts forward a phonological account where the suffix contains an underlying back vowel which is fronted after a velar and subsequently, as a front vowel, causes palatalization of that velar. Rubach (1984: 186) seems to assume the existence of two separate suffixes, one with a front vowel appearing after velars and causing their palatalization and one with a back vowel appearing elsewhere. This is done despite the fact that otherwise, both morphologically and semantically, the two units display identical patterns of behaviour.

The phonologically non-palatalizing nature of the suffix can be seen rather dramatically in a phenomenon which, while quite general, has only marginally been discussed in the literature (Gussmann 1980a: 57–9, 1992b: 52–4), namely, in what might at first glance be called depalatalization. The attachment of the suffix in question to soft-stemmed nouns leads to the undoing of the palatalization effect with anterior consonants. Consider some examples:

(29) gołębi-a [gɔwɛmbʲa] 'pigeon, gen. sg.'   gołąb-ek [gɔwɔmbɛk] 'dim.'
      liść [liɕtɕ] 'leaf'   list-ek [listɛk] 'dim.'
      kość [kɔɕtɕ] 'bone'   kost-ek [kɔstɛk] 'dim. gen. pl.'
      pacierz-a [patɕɛʒa] 'prayer, gen. sg.'   pacior-ek [patɕɔrɛk] 'dim.'
      pasterz-a [pastɛʒa]   paster-ek [pastɛrɛk]
      'shepherd, gen. sg.'   'shepherdess, gen. pl.'
      niedźwiedzi-a [ɲɛdʑvʲɛdʑa]   niedźwiad-ek [ɲɛdʑvʲadɛk] 'dim.'
      'bear, gen. sg.'
      jeleń [jɛlɛɲ] 'stag'   jelon-ek [jɛlɔnɛk] 'dim.'
      kmieć [kmʲɛtɕ] 'peasant'   kmiot-ek [kmʲɔtɛk] 'id., expr.'
      dzień [dʑɛɲ] 'day'   dzion-ek [dʑɔnɛk] 'dim.'
      gęś [gɛʲɕ] 'goose'   gąs-ek [gɔʷsɛk] 'dim. gen. pl.'
      ćwierć [tɕfʲɛrtɕ] 'quarter'   ćwiart-ek [tɕfʲartɛk] 'gen. pl.'

The absence of palatalized consonants before the suffix -ek is almost completely general.[7]

Thus we face the question of how to account for the alternations between palatalized and plain consonants before the suffix -ek. The traditional concept of depalatalization seems both infelicitous and implausible: under this interpretation a palatalized consonant is acceptable, say, word-finally (e.g. kmieć [kmʲɛtɕ]) but is turned into its non-palatalized congener before a suffix beginning with the front vowel [ɛ] (e.g. kmiot-ek [kmʲɔtɛk]). This view is ultimately based on assumptions concerning the mechanism of the morphological derivation: the -ek derivative is formed by appending this suffix to the phonetic (phonological) form of the base. The morphological derivative is the mechanical consequence of concatenating a suffix with an existing lexical noun. The effect of this view is that given the lexical items kot [kɔt] 'cat' and liść [liɕtɕ] 'leaf', the suffix is attached in the same way to both nouns; since the results are kot-ek, list-ek we would have to conclude that in the case of the second noun some sort of morphophonological depalatalization must have applied. This view is not necessarily the correct one.

The above reasoning is based on the assumption that the shorter form is the base for the longer one, hence the mechanism of appending a suffix to a base must be at work. The question is whether the base is indeed a simplex or whether it could be argued to be in some way complex. The noun liść—and all others

---

[7] Exceptions include hypocoristics like Jasi-ek [jaɕɛk] (also as a common name jasiek 'small pillow'), Stasi-ek [staɕɛk], the nouns misi-ek [mʲiɕɛk] 'bear, dim.', pieni-ek [pʲɛɲɛk] 'stump, dim.', and ogieni-ek [ɔɟɛɲɛk] 'fire, blaze' (although the last word appears also regularly with depalatalization as ogien-ek [ɔɟɛnɛk]).

displaying the alleged depalatalization effects—belongs to a class of so-called soft-stemmed nouns, that is, nouns whose stem-final palatalized consonant remains constant throughout the paradigm. It is possible to assume that what is responsible for the softness of these stems is a morphophonological diacritic which dictates the appropriate replacement of the consonant. Since the diacritic is a permanent element of the noun, it is only to be expected that the noun will maintain the palatalized consonant throughout the paradigm. Viewed in this way the stems in both the noun *liść* and the noun *listek* are morphologically complex: in the former case the bare root /list/ is accompanied by the diacritic <PR1>, while in the latter case the root is combined with the suffix *-ek*. No depalatalization needs to be invoked since the morphological process which appears to call for it—*list-ek*—never acted on a base containing a palatalized segment in the first place.

The view of soft-stemmed nouns (and adjectives, see below) as being morphologically complex through derivation involving the addition of a diacritic is novel and somewhat unorthodox. The alternative entailing depalatalization is hopelessly complex: in the case of our *liść* depalatalized before *-ek* to *listek* we would also need to involve depalatalization in the same root before other suffixes, sometimes relatively isolated. The noun *list-owi-e* [listɔvʲɛ] 'foliage' is a case in point; here depalatalization would be called for by the suffix *-owi-e*; similarly *list-opad* [listɔpat] 'November' is clearly felt as related to *liść* and the verb *opaść* 'fall' and would evidently call for depalatalization. Even worse, since the noun *liść* 'leaf' is felt synchronically to be related to the noun *list* [list] 'letter' and its numerous derivatives, depalatalization would have to be postulated there as well. But in that case depalatalization would not be induced by (classes of) affixes, but would be a property of individual lexical items. Our proposal amounts to the claim that soft-stemmedness of nominals translates into the presence of a specific diacritic attached to a stem and is therefore found throughout a given paradigm—but not in derivationally related forms.

As an additional illustration, consider the soft-stemmed adjective *glup-i* [gwupʲi] 'stupid'[8] and a number of words derived from it: *glup-ek* [gwupɛk] 'fool', *glup-awy* [gwupavɨ] 'foolish', *glup-ol* [gwupɔl] 'imbecile', *glup-ota* [gwupɔta] 'stupidity', *glup-owaty* [gwupɔvatɨ] 'moronic'. The examples show that the final consonant of the base adjective has no palatalizations (or: is depalatalized), not only before *-ek* but also before several other suffixes. On the other hand, the consonant is palatalized in the adverbial form *glupi-o* [gwupʲɔ] 'stupidly'. On our interpretation it is only in the case of the adjective *glup-i* and the adverb *glupi-o* that we invoke diacritic marking as a way of representing the morphological category of soft stems.

---

[8] As argued in the preceding chapter, the final [i] is due to I-alignment and can in no way be regarded as responsible for the palatalization of the labial. Note that the labial remains palatalized throughout the paradigm, hence also before a back vowel, e.g. *glupi-ą* [gwupʲɔ̃ʷ] 'acc. sg. fem.'.

Before leaving the suffix -*ek* we have to consider the alternations, illustrated above, between dental and palatal (alveolar) affricates. They are repeated here for convenience with additional evidence supplied. For reasons which are presumably coincidental, most of the lexical support of the alternations comes from voiceless consonants.

(30) zając [zajɔnts] 'hare'   zającz-ek [zajɔntʃɛk] 'dim.'
      pieniądz-e [pʲɛɲɔndzɛ] 'money'   pieniąż-ek [pʲɛnɔʷʒɛk] 'coin'
      ulic-a [ulitsa] 'street'   ulicz-k-a [ulitʃka] 'dim.'
      lic-o [litsɔ] 'face'   licz-k-o [litʃkɔ] 'dim.'
      tysiąc [tʲiɕɔnts] 'thousand'   tysiącz-ek [tʲiɕɔntʃɛk] 'dim.'
      łasic-a [waɕitsa] 'stoat'   łasicz-k-a [waɕitʃka] 'dim.'
      owiec [ɔvʲɛts] 'sheep, gen. pl.'   owiecz-ek [ɔvʲɛtʃɛk] 'dim. gen. pl.'
      gorąc-y [gɔrɔntsɨ] 'hot'   gorącz-k-a [gɔrɔntʃka] 'temperature'
      ucie-(?)c [utɕɛts] 'escape, vb.'   uciecz-k-a [utɕɛtʃka] 'escape, n.'

In connection with list (27) we suggested that the alternations can be handled by substituting the affricate in the base in accordance with the replacement pattern PR7. Before this conclusion can be accepted, we need to observe some additional facts which complicate the picture. The examples below display a pattern departing from what we would expect.

(31) kloc [klɔts] 'block'   kloc-ek [klɔtsɛk] 'dim.'
      cyc [tsɨts] 'boob'   cyc-ek [tsɨtsɛk] 'dim.'
      noc [nɔts] 'night'   noc-ek [nɔtsɛk] 'dim., gen. pl.'
      płuc-o [pwutsɔ] 'lung'   płuc-ek [pwutsɛk] 'dim., gen. pl.'
      tac-a [tatsa] 'tray'   tac-ek [tatsɛk] 'dim., gen. pl.'
      mac-a-ć [matsatɕ] 'feel, grope, vb.'   mac-ek [matsɛk] 'tentacle, gen. pl.'
      onuc-a [ɔnutsa] 'footwrapping'   onuc-ek [ɔnutsɛk] 'dim., gen. pl.'
      kiec-a [cɛtsa] 'dress, n., expr.'   kiec-ek [cɛtsɛk] 'dim., gen. pl.'

A comparison of the two groups of examples leads us to the conclusion that the alveolar fricative [ts] is an ambiguous segment or, that its identity in the set where it alternates with [tʃ] must in some way differ from that in the other set, where identical phonological and morphological contexts evince no alternations. It should be added here that it is not just the suffix -*ek* that produces such effects—the same is true about the suffix -*ik/-yk*, as shown by the following contrasts with alternations in (a) and no alternation in (b).

(32) (a) samiec [samʲɛts] 'male'   samcz-yk [samtʃɨk] 'dim.'
           chłopi-ec [xwɔpʲɛts] 'boy'   chłop-cz-yk [xwɔptʃɨk] 'dim.'
           księdz-a [kɕɛndza] 'priest, gen. sg.' księż-yk [kɕɛʷʒɨk] 'dim.'

      (b) pajac [pajats] 'clown'   pajac-yk [pajatsɨk] 'dim.'
           koc [kɔts] 'blanket'   koc-yk [kɔtsɨk] 'dim.'
           rydz-a [rɨdza] 'kind of mushroom,   rydz-yk [rɨdzɨk] 'dim.'
           gen. sg.'

The evidence allows no room for doubt: morphophonologically, Polish alveolar affricates display ambiguous behaviour. An adequate description must reflect the ambiguity in some way.

Let us reiterate the basic observation we made with reference to the suffix -ek: PR5 replacements of velars are evinced by its attachment while non-velar consonants remain unaffected. If we were to extend this observation to the alternating and non-alternating dental affricates we would have to conclude that the non-alternating dental affricates are exactly what they appear to be, namely, dental consonants, and as such do not undergo the replacements which -ek enforces on velars only. By the same token the alternating dental affricates are not dental but have to be velar. Note that we already have a replacement pattern which substitutes dental affricates for velar plosives, namely, PR2. Let us assume that PR2 is attached to the stem-final velar; the diacritic will ensure that the velar is consistently replaced by a dental affricate throughout the paradigm of the base noun, as in zając [zajɔnts] 'hare'. In traditional terminology the final affricate is referred to as a functionally palatalized consonant. The suffix -ek will then be attached to a base ending in a velar consonant and regularly replace it in accordance with PR5 overriding the noun's inherent diacritic and yielding zającz-ek [zajɔntʃɛk] 'hare, dim.'.[9] Thus there is no alternation [ts ~ tʃ] but rather the independently necessary alternations [k ~ ts] and [k ~ tʃ] enforced by the replacement patterns PR2 and PR5, respectively. We conclude, then, that underlying the [ts ~ tʃ]—and also [dz ~ dʒ]—alternations we have velar consonants which are morphophonologically replaced by either the dental or the alveolar affricates as dictated by the accompanying diacritic; the diacritic may be attached as part of the stem and then its effects will be transparent throughout the paradigm or it may be associated with the suffix so that whenever the suffix is present, so will its diacritic requirements. The same reasoning holds for the suffix -ik/-yk illustrated in (27) and (30): when attached to dental affricates it either leaves them unaffected (because they are dentals) or turns them into palatals (because they are velars with a diacritic in non-suffixed nouns). On this analysis neither the suffix -ek nor -ik/-yk requires reference to the specification PR7, whose very existence is thereby undermined.

As a final illustration of the way we envisage the working of morphology and morphophonology with reference to velar alternations, consider the suffixes -ek, -nik, and -nic-a as attached to the noun cukier [tsucɛr] 'sugar':

---

[9] We deliberately gloss over a potentially important issue here, namely a clash of diacritics. One can easily imagine a few ways of handling the problem but it seems safer to leave it open since what is really at stake are the poorly understood morphological and morphophonological mechanisms of word coinage. For example, if the diminutive were to be included in the lexicon and only analyzed by the morphology, the base noun would contain one diacritic while the derivative could have none and could be affected only by whatever the following suffix might require. The moot question is the nature of lexicalization and the structure of lexical items, including their idiosyncratic properties.

(33) cukier-nik [tsucɛrɲik] 'confectioner'
      cukier-nic-a [tsucɛrɲitsa] 'sugar bowl'
      cukier-nicz-k-a [tsucɛrɲitʃka]   1. 'female confectioner'
                                       2. 'sugar bowl, dim.'

The velar in the suffix -nik [ɲik] and also in -ek [ɛk] is not associated with any diacritics, so it remains unaffected. The suffix -nic-a (with numerous functions) also contains a velar with the diacritic <PR2> which enforces the replacement of the velar plosive by the dental affricate. The further attachment of the suffix -ek carrying the diacritic <PR5> to either -nik or -nic-a produces the same effect since both suffixes end in a velar.[10]

It is worth noting that the case of the surfacy [ts ~ tʃ] alternation is interesting also because it shows that the source of an alternation need not be overtly present in any of its realizations. The claim then that the alternation in focus derives from different diacritics attached to the voiceless velar plosive has only system-internal support and follows from the logic of the system. One may occasionally find supporting evidence in other parts of the system. In our list of -ek derivatives, above, the bases were predominantly nominal. There are two striking exceptions which we repeat here, where the base must be verbal, if only because there are no nominals which could serve as the input to the derivational process. These are:

(34) ucie-(?)c [utɕɛts] 'escape, vb.'   uciecz-k-a [utɕɛtʃka] 'escape, n.'
      mac-a-ć [matsatɕ] 'feel, grope'   mac-k-a [matska] 'tentacle'

The assumed bases are given here in the infinitive, hence the first pair appears to give the impression of illustrating a [ts ~ tʃ] alternation. In actual fact the final affricate of the infinitive is a form of the stem-final velar, presumably a merger of a velar and the infinitive marker -ć [tɕ] found elsewhere. The velar itself is seen in the present and the past forms of the verb: uciek-am [utɕɛkam] 'I escape', uciek-l-e-m [utɕɛkwɛm] 'I (masc.) escaped', and that is why the morpheme boundary before -c in the infinitve ucie-c is artificial as it should really appear in the middle of the affricate...The other verb—macać—has no forms with the velar. Thus the

---

[10] As remarked in a number of places, progress in the understanding of Polish phonology and, in particular, its morphophonology is hampered by the absence of a theoretically adequate account of Polish morphology. The suggestions we offer here come from what the sound structure seems to be saying. Viewed in this way words are formed by combining morphemes with morphophonological diacritics. Such formations become members of the lexicon and are subject to its properties and idiosyncrasies; alternatively one may view lexical units as combinations of morphemes and morphophonological diacritics. Consider here the openly arbitrary and unpredictable functions that the suffix -nic-a performs in the different derivatives: cukier [tsucɛr] 'sugar' ~ cukier-nic-a [tsucɛrɲitsa] 'sugar bowl', Bóg [buk] 'God' ~ boż-nic-a [bɔʒɲitsa] 'synagogue', rok [rɔk] 'year' ~ rocz-nic-a [rɔtʃɲitsa] 'anniversary', poziom [pɔʑɔm] 'level' ~ poziom-nic-a [pɔʑɔmɲitsa] 'spirit level', służb-a [swuʒba] 'service' ~ służeb-nic-a [swuʒɛbɲitsa] 'handmaid'. The suffix -nic-a [ɲitsa] is clearly identifiable but the meaning of the unit that it appears in is non-compositonal and has to be specified in individual entries. Similarly the distribution of affixes may be a lexical matter to a greater or lesser extent: koc [kɔts] 'blanket' and kloc [klɔts] 'block' (with a final dental) form their diminutives by arbitrarily attaching -yk [ɨk] and -ek [ɛk]: koc-yk, kloc-ek; in the same way, nouns ending with a velar, similarly, arbitrarily attach the same suffixes, e.g. hak [xak] 'hook' ~ hacz-yk [xatʃɨk] vs. rok [rɔk] 'year' ~ rocz-ek [rɔtʃɛk]. Apart from morphology itself it is the structure of the lexicon and its place in the morphology of the language that remain an urgent task to be faced by both morphological and lexical studies.

isolated example of a de-verbal derivative in -ek supports the contention that the alternations [ts ~ tʃ, dz ~ dʒ] are spurious since what we have are alternations of velars and dentals [k ~ ts, g ~ dz] and velars and alveolars [k ~ tʃ, g ~ ʒ]. In view of this conclusion we need to revise one of our replacement patterns, namely, PR7; it seems that it may just be restricted to the irregular [t ~ tʃ, ʃ ~ ɕ] alternations while the other two pairs may be deleted since they are handled by PR2 and PR5.

The decision to do away with pattern PR7 means of course that in all those instances presented above where this particular replacement was invoked we really have a lexical velar plosive associated with either <PR2> or <PR5>. This possibility was already briefly mentioned for the suffix -ik/-yk in chłop-iec [xwɔpʲɛts] ~ chłop-cz-yk [xwɔptʃɨk]; the same would hold for the other suffixes illustrated in (27): -ist-y/-yst-y in ojc-a [ɔjtsa] 'father, gen. sg.' ~ ojcz-yst-y [ɔjtʃistɨ] 'paternal', -ast-y in palec [palɛts] 'finger' ~ palcz-ast-y [paltʃastɨ] 'fingery', -nik in miesiąc [mʲɛɕɔnts] 'month' ~ miesięcz-nik [mʲɛɕɛntʃɲik] 'a monthly', -arz in owc-a [ɔftsa] 'sheep' ~ owcz-arz [ɔftʃaʃ] 'shepherd'. The interpretation adopted here arises out of an attempt to break down the existing alternations into a small number of well-established patterns and to eliminate excessive markings. Note that since phonetically (phonologically) we have the same segment [ts] in noc [nɔts] 'night' and owc-a [ɔftsa] 'sheep', to get the different effects before the diminutive -ek in noc-k-a [nɔtska] vs. owiecz-k-a [ɔvʲetʃka], we would have to distinguish them in some way. We could of course mark one of them as [ts]₁, the other as [ts]₂, and modify the replacement pattern PR6 appropriately. What would remain unexpressed in such an account would be the fact that both [ts] and [tʃ] alternate with velars in Polish, sometimes even within the same morpheme, for example, ręk-a [rɛnka] 'hand' ~ ręc-e [rɛntsɛ] 'dat. sg.' ~ rącz-k-a [rɔntʃka] 'dim.' ~ ręcz-n-y [rɛntʃnɨ] 'adj.'; thus the [ts ~ tʃ] alternation found here would have to be viewed as independent of and unrelated to the same alternation found in owc-a [ɔftsa] ~ owiecz-k-a [ɔvʲetʃka]. Our account says that this alternation is due to the velar being subject to identical replacement patterns; what is striking is that some of the alternations are not directly supported by the appearance of the velar; recall, however, that in isolated cases such support is available (e.g. uciek-am [utɕɛkam] 'escape' ~ uciecz-k-a [utɕɛtʃka] 'escape, n.'). Our account attempts to bring coherence into the system by making morphophonology less dependent on arbitrary diacritics.

4.4.2.1.2 The suffix -n-y

The suffix -n-y provides us with an opportunity to explore further the nature of morphophonological mechanisms, and, implicitly, the differences between such operations and phonological regularities. Let us look again at the examples we introduced above.

(35) -ny <PR4, PR5, P7>
glos [gwɔs] 'voice'   głoś-n-y [gwɔɕnɨ] 'loud'
wiatr [vʲatr̥] 'wind'   wietrz-n-y [vʲɛt-ʃnɨ] 'windy'
piekł-o [pʲɛkwɔ] 'hell'   piekiel-n-y [pʲɛcɛlnɨ] 'hellish'

nog-a [nɔga] 'leg'   noż-n-y [nɔʒnɨ] 'adj.'
granic-a [graɲitsa] 'boundary'   granicz-n-y [graɲitʃnɨ] 'adj.'

Let us start with the last example and extend it a bit; side by side with the
alternations illustrated (a) we also find forms such as (b):

(36) (a) granic-a [graɲitsa] 'boundary'   granicz-n-y [graɲitʃnɨ] 'adj.'
          mosiądz-u [mɔcɔndzu] 'brass, gen. sg.' mosięż-n-y [mɔcɛᵂʒnɨ] 'brassy'
      (b) moc [mɔts] 'strength'   moc-n-y [mɔtsnɨ] 'strong'
          nędz-a [nɛndza] 'misery'   nędz-n-y [nɛndznɨ] 'miserable'.

The contrast whereby some [ts]s alternate with [tʃ] before the suffix -n-y while
others remain unaffected is identical to the pattern we discussed earlier in connection with the suffix -ek in forms such as uciecz-ka 'escape, n.' vs. mac-ka 'tentacle'.
Since there is nothing to indicate differences, we adopt the same interpretation as
there: the alternating segments go back to velars, hence they follow from PR2 and
PR5, while the non-alternating ones are simple dental affricates. Thus, yet again,
PR7 is shown to be superfluous. We are thus left with velar alternations due to PR5
and the restricted class of alternations arising out of PR4.

It is the restricted nature of the second group that is striking. Note that
according to PR4 just three plain consonants are replaced by their palatalized
congeners: [w, s, z]; all other consonants are either unaffected or they in fact
display effects of depalatalization. This is not surprising only with labials, which
cannot be palatalized before a consonant for phonological reasons. With the
other anterior consonants the absence of palatalization replacements is less
obvious, the most characteristic case being the sonorant [r]. There are two
reasons to be surprised by this consonant. First, the palatalized congener of
this consonant coincides with that of [g] when it is affected by PR5; it is [ʒ].
Before the suffix -n-y, the consonants [r] and [g] behave differently in that the
former is unaffected by it; compare:

(37) kar-a [kara] 'punishment'   kar-n-y [karnɨ] 'punitive'
      nog-a [nɔga] 'leg'   noż-n-y [nɔʒnɨ] 'adj.'

In other words, there would be nothing phonologically odd about having
consistently either *każ-n-y [kaʒnɨ] as we have noż-n-y [nɔʒnɨ] or *nog-n-y
[nɔgnɨ] as we have kar-n-y [karnɨ] (cf. also wilg-ny [vʲilgnɨ] 'moist', which shows
that there is nothing wrong about the sequence [gn]). What happens is that while
the velar plosive undergoes the replacement, the sonorant fails to do so.

The other surprise factor is the restricted existence of alternations of [r] with [ʒ]
before the suffix -n-y, despite what has just been shown. The examples are
infrequent but totally unambiguous:

(38) wiatr-u [vʲatru] 'wind, gen. sg.'   wietrz-n-y [vʲɛt-ʃnɨ] 'windy'
      powietrz-e [povʲɛt-ʃɛ] 'air'   powietrz-n-y [pɔvʲɛt-ʃnɨ] 'adj.'
      szkaplerz-a [ʃkaplɛʒa] 'scapular, gen. sg.' szkaplerz-n-y [ʃkaplɛʒnɨ] 'adj.'

The last example seems to have no alternants with [r], but the two other ones show that [r] in the context of the suffix -n-y can emerge as [ʒ]. It transpires then that one cannot make a categorical statement about the way the suffix influences the preceding consonants, and our claim about the replacement patterns PR4 and PR5 characterizing the suffix must be viewed as a tendency, even if it occasionally is a predominant and almost exceptionless tendency. Whether a replacement will take place in a given derivative is a matter for the lexicon and the specific diacritic, if any, which appears in the lexical entry. As a final piece of evidence in favour of this position, consider the following set:

(39) mięs-o [mʲɛ̃ʷsɔ] 'meat'   mięs-n-y [mʲɛ̃ʷsnɨ] 'meaty'
      żelaz-o [ʒɛlazɔ] 'iron'   żelaz-n-y [ʒɛlaznɨ] 'adj.'
      bez-kres [bɛskrɛs] 'boundlessnes' bez-kres-n-y [bɛskrɛsnɨ] 'boundless'
      bez rzęs [bɛz ʒɛ̃ʷs] 'without eyelashes' bez-rzęs-n-y [bɛzʒɛ̃ʷsnɨ] 'adj.'
      czas [tʃas] 'time'   w-czes-n-y [ftʃɛsnɨ] 'early'

Examples are again not very numerous but mostly uncontroversial (the relationship between czas [tʃas] 'time' and wczesny [ftʃɛsnɨ] 'early' might be questioned but the first three -n-y words belong to everyday vocabulary with completely transparent morphology and compositional semantics). What we have is the dental fricatives [s, z] which remain unaffected by the following suffix despite the fact that, overwhelmingly, the replacement of these consonants takes place before this suffix. What is more, when these adjectives appear in the first-person plural masculine personal, before the ending -i <P1, P2>, then the clusters are uniformly palatalized, as in mięś-n-i [mʲɛ̃ʲɕɲi], żelaź-n-i [ʒɛlaʑɲi], bezkreś-n-i [bɛskrɛɕɲi], in accordance with the properties of the ending. Thus the failure in the remaining case forms of the adjectives must be due to the fact that the suffix carries no diacritic requiring a replacement to come into effect. The conclusion that we reluctantly have to draw is that morphophonological operations are conditioned by diacritically marked suffixes where the presence of a diacritic on a suffix is not invariant and may be subject to lexical fluctuations.

Another lexically governed property relating to the suffix at hand is the suppression (deletion) of the consonant [t] of the base in some -n-y derivatives. The deleted consonant of the noun appears as [tɕ], that is, as the PR1 congener of [t]—this is a case of soft stems carrying a morphophonological diacritic, as discussed earlier. In (a) we show cases of such t-suppression, whereas in (b), an identical context evinces no suppression.

(40) (a) mił-ość [mʲiwɔɕtɕ] 'love'   mił-os-n-y [mʲiwɔsnɨ] 'amorous'
           rad-ość [radɔɕtɕ] 'joy'   rad-os-n-y [radɔsnɨ] 'joyful'
           szczęści-e [ʃtʃɛ̃ʲɕtɕɛ] 'happiness' szczęs-n-y [ʃtʃɛ̃ʷsnɨ] 'happy'
           litość [litɔɕtɕ] 'pity'   litos-n-y [litɔsnɨ] 'pitiful'
           bol-eść [bɔlɛɕtɕ] 'pain'   boles-n-y [bɔlɛsnɨ] 'painful'

      (b) kość [kɔɕtɕ] 'bone'   kost-n-y [kɔstnɨ] 'adj.'
           korzyść [kɔʒɨɕtɕ] 'profit, n.'   korzyst-n-y [kɔʒɨstnɨ] 'profitable'

liść [liɕtɕ] 'leaf'   list-n-y [listnɨ] 'adj.'
ust-a [usta] 'mouth'   ust-n-y [ustnɨ] 'oral'
post [pɔst] 'fast, n.'   post-n-y [pɔstnɨ] 'adj.'

The suppression of [t] is evidently a lexeme-individual matter: it takes place when e.g. *miłość* but not *kość* is combined with the adjectival suffix. Thus it is a property of a combination of a specific base and the suffix, encoded in the lexical representation of the derivative. We may formulate it as a morphophonological suppression (S) process in the following way:

S1 stn ⟹ sn

The formula is a reflection of the morphological and morphophonological relatedness of two classes of words rather than of a live phonological regularity.

4.4.2.1.3 The suffix -*sk-i*

This is the most complex of the suffixes we have looked at so far. It actually appears in two shapes: -*sk-i* [sci] and -*ck-i/-dzk-i* [tsci], but we will continue to refer to just one variant for short. The suffix is used to derive de-nominal adjectives; its behaviour has been viewed in derivational-generative terms (Gussmann 1978: 103–8) as a result of a complex interplay of phonological factors in an abstract analysis. In this book we develop a view of morphophonology which is not reducible to or dependent on elementary phonological operations but operates in terms of segments, their replacements and deletions. For this reason we will take the opportunity not only of surveying the relevant data but also of comparing the two analyses. As can be expected, each analysis can claim its merits and de-merits but these only make sense within a more comprehensive view of the phonological organization. We will try to indicate what the two analyses, and hence two very different views of morphophonology, regard as their particular forte and aspects worth preserving. Consider the facts first.

The denominal suffix -*sk-i*, when attached to final labials, emerges unchanged; if the labial happens to be palatalized, it loses its palatality:

(41) ziemi-a [ʑɛmʲa] 'earth'   ziem-sk-i [ʑɛmsci] 'earthly'
      chłop [xwɔp] 'peasant'   chłop-sk-i [xwɔpsci] 'adj.'
      bab-a [baba] 'crone'   bab-sk-i [bapsci] 'adj.'
      myśliw-y [mɨɕlivɨ] 'hunter'   myśliw-sk-i [mɨɕli(f)sci] 'adj.'
      Wrocławi-a [vrɔtswavʲa]   wrocław-sk-i [vrɔtswa(f)sci] 'adj.'
      'place name, gen. sg.'

The loss of palatalization can be accounted for in two ways. One is to invoke the general palatalized labials licensing, which requires that to stay palatalized a labial has to be followed by a full (pronounced) vowel, hence the absence of such consonants preconsonantally and word-finally. Alternatively we may adopt the view of soft-stemmed nouns as formed from bases by the addition of a diacritic which triggers a palatalization replacement in every form of the paradigm;

adjectives would be derived from the same bases by the addition of the appropriate suffix (-sk-i in our case) but of course without the diacritic, the result being the presence of a palatalized consonant in the noun and its absence in the adjective. An argument in favour of the latter approach is connected with a class of nouns ending in the voiced alveolar fricative [ʒ]: some nouns ending in this consonant replace it with [r] before our suffix (a), whereas others delete it altogether (b).

(42) (a) morz-e [mɔʒɛ] 'sea'   mor-sk-i [mɔrsci] 'maritime'
        żołnierz-a [ʒɔwɲɛʒa] 'soldier, gen. sg.'   żołnier-sk-i [ʒɔwɲɛrsci] 'adj.'
        rycerz-a [rɨtsɛʒa] 'knight, gen. sg.'   rycer-sk-i [rɨtsɛrsci] 'chivalrous'
        harcerz-a [xartsɛʒa] 'scout, gen. sg.'   harcer-sk-i [xartsɛrsci] 'adj.'

     (b) papież-a [papʲɛʒa] 'pope, gen. sg.'   papie-sk-i [papʲɛsci] 'papal'
        męż-a [mɛ̃ʷʒa] 'man, gen. sg.'   mę-sk-i [mɛ̃ʷsci] 'valiant'
        Paryż-a [parɨʒa] 'Paris, gen. sg.'   pary-sk-i [parɨsci] 'Parisian'
        Zaporoż-e [zapɔrɔʒɛ] 'place name'   zaporo-sk-i [zapɔrɔsci] 'adj.'

The [ʒ] in nouns which alternates with [r] in adjectives can be interpreted as lexical [r] with the diacritic <PR1>, assigning it to the class of soft-stemmed nouns; adjectives are derived by adding the suffix to the base, not to a particular inflectional class. Thus there is no 'depalatalization' and no change of some [ʒ]s into [r] but a superficial alternation whose roots are in the morphology, or, more adequately, in the principles of word formation. For this reason it comes as no surprise that hard-stemmed nouns in [r], those containing no palatalization diacritic, combine with the suffix without morphophonological side effects:

(43) kawaler [kavalɛr] 'bachelor'   kawaler-sk-i [kavalɛrsci] 'adj.'
     szuler [ʃulɛr] 'swindler'   szuler-sk-i [ʃulɛrsci] 'adj.'
     autor [awtɔr] 'author'   autor-sk-i [awtɔrsci] 'authorial'
     gór-a [gura] 'mountain'   gór-sk-i [gursci] 'mountainous'

We can conclude that when [ʒ] alternates with [r] it is part of a soft stem; the soft stem contains a diacritic which triggers a replacement procedure.

The other group of nouns ending in [ʒ] are those that delete it before the suffix -sk-i. They belong together with a large group of consonants which all behave in the same way—they are suppressed before the suffix. Consider some data:

(44) Hindus [çindus] 'Hindu, n.'   hindu-sk-i [çindusci] 'adj.'
     Francuz-a [frantsuza] 'Frenchman,   francu-sk-i [frantsusci] 'French'
     gen. sg.'
     Ruś [ruɕ] 'Old Russia'   ru-sk-i [rusci] 'Russian'
     towarzysz [tɔvaʒɨʃ] 'comrade'   towarzy-sk-i [tɔvaʒɨsci] 'sociable'
     Włoch [vwɔx] 'Italian, n.'   wło-ski [vwɔsci] 'adj.'
     Haga [xaga] 'The Hague'   ha-ski [xasci] 'adj.'

There seem to be no examples of appropriate nouns ending in [ʐ], clearly an accidental gap; together with [ʒ] illustrated above we have here a class of non-labial fricatives that are all deleted before the suffix. There is a single but a major glitch: apart from the fricatives we also have examples of the voiced velar stop [g] which disappears in the same context. Apart from the pair *Hag-a* ∼ *ha-sk-i* there are other examples which make the case non-accidental:

(45) Bog-a [bɔga] 'God, gen. sg.'   bo-sk-i [bɔsci] 'divine'
      Norweg-a [nɔrvɛga] 'Norwegian, gen. sg.'   norwe-sk-i [nɔrvɛsci] 'adj.'

We are therefore unable to form a single elegant generalization but have to resort to a disjunction: non-labial fricatives *and* the voiced velar plosive delete before the suffix -*sk-i*.

The two sonorants [w, n] undergo a palatal replacement in accordance with PR1, as shown by the following cases:

(46) Londyn [lɔndɨn] 'London'   londyń-sk-i [lɔndɨɲsci] 'adj.'
      młyn [mwɨn] 'mill, n.'   młyń-sk-i [mwɨɲsci] 'adj.'
      diabeł [dʲjabɛw] 'devil'   diabel-sk-i [dʲjabɛlsci] 'devilish'
      generał [gɛnɛraw] 'general, n.'   general-sk-i [gɛnɛralsci] 'adj.'

The problem with the palatal replacement is that it holds only in the case of the two sonorants, so we cannot say that it is the suffix -*sk-i* that is supplied with the diacritic <PR1>. Rather, we need an additional subclause of PR1, call it PR1a, which would be restricted to just these two consonants:

PR1a w   n
      | |
      1   ɲ

The need for additional replacement patterns is unfortunate and may indicate that a more satisfactory method should be sought.

The remaining obstruents select another allomorph, -*ck-i*/-*dzk-i*. These are two orthographic variants since phonetically they are homophonous [tsci]. Consider the data in (47).

(47) student [studɛnt] 'student'   studen-ck-i [studɛntsci] 'adj.'
      inwalid-a [invalida] 'cripple'   inwali-dzk-i [invalitsci] 'adj.'
      jeniec [jɛɲɛts] 'captive, n.'   jenie-ck-i [jɛɲɛtsci] 'adj.'
      partacz [partatʃ] 'bungler'   parta-ck-i [partatsci] 'adj.'
      Noteć [nɔtɛtɕ] 'name of a river' note-ck-i [nɔtɛtsci] 'adj.'
      Wdzydze [vdzɨdzɛ] 'name of a lake' wdzy-dzk-i [vdzɨtsci] 'adj.'
      ludzi-e [ludʑɛ] 'people'   lu-dzk-i [lutsci] 'humane'
      ryb-ak [rɨbak] 'fisherman'   ryba-ck-i [rɨbatsci] 'adj.'

The temptation to restrict the variant -*ck-i* to nouns ending in a non-continuant (plosives or affricates) cannot succeed for the same reason as above, namely, the non-continuants would have to exclude the voiced velar plosive; hence another disjunction is called for: non-continuants except for [g] merge with the fricative of the suffix to yield an affricate.

All in all we have two allomorphs and two phonetic effects: palatal replacement PR1a in the case of coronal sonorant stops, consonant deletion with fricatives and the voiced velar plosive. For the sake of completeness we need to mention several other forms which further remove the suffix from the domain of phonological or morphophonological regularity. Consider some examples involving proper (place) names and adjectives derived from them:

(48) Gdańsk [gdaɲsk]   gdań-sk-i [gdaɲsci]
      Bydgoszcz [bɨdgɔʃtʃ]   bydgo-sk-i [bɨdgɔsci]
      Śląsk [ɕlɔ̃ʷsk] 'Silesia'   ślą-sk-i [ɕlɔ̃ʷsci]
      Polsk-a [pɔlska] 'Poland'   pol-sk-i [pɔlsci]
      Otwock [ɔtfɔtsk]   otwo-ck-i [ɔtfɔtsci]
      Brześć [bʒɛɕtɕ]   brze-sk-i [bʒɛsci]

The exact nature of these simplifications is not unambiguous: the contrast *Gdańsk ~ gdań-sk-i, Otwock ~ otwo-ck-i* indicates that the same final consonant [k] can select either of the two allomorphs. No matter what ingenious interpretation one might come up with, these examples show clearly that individual marking would have to be involved. The alternative, which we wish to support, is to eliminate the two final consonants of the base lexically in adjectival derivatives, in other words, we want to treat them as partially irregular. The number of such forms is quite small for one thing; secondly, there are other changes, restricted to single items, when listing is the only available method in any way. Three such examples involving the suppression of the stem final consonant worth recording here are listed in (49).

(49) Egipt [ɛɟipt] 'Egypt'   egip-sk-i [ɛɟipsci], not *egip-cki 'Egyptian'
      szewc [ʃɛfts] 'shoe-maker'   szew-sk-i [ʃɛfsci], not *szew-cki 'adj.'
      Malbork [malbɔrk]   malbor-sk-i [malbɔrsci], not *malbor-ck-i 'adj.'
      'place name'

The morphophonological solution involving three major operations plus a few minor adjustments can be compared with a classical generative analysis couched in purely phonological terms. Comparisons across frameworks are both complex and risky since, naturally, individual notions and interpretations make sense within a specific set of assumptions and acceptable procedures, that is, within individual models. Nonetheless there are certain general observations which can usefully be made.

Unlike the morphophonological description developed above, a phonological account views the alternations as resulting from regularities specifiable in terms of phonological distinctive features. The suffix has been argued to begin with a phonological front vowel which palatalizes the preceding consonant and is subsequently deleted. The palatalized consonants—with the exception of the coronal sonorant stops (*londyń-sk-i* [lɔndɨɲsci], *diabel-sk-i* [dʲjabɛlsci])—undergo depalatalization (e.g. *gór-sk-i* 'mountainous' from earlier /gor'ski/, *let-n-i* 'summery' from earlier /let'n'i/), assimilations and simplifications (e.g. *hindu-sk-i* from earlier /xindusskɨ/, from /xinduśskɨ/, from underlying /xindusīskɨ/). In some cases the intermediate stages are quite complex: *haski* is underlyingly /hagīskɨ/, which becomes /hadʒīskɨ/ through palatalization, becomes /haʒīskɨ/ through spirantisation, becomes /haʒskɨ/ through vowel deletion, becomes /hazskɨ/ through palatal assimilation, becomes /hasskɨ/ through voice assimilation, and surfaces as [hasci] through degemination, surface palatalizations, and vowel adjustment. The intermediate stages are nothing unexpected within the derivational framework, indeed they are an inherent property of the model. All the operations, or rules, which convert one intermediate stage into another are said to be extrinsically ordered; they themselves manipulate not so much segments as our simplified summary might suggest but distinctive features that are the proper building blocks of phonological expressions. An obvious general property of representations and derivations is the presence of segments that are only indirectly relatable to phonetic units, at times feature combinations which never occur in the language. Both of these formal aspects of generative phonology—highly abstract representations and ordered rules deriving intermediate stages—have met with a lot of criticism as unconstrained and extremely costly devices, unlikely to be available to the language learner and unsupported by convincing cases of historical development. This is not the place to enter into a discussion of the nature of the models. If the typical generative mechanisms were to characterize phonology, a description of the alternations evoked by our suffix would presumably follow the lines we summarized above. If such devices are illegitimate, an alternative has to be sought. The morphophonological replacements and simplifications constitute one such possibility.

There is one aspect of the analysis where the generative model clearly wins out. Recall our anxiety, when it was observed that nouns ending in *-g* emerge with the suffix *-sk-i*, such as *Bog-a* [bɔga] 'God, gen. sg.' ~ *bo-sk-i* [bɔsci] 'divine', while those terminating in *-k* end up with *-ck-i*, for instance *ryb-ak* [rɨbak] 'fisherman' ~ *ryb-a-ck-i* [rɨbatsci] 'adj.'. It was this asymmetry which prevented us from arriving at a neat generalization connecting the suffix with the continuant or non-continuant nature of the final consonant of the base. The generative interpretation supplies a reason for this state of affairs: the output of the palatalization of underlying /g/, that is to say that /dʒ/ undergoes a process called *spirantization* and emerges in most contexts as /ʒ/; therefore it is subsequently processed phonologically as a fricative and it is not unusual that it patterns as a fricative with respect to the suffix in question. The morphophonological analysis has to treat this patterning as an irregularity. The generative success is paid for by a highly intricate analysis and it remains a matter of metatheoretical evaluation whether the particular point is worth the price it requires. To this it must be added that there are aspects of the generative analysis which are either unclear or ambiguous (non-unique). Take the noun *mąż* [mɔ̃ʷʃ] 'man, husband' and the adjective *mę-sk-i* [mɛ̃ʷsci] 'valiant', for example. It is not clear whether the final consonant of the noun should be derived from /gi, gj/ or /zj/ through palatalizations and segment deletions or whether the underlying form should be more or less identified with the surface form. Each option spawns its own derivation so that with underlying /ʒ/ we would presumably have /ʒʲisk/ by palatalization, /ʒ́sk/ by vowel deletion, /z-sk/ by palatal assimilation, /s-sk/ by voice assimilation, and finally /sk/ by degemination. The morphophonological analysis bypasses all the intermediate representations but is then forced to treat the distribution of the allomorphs as a matter of chance or irregularity. It must be pointed out, however, that irregularities do exist on any analysis: a form like *szewc* [ʃɛfts] 'shoemaker' should result in an adjective **szew-ck-i* [ʃɛftsci] on both interpretations. It does so on neither.

There is the additional matter of intermorphs preceding the suffix *-sk-i*. As far as we can judge these are morpheme-like sequences which are inserted between the base and the suffix. Consider a few cases:

(50) Kanad-a [kanada] 'Canada'   kanad-yj-sk-i [kanadɨjsci] 'Canadian'
                                  *kana-dzk-i
      Hamlet [xamlɛt]   hamlet-ow-sk-i [xamlɛtɔ(f)sci] 'Hamlet-like'
                                  *hamle-ck-i
      Afryk-a [afrɨka] 'Africa'   afryk-ań-sk-i [afrɨkaɲsci] 'African' *afry-ck-i
      tchórz-a [txuʒa]   tchórz-ow-sk-i [txuʒɔ(f)sci] 'cowardly'
      'coward, gen. sg.'   *tchór-sk-i, *tchó-sk-i
      Chile [tʃʲilɛ] 'Chile'   chil-ij-sk-i [tʃʲilijsci] 'Chilean' *chil-sk-i,
                                  *chilań-sk-i

The very existence of the intermorphs in individual adjectives (cf. *Kanada* ~ *kanad-yj-sk-i* vs. *Hag-a* ~ *ha-sk-i*) and the specific shape (i.e. *kanad-yj-sk-i* rather than the equally well-formed *kanad-ow-sk-i* or *kanad-ań-sk-i*) are an idiosyncratic property of the adjectives themselves, hence must be included in the lexicon.[11] Thus a comprehensive description of the *-sk-i* derivatives must rely heavily on the repository of forms and their unpredictable properties. There is nothing in the data themselves that favours a derivational, feature-based phonological, rather than an enumerative, morphophonological model. The decision must come from general theoretical considerations.[12]

4.4.2.1.4 The suffix *-ist-a/-yst-a*

Our discussion of the selected suffixes leads to the conclusion that the operation of morphophonological palatalization replacements in Polish is to a greater or lesser extent a matter of the lexicon. While individual suffixes may show a

---

[11] The appearance and distribution of intermorphs is the domain of morphology as there are some partial regularities and tendencies there as well. The suffix *-sk-i*, for example, when attached to personal nouns tends to be preceded by the intermorph [ɔv] when the base is monomorphemic, e.g. *kat* [kat] 'executioneer' ~ *kat-ow-sk-i* [katɔ(f)sci] 'adj.', *szpieg* [ʃpʲɛk] 'spy' ~ *szpieg-ow-sk-i* [ʃpʲɛgɔ(f)sci] 'adj.'. See Szymanek (1985: 150 ff.) for some discussion.

[12] A problem we have bypassed in the preceding sections is that of the alternation between the vowel [ɛ] and zero. Within the generative model this particular issue is crucial and critically related to the palatalization properties of affixes. We take up the problem of vowel–zero alternations in present-day Polish in Ch. 5.

proclivity towards palatalization, it is the idiosyncratic information in the lexical entry of a given derivative, the ultimate arbiter, that settles the issue. This stands in sharp contrast to the situation found with inflectional endings where morpho-phonological regularities appear to apply across the board. As might be expected, derivational suffixes display a gamut of possibilities varying between near com-plete to highly restricted applicability. As a final instance of a suffix that comes close to achieving a full palatalizing potential but does not quite make it, we will now consider again derivatives ending in *-ist-a/-yst-a* which we studied from a somewhat different point of view in the preceding chapter. The differentiation of the initial vowel is due to the phonology while the suffix itself is, of course, a borrowing, corresponding to the English *-ist* in, for example, *Marx-ist*. It has been investigated in detail by Kreja (1989: 63–70), on whose findings we will base our presentation. The suffix can productively be attached to nouns although other bases can also be occasionally found. We restrict ourselves to cases of unambiguous nominal bases.

Consider examples of the suffix attached to bases ending in most of the anterior consonants in (51).

(51) WOP [vɔp] 'Border Defence Army'   wop-ist-a [vɔpʲista] 'soldier of WOP'
      trąb-a [trɔmba] 'trumpet'   trąb-ist-a [trɔmbʲista] 'trumpeter'
      harf-a [harfa] 'harp'   harf-ist-a [harfʲista] 'harp player'
      aktyw-u [aktɨvu] 'active members,   aktyw-ist-a [aktivʲista] 'activist'
      gen. sg.'
      atom [atɔm] 'atom'   atom-ist-a [atɔmʲista] 'atomist'
      bas [bas] 'bass'   bas-sit-a [baɕista] 'bass player'
      puzon [puzɔn] 'trombone'   puzon-ist-a [puzɔɲista] 'trombone
                                           player'
      finał [fʲinaw] 'finish'   final-ist-a [fʲinalista] 'finalist'

There are very few clear examples where the suffix fails to enforce a palatal replacement but some can be found, e.g. *hobby* [xɔbbɨ] 'hobby' ~ *hobb-yst-a* [xɔbbista], even though Markowski's (1999) dictionary admonishes against the variant *hobb-ist-a* [xɔbbʲista], which evidently means that it does occur. The situation is very different with the dental plosives and [r], where both the presence (a) and absence (b) of palatalization are regularly attested.

(52) (a) afer-a [afera] 'scandal'   aferz-yst-a [afeʒɨsta] 'racketeer'
           rower [rɔvɛr] 'bicycle'   rowerz-yst-a [rɔvɛʒɨsta] 'cyclist'
           chór [xur] 'choir'   chórz-yst-a [xuʒɨsta] 'chorister'
           flet [flɛt] 'flute'   flec-ist-a [flɛtɕista] 'flautist'
           rent-a [rɛnta] 'pension'   renc-ist-a [rɛɲtɕista] 'pensioner'
           portret [pɔrtrɛt] 'portrait'   portrec-ist-a [pɔrtrɛtɕista]
                                            'portrait painter'

           hazard-u [xazardu] 'gambling,   hazardz-ist-a [xazardʑista]
           gen. sg.'   'gambler'

rekord-u [rɛkɔrdu] 'record, gen. sg.'	rekordz-ist-a [rɛkɔrdʑista] 'record holder'
(b) terror [tɛrrɔr] 'terror'	terror-yst-a [tɛrrɔrista] 'terrorist'
folklor [fɔlklɔr] 'folklore'	folklor-yst-a [fɔlklɔrista] 'folklorist'
Molier [mɔljɛr] 'Molière'	molier-yst-a [mɔljɛrista] 'Molière scholar'
esperanto [ɛspɛrantɔ] 'Esperanto'	esperant-yst-a [ɛspɛrantista] 'specialist in Esperanto.'
Kant [kant]	kant-yst-a [kantista] 'follower of Kant'
Bonaparte [bɔnapartɛ]	bonapart-yst-a [bɔnapartista] 'follower of Bonaparte.'
Freud-a [frɔjda] 'gen. sg.'	freud-yst-a [frɔjdista] 'follower of Freud'
stypend-ium [stipɛndʲum] 'scholarship'	stypend-yst-a [stipɛndista] 'scholarship holder'
parodi-a [parɔdʲja] 'parody'	parod-yst-a [parɔdista] 'parodist'

Although statistically the number of cases where palatalization is found is greater than those without the replacement, the existence of both patterns cannot be denied with respect to the three consonants. We are dealing here with a clearly non-native suffix that sometimes does and sometimes does not force the final consonant of the base to be modified. The bases themselves are practically always non-native. Although one could perhaps point out that it is the more assimilated words that tend to display palatalization effects in combination with the suffix, the degree of assimilation is a weak criterion and subject to impressionistic judgements. As evidence of this, consider the fact that the three foreign names—*Molière*, *Kant*, and *Freud*—that resist palatalization before the suffix in question, allegedly because of their weak nativization, have no problems in yielding to it before the locative singular ending -*e*: *Molierze* [mɔljɛʒɛ], *Kanci-e* [kaɲtɕɛ], *Freudzi-e* [frɔjdʑɛ]. Whatever intuitive appeal the concept of nativization may possess, predictive power it has none. Or almost none. What is more, there are derivatives that admit of both variants with no difference between them:

(53) propagand-a 'propaganda'   propagand-yst-a or propagandz-ist-a
     [prɔpaganda]   [prɔpagandista] [prɔpagaɲdʑista]
                                  'propagandist'

     ballad-a 'ballad'   ballad-yst-a or balladz-ist-a 'balladist'
     [ballada]   [balladista] [balladʑista]

The existence of such free variants is an unmistakable indication that the presence or absence of a palatalization replacement is decided upon in the lexicon. We may envisage it in the following way: the suffix -*ist-a* normally carries

the diacritic <PR1> which produces the required morphophonological replacements; with those lexical items where such replacements are not observed, the
suffix will be regarded as not carrying the diacritic, hence the stem-final consonant will emerge phonologically as non-palatal(ized). The initial vowel of the suffix
will be subject to the phonological alignment, the result being I-aligned -iyst-a
[ista] after an I-headed palatalized consonant and -yst-a [ɨsta] elsewhere. The free
variants will display the same behaviour: if palatalization is found, this means
that the suffix carries a diacritic, otherwise we get the form without replacement.

Another instance of the interaction between morphophonology and phonology comes from the suffix attached to nouns ending in the glide [j]. Examples:

(54)   hokej [xɔkɛj] 'hockey'   hoke-ist-a [xɔkɛista] or [xɔkɛjista] 'hockey player'
       pięci-o-bój [pʲɛɲtɕɔbuj]   pięci-o-bo-ist-a [pʲɛɲtɕɔbɔista] or [pʲɛɲtɕɔbɔjista]
       'pentathlon'   'pentathlete'
       Himalaje [ɕimalajɛ]   himalaista [ɕimalaista] or [ɕimalajista]
       'the Himalayas'   'Himalaya climber'

There are alternative pronunciations of the seuquence arising at the juncture
either [ji] or with the glide suppressed. We showed in Chapter 3 that the sequence
[ji] is disallowed due to the constraint we called Operators Required. This
constraint holds true for the word-initial position but can be relaxed word-
internally and suspended word-finally (see Ch. 3, examples (37) and the attending
discussion). Here we have another instance where the constraint can be relaxed
and this results in the two phonetic variants.

The approach to alternations we have just sketched carries an important
implication which deserves to be spelt out. The existence of an alternation
amounts to the addition of a diacritic to a lexical representation of a form: it is
the diacritic which is responsible for the presence of an alternation. This is best
seen in the case of the morphological free variants: the absence of a diacritic on a
suffix entails a mechanical concatenation of the base with the suffix with just
phonological modifications, if any. If a diacritic is present, it triggers a replacement which results in alternations of consonants. In this view, morphophonological alternations are complications of the grammar and complications
(enrichment) of the lexicon. What is more, and the free variants yet again show
it clearly, the alternations serve no particular function: they are a useless piece of
embellishment which the language decides to adopt, possibly in an attempt to
make the forms appear more native. The price paid for this indulgement is an
added lexical (diacritic) specification because—as we have argued above—
morphophonological alternations are not enforced by the segmental (phonological) structure but are predominantly (always?) due to the presence of
arbitrary diacritics. Thus, to effect morphophonological alternations recourse
must be had to arbitrary, non-phonological, features; as arbitrary properties they
may but do not have to be present among the other arbitrary properties of words.
In other words, and completely generally: morphophonological alternations are
facultative or non-necessary. Affording them denotes a readiness to pay a price.

There is a major question which the preceding discussion raises, a question we must ask but cannot answer in a satisfactory manner. As we have seen, the suffix -ist-a enforces palatal morphophonological reflexes with anterior consonants. There are no convincing examples of velars being affected[13] while the dentals [t, d, r] are replaced inconsistenly, as we have seen. The question of course is whether the group of segments which regularly displays replacements should in some way be set off from the rest of the consonants. Let us consider again the plain consonants and their morphophonologically palatalized congeners: [p, b, f, v, m, s, z, w, n] alternate with [pʲ, bʲ, fʲ, vʲ, mʲ, ɕ, ʑ, l, ɲ], in other words, the plain and the palatalized consonants are relatively similar or close in terms of their phonological make-up. The suffix -ist-a replaces [t, d, r] by [tɕ, dʑ, ʒ] either irregularly or not at all; in the latter cases—and also with velar plosives if they were to be involved in the replacement—the segmental change is quite substantial and hence, perhaps, considered not worth the facultative embellishment we noted above. This account is openly flippant, but on a more serious note it means, quite simply, that morphophonological alternations are neither necessary nor necessarily regular, with irregularities and inconsistencies galore.[14] The lesson that the suffix teaches, then, is not to demand regularity or neatness of the pattern in morphophonological alternations. These, by their very nature, can only be regular up to a point, a point which cannot be defined with any certainty. Morphophonological alternations are resultants of segmental changes and lexical idiosyncracies.

4.5 PARADIGMATIC DERIVATION, SOFT STEMS, AND BACKFORMATIONS: MORPHOLOGY AND MORPHOPHONOLOGY

'Paradigmatic derivation' is a notion developed within structuralist studies of Polish (Laskowski and Wróbel 1964; Waszakowa 1996) and it corresponds quite closely to *conversion* and *zero derivation* in English word formation (in fact, the term

---

[13] There is just one showing the alternation [k ~ ts] which could be derived from a noun, namely, *klinic-yst-a* [kliɲitsɨsta] 'doctor working in a clinic' (cf. *klinik-a* [kliɲika] 'clinic); the other potential example *public-yst-a* [publitsɨsta] 'feature writer' would have to be derived from the verb *publik-ow-a-ć* [publikɔvatɕ] 'publish'. There is little to support the view that these are genuine alternations rather than accidental juxtapositions of borrowings (cf. German *Klinizist, Publizist*). Apart from the extreme scantiness of the examples it must be noted that there are others where the alternation is not attested and only phonological effects are found, e.g. *Franco* [frankɔ] ~ *frank-ist-a* [francista] 'follower of Franco', *czołg-u* [tʃɔwgu] 'tank, gen. sg.' ~ *czołg-ist-a* [tʃɔwɟista] 'tank driver'. The spirant alternation in *szach-y* [ʃaxɨ] 'chess' ~ *szach-ist-a* [ʃaçista] 'chess player' is presumably glottal rather than velar phonologically, as argued in Ch. 3.

[14] A simple but telling example of the inconsistencies involved in alternations can be seen by considering the two adjectives ending in a velar: *dzik-i* [dʑici] 'savage' and *srog-i* [srɔɟi] 'severe'. The comparative degree of these formed by the addition of the suffix *-sz-y* [ʃɨ] are *dzik-sz-y* [dʑikʃɨ] and *sroż-sz-y* [srɔʃʃɨ]: no change in the case of the voiceless plosive but a palatal replacement PR5 and voice assimilation in the latter. One may well wonder which option is more absurd to entertain: palatalization replacement of velar plosives in the comparative degree of adjectives depends on the voicing of the plosives, or adjectives ending in a velar plosive have their comparative allomorphs listed lexically.

konwersja is also used); the derivation is said to be paradigmatic since it is only a specific paradigm regarded as a set of desinences that distinguishes the lexemes in question. Thus the adjective *dobr-y* 'good' has its set of (theoretically as many as thirty-five) inflectional endings (*-a*, *-e*, *-ego*, *-emu*, *-ej*, etc.), while the abstract noun derived from it *dobr-o* 'goodness' has its own set of inflectional endings of (theoretically) fourteen nominal endings; thus the two forms differ only in that they belong to different grammatical categories, not through differences in affixation but through the endings they carry (or take). There are purely morphological problems connected with deciding what constitutes the base and what is the derivative. Side by side with deriving the noun *dobr-o* from the adjective *dobr-y* it is claimed that the adjective *zlot-y* 'golden' is derived from the noun *zlot-o* 'gold'. This is the problem of the so-called motivation; it involves both formal and semantic criteria (for some illuminating discussion see Grzegorczykowa and Puzynina 1979). In the case of the adjective–noun pair *dobr-y/dobr-o* or *zlot-y/zlot-o* the issue of motivation need not concern us here since the stems of the words are identical: thus it is *dobr-* both in the case of the noun and the adjective, so morphophonologically changes will take place in accordance with the properties of the desinences. The situation is seldom as simple as that, though.

Consider a number of adjectives derived from nouns where the only difference between the stem of the noun base and the derivative adjective is the replacement of the stem-final consonant in accordance with the patterns of palatalization which we have identified earlier; the adjectives are supplied in the nominative singular feminine taking the ending *-a*, and information is provided as to the specific palatalization replacement involved.

(55)   kret [krɛt] 'mole'   kreci-a [krɛtɕa] 'adj.' <PR1>
       orł-a [ɔrwa] 'eagle, gen. sg.'   orl-a [ɔrla] 'aquiline' <PR1>
       sow-a [sɔva] 'owl'   sowi-a [sɔvʲa] 'adj.' <PR1>
       kur-a [kura] 'hen'   kurz-a [kuʒa] 'adj.' <PR1>
       kobiet-a [kɔbʲɛta] 'woman'   kobiec-a [kɔbʲɛtsa] 'feminine' <PR3>
       sierot-a [ɕɛrɔta] 'orphan'   sieroc-a [ɕɛrɔtsa] 'adj.' <PR3>
       ochot-a [ɔxɔta] 'willingness'   ochocz-a [ɔxɔtʃa] 'willing' <PR7>
       człowiek-a [tʃwɔvʲɛka] 'man,   człowiecz-a [tʃwɔvʲɛtʃa] 'human'
       gen. sg.'   <PR5>
       Bog-a [bɔga] 'God, gen. sg.'   boż-a [bɔʒa] 'divine' <PR5>
       mnich [mɲix] 'monk'   mnisz-a [mɲiʃa] 'adj.' <PR5>

The examples reveal that the morphological process deriving adjectives from nouns is accompanied not only by a change of paradigmatic allegiance—replacing noun desinences by those of the adjective paradigm—but also by morphophonological modifications. The latter consist in the addition of a diacritic to the final consonant of the stem; an adjectival stem therefore differs from the nominal one in accordance with the patterns of morphophonological replacement which a given diacritic requires. What is striking and what accounts for the traditional appellation *soft-stemmed adjectives* is the fact that the diacritic (and the morphophonological replacement) is present throughout the paradigm, hence it constitutes an indispensable part of the stem. To see it clearly, consider the first noun in the list above, *kret* [krɛt] 'mole', and the adjective *kreci-a* [krɛtɕa]. Before the locative singular ending -*e* of the noun, the stem-final consonant is replaced in the regular way, so that the stem of the noun is homophonous with the adjectival stem: *kreci-* [krɛtɕ]; the difference between the nominal and the adjectival stem is that the noun in other cases (before other desinences) displays the voiceless non-palatalized plosive, e.g. *kret-em* [krɛtɛm] 'instr. sg.', *kret-om* [krɛtɔm] 'dat. pl.', *kret-a* [krɛta] 'gen. sg.', *kret-ami* [krɛtamʲi] 'instr. pl.', while the adjectival stem maintains the palatal reflex no matter what ending follows: *kreci-ą* [krɛtɕɔ̃] 'instr. sg. fem.', *kreci-ej* [krɛtɕɛj] 'gen. sg. fem.', *krec-im* [krɛtɕim] 'instr. sg. masc', etc. Thus, while in the noun the stem-final consonant can be morphophonologically affected by the inflectional vowel, the consonant terminating the adjectival stem remains intact (always palatalized) before inflectional endings. Morphophonologically the cross-paradigm alternations translate into the presence of a diacritic in the adjectival class and its absence in the nominal one.[15]

Apart from soft-stemmed adjectives, traditional Polish grammar recognizes also the category of soft-stemmed nouns: these are nouns that preserve the same palatal or palatalized consonant throughout the paradigm. Since quite often these nouns are related to forms which have a plain consonant, it seems plausible to extend the analysis proposed above and regard the soft-stemmed nouns as containing a diacritic specifying the replacement pattern attached to the stem. Consider some examples:

(56) dzik-a [dʑika] 'wild, fem.'   dzicz [dʑitʃ] 'savages, barbarians' <PR5>
      żółt-y [ʒuwtɨ] 'yellow'   żółć [ʒuwtɕ] 'bile' <PR1>
      ostr-y [ɔstrɨ] 'sharp'   ostrz-e [ɔst-ʃɛ] 'blade' <PR1>
      zdrow-y [zdrɔvɨ] 'healthy'   zdrowi-e [zdrɔvʲɛ] 'health' <PR1>
      obyt-y [ɔbɨtɨ] 'refined'   obyci-e [ɔbɨtɕɛ] 'refinement' <PR1>
      biał-y [bʲawɨ] 'white'   biel [bʲɛl] 'whiteness' <PR1>
      zielon-y [ʑɛlɔnɨ] 'green'   zieleń [ʑɛlɛɲ] 'greenness' <PR1>

An adequate description should at least meet two conditions in such cases; (1) it should reflect the fact that the pairs of words are related not just in semantic or morphological terms, which is the domain of derivational morphology, but also in terms of their sound structure; (2) the soft-stemmed nouns should be set off

---

[15] At this stage one might ask about the representation of non-alternating forms, those where no cross-paradigm alternations seem to exist. A case in point is the adjective (numeral) *trzec-i* [t-ʃɛtɕi] 'third'; here the stem-final affricate always appears in this particular shape and there are no shapes of the root with a plosive. Two possible approaches can be envisaged with data of this kind. One is to assume that the absence of any alternations indicates the absence of evidence for a representation differing from the surface one. Alternatively we might find the massive evidence for the existence of a morphophonological replacement of [t] by [tɕ] in the language at large as sufficient to guarantee the secondary status of any [tɕ]. If the latter were to be adopted, the stem-final consonant in the numeral *trzeci* would be /t/ with the diacritic <PR1>, in the same way as the cross-paradigm alternating adjectives discussed above.

from hard-stemmed ones in such a way as to ensure the proper selection of desinences.

The first condition is met in a straightforward way since both members of such pairs are morphophonologically either very close or downright identical and end in the same consonant; they differ in that the soft stem contains a specification of the type of replacement its final consonant undergoes. The second condition is met since the class of soft stems is separated from the class of hard stems in the diacritic it contains; it is the presence of the diacritic that ensures the correct selection of the desinences.[16]

It goes without saying that both the adjectival bases and the derived nouns have to be entered in the lexicon and the allegedly derivational morphological process performs the function of analyzing existing lexical items. The lexicalized nature of the 'derived' nouns can best be seen in their frequently non-compositional semantics, as in *żółt-y* [ʒuwtɨ] 'yellow' ~ *żółć* [ʒuwtɕ] 'bile'.

Another problem which arises in connection with the diacritic method of encoding palatalization replacements concerns certain back-formations. A morphophonological by-product of chopping off parts of words is frequently something that looks like a reversal of palatalization. Consider some examples:

(57) po-słusz-n-y [pɔswuʃnɨ] 'obedient'   po-słuch [pɔswux] 'respect'
      wy-top-i-ć [vɨtɔpʲitɕ] 'smelt'   wy-top [vɨtɔp] 'smelting'
      olbrzym-i [ɔlbʒɨmʲi] 'enormous'   olbrzym [ɔlbʒɨm] 'giant'
      flasz-k-a [flaʃka] 'flask'[17]   flach-a [flaxa] 'expr.'
      beczk-a [bɛtʃka] 'barrel'   bek-a [bɛka] 'expr.'

The back-formations morphologically amount to the chopping off of a suffix, a suffix combination, or a suffixoid. As our examples indicate this is not the end of the story since the final consonant in the truncated form undergoes what looks like depalatalization. This is found not only with consonants which otherwise might be argued to display depalatalization effects, but also with palatals that never undo their palatal properties—there are no contexts in Polish where, say, [tʃ], emerges as [k] in some specific phonological or morphophonological environments. This happens with back-formations, when *beczk-a* [bɛtʃka] gives rise to *bek-a* [bɛka]. In morphophonological terms, the alleged depalatalizations are quite complex since they involve a reversal of palatalization replacements, that is to say, when PR1 turns [r] into [ʒ], depalatalization would require a replacement of [ʒ] by [r]. If we adopt the approach to morphophonological palatalizations as it

---

[16] The last statement disguises a problem since the selection of the desinences is now controlled by a disjunction: phonological palatality, i.e. {I}, and the diacritics. We leave it at what may look like an unsatisfactory stage; however, the selection of desinences is conditioned not only by morphophonological factors but also grammatical ones such as gender, animacy, etc. and even lexical (foreign vs. native words). Clearly there is no way—and no reason—to try and bring them all to a common denominator.

[17] The word is a loan of the German *Flasche* with the addition of the diminutive suffix (or suffixoid) *-ek* (cf. *flasz-ek* 'gen. pl.') and the feminine gender marker *-a*. The backformation *flacha* [flaxa] indicates that the consonant [ʃ] in *flaszka* [flaʃka] is analyzed as [x] with the diacritic <PR5>.

emerges from the discussion above, as the presence of a diacritic that triggers a specific replacement, we arrive at a simple statement of the depalatalizations attending back-formations: what is chopped off is not only a suffix or a suffixoid but also the palatalization-specifying diacritic, which is part of the suffix or suffixoid. Once the diacritic is removed, the 'bare' consonant comes to the surface.

4.6 MORPHOPHONOLOGICAL DEPALATALIZATION

The mechanism of diacritic removal is a good opportunity to take another look at depalatalization. We examined one possibility of handling the absence of palatalizations in connection with the suffix -n-y [nɨ] (c. the brief discussion at examples (20) and (21); see also the examples in (58a)). The noun chęć [xɛɲtɕ] 'willingness' is clearly related, morphologically and semantically, with the adjective chęt-n-y [xɛntnɨ] 'willing'; the outstanding problem is the nature of the morphophonological alternation [tɕ ~ t]. We tentatively concluded that cases such as these can be interpeted by placing the diacritics <PR1>, <PR2> with the palatal(ized) consonants. The diacritics in their relational function could be used to relate these consonants with their plain congeners, with no need for a distinct depalatalization regularity.

In the preceding section we argued for a diacritic encoding of soft-stemmed nominals, so that chęć [xɛɲtɕ] 'willingness' would end in [t <PR1>]. That means that the diacritic <PR1> discharges its replacement function here, while the adjective chęt-n-y [xɛntnɨ] 'willing' and words of other categories derived from the same root (chętni-e [xɛntɲɛ] 'willingly, adv.', chęt-k-a [xɛntka] 'whim, n.') are entered lexically without the diacritic, so the consonant emerges as plain [t].[18] This morphophonological reinterpretation of soft-stemmed nominals yields a similar conlusion with respect to depalatalization as an unnecessary or flawed generalization. There are facts, however, which force us to revise this conclusion. In (58) we list four sets of examples, starting with a few more cases which can be handled by an interpretation doing away with depalatalization.

(58) (a) kość [kɔɕtɕ] 'bone'   kost-n-y [kɔstnɨ] 'adj.'
         morze [mɔʒɛ] 'sea'   mor-sk-i [mɔrsci] 'maritime'
         żołnierz-a [ʒɔwɲɛʒa]   żołnier-sk-i [ʒɔwɲɛrsci] 'adj.'
         'soldier, gen. sg.'

---

[18] The lexicalized nature of the adjectives is beyond doubt and is best seen in the fact that the semantics of certain adjectival forms does not amount to a mere conversion of a noun into an adjective. Thus while the noun żądza [ʒɔndza] 'lust, concupiscence' has very clear sexual associations and only secondarily is felt to be metaphorical (żądza władzy 'lust for power'), the adjective żądny [ʒɔndnɨ] has no sexual connotations whatsoever; its primary reading is that of 'avid, greedy, desirous (of something other than sex)'. Similarly, while the noun żołądź [ʒɔwɔɲtɕ] can denote 'acorn' or 'clubs' (a card suit), the adjective żołędny [ʒɔwɛndnɨ] refers to the latter reading only, with a different derivative (żołędziowy [ʒɔwɛɲdʑɔvɨ]) forming an adjectival pair with the first reading.

(b) dzień [dʑɛɲ] 'day'   dni-em [dɲɛm] 'loc. sg.'
    godzien [gɔdʑɛn] 'worthy'   godn-ego [gɔdnɛgɔ] 'gen. sg.'
    wy-cier-a-m [vitɕɛram]   wy-tr-ę [vitrɛ] 'perf.'
    'I wipe out, der. imperf.'
    kocioł [kɔtɕɔw] 'cauldron'   kotł-y [kɔtwɨ] 'nom. pl.'
    marzec [maʒɛts] 'March'   marc-a [martsa] 'gen. sg.'
    karzeł [kaʒɛw] 'dwarf'   karł-y [karwɨ] 'nom. pl.'
    orzeł [ɔʒɛw] 'eagle'   orl-i [ɔrli] 'aquiline'
    wanien [vaɲɛn] 'tub, gen. pl.'   wann-a [vanna] 'nom. sg.'

(c) dźg-a-ć [dʑgatɕ] 'stab, vb.'   dźwig [dʑvʲik] 'crane'
    ćm-a [tɕma] 'moth'   ćwok [tɕfɔk] 'jerk, n.'

(d) czyści-ec [tʃiɕtɕɛts] 'purgatory'   czyść-c-a [tʃiɕtɕtsa] 'gen. sg.'
    udzi-ec [udʑɛts] 'haunch'   udź-c-a [utɕtsa] 'gen. sg.'
    wieni-ec [vʲɛɲɛts] 'wreath'   wień-c-e [vʲɛɲtsɛ] 'nom. pl.'

The examples in (a) could be handled along the lines developed above, that is to say, without any depalatalization mechanism but either with different consonants and a relational use of the replacement statements or the same consonants and a derivational use of the replacement procedure. The examples in (b) demonstrate, however, that an approach along these lines cannot be generally true. Here we face alternations morpheme-internally: the palatalized consonant appears before an attached vocalic melody while its plain congener emerges with the melody unattached (floating) and the adjacent consonant being a coronal. As argued in Chapters 3 and 5, the vocalic melody has a highly specified influence on the nature of the consonant: in the case at hand, side by side with the consonantal alternation in *dzień* [dʑɛɲ] 'day' ~ *dni-em* [dɲɛm] 'loc. sg.', we have no alternation in *den* [dɛn] 'bottom, gen. pl.' ~ *dn-em* [dnɛm] 'loc. sg.'. Consequently, there can be little doubt that the presence of a palatalized consonant has to be lexically specified in some words and not others. The intramorphemic alternations between the palatal(ized) and plain consonants must result from depalatalization. If palatalized consonants contain a diacritic <PR1>, then we need a morphophonological regularity we shall call Palatalization Loss (PL), which will remove it before a following coronal.[19]

Palatalization Loss
Remove <PR1> from [t, d, r, n] before a coronal consonant.

Deprived of the diacritic before a coronal, the consonants remain plain while those followed by an attached melody are subject to replacement;[20] the result is an alternation between palatal(ized) and plain consonants which is found morpheme internally, as in (59b), but which can also function at morpheme junctures,

[19] As throughout, the phonetic semivowel [w] is taken to be a lateral, hence a coronal.
[20] This interpretation, if correct, clearly indicates that some morphophonological regularities take precedence over others. The concept of a descriptive order in morphophonology is explicit in Bloomfield (1939) and was adopted as rule order in derivational-generative phonology.

as in (59a) and other examples discussed above. The examples in (59c) show that the coronal conditioning is required since before non-coronals palatalized consonants can freely occur.

Finally, the absence of alternations in (58d) is intriguing: the suffix -ec [ɛts] has a floating vowel which is regularly attached or unattached (see Ch. 5). We might thus expect the final consonant(s) of the base to emerge depalatalized when the consonants of the base become directly adjacent to the consonant of the suffix. Note that this is what happens with the fricative [ʒ] in *marzec* [maʒɛts] 'March' when it appears before the consonant [ts] in *marc-a* [martsa] 'gen. sg.'. No depalatalization takes place in (58d) and heavy consonantal clusters are found, e.g. *czyść-c-a* [tʃiɕtɕtsa] 'purgatory, gen. sg.'—even though the same root morpheme is found with the consonant sequence [st] elsewhere: *czyst-y* [tʃisti] 'pure', *czyst-ość* [tʃistɔɕtɕ] 'purity', *czyst-k-a* [tʃistka] 'purge, n.'. Judging by the behaviour with respect to depalatalization we could say that [ts] in *marzec* [maʒɛts] is coronal whereas that in *czyci-ec* [tʃiɕtɕɛts] 'purgatory' is not. The conclusion might be surprising had we not arrived at it in a different context earlier on: discussing the [ts ~ tʃ] alternation above (see examples in (32)), we concluded that it results from two different replacements of the velar plosive; the [ts] which does not alternate with [tʃ] was regarded as a coronal. The involvement or not in an alternation testifies to the distinct morphophonological status of a segment. Depalatalization offers additional support for this conclusion since the segment either conditions the regularity (when it is coronal) or does not (when it is velar). The coincidence of the phonological effects is a welcome confirmation of the reality of the morphophonological distinction.

In this section we have considered evidence for a depalatalization regularity as an alternative interpretation to the relational function of diacritic marking. It is not the case, however, that the two solutions are mutually exclusive. While the PL morphophonological analysis seems better suited to handle the intramorphemic situation in addition to the intermorphemic one, we have restricted it just to one type of replacements, namely, PR1. The examples in (20) embrace also instances of PR3 (e.g. *wladz-a* [vwadza] 'authority' ~ *wlad-n-y* [vwadni] 'having authority', *ambicj-a* [ambʲitsʲja] 'ambition' ~ *ambit-n-y* [ambʲitni] 'ambitious'), which the PL solution does not cover. It could easily be made to cover it but since the number of such examples is very small it might be prudent to suspend judgement and to admit a possiblility that the relational solution which is undeniably needed elsewhere in the language might also be at work here.

4.7 NOTES ON THE VERBAL SYSTEM; THE IMPERATIVE

The Polish verbal system displays considerable complexity in both its derivational and inflectional parts. Nothing approaching a description can be attempted here; at most we can make a number of observations and suggestions with reference to the morphophonological implications the system leads to.

A comprehensive study of the morphology of the Polish verb remains a pressing challenge for the future. Indeed, what is least understood is not so much the phonology or morphophonology but precisely the morphology of the category.

To begin with, one of the major problems concerns the nature of the verbal bases that need to be recognized. Traditionally, two such bases are normally posited from which the various finite and non-finite forms are derived by addition of suffixes and various morphophonological modifications. Verbs are grouped into three conjugational types on the basis of the inflectional endings of the present tense and each further into a number of sub-groups depending on the nature of the thematic vowel, if any, and the choice of other suffixes and types of alternation in verbal bases. As a result, the academic grammar of Polish identifies as many as twenty-one distinct groups or classes in addition to irregular patterns (Laskowski 1998: 248–9); Tokarski's (1973, 2001: 219) somewhat different classification distinguishes eighteen types. These classifications and attempts at a comprehensive account, leaving aside obvious redundancies and lack of concern for systematic generalizations, are a telling example of the complexity and richness of the verbal system. A very different view was inspired by Jakobson's (1948) original interpretation of the Russian verbal system with its assumption of a single verbal base from which the surface richness is derived by the selection of affixes and the application of morphophonological rules. Polish was subjected to this analysis by Schenker (1954) and the basic insights were subsequently adopted by the generative tradition (Laskowski 1975a; Gussmann 1980a; Rubach 1984; Bethin 1992; Czaykowska-Higgins 1998). Unfortunately, the generative descriptions usually concentrate on selected issues, very often on problems that are consequences of the single base hypothesis, the result being that there is no comprehensive account of the morphology of the verbal system as a whole. Czaykowska-Higgins goes some way towards rectifying the situation, but her scope of data is curtailed in such a way that what emerges is nothing but an outline of the system. As mentioned above, a full account is a task which the morphology of Polish must yet face as otherwise we will be dealing either with dozens of atomistic paradigms or tantalizing but sketchy outlines of theoretical possibilities.

One of the verbal forms that attracted considerable attention in the generative tradition is the imperative: it is formed by combining the verbal base with the imperative suffix. The important point is that the imperative suffix is either zero phonetically (the predominant case) or it appears as -ij [ij]. Attempts have been made to reduce the two allomorphs to a single input base, attempts which despite the rich theoretical machinery they require do only partial justice to the facts of the language. One general property of the derivational approach to the Polish imperative is the view that this category is independent of the rest of the system and can be studied in isolation; thus the imperative is said to consist of the verbal root, followed by the verbalizing suffix, if any, and followed in turn by the imperative ending (Gussmann 1980a, b, Bethin 1987, 1992). Whatever (morpho)phonological modifications are required follow mechanically from this structure. A case in point could be the root *pis* 'write' combined with the verbalizing suffix *-a* and the imperative marker -ĭ yielding the underlying form /pis+a+ĭ/; a rule of j-insertion derives the stage /pisj+a+ĭ/, which is followed by the palatalization of the fricative (and presumably also the initial plosive) to derive /pʲiʃj+a+ĭ/; the glide is subsequently deleted, /pʲiʃ+a+ĭ/, a general rule simplifying vowel sequences derives /pʲiʃ +ĭ/, the final lax vowel is removed and thus the chain of operations results in the phonetic *pisz* [pʲiʃ]. Once the derivational model comes to be questioned, the view sketched here is no longer a necessary approach either to the phonological structure of the imperative or to the phonology of the verbal system at large.

There are two morphophonological observations we wish to make here with respect to the imperative, one of which is quite traditional but overlooked by the generative models and another one which is perhaps somewhat original.

Traditionally, the shape of the imperative is not a matter isolated from the rest of the verbal system; quite conversely, the stem which appears in the imperative is regarded as identical with the one which is found in the present tense. Specifically, the verbs of the first and second conjugation identify the imperative stem with the stem of the third-person singular present tense, whereas those of the third conjugation identify it with the third-person plural (Laskowski 1998: 264). In other words, forming the imperative as a morphological process is not an operation isolated from the rest of the verbal system, but in its morphophonological modifications it coincides with what emerges in the present tense. Consider the following list of verbs, where the left-hand column provides forms of the verb in the third-person present singular (a) or plural (b), while the middle column supplies the imperative. In the right-hand column we provide alternations of the stem-final consonant, coming either from a different verbal form of the paradigm or from a derivationally related word; these are not available in every case.

(59) (a) każ-e [kaʒɛ] 'order'   każ [kaʃ]   kaz-a-ć [kazatɕ] 'inf.'
           pisz-e [pʲiʃɛ] 'write'   pisz [pʲiʃ]   pis-a-ć [pʲisatɕ] 'inf.'
           skacz-e [skatʃɛ] 'jump'   skacz [skatʃ]   skok [skɔk] 'n.'
           pomoż-e [pɔmɔʒɛ] 'help'   pomóż   pomog-ę [pɔmɔgɛ]
                                       [pɔmuʃ]   'I will help'

           wierz-y [vʲɛʒɨ] 'believe'   wierz [vʲɛʃ]   wiar-a [vʲara] 'faith'
           krzycz-y [kʃitʃɨ] 'shout'   krzycz [kʃitʃ]   krzyk [kʃɨk] 'n.'
           gryzi-e [grɨʑɛ] 'bite'   gryź [grɨɕ]   gryz-ę [grɨʑɛ] 'I bite'
           niesi-e [ɲɛɕɛ] 'carry'   nieś [ɲɛɕ]   nios-ę [ɲɔsɛ] 'I carry'
           pędz-i [pɛndʑi] 'rush'   pędź [pɛɲtɕ]   pęd [pɛnt] 'n.'
           pros-i [prɔɕi] 'request'   proś [prɔɕ]
           groz-i [grɔʑi] 'threaten'   groź [grɔɕ]   groz-a [grɔza] 'dread, n.'
           nęc-i [nɛɲtɕi] 'lure'   nęć [nɛɲtɕ]   po-nęt-n-y [pɔnɛntnɨ]
                                                          'alluring'

           zwycięż-y [zvitɕɛ^wʒɨ]   zwycięż   zwycięz-c-a [zvitɕɛ^wstsa]
           'conquer'   [zvitɕɛ^wʃ]   'conqueror'
           marz-y [maʒɨ] 'dream'   marz [maʃ]   ?mar-a [mara] 'apparition'
           marszcz-y [marʃtʃɨ] 'crease' marszcz [marʃtʃ]

(b) koch-aj-ą [kɔxajɔ̃ʷ] 'love'   koch-aj [kɔxaj]
    znaj-ą [znajɔ̃ʷ] 'know'   znaj [znaj]
    klej-ą [klɛjɔ̃ʷ] 'glue'   klej [klɛj]
    stoj-ą [stɔjɔ̃ʷ] 'stand'   stój [stuj]

What clearly transpires from such juxtapositions is the identity of the imperative with the present tense stem. This holds also for the palatal and palatalized consonants that appear in both forms: no matter whether and to what extent they may otherwise be related, with the relatedness attested through alternations, the forms of the present tense and those of the imperative have the same palatal(ized) consonant. Since the stem-final consonants in these forms are invariably either palatal or palatalized, their relatedness to the plain consonants found elsewhere can be expressed by including the palatalization replacement specification into the relevant forms of the paradigm. In this way the information about the specific replacement becomes part of the relevant forms of the present tense and the imperative, be it <PR3> in the case of verbs like *pisz-e* [pʲiʃɛ], *pisz* [pʲiʃ], or <PR1> with verbs like *gryzi-e* [grʲiʑɛ], *gryź* [grʲiʑ], or <PR5> with verbs ending in a velar consonant like *krzycz-y* [kʃɨtʃɨ], *krzycz* [kʃɨtʃ]. The diacritic becomes the marker of the imperative, rather than some abstract vowel like /ɨ/. This conclusion tallies with our view of the so-called soft-stemmed nouns and adjectives discussed above, where it is also the presence of a diacritic that identifies morphological classes.

Two additional points need to be made about the view of the zero imperative affix. If we are to assume that the imperative (and the relevant present tense forms) are formed by adding the diacritic in forming a given verbal category, then we would expect it to be present with verbs irrespectively of the nature of the final consonant of their stems. In the list above there are no labials; recall that this class of consonants, when palatalized, is subjected to a constraint that fails to license them word-finally and before a consonant. This brings about phonological rather than morphophonological alternations whereby in the third-person singular present tense we find palatalized labials but plain labials in the imperative; see (60).

(60)   łami-e [wamʲɛ] 'break'   łam [wam]
       kopi-e [kɔpʲɛ] 'kick'   kop [kɔp]
       rob-i [rɔbʲi] 'do'   rób [rup]
       traw-i [travʲi] 'digest' traw [traf]
       traf-i [trafʲi] 'hit'   traf [traf]

The absence of palatalization in this class of consonants is thus due to a phonological regularity which does not affect the diacritic nature of forming the imperative.

The other point that deserves mention concerns verbs which do not appear to have any alternations which might reveal the morphophonological origin of a given palatal. A case in point are the verbs *proś* [prɔɕ], *zwycięż* [zvɨtɕɛ̃ʷʃ], and *marz* [maʃ]. The first is relatively uncontroversial since the palatalized consonant [ɕ] emerges as a result of the PR1 replacement of [s], so we might extend the analysis also to non-alternating words. We might but perhaps we need not since we gain nothing by it: our framework is not focussed on individual segments and we do not aim to reduce their number. The remaining two verbs—*zwycięż* [zvitɕɛ^wʃ] 'conquer' and *marz* [maʃ] 'dream'—provide some indirect evidence why we should not extend the analysis to ambiguous cases.

These two verbs show no alternations which would allow us to uncover their simple morphophonological identity. Note that in Polish the consonant [ʒ] can be related to—can morphophonologically be derived from—as many as three sources. These have appeared in our examples above:

(61)   pomog-ę [pɔmɔgɛ] 'I will help'   pomoż-e [pɔmɔʒɛ] '(s)he will help'
        maz-a-ć 'wipe, inf.'   maż-e [maʒɛ] '(s)he wipes'
        wiar-a [vʲara] 'faith'   wierz-y [vʲɛʒɨ] '(s)he believes'

Given a non-alternating verb such as *zwycięż* [zvitɕɛ^wʃ] or *marz* [maʃ], we have absolutely no evidence to help us decide whether the stem-final consonant is [g], [z], or [r]. The selection of any one of them, along with the diacritic <PR5>, <PR3>, or <PR1> would be a totally arbitrary decision. The most direct approach is to assume that in the face of the absence of any indication to the contrary, the phonological form does not depart from the attested one, in other words, it is simply [ʒ]. The palatalization diacritic, an exponent of the imperative, would leave this segment unaffected since no replacement pattern has it as its input; the same is true about [ɕ] of *proś* [prɔɕ] 'ask', or, indeed, about [j] of *kochaj* 'love'.

To conclude, the imperative and defined parts of the verbal paradigm at large are formed by attaching diacritics specifying palatal replacements. Labials are phonologically depalatalized while non-alternating palatals remain unaffected by any replacement since no pattern takes them as its input. This concludes our brief survey of the zero suffix as an exponent of the imperative marker. We are still left with the other allomorph, *-ij* [ij], to which we now turn our attention.

Basically, the suffix *-ij* [ij]—with the phonologically conditioned variant *-yj* [ɨj]—is said to attach to stems meeting specific phonological conditions. Thus Kreja (1989: 88–9) and Laskowski (1998: 264–5) supply lists of contexts embracing the following three groups whose verbs select the allomorph in question:

(62)   (a) non-syllabic stems, i.e. those whose roots in the third-person singular present tense (left-hand column) contain no vowel:
             drż-y [drʒɨ] 'shudder'   drż-yj [drʒɨj]
             dmi-e [dmʲɛ] 'blow'   dm-ij [dmʲij]
             mśc-i [mɕtɕi] 'avenge'   mśc-ij [mɕtɕij]
             śp-i [ɕpʲi] 'sleep'   śp-ij [ɕpʲij]
             śn-i [ɕɲi] 'dream'   śn-ij [ɕɲij]

lśn-i [lɕɲi] 'glow'   lśn-ij [lɕɲij]
trz-e [t-ʃɛ] 'rub'   trz-yj [t-ʃɨj]
rż-y [rʒɨ] 'neigh'   rż-yj [rʒɨj]
drw-i [drvʲi] 'mock'   drw-ij [drvʲij]
czc-i [tʃtɕi] 'venerate'   czc-ij [tʃtɕij]
lż-y [lʒɨ] 'slander'   lż-yj [lʒɨj]
tkw-i [tkfʲi] 'stick'   tkw-ij [tkfʲij]
rżni-e [rʒɲɛ] 'saw'   rżn-ij [rʒɲij]
(od)pchl-i [ɔtpxli] '(de-)flea'   (od)pchl-ij [ɔtpxlij]
pstrz-y [pst-ʃɨ] 'splatter'   pstrz-yj [pst-ʃɨj]
(pode)jmi-e [pɔdɛjmʲɛ] 'entertain'   (pode)jm-ij [pɔdɛjmʲij]

(b) roots ending in a consonant followed by the palatal nasal [ɲ],
    where the nasal is most frequently part of a verbalizing suffix:
    ciąg-ni-e [tɕɔŋgɲɛ] 'pull'   ciąg-n-ij [tɕɔŋgɲij]
    kop-ni-e [kɔpɲɛ] 'kick'   kop-n-ij [kɔpɲij]
    sięg-ni-e [ɕɛŋgɲɛ] 'reach'   sięg-n-ij [ɕɛŋgɲij]
    na-pełn-i [napɛwɲi] 'fill'   na-pełn-ij [napɛwɲij]
    u-moral-n-i [umɔralɲi] 'moralize'   u-moral-n-ij [umɔralɲij]
    z-drzem-ni-e [zd-ʒɛmɲɛ] 'snooze'   z-drzem-n-ij [zd-ʒɛmɲij]
    za-ogn-i [zaɔgɲi] 'enflame'   za-ogn-ij [zaɔgɲij]
    u-co-dzien-n-i [utsɔdʑɛnɲi]   u-co-dzien-n-ij [utsɔdʑɛnɲij]
    'make ordinary'
    drażn-i [draʒɲi] 'irritate'   drażn-ij [draʒɲij] or drażń [draʃn̥]
    za-trud-n-i [zatrudɲi] 'employ'   za-trud-n-ij [zatrudɲij]
    bębn-i [bɛmbɲi] 'drum'   bębn-ij [bɛmbɲij]
    za-milk-ni-e [zamʲilkɲɛ] 'grow   za-milk-n-ij [zamʲilkɲij]
    silent'
    uszczkni-e [uʃtʃkɲɛ] 'nibble'   uszczkn-ij [uʃtʃkɲij]
    marz-ni-e [marzɲɛ] 'freeze'   marz-n-ij [marzɲij]
    wz-moc-n-i [vzmɔtsɲi] 'strengthen'   wz-moc-n-ij [vzmɔtsɲij]
    wahni-e [vaxɲɛ] 'swing'   wahn-ij [vaxɲij]
    bujni-e [bujɲɛ] 'rock'   bujn-ij [bujɲij]
    o-czern-i [ɔtʃɛrɲi] 'blacken'   o-czern-ij [ɔtʃɛrɲij] or
                                                       o-czerń [ɔtʃɛrɲ]

    szur-ni-e [ʃurɲɛ] 'shuffle'   szurn-ij [ʃurɲij]
    chluś-ni-e [xluɕɲɛ] 'splash'   chluś-n-ij [xluɕɲij]
    kwit-ni-e [kfʲitɲɛ] 'bloom'   kwit-n-ij [kfʲitɲij]
    kiw-ni-e [civɲɛ] 'beckon'   kiw-n-ij [civɲij]
    od-pocz-ni-e [ɔtpɔtʃɲɛ] 'rest'   od-pocz-n-ij [ɔtpɔtʃɲij]
    u-ze-wnętrz-n-i [uzɛvnɛnt-ʃɲi]   u-ze-wnętrz-n-ij [uzɛvnɛnt-ʃɲij]
    'externalize'
    s-późn-i [spuʑɲi] 'be late'   s-późn-ij [spuʑɲij]

(c) roots ending in a consonant followed by a sonorant other than [ɲ], although fluctuations must also be noted here:

roze-źl-i [rɔzɛʑli] 'infuriate'   roze-źl-ij [rɔzɛʑlij]
u-sidl-i [uɕidli] 'ensnare'   u-sidl-ij [uɕidlij]
za-okrągl-i [zaɔkrɔŋgli] 'round'   za-okrągl-ij [zaɔkrɔŋglij]
  or za-okrągl [zaɔkrɔŋkl̩]
u-szczupl-i [uʃtʃupli] 'deplete'   u-szczupl-ij [uʃtʃuplij] or
  u-szczupl [uʃtʃupl̩]
mądrz-y [mɔnd-ʒɨ] 'mouth off'   mądrz-yj [mɔnd-ʒɨj] or
  mądrz [mɔnt-ʃ]
orzeźw-i [ɔʒɛʑvʲi] 'sober up'   orzeźw-ij [ɔʒɛʑvʲij] or
  orzeźw [ɔʒɛɕf]
pastw-i [pastfʲi] 'torment'   pastw-ij [pastfʲij] or pastw [pastf]
roz-świetl-i [rɔɕɕfʲɛtli] 'lighten'   roz-świetl-ij [rɔɕɕfʲɛtlij] or
  roz-świetl [rɔɕɕfʲɛtl̩]
u-jarzm-i [ujaʒmʲi] 'subjugate'   u-jarzm-ij [ujaʒmʲij] or u-jarzm
  [ujaʃm̩]

The tacit assumption behind this grouping is the belief in the relevance of consonantal clusters. Thus, group (a) takes the allomorph -ij since otherwise we would be dealing with words consisting only of consonants, something that Polish does not tolerate apart from prepositions. The syllabic -ij suffix prevents such a situation, hence we have rżnij [rʒɲij] 'saw' rather than *rżń [rʃɲ̩]. Group (b) implies that the selection of syllabic rather than zero variant is motivated by the avoidance of final consonantal clusters ending in [ɲ], hence bębnij [bɛmbɲij] 'drum' rather than *bębń[bɛmpɲ̩]. This argument, unlike the previous one about the non-existence of words consisting of consonants only, is not water-tight since some word-final sequences of a consonant plus [ɲ̩] do exist, such as cierń [tɕɛrɲ] 'thorn', darń [darɲ] 'sod', baśń [baɕɲ̩] 'fairy tale', pleśń [plɛɕɲ̩] 'mold, n.', and przyjaźń [pʃijaɕɲ̩] 'friendship'. Thus, since we have cierń, the presence of szurnij [ʃurɲij] 'shuffle' and the non-existence of *szurń [ʃurɲ] cannot be mechanically assigned as due to the avoidance of a certain consonantal cluster. At best this can be regarded as a tendency, which may account for occasional double forms such as oczerń [ɔtʃɛrɲ] 'blacken' ~ oczernij [ɔtʃɛrɲij].

Group (c) imperatives can be similarly motivated as a tendency to avoid consonant sequences whose last member is a sonorant. The sonorant as being more sonorous than the preceding obstruent in *rozeźl [rɔzɛɕl], for instance, would score poorly as a word-final cluster (traditional coda), hence the preferred syllabic allomorph yielding rozeźlij [rɔzɛʑlij], arguably with the sonorant [l] (or the cluster [ʑl]) in the onset position. This interpretation must again be viewed as specifying a tendency since we can easily find cases of the imperative with sequences which the tendency disfavours; see (63).

(63) martw-i [martfʲi] 'worry'   martw [martf]
  załatw-i [zawatfʲi] 'arrange'   załatw [zawatf]

karm-i [karmʲi] 'feed'	karm [karm]
modl-i [mɔdli] 'pray'	módl [mutl̩]
srebrz-y [srɛbʒɨ] 'silver'	srebrz [srɛpʃ]
marszcz-y [marʃtʃɨ] 'crease'	marszcz [marʃtʃ]
wątp-i [vɔntpʲi] 'doubt'	wątp [vɔntp]

In addition, outside the verbal system we find numerous violations of the tendency, hence there are words like *sejm* [sɛjm] 'parliament', *rozejm* [rozɛjm] 'truce', *wieprz* [vʲɛpʃ] 'hog', and *jarzm* [jaʃm̩] 'yoke, gen. pl.'. As before, the nature of the constraint as a tendency can explain why some verbs admit of two variants, e.g. *mądrzyj* [mɔnd-ʒɨj] or *mądrz* [mɔnt-ʃ], *rozświetlij* [rɔɕɕfʲɛtlij] or *rozświetl* [rɔɕɕfʲɛtl̩], and why, side by side with *mądrzyj*, we have the imperatives in (64) with one variant only.

(64)   ostrz-y [ɔst-ʃɨ] 'sharpen'   ostrz [ɔst-ʃ]
        patrz-y [pat-ʃɨ] 'look'   patrz [pat-ʃ]
        pieprz-y [pʲɛpʃɨ] 'bullshit'   pieprz [pʲɛpʃ]
        mizdrz-y [mʲizd-ʒɨ] 'simper'   mizdrz [mʲist-ʃ]

The traditional account therefore provides two separate reasons for the selection of the -*ij* allomorph: the strong claim is that it is always selected if the emerging form of a word were to consist of consonants only; the weaker claim is that it tends to be selected when an undesirable final cluster of consonants were to arise. The motivation is phonological, if different, in the two classes and rests fundamentally with the avoidance of certain consonantal clusters. As an explanatory account this does not carry much obvious plausibility in view of the heavy clusters that Polish abounds in. An account going beyond lists of offending consonantal sequences should therefore be considered.

As a starting point, let us consider the motivation behind group (a) examples, that is, the existence of consonant only stems. While some roots are indeed fully consonantal in all combinations, others appear as such in some forms of the paradigm while in other forms or in derivationally related words they display a vowel in the stem. Consider the examples, where verbs are all in the third-person singular present:

(65)   dmi-e [dmʲɛ] 'blow'   na-dym-a [nadɨma] 'inflate'
        śp-i [ɕpʲi] 'sleep'   sypi-a [sɨpʲa] 'der. imperf.
        śn-i [ɕɲi] 'dream'   sen [sɛn] 'n.'
        trz-e [t-ʃɛ] 'rub'   na-cier-a [naɕɛra] 'der. imperf.'
        czc-i [tʃtɕi] 'venerate'   cześć [tʃɛɕtɕ] 'honour, n.'
        (od)pchl-i [ɔtpxli] 'de-flea'   pcheł [pxɛw] 'flea, n. gen. pl.'

These data clearly indicate that the root consists of consonants in certain verbal forms only; in other verbal forms and elsewhere the same morphemes have the vowel [ɛ] or [ɨ] corresponding to the phonetic zero. This observation raises doubts as to the existence of non-syllabic or consonant-only root morphemes. If we adopt the view that all roots must have nuclei but some nuclei remain phonetically empty, we can suggest that the allomorph -*ij* is attached to those with empty nuclei. This conclusion means that all remaining 'non-syllabic' roots in our group (a), from *drż-y* [drʒɨ] 'shudder' to *pstrz-y* [pst-ʃɨ] 'splatter', must contain one empty nucleus, hence they are *drØż-y*, *pØstrz-y*, etc. It is this empty nucleus that conditions the selection of the syllabic imperative allomorph.

If this suggestion is on the right track, we should be able to extend it to the two remaining groups that select the syllabic allomorph. It seems that a case can be made for this conclusion. For one thing, some verbs display alternations where a vowel appears between the two consonants that are traditionally taken to condition the suffix -*ij*. Consider

(66) na-pełn-i [napewɲi] 'fill'   pełen [pɛwɛn] 'full'
      (za)ogn-i [zaɔgɲi] 'enflame'   ogień [ɔɟɛɲ] 'fire'
      bębn-i [bɛmbɲi] 'drum'   bęben [bɛmbɛn] 'n.'
      milk-ni-e [mʲilkɲɛ] 'grow silent'   milcz-eni-e [mʲiltʃɛɲɛ] 'silence'
      od-pocz-ni-e [ɔtpɔtʃɲɛ] 'rest'   od-pocz-yn-ek [ɔtpɔtʃɨnɛk] 'n.'
      roze-źl-i [rɔzɛʑli] 'irritate'   zeł [zɛw] 'evil, n. gen. pl.'
      u-sidl-i [uɕidli] 'ensnare'   sideł [ɕidɛw] 'snare, n. gen. pl'
      wz-moc-n-i [vzmɔtsɲi] 'strengthen'   mocen [mɔtsɛn] 'powerful'

Some of the verbal bases are morphologically complex and can be claimed to contain suffixes which begin with an empty nucleus, as in -*n*-, i.e. -*Øn*-. This could be the case with verbs such as *umoraln-i* (<u+moral+Øń-i), *ucodzienn-i* (<u+co +dzien+Øń-i), *zatrudn-i* (<za+trud+Øń-i), and *uzewnętrzni-a* (<u+ze+wnętrz+ Øń+a). The absolute majority of verbs remaining in group (b) contain the verbalising suffix -*ną*-, which is reduced to the palatal nasal [ɲ] in the present tense; compare the -*ną*- forms of verbs with those without this suffix – all verbs are in the third person singular present tense:

(67) ciąg-ni-e [tɕɔŋgɲɛ] 'pull'   ciąg-a [tɕɔŋga]
      kop-ni-e [kɔpɲɛ] 'kick'   kopi-e [kɔpʲɛ]
      sięg-ni-e [ɕɛŋgɲɛ] 'reach'   sięg-a [ɕɛŋga]
      z-drzem-ni-e [zd-ʒɛmɲɛ] 'snooze'   drzemi-e [d-ʒɛmʲɛ]
      marz-ni-e [marzɲɛ] 'freeze'   (za)marz-a [zamarza]
      wah-ni-e [vaxɲɛ] 'swing'   wah-a [vaxa]
      buj-ni-e [bujɲɛ] 'rock'   buj-a [buja]
      szur-ni-e [ʃurɲɛ] 'shuffle'   szur-a [ʃura]
      chluś-ni-e [xluɕɲɛ] 'splash'   chlust-a [xlusta]
      kwit-ni-e [kfʲitɲɛ] 'bloom'   (za)kwit-a [zakfʲita]
      kiw-ni-e [civɲɛ] 'beckon'   kiw-a [civa]

The verbs in (62b) for which no alternant without the nasal [ɲ] is available are *drażn-i* [draʒɲi] 'irritate', *uszczkni-e* [uʃtʃkɲɛ] 'nibble' and *oczern-i* [ɔtʃɛrɲi] 'blacken'; of these, two admit both the zero and the suffix as imperative exponents: *draźń* [draʃɲ̊] ~ *drażn-ij* [draʒɲij], *oczerń* [ɔtʃɛrɲ] ~ *oczern-ij* [ɔtʃɛrɲij].

Since the -ną verbs are derived from the more basic forms without this suffix, it is perfectly natural to assume that the process of morphological derivation involves gluing the suffix to the base by means of an intervening empty nucleus. In such a case the [ɲ] of the present tense would in every case be separated from the preceding consonant by an empty nucleus which, just like in the case of the so-called asyllabic stems conditions the selection of the -ij allomorph of the imperative.

The verbs in group (c) have been partly accounted for; we are left with a few that admit of two possibilities, some of which are normatively marked. The co-existence of the variants means in our terms that the consonant sequences ending in a sonorant are regarded as clusters, in which case the zero variant of the imperative is selected, or as separated by an empty nucleus, which calls for the syllabic allomorph. Such variation in syllabic affiliation is not infrequent and in our case leads to alternative allomorphy selection in the imperative.

Before leaving the imperative allomorphy we would like to return to the existence of variation between the zero and the syllabic suffix and consider some implications of the variation for the syllable theory. Above we noted in several instances that two imperative forms could be found with some verbs. Typically, this happens when the stem ends in two consonants and when there is a vowel in the stem; thus there is never any variation with the so-called asyllabic stems, so that śpij never co-exists with *śp and, more interestingly, goń [gɔɲ] 'chase' or módl [mutl̩] 'pray' do not admit of the variants *gonij [gɔɲij] or *modlij [mɔdlij]. We find the two variants in some verbs that have been noted above (62c):

(68)   za-okrągl-i [zaɔkrɔŋgli] 'round'   za-okrągl-ij [zaɔkrɔŋglij] or za-okrągl
                                            [zaɔkrɔŋkl̩]
        u-szczupl-i [uʃtʃupli] 'deplete'   u-szczupl-ij [uʃtʃuplij] or u-szczupl
                                            [uʃtʃupl̩]
        mądrz-y [mɔnd-ʒɨ] 'mouth off'   mądrz-yj [mɔnd-ʒɨj] or mądrz [mɔnt-ʃ]
        pastw-i [pastfʲi] 'torment'   pastw-ij [pastfʲij] or pastw [pastf]
        roz-świetl-i [rɔɕɕfʲɛtli] 'lighten' roz-świetl-ij [rɔɕɕfʲɛtlij] or roz-świetl
                                            [rɔɕɕfʲɛtl̩]

Similar variation is also attested with other verbs, although the evidence is not always clear-cut or unambiguous. The difficulty is enhanced by the fact that normative dictionaries (e.g. Markowski 1999), acting as mystagogues, decide, without revealing the reasons for or sources of their arcane knowledge, that some forms are rare while others are simply bad and to be shunned in polite imperative society. From our point of view the existence of forms marked as 'rare' or branded as 'bad' is evidence of the fact that such forms can and do occur. We need to try and understand the nature of the variation. Consider some more examples of imperative variation where the first form is the one I would prefer or accept exclusively.

(69)   wy-wyższ-y [vɨvɨʃʃɨ] 'extol'   wy-wyższ-yj [vɨvɨʃʃɨj] or wy-wyższ [vɨvɨʃʃ]
        u-jarzm-i [ujaʒmʲi] 'harness'   u-jarzm-ij [ujaʒmʲij] or u-jarzm [ujaʃm̩]

po-większ-y [pɔvʲɛŋkʃɨ]   po-większ [pɔvʲɛŋkʃ] or po-większ-yj

'enlarge'   [pɔvʲɛŋkʃɨj]

iskrz-y [iskʃɨ] 'sparkle'   iskrz [iskʃ] or iskrz-yj [iskʃɨj]

wątp-i [vɔntpʲi] 'doubt'   wątp [vɔntp] or wątp-ij [vɔntpʲij]

martw-i [martfʲi] 'worry'   martw [martf] or martw-ij [martfʲij]

trzeźw-i [t-ʃɛʑvʲi] 'sober up'   trzeźw-ij [t-ʃɛʑvʲij] or trzeźw [t-ʃɛɕf]

wielb-i [vʲɛlbʲi] 'venerate'   wielb-ij [vʲɛlbʲij] or wielb [vʲɛlp]

spo-jrz-y [spɔjʒɨ] 'glance'   spó-jrz [spujʃ] or spo-jrz-yj [spɔjʒɨj]

zajrz-y [zajʒɨ] 'peep'   zajrz-yj [zajʒɨj] or zajrz [zajʃ]

karm-i [karmʲi] 'feed'   karm [karm] or karm-ij [karmʲij]

chełp-i [xɛwp] 'brag'   chełp [xɛwp] or chełp-ij [xɛwpʲij]

If the interpretation of the imperative allomorphy we defended above is on the right track, then the variation must be interpreted as pointing to the ambiguity of representations. Specifically, if the presence of the syllabic variant presupposes a preceding empty nucleus, then the variants with -ij show that members of the stem final consonantal cluster belong to two separate onsets. The absence of the syllabic variant argues that the two consonants constitute either a coda–onset contact or a branching onset. The existence of this sort of differences in the morphophonological representation of words is no more surprising than the existence of surface variants of the imperative, a fact that cannot be denied. In actual fact, the two different representations can be regarded as a reflection of the distinct 'surface' forms or vice versa, the two surface forms point to distinct representations.

What remains an interesting question is the nature of the consonantal clusters which allows this sort of representational ambiguity. Note that imperatives like *ciągnij* [tɕɔŋgɲij] 'pull', *kopnij* [kɔpɲij] 'kick' do not allow the zero allomorph: forms such as *ciągń [tɕɔŋkɲ̩], *kopń [kɔpɲ̩] are not found. The zero allomorph should be possible when the two consonants can form a coda–onset sequence, hence imperatives such as *wielb* [vʲɛlp] 'venerate', *chełp* [xɛwp] 'brag' with a sonorant–obstruent contact are in principle well formed. The existence of the syllabic variants *wielb-ij* [vʲɛlbʲij], *chełp-ij* [xewpʲij] indicates that some speakers analyse these forms with a nucleus between the two consonants, a situation which is not particularly disturbing since the very possibility of a constituent relation is no guarantee of its presence. The syllabic variant should attach to a consonant combination which cannot form such a contact: in *po-większ* [pɔvʲɛŋkʃ] 'enlarge' a fricative should not govern a plosive, the two consonants should be separated by a nucleus and thus we would expect the form *po-większ-yj* [pɔvʲɛŋkʃɨj]; the shorter form does occur (in this particular case it happens to be the dominant variant), which means that contrary to our assumptions a fricative can govern a plosive, or at least the fricative [ʃ] can govern the plosive [k]. Looked at in this way, the imperative allomorphy can be used to determine the governing properties of consonants and their syllabic affiliation.

A particularly interesting instance of the syllabic affiliation can be found in the zero-allomorph imperatives: *roz-świetl* [rɔçcfʲɛtl̩] 'lighten up', *u-jarzm* [ujaʃm̥] 'yoke', and *iskrz* [iskʃ] 'sparkle', which are derivationally related to the nouns *światl-o* [çfʲatwɔ] 'light', *jarzm-o* [jaʒmɔ] 'yoke', and *iskr-a* [iskra] 'sparkle'. The consonantal clusters [tw, ʒm, kr] can be argued to belong to separate onsets on the basis of their genitive plural forms: *świateł* [çfʲatɛw], *jarzem* [jaʒɛm], *iskier* [iscɛr] (*jarzem* appears side by side with *jarzm* [jaʃm]) and on the basis of their diminutives: *światel-k-o* [çfʲatɛwkɔ], *jarzem-k-o* [jaʒɛmkɔ], *iskier-k-a* [iscɛrka]. Despite the unquestionable presence of a nucleus separating the consonants in what may be regarded as the nominal derivational bases of the verbs, the zero imperative allomorph is found (for me it is the preferred form, at least for *rozświetl* and *iskrz*). The conclusion that suggests itself is that the representational shape of a word is not a sum total of the representations of its constituent morphemes but may have to be determined independently for different words sharing a particular morpheme. Simply put: constituent structure is not established for morphemes once and for all and maintained in all of their occurrences. Morphology, unsurprisingly, leads to shifts in grammatical categories (hence denominal verbs, de-adjectival nouns, etc.) and to non-compositional semantics and lexicalizations; in view of this, the generative and post-generative assumption that syllabic structure of morphemes remains intact or that a morpheme must have the same syllabic structure no matter what combination it appears in is both disturbing and non-obvious. The evidence seems to point to the contrary, namely, that syllabification holds for words rather than morphemes hence it is perfectly possible for a given consonant clutter to form two onsets in one word and a constituent in another one.[21]

The existing variability in the imperative allomorphy is indicative of the ambiguities found in some consonant combinations and also of the different options speakers take in dealing with those ambiguities. Rather than undermine our interpretation of the imperative, the existence of variation makes it more realistic. What is crucial to the interpretation is the distinction between a branching constitutent (onset, coda–onset contact) and a sequence of two onsets separated by an empty nucleus.

To conclude, the imperative allomorphy in Polish embraces a phonetic zero with specified morphophonological palatalization replacements and the suffix *-ij* attached when the last nucleus of the base contains an empty nucleus.

---

[21] An additional piece of evidence comes from the noun *światl-o* [çfʲatwɔ] 'light' with a nucleus between the two last consonants as shown by the genitive plural *świateł* [çfʲatɛw] and the diminutive *światel-k-o* [ʃfʲatɛwkɔ]; as we have seen it may contain a cluster (a branching onset?) stem-finally in the verb and hence the imperative selects the zero allomorph: *roz-świetl* [rɔçcfʲɛtl]. It is striking that the same root also seems to appear without the nucleus in the adjective *świetlny* [çfʲɛtlni] 'light' since if the nucleus were there we would expect *świetelny* [çfʲɛtɛlni] (cf. *sen* [sɛn] 'sleep' ~ *sn-u* [snu] 'gen. sg' ~ *sen-n-y* [sɛnni] 'sleepy').

4.8 CONCLUSION

Morphophonological palatalization in contemporary Polish embraces two major parts: there are diacritics associated lexically with specific segments, morphemes, and words, and also there are replacement patterns formulated for the language at large. The replacement patterns can be used dynamically (derivationally) to convert segments in specified contexts or statically to analyze morphophonological relations among words. Morphophonology may also remove diacritics in particular positions. These operations may be augmented by additional regularities relating to cluster simplifications and alternations of vowels with zero.

STRUCTURE OF THE SYLLABLE
AND THE VOWEL PRESENCE

5.1 OVERVIEW

Polish consonantal clusters that have bedevilled phonologists of all sorts of theoretical persuasion are studied within the highly constrained GP theory of syllabic constituents. Existing consonant combinations result from licit constituents such as a branching onset or a coda and a branching-onset contact, but they also arise as a result of the vowel–zero alternations. These are interpreted as a consequence of a morphophonological mechanism which attaches floating melodies in some contexts but not in others. In addition to a phonetic zero resulting from an unattached floating melody we also recognize empty nuclei; these are subject to the condition that domain-internally no sequences of such nuclei are tolerated. The interaction of floating melodies and empty nuclei is analyzed on the basis of the behaviour of certain prepositions and prefixes; morphology is claimed to play an indirect role in the pattern by supplying or adjusting domain boundaries. The absolute majority of consonantal clusters—initial, medial, and final—are shown to arise due to unattached floating melodies and empty nuclei.

The mechanisms controlling floating melodies and empty nuclei are predominantly morphophonological. An additional type of morphophonological regularity is developed which relates lexical items rather than transforming or replacing segments in specified contexts.

5.2 VOWEL~ZERO ALTERNATIONS

5.2.1 *Introduction*

The structure of the Polish syllable seems to hold a particular fascination for phonologists not directly concerned with Slavic languages almost exclusively on account of the consonantal clusters that the language allows. These can not only reach four or five elements but, fundamentally, the arrangement or order of the consonants in a sequence appears to defy principles established on the basis of well- (or, at least, better-) behaved languages. There are words galore of the type *lgarstw* [wgarstf] 'lie, gen. pl.', which are traditionally held to be monosyllabic and where the nucleus is surrounded by consonantal sequences violating established sonority norms. Since Polish has no complex nuclei (long vowels or diphthongs), it is consonant combinations that constitute the scope of what can be regarded as syllabic issues; in other words, attention is focussed on the structure of the onset and the coda.

The traditional Polish linguistic parlance identifies syllables with vowels, so the number of vowels in a word defines the number of syllables. As a corollary, the absence of vowels denotes non-syllabic units, hence the morphology of Polish speaks of asyllabic roots such as *sp-* in *sp-a-ć* [spatç] 'sleep, vb.' or consonant-only prepositions such as *z* [s] 'with' as against their syllabic variants *syp-* in *sypi-a-ć* [sɨpʲatç] 'sleep, iterat.' or *ze* [zɛ] 'with'. Syllabification on this view amounts to assigning consonants to onsets and codas, since vowels obviously constitute nuclei. This traditional view was adopted by the classical generative tradition and most of its offshoots, such as Optimality Theory (Féry and van de Vijver 2003). The procedure starts with phonetic—or phonemic—chunks of an utterance being chopped up into basic units (vowels and consonants). Syllabification then projects units of the melody onto the higher level units: nuclei, onsets, and codas; in other words, syllabification is melody driven. Since syllabification is nothing more than putting—or forcing—segment sequences into structural positions, the emerging configurations amount to a mere reflection of the segmental sequences. It is thus perfectly possible to relate a given phonological regularity to either a syllabic structure or a purely segmental sequence: something happens in the coda or before two consonants. It proved feasible to provide a comprehensive description of English without the notion of the syllable or its parts (Chomsky and Halle 1968). The syllableless approach may be more cumbersome at times or may involve repetitions but the gains from a mechanical translation of segments into syllabic units are not necessarily very impressive or far-reaching. Obviously the enrichment of the model by inclusion of the syllable construed along the traditional lines breeds consequences and difficulties of its own. The problems which arise in relation to Polish concern the degree of acceptable complexity for onsets and codas, the sequencing of consonants within these constituents and ways of handling segments that either do not conform to or exceed the acceptable sequencings (consult Rubach and Booij 1990; Bethin 1992; Gussmann 1992*b*; Gladney 2004 for an overview of positions). The derivational approach spawned a host of other problems such as the distinction between a phonological and a phonetic syllable (Bogusławski 1990; Szpyra-Kozłowska 1998), possible resyllabifications in the course of the derivation, ambisyllabicity, interaction with other phonological regularities, unsyllabified (unpedified) segments, and so forth. These are theory-internal problems of little or no interest within a model adhering to other assumptions. Government Phonology offers an alternative approach where most of these problems never emerge, which is not to say that other theory-internal difficulties will not make themselves felt (for surveys of the GP theory of the syllable see Kaye, Lowenstamm, and Vergnaud 1990; Harris 1994; Cyran 1998; Gussmann 2002; Scheer 2004).

As discussed in Chapter 2, the most significant innovation introduced by the GP theory of the syllable is the recognition of the syllabic level which is independent of the melodic level. Thus the syllabic level consists of sequences of onsets and rhymes, each of which can branch; branching onsets are subject to largely universal conditions on what can constitute the head and the dependent of the domain. Similarly the consonant appearing in the coda position must be licensed by the following onset, the result being that word-final codas are non-existent as there would be no consonant to license them (see Kaye 1990; Harris 1994; Harris and Gussmann 1998, 2002; Gussmann 2002 for more discussion). In most general terms and subject to additional constraints (to be made precise below; see also the literature referred to above) a branching onset consists of an obstruent followed by a sonorant while a coda–onset contact consists of a weaker or more sonorous consonant followed by a stronger or less sonorous one. Since the level of onsets and rhymes is not derived from the melodic level, it is perfectly possible for both onsets and nuclei to have no melody attached, in other words, to be empty. The category of empty nuclei in particular plays an important role in the model. Furthermore, since both onsets and rhymes can be maximally binary branching structures, both of them can dominate at most two skeletal positions. The nucleus is an indispensable part of any rhyme and this means in turn that complex codas are in principle impossible (for the notion of a superheavy rhyme, see Cyran 1994; Harris 1994). The concepts of extrasyllabicity and ambisyllabicity are incoherent within this framework. As GP is a non-derivational model, resyllabification is also a meaningless notion: a linguistic form has one and only one representation, which also holds for its syllabic structure. The GP model of syllabic constituents is thus highly restricted and quite challenging for a language such as Polish, its consonants in particular. Nuclei are invariably non-branching since there are no long vowels or diphthongs in the language. We run into problems once we confront the syllabic constituents which admit at most two consonants in the onset and three consonant at the coda–onset juncture as predicted by the theory with the actually recorded consonantal sequences. The response of the model to such difficulties can be initially illustrated by the words *łza* [wza] 'tear, n.' and *łgać* [wgatɕ] 'lie'.

A consonantal sequence such as [wz] or [wg], or more generally [w] plus an obstruent, can never constitute a branching onset since a glide cannot be head of an obstruent. The claim remains true even if we treat the glide, as throughout this book, as phonologically a velarized lateral in Polish. Since the two consonants cannot belong to a single constituent (the onset), they obviously must belong to two separate onsets; to be in the onset position they must be followed by a nucleus, which follows from the assumption that every onset must be licensed by a nucleus. The first nucleus has no melody attached to it: it is empty. Thus the representation of relevant parts of the two words is as follows, where the rhyme node dominating the nucleus has been omitted:

(1)
```
O   N   O   N   O   N   O   N
|   |   |   |   |   |   |   |
x   x   x   x   x   x   x   x
|       |   |   |       |   |
w       z   a   w       g   a
```

The representations show that both words would qualify as bisyllabic, since they each contain two syllable nuclei. No such interpretation would be possible if the input to syllabification were to be restricted to the phonetic signal where one vowel is found in each word. As we noted above, units such as onsets and nuclei within GP are elements of a level that is constructed independently of the melodic level. Hence it is perfectly possible for a nucleus to exist without any melody attached to it. The two levels are connected but to be attached to a constituent, melodic units must meet specific and well-defined conditions; otherwise units of the melody must belong to separate constituents. This follows mechanically from basic tenets of the model. A question that arises is whether there is any independent evidence for the empty nuclei or whether they are inserted into the structure in order to meet assumptions made in advance. In other words, is there evidence which could be described as theory-independent? The answer is that Polish supplies such evidence in substantial if not massive amounts.

The evidence comes from alternations of vowels with zero. In the case at hand, corresponding to the zero melody in the first nucleus of *lza* [wza] there is the vowel [ɛ] in the gen. pl. *lez* [wɛs] and also the diminutive *lez-k-a* [wɛska] 'nom. sg.', *lez-ek* [wɛzɛk] 'gen. pl.'. This shows that the recognition of an empty nucleus between the two consonants is not just a theory-internal requirement but is supported by other facts of Polish: no matter how the initial sequence [wz] is syllabified, every description must cover the alternation of this sequence with [wɛz]. What our description needs to do is provide a systematic account of cases when the nucleus is empty and when it is filled by melody. This we propose to do in the first section of this chapter.

The second section will scrutinize cases where empty nuclei have to be recognized to meet the requirement of the theory. We will consider heavy or otherwise unusual consonantal clusters and try to see what they tell us about the need for empty nuclei and their distribution. We will take into account both phonological and morphophonological aspects of the stable and alternating consonant sequences. Before starting we would like to clarify a terminological issue which figures prominently in past discussions of the problem.

Proto-Slavic developed a pair of vowels called *jers* (or *yers*) out of the Indo-European short *i* and *u*; the precise phonetic nature of these segments is a matter of some controversy. Shevelov (1964: 436) objects to labelling them *reduced vowels* or to recognizing a three-way contrast in length: long, short, and extra short (or jers). The relevant point is that the jers in all Slavic languages developed in a characteristic and uniform fashion, being lost in some positions and turned into non-high vowels in others. The result is the emergence of a pattern of vowels alternating with zero. What vowels emerged depends upon the specific dialect (Shevelov 1964: 434) and there were also some differences in the pattern of jer loss, all of which were subject to subsequent developments in individual languages. The loss of jers was a lengthy period; historians of Slavic place it between the beginning of the tenth and the middle of the thirteenth century (Shevelov 1964: 459). Predictably enough, reflexes of the original jers in Slavic today offer a number of distinct patterns. Polish turned the non-lost jers into the vowel [ε], which thus merged with [ε]s from other historical sources. This is the source of the alternations of the vowel [ε] with zero in the present-day language. Since obviously it is only some [ε]s that alternate with zero, the phonological segment(s) 'underlying' the alternation have been termed *jers* in some, mostly generative, descriptions. We find this usage highly objectionable and will not follow it here reserving the term *jer* for the historical context only. Talking about jers in present-day Polish (or Slavic at large) appears to give the impression that the synchronic description recapitulates history. Apart from being irrelevant this conclusion is false and produces a distorted picture of history.

For one thing, many of the historical jers are not reflected in any phonetic vowel or vowel–zero alternation in the present language. This is to be expected since jers were lost in some positions without leaving a trace in the form of a residue. In other cases, however, the historical jers have been restructured and today they are just the 'ordinary' vowel [ε]: the vowel in the word *szewc* [ʃɛfts] 'shoe-maker' shows no alternations with zero (e.g. *szewc-y* [ʃɛftsɨ] 'nom. pl.') despite the fact that historically it contained three jers (Klemensiewicz *et al.* 1965: 115). Worst of all, there are cases of the vowel [ε] alternating with zero in the present-day language that do not go back to historical jers. An obvious case are borrowings such as those in (2) (taking examples from English, German, and French).

(2)   rober [rɔbɛr] 'rubber'   robr-a [rɔbra] 'gen. sg.'
       sweter [sfɛtɛr] 'sweater'   swetr-a [sfɛtra] 'gen. sg.'
       Luter [lutɛr] 'Luther'   Lutr-a [lutra] 'gen. sg.'
       fiakier [fʲjacɛr] 'cabman'   fiakr-a [fʲjakra] 'gen. sg.'

In no way can these be regarded as continuing historical jers. Less glaringly, consider the word *mgl-a* [mgwa] 'mist, fog', to which we will be returning below. In today's language there is the alternant *mgiel* [mjɛw] 'gen. pl.' (also *mgiel-k-a* [mjɛwka] 'dim.' *mgiel-n-y* [mjɛlnɨ] 'misty', etc.), which should point to the presence of a jer between the two last consonants. In fact, a jer was present between the first two consonants: *mĭgla* in Old Slavic and, for example, *magla* in Croatian today (in fact, the jer corresponds to the first vowel in the English *mist* with which it is etymologically related, see Klein 1971: 469; Vasmer 1986: 587). Thus the original jer in the word was lost and the alternation *mgla* ∼ *mgiel* does not go back to a historical jer but to what used to be a branching onset. For all these reasons and in agreement with tradition we restrict the term *jer* to a historical context only and will continue to talk about vowel∼zero alternations in the modern language. Historical accounts of the origin and the rise of jers can be found in standard histories of Slavic (e.g. Stieber 1958, 1966, 1979; Shevelov 1964; Moszyński 1984) and their subsequent developments in the histories of individual Slavic languages (for Polish, see Łoś 1922; Klemensiewicz *et al.* 1965; Stieber 1973).

Polish vowel~zero alternations form the centre of attention in generative phonological descriptions of Polish (Laskowski 1975*a*; Gussmann 1980*a*; Rubach 1984, 1992; Bethin 1992, 1998; to name just the major book-length attempts). Listing individual papers and other contributions, to say nothing of unpublished dissertations, would result in a very long list of which the most significant (or intriguing) and influential studies are Spencer (1986), Rubach (1986), Piotrowski (1988, 1992), Piotrowski, Roca, and Spencer (1992), and Szpyra (1992*a*). Outside the standard generative framework there is Rowicka's (1999) attempt to combine GP and OT; a purely GP approach is followed by Gussmann and Kaye (1993), Gussmann (1997*b*), Cyran and Gussmann (1999), and Scheer (2004). A review of the different proposals would amount to a veritable survey of phonological anxieties in the second half of the twentieth century, a review which cannot be attempted here. One thread which cuts across all the disparate studies is the conviction in the phonological nature of the phenomenon; the vowel~zero alternation in modern Polish is believed to be phonologically controlled. This stands in sharp contrast to the earlier or structural approach which regarded the alternations as due to the morphophonology of the language. It is this more traditional view that we wish to uphold in the current account. Before we delve into this issue we need to look at some basic data.

5.2.2 *Basic facts*

The vowel [ɛ] alternates with zero in numerous stems within the same paradigm and also in derivationally related forms. Typical of the alternations are the following:

(3) łeb [wɛp] 'head' łb-a [wba] 'gen. sg.'
    dech [dɛx] 'breath' tch-u [txu] 'gen. sg.'
    łokieć [wɔcɛtɕ] 'elbow' łokci-a [wɔktɕa] 'gen. sg.'
    szczygieł [ʃtʃɨɟɛw] 'goldfinch' szczygł-a [ʃtʃɨgwa] 'gen. sg.'
    taniec [taɲɛts] 'dance' tańc-e [taɲtsɛ] 'nom. pl.'
    kropel [krɔpɛl] 'drop, gen. pl.' kropl-a [krɔpla] 'nom. sg.'
    desek [dɛsɛk] 'board, gen. pl.' desk-a [dɛska] 'nom sg.'
    wiader [vʲadɛr] 'bucket, gen. pl.' wiadr-o [vʲadrɔ] 'nom. sg.'
    wioseł [vʲɔsɛw] 'oar, gen. pl.' wiosł-o [vʲɔswɔ] 'nom. sg.'
    węzeł [vɛ̃ʷzɛw] 'knot' węzł-em [vɛ̃ʷzwɛm] 'instr. sg.'
    żeber [ʒɛbɛr] 'rib, gen. pl.' żebr-o [ʒɛbrɔ] 'nom. sg.'
    igieł [iɟɛw] 'needle, gen. pl.' igł-a [igwa] 'nom. sg.'
    świateł [ɕfʲatɛw] 'light, gen. pl.' światł-o [ɕfʲatwɔ] 'nom. sg.'
    kukieł [kucɛw] 'puppet, gen. pl.' kukł-a [kukwa] 'nom. sg.'
    wafel [vafɛl] 'waffle' wafl-e [vaflɛ] 'nom. pl.'
    pełen [pɛwɛn] 'full' pełn-ego [pɛwnɛgɔ] 'gen. sg.'

magister [maɟistɛr] 'holder of MA'   magistr-em [maɟistrɛm] 'instr. sg.'
pode mną [pɔdɛ mnɔ̃ʷ] 'under me'   pod tobą [pɔt tɔbɔ̃ʷ] 'under you'
pode-prz-e-ć [pɔdɛpʃɛtɕ] 'support'   pod-pier-a-ć [pɔtpʲɛratɕ] 'imperf.'

As always in the case of an alternation of a segment with zero, the facts can be interpreted either as an instance of deletion or insertion, or both. The Polish structuralist tradition tilts in the direction of insertion while the predominant generative trend supports deletion. Reasons for the latter position were discussed at length and made explicit in Laskowski (1975a); these were endorsed and repeated by subsequent research. Unfortunately, results of the research have not percolated down into the received wisdom of standard Polish grammatical presentation: Kowalik (1997, 1998) treats the alternation as epenthesis where the inserted vowel splits up consonantal clusters. The inadequacy of the reasoning can be found among the examples which Kowalik (1997: 146) herself supplies. Consider three pairs of nouns, each in the nominative singular and the genitive plural, where the same consonantal cluster is broken up by the alleged epenthesis in one but not the other case.

(4) (a) trumn-a [trumna] 'coffin'   trumien [trumʲɛn]
         vs. kolumn-a [kɔlumna] 'column'   kolumn [kɔlumn]

     (b) bagn-o [bagnɔ] 'swamp'   bagien [baɟɛn]
         vs. malign-a [maligna] 'delirium'   malign [malikn] 'gen. pl.'

     (c) łask-a [waska] 'stoat'   łasek [wasɛk]
         vs. łask-a [waska] 'grace'   łask [wask]

The relevance of such examples cannot be overstated: it is simply not the case that some clusters, say [mn] or [sk], have to be broken up by an epenthetic vowel in word-final positions—the last example is particularly telling. Such clusters are perfectly capable of remaining intact there as the second example in each pair shows. The best that can be done is to list the forms where the alleged insertion takes place, which is another way of saying that insertion is not conditioned by consonantal clustering; it is individual items which decide whether a vowel will appear in them or not. In other words, no epenthesis is at work because no epenthesis is predictable.

It is not difficult to see why Kowalik and the tradition she follows must be forced into the epenthesis corner, despite the fact that the solution obviously does not work. In a nutshell, the conundrum can be illustrated by the following pair of nouns (again in the nominative and the genitive singular):

(5) pies [pʲɛs] 'dog'   ps-a [psa]
     bies [bʲɛs] 'devil'   bies-a [bʲɛsa]

If deletion were to be assumed to apply to the first noun, we would need to distinguish it in some way from the second noun since in phonological, morphophonological, and morphological contexts the vowels in the two words in the relevant sense are identical. This could only be done by marking individual forms. On the epenthesis solution, the first noun would be morphophonologically consonantal, something like {pʲs}, with epenthesis deriving the phonological form /pʲɛs/; the other noun would appear, both morphophonologically and phonologically, in an unalterable form {bʲɛs}. If the epenthesis account seems preferable, it is because it resorts to the concept of breaking up consonantal clusters, the implication being that were epenthesis not to be operative, we would end up with words consisting of consonants only. Although not resorting to explicit marking, the view is not really different from it since it starts with the assumption that lexically there are consonant-only stems. At most, then, the insertion analysis appears to provide some rationale for what is found to occur and thus seems the lesser of the two evils. Note, however, that this view starts with the assumption that there are lexical consonant-only major lexical categories, hence their representations need to be rectified by a morphophonological regularity inserting a vowel.

The fundamental failing behind this sort of reasoning follows from the tacit—or perhaps explicit—assumption that phonetic identity entails linguistic or structural identity. As the vowels in the two words *pies* [pʲɛs] and *bies* [bʲɛs] are undoubtedly identical, the assumption of their (morpho)phonological identity means that we cannot distinguish between them and that diacritic marking is therefore the only way of distinguishing cases of deletion from non-deletion. Once the initial assumption is abandoned, the difficulty disappears and deletion, rather than epenthesis, remains a viable option. We see no reason to argue against the absurd view that surface phonetics exhausts the linguistic potential of a form. Quite conversely, it is the pattern of behaviour that reveals the linguistically significant properties of forms and segments. With reference to the issue at hand, the vowel [ɛ] which alternates with zero is simply a separate structural object from the vowel [ɛ] which stays put. It is an entirely different question to decide what the difference between the two objects consists in but their distinctness cannot be questioned.

Consider now more examples with the alternating [ɛ].

(6) bez [bɛs] 'lilac'   bz-y [bzɨ] 'nom. pl'
     sen [sɛn] 'sleep, n.'   sn-em [snɛm] 'instr. sg.'
     lew [lɛf] 'lion'   lw-y [lvɨ] 'nom. pl'
     den [dɛn] 'bottom, gen. pl.'   dn-o [dnɔ] 'nom. sg.'
     len [lɛn] 'linen'   ln-u [lnu] 'gen. sg.'
     wesz [vɛʃ] 'louse'   wsz-y [fʃɨ] 'nom. pl.'
     wieś [vʲɛɕ] 'village'   ws-i [fɕi] 'gen. sg.'
     cześć [tʃɛɕtɕ] 'honour'   czc-i [tʃtɕi] 'gen. sg.'
     mech [mɛx] 'moss'   mch-em [mxɛm] 'instr. sg.'
     ciem [tɕɛm] 'moth, gen. pl.'   ćm-a [tɕma] 'nom. sg.'
     łez [wɛs] 'tear, gen. pl.'   łz-y [wzɨ] 'nom. pl.'
     kiep [cɛp] 'halfwit'   kp-a [kpa] 'gen. sg.'
     szew [ʃɛf] 'seam'   szw-y [ʃfɨ] 'nom. pl.'
     pień [pʲɛɲ] 'stump'   pni-a [pɲa] 'gen. sg.'

ceł [tsɛw] 'customs duty, gen. pl.'   cł-o [tswɔ] 'nom. sg.'
giez [ɟɛs] 'gadfly'   gz-y [gzɨ] 'nom. pl.'

The examples—and also the alternations *leb* [wɛp] 'head' ~ *lba* [wba] 'gen. sg.', *dech* [dɛx] 'breath' ~ *tchu* [txu] 'gen. sg.', *pies* [pʲɛs] 'dog' ~ *psa* [psa] 'gen. sg.' above—are typical of the pattern where a vowel of the stem is deleted before an inflectional ending. Note that the left-hand column forms are syllabically totally uninteresting as they involve a single consonant in the onset; the word-final consonant, when single, invariably occupies the onset, too, and is licensed by the empty nucleus in accordance with the coda-licensing principle (Kaye 1990; Harris and Gussmann 1998, 2002). The right-hand-column words differ from these in having the [ɛ] vowel suppressed and in the final nucleus having a melody attached to it. The final melody represents some inflectional ending. Consider the representations *dech* ~ *tchu* (and disregard for the moment the voicing of the initial plosive):

(7)   O   N   O   N   O   N   O   N
      | | | | | | | |
      x   x   x   x   x   x   x   x
      | | | | | |
      d   ɛ   x   t   ɛ   x   u

The suppressed vowel is represented as delinked from its skeletal position and hence not pronounced. In terms of syllable structure both forms are identical; the same applies to all other words in (6). Much more significantly, the clusters that emerge with the suppression of the vowel are in reality spurious clusters; in fact they are single consonants associated with different onsets and separated by a nucleus. As such, the typically Polish initial sequences which either openly violate universal constraints on well-formed onsets, such as combinations of two obstruents [bz, ps, fs, fʃ, tʃtɕ, fɕ, kp, tx, ʃf, gz], or sequences whose status as a possible branching onset is suspect or dubious either because wrong consonants are combined (sequences of sonorants [ln]) or the order of the consonants is wrong (a sonorant followed by an obstruent [wb, mx, wz]), are eliminated with one fell swoop from the class of offending candidates. The simple reason for this is that they are not clusters or single onsets but two separate, one-consonant onsets which happen to be placed together by the suppression of the melody of the first nucleus.

The same mechanism allows us to account for some three-consonant sequences which emerge as a result of vowel suppression. Some examples follow:

(8)   krew [krɛf] 'blood'   krw-i [krf ʲi] 'gen. sg.'
      brew [brɛf] 'brow'   brw-i [brvʲi] 'gen. sg.'
      drew [drɛf] 'firewood, gen. pl.'   drw-a [drva] 'nom. pl.'
      sechł [sɛx(w)] 'he dried up'   schł-a [sxwa] 'she dried up'

Within GP, an onset can be maximally binary branching, therefore three consonants (understood as three melodies attached to skeletal positions) can never form an onset. Sequences such as those above, [krf ʲ, brvʲ, drv, sxw], by definition must be split up between at least two constituents. This theory-internal requirement is neatly confirmed by the existence of alternations with a vowel appearing within such three-member sequences so that we end up with a well-formed branching onset consisting of an obstruent and a sonorant [kr, br, dr] and another onset consisting of a single consonant; or, conversely, we have an onset consisting of a single consonant followed by a well-formed branching onset [s+ xw]. The three-member initial sequences are no more surprising than the unusual looking two-member units: they all arise out of a combination of two well-formed onsets.

The preceding observations lead to a conclusion that is seldom noted: word-initial consonant sequences cannot be identified with syllable onsets. This view runs against the traditional wisdom which sees the word-initial position as the prime manifestation of the syllable initial position, so whatever consonantal combination can be found initially must be an onset. GP categorically rejects this simple identification: while an onset of the syllable should be manifested at the beginning of the word, the reverse is not true (for examples see all the right-hand-column words above). The same rejection holds for word-final position: contrary to the traditional lore, word-final consonants or consonant sequences cannot be identified with consonantal codas (a position somewhat anticipated in the generative notion of extrasyllabic consonants); in fact, GP maintains that a word-final consonant is never a coda but either an onset or a coda–onset contact (Kaye 1990; Harris and Gussmann 1998, 2002). The syllabic level is constructed independently of other levels; as GP upholds, there is no a priori reason why the structure of a word should begin with an onset filled melodically rather than empty. If, additionally, empty categories are recognized as an integral part of linguistic (phonological) representations, then a word can begin with an empty onset followed by a filled nucleus, in the same way as it can begin with a filled onset followed by an empty nucleus. The former case is of course widely illustrated by words beginning with a vowel. We conclude that the existence of the vowel~zero alternation in Polish explains away a large number of consonant sequences that from the point of view of other languages may look implausible or downright impossible. The alternation makes the Polish onset look like the objects familiar from other, less syllabically exotic, languages.

The examples we provided above illustrate a situation where vowel suppression affects the first nucleus in a word, hence the heavy word-initial sequence. This was done for ease of exposition since a similar situation can be observed word-internally. Consider the following examples.

(9) oset [ɔsɛt] 'thistle'   ost-y [ɔstɨ] 'nom. pl.'
     ocet [ɔtsɛt] 'vinegar'   oct-u [ɔtstu] 'gen. sg.'
     chłopi-ec [xwɔpʲɛts] 'boy'   chłop-c-y [xwɔptsɨ] 'nom. pl.'
     żagiel [ʒaɟɛl] 'sail, n.'   żagl-e [ʒaglɛ] 'nom. pl.'
     paznokieć [paznɔcɛtɕ] 'nail'   paznokci-e [paznɔktɕɛ] 'nom. pl.'
     toreb [tɔrɛp] 'bag, gen. pl.'   torb-a [tɔrba] 'nom. sg.'

pozew [pɔzɛf] 'summons'   pozw-u [pɔzvu] 'gen. sg.'
szaniec [ʃaɲɛts] 'entrenchment'   szańc-e [ʃaɲtsɛ] 'nom. pl.'
najem [najɛm] 'hiring'   najm-u [najmu] 'gen. sg.'
bochen [bɔxɛn] 'loaf'   bochn-a [bɔxna] 'gen. sg.'
kropel [krɔpɛl] 'drop, gen. pl.'   kropl-a [krɔpla] 'nom. sg.'
wanien [vaɲɛn] 'tub, gen. pl.'   wann-a [vanna] 'nom. sg.'
udziec [udʑɛts] 'haunch, leg'   udźc-a [utɕtsa] 'gen. sg.'

These examples are not really different from the first set of word-initial
clusters produced by vowel suppression. From our point of view the existence
of the word-internal vowel~zero alternation achieves two objectives. For one
thing it eliminates the need for resyllabifications, even in those cases where a
resyllabification could produce a well-formed constituent: in *żagle* [ʒaglɛ] 'sail,
nom. pl.' the sequence [gl] is a possible onset with an obstruent preceding (being
head of) a non-homorganic sonorant. Since resyllabification is not a possibility
within our model, such ostensibly well-formed branching onsets have to continue
to be regarded as a sequence of two onsets with an intervening nucleus. We have
direct evidence for it in the form of the alternation: *żagiel* [ʒaɟɛl] 'nom. sg.'. At the
other end, some of the clusters that would arise could be neither a well-structured
branching onset nor a plausible coda–onset contact; a case in point is offered by
words like *octu* [ɔtstu] 'vinegar, gen. sg.', *udźca* [utɕtsa] 'haunch, gen. sg.', where
the [ts-t, tɕ-ts] combinations fail to meet conditions for either of the structures.
The ban against resyllabification disposes of such possible worries: both the
affricates [ts, tɕ] and the plosive [t] occupy the onset position in the nominative
and the oblique cases while the nucleus is filled or suppressed. Also, as above,
sequences of three consonants observe conditions on onsethood or on coda–
onset contacts. Consider:

(10)   marchew [marxɛf] 'carrot'   marchw-i [marxfʲi] 'gen. sg.'
       czerwiec [tʃɛrvʲɛts] 'June'   czerwc-a [tʃɛrftsa] 'gen. sg.'
       pluskiew [pluscɛf] 'bed bug, gen. pl.' pluskw-a [pluskfa] 'nom. sg.'
       cerkiew [tsɛrcɛf] 'Orthodox church' cerkw-i [tsɛrkfʲi] 'gen. sg.'

The right-hand column consonantal sequences observe the same syllabic affiliation as the left-hand ones. This can be made clear by the representations of the
nouns *marchew*, *marchwi*, where we suppress irrelevant details (such as voicing
and palatalization) but include a full structure of the rhyme.

(11)

As can be seen, syllabically the two forms do not differ. The differences lie in the melodies in that the alternating vowel is phonetically present in one of them, while the other contains an empty nucleus and an inflectional ending with a full vocalic melody.

In line with the picture sketched above, the vowel∼zero alternation provides a straightforward account of some of the unusual consonantal clusters found in Polish. It furthermore confirms the restricted structure of syllabic constituents: branching onsets and non-branching codas as the only possible consonant combinations. A crucial aspect of this approach to the syllabic organization is the claim that codas have to be licensed by onsets, hence word-final consonants cannot be codas but onsets, and as such they must be followed by a nuclear position with no melody attached to it (an empty nucleus). This particular claim will be shown to play a part in the formalization of the vowel∼zero regularity which so far has been referred to in an informal way.

5.2.3 Vowel∼zero alternations: determining the pattern

We pointed out above that the vowel [ɛ] in Polish is an ambiguous object, a *double agent* in the terminology of Gussmann (2002) in that it sometimes does and sometimes does not alternate with zero. The [ɛ] which is susceptible to alternations is not conditioned in any way by the phonological or morphological context—rather, this is an unpredictable property of individual morphemes and as such has to be included in the lexical specification of each item. There are two questions which have to be faced: how exactly does the alternating [ɛ] differ from the non-alternating one, and what controls the appearance and the suppression of the vowel. Ideally, the answer given to one question should facilitate or tally with that supplied to the other one.

The alternating vowel can be seen as unstable in that its presence or absence depends on what follows. A survey of the alternating forms shows that the vowel is suppressed when the following nucleus is filled by some melody and is phonetically present when the following nucleus has no melody attached to it, in other words, it is empty. A possible description of the alternation might involve a vocalic melody for [ɛ] which is lexically unattached—it is floating; when followed by another nucleus with no melody associated with it, this floating melody gets associated with the nuclear position. In other words we have a case of melody association:

(12) *Melody Association*
      Attach floating [ɛ] to the nucleus when the following nucleus has no melody attached to it.

Consider again the forms *dech, tchu* in a slightly more detailed way. After the operation of the morphology, which attaches the required inflectional endings, the two words may be envisaged as follows:

(13) O   N   O   N   O   N   O   N

```
(13)   O   N   O   N        O   N   O   N
       |   |   |   |        |   |   |   |
       x   x   x   x        x   x   x   x
       |       |            |       |   |
       d   ε   x            d   ε   x   u
```

Melody Association applies to the left-hand form since the floating vowel is followed by a melody-less nucleus, while it does not affect the right-hand one since the nucleus following the floating melody is filled. An unassociated melody is not pronounceable and can be regarded as eliminated or invisible to the phonology. Coupled with voicing assimilation this leads to representations such as those in (14).

```
(14)   O   N   O   N        O   N   O   N
       |   |   |   |        |   |   |   |
       x   x   x   x        x   x   x   x
       |   |   |            |       |   |
       d   ε   x            t   ε   x   u
```

These are syllabically identical but differ in melody association. The vowel–zero alternation pattern emerges thus as a result of associating a floating melody in a weak context, that is, before a following empty nucleus. In a strong context, before a nucleus filled by a vocalic melody, the association fails to take place.[1]

It should be stressed that the pattern of alternations holds not just for different inflectional cases of nominals but also for derivationally related forms. In (15) we offer several examples of the vowel~zero alternation in nouns or adjectives as contrasted with the absence of such direct alternations in related verbs.

(15)	(a) Noun		(b) Verb
	sen [sɛn] 'dream'	sn-u [snu] 'gen. sg'	śn-i-ć [ɕɲitɕ] 'dream, vb.'
	pełen [pɛwɛn] 'full'	pełn-a [pɛwna] 'fem.'	(na)pełn-i-ć [napɛwɲitɕ] 'fill'
	ceł [tsɛw] 'customs duty, gen. pl.'	cł-o [tswɔ] 'nom. sg.'	cl-i-ć [tslitɕ] 'impose duty'
	cześć [tʃɛɕtɕ] 'honour'	czc-i [tʃtɕi] 'gen. sg'	czc-i-ć [tʃtɕitɕ] 'vb.'
	kropel [krɔpɛl] 'drop, gen. pl.'	kropl-a [krɔpla] 'nom. sg.'	(s)kropl-i-ć [skrɔplitɕ] 'liquefy'

---

[1] The interpretation put forward here makes a certain tacit theoretical assumption, namely, that lexical representations of forms contain not only melodies but also that the melodies are associated to skeletal positions. This allows us to make a distinction between the stable [ɛ], which is associated to a position, and a fleeting [ɛ] which, while melodically identical, differs from the previous one in its failure to be associated. The need to incorporate skeletal positions into representation follows from the multi-tiered model of phonology and has been part of different traditions; this mechanism was originally employed to capture phonologically the distinction between long and short vowels and also between single and geminate consonants (Prince 1984).

błazen [bwazɛn]	błazn-a [bwazna]	błazn-ow-a-ć [bwaznɔvatɕ]
'clown'	'gen. sg.'	'act the fool'
		błaźn-i-ć [bwaʑɲitɕ]
		'make a fool'
szkieł [ʃcɛw] 'glass, gen. pl.'	szkł-o [ʃkwɔ] 'nom. sg.'	szkl-i-ć [ʃklitɕ] 'glaze'
bęben [bɛmbɛn] 'drum'	bębna [bɛmbna] 'gen. sg.'	bębn-i-ć [bɛmbɲitɕ] 'vb.'
pluskiew [pluscɛf]	pluskw-a [pluskfa]	(od)pluskw-i-ć [ɔtpluskfʲitɕ]
'bed bug, gen. pl.'	'nom. sg.'	'debug'

The verbs in the right-hand column show no traces of the floating vowel in any of their forms because in every case this vowel is followed by an associated vowel in the next nucleus, which represents the suffix of some verbal category of inflectional ending. In this way the conditions for Melody Association are not met and the root vowel has no chance to get attached. The phonological presence of the floating vowel, and hence also the absence of consonant only roots, is confirmed through existing alternations involving other lexical categories. It should also be pointed out that the interpretation of the imperative allomorphy discussed in Chapter 4 is confirmed here: the allomorph -ij argued to be attached when the final nucleus of the base is not filled is found with most verbs in the list at (6): *śnij* [ɕɲij] 'dream', *napełnij* [napɛwɲij] 'fill', *clij* [tslij] 'impose duty', *czcij* [tʃtɕij] 'honour', *skroplij* [skrɔplij] 'liquefy', *błaźnij* [bwaʑɲij] 'make a fool',[2] *szklij* [ʃklij] 'glaze', *bębnij* [bɛmbɲij] 'drum', *odpluskwij* [ɔtpluskfʲij] 'de-bug'.

Derivationally related words display a characteristic pattern of alternations: the vowel [ɛ] appearing before the final empty nucleus is suppressed when the suffix begins with a full vowel. It makes no difference whether the emerging category is a verb, as in the case just illustrated, or some other part of speech. Consider more examples of the morphological relatedness accompanied by the vowel~zero alternation:

(16) pies [pʲɛs] 'dog'   ps-a [psa] 'gen. sg.'
                                            ps-ina [pɕina] 'expr.'
                                            psi-ak [pɕak] 'puppy'
      łez [wɛs] 'tear, gen. pl.'   łz-a [wza] 'nom. sg.'
                                            łz-aw-y [wzavɨ] 'maudlin'
                                            łz-ow-y [wzɔvɨ] 'lacrimal'
                                            łz-aw-i-ć [wzavʲitɕ] 'water (of eyes), vb.'

---

[2] Note that in *blazn-owa-ć* [bwaznɔvatɕ] 'act the fool', based on the same noun, but with a different verbalizing suffix -*ow*- [ɔv], the floating vowel in the nominal base is not the final nucleus of the stem, hence the imperative *blaznuj* [bwaznuj].

krew [krɛf] 'blood'

krw-i [kr̥fʲi] 'gen. sg.'
krw-aw-y [kr̥favɨ] 'bloody'
krw-ink-a [kr̥fʲinka] 'blood cell'
krw-o-tok [kr̥fɔtɔk] 'haemorrhage'
krwi-ak [kr̥fʲak] 'heamatoma'
krw-ist-y [kr̥fʲistɨ] 'blood-red'
krw-aw-i-ć [kr̥favʲitɕ] 'bleed'

len [lɛn] 'linen'

ln-u [lnu] 'gen. sg.'
lni-an-y [lɲanɨ] 'adj.'
lni-ar-sk-i [lɲarsci] 'of linen industry'

cegieł [tsɛjɛw] 'brick, gen. pl.'

cegł-a [tsɛɡwa] 'nom. sg.'
cegl-an-y [tsɛɡlanɨ] 'of brick, adj.'
cegl-ast-y [tsɛɡlastɨ] 'brick-red'

pereł [pɛrɛw] 'pearl, gen. pl.'

perł-a [pɛrwa] 'nom. sg.'
perl-ist-y [perlistɨ] 'pearly'
perł-ow-y [pɛrwɔvɨ] 'of pearl'

cukier [tsucɛr] 'sugar'

cukr-u [tsukru] 'gen. sg.'
cukr-ow-y [tsukrɔvɨ] 'sugary'
cukrz-yc-a [tsukʃɨtsa] 'diabetes'
cukrz-yk [tsukʃɨk] 'diabetic, n.'

nikiel [ɲicɛl] 'nickel'

nikl-u [ɲiklu] 'gen. sg.'
nikl-ow-y [ɲiklɔvɨ] 'adj.'
nikl-ow-a-ć [ɲiklɔvatɕ]
'nickel-plate, vb.'

plotek [plɔtɛk] 'rumour, gen. pl.'

plotk-a [plɔtka] 'nom. sg.'
plotk-ow-a-ć [plɔtkɔvatɕ] 'vb.'
plotk-arz [plɔtkaʃ] 'a gossip'

poseł [pɔsɛw] 'deputy'

posł-a [pɔswa] 'gen. sg.'
posł-ank-a [pɔswanka] 'woman deputy'
posł-ow-a-ć [pɔswɔvatɕ] 'be a deputy'

więzień [vʲɛʲʑɛɲ] 'prisoner'

więźni-a [vʲɛʲʑɲa] 'gen. sg.'
więźni-arsk-i [vʲɛʲʑɲarsci]
'prison-related'
więźni-ark-a [vʲɛʲʑɲarka] 'prisoner van'

walec [valɛts] 'cylinder'

walc-a [valtsa] 'gen. sg.'
walc-ow-at-y [valtsɔvatɨ] 'cylindrical'
walc-ow-a-ć [valtsɔvatɕ] 'roll'

Polish derivational morphology is replete with examples like these—they point to the reality of the floating vowel and its regular behaviour when followed directly by a nucleus with a filled melody. The derivative can be quite complex; consider here the imperative *krw-aw* [kr̥faf] 'bleed' based on the noun *krew* [krɛf] 'blood' with a floating root vowel; the noun forms the base for the adjective *krw-aw-y* [kr̥favɨ] 'bloody' which in turn feeds verb formation yielding *krw-aw-i-ć* [kr̥favʲit͡ɕ] 'bleed'. The floating vowel of the root noun is irrelevant to the imperative allomorphy since it is the *final* nucleus that determines it. To see this, consider the representation of *krw-aw* [kr̥faf]:

(17)

Since the first nucleus is followed by an associated nucleus, its vowel remains unattached. The imperative allomorph is zero because the final vowel of the base is the attached [a] rather than the floating vowel.

The suffixes illustrated above all begin with a full vowel. Consider now several suffixes beginning with a consonant. Below we present bases with an alternating vowel which are combined with consonant-initial suffixes: *-nik, -n-y, -nic-a, -niak, -sk-i/-ck-i, -stw-o/-(ni)ctw-o*.

(18) sen [sɛn] 'dream'   sn-y [snɨ] 'nom. pl.'
                                   sen-n-y [sɛnnɨ] 'sleepy'
                                   sen-nik [sɛnɲik] 'dream-book'

      cukier [tsucɛr] 'sugar'   cukr-u [tsukru] 'gen. sg.'
                                   cukier-nik [tsucɛrɲik] 'confectioner'
                                   cukier-nic-a [tsucɛrɲitsa] 'sugar bowl'
                                   cukier-nictw-o [tsucɛrɲitstfɔ]
                                   'confectionery'

      dzień [d͡ʑɛɲ] 'day'   dn-i [dɲa] 'gen. pl.'
                                   dzien-ny [d͡ʑɛnnɨ] 'daily'
                                   dzien-nik [d͡ʑɛnɲik] 'diary'
                                   dzien-nik-arz [d͡ʑɛnɲikaʃ] 'journalist'

      piekieł [pʲɛcɛw] 'hell, gen. pl.'   piekł-o 'nom. sg.'
                                   piekiel-nik [pʲɛcɛlɲik] 'spitfire'
                                   piekiel-nic-a [pʲɛcɛlɲitsa] 'battleaxe'
                                   piekiel-n-y [pʲɛcɛlnɨ] 'of hell'

      chrzest [xʃɛst] 'baptism'   chrzt-u [xʃtu] 'gen. sg.'
                                   chrzest-n-y [xʃɛstnɨ] 'adj.'
                                   chrześni-ak [xʃɛɕɲak] 'god child'

      wieś [vʲɛɕ] 'village'   ws-i [fɕi] 'gen. sg.'
                                   wieś-niak [vʲɛɕɲak] 'villager'

      okien [ɔcɛn] 'window, gen. pl.'   okn-o [ɔknɔ] 'nom. sg.'
                                   okien-n-y [ɔcɛnnɨ] 'adj.'
                                   okien-nic-a [ɔcɛnɲitsa] 'window shutter'

poseł [pɔsɛw] 'deputy'   posł-a [pɔswa] 'gen. sg.'
                                    posel-stw-o [pɔsɛlstfɔ] 'mission'
                                    posel-sk-i [pɔsɛlsci] 'parliamentary'
jeniec [jɛɲɛts] 'captive'   jeńc-a [jɛɲtsa] 'gen. sg.'
                                    jenie-ck-i [jɛɲɛtsci] 'adj.'
                                    jenie-ctw-o [jɛɲɛtstfɔ] 'captivity'

In all instances where the suffix begins with a phonetic consonant, the floating vowel of the base is phonetically realized. If we are to take seriously the formulation of Melody Association as given above, this must mean that the nucleus with the floating vowel is followed by one with no melody attached to it. There are a few ways in which this conclusion can be translated into a morphological statement. One is to claim that a consonant-initial suffix when attached to a consonant final base is invariably separated from it by an empty nucleus. This empty nucleus would constitute the context for Melody Association. Alternatively we could claim that the suffixes all begin with an empty nucleus, there being no—or very few—truly consonant-initial suffixes. With either of these assumptions a sequence of a floating vowel and a following empty nucleus would result in melody attachment. Consider the representation of *senny cukiernik* 'sleepy confectioner' (with palatalization relations omitted):

(19) O   N   O   N   O   N
      | | | | | |
      x   x   x   x   x   x
      | | | |
      s   ɛ   n   n   ɨ

      O   N   O   N   O   N   O   N   O   N
      | | | | | | | | | |
      x   x   x   x   x   x   x   x   x   x
      | | | | | | |
      ts u   c   ɛ   r   ɲ   i   k

The unassociated melody in both words is followed by an empty nucleus, hence association must be established. The middle nucleus in the adjective and the final one in the noun, being empty, remain without any phonetic content. In this way the fact that bases with a floating vowel always end up attaching the vowel before a consonantal suffix is shown not to follow from the consonantality of the suffix: it is difficult to see any rational connection between the pronounceability of a vocalic melody and the presence of a consonant in the following suffix.[3] On our interpretation it is a sequence of two unfilled nuclei that requires a repair strategy: in accordance with Melody Association when the first nucleus contains a floating

---

[3] It is worth noting that the addition of a consonant-initial suffix does not lead to a vowel splitting up genuine consonantal clusters, that is, adjacent consonantal melodies. The vowel emerges only when the base displays alternations of the familiar type; otherwise, when a cluster-final base precedes a consonant-initial suffix, we end up with a heavy cluster: *skarb* [skarp] 'treasure'+ *-nik* yields *skarbnik* [skarbɲik] 'treasurer' and never *skarebnik* [skarɛbɲik]. For more examples see Gussmann (1980a: 32–3).

melody, an association is established between the melody and the skeletal position. The phonetic pattern that emerges is due to internuclear relations. More evidence for the internuclear relation will transpire from the behaviour of the suffix -*ek*, to which we now turn.

5.2.4 *The suffix* -ek *again*

The morpheme -*ek* is described for short as the diminutive suffix, even though it has a number of distinct functions. We will not be concerned with its semantics but rather with the patterns of vowel~zero alternations that it displays.

The nominal suffix appears in three genders but it starts with the floating vowel which emerges as predicted before a following empty nucleus. Consider examples of nouns in the three genders:

(20) dom [dɔm] 'house, masc.'
      dom-ek [dɔmɛk] 'dim.'   dom-k-i [dɔmci] 'nom. pl.'
      skał-a [skawa] 'rock, fem.'
      skał-ek [skawɛk] 'dim. gen. pl.'   skał-k-a [skawka] 'nom. sg.'
      koł-o [kɔwɔ] 'wheel, neut.'
      kół-ek [kuwɛk] 'dim. gen. pl.'   kół-k-o [kuwkɔ] 'nom. sg.'

As can be seen, the pattern of alternations is exactly as predicted, while the differences arise because the different paradigms have distinct inflectional endings; for instance, a zero ending (i.e. an empty nucleus) tends to appear in the nominative singular of masculine nouns and the genitive plural of feminine and neuter nouns. It should be understood that when the suffix -*ek* is evoked, it is the pattern which is relevant rather than the gender of the noun to which the suffix is attached. The representation of the diminutive suffix is then:

(21) N   O   N
      | | |
      x   x   x
            |
      ɛ   k

Melody Association links the floating melody with the skeletal position. This is also the representation of the suffix in cases where the inflectional ending is zero (i.e. nom. sg. masc., gen. pl. fem. and neut.). With the inflectional ending being -*a*, for example, the representation remains intact at the syllabic and skeletal levels:

(22) N   O   N
      | | |
      x   x   x
            | |
      ɛ   k   a

This time, however, the floating melody is not followed by an empty nucleus so it fails to get attached and is not audible.

A novel situation arises when a base containing a floating vowel is combined with the diminutive suffix. A case in point is the noun *pies* [pʲɛs] 'dog' whose nom. pl. *ps-y* [psɨ], shows the regular floating vowel pattern. If we now combine this noun with the diminutive suffix in the nominative singular and the nominative plural, we end up with the following representations (irrelevant details omitted):

(23)
```
 O    N    O    N    O    N
 |    |    |    |    |    |
 x    x    x    x    x    x
 |    |    |    |    |
 pʲ   ɛ    s    ɛ    k

 O    N    O    N    O    N
 |    |    |    |    |    |
 x    x    x    x    x    x
 |    |    |    |    |    |
 pʲ   ɛ    s    ɛ    k    i
```

In the singular, where we have two floating melodies followed by an empty nucleus, they both get attached, hence *pies-ek* [pʲɛsɛk]. In the plural they are followed by a filled nucleus so only the first is pronounced: *pies-k-i* [pʲɛsci]. The plural situation is exactly what we expect: the second floating nucleus does not meet the conditions for Melody Association while the first one does. In the singular the reasons for both floating melodies to be attached are less clear. Before proposing a solution, let us consider a situation where we have three floating vowels in a row: as it happens, Polish admits a doubling of diminutive suffixes so 'a very small dog' is *pies-ecz-ek* [pʲɛsɛtʃɛk] in the singular and *pies-ecz-k-i* [pʲɛsɛtʃci] in the plural.[4] Consider the representations in (24):

(24)
```
 O    N    O    N    O    N    O    N
 |    |    |    |    |    |    |    |
 x    x    x    x    x    x    x    x
 |    |    |    |    |    |    |
 pʲ   ɛ    s    ɛ    tʃ   ɛ    k

 O    N    O    N    O    N    O    N
 |    |    |    |    |    |    |    |
 x    x    x    x    x    x    x    x
 |    |    |    |    |    |    |    |
 pʲ   ɛ    s    ɛ    tʃ   ɛ    k    i
```

In the singular all three floating melodies are attached, in the plural only the first two. Without offering the actual proof we can be confident that any iterative

---

[4] The morphophonological palatalization of the velar in the first suffix is discussed in Ch. 4.

mechanism would be doomed to failure since it should produce an alternating pattern. The regularity we observe seems quite simple: a floating vowel is attached unless it is immediately followed by a filled nucleus. This translates into a simple algorithm for Melody Association: attach the floating melody *unless the next nucleus* contains an attached melody; all melodies meeting the condition are identified in representations such as the ones above and the linking is carried out simultaneously. No iteration is allowed, hence no interaction between consecutive stages can take place, if only because there are no stages, consecutive or otherwise.[5]

The suffix *-ek* confirms the fundamental insight of the model we have adopted in our description, namely, the non-derivational nature of phonological relations; it is not the case that one application of a regularity creates the context for a successive application of either the same or a different regularity. Phonology interprets representations and whatever is significant phonologically is not derived, produced, or processed by lexical or cyclic rules, but is statically available 'all the time'. An interpreted representation shows all the phonological relations and regularities—in other words, whatever is phonological can be read off the representations without underlying, intermediate and derived stages. The indirect conclusion is that Melody Association is a phonological regularity, performing a phonological operation—linking a melody with a skeletal position—in a phonologically defined environment (before a melodically empty nucleus). The conclusion can be upheld only if appropriate morphophonological assumptions are made. As will be shown below, vowel~zero alternations are no monolith but need to be seen as emerging in part out of morphophonology and the lexicon. Before considering these aspects of the vowel~zero alternation we need to concentrate on other consonantal clusters for which no account along the lines adopted above can be easily envisaged. The theoretical issue bearing on it is the existence of empty nuclei—nuclei without any melody—floating or attached.

5.3 EMPTY NUCLEI AND HEAVY CONSONANTAL CLUSTERS

Our discussion of the vowel~zero alternations points to the existence of two types of nuclei without an associated melody. On the one hand there are nuclei with a floating melody, which can be attached or not depending on the shape of

[5] The ban on iteration allows the most direct account of forms containing more than one floating nucleus. Given a representation of *pieseczek* as [pʲEsEtʃEkø] (where E stands for a floating melody and ø denotes a domain-final empty nucleus), a leftward iterative application of Melody Association would yield *[pʲɛstʃɛk]; to be in accordance with the facts the application would have to be rightward. Directionality specification would thus have to be included in the formulation of the regularity, a step we regard as unnecessarily enriching the power of the model reminiscent of rule ordering. The mode of accounting for the vowel~zero alternations adopted above goes back to a proposal made within a very different framework by Anderson (1974). For earlier ways of handling the alternation in the context of the historical predecessors of Melody Association, see Isačenko (1970). Gussmann and Kaye (1993) propose an account which crucially depends on domain structures.

the following nucleus; on the other hand there are nuclei without any melody at all and these always remain empty. A case in point illustrating the latter type are the domain-final nuclei: these not only license the word-final onset but also create the context for the vowel~zero alternation, as we have seen. The evidence for such truly empty nuclei is much greater than this. Polish inalterable consonantal clusters supply ample evidence.

We noted above our rejection of the traditional view, which identifies word positions with syllabic constituents: it is not the case that a consonantal sequence appearing at the beginning of the word is necessarily an onset; even worse, a consonant cluster word-finally is never a coda. This follows from our assumptions about syllabic constituency (Kaye, Lowenstamm, and Vergnaud 1990; Kaye 1990):

- branching onsets must conform to complexity conditions with the governor, or head, being more complex than the governee or dependent;
- branching onsets can be maximally binary;
- onsets must be licensed by nuclei;
- codas must be licensed by following onsets.

These conditions not only rule out three consonants in the onset but equally they disallow, for example, sequences consisting just of obstruents or just of sonorants there. Such sequences do appear quite frequently word-initially in Polish, both when it comes to exceeding two consonants and to admitting sequences barred by the constraints. In the preceding sections we showed how the existence of the vowel~zero alternation removes a number of such cases from the potential offending forms: *krw-i* [krfʲi] 'blood, gen. sg.' has a floating melody after the first two consonants (*krew* [krɛf] 'nom. sg.'), impossible onsets of two obstruents (*tch-u* [txu] 'breath, gen. sg.'), of two sonorants (*ln-u* [lnu] 'linen, gen. sg.'), or a sonorant followed by an obstruent (*lb-a* [wba] 'head, gen. sg.') all turn out to be sequences of two non-branching onsets (*dech* [dɛx], *len* [lɛn], *leb* [wɛp] 'nom. sg.'). Superficial violations of syllable-structure constraints are nothing but a mechanical consequence of the vowel~zero regularity. If empty nuclei are taken seriously as having a genuine role to play in the structure of the language, then they can be seen at work in admitting ostensible departures from what is syllabically expected or admissible. Let us consider the consonant combinations found at the beginning of the word from the point of view of the syllabic well-formedness and the evidence they supply for empty nuclei.

Initially, Polish admits up to four consonants, which uncontroversially cannot make up single onsets. Two consonants can form a branching onset if the first of them is an obstruent, preferably a plosive, and the second a sonorant, preferably a lateral or the trill. The lateral can be phonetically either [l] or the semivowel [w], as generally accepted in this book. Thus we find:

(25)   plac [plats] 'square'   płacz [pwatʃ] 'weeping'
        blisk-o [bliskɔ] 'close by'   błąd [bwɔnt] 'error'

prąd [prɔnt] 'current'   bram-a [brama] 'gate'
tlen [tlɛn] 'oxygen'   dla [dla] 'for'
tłams-i-ć [twamɕitɕ] 'suppress'   dłoń [dwɔɲ] 'palm'
trąd [trɔnt] 'leprosy'   drog-a [drɔga] 'road'
klucz [klutʃ] 'key'   gleb-a [glɛba] 'soil'
kłopot [kwɔpɔt] 'trouble'   głos [gwɔs] 'voice'
krow-a [krɔva] 'cow'   grób [grup] 'grave'
chleb [xlɛp] 'bread'   chłod-n-y [xwɔdnɨ] 'cool'
chrom-y [xrɔmɨ] 'lame'

The status of obstruent plus nasal sequences is more difficult to define. Theoretically, it is sometimes claimed that nasals are too complex to be governed by obstruents or that the complexity curve is not steep enough for them to form a governing domain. The Polish evidence partly corroborates these positions. For one thing, there are no bilabial plosives followed by a bilabial nasal, which could perhaps be due to a homorganicity ban disallowing such sequences. Additionally, there are very few cases of other obstruents plus nasals:

(26)   dmuch-a-ć [dmuxatɕ] 'blow'   kmin-ek [kmʲinɛk] 'cumin'
       kmieć [kmʲɛtɕ] 'peasant'   knu-ć [knutɕ] 'plot, vb.'
       kniaź [kɲaɕ] 'prince'   knot [knɔt] 'wick'
       gmach [gmax] 'building'   gmer-a-ć [gmɛratɕ] 'fumble'
       gnat [gnat] 'bone'   gniew [gɲɛf] 'anger'
       gniazd-o [gɲazdɔ] 'nest'   chmur-a [xmura] 'cloud'
       chmiel [xmʲɛl] 'hop, n.'

A few more examples could be added but their number, while not exactly negligible, is not impressive, either. Some combinations simply do not appear at all, e.g. [tm, xn], even though no homorganicity ban could be brought to bear here. In a few cases with a superficial obstruent–nasal sequence there is evidence for the vowel~zero alternation, e.g. *tn-ę* [tnɛ] 'I cut' ~ *cię-t-y* [tɕɛntɨ] 'past part.', *dn-o* [dnɔ] 'bottom'~ *den* [dɛn], 'gen. pl.'. Thus we might uphold the view that nasals cannot appear as dependents in branching onsets, which would mean that in sequences without alterations the nasal occupies an onset separate from the preceding obstruent in the same way as it does with vowel~zero alternations.

There is a whole group of initial sequences starting with a segment of the 's-group'—[s, z, ɕ, ʑ, tɕ, dʑ, ʃ, ʒ, tʃ, dʒ]—and also the affricates [ts, dz]. As for the s-sounds, it is generally assumed within GP that these cannot be heads of branching onsets (Kaye 1991/2; Harris 1994; Gussmann 2002),[6] hence they are either rhymal complements (codas) or simplex onsets. The

---

[6] The special status of the s-group of sounds within Polish—and Indo-European in general—was stressed by Kuryłowicz (1952).

latter situation can easily be defended when vowel~zero alternations occur; see (27).

(27) st-o [stɔ] 'hundred'   set [sɛt] 'gen. pl.'
      wiosn-a [vʲɔsna] 'spring'   wiosen [vʲɔsɛn] 'gen. pl.'
      szł-a [ʃwa] 'she went'   szedł [ʃɛt(w̥)] 'he went'
      łyż-a [wiʒva] 'skate'   łyżew [wiʒɛf] 'gen. pl.'
      błazn-a [bwazna] 'fool, gen. sg.'   błazen [bwazɛn] 'nom. sg.'
      ćm-a [tɕma] 'moth'   ciem [tɕɛm] 'gen. pl.'
      dn-i [dɲi] 'day, nom. pl.'   dzień [dʑɛɲ] 'nom. sg.'
      cł-o [tswɔ] 'duty'   ceł [tsɛw] 'gen. pl.'
      beczk-a [bɛtʃka] 'barrel'   beczek [bɛtʃɛk] 'gen. pl.'

When no alternations are available, all such combinations are inherently ambiguous and may be interpreted either as coda–onset contacts or as onset sequences. Consider more examples of such sequences:

(28) słoń [swɔɲ] 'elephant'   slawist-a [slavʲista] 'Slavist'
      snop [snɔp] 'sheaf'   smut-n-y [smutnɨ] 'sad'
      srok-a [srɔka] 'magpie'   stok [stɔk] 'slope'
      spor-y [spɔrɨ] 'sizeable'   skał-a [skawa] 'rock, n.'

      złot-y [zwɔtɨ] 'golden'   zlew [zlɛf] 'sink, n.'
      znak [znak] 'sign'   zmian-a [zmʲana] 'change, n.'
      zrąb [zrɔmp] 'hem, n.'   zdoln-y [zdɔlnɨ] 'capable'
      zbój [zbuj] 'thug'   zgon [zgɔn] 'demise'

      ślad [ɕlat] 'trace'   śmiał-y [ɕmʲawɨ] 'bold'
      śnieg [ɕɲɛk] 'snow, n.'   środ-a [ɕrɔda] 'Wednesday'
      śpiew-a-ć [ɕpʲɛvatɕ] 'sing'   ździr-a [ʑdʑira] 'tart, n.'
      źródł-o [ʑrudwɔ] 'source'   ćpun [tɕpun] 'junkie'
      ćm-i-ć [tɕmʲitɕ] 'smoke, vb.'   dźg-a-ć [dʑgatɕ] 'stab, vb.'
      czter-y [tʃtɛrɨ] 'four'   czka-wk-a [tʃkafka] 'hiccups'
      człon [tʃwɔn] 'member'   dżdż-yst-y [dʒdʒɨstɨ] 'rainy'

The amount of lexical support for individual combinations is quite varied, and declining with the complexity of the consonant. The palatalized, palatal, and the affricates appear in relatively few combinations while the plain fricatives [s, z] are quite frequent. As noted above the dental fricative—and, by extension, the s-group of consonants—is assumed to be universally unable to govern, in other words to be onset head. For this reason it can be either in the coda and licensed by the following consonant (the onset) or both elements of the consonant combination appear in separate onsets. Consider the alternative representations of the noun *słoń* 'elephant':

(29) (a)

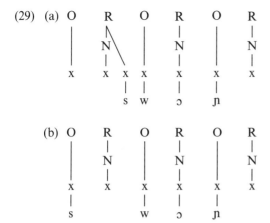

(b)

In the first representation, (29a), both the first onset and the first nucleus have no melody attached while the fricative forms a contact with the following onset. Empty nuclei—just as empty onsets—remain phonetically silent. The alternative representation, (29b), separates the fricative and the lateral with an empty nucleus, which likewise remains uninterpreted phonetically.

A question which must be asked is whether there is any evidence that could help us choose between the two alternatives. No simple answer seems available in view of the absence of direct alternations. However, the existence of the relevant alternations elsewhere in the language (see (27)) might in itself argue in favour of the two-onset interpretation. Additionally, the coda–onset contact would suggest a situation where a weak consonant, such as a sonorant, can govern a relatively stronger one, such as an obstruent; while this cannot be ruled out in advance, it certainly does not strengthen the case. We would also have to question the legitimacy of the structure with an empty onset and an empty nucleus, since this would theoretically allow words consisting of sequences of such empty constituents, a patently absurd conclusion. Finally there are some consonant combinations which must be split between successive onsets, e.g. [dʐg] in *dźg-a-ć* 'stab', since it is implausible to assume that a strong and complex consonant such as [dʐ] could be governed by a simplex such as [g]. All these pieces taken together seem to provide some support in favour of a two-onset solution, so we will adopt a position that a structure like (29a) should be either disallowed, or at least disfavoured (see also Rowicka 2001).

Words like *dźg-a-ć* [dʐgatɕ] 'stab' illustrate a frequent instance of melodic adjacency of consonants which cannot form a branching onset and are unlikely to form a coda-onset contact. Since these two situations exhaust the syllabic relations that two neighbouring consonants can contract, the recognition of an intervening empty nucleus brings such forms into conformity with cases of vowel~zero alternations and at the same time makes Polish consonantal clusters well-behaved phonological objects, and, therefore, relatively uninteresting as potential violators of universal principles. Where Polish departs from other languages is in admitting a more generous use of empty nuclei. As another illustration of this possibility, consider the representation of the word *ptak* [ptak] 'bird' with the unusual-looking initial consonantal sequence.

(30)
```
O   N   O   N   O   N
|   |   |   |   |   |
x   x   x   x   x   x
|       |   |   |
p       t   a   k
```

The first and the last nucleus have no melody attached to them, so they remain phonetically inaudible. Syllabically, however, the word does not differ from the totally unremarkable word *potok* [pɔtɔk] 'stream'.

Below we offer examples of such two-onset initial sequences where the presence of an empty nucleus renders them an impossible surface constituent.

(31) (a) *Two obstruents*

psot-a [psɔta] 'prank'   bzyk-a-ć [bzɨkatɕ] 'bonk, vb.'
ptyś [ptɨɕ] 'choux'   tk-acz [tkatʃ] 'weaver'
db-a-ć [dbatɕ] 'care, vb.'   tchórz [txuʃ] 'coward'
czter-y [tʃterɨ] 'four'   Tczew [ttʃɛf/tʃtʃɛf] 'place name'
kto [ktɔ] 'who'   gdy [gdɨ] 'when'
ksyw-a [ksɨva] 'nickname'   gzyms [gzɨms] 'mantelpiece'
księg-a [kɕɛŋga] 'book'   gz-i-ć [gʑitɕ] 'fornicate'
kp-i-ć [kpʲitɕ] 'deride'   gbur [gbur] 'boor'
chc-e [xtsɛ] '(s)he wants'   chci-e-ć [xtɕɛtɕ] 'want, vb.'
czcz-y [tʃtʃʃɨ] 'futile'   dżdżownic-a [dʒdʒɔvɲitsa] 'earthworm'

(b) *Sonorant+obstruent*

lż-y-ć [lʒɨtɕ] 'slander, vb.'   łg-a-ć [wgatɕ] 'lie, vb.'
łż-e [wʒɛ] '(s)he lies'   łk-a-ć [wkatɕ] 'sob, vb.'
msz-a [mʃa] 'Mass'   mż-awk-a [mʒafka] 'drizzle'
mgiel-n-y [mʲɛlnɨ] 'misty'   rtęć [rtɛɲtɕ] 'mercury'
rdest [rdɛst] 'knot-grass'   rdzeń [rdzɛɲ] 'root'
rż-e-ć [rʒɛtɕ] 'neigh'

(c) *Sonorant+sonorant*

młod-y [mwɔdɨ] 'young'   mlek-o [mlɛkɔ] 'milk'
mnog-i [mnɔɟi] 'plural'   mnich [mɲix] 'monk'
mrówk-a [mrufka] 'ant'

The examples lead to several observations. The amount of lexical support for the various consonant sequences differs, which is hardly surprising. Sequences of initial obstruents, while not confirmed lexically for every conceivable combination, seem not only generally acceptable but also largely unconstrained. This can be seen in the fact that most of the combinations allow their mirror-image reflections—e.g. [tk - kt, ps - sp, bz - zb]—and even in cases where no words exist, the reversed combination seems possible, as in [dg]. The possibility of combining consonants is constrained by the phonology in that, for example, obstruents differing in voicing are not admissible *[bt] (for reasons, see Ch. 7) or obstruents displaying palatalization combinations which are not tolerated in the language, e.g. *[ct, pʲs] (see Ch. 3). The possibility of combining obstruents word-initially is a simple reflection of the existence of nuclei without melodies; the syllabic well-formedness of a word is ensured by assigning each obstruent to a separate onset.[7]

The initial sequences of a sonorant and an obstruent show two remarkable gaps, namely, the sonorant cannot be the palatal glide [j] or the dental nasal [n]. The disallowed sonorant sequences include also [r], which means that they can only start with [m]. With the nasals it is additionally striking that no homorganic clusters are allowed. These facts should presumably yield an insightful phonological analysis: we want to know whether the possibility of an initial [mg] or [mӡ] and the absence of [mp] or [nd] is a lexical accident or whether this derives from some systematic principles (see Gussmann and Cyran 1998). At this stage, apart from noting the facts, we are unable to supply a non-ad hoc account.

The essence of the above account reduces to a claim that two consonant sequences initially are either well-formed branching onsets, in a nutshell combinations of an obstruent and a sonorant [tr, kl, fl,...], or combinations of non-branching onsets separated by an empty nucleus. As an illustration, consider the *wh*-pronoun *gdy* [gdɨ] 'when' and contrast it with the presumably related question form *kiedy* [cɛdɨ] 'when':

(32)
```
     O    N    O    N         O    N    O    N
     |    |    |    |         |    |    |    |
     x    x    x    x         x    x    x    x
     |         |    |         |    |    |    |
     g         d    ɨ         k    ɛ    d    ɨ
```

Syllabically the two forms are identical; they differ in that the first has an empty first nucleus, whereas the second has the melody [ɛ] attached to it. Since empty nuclei correspond to phonetic silence, the two consonants in the onsets end up adjacent and consequently have to be uniform in voicing with the voice of the second onset determining the first one (as discussed in Ch. 7). In the second word, the front vowel [ɛ], separating the two onsets, produces palatalization effects in the first one, as discussed in Chapter 3.

---

[7] There are major theoretical issues involved in this proposal but their extended discussion goes beyond the scope of a descriptive study. In brief, the question is whether syllabification of a linguistic form is segment-driven or whether it is given in advance (underlying, unpredictable). If the former or dominant view is taken to be legitimate we must conclude that empty nuclei—unlike floating melodies—are not part of the lexical representation of words but rather that they are introduced through syllabification: given an initial melodic sequence like /kp/, the syllabification algorithm must introduce a nucleus between the two consonants since they obviously fail to meet the criteria for a branching onset. On this view, syllabification is the construction of onsets and rhymes on the basis of the existing melody units, which constitute the irreducible minimum of linguistic form.

Empty nuclei differ crucially from floating melodies: while the latter correspond to a phonetic melody in specified contexts, empty nuclei remain always
empty and are never turned into sound. The two types of entity can co-exist
within words, a case best illustrated by the adjective supplied above as an instance
of a sonorant plus obstruent initial sequence: *mgiel-n-y* [mɟɛlni] 'misty'. The
vowel [ɛ] in the word is a realization of the floating melody, as evidenced by the
derivational base noun *mgl-a* [mgwa] 'mist'– *mgiel* [mɟɛw] 'gen. pl.'; the adjectival
suffix *-n-y* starts with an empty nucleus, as argued in an earlier part of this
chapter. Consider first the representations of the two forms of the noun shown
in (33):

(33)
O	N	O	N	O	N		O	N	O	N	O	N
x	x	x	x	x	x		x	x	x	x	x	x
m		g	ɛ	w	a		m		g	ɛ	w	

In the nom. sg. *mgl-a* [mgwa] the floating melody remains unattached because
the context for its attachment—the presence of another unattached melody in the
following nucleus—is not met. The context for melody attachment is met in
the gen. pl. *mgiel* where the inflectional ending has an empty nucleus as its
exponent; additionally, palatalization effects set in as expected—recall that
the suffix *-n-y* carries the diacritic <PR4>. Consider now the derived adjective
mgiel-n-y (misty):

(34)
O	N	O	N	O	N	O	N
x	x	x	x	x	x	x	x
m		g	ɛ	l		n	ɨ

Here the floating [ɛ] is followed by an empty nucleus, so it is attached to its
skeletal point; the two empty nuclei remain silent phonetically, hence with
palatalization of the velar the word appears as [mɟɛlni].

A different adjectival derivative from the same base allows us to launch the
issue of three- and four-consonant-initial sequences. The suffix is *-ist-y* and the
adjective is *mgl-ist-y* [mglistɨ] 'misty', with the representations as in (35).

(35)
O	N	O	N	O	N	O	N	O	N[8]
x	x	x	x	x	x	x	x	x	x
m		g	ɛ	l	i	s		t	ɨ

---

[8] The consonant [s] in this representation could be placed within the rhyme with the preceding vowel
and be itself licensed by the plosive of the final onset; since nothing depends upon the specific decision,
we leave the representation in this form.

Since the floating melody is followed by a filled nucleus, it remains unassociated and therefore unpronounced. With the two other empty nuclei likewise silent and palatalization replacement of [w] by [l] in accordance with PR4, the adjective is pronounced as [mglistɨ], with the initial three-consonant sequence [mgl]. Note that the impossible-looking initial cluster is in syllabic terms nothing more than a sequence of three separate non-branching onsets, a totally unremarkable situation not different in kind from what appears in the word (po)magała [(pɔ)magawa] 'she helped'; the difference is that in this latter word the nuclei are filled by melodies. Thus what is remarkable is the use of empty nuclei, a fact which characterizes the phonology of Polish in general.

The idea that word-initial consonant sequences are in fact combinations of onsets, either non-branching or branching, follows naturally from the Government Phonology view of syllabic constituents. It coincides in general assumptions and in many details with a proposal made in the middle of last century by Kuryłowicz (1952) in a paper which can only be described as a theoretical and descriptive tour de force. The basic idea of the proposal, revived in Gussmann (1992b), entails a claim that a word-initial consonant sequence in Polish potentially embraces two well-formed onsets. Kuryłowicz makes the specific proviso for the consonant [s] and its congeners as being outside branching onsets and puts forward a few additional modifications which we will take up below. In our terms, an onset has to be followed by a nucleus, which means that a consonant sequence embracing two well-formed onsets must be separated either by a nucleus with a floating melody or an empty nucleus. The proposal that word-initial consonant sequences are in fact remains of two—and not more than two—onsets separated by a nucleus without melody allows us to capture all existing facts in a neat system. It requires certain additional assumptions tacitly made by Kuryłowicz, which we shall inspect below. Before doing that let us note what the proposal systematically excludes.

Although Polish admits initial sequences of up to four consonants, there are some combinations of three or four consonants that are totally impossible. A case in point is any sequence of three, let alone four, sonorants: nothing like *[mlr, nml, wmr, lrl, nwlr] is even vaguely possible. Similarly, with qualifications to be discussed presently, sequences of three or four obstruents are categorically ruled out: *[ptk, pfk, bgd, xptk].[9]

The reasons for this restriction are not difficult to see: a sequence of three sonorants or three obstruents necessarily entails three separate onsets since neither two sonorants nor two obstruents can constitute a branching onset. This violates the restriction which tolerates only two such events when the intervening nucleus is not filled. In this way the impossibility of three or more

---

[9] Note that some of these clusters are found word-internally, e.g. [ptk] in neptka [nɛptka] 'halfwit, gen. sg.', [ktk] in subiektka [subʲɛktka] 'female shop assistant', architektka [arçitɛktka] 'woman architect'. We return to these later.

adjacent sonorants or obstruents is another way of saying that Polish bans two consecutive empty nuclei domain-internally. Note that this particular ban is quite similar in its effects to the regularity we referred to above as Melody Association: a floating melody must be attached if the next nucleus is not filled, in other words, a sequence of two floating melodies (= empty nuclei) is not tolerated. The two objects—a floating melody and an empty nucleus—are thus seen to be controlled by the same constraint which disallows two adjacent nuclei without an attached melody. The initial observation concerning possible consonant combinations at the beginning of the word turns out to derive from the ban on empty nuclei sequences: we can have no more than four consonants since this is what two branching onsets with an intervening empty nucleus add up to. We will argue below that this conclusion is not quite correct but before doing this we would like to buttress it by several clarifications. The data we discuss below exclude specifically the consonants [s, z, f, v] in the prefixes z-/s- and w-, as we consider them in greater detail separately.

5.3.1 *The obstruent/sonorant status of [ʃ, ʒ, f, v]*

The contention that two obstruents cannot form a branching onset seems unassailable. Against this conclusion we need to take a close look at the numerous instances in Polish where an initial obstruent is followed by what is normally regarded as another obstruent, namely [ʃ, ʒ, f, v]:

(36) przód [pʃut] 'front'   brzeg [bʒɛk] 'coast'
       trzon [t-ʃɔn] 'core'   drzew-o [d-ʒɛvɔ] 'tree'
       krzak [kʃak] 'bush'   grzech [gʒɛx] 'sin'
       chrzan [xʃan] 'horseradish'   zrzęd-a [zʒɛnda] 'grouch'
       twój [tfuj] 'your'   dw-a [dva] 'two'
       kwiat [kfʲat] 'flower'   gwiazd-a [gvʲazda] 'star'
       chwil-a [xfʲila] 'moment'   dzwon [dzvɔn] 'bell'
       dźwig [dʑvʲik] 'crane'   szwagier [ʃfajɛr] 'brother-in-law'
       swobod-a [sfɔbɔda] 'freedom'   zwykł-y [zvɨkwɨ] 'ordinary'
       święt-y [ɕfʲɛntɨ] 'holy'   zwierz-ę [zvʲɛʒɛ] 'animal'
       żwaw-y [ʒvavɨ] 'brisk'

Taken in isolation, such obstruent combinations need not be particularly disturbing: we have seen above similar cases such as *ptak* [ptak] 'bird' and have interpreted the two consonants as two non-branching onsets separated by a nucleus. The same mechanism could be extended to the forms above and in some cases it would presumably have to be applied: since strident sibilants cannot combine with anything to form an onset, the combinations of [s, z, ɕ, ʃ, ʒ] and [ʃ, ʒ, f, v] may have to be separated by an empty nucleus. The real difficulty arises when we consider sequences of three or four consonants as in the following examples:

(37) prztyczek [pʃtɨtʃɛk] 'fillip'   brzdąc [bʒdɔnts] 'toddler'
      brzmieni-e [bʒmʲɛɲɛ] 'sound'   bżdż-ąc-y [bʒdʒɔntsɨ] 'farting'
      krzt-a [kʃta] 'ounce'   grzbiet [gʒbʲɛt] 'back, n.'
      grzmot [gʒmɔt] 'thunder'   chrzt-u [xʃtu] 'baptism, gen. sg.'
      chrzci-e [xʃtɕɛ] 'baptism, loc. sg.'   skrzat [skʃat] 'sprite'
      strzech-a [st-ʃɛxa] 'thatch'   skwar [skfar] 'heat'
      tkw-i-ć [tkfʲitɕ] 'stick, vb.'

Empty nuclei, which could be called upon to help out, are not necessarily a solution since we argued above that Polish disallows sequences of such objects within a single domain. Although in some instances a representation could be found which would circumvent the need for two consecutive empty nuclei, this could not be extended to all cases. A word such as *tkwić* [tkfʲitɕ] 'stick' would need to allow two nuclear positions without a melody, with a representation something like that in (38).

(38) O   N   O   N   O   N   O   N
      | | | | | | | |
      x   x   x   x   x   x   x   x
      | | | | |
      t   k   fʲ   i   tɕ

Before abandoning the restriction disallowing sequences of empty nuclei it is worth considering an alterative adopted somewhat cryptically by Kuryłowicz. The class of consonants that produce the hurdle embraces, as we have just seen, [ʒ, v] after voiced obstruents and their voiceless congeners after voiceless ones. The fricative [ʒ] within Polish morphophonology can be a reflex of the sonorant [r] (see Ch. 4), which devoices after a voiceless obstruent (cf. *Piotr-a* [pʲɔtra] 'Peter, gen. sg.'~ *Piotrz-e* [pʲɔt-ʃɛ] 'loc. sg.'). Likewise the spirant [v] has been argued to act as a sonorant (Gussmann 1981, 2002; for Russian, see Andersen 1969*b*, Flier 1974*a, b*; for Slavic in general, Cyran and Nilsson 1998; we discuss this in Ch. 7). On the assumption that [ʒ, ʃ] and [v, f] are morphophonologically something like [r] and [w], respectively, the syllabification problem above disappears since these sonorants can readily combine with the preceding obstruent to form a branching onset. The word *tkw-i-ć* [tkfʲitɕ] would then receive the following representation:

(39) O   N   O   N   O   N
      | | |\ | | |
      x   x   x x   x   x   x
      | | | | |
      t   k w   i   tɕ

On this interpretation the initial sequence in the word *brzdąc* [bʒdɔnts] 'toddler' does not differ from the sequence in *brdys-a-ć* [brdɨsatɕ] 'frolic, vb.' since both break up into a branching and a non-branching onset. The sonorant of the branching onset is [r] with the specification <PR1> in the former case while it is a 'simple' [r] without any diacritic in the latter. The existence of a phonetic fricative that corresponds to the morphophonological trill [r] is independently justified as is the special status of the labio-dental fricatives. For these reasons we will adopt the sonorant interpretation of these fricatives in our analysis of the syllabic constituents.

5.3.2 *The fricative [s] and its congeners in the syllabic organization*

As mentioned earlier several times, the consonant [s] occupies a special place in Government Phonological studies. This has been discussed at length in the literature (Kaye 1991/2; Harris 1994; Gussmann 2002); in brief, while [s] can occupy the onset position on its own, it cannot govern a dependent in a branching onset. It can appear as the rhymal complement when governed by a following onset. These restrictions apply not only to the voiceless dental [s] but also to its voiced, palatal, and palatalized congeners. We showed above that an initial s-consonant sequence should preferably be interpreted as a two-onset structure with an intervening floating melody or an empty nucleus; thus *s-to* [stɔ] 'hundred' contains a floating melody as seen in the form *set* [sɛt] 'gen. pl.', whereas *stół* [stuw] 'table', showing no alternations, is best assumed to contain an empty nucleus between the two consonants.

The fact that the consonant of the type [s] can only appear in a non-branching onset or as a rhymal complement has its implications for the syllabification of heavy consonantal sequences.

Three member sequences beginning with an s-type consonant can be interpreted naturally as a non-branching onset followed by a branching one. This is the case for [spr, str, skr, skn, ʃpr, zbr, zdr, zgr, zgl, skw, ʃkw, sxl]:

(40) spraw-a [sprava] 'matter'   stron-a [strɔna] 'page'
      skromn-y [skrɔmnɨ] 'modest'   skner-a [sknɛra] 'miser'
      szprot [ʃprɔt] 'sprat'   zbrodni-a [zbrɔdɲa] 'crime'
      zdrad-a [zdrada] 'treason'   zgliszcz-a [zgliʃtʃa] 'ruins'
      składni-a [skwadɲa] 'syntax'   szkł-o [ʃkwɔ] 'glass'
      schludn-y [sxludnɨ] 'spruce, adj.' zgred [zgrɛt] 'old buffer'

Some of the clusters appearing to challenge the above description vanish as counterexamples if the suggestion of the preceding section is followed, namely, if we interpret the fricatives [ʒ, ʃ] as the sonorant [r], e.g. *zgrzyt* [zgʒɨt] 'gnashing'. Note that unless [ʒ] in its shape as [r] <PR1> forms a branching onset with the preceding plosive, we would need to introduce two empty nuclei. The disfavoured and the preferred representations would take the following shapes:

(41)

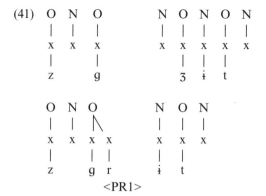

If an initial sequence of two empty nuclei is disallowed, the first of two representations in (41) has to be regarded as ill-formed.

Consonants of the *s*-type appear not only as the first but also as the second member of three-member initial sequences. An interpretation which tallies with what we have developed so far will treat the s-type consonant as the rhymal complement attached to the first nucleus and governed by the following onset. Thus the initial cluster in the word *wstęga* [fstɛŋga] 'ribbon' reflects the following structure:

(42)

It contains a single empty nucleus; whether the first consonant is voiced with subsequent phonological voice assimilation or whether it is voiceless throughout is a marginal issue.

Examples of such sequences with the s-type consonant in the middle can be illustrated by the following examples:

(43) wspaniał-y [fspaɲawɨ] 'wonderful'   wskaz-a-ć [fskazatɕ] 'indicate'
      wściek-ł-y [fɕtɕɛkwɨ] 'furious'   mśc-i-ć [mɕtɕitɕ] 'avenge'
      lśn-i-ć [lɕɲitɕ] 'shine'   pszczoł-a [pʃtʃɔwa] 'bee'
      kształt [kʃtawt] 'shape'   szczwan-y [ʃtʃfanɨ] 'sly'

The middle consonant in the initial clusters is in the coda position and as such forms a contact with the following onset. In any case, the three-consonant cluster contains one empty nucleus after the first consonant.

Two further points deserve mention here. The last example—*szczwan-y* [ʃtʃfanɨ] 'sly'—must treat the final fricative of the cluster as the sonorant [w] which forms a branching onset with the preceding affricate, a move that allows us to maintain the hypothesis about one empty nucleus, in line with the examples analyzed in the preceding section.

Second, it has to be admitted that certain instances are ambiguous or non-unique: the words *pszczol-a* [pʃtʃɔwa] 'bee' and *ksztalt* [kʃtawt] 'shape' are a case in point. The middle fricative can be seen either as a palatalized sonorant forming a branching onset with the preceding plosive or as a rhymal complement licensed by the following plosive. Both possibilities are represented below:

(44)

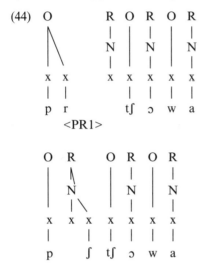

Both interpretations conform to the one-empty nucleus requirement and there is no evidence to indicate which one should be the preferred solution. This in itself is no cause for concern—quite conversely, the existence of ambiguous structures merely indicates that different speakers may analyze individual forms in different ways. What remains crucial is that all such alternative interpretations observe constraints on well-formed structures.

It was mentioned above that the *s*-type consonant can appear as the first or the second but not the third member of the cluster. We have seen how the attested situations arise so it is interesting to consider the non-existing case; in other words, if we can have, say, [mɕtɕ] in *msc-i-ć* [mɕtɕitɕ] 'avenge' or [fsp] in *wspanialy* [fspaɲawɨ] 'wonderful', why is it that a slight modification of such clusters— *[mtɕɕ] or *[fps]—is categorically ruled out? The answer seems to lie in the number of empty nuclei: if such sequences were to be syllabified we would need an empty nucleus between the first two and the last two consonants. Neither [mtɕ] nor [tɕɕ] qualify as well-formed branching onsets, nor does [tɕɕ] appear a viable coda–onset contact, hence each consonant would have to be a sole occupant of an onset. The same holds for the consonants in the cluster [fps] so that these two clusters would require the representations in (45), where they are followed by a full vowel:

(45) O   N   O   N   O   N   O   N   O   N   O   N
      | | | | | | | | | | | |
      x   x   x   x   x   x   x   x   x   x   x   x
      | | | | | |
      m   tɕ   ɕ   V   f   p   s   V

The ungrammatical sequences *[mtɕɕ] and *[fps] arise only if the ban against two consecutive empty nuclei is violated. To put it differently, the impossible sequences are exactly the ones what we cannot expect to find, given our understanding of the distribution of empty nuclear positions.

Finally, we are left with four-member initial sequences. There are very few such clusters which would additionally meet the requirement of belonging to a single domain, that is, not include prefixes. The near-complete listing of such items includes: [pstr, pst-ʃ, fskʃ, fstr, ʐdʐbw, drgn]:

(46) pstryk-a-ć [pstrɨkatɕ] 'snap, vb.'   pstr-y [pstrɨ] 'speckled'
      pstrz-y-ć [pst-ʃɨtɕ] 'make gaudy'   wskrzes-i-ć [fskʃɛɕitɕ] 'resurrect'
      wstręt [fstrɛnt] 'repulsion'   źdźbł-o [ʐdʐbwɔ] 'blade (of grass)'
      drgn-ę [drgnɛ] 'I will shudder'

Leaving aside for a moment the last two sequences, let us consider the first four beauties: [pstr, pst-ʃ, fskʃ, fstr]. We can immediately reduce their number to two by observing that the fricative [ʃ] can be regarded as realization of the sonorant [r] after a voiceless plosive with which it forms a branching onset. In fact, the pair *pstr-y* [pstrɨ] ~ *pstrz-y-ć* [pst-ʃɨtɕ] is an instance of direct morphophonological alternation where the [ʃ] of the verb corresponds to (= <PR1>) the [r] of the adjective. Thus [pst-ʃ, fskʃ] can be interpreted as [pstr, fskr] where the final [r] is marked <PR1>. To account for sequences such as [pstr, fstr] we need one empty nucleus. Consider the adjective *pstr-y*:

(47)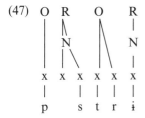

The rhymal [s] is governed by the plosive of the well-formed branching onset, so the impossible looking four-element cluster requires no additional mechanism apart from what we need independently in any case.[10]

The initial sequence [fskʃ] would be handled analogously, the only controversial issue being the nature of the first consonant: is it the fricative [v] which

---

[10] The representation of *pstr-y* is based on theory-internal considerations only. It comes as no surprise, however, that other Slavic languages, less eager to tolerate such heavy clusters, have a full vowel corresponding to the empty nucleus in Polish: Russian *pëstr-yj*, Czech *pestr-ý*. Likewise for *wskrzes-i-ć* 'resurrect' with [fskʃ] we find the Russian *voskresit'* with [voskr]; note additionally that this example provides a perfect fit for our decision to interpret the Polish [kʃ] as [kr<PR1>].

assimilates in voice to the following cluster or is it quite simply voiceless [f] with no assimilation? Deciding this particular issue has no bearing upon the syllabification of the sequence: the first consonant is separated from the rest by an empty nucleus—the representation is exactly the same as that for *pstr-y*, above.

For the words *źdźbl-o* [ʐdʐbwɔ] 'blade of grass' and *drgn-ę* [drgnɛ] 'I will shudder' we suggest the following representations.

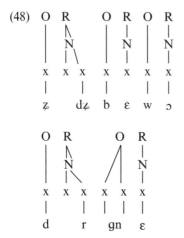

(48)

The representations are perhaps somewhat controversial. The floating vowel is justified by the genitive plural form of the noun, *źdźbeł* [ʐdʐbɛw], where Melody Association works in a regular fashion. A contact is established between the rhymal complex affricate [dʐ] and the plosive [b], a rare but not impossible situation, cf. *swadźb-a* [sfadʐba] 'match-making' where the gen. pl. *swadźb* [sfatɕp] indicates that the two obstruents are not separated by a floating melody. The word *źdźbl-o* appears to cause problems for native speakers since normative dictionaries warn against the ungrammatical, hence obviously occurring, form *ździeblo* [ʐdʐɛbwɔ]. This particular form requires a nucleus between the members of what the standard representation treats as a rhyme–onset contact [dʐb] in (48). Possibly, speakers who regard such a contact as ill-formed reinterpret its two consonants are separate onsets, since they obviously could not form a branching onset.

The word *drgn-ę* [drgnɛ] 'I will shudder' presents a different problem since the cluster [dr] is a perfect example of a branching onset, hence the four-consonant cluster should naturally break up into two branching onsets [dr + gn]. Our representation above takes [r] to be the rhymal complement governed by the plosive of the branching onset. The reason for this decision is that contrary to Kuryłowicz and others we do not believe that Polish allows sequences of branching onsets (of course when separated by an empty nucleus). We thus believe that the following structure is disallowed in Polish:

(49)   O   N   O   N
       ⋀ | ⋀ |
       X X X   X X X

where the first nucleus is empty while the second is melodically filled (a sequence of two empty nuclei is independently barred). Thus a word such as *brkla* is ruled out if the consonants are all in two branching onsets.

Admitting the possibility of two branching onsets would lead to massive over-generation since, leaving aside voice agreement, practically any two branching onsets could be combined. We would then expect numerous initial sequences such as *[tfkr, krtf, plfr, frpl, grdw, dwgr, dẓvbr, brdẓv, klpl, plkl, gngr, grgn, . . .], to say nothing of sequences of identical onsets which should also be possible: *[grgr, klkl, frfr]. None of these is found and none seems well-formed. In actual fact we have just one word—*drg-nᶐ-ć* [drgnɔɲtɕ] 'shudder'—where the initial consonantal sequence can be broken up into two branching onsets. If we accept this conclusion at face value, that is to say, if we admit that two branching onsets constitute a well-formed structure, then we have to explain while there is only one attested form out of dozens if not hundreds of theoretical possibilities. Leaving aside the one example, which can be provided a straightforward alternative representation in (48), we conclude that a branching onset can only be followed by a non-branching one and vice versa. Thus a combination of two branching onsets is not allowed. This explains the paucity of four-consonant sequences word-initially, since the occurring sequences invariably involve a consonant as a rhymal coda, hence practically a consonant of the s-type.

To sum up the situation with respect to initial consonant sequences, this is what we find:

- We can have non-branching onsets consisting of a single consonant or branching onsets comprising two consonants, e.g. *bat* [bat] 'whip', *brat* [brat] 'brother'.
- We can have two non-branching onsets, e.g. *d-b-ać* [dbatɕ] 'care, vb.', *mróz* [mrus] 'frost', *rtęć* [rtɛɲtɕ] 'mercury', *stal* [stal] 'steel'.
- We can have three consonants which break up into a non-branching onset followed by a branching one, e.g. *stron-a* [strɔna] 'side', *wbrew* [vbrɛf] 'against'.
- We can have a branching onset followed by a simplex one: *krnᶐbrn-y* [krnɔmbrnɨ] 'unruly', *plc-i* [pwtɕi] 'gender, gen. sg.', *brdys-a-ć* [brdɨsatɕ] 'frolic, vb.'.

The above descriptive statements result from two constraints. One of them disallows two consecutive domain-internal empty nuclei, which explains the absence of three sonorants, (*mlra*), three obstruents (*bgdać*), a sonorant followed by two obstruents (*mgda*), and other combinations. To remain grammatical these consonants would have to be separated by two empty nuclei. Further disallowed is a sequence of two branching onsets, which explains the near-total absence of clusters such as *krpla*.

Before leaving the initial consonant sequences we need to return to an issue which was mentioned in passing, namely, the clusters that arise when a consonantal prefix is attached to a word beginning with a sequence. Two such consonant-only prefixes are found: *w-* [v, f] and *s-/z-* [s, z], bypassing the issues of voicing which will be discussed in Chapter 7. In most cases these prefixes produce no problems for a syllabic interpretation since the consonant of the prefix could be separated from the branching or non-branching onset by a floating melody. This melody is unattached since it is followed by an attached melody, although we will see numerous cases below where the vowel of the prefix is actually pronounced. Thus we find for example *s-fru-nq-ć* [sfrunɔntɕ] 'fly down' (cf. *fru-nq-ć* [frunɔntɕ] 'fly'), and *w-prowadz-i-ć* [fprɔvadʑitɕ] 'lead into' (cf. *pro-wadz-i-ć* [prɔvadʑitɕ] 'lead'). The initial [sfr] and [fpr] are obviously combinations of an initial fricative and a branching onset, hence could be represented as in (50).

(50)

```
O   N   O       N       O   N   O       N
|   |    \      |        |   |    \      |
x   x   x x     x        x   x   x x     x
|       | | |            |       | | |
s   ɛ   f r u            f   ɛ   p r ɔ
```

While operational, in such cases we believe that the interpretation is on the wrong track; to see this, take an onset with an empty nucleus in its structure and combine it with the prefixes. Some examples follow:

(51)   trwon-i-ć [tr̥fɔɲitɕ] 'squander'   s-trwon-i-ć [str̥fɔɲʲitɕ] 'perf.'
        psoc-i-ć [psɔtɕitɕ] 'play pranks'   s-psoc-i-ć [spsɔtɕiɕ] 'perf.'
        tchórz-y-ć [txuʒɨtɕ] 'chicken out'   s-tchórz-y-ć [stxuʒɨtɕ] 'perf.'
        mroz-i-ć [mrɔʑitɕ] 'freeze'   z-mroz-i-ć [zmrɔʑitɕ] 'perf.'
        mniej-sz-y [mɲɛjʃɨ] 'smaller'   z-mniej-sz-y-ć [zmɲɛjʃɨtɕ] 'reduce'
        sta-ć [statɕ] 'stand'   w-sta-ć [fstatɕ] 'stand up'
        sław-i-ć [swavʲitɕ] 'praise'   w-sław-i-ć [fswavʲitɕ] 'make known'

Since the two- or three-segmental sequence at the beginning requires an empty nucleus separating the consonants, the attachment of the prefix ending in a floating melody would end up with the melody being attached (and pronounced). Consider such a potential violation in the case of [zmrɔ] in *zmro(zić)* [zmrɔʑitɕ] and [str̥fɔ] in *strwo(nić)* [str̥fɔɲitɕ]:

(52)

```
O   N   O       N   O   N
|   |   |       |   |   |
x   x   x       x   x   x
|       |           |   |
z   ɛ   m           r   ɔ
```

```
O   N   O       N   O   N
|   |   | \     |   |   |
x   x   x x     x   x   x
|       | |         |   |
z   ɛ   t r̥        f   ɔ
```

Melody Association requires attachment of a floating melody if the following nucleus contains no attached melody. The two verbs would have to be pronounced *[zɛmrɔʑitɕ] and *[zɛtrfɔɲitɕ]. Of course, Melody Association as formulated in (12) could itself be flawed so we might conclude that it should be abandoned or revised. What is striking, however, is the fact that the alleged failure of Melody Association appears to involve a prefix rather than the morpheme internal situation.[11] For this reason an alternative is worth exploring.

An alternative which suggests itself is connected with the fact that the consonants in focus are live prefixes, hence the words they appear in are morphologically complex. Morphological complexity may—although it does not have to—translate into domain structure (see Kaye 1995 for a discussion of the issue within GP). The prefix remains outside the domain for the basic verb, so its final nucleus does not affect—or is interpreted independently of—the nuclei of the base. With E as a marker of the floating melody, the words *zmrozić* and *strwonić* might have the following (simplified) representation [zE[mørozićø]], [zE[trøwonićø]]. No violation of Melody Association is incurred since the potential candidates do not belong to the same innermost domains as the following empty nuclei which would condition their attachment. Thus the structures are not different in kind from sequences of homophonous prepositions *z* 'with', *w* 'in': *z mrozem* [zmrɔzɛm] 'with frost', *w trwonieniu* [ftrfɔɲɛɲu] 'in squandering': as prepositions they are separated from their nominals by domain boundaries; phonetically they produce the clusters [zmr, f̥tr̥f], but these are mechanical consequences of morphological concatenations.[12]

The possibility of some complex words displaying domain structure with phonological consequences thereof is a well-established tradition in phonology. We adopt it here for clusters that appear to violate a condition commonly adhered to and, generally, where (morpho)phonological evidence appears to override morphological divisions. In fact, the phonology–morphology re-alignments may need to be taken further than that since a case can be made for domain structure which does not correspond to morphological divisions. Kuryłowicz (1952) offers an interesting interpretation of an instance where morphological re-analysis goes against the grain of a (morpho)phonological account and has to be subordinated to it. While there are minor differences between his account and the one put forward here, the gist of the matter remains unaffected. It concerns the largely unproductive prefix *wz-* [vz/fs], which in some cases is lexicalized with the verbal base, whereas in others it is reasonably transparent, both formally and

---

[11] It must be admitted that there is a handful of words for which no synchronically motivated morphological complexity could be defended and which display similar clusters involving the two fricatives. Their list is not impressive: *smród* [smrut] 'stench', *smrek* [smrɛk] 'spruce', *wzwyż* [vzvɨʃ] 'upwards', *wzwód* [vzvut] 'erection'. It is remarkable that the offending forms involve the consonants which elsewhere appear as prefixes. In this context it could be pointed out that the English violations of the coda constraint also involve consonants that elsewhere function as clear-cut morphological markers (Harris 1994: 82).

[12] The same sort of mechanical concatenation can produce initial consonant sequences of four consonants in *z Wprost* [sfprɔst] 'with Wprost' (*Straight on*—title of a magazine) or five consonants in [spstr], e.g. *z pstrągiem* [spstrɔŋɟɛm] 'with a trout'.

semantically. When attached to verbs starting with a non-branching onset it yields three, to a branching onset, four consonants, as in the following examples:

(53) ws-pią-ć [fspʲɔɲtɕ] 'climb'
      wz-burz-y-ć [vzbuʒitɕ] 'agitate'
      wz-brani-a-ć [vzbraɲaɕ] 'forbid'
      ws-trzym-a-ć [fst-ʃɨmatɕ] 'refrain'
      ws-kaz-a-ć [fskazatɕ] 'indicate'
      wz-gardz-i-ć [vzgardʑitɕ] 'spurn'
      wz-leci-e-ć [vzlɛtɕɛtɕ] 'fly up'
      wz-mó-c[13] [vzmuts] 'intensify'
      wz-nieś-ć [vzɲɛɕtɕ] 'lift'
      wz-rusz-y-ć [vzruʃitɕ] 'move'
      wz-drag-a-ć [vzdragatɕ] 'shy away'
      wz-dłuż-a-ć [vzdwuʒatɕ] 'elongate'

Kuryłowicz claims that the phonologically adequate syllabification separates the initial spirant from the following cluster despite the morphology (where *wz-*, *ws-* are morphemes). In the model adopted in this book this would entail a modification of syllabic structure since the initial spirant of the verb [z] would now require a following empty nucleus. Consider the possible structure of the sequence [vzbra] of *wzbra(niać)* [vzbraɲatɕ] 'forbid':

(54)
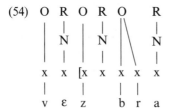

The morphophonological analysis and its consequences need not be viewed as particularly disturbing or more off-putting that the semantic differences between derivatives from a single base (e.g. *kaz-a-ć* 'tell, order' ∼ *ws-kaz-a-ć* 'indicate' and more examples in (53)). A similar analysis would extend to words where morphological division is tenuous or at least not obvious and to those where it is downright implausible but where the consonants have to be grouped into two onsets. Most of the words, or perhaps all of them, would have to be entered in the lexicon on account of their non-compositional semantics. The relevant examples are:

(55) wz-górz-e [vzguʒɛ] 'hill' (cf. po-górz-e [pɔguʒɛ] 'plateau', pod-górz-e [pɔdguʒɛ] 'piedmont')

---

[13] Here, *-c* as the marker of the infinitive is a form of a portmanteau morph as it combines the final velar of the stem (cf. *wz-mog-ę* [vzmɔgɛ] 'I will intensify') with the infinitival ending *-ć* [tɕ] found after non-velar stems (as in all other examples in (53)).

wz-gląd [vzglɔnt] 'consideration' (cf. o-gląd [ɔglɔnt] 'inspection', prze-gląd [pʃɛglɔnt] 'survey', wy-gląd [vɨglɔnt] 'looks')

wz-ględ-n-y [vzglɛndnɨ] 'relative' (cf. o-ględ-n-y [ɔglɛndnɨ] 'moderate')

wz-rost [vzrɔst] 'growth' (cf. po-rost 'lichen', za-rost [zarɔst] 'facial hair, stubble')

wz-wód [vzvut] 'erection' (cf. roz-wód [rɔzvut] 'divorce', prze-wód [pʃɛvut] 'cable')

ws-tręt [fstrɛnt] 'disgust' (cf. na-(?)tręt [natrɛnt] 'nuisance', w-(?)tręt [ftrt] 'interpolation')

wz-wyż [vzvɨʃ] 'upward' (cf. wyż [vɨʃ] 'high, n.')

wz-dłuż [vzdwuʃ] 'along'

wz-rok [vzrɔk] 'eye-sight'

With the structure adopted for the *wzbr-* [vzbr] sequence in (54), we can plausibly deal with these cases even if it has to be admitted that Kuryłowicz's proposal forces us to separate the first fricative from the rest by domain boundary against the evidence supplied by morphological analysis. Thus the [vzlɛ] sequence in *wz-leci-e-ć* [vzlɛtɕɛtɕ] 'fly up' and [vzrɔ] in *wz-rost* [vzrɔst] 'growth' could be represented as follows:

(56)
```
      O    N    O    N    O    N
      |    |    |    |    |    |
     [x    x   [x    x    x    x . . .]]
      |    |    |         |    |
      v    ɛ    z         l    ɛ
      v    ɛ    z         r    ɔ
```

The first nucleus contains a floating melody which remains unattached because it does not belong to the same domain as the second or empty nucleus. In other words, while the evidence is not overwhelming, the domain-based interpretation remains an option which cannot be easily dismissed.[14]

To sum up, four consonant sequences embrace two types of structure:

- a non-branching onset followed by branching rhyme (an empty nucleus plus a coda) and a following branching onset, e.g. *pstr-y* [pstrɨ] 'speckled', *wstręt* [fstrɛnt] 'revulsion';
- the fricatives [s/z, f/v] representing prefixes and separated from the base by a domain boundary, e.g. *s-krw-aw-i-ć* [skr̥favʲitɕ] 'bleed', *s-trwon-i-ć* [str̥fɔɲitɕ] 'squander'.

It remains a task for future studies to determine whether the order of branching and non-branching onsets is relevant—and if it is, then why?—and whether the melodic structure of the onsets is in any way connected with the melodies of the prefixes. Another problem which calls for a systematic account is the absence of

---

[14] One example that Kuryłowicz admits would not fit into his model is the somewhat strained but perfectly well-formed derivative *w-sznur-owa-ć* [fʃnurɔvatɕ] 'tie a shoelace into'—the sequence [fʃn] in our terms would require a domain boundary between the first two consonants, something like [fE[ʃønurɔvatɕ], hence the floating melody would not see the empty nucleus.

certain consonant combination: *j+consonant* or *n, m+ homorganic consonant* are not only absent but they appear totally impossible. Since in principle there is nothing implausible about separating such consonants by an empty nucleus, e.g. *jøpać, møpolać* (yielding **jpać, *mpolać*), the non-existence and impossibility of such initial occurrences indicates that our analysis is in some ways incomplete or inadequate. For reasons we do not fully understand, an empty nucleus is not an appropriate licensor for these consonants when another onset follows.

5.3.3 *Medial and final clusters*

These two types of cluster—medial and final—are traditionally distinguished as separate groups. Within the framework adopted in this book they must be viewed as coterminous since word-final clusters do not exist as an independent entity. Recall that a final consonant must invariably be assigned to an onset which is licensed by the final empty nucleus; final clusters, on the other hand, must be either branching onsets or coda–onset contacts. Thus, the so-called final clusters are, in fact, medial clusters and differ from them in the absence of the melody in the following nucleus. In Polish this is particularly well documented since certain inflectional desinences are represented as zero endings. Consider representations of the nom. sg. *państwo* [paɲstfɔ] 'state' and its gen. pl. *państw* [paɲstf]:

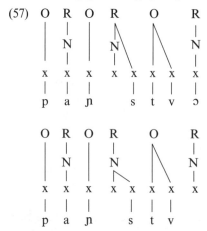

(57)

As can be seen, the only difference between these two forms is the presence of a melody on the final nucleus in the nominative singular and its absence in the genitive plural. As far as constituent structure is concerned, the two forms are identical. It might seem, then, that the medial and final onsets will not differ, a conclusion we will argue is largely but not completely true. We will be interested in ascertaining whether the onsets we find initially are fully identical with these that appear medially (and finally).

One obvious place where our non-initial clusters can differ from onsets is that they can be preceded by a rhymal complement (a coda). In the example above the head of the branching onset [tv] licenses the fricative [s] in the coda and this, in combination with the preceding non-branching onset, yields a four-member consonant sequence. It is hardly worth stressing, though, that the consonant sequence is structurally quite unremarkable consisting as it does of a non-branching onset, a coda and a branching onset with a single internal empty nucleus. Structurally the sequence is identical to what we find initially in the word *pstr-y* 'speckled' (see (47)).

In general, combinations of a coda consonant and a non-branching onset are commonplace before a final empty nucleus:

(58) cierń [tɕɛrɲ] 'thorn'   kark [kark] 'nape'   pierś [pʲɛrɕ] 'breast'
      skurcz [skurtʃ] 'spasm'   wierch [vʲɛrx] 'peak'   wart [vart] 'worthy'
      wilk [vʲilk] 'wolf'   milcz [mʲiltʃ] 'be quiet!' strzelb [st-ʃɛlp] 'pistol,
                                                          gen. pl.'
      odwilż [ɔdvʲilʃ] 'thaw'   film [fʲilm] 'film'   olch [ɔlx] 'alder tree,
                                                          gen. pl.'
      żółw [ʒuwʃ] 'tortoise'   gwałt [gvawt] 'rape'   pułk [puwk] 'regiment'
      hełm [xɛwm] 'helmet'   zamsz [zamʃ] 'suede'   czeremch [tʃɛrɛmx]
                                                          'bird cherry, gen. pl.'
      band [bant] 'gang,   lamp [lamp] 'lamp,   hańb [xaɲp] 'shame,
      gen. pl.'   gen. pl.'   gen. pl.'
      sejm [sɛjm] 'parliament'   wójt [vujt] 'alderman'   spójrz [spujʃ] 'look!'

Since the coda position is taken by a sonorant, the emerging consonantal cluster is a sonorant–obstruent contact typical of the position. In word-initial position such consonant sequences would have to be split by an empty nucleus, e.g. *lk-a-ć* [wkatɕ] 'sob', *rtęć* [rtɛɲtɕ] 'mercury', *msz-a* [mʃa] 'mass'. As noted above, some combinations are not allowed initially (the glide *j* + a consonant, a nasal and a homorganic obstruent).

Apart from sonorants, obstruents, too, can occupy the coda position, although these are usually subject to the requirement of being weaker than the licensing onset. A case in point is the labio-dental fricative [v] which, as we have seen, can be regarded as a sonorant; this is the case with words like *prawd* [praft] 'truth, gen. pl.' and *krzywdź* [kʃiftɕ] 'harm, imper.' (both with terminal devoicing). In other combinations the coda consonant seems to be equally complex as the licensing onset, e.g. *hymn* [xɨmn] 'hymn', *szept* [ʃɛpt] 'whisper'; in such cases it might be argued that the two consonants belong to separate onsets and are separated by an empty nuclear position. This is a possibility we will not follow here as we believe that empty nuclei should be recognized where necessary rather than where merely possible.[15]

---

[15] The full use of empty nuclei is advocated by proponents of the strict CV approach (Lowenstamm 1996; Rowicka 1999; Szigetvári 1999; Cyran 2003; and, most forcefully, Scheer 2004). Its most direct effect is the dismantling of syllable structure since phonological representations in this view are nothing more than consonant–vowel sequences.

Since onsets can be branching we would predict the existence of two-consonant clusters that form onsets and three-consonant groups conforming to the requirements of a combined single coda and a branching onset. This is indeed what we find: word-final branching onsets (a) and coda-branching onset contacts (b):

(59) (a) wiatr [vʲatr̥] 'wind'   cyfr [tsɨfr̥] 'figure, gen. pl.'
           trefl [trɛfl̥] 'clubs'   Cypr [tsɨpr̥] 'Cyprus'
           cykl [tsɨkl̥] 'cycle'   wydm [vɨtm̥/vɨdm] 'dune, gen. pl.'

      (b) blichtr [blixtr̥] 'tinsel'   filtr [fʲiltr̥] 'filter'
           sióstr [ɕustr̥] 'sister, gen. pl.'   chandr [xantr̥/xandr] 'doldrums, gen. pl.'
           ostrz [ɔst-ʃ] 'sharpen, imper.'   bóstw [bustf] 'deity, gen. pl.'
           ([r] <PR1>)   ([f] = [v] = [w])
           martw [martf] 'worry, imper.'
           ([f] = [v] = [w])

Below we provide representations of the words *wiatr* [vʲatr̥] 'wind' and *blichtr* [blixtr̥] 'tinsel': in both cases the final empty nucleus licenses a branching onset. Otherwise the first word has no rhymal complement.

(60)
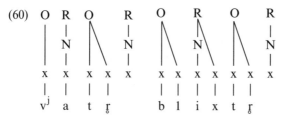

Although segmentally (melodically) somewhat complex, the two words are precisely what we would expect given our assumptions about constituent structures: rhymes can branch and onset can branch. Nuclei while empty can license a preceding onset. We must now turn to other structures which force us to recognise empty nuclei internal to the consonant sequence.

Cases where no coda–onset contact can be plausibly postulated involve primarily situations where the second of the two consonants, in other words, the onset is less complex than the coda. These would involve, for instance, sequences of an affricate and a plosive, a plosive and a spirant, a spirant and a sonorant, etc. In such cases we are forced to assign both of these consonants to consecutive onsets with an intervening empty nucleus:

(61) uczt [utʃt] 'feast, gen. pl.'   liczb [litʃp] 'number, gen. pl.'
      wieprz [vʲɛpʃ] 'hog'[16]   kobz [kɔps] 'bagpipes, gen. pl.'
      kleks [klɛks] 'ink blot'   biceps [bʲitsɛps] 'muscle'
      klaps [klaps] 'spank, n.'

---

[16] Unless the final [ʃ] is taken to be [r] <PR1>, in which case we would be dealing with a final branching onset [pr].

Another place where an empty nucleus has to be recognized involves situations where a coda consonant is followed by two more segments which cannot form a branching onset. Thus, while in *sióstr* [ɕustr̩] 'sister, gen. pl.' the final cluster can naturally be broken into a coda and a branching onset, the same cannot be done in numerous other instances:

(62) kunszt [kunʃt] 'art'   garść [garɕtɕ] 'handful'
      miejsc [mʲɛjsts] 'place, gen. pl.' tekst [tɛkst] 'text'
      herszt [hɛrʃt] 'ringleader'   zemst [zɛmst] 'revenge, gen. pl.'
      asumpt [asumpt] 'cause, n.'   sfinks [sfʲiŋks] 'sphinx'
      wojsk [vɔjsk] 'army, gen. pl.'   łapsk [wapsk] 'paw, gen. pl.'
      pilśń [pʲilɕɲ] 'felt, n.'   bractw [bratstf] 'fraternity, gen. pl.'
      barszcz [barʃtʃ] 'borsch'   polszcz [pɔlʃtʃ] 'translate into Polish, imp.'

Not surprisingly many—or most—of the clusters contain an *s*-type consonant with its highly restricted possibilities of contracting relations; while arguably as an onset it could govern the preceding sonorant in the coda, it cannot do so with reference to a preceding obstruent. Thus the word *garść* [garɕtɕ] 'handful' is potentially ambiguous, *łapsk* [wapsk] is not. Consider the two possible representations of the former and one of the latter word.

(63)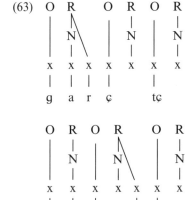

As indicated, the existence of alternative representations—of forms which must be viewed as ambiguous—is not in itself either surprising or worrying. It is perfectly possible that different speakers may reconstruct the phonological form of a word in different ways, and this holds, as we have seen before, both for the melodic and syllabic organization. What is crucial is that the alternative representations conform to what is dictated by the theoretical model, and this is the case with the two possible shapes of *garść*.

The final onset in the three-consonant clusters in (62) is non-branching; if it were branching we would expect a sequence of four consonants. Such sequences are also attested.

(64)   warstw [varstf] 'layer, gen. pl.'   głupstw [gwupstf] 'nonsense, gen. pl.'
        zabójstw [zabujstf] 'manslaughter,   kłamstw [kwamstf] 'lie, gen. pl.'
        gen. pl.'
        intryganctw [intrɨgantstf]   państw [paɲstf] 'state, gen. pl.'
        'scheming, gen. pl.'

Admittedly, the clusters seem restricted to the suffix -stwo/-ctwo and, just as in the case of word-initial four-consonant sequences their number is quite small. But their structure and phonological well-formedness are beyond dispute (see (57) for the representation of państw). We might also mention one more instance where phonetically a sequence of five consonants can be heard, namely, derivatives such as na-stęp-stw [nastɛmpstf] 'consequence, gen. pl.', za-stęp-stw [zastɛmpstf] 'replacement, gen. pl.', and od-stęp-stw [ɔtstɛmpstf] 'departure, gen. pl.' The sequence [ɛm] can be interpreted as a realization of the front nasal vowel, hence the words do not differ from those listed earlier. Here is a representation of the lexeme na-stęp-stw:

(65)
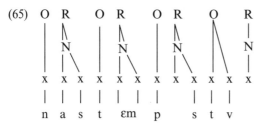

In the same way as we summarized the initial situation, we can offer a similar account of the word-final possibilities:

- We can have non-branching onsets consisting of a single consonant or branching onsets comprising two consonants: bat [bat] 'whip', wiatr [vʲatr̩] 'wind, n.'.
- We can have two non-branching onsets: uczt [utʃt] 'feast, gen. pl.'.
- We can have three consonants which break up into a coda and a branching onset: blichtr [blixtr̩] 'tinsel' or a non-branching and a branching onset, e.g. dom-o-stw [dɔmɔstf] 'homestead, gen. pl.'
- We can have a four-consonant sequence which results from a non-branching onset followed by a coda and a branching onset, e.g. pań-stw [paɲstf] 'state, gen. pl.' or from a coda, a non-branching onset and a branching onset: intryganctw [intrɨgantstf] 'scheming, gen. pl.'.

The five-consonant possibility emerges when a nasal vowel (i.e. a vowel and a nasal consonant; see Ch. 6) appears before a plosive in the onset and is followed by a coda and a branching onset as in na-stęp-stw [nastɛmpstf] 'consequence, gen. pl.'

In structural terms then, the initial and medial/final situations are essentially parallel. This is not to say that they are completely identical or fully coterminous, starting with the trivial restriction on voiced obstruents which are not licensed by the domain-final nucleus. There are also melodic gaps in both positions which can only be described as fortuitous; thus both initially and finally we find [pt]—*ptak* [ptak] 'bird', *szept* [ʃɛpt] 'whisper, n.'—while its voiced counterpart is found word-internally in e.g. *chebdu* [xɛbdu] 'kind of lilac, gen. sg.' (hence also word-finally subject to voice neutralization *chebd* [xɛpt][17]) but is absent word-initially. This is an accidental gap which does not affect the basic structural regularities we find in the data. There are more important observations to be made.

In discussing the initial combinations we noted the strange absence, which we believe is systematic rather than accidental, of the palatal glide followed by a consonant *jC and a nasal homorganic with the following obstruent *nd, *mp, etc. (note the presence of non-homorganic sequences *mdł-y* [mdwɨ] 'bland', *mgł-a* [mgwa] 'mist'). While totally impossible initially, these clusters are quite common—or at least unremarkable—word-finally (and, of course, word-medially):

(66) strajk [strajk] 'strike, n.'
      sejm [sɛjm] 'parliament'
      pejs [pɛjs] 'sidelock'
      lump [lump] 'vagrant'
      sierżant [ɕɛrʒant] 'sergeant'
      cynk [tsɨŋk] 'tip-off, n.'

What we have here are coda–onset contacts where a sonorant is governed by a strong obstruent in the onset. In contradistinction to the putative word-initial position, the codas accompany melodically filled nuclei; word-initially a *jd*-sequence, for instance, would necessarily call for an intervening empty nucleus. Empty nuclei appear to be weak licensors although why they should fail to license the palatal glide (*jC) and a nasal homorganic with the following onset (*mp, nd) while licensing the trill (*rdzeń* [rdzɛɲ] 'root') remains unclear.

Although we have been trying to stress the essential identity of word-initial and word-final consonant sequences in terms of the structural syllabic units admitted there, there is no denying that the final position is more restrictive. A case in point is the distribution of branching onsets: while undoubtedly they do occur word-finally, both their frequency and the range of possibility is far richer in the initial position. There are onsets galore ending in a liquid word-initially, while finally they are few and far between. Even more so, the non-palatalized lateral realized as the labio-velar semivowel [w] when appearing as the marker of the past tense is usually suppressed after a consonant. Consider pairs of the third-person singular feminine and masculine, where the former takes the gender marker *-a*, while the latter takes an empty nucleus. The masculine form contains the lateral only in very stilted styles—normally the consonant deletes, so we place it in brackets.

(67) wlok-ł-a [vlɔkwa] 'drag'   wlók-ł [vluk(w̥)]
      plot-ł-a [plɔtwa] 'spin'   plót-ł [plut(w̥)]
      wiod-ł-a [vʲɔdwa] 'lead'   wiód-ł [vʲut(w̥)]

---

[17] Since the word is quite rare, it would probably be pronounced in a self-conscious way as [xɛbd].

strzeg-ł-a [st-ʃɛgwa] 'guard'   strzeg-ł [st-ʃɛk(w̥)]
zmar-ł-a [zmarwa] 'die'   zmar-ł [zmar(w̥)]
ros-ł-a [rɔswa] 'grow'   rós-ł [rus(w̥)]

In a clear sense, the final empty nucleus is a weaker licensor than both a full vowel and an empty nucleus at the left edge of the word. This accounts for the frequently observed special property of the right edge of the word, which in our terms translates into the weaker licensing potential of the final nucleus (for an extensive discussion and specific proposals concerning the strength of nuclei, see Cyran 2003). In our case this tendency also accounts for certain differences between word-internal and word-final position: word-medially a cluster being followed by a full vowel—a stronger licensor—admits more consonantal combinations than the final position with its weak empty nuclei. Consider some examples with internal clusters which do not appear word-finally.

(68)   [mkn]   zamk-ną-ć [zamknɔɲtɕ] 'close, vb.'
        [brn]   srebr-n-y [srɛbrnɨ] 'silver, adj.'
        [wpl]   chełp-liw-y [xɛwplivɨ] 'boastful'
        [stn]   ust-n-y [ustnɨ] 'oral'

The non-existence and impossibility of such sequences in the final position reflects therefore a more general property of phonological units, namely, the weaker licensing potential of empty nuclei.

One of the examples above, *srebr-n-y* [srɛbrnɨ] 'silver', may be another indication of the diminished potential of the final nucleus. This can be seen in the fact that while branching onsets do occur word-finally and can be preceded by a code consonant, e.g. *wiatr* [vʲatr̥] 'wind', *blichtr* [blixtr̥] 'tinsel', *dom-o-stw* [dɔmɔstf] 'homestead, gen. pl.', the reverse order of constituents seems ruled out: words ending in *-krt*, *-klt* seem ungrammatical. This stands in sharp relief to the initial position where both orders of onsets are tolerated, e.g. *trw-a-ć* [trfatɕ] 'last, vb.', *tkw-i-ć* [tkfitɕ] 'stick, vb.', but where the cluster is followed by a full vowel. In general then, the domain-final empty nucleus can support less segmental material and constituent structure than the same nucleus in other positions.

The single most important exceptional property of the final empty nucleus comes from a constraint we adopted earlier but which at first glance appears to be violated in final clusters. The constraint refers to the ban on sequences of two empty nuclei: we argued in connection with initial clusters that whatever consonantal combinations exist can be described by admitting one and one only domain-internal empty nucleus. The single nucleus in conjunction with the restrictive model of constituent structure allows us to capture most—or perhaps all—of the observable combinations. Admitting two such empty nuclear positions would increase the generative potential of the model and necessitate additional conditions, filters, and the like. To take just one in place of a possible plethora of examples, by admitting one internal empty nucleus we have a ready account for the absence of three initial sonorants (in a language which tolerates up to four initial consonants), e.g. *mln-, *rlm-. To be grammatical such a sequence would require two empty nuclei since each sonorant would need to be an onset. The same holds for three plosives, e.g. *ptk-. The fact that such and numerous other combinations are not found does not follow from any particular restriction on the combinability of segments but from an impossible syllabic combination involving two consecutive empty nuclei.

Against this background we need to comment on the fact that some of our more complex final consonant combinations do contain two empty nuclei (see the representations of *garść*, *lapsk*, *następstw* in (63) and (65), above). The major difference between the initial and final situation is that finally the second or last nucleus is not enforced by the specific melodic sequence but, rather, is part of the universal condition on constituent structure. As discussed in Chapter 2 and adopted throughout this book, the coda must be licensed by a following onset, hence word-final consonants are never codas, and on onsets must be licensed by nuclei, hence word final consonants must be licensed by an empty nucleus. In this way the second nucleus found in our representations (63) and (65), above, forms part of the universal structure of the syllable. Note that the initial heavy clusters, while containing one internal empty nucleus, are always and invariably followed by a second full vowel, e.g. *pstr-y* [pstri] 'speckled' is syllabically {pøstri} with two nuclei, one empty and one filled. Word-finally, the second nucleus is also empty because it has to be empty by universal assumptions. What is crucial is that internally—one might say, lexically—there is only one empty nucleus in both categories. The fact that the second nucleus is domain-final, hence weak, explains restrictions on its licensing potential and thus accounts for the restricted set of combinations it can support. This reasoning is incorporated in our formulation of the ban on two consecutive empty nuclei domain-internally, so the final nucleus is excluded from consideration.

5.4 MORPHOPHONOLOGY AND LEXICAL UNDERPINNINGS OF MELODY ASSOCIATION

Our discussion of the Polish syllable structure has centred round the licit and illicit ways of combining consonants; the crucial role in the account has been assigned to nuclei without an attached melody. Some of these have a floating melody which gets associated to its skeletal point due to a regularity we called Melody Association—basically a floating melody remains floating when the successive nucleus contains an associated melody; otherwise it is attached and pronounced in most cases as [ɛ]. This is our account of the vowel~zero alternation in Modern Polish. The other type of nucleus has no floating melody and thus no attachment is possible—such nuclei always remain silent.

The alternation of the vowel is conditioned by the phonological context and is quite mechanical: the floating vowel is silenced, that is to say that it is not attached to the skeletal point when there is a vowel melody attached to the very next nucleus. The regularity looks fully phonological and has been claimed to belong to the phonology of the language by derivational-generative and post-generative models alike (Laskowski 1975a; Gussmann 1980a; Rubach 1984; Bethin 1992; Gussmann and Kaye 1993; Rowicka 1999; Scheer 2004, to mention just a few studies). In what follows we wish to challenge this assumption and revert to the structuralist position, which holds that the regularity is morpho-phonological rather than phonological. We start by considering cases where the conditions for the melodic association or its failure are not provided by the phonology but relate to the phonology–morphology–lexicon interface.

Consider first a simple case of the noun we used above to illustrate the vowel–zero alternation and a few derivatives based on the noun.

(69)   dech [dɛx] 'breath'   tch-u [txu] 'gen. sg.'
        od-dech [ɔddɛx] 'breathing'   od-dech-u [ɔddɛxu] 'gen. sg.'
        wy-dech [vɨdɛx] 'exhalation'   wy-dech-u [vɨdɛxu] 'gen. sg.'
        w-dech [vdɛx] 'inhalation'   w-dech-u [vdɛxu] 'gen. sg.'
        przy-dech [pʃɨdɛx] 'aspiration'   przy-dech-u [pʃɨdɛxu] 'gen. sg.'
        bez-dech [bɛzdɛx] 'apnoea'   bez-dech-u [bɛzdɛxu] 'gen. sg.'

The morpheme *dech* [dɛx], which appears in all the derivatives, contains the floating vowel when the morpheme stands on its own as an independent word. Hence the vowel disappears—that is, is not attached to the skeletal position—before a full melody in the nucleus of the inflectional ending. In the derivatives, however, the floating vowel of the basic morpheme stays put irrespectively of the nature of the following nucleus (full or empty). Thus the nucleus of the derivatives no longer contains a floating but an attached melody. Before connecting this fact with the derived or non-derived nature of the word, let us observe a somewhat different situation in the morpheme *zew* [zɛf] and its derivatives:

(70)   zew [zɛf] 'call, n.'   zew-u [zɛvu] 'gen. sg.'
        od-zew [ɔd-zɛf] 'response'   od-zew-u [ɔdzɛvu] 'gen. sg.'
        po-zew [pɔzɛf] 'summons'   po-zw-u [pɔzvu] 'gen. sg.'

Here the floating vowel appears not in the basic word but in just one of the derivatives. Thus, whether a vowel is floating or attached has nothing to do with simplex or complex morphology of the word. The only alternative is to claim that the distinction belongs to the lexicon: in some words the melody for [ɛ] is attached, in others it is not. In effect, the same morpheme in different words—that is, when combined with other morphemes—may have different phonological representations. This leads to two conclusions; first, it constitutes yet another piece of evidence against the often assumed but hardly ever defended view of a single phonological representation for each morpheme. A corollary is the impossibility of regarding alternations of the vowel [ɛ] with zero as a phonological phenomenon. Since, however, the different shapes of the morpheme are felt to constitute one unit, a way has to be found to capture their relatedness. Note that we are not talking about phonologically or morphologically conditioned relatedness since in the examples above there is no relevant phonological or morphological context that could be connected with the segmental shape of the morpheme. Thus given *dech* [dɛx] and *zew* [zɛv] there is no phonological or morphological reason why their genitive singular forms should not be, respectively, *dech-u* [dɛxu] and *zw-u* [zvu], rather than the actual *tch-u* [txu] and *zew-u* [zɛvu]. Additionally, the simple nouns can be combined with prefixes homophonous with prepositions, such as *od-* [ɔd], *bez-* [bɛz], *po-* [pɔ] and in such cases the behaviour of a noun with a prefix may differ from a situation when the noun appears after a preposition. This produces surface 'minimal pairs':

(71)   od-dech-u [ɔddɛxu] 'breathing, gen. sg.'   od tch-u [ɔttxu] 'from breathing'
       bez-dech-u [bɛzdɛxu] 'apnoea, gen. sg.'   bez tch-u [bɛstxu] 'breathless'
       po-zw-u [pɔzvu] 'summons, gen. sg.'   po zewi-e [pɔzɛvʲɛ] 'after the call'

Thus the relatedness between the floating vowel in, say, *tch-u* [txu] and the attached one in *od-dech-u* [ɔddɛxu] is not statable as either a phonological or even a morphophonological regularity. Rather the relatedness is lexical and needs to be captured as such. To achieve this, we propose an additional lexical mechanism which we shall call statements of Lexical Relatedness (LR).

Such statements are intended to connect different phonological shapes without assigning any directionality to them, that is, without deriving one from the other in any way. By connecting the floating vowel in some words with the non-floating one in others we are simply making a statement that the words share some parts despite the unpredictable differences between them. The LR information can be regarded as contained in the specification of the vowel in the same way as other morphophonological instructions contained there. To be concrete, the link between floating and stable vowels in the morphemes *dech, zew* will be reflected in the diacritic <LR1> attached to the nucleus in the lexicon. The lexical statement itself may take the following form:

LR1 x   ~   x
    |
    ɛ   ɛ

with a self-explanatory meaning: relate the floating and non-floating [ɛ]. This formulation indicates that a vowel with the diacritic <LR1> may be related to an otherwise identical morpheme differing from it in the property specified. Thus, for example, the vowel [ɛ] of the morpheme *dech* [dɛx] will be provided with the diacritic <LR1> in *wy-dech, w-dech, przy-dech, bez-dech* (see (69)), but not when it appears on its own as the independent word *dech* alternating with *tch-u*. This independent word bears testimony to and is a product of the prevailing morphophonological regularities of the language resulting in the vowel-zero alternation—recall that the prefixed words in (69) show no vocalic alternations within their paradigms. There seems to be no justification for burdening the basic word with information about properties of the more complex words which are lexically related to it. LR statements reflect links between and among words rather than reflect phonological, morphophonological, or morphological processes. The need to incorporate such statements into the lexicon confirms the view that the phenomena they cover—vowel~zero alternations in our case—have little to do with the phonology of the language.

The existence of two or more somewhat different phonological representations of the same morphemes and, hence, the existence of LR statements, will now be shown to have a much broader applicability. To begin with, we need a way of handling morphological free variants. A case in point is the appearance in Polish of nouns whose oblique forms either do or do not contain the floating vowel:

(72)   bitw-a [bʲitfa] 'battle'   bitew [bʲitɛf] / bitw [bʲitf] 'gen. pl.'
        pasm-o [pasmɔ] 'wisp'   pasem [pasɛm] / pasm [pasm̩] 'gen. pl.'
        brzytw-a [bʒitfa] 'razor'   brzytew [bʒitɛf] / brzytw [bʒitf] 'gen. pl.'
        ziarn-o [ʑarnɔ] 'grain'   ziaren [ʑarɛn] / ziarn [ʑarn] 'gen. pl.'
        sarn-a [sarna] 'roe deer'   saren [sarɛn] / sarn [sarn] 'gen. pl.'
        wydr-a [vɨdra] 'otter'   wyder [vɨdɛr] / wydr [vɨtr̩, vɨdr] 'gen. pl.'
        kalk-a [kalka] 'carbon paper'   kalek [kalɛk][18]/ kalk [kalk] 'gen. pl.'

The forms can be handled in two different ways, either of which is partially irregular. We can assume that the stems contain the floating vowel, in which case we shall have an account due to Melody Association of the nominative singular and the first variant of the genitive plural (with the vowel [ɛ]); what will remain puzzling is the variant without the vowel. Alternatively we can assume that consonant clusters form either branching onsets (*bitw-a*, *brzytw-a*, *wydr-a*) or a coda–onset contact (in the remaining cases); if that is the case, the variant with the vowel will be unexpected and will require some additional mechanism. One way or the other, some forms will remain exceptional. The way the exceptionality has to be handled can come from an observation that when the nouns become the input to further derivatives, the floating vowel normally appears in them. Consider again the nouns of (72) and words derived from them:

(73)   bitew [bʲitɛf]/bitw [bʲitf]   bitew-n-y [bʲitɛvnɨ] 'of the battle, adj.'
        pasem [pasɛm]/pasm [pasm̩]   pasem-k-o [pasɛmkɔ] 'wisp, dim.'
        brzytew [bʒitɛf]/brzytw [bʒitf]   brzytew-k-a [bʒitɛfka] 'razor, dim.'
        ziaren [ʑarɛn]/[ʑarn]   ziaren-k-o [ʑarɛnkɔ] 'grain, dim.'
        saren [sarɛn]/sarn [sarn]   saren-k-a [sarɛnka] 'roe deer, dim.'
        wyder [vɨdɛr]/wydr [vɨtr̩, vɨdr] wyder-k-a [vɨdɛrka] 'otter, dim.'
        kalek [kalɛk]/kalk [kalk]   kalecz-k-a [kalɛtʃka] 'carbon paper, dim.'

---

[18]   The form *kalek* is regarded as incorrect by the normative dictionary (Markowski 1999: 315) but quoted as a possibility by Gussmann (1980a: 40) and Kowalik (1997: 147). What all sources agree on is that the forms do occur.

The representations of *sarenka* [sarɛnka] 'roe deer' and its gen. pl. *sarenek* [sarɛnɛk] take the following shape:

(74)
```
O   N   O   N   O   N   O   N
|   |   |   |   |   |   |   |
x   x   x   x   x   x   x   x
|   |   |   |   |       |   |
s   a   r   ɛ   n   ɛ   k   a


O   N   O   N   O   N   O   N
|   |   |   |   |   |   |   |
x   x   x   x   x   x   x   x
|   |   |   |   |   |   |
s   a   r   ɛ   n   ɛ   k
```

In the top form the first floating [ɛ] is attached because it is followed by an unattached one while the second remains silent. In the lower representation the second one gets attached as well because the final nucleus is empty. The fact that the vowel in the root appears before the floating vowel of the suffix could be used as an argument in favour of the solution which regards the absence of the vowel in the genitive plural as an exception. The situation is more complex, however, since there are also numerous nouns which show no variable vowel alternation in different inflectional forms but which nonetheless require the vowel before certain derivational suffixes. Consider the examples in (75).

(75) (a) form-a [fɔrma] 'form'   form [fɔrm] 'gen. pl.'
          forem-k-a [fɔrɛmka] 'dim.'   forem-n-y [fɔrɛmnɨ] 'shapely'

      (b) walk-a [valka] 'strife'   walk [valk] 'gen. pl.'
          walecz-n-y [valɛtʃnɨ] 'valiant'

      (c) pasm-o [pasmɔ] 'wisp'   pasm [pasm̥] 'gen. pl.'
          pasem-k-o [pasɛmkɔ] 'dim.'   pasem-ek [pasɛmɛk] 'gen. pl.'

      (d) wróż-b-a [vruʒba] 'n.'   wróżb [vruʃp] 'gen. pl.'
          zło-wróż-b-n-y [zwɔvruʒbnɨ]   wróż-eb-n-y [vruʒɛbnɨ]
          'portending ill'   'portentous'

      (e) służ-b-a [swuʒba] 'service'   służ-b [swuʃp] 'gen.pl.'
          służ-eb-n-y [swuʒɛbnɨ] 'ancillary'   służ-eb-nic-a [swuʒɛbɲitsa]
                                                        'handmaid'

      (f) licz-b-a [lidʒba] 'number'   licz-b [litʃp] 'gen. pl.'
          licz-eb-n-y [litʃɛbnɨ] 'numerical'   licz-eb-nik [litʃɛbɲik] 'numeral'

      (g) świń-stw-o [ɕfʲiɲstfɔ] 'dirty trick'   świń-stw [ɕfʲiɲstf] 'gen. pl.'
          świń-stew-k-o [ɕfʲiɲstɛfkɔ] 'dim.'   świń-stew-ek [ɕfʲiɲstɛvɛk] 'gen. pl.'

      (h) modl-itw-a [mɔdlitfa] 'prayer'   modl-itw [mɔdlitf] 'gen. pl.'

modl-itew-ka [mɔdlitɛfka] 'dim.'   modl-itew-n-y [mɔdlitɛvnɨ]
                                        'prayerful'
modl-itew-nik [mɔdlitɛvɲik]
'prayer book'

(i) pań-stw-o [paɲstfɔ] 'state'   pań-stw [paɲstf] 'gen. pl.'
    pań-stewk-o [paɲstɛfkɔ] 'dim.'   pań-stew-ek [paɲstɛvɛk] 'gen. pl.'
    pań-stew-ecz-ko [paɲstɛvɛtʃkɔ]   pań-stew-ecz-ek [paɲstɛvɛtʃɛk]
    'dim.'   'gen. pl.'

Unlike the previous set of examples, here we encounter no variation within the inflectional paradigm of the derivational base. Thus the gen. pl. of *form-a* [fɔrma] is *form* [fɔrm] and never **forem* [fɔrɛm]. Nonetheless, when the diminutive suffix *-k-* or the adjective forming suffix *-n-* are attached, the floating vowel emerges between the two sonorants. The same is true about other suffixes, such as *-nik*, *-nic-a*, *-stw-o*, some of which have explicitly been argued above to contain branching onsets (e.g. [tf] = [tv] = [tw]). Consider example (75i), where the suffix *-stw-o* is attached to the basic morpheme *pan* [pan] 'lord, master': the initial fricative of the suffix occupies the coda position and is governed by the plosive of the branching onset. The genitive plural has an empty nucleus as its marker, hence the representations of the two forms are as given in (57). Before the diminutive suffix *-k-* and also before the double diminutive *-ecz-k-* the branching onset is broken up by the vowel [ɛ]. Here is the representation of the genitive plural of the double diminutive *pań-stew-ecz-ek* [paɲstɛvɛtʃɛk]:

(76) O R   O R   O R   O R   O R   O R
     | | | \ | | | | | | | |
     | N_1 | N_2 | N_3 | N_4 | N_5 | N_6
     | | | |\ | | | | | | | |
     x x   x x x x x   x x   x x   x x
     | | | | | | | | | | | |
     p a   ɲ s t ɛ v   ɛ tʃ   ɛ k

N_2 is an empty nucleus and always remains such; N_4 and N_5 are floating in a way that is typical of the vowel of the diminutive suffix and their appearance or non-appearance (being attached or not) is par for the course. It is N_3 that is problematic compared to the non-diminutive forms: it appears that the nucleus is inserted.

Within the standard model of Government Phonology, resyllabification is strictly disallowed as a phonological operation.[19] This tenet holds as long as we are dealing with a representation of a single form. It has never been claimed that a morpheme must have the same representation whenever it occurs, along the lines of the derivational-generative shibboleth, *one morpheme–one representation*. Quite conversely, cases have been explicitly recognized where a

---

[19] Note, however, that certain attempts have been made under the term *reduction* (Gussmann and Kaye 1993) or *syllable superimposition* (Yoshida 1993), where chunks of syllables (i.e. onsets and rhymes) were eliminated from representations.

given morpheme may have a different representation depending upon the environment—in such cases no violation of the resyllabification ban is found.[20] Thus, lexicalized formations are not a reliable source of evidence about the phonological representations of the constituent chunks.

If a morpheme can be syllabified in different ways when combined with other morphemes, then the presence of an additional nucleus in the forms above need not worry us. The examples show clearly that the forms have to be lexicalized if only because their semantics is non-compositional and partly unpredictable. The very notion of a floating melody with reference to nuclei like N_3 above is gratuitous: it assumes that the phonological representation of the component morpheme is the same wherever the morpheme occurs. Since we explicitly reject this assumption, we may regard what looks like an inserted vowel (N_3) as the melody [ɛ] attached to a skeletal position. In other words, alternations like *państw-o* [paɲstfɔ] 'state' ~ *pań-stew-k-o* [paɲstɛfkɔ] 'dim.' are not instances of the floating vowel as controlled by Melody Association. Rather, the superficially similar vowel~zero alternation is due to different phonological representations. What we might want to capture lexically is the information that the inserted vowel corresponds to nothing in the base morpheme; this we can do by recognizing an LR statement along the following lines:

LR2 X

    | ~∅

  ɛ

The diacritic <LR2> attached to N_3 of *państeweczek* (see (76)) indicates that the vowel corresponds to no segment in other words. An interpretation which relies on diacritic marking accounts for the non-necessary or stipulatory character of their morphophonological effects and gives the lie to any phonologically based approach to the issue, no matter how rich the theoretical machinery it employs. This is confirmed rather dramatically by some examples in (75d):

(77) wróżb [vruʃp] 'prophesy, gen. pl.'   zło-wróż-b-n-y [zwɔvruʒbnɨ] 'portending ill'
   wróż-eb-n-y [vruʒɛbnɨ] 'portentous'

In one adjective derived from the same nominal base by means of the same suffix -*n-y* an inserted nucleus appears while in the other it does not. Obviously, phonologically, morphophonologically, and morphologically the reverse could just as well be true, that is, *złowróżebny* [zwɔvruʒɛbnɨ], *wróżbny* [vruʒbnɨ] are

---

[20] In English, [p] is an onset in *sleep* [sli:p] with a preceding branching nucleus but a coda with a non branching nucleus in *slept* [slept]. Likewise, there are numerous derivationally related forms like *heal–health, deep–depth, wise–wisdom*, which have to be represented differently if only because the generative rules of vowel shortening or vowel shift are no longer a going concern—they do not belong to the phonology of the language (Kaye 1995; Harris 1994: 79–81).

non-existent but well-formed; the occurring forms have the shape they do because that is what is dictated by the lexicon. A description merely relates the forms by statements like <LR2> without deriving one from the other or both from a common source.

A distinct phonological and morphophonological implication is that alternations of sounds are no raw data of analysis—they have to be interpreted, fitted into the emerging linguistic system, and related to what is understood about its working. In principle, the same vowel~zero alternation can instantiate a phonological, a morphophonological, or a lexical regularity. In our case, phonology merely receives structures supplied by the lexicon and morphophonology while the alternation itself is outside the purview of phonology or its mechanisms. However, segments can be ambiguous and may reflect different linguistic properties. A case where interaction of different components can be seen very clearly involves some prefixes and prepositions, to which we now turn.

5.5 PREFIXES AND PREPOSITIONS

The phonological properties of certain prefixes and prepositions, alluded to above in a few places, have attracted the attention of phonologists for a long time (Laskowski 1975a; Gussmann 1980a; Nykiel-Herbert 1985; Rubach 1984, 1985; Szpyra 1989, 1992b; Bethin 1992; Ruszkiewicz 1992). These form an interesting area in itself in that they reveal the potential of different theoretical mechanisms and systems; hence, they document in a way the development of phonological theory. We cannot delve into these partially conflicting accounts here but propose instead to review the relevant facts and show how they fit the framework we used above to describe the vowel~zero alternations. Let us start with prepositions.

Several prepositions appear in two shapes: one with the final vowel -*e* [ɛ], and one without it: *w*(*e*) [vɛ] 'in', *od*(*e*) [ɔdɛ] 'from', *bez*(*e*) [bɛzɛ] 'without', *z*(*e*) [zɛ] 'with' *przez*(*e*) [pʃɛzɛ] 'by', *pod*(*e*) [pɔdɛ] 'under', *nad*(*e*) [nadɛ] 'above', *spod*(*e*) [spɔdɛ] 'from beneath' as in the following examples:[21]

(78)   we włosach [vɛ vwɔsax] 'in the hair'   w mroku [v mrɔku] 'in the darkness'

we krwi [vɛ kr̥fʲi] '(running) in the blood'   w krwi [f kr̥fʲi] 'in blood'

we śnie [vɛ ɕɲɛ] 'while asleep'   w snach [f snax] 'in dreams'

ode złego [ɔdɛ zwɛgɔ] 'from evil'   od złości [ɔd zwɔɕtɕi] 'from anger'

beze mnie [bɛzɛ mɲɛ] 'without me'   bez mnicha [bɛz mɲixa] 'without a monk'

---

[21] Since in this section we are interested in the phenomena arising at the juncture of the prefix/ preposition and the following word, the morphological composition of that word is irrelevant and morpheme boundaries outside the prefix are disregarded.

ze Lwowa [zɛ lvɔva] 'from Lvov'	z lwem [z lvɛm] 'with a lion'
ze wsi [zɛ fçi] 'rustic, from the country'	z wsiadaniem [s fçadaɲem] 'with embarkation'
ze względu [zɛ vzglɛndu] 'on account of'	z względnym [z vzglɛndnɨm] 'with relative...'
ze wstydu [zɛ fstɨdu] 'for shame'	z wstępem [s fstɛmpɛm] 'with an introduction'
ze wzruszeniem [zɛ vzruʃɛɲɛm] 'with emotion'	z wzrostem [z vzrɔstɛm] 'with growth'
przeze mnie [pʃɛzɛ mɲɛ] 'by me'	przez mnogie [pʃɛz mnɔjɛ] 'through numerous'
pode drzwiami [pɔdɛ d-ʒvʲamʲi] 'by the door'	pod drzwiami [pɔd d-ʒvʲamʲi] 'under a door'
nade wszystko [nadɛ fʃɨstkɔ] 'above all'	nad wszystkim [nat fʃɨstcim] 'over everything'
spode łba [spɔdɛ wba] '(look) angrily'	spod pstrych [spɔt pstrɨx] 'from under speckled...'

We need to introduce some order into the apparent chaos prevailing here. A striking fact about most of the prepositions is that they appear in both shapes before what is the same consonant sequences. For this reason, one tentative generalization that suggests itself needs to be discarded out of hand: it might seem that the final vowel of the preposition appears before heavy consonantal clusters. That this is not the case is documented rather eloquently by the last example: *spod pstrych* [spɔt pstrɨx] rather than **spode pstrych* [spɔdɛ pstrɨx], also *w pstrągu* [fpstrɔŋgu] 'in the trout', *z pstrągiem* [spstrɔɲjɛm] 'with a trout' and never **we pstrągu* [vɛ pstrɔŋgu], **ze pstrągiem* [zɛ pstrɔɲjɛm]. Having said this we must also observe that the final vowel of the preposition never occurs before a single consonant in the following word. In other words, a two-member consonant sequence is a necessary but not a sufficient condition for the final vowel to appear. The preposition itself ends with a vowel alternating with zero, that is, a floating melody.[22]

The appearance of the final vowel before a consonantal cluster suggests that the cluster is itself an onset sequence separated by an empty nucleus or a nucleus without an attached melody. Thus, on the assumption that the final vowel of the preposition is a floating melody, we can identify its behaviour with what Melody Association predicts: a floating melody is attached before an unattached melody or an

---

[22] Another point that has to be made is that there is a certain amount of variation in some cases. Some speakers prefer a syllabic variant in, for example, *ze względnym* [zɛ vzglɛndnɨm] 'with relative...', *ze wstępem* [zɛ fstɛmpɛm] 'with an introduction', *ze wzrostem* [zɛ vzrɔstɛm] 'with growth'. The forms described in the body of the text are the ones I would use and for which I have found sufficient support from other speakers. It should also be pointed out that there is some regional variation affecting the prepositions *w* and *z* before single but similar onsets. Thus, side by side with the standard *w wodzie* [v vɔdʑɛ] 'in water' and *z sokiem* [s sɔcɛm] 'with juice' one finds regional variants, regarded as substandard, *we wodzie* [vɛ vɔdʑɛ], *ze sokiem* [zɛ sɔcɛm].

empty nucleus. This conclusion is particularly plausible in view of the fact that practically none of the consonant sequences can qualify as a well-formed onset for either universal or theory-internal reasons; in *mnie* [mɲɛ] 'me, gen. acc.' a sequence of two nasals can never form an onset by a universal assumption, while in *zlego* [zwɛgɔ] 'evil, adj., gen. sg.' the dental fricative can never be the head of a branching onset by an additional GP assumption. The two phrases *ode zlego* 'from evil' and *beze mnie* 'without me' are therefore represented as follows:

(79)
```
    O   N   O   N       O   N   O   N   O   N
    |   |   |   |       |   |   |   |   |   |
    x   x   x   x       x   x   x   x   x   x
        |   |   |       |       |   |   |   |
        ɔ   d   ɛ       z       w   ɛ   g   ɔ


    O   N   O   N       O   N   O   N
    |   |   |   |       |   |   |   |
    x   x   x   x       x   x   x   x
    |   |   |   |       |       |   |
    b   ɛ   z   ɛ       m       ɲ   ɛ
```

These representations, self-explanatory as they are, make a tacit assumption, namely that the floating final nucleus of the preposition can see the empty nucleus of the following word. This means that the phrases form a single phonological domain with no boundary separating the preposition and the following word. While arbitrary at first glance this interpretation makes perfect sense and is independently supported.

Most of the left-hand column expressions in (78) are set phrases or petrified collocations. The form *ode zlego* [ɔdɛ zwɛgɔ] appears exclusively in the context of *nas zbaw ode zlego* 'deliver us from evil'; *beze* [bɛzɛ], just like *przeze* [pʃɛzɛ], appears in the modern language almost exclusively before the pronoun *mnie* [mɲɛ] 'me, gen. acc.'. Additionally, in combinations with this pronoun it is the last vowel of the prepositions which receives stress, [bɛˈzɛmɲɛ], [pʃɛˈzɛmɲɛ], which further strengthens the case for a single phonological domain and the working of Melody Association. A case for semantic non-compositionality can be made for the other expressions as well: *pode drzwiami* [pɔdɛ d-ʒvʲamʲi] 'by the door' is literary or bookish, *nade wszystko* [nadɛ fʃistkɔ] 'above all' is idiomatic, as is *spode lba* [spɔde wba] (lit. 'from beneath the noggin') in the expression *spojrzeć spode lba* 'look angrily, glower', *we znaki* [vɛ znaci] in the phrase *dać się we znaki* 'make oneself felt, be difficult'.[23] Such forms can be assumed to form a single domain not only on phonological grounds, in other words, with reference to Melody Association, but also because they tend to be morphologically isolated and semantically idiosyncratic. Since semantic or morphological idiosyncracy

---

[23] For more examples and discussion with a basically commensurate way of thinking, see Rubach (1985).

refers to a gradable and occasionally vague phenomenon, it is not surprising that it may lead to variation and vacillation.

The outstanding question concerns the absence of the final vowel before very similar or identical consonant sequences, as in the right-hand-column words in (78); a straightforward mechanism for handling these cases is available, however, namely, domain boundary.

Unlike the petrified or idiomatic expressions which constitute single domains, ordinary, syntax-derived prepositional phrases contain a domain boundary between the preposition and the following nominal. This leads to tangible phonological consequences since each domain is processed independently—in our terms, the final floating vowel of the preposition remains unattached because it is not followed by an empty nucleus which would license its attachment. The first nucleus of the nominal similarly remains unattached or empty. Consider *z lwem* [zlvɛm] 'with a lion', with a floating vowel (cf. *lew* [lɛf] 'lion, nom. sg.'), and *z mnichem* [zmɲixɛm] 'with a monk', with an empty nucleus.

```
(80)  O   N     O   N   O   N   O   N
      |   |     |   |   |   |   |   |
      x   x    [x   x   x   x   x   x]
      |   |     |       |   |   |
      z   ε     l   ε   v   ε   m


      O   N     O   N   O   N   O   N   O   N
      |   |     |   |   |   |   |   |   |   |
      x   x    [x   x   x   x   x   x   x   x]
      |   |     |       |   |   |   |
      z   ε     m   ɲ   i   x   ε   m
```

The nucleus of the prefix, pronounced without any vowel, is the unmarked case and this is the variant we find before consonantal clusters of any complexity, or indeed before an empty onset (*z osą* [z ɔsɔ̃ʷ] 'with a wasp') or a non-branching onset (*z wodą* [z vɔdɔ̃ʷ] 'with water'). Our interpretation thus remains purely phonological as long as appropriate morphophonological clearing of the stage has been performed and adequate domain structure bracketing supplied.[24]

One case where phonological—or, more specifically, melodic—considerations override those of domain structure deserves mention. The two prepositions *z* [z], *w* [v] always appear in their syllabic versions *ze* [zɛ], *we* [vɛ] when the following

---

[24] It might be suggested that rather than adjust domain structure, a different phonological representation might be posited for prepositions in non-lexicalized structures, namely, one with an empty nucleus in place of the floating melody. We believe that manipulating domains is more in keeping with what is known about the nature of petrified and otherwise idiosyncratic expressions, which tend to lose their internal structure and, concomitantly, often also the phonological transparency of their constituent parts—English *cupboard* [kʌbəd] or *boatswain* [bəusən] today reveal their historical complexity only because of the spelling. Additionally, the alternative proposal would force us to relinquish the ban against more than one empty nucleus domain internally, as *z mnichem* above would require two such nuclei: [zəmøɲixhɛm].

nominal begins with a cluster whose first consonant is similar to that of the preposition:

(81) we władzy [vɛ vwadzɨ]   ze złości [zɛ zwɔ¢tɕi]
      'in the power'   'out of fury'
      we Wrocławiu [vɛ vrɔtswavʲu]   ze Szwecji [zɛ ʃfɛtsji]
      'in Wrocław'   'from Sweden'
      we Włoszech [vɛ vwɔʃɛx]   ze źródła [zɛ ʐrudwa]
      'in Italy'   'from a spring'

It hardly needs pointing out that what is at stake is the melodic similarity rather than mere segmental complexity; when the consonants are not similar, no vowel appears on the preposition:

(82) we Wrzeszczu [vɛ vʒɛʃtʃu] but z Wrzeszcza [z vʒɛʃtʃa]
      'in Wrzeszcz'   'from Wrzeszcz'
      ze strzelby [zɛ st-ʃɛlbɨ] but w strzelbie [f st-ʃɛlbʲɛ]
      'from a rifle'   'in a rifle'

Also, a single consonant does not influence the pronounceability of the final vowel of the preposition:

(83) w wodzie [v vɔdʑɛ]   z sokiem [s sɔcɛm]
      'in water'   'with juice'
      w wannie [v vanɲɛ]   z zazdrością [z zazdrɔ¢tɕɔʷ]
      'in a bath-tub'   'with jealousy'

Likewise, no final vowel appears when the preposition contains a pronounced vowel:

(84) bez strzelby [bɛs st-ʃɛlbɨ]   przez strzelbę [pʃɛs st-ʃɛlbɛ]
      'without a rifle'   'because of a rifle'
      pod trawą [pɔt travɔʷ]   nad drogą [nad drɔgɔʷ]
      'under the grass'   'over the road'

The conditioning seems somewhat convoluted but clear-cut: if a preposition consisting of a fricative and a floating vowel is followed by a consonantal cluster in the next word whose first consonant is similar to the consonant of the preposition, then the floating vowel gets attached to its skeletal position. The structure then has the following shape:

(85)
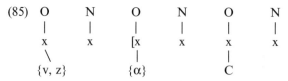

where α is similar to {v, z}

although it should probably be simplified to just melodic considerations. Traditionally (Kowalik 1997: 148), the appearance of the vowel is understood as a case of epenthesis motivated by the avoidance of certain consonantal clusters.

To sum up so far: prepositions ending in a floating nucleus are governed by Melody Association very much like the rest of relevant cases. The factors which somewhat obscure the picture are the presence or absence of domain boundaries and possible melodic similarity between the preposition and the beginning of the next word. Expressions without phonological domains are listed in the lexicon and constitute a minority of eligible forms.

We will now use the conclusions arrived at by our survey of prepositions to deal with prefixes, which are often—non-accidentally—identical with prepositions. Below we list verbs with the prefixes *roz-(e)* [rɔzɛ], *od(e)-* [ɔdɛ], *pod(e)-* [pɔdɛ], *w(e)-* [vɛ], *z(e)-* [zɛ], where the prefix ends in the vowel [ɛ] in the left-hand column, whereas the vowel is not present in the right-hand one although the verb begins with the same or very similar consonant sequence.

(86) roze-brać [rɔzɛbratɕ] 'undress'   roz-bryzgać [rɔzbrɨzgatɕ] 'splash out'

    roze-drzeć [rɔzɛd-ʒɛtɕ] 'tear out'   roz-drapać [rɔzdrapatɕ] 'scratch'
    roze-mleć [rɔzɛmlɛtɕ] 'crush into pulp'   roz-ławić [rɔzwzavʲitɕ] 'draw tears'
    roze-źlić [rɔzɛʑlitɕ] 'make angry'   roz-złościć [rɔzzwɔɕtɕitɕ] 'make angry'

    ode-pchnąć [ɔdɛpxnɔɲtɕ] 'push out'   od-pchlić [ɔtpxlitɕ] 'de-flea'
    ode-spać [ɔdɛspatɕ] 'sleep off'   od-sprzedać [ɔtspʃɛdatɕ] 'sell off'
    ode-zwać [ɔdɛzvatɕ] 'respond'   od-dzwonić [ɔddzvɔɲitɕ] 'phone back'

    ode-przeć [ɔdɛpʃɛtɕ] 'repulse'   od-prząc [ɔtpʃɔnts] 'unharness'
    pode-przeć [pɔdɛpʃɛtɕ] 'support'   pod-prowadzić [pɔtprɔvadʑitɕ] 'lead'
    pode-słać [pɔdɛswatɕ] 'send'   pod-słuchać [pɔtswuxatɕ] 'overhear'
    pode-trzeć [pɔdɛt-ʃɛtɕ] 'wipe'   pod-trzymać [pɔtt-ʃɨmatɕ] 'support'
    we-gnać [vɛgnaɕ] 'drive in'   w-gnieść [vɡɲɛɕtɕ] 'crush in'
    we-drzeć [vɛd-ʒɛtɕ] 'force into'   w-drapać [vdrapatɕ] 'climb'
    we-przeć [vɛpʃɛtɕ] 'push into'   w-przęgać [fpʃɛŋgatɕ] 'harness'
    ze-psuć [zɛpsutɕ] 'spoil'   s-psocić [spsɔtɕitɕ] 'play a prank'
    ze-tleć [zɛtlɛtɕ] 'smoulder'   s-tlenić [stlɛɲitɕ] 'make oneself scarce'
    ze-tlić [zɛtlitɕ] 'burn to cinders'   s-tlić [stlitɕ] 'burn to cinders'
    ze-psieć [zɛpɕɛtɕ] 'go to the dogs'   s-psieć [spɕɛtɕ] 'go to the dogs'

Thus, yet again, it is not the consonantal complex following the suffix that determines the appearance or non-appearance of the final vowel although, of course, before a single consonant of the root, the vowel never emerges: *roz-pisać* [rɔspʲisatɕ] 'write out', *od-gałęzić* [ɔdgawɛ́ʷʑitɕ] 'branch off'.

The last two sets of examples in (86) are particularly telling since the two possibilities are free variants, showing that it is not the nature of the cluster that determines the vowel of the prefix. Similarly the presence of a floating vowel or empty nucleus is not a sufficient condition: although all the left-hand stems can be shown to contain such nuclei, so can most of the right-hand ones: *roz-łzawić* [rɔzwzavʲitɕ] 'draw tears' and *od-pchlić* [ɔtpxlitɕ] 'de-flea' are morphologically derived from *łz-a* [wza] 'tear, n.' and *pchł-a* [pxwa] 'flea', whose floating vowel appears quite regularly in the genitive plural forms: *łez* [wɛs], *pchel* [pxɛw]. Thus, although an unattached vowel or an empty nucleus in the root is necessary for the vowel of the prefix to emerge, this does not exhaust the conditioning. What is additionally necessary is neighbourhood within a domain, in the same way as in the prepositional phrases above.

The analysis we adopt is that in some cases the prefixes form single domains with the verb to which they are attached. There is no way of predicting which roots with a floating vowel or an empty nucleus will form a single domain and which ones will be separated from it by a domain boundary. This is the dominion of the lexicon and lexical idiosyncrasy although on the whole, single domains tend to be less semantically compositional than complex structures: between *brać* [bratɕ] 'take' and *roze-brać* [rɔzɛbratɕ] 'undress' (also 'take apart') there is a vast difference which cannot be meaningfully or systematically bridged and has to be placed in the lexicon in the same way as in English the difference between *take* and *take off*. Our representations of *roze-brać* [rɔzɛbratɕ] and *roz-łzawić* [rɔzwzavʲitɕ] take the following shapes:

(87)
O	N	O	N	O	N	O	N	O	N
x	x	x	x	x	x	x	x	x	x
r	ɔ	z	ɛ	bʲ	ɛ	r	a	tɕ	

O	N	O	N	O	N	O	N	O	N	O	N
x	x	x	x	[x	x	x	x	x	x	x	x]
r	ɔ	z	ɛ	w	ɛ	z	a	vʲ	i	tɕ	

Just like with prepositional phrases discussed above, the floating vowel in the prefix of the first verb is within a single domain with the following stem, which is why it is attached before the next unattached nuclear melody (see (79)). The final vowel of the prefix in the second verb cannot be regarded as followed by any nucleus because of the intervening domain boundary and for this reason it remains unattached (see (80)). The co-existence of two possible patterns of interpreting prefixed verbs naturally suggests that alternative analyses of individual forms may also exist. This does happen as evidenced by the frequent admonitions in normative dictionaries against forms such as **ode-grzać* [ɔdɛgʒatɕ] for *od-grzać* [ɔdgʒatɕ] 'warm up', or **roze-grywać* [rɔzɛgrɨvatɕ] for *roz-grywać* [rɔzgrɨvatɕ] 'play out'. It transpires then that specific prefix-verbal root combinations have to be marked lexically for single domainhood. When not marked in this way, prefixes are processed independently of the following verbal stem. It should be stressed, however, that the number of roots involved in such lexicalized prefixal formations does not exceed thirty (Szpyra 1989: 214) of which a part only takes the prefixes of the required shape.[25] Thus in real terms the number of such arbitrarily combined prefixed verbs is significantly smaller than the number of strong verbs in modern Germanic languages.

Most of the left-hand column's verbal roots in (86) contain a floating vowel which remains unattached because it is followed by an attached nuclear melody. There is a morphological process, forming derived imperfectives, whereby the floating vowel gets attached to its position. In such a case we predict that the final vowel of the prefix must be subject to changes since it is now followed by an attached vowel: the vowel of the prefix is expected to remain floating. This is exactly what happens as shown by the different verbal forms of the left-hand column verbs.

(88) roze-brać [rɔzɛbratɕ] 'undress'   roz-bierać [rɔzbʲɛratɕ] 'imperf.'
      roze-drzeć [rɔzɛd-ʒɛtɕ] 'tear out'   roz-dzierać [rɔzdʑɛratɕ] 'imperf.'
      roze-mleć [rɔzɛmlɛtɕ] 'crush into pulp' roz-mielę [rɔzmʲɛlɛ] '1 sg. pres.'
      ode-pchnąć [ɔdɛpxnɔɲtɕ] 'push out'   od-pychać [ɔtpɨxatɕ] 'imperf.'
      ode-spać [ɔdɛspatɕ] 'sleep off'   od-sypiać [ɔt-sɨpʲatɕ] 'imperf.'
      ode-zwać [ɔdɛzvatɕ] 'respond'   od-zywać [ɔd-zɨvatɕ] 'imperf.'
      ode-przeć [ɔdɛpʃɛtɕ] 'repulse'   od-piera [ɔtpʲɛra] '3 sg. pres.'
      pode-przeć [pɔdɛpʃɛtɕ] 'support'   pod-pierać [pɔtpʲɛratɕ] 'imperf.'
      pode-słać [pɔdɛswatɕ] 'send'   pod-syłać [pɔt-sɨwatɕ] 'imperf.'
      pode-trzeć [pɔdɛt-ʃɛtɕ] 'wipe'   pod-cierać[pɔttɕɛratɕ] 'imperf.'
      we-zwać [vɛzvatɕ] 'summon'   w-zywać [vzɨvatɕ] 'imperf.'
      we-ssać [vɛssatɕ] 'suck in'   w-sysać [vsɨsatɕ] 'imperf.'

When the nucleus in the root is filled, the floating vowel of the prefix must remain unassociated and therefore is not pronounced. As before, once the proper context is produced by morphological or lexical operations, phonology can apply across the board. The morphological or lexical operations may attach a vowel other than [ɛ], an issue to which we return below, but its behaviour is the same as of other attached an unattached nuclei. Consider the last examples in the list above based on the verb ss-a-ć [ssatɕ] 'suck'; the initial geminate consonant indicates that a nucleus must intervene since a geminate is not a possible onset and Polish, in general, does not tolerate geminates morpheme internally. The nucleus actually emerges in the imperfective form as [ɨ] so we assume this is the floating melody of the perfective form. Given these observations note the representations of both verbal forms.

---

[25] There are prefixes that end in an attached vowel, hence no vowel alternation in the prefix can take place. Examples are the prefixes *na- wy- za-*, e.g. *na-brać* [nabratɕ] 'take a lot', *wy-brać* [vɨbratɕ] 'choose', *za-brać* [zabratɕ] 'take away'.

(89)

```
O   N   O   N   O   N   O   N
|   |   |   |   |   |   |   |
x   x   x   x   x   x   x   x
|   |   |   |   |   |   |
v   ɛ   s   ɨ   s   a   tɕ
```

```
                        R
                        |\
O   N   O   N   O   N     O   N²⁶
|   |   |   |   |   |     |   |
x   x   x   x   x   x x   x   x
|   |   |   |   |   |     |
v   ɛ   s   ɨ   s   a j   tɕ
```

In the top form the floating [ɨ], being followed by a filled nucleus, is not pronounced, while the floating [ɛ] of the prefix is attached since it is not followed by a filled nucleus. In the derived imperfective where the floating melody of the root is attached as part of the morphological process, the vowel of the prefix is regularly silent as required by Melody Association.

Just as the preposition z [z], which before a cluster beginning with a similar consonant emerges with a vowel, the prefix z- likewise appears as ze- [zɛ] in that context. This can be seen in the following examples:

(90) ze-skoczyć [zɛskɔtʃitɕ] 'jump down'   ze-słać [zɛswatɕ] 'send into exile'
      ze-szlifować [zɛʃlifɔvatɕ] 'grind, polish'   ze-szmacić [zɛʃmatɕitɕ] 'become
                                                    a rag'
      ze-ślizgnąć [zɛɕlizgnɔɲtɕ] 'glide down'   ze-świnić [zɛɕfʲiɲitɕ] 'act like
                                                    a swine'
      ze-złościć [zɛzwɔɕtɕitɕ] 'make angry'   ze-żreć [zɛʒrɛtɕ] 'devour'
      ze-zwierzęcić [zɛzvʲɛʒɛɲtɕitɕ]
      'turn a beast'

The constraint we formed above for the prepositions (85) holds also in the case of such verbs, the difference being that there are no cases of the other preposition/ prefix w [v]. This seems an accidental gap as there happen to be no verbs beginning with v+C to which the prefix could be attached.[27]

Another prefix which we discussed above in connection with our Kuryłowicz-inspired reinterpretation is ws-/wz- (see (53)). There we claimed that this historical prefix, unproductive today and often hardly identifiable as such, is reinterpreted to

---

[26] The suffix -aj is one of the markers of the category of derived imperfectives and appears without the final glide before a consonant; for this reason we leave the glide unassociated to the skeletal position. The functioning and distribution of the suffix -aj must be described in the morphology of the language.

[27] The particular combination of consonants is rare in Polish but when it does occur the results are exactly as we expect. Thus the noun wnętrze [vnɛnt-ʃɛ] 'the interior' can take the prefix w- which emerges as we-: wewnętrzny [vɛvnɛnt-ʃni] 'internal'.

contain a domain boundary falling between two consonants. The boundary prevents a sequence of two empty nuclei from arising within a single domain. For the sake of completeness we note the existence of three verbs with the prefix *wez-* [vɛz]/*wz-* [vz] (*wes-* [vɛs]/*ws-* [vs]) whose behaviour falls into the group discussed here. Unlike the re-analyzed variants with doctored domain structures (see (54)), the three verbs display a floating vowel in the prefix and analyze it jointly with the verbal stems:

(91)   wez-br-a-ć [vɛzbratɕ] 'surge'   wz-bier-aj-ą [vzbʲɛrajɔ̃ʷ]
                                                            'imperf. 3 pl. pres.'
        wes-prz-e-ć [vɛspʃɛtɕ] 'support'   ws-pier-aj-ą [fspʲɛrajɔ̃ʷ]
                                                            'imperf. 3 pl. pres.'
        wes-tch-ną-ć [vɛstxnɔɲtɕ] 'sigh'   wz-dych-aj-ą [vzdɨxajɔ̃ʷ]
                                                            'imperf. 3 pl. pres.'

Being within a single domain with the root, the final fricative of the prefix occupies the coda position and is governed by a strong obstruent, a plosive. The prefix contains a floating melody and is subject to Melody Association in the regular way. Thus the vowel of the prefix is pronounced in the left-hand column's verbs where the root's floating vowel cannot be pronounced as it is followed by an attached melody. The right-hand column's verbs are so-called derived imperfectives; the morphological process of their formation consists in the addition of the suffix *-aj-* [aj] and the attachment of the root's floating vowel to its skeletal position. When this happens, the floating vowel of the prefix remains unpronounced since it cannot be attached. The glide of the derived imperfective suffix is morphophonologically suppressed (cf. n. 26). The resulting vowel alternation in the prefix is accountable only when a single domain is assumed for the prefixed verbs. Consider representations of the first example:

(92)

```
O   R        O   R   O   R        O   R
|   |\       |   |   |   |        |   |
|   N \      |   N   |   N        |   N
|   |   \    |   |   |   |        |   |
x   x    x   x   x   x   x        x   x
|   |    |   |   |   |   |        |
v   ɛ    z   b   ɛ   r   a        tɕ


O   R        O   R   O   R            O   R
|   |\       |   |   |   |            |   |
|   N \      |   N   |   N \          |   N
|   |   \    |   |   |   |   \        |   |
x   x    x   x   x   x   x    x       x   x
|   |    |   |   |   |   |    |       |
v   ɛ    z   b   ɛ   r   a    j       tɕ
```

In the above discussion we concentrated on verbs, since it is there that the alternations and constraints can be seen most clearly and exemplified most readily. It is not the case, however, that either the alternations or the constraints are verb-specific. Since outside the verbal system the regularities are the same, we limit ourselves here to mentioning a few examples of denominal adjectives; the base noun contains a floating melody as shown by the alternations:

(93) krew [krɛf] 'blood'   krw-i [kr̥fʲi] 'gen. sg.'   bez-krw-aw-y [bɛskr̥favɨ]
                                                             'bloodless'

      płeć [pwɛtɕ] 'sex'   płc-i [pw̥tɕi] 'gen. sg.'   bez-płc-iow-y [bɛspw̥tɕɔvɨ]
                                                             'sexless'

      cł-o [tswɔ] 'customs'   ceł [tsɛw] 'gen. pl.'   bez-cł-ow-y [bɛstswɔvɨ]
                                                             'duty-free'

      brew [brɛf] 'brow'   brw-i [brvʲi] 'gen. sg.'   nad-brwi-owy [nadbrvʲɔvɨ]
                                                             'over the brow'

      den [dɛn] 'pit, gen. pl.'   dn-o [dnɔ] 'nom. sg.'   bez-den-n-y [bɛzdɛnnɨ]
                                                             'bottomless'

The prefixes are separated from the base by domain boundary, hence their final vowel remains unattached. Note that this happens, predictably enough, irrespective of whether the root vowel is attached or floating. Thus compare the representations of the first and the last example in our list:

(94)

O	N	O	N	O	N	O	N	O	N
|	|	|	|	$\wedge$	|	|	|	|	|
x	x	x	x	[x x x		x	x	x	x]
|	|	|		| |		|	|	|	|
b	ɛ	z	ɛ	k r ɛ		v	a	v	ɨ

O	N	O	N	O	N	O	N	O	N
|	|	|	|	|	|	|	|	|	|
x	x	x	x	[x	x	x	x	x	x]
|	|	|		|	|	|		|	|
b	ɛ	z	ɛ	d	ɛ	n		n	ɨ

The final vowel of the prefix is processed in the same way as it would be in expressions *bez krwi* [bɛs kr̥fʲi] 'without blood' and *bez dna* [bɛz dna] 'without the bottom'; similarly the nominal bases are processed in the same way as they would be in prepositional phrases.

The denominal prefixed adjectives can be seen to correspond structurally to the majority of prefixed verbs in that both categories analyze prefixes independently of the following roots and separate them by domain boundaries. We noted that only about thirty verbal roots are lexicalized into single domains with the prefixes. Adjectives are likewise predominantly derived with internal domain structure. One counter-example, much discussed in the literature, is the word *beze-cn-y* [bɛzɛtsnɨ] 'disgraceful', which is based on the obsolete adjective *cn-y* [tsnɨ] 'noble, virtuous' (cf. also *nie-cn-y* [ɲɛtsnɨ] 'wicked'). The appearance of the prefix with a final vowel indicates that the prefix forms a single domain with the adjectival base;

the same vowel also confirms the existence of a nucleus in the adjectival root, -cn-
[tsn]. This follows not only from the non-existence of consonant only roots in
Polish, but also from that fact that—given appropriate condition—a vowel will
emerge between the two consonants in total agreement with what is found generally
in the language. It so happens that the adjective *beze-cn-y* [bɛzɛtsnɨ] 'disgraceful' can
be combined with the nominalizing suffix *-stw-o*, which we argued above begins
with an empty nucleus and carries the diacritic <PR1>. The derived noun is *beze-
ceń-stw-o* [bɛzɛtsɛɲstfɔ] 'ignominy'. Consider the representation of the prefixed
adjective and the derived nominal.

(95)

```
O   N   O   N   O   N   O   N
|   |   |   |   |   |   |   |
x   x   x   x   x   x   x   x
|   |   |   |   |       |   |
b   ɛ   z   ɛ   ts  ɛ   n   ɨ
```

```
                                R
                               /\
O   N   O   N   O   N   O   N  /    \  O        N
|   |   |   |   |   |   |   | /      \ /\       |
x   x   x   x   x   x   x   x  x     x  x       x
|   |   |   |   |   |   |             |  |  |   |
b   ɛ   z   ɛ   ts  ɛ   ɲ             s  t  f   ɔ
```

The floating melody in the prefix in both the adjective and the noun and also the
floating melody in the nominal are selected as meeting the conditions for association since they are followed by non-associated melodies; the association is
carried out simultaneously, as discussed in an early part of this chapter in
connection with sequences of floating melodies (cf. also n. 5). The crucial point
about the adjective *beze-cn-y* and the noun *beze-ceń-stw-o* is the absence of
domain boundary after the prefix *beze-*.

5.6 OTHER FLOATING MELODIES

As indicated on a few occasions above, there are other floating vowels than just
[ɛ] and they can be attached in different ways. One case referred to earlier is found
in a class of derived imperfective verbs taking the suffix *-aj*. The morphophonological consequence of the presence of this suffix is the attachment of floating
nucleur melody of the root which thus acts as an attached melody for the
purposes of phonology. The floating vowels are {ɛ} and {I}, where the latter is
realized as either [i] or [ɨ] depending upon the palatality of the preceding consonant. Consider a few cases where the right-hand examples are all imperfectives,
third-person plural present tense:

(96) wy-br-a-ć [vɨbratɕ] 'choose'   wy-bier-aj-ą [vɨbʲɛrajɔʷ]
      tr-ą [trɔʷ] 'rub, 3 pl. pres.'   wy-cier-aj-ą [vɨtɕɛrajɔʷ]
      na-zw-a-ć [nazvatɕ] 'name'   na-zyw-aj-ą [nazɨvajɔʷ]
      prze-tk-a-ć [pʃɛtkatɕ] 'thread'   prze-tyk-aj-ą [pʃɛtɨkajɔʷ]
      kl-n-ą [klnɔʷ] 'swear, 3 pl. pres.'   prze-klin-aj-ą [pʃɛklinajɔʷ]

The nature of the floating vowel is a lexical matter, while its attachment is conditioned by the presence of a following derived imperfective suffix [aj]. The presence of the floating or unattached vowel interacts with the floating nucleus in the preceding prefix in the usual way, as we have seen in the section above. The morphophonological operation of the morphologically conditioned vowel attachment prepares the ground for phonological interpretation which conforms to the simple mechanism of Melody Association.

The mechanism of floating melodies may be extended to cover other alternations of vowels with zero. These are not very frequent or systematic but nonetheless have to be included in a comprehensive description. Consider the following cases:

(97) kozioł [kɔʑɔw] 'he-goat'   kozł-a [kɔzwa] 'gen. sg.'   koźl-i [kɔʑli] 'adj.'
      koźl-ę [kɔʑlɛ] 'kid'   kozioł-ek [kɔʑɔwɛk] 'dim.'

      osioł [ɔɕɔw] 'donkey'   osł-a [ɔswa] 'gen. sg.'[28]   ośl-i [ɔɕli] 'adj.'
      ośl-ic-a [ɔɕlitsa] 'jenny' ośl-ę [ɔɕlɛ] 'dim.'   ośl-isk-o [ɔɕliskɔ]
                                                                 'expr.'

      osioł-ek [ɔɕɔwɛk] 'dim.'

      kocioł [kɔtɕɔw]   kotł-a [kɔtwa] 'gen. sg.'   kocioł-ek
      'cauldron'   [kɔtɕɔwɛk] 'dim.'
      kotł-owni-a [kɔtwɔvɲa]   kotl-arz [kɔtlaʃ]
      'boiler room'   'boiler-smith'

The alternating vowel in these examples is [ɔ]. Apart from this difference its behaviour is exactly the same as the behaviour of the alternating [ɛ] we have discussed at length above. It disappears before a following full melody but is pronounced if followed by another unattached melody or empty nucleus. Hence, before the diminutive suffix -ek [ɛk] it is invariably pronounced. All these properties fall out from the view of floating melodies and regularities on the attachment as specified in Melody Association. Consider the representations of kozioł, osiołek, kotlarz, where palatalization effects are overlooked and the floating melodies underlined:

(98)   O   N   O   N   O   N
       | | | | |
       x   x   x   x   x   x
       | | | | |
       k   ɔ   ʑ   ɔ   w

---

[28] The nouns kozioł [kɔʑɔw] 'he-goat' and osioł [ɔɕɔw] 'donkey' are further irregular in that the spirants [ɕ] and [ʑ] depalatalize in oblique cases.

```
O   N   O   N   O   N   O   N
|   |   |   |   |   |   |   |
x   x   x   x   x   x   x   x
|   |   |   |   |   |
ɔ   ɕ   ɔ   w   ɛ   k
```

```
O   N   O   N   O   N   O   N
|   |   |   |   |   |   |
x   x   x   x   x   x   x   x
|   |   |       |   |   |
k   ɔ   t   ɔ   l   a   3
```

The floating [ɔ] is attached before a following empty nucleus in the first form, it is likewise attached before a following floating nucleus in the middle form and remains unassociated, hence unpronounced, before a full vowel of the last word. The effects are exactly those we would expect of the floating vowel [ɛ], and the current examples show that they are properties of floating Polish vowels in general, rather than of any specific individual vowel. What confirms the phonological regularity of the mechanism is the fact that there are just three morphemes displaying the alternation of [ɔ] with zero: despite their extreme paucity these examples behave as regularly as those of the main alternation, supported by dozens of morphemes. What is irregular here is the melody, while the patterning conforms to the established mechanism.

Before closing let us note some cases that are occasionally regarded as instantiating floating vowels but which have received a different interpretation in this book. Consider examples, some of which have been used before:

(99) utopi-a [utɔpʲja] 'utopia'   utopij-n-y [utɔpʲijnɨ] 'utopian'
      Bibli-a [bʲiblja] 'the Bible'   biblij-n-y [bʲiblijnɨ] 'biblical'
      religi-a [rɛliɟja] 'religion'   religij-n-y [rɛliɟijnɨ] 'religious'
      parti-a [partʲja] 'party'   partyj-k-a [partɨjka] 'dim.'
      gwardi-a [gvardʲja] 'guard'   gwardyj-sk-i [gvardɨjsci] 'adj.'
      pasj-a [pasʲja] 'passion'   pasyj-n-y [pasɨjnɨ] 'adj.'
      aluzj-a [aluzʲja] 'hint'   aluzyj-n-y [aluzɨjnɨ] 'adj.'
      teori-a [tɛɔrʲja] 'theory'   teoryj-k-a [tɛɔrɨjka] 'dim.'
      kolacj-a [kɔlatsʲja] 'supper'   kolacyj-k-a [kɔlatsɨjka] 'dim.'

A cursory glance might lead us to conclude that the vowels [i, ɨ] alternating with zero indicate the presence of floating melodies. We discussed this issue at length in Chapter 3 in connection with palatalization phenomena in loan words (examples (93) and following). There a phonological interpretation was offered where a connection is established between the palatal glide found in these loans and the nature of the preceding consonant.

6

MORPHOPHONOLOGY OF VOWEL ALTERNATIONS

6.1 OVERVIEW

The mid vowel [ɛ] alternates with the back vowel [ɔ] and the low [a] before a non-palatalized coronal. The alternations are morphophonological as shown by the fact that the context of the alternations is often made opaque: the alternation is found in forms contradicting the context and is not found in others which meet the conditions specified. It is argued that the best method of handling the facts is by introducing relatedness statements into appropriate lexical entries.

The back vowel [ɔ] is raised in numerous contexts to [u], a morphophonological replacement which is quite well established within inflectional morphology but is much less stable within derivationally related forms. For this reason a replacement statement is recognized and also one relating lexemes.

Nasal vowels are regarded as phonological units which are adjusted depending on the phonological environment. The adjustment involves what appears to be a fissure of the nasal nucleus into an oral vowel and a nasal rhymal complement; we treat this as a phonological equivalence relation. Alternations of morphophonological nasal nuclei again represent both replacements and lexical relatedness statements.

An interesting productive alternation connects the vowel [ɔ] with [a] in a morphologically delimited context, namely, in imperfective verbs derived from perfective ones.

6.2 INTRODUCTORY

In the preceding chapters we described the phonological behaviour of Polish vowels. The scope for variation is quite restricted and embraces basically the alterations between [i] and [ɨ] in the context after consonants of differing palatal qualities. The alternations between some vocalic melody and zero, despite their frequency in the language, can be viewed as phonological only superficially since they result from the interpretation of representations prepared by the lexicon and the morphology of the language through the intermediary of morphophonology.

We have seen that floating melodies get attached under well-defined conditions, exhausting the domain of phonological processing; the incidence of the floating melodies and the required context for their attachment are phonologically unpredictable and additionally involve a modicum of diacritic marking. For this reason we have claimed that phonology merely cleans up the stage arranged and/or cluttered by the combined workings of morphology, the lexicon, and morphophonology. We have also recognized nuclei without melodies as they have an impact on preceding floating melodies and also on the nature of consonantal clusters.

The [i ~ ɨ] and the vowel~zero alternations constitute but a small part of vocalic exchanges found in the language. There are others but their regularity is quite restricted to specified lexical items and often further constrained to individual cases within a paradigm with unpredictable results within derivationally related forms. The existence of such alternations means that despite a degree of regularity found both in the changes and in the contexts they occur in (Laskowski 1975*b*), they have to be regarded as morphophonological. As a case in point consider the alternation [ɛ ~ a] found in a number of nominal stems after a palatal(ized) consonant; the vowel [ɛ] appears before a following soft dental consonant, while [a] before a hard one; see (1).

(1) kwieci-e [kfʲɛtɕɛ] 'flower, loc. sg.' kwiat [kfʲat] 'nom. sg.'
     cieści-e [tɕɛɕtɕɛ] 'dough, loc. sg.' ciast-o [tɕastɔ] 'nom. sg.'

The left-hand-column nouns show the vowel [ɛ] between palatalized consonants; when the second of the consonants for whatever reason is non-palatalized, the preceding vowel is lowered to [a].

The same regularity can be found in derivationally related words based on stems showing the alternation within the inflectional paradigm. Examples:

(2) kwiat [kfʲat]   kwieci-e [kfʲɛtɕɛ]   kwieci-eń [kfʲɛtɕɛɲ]
     'flower'   'blossom'   'April'
                          kwiat-ek [kfʲatɛk]   kwiat-uszek [kfʲatuʃɛk]
                          'flower, dim.'   'tiny flower'
     miast-o [mʲastɔ]   mieśc-in-a [mʲɛɕtɕina]   miast-k-o [mʲastkɔ]
     'city'   'small place'   'small town'
     jazd-a [jazda]   jeździ-eck-i [jɛʑdʑɛtsci] jeźdz-i-ć [jɛʑdʑitɕ]
     'ride, n.'   'adj.'   'vb.'

One might speculate about whether the environment of flanking palatalized consonants can be held responsible for making the intervening nucleus more palatal, hence [ɛ], or, conversely, whether the following non-palatalized consonant can be linked causally with the less palatal vowel, [a]. This sort of speculation—or an attempt at a phonetic explanation—is pointless in view of the fact that there are words with identical contexts where no such change takes place. Consider:

(3)   grzbieci-e [gʒbʲɛtɕɛ] 'back, loc. sg.'   grzbiet [gʒbʲɛt] 'nom. sg.'
      biesi-e [bʲɛɕɛ] 'devil, loc. sg.'   bies [bʲɛs] 'nom. sg.'
      kobieci-e [kɔbʲɛtɕɛ] 'woman, loc. sg.'   kobiet-a [kɔbʲɛta] 'nom. sg.'
      siaci-e [ɕatɕɛ] 'net, expr. loc. sg.'   siat-a [ɕata] 'nom. sg.'

The first three nouns could be expected to be *grzbiat [gʲʒbʲat], bias [bʲas], and
*kobiata [kɔbʲata] in the nominative singular while the fourth should be *sieci-e
[ɕɛtɕɛ] in the locative singular, since these are the contexts where the two vowels
appear in (3). As we see, nothing of the sort happens with results contrary to
those expected: the vowel [ɛ] is able to appear before a non-palatalized consonant
and [a] before a palatalized one.

The expected distribution of the vowels after a palatalized consonant—[ɛ]
before a palatalized (including functionally palatalized) and [a] before a non-
palatalized segment—is contradicted not only within paradigms as in (3) but also
in derivationally related words. A few examples will illustrate the point: there are
cases when the [ɛ ~ a] alternation found within a morphological paradigm is
flouted in derivationally related words.

(4)   kwieci-e [kfʲɛtɕɛ] 'flower, loc. sg.'   kwiat [kfʲat] 'nom. sg.'
                                               kwiet-n-y [kfʲɛtnɨ] 'floral'
                                               kwiet-nik [kfʲɛtɲik] 'flower bed'
                                               kwiaci-ar-k-a [kfʲatɕarka] 'florist, fem.'
                                               kwiaci-ar-ni-a [kfʲatɕarɲa] 'florist's'
                                               kwiac-iast-y [kfʲatɕastɨ] 'flowery'

The predicted behaviour is that of the base noun in the first line, with [ɛ]
between palatalized consonants and [a] before a non-palatalized one; the derived adjective and the derived noun with the following non-palatalized dental
plosive should yield *kwiatny [kfʲatnɨ] and *kwiat-nik [kfʲatɲik], just as we have
kwiat [kfʲat]. The two other derived nouns and the adjective should have the
front vowel between two palatalized consonants: *kwieci-ar-ka [kfʲɛtɕarka],
*kwieci-ar-ni-a [kfʲɛtɕarɲa], *kwieci-ast-y [kfʲɛtɕastɨ], just as we get kwieci-e
[kfʲɛtɕɛ]. In fact, the last example in (4) is instructive since side by side with
the unexpected kwiaci-ast-y [kfʲatɕastɨ] 'flowery' there is a different derivative
with the expected phonology and a slight difference in meaning: kwiec-ist-y
[kfʲɛtɕistɨ] 'flowery, ornate'. It is not the case, then, that some morphemes are
marked so that they do not undergo the change in the expected context (grzbiet
[gʒbʲɛt] 'back', kobiet-a [kɔbʲɛta] 'woman') or that some derivatives always
display its effects (kwieci-eń [kfʲɛtɕɛɲ] 'April'). The real complication is that
some derivatives based on an alternating morpheme (kwiat [kfʲat] ~ kwieci-e)
do not show the expected effects—in kwiet-n-y [kfʲɛtnɨ] 'floral' the front vowel
appears before a hard dental—or show them in contexts reserved for the opposite
effect (in kwiaci-ar-ni-a [kfʲatɕarɲa] 'florist's', kwiaci-ar-k-a [kfʲatɕarka] 'florist,
fem.', and kwiaci-ast-y [kfʲatɕastɨ] 'flowery', we have a low vowel before a palatal
consonant).

Numerous bases exist which show one and the same shape within their paradigms but where forms derivationally related to them display alternations. Consider:

(5) strzał-a [st-ʃawa] 'arrow' strzal-e [st-ʃalɛ] 'loc. sg.'
  strzel-a-ć [st-ʃɛlatɕ] 'shoot'
  strzel-nic-a [st-ʃɛlɲitsa] 'shooting range'
  strzel-b-a [st-ʃɛlba] 'rifle'

 podział [pɔdʑaw] 'division' podzial-e [pɔdʑalɛ] 'loc. sg.'
  podziel-i-ć [pɔdʑɛlitɕ] 'divide'
  podziel-n-y [pɔdʑɛlnɨ] 'divisible'
  podziel-nik [pɔdʑɛlɲik] 'factor'
  podział-k-a [pɔdʑawka] 'scale'

 pian-a [pʲana] 'foam' piani-e [pʲaɲɛ] 'loc. sg.'
  pien-i-ć [pʲɛɲitɕ] 'vb.'
  pien-ist-y [pʲɛɲistɨ] 'frothy'

 zamiar [zamʲar] 'intention' zamiarz-e [zamʲaʒɛ] 'loc. sg.'
  zamierz-a-ć [zamʲɛʒatɕ] 'intend'

 ścian-a [ɕtɕana] 'wall' ściani-e [ɕtɕaɲɛ] 'loc. sg.'
  ścien-n-y [ɕtɕɛnnɨ] 'adj.'

 sian-o [ɕanɔ] 'hay' siani-e [ɕaɲɛ] 'loc. sg.'
  sien-ny [ɕɛnnɨ] 'adj.'
  sien-nik [ɕɛɲɲik] 'pallet'

The nominal derivational base displays no intraparadigmatic alternations but maintains the low vowel throughout, including the position before a palatalized consonant; in derived words we find the vowel [ɛ] both before a palatalized consonant (or palatal, as long as [l, ʒ] are treated as such) and before a non-palatal(ized) one where the low vowel would be expected (as in the last three examples). As an extreme illustration of the arbitrariness involved consider the pair of nouns *wiar-a* [vʲara] 'faith' and *ofiar-a* [ɔfʲara] 'sacrifice', their dative singular forms and derived adjectives:

(6) wiar-a [vʲara] wierz-e [vʲɛʒɛ] 'dat. sg.' wier-n-y [vʲɛrnɨ] 'faithful'
 ofiar-a [ɔfʲara] ofierz-e [ɔfʲɛʒɛ] 'dat. sg.' ofiar-n-y [ɔfʲarnɨ] 'sacrificial'

While the base noun shows the expected [ɛ ~ a] pattern within the inflectional paradigm, the adjective derived by means of the suffix -n-y has [ɛ] in one case and [a] in the other. Since the phonological, morphological, and morphophonological environment is identical in both cases, the conclusion can only be that the presence or absence of the alternation results from an arbitrary diacritic.

Examples of this sort, which are legion, remove this alternation and others, to be discussed below, from the purview of phonology proper. Rather, they belong to morphophonology and the lexicon in very much the same way as most alternations of plain and palatal(ized) consonants, as discussed in Chapter 4. We would like to be able to relate the vowels [ε] and [a] in the words where they alternate without deriving one from the other or giving priority to any of them. At the same time it seems that our description would be incomplete if we did not include the information that (1) the alternation takes place predominantly after a palatalized consonant and (2) the vowel [ε] tends to appear before another palatalized segment while [a] tends to appear before a non-palatalized one. Our formulation should be sufficiently general to allow offending cases such as those described above, but should nonetheless reflect the predominant pattern. In Chapter 5 we developed a mechanism of Lexical Relatedness for connecting words along these lines which appears to meet the two requirements specified here. As a lexical mechanism it should also be applicable to the vocalic alternations at hand. We suggest that the vowels in morphemes showing alternations should be supplied with a diacritic RV (Relate Vowels) of the general very simple format:

<RV1> (C^j) ε (palatalized coronal) ~ (C^j) a (non-palatalized coronal).

The elements in brackets represent the most general pattern specifying the most typical morphophonological conditioning of the alternation; with the bracketed material excluded, we are left with a very broad formula which covers the infrequent or rare instances of the alternation.

The general formulation covers alternations that seem to be contextually determined in that the vowel [a] appears after a palatalized consonant and before a non-palatalized coronal, e.g. *obiad* [ɔbʲat] 'dinner' whereas [ε] requires flanking palatalized consonants, as in *obiedzi-e* [ɔbʲɛdʑɛ] 'loc. sg.'. We have seen, however, that these conditions are not sufficient, since [a] can just as well appear between palatalized segments, as in *siani-e* [ɕaɲɛ] 'hay, loc. sg.'—in such a case the right-hand non-palatalized consonant will be overlooked; it will also be overlooked when [ε] can be followed by non-palatalized consonants, as in *sien-n-y* [ɕɛnnɨ] 'hay, adj.'.

In most cases the consonant preceding the alternating vowel needs to be palatalized, but even this is not inviolable. Consider the following cases which meet the conditions only up to a point:

(7)   dzisiaj [dʑiɕaj] 'today'   dzisiej-sz-y [dʑiɕɛjʃɨ] 'today's'
       tutaj [tutaj] 'here'   tutej-sz-y [tutɛjʃɨ] 'local'

What complicates the picture of the alternation in both words even further is the fact that the vowel [a] appears before the palatal glide [j], contrary to the predominant pattern where [ε] is required before a palatalized consonant. In the second word the consonant preceding the alternation site is additionally not palatalized and thus the word contravenes the regularity on two counts: it takes place after a non-palatalized consonant and it admits the low vowel before a palatal. Thus it reflects the formula above stripped of all bracketed material.

RV1 captures lexical relatedness and imposes no derivational primacy but does so at a price of a diacritic attached to representations of individual word-forms. An implication of such a mechanism is that speakers may fail to relate words, for example when they are sufficiently distant semantically even if historically they can be traced back to the same source. Given the non-alternating noun *czas* [tʃas] 'time' ∼ *czasi-e* [tʃaɕɛ] 'loc. sg.' we may well wonder whether the adjectives *w(-?)czes-n-y* [ftʃɛsnɨ] 'early', *do(-?)czes-n-y* [dɔtʃɛsnɨ] 'temporal' are derived from or related to it; were we to answer the question in the affirmative, the conclusion would be that the vowels [a] and [ε] in these items are related by RV1. A negative answer would mean not only that the words have separate representations but also that no lexical relatedness is established among them, a conclusion that might be in accordance with semantic intuitions.

In what follows we will survey instances of vocalic alternations in what appear to be firmly related lexical groups. We have seen that there are no (morpho)phonological contexts where a directional change—either [ε] > [a] or [a] > [ε]—can take place. Likewise it is not individual morphemes that determine specific effects. Rather, individual, lexically specified combinations of morphemes, diacritically marked, constitute the domain where such alternations are attested. Generally, the alternations are more frequent within the derivational component than within flection. It should be kept in mind that lexical relatedness is a muzzy notion and hence diacritic presence is a wavering property of individual words, and perhaps even individual speakers.

6.3 THE ALTERNATION [ε ∼ a]

As stated above, the most typical context determining the alternation is the nature of the following coronal: if palatalized, then the vowel is [ε], if nonpalatalized, then the vowel is [a]. For this reason palatalizing suffixes are likely to be preceded by morphemes containing the mid vowel, where the palatalizing property of suffixes is the diacritic <PR1> attached to them (see Ch. 4). This situation is reflected most prominently within inflectional paradigms. Consider the vowel *-e* [ε], which represents a few morphological categories, namely: locative singular of masculine and neuter nouns, dative and locative singular of feminine nouns, and vocative singular of masculine nouns. Most nouns containing the diacritic <RV1> will have the mid vowel before the stem-final, palatalized consonant. More examples follow:

(8) obiad [ɔbʲat] 'dinner'   obiedzi-e [ɔbʲɛdʑɛ] 'loc. sg.'
     ciast-o [tɕastɔ] 'dough'   cieśći-e [tɕɛɕtɕɛ] 'loc. sg.'
     na-jazd [najast] 'invasion'   na-jeździ-e [najɛʑdʑɛ] 'loc. sg.'
     jazd-a [jazda] 'ride'   jeździ-e [jɛʑdʑɛ] 'dat., loc. sg.'
     gwiazd-a [gvʲazda] 'star'   gwieździ-e [gvʲɛʑdʑɛ] 'dat., loc. sg.'
     świat [ɕfʲat] 'world'   świeci-e [ɕfʲɛtɕɛ] 'loc., voc. sg.'

There are two major problems besetting this sort of description. One is connected with the fact that the alternation is restricted to diacritically-marked items only; this means that the vowels [ε] and [a] can occur throughout the paradigm irrespective of the nature of the following consonant. Thus we find the vowel [ɛ] both in *biesi-e* [bʲɛɕɛ] 'devil, loc. sg.' and *bies* [bʲɛs] 'nom. sg.' and the vowel [a] in *siar-a* [ɕara] 'colostrum' as well as in *siarz-e* [ɕaʒɛ] 'loc. sg.'. These nouns carry no diacritic relating them to anything else. More importantly, however, diacritic marking must accompany different phonological shapes of the same morpheme. This was noted above but in view of the relevance of the issue we will recall it briefly: there are nouns uniform with reference to the vowel within their paradigms but displaying alternations in derivationally related words. Consider again:

(9) pian-a [pʲana]   piani-e [pʲaɲɛ]   pien-ist-y [pʲɛɲistɨ]
     'foam'   'dat., loc. sg.' 'foamy'
     dział [dʑaw]   dzial-e [dʑalɛ]   dziel-i-ć [dʑɛlitɕ]
     'division'   'loc. sg.'   'divide'
     ślad [ɕlat]   śladzi-e [ɕladʑɛ] śledz-i-ć [ɕlɛdʑitɕ]
     'trace'   'loc. sg.'   'vb.'

Since the right-hand column's adjective and verbs with the vowel [ɛ] are morphologically complex and unmistakeably derived from the nouns with the vowel [a], we would like to be able to view the alternation of vowels as due to RV1. The relatedness of the words is so obvious that we would like to do it despite the fact that the nouns themselves show no alternations within their paradigms: *pian-a* [pʲana] 'foam' ~ **pieni-e* [pʲɛɲɛ], *dzial* [dʑaw] 'division' ~ **dziel-e* [dʑɛlɛ], *ślad* [ɕlat] 'trace' ~ **śledzi-e* [ɕlɛdʑɛ].[1] A way of ensuring that the relatedness is captured is to supply both the phonologically invariant base noun and the phonologically invariant adjective or verb with the diacritic <RV1>. Thus the same morpheme will have different phonological representations but these will be connected through the presence of the diacritic <RV1> in the lexical entries of the words.

An implication which suggests itself from such examples is that alternations tend to be eliminated within paradigms. As a further exemplification of the role of the paradigm, consider the nominative plural of personal masculine nouns as marked by the ending -*i* [i], which morphophonologically palatalizes the preceding consonant:

(10) sąsiad [sɔ̃ʷɕat] 'neighbour'   sąsiedz-i [sɔ̃ʷɕɛdʑi] 'nom. pl.'

with the vowels alternating as expected. The nominative plural masculine personal of the adjectival paradigm displays a failure of the alternation with [a] appearing throughout, although elsewhere in the lexicon the same root shows the expected variation:

(11) biał-y [bʲawɨ] 'white'   bial-i [bʲali] 'nom. pl.'   biel-i-ć [bʲɛlitɕ] 'whiten'
      blad-y [bladɨ] 'pale'   bladz-i [bladʑi]   bled-ną-ć [blɛdnɔɲtɕ]
                               'nom. pl.'   'grow pale'

---

[1] The starred forms are not only well-formed phonologically but they actually occur, as different lexical items: *pieni-e* 'singing', *dziel-e* 'work, loc. sg.', *śledzi-e* 'herring, nom. pl.'

śniad-y [ɕɲadɨ]   śniadz-i [ɕɲadʑi]   śniedzi-e-ć [ɕɲɛdʑɛtɕ]
'swarthy'   'nom. pl.'   'tarnish, vb.'

The significance of such facts is irresistible: given, for example, the adjective *biał-y* [bʲawɨ] 'white' we would expect its nominative plural to be *biel-i* [bʲɛli], just as we have the verb *biel-i* [bʲɛli] 'whiten, 3 sg. pres.'. The fact that the adjectival paradigm shows no alternations must mean that the shape of the paradigm overrides any phonological or morphophonological considerations.[2]

The other issue which needs to be mentioned concerns the interaction of different morphophonological regularities. Specifically, the paradigmatic alternations illustrated above require the presence of the palatalized consonant following the vowel [ɛ] in the most general formulation of RV1; this context is created by the application of the replacement palatalization operation PR1 hence, for the vowel alternation to manifest itself fully, the effects of palatalization replacement need to be taken into account. Note that we are not proposing rule ordering or constraint interaction familiar from other frameworks since the vocalic alternations in focus are in no sense derived but rather supplied by the morphology and the lexicon. Instead, the static vocalic relation is found in a specific context as reflected in our formulae like RV1.

The alternation under discussion is characteristically found in the nominal paradigm and it hardly exists in the verbal system. Two partly irregular verbs exhaust its scope there:

(12)   jad-ę [jadɛ] 'I go'   jedzi-e-sz [jɛdʑɛʃ] 'you go'
       jad-ł-y [jadwɨ] 'they (fem.) ate'   jed-l-i [jɛdli] 'they (masc.) ate'

The forms must be supplied by the morphology and the vocalic alternations related by RV1; note that in the case of *jedli* the incomplete version of the regularity holds since the vowel [ɛ] appears before a non-palatalized coronal.

The alternation, while scantily attested within morphological paradigms, finds a lot of lexical support in derivationally related forms. The vowel [ɛ] is most frequently found when a palatalizing suffix is attached, where by a palatalizing suffix we understand one with the diacritic <PR1> appended in the lexical representation; the word without the suffix, that is, without the diacritic, normally displays the vowel [a]. The suffix can also be realized as phonetic zero, which means that it manifests itself through the addition of the diacritic to the base (see Ch. 4). The evidence is quite rich and involves suffixes deriving nouns (a), adjectives (b), and verbs (c). We illustrate each of the groups by several examples:

(13)   (a) ciasn-y [tɕasnɨ] 'tight'   cieśn-in-a [tɕɛɕɲina] 'strait'
           biał-y [bʲawɨ] 'white'   biel-izn-a [bʲɛlizna] 'underwear'

---

[2] Although paradigms are not usually accorded a place in phonological and morphophonological descriptions, their role needs to be re-assessed. See Downing *et al.* (2005), a collection of papers, examining the role of the paradigm with reference to Optimality Theory.

biel-m-o [bʲɛlmɔ] 'leucoma'
biel-ik [bʲɛlik] 'white rust'
biel-ak [bʲɛlak] 'mountain hare'
biel-idł-o [bʲɛlidwɔ] 'bleach'
biel [bʲɛl] 'whiteness'

czarn-y [tʃarnɨ] 'black'
czern-idł-o [tʃɛrɲidwɔ] 'blacking'
czerni-ak [tʃɛrɲak] 'melanoma'
czern-in-a [tʃɛrɲina] 'duck blood soup'
czerń [tʃɛrɲ] 'blackness'

ciał-o [tɕawɔ] 'body'
ciel-sk-o [tɕɛlskɔ] 'hulk'

rumian-y [rumʲanɨ] 'ruddy'
rumieni-ec [rumʲɛɲɛts] 'blush'

powiast-k-a [pɔvʲastka] 'story'
powieść [pɔvʲɛɕtɕ] 'novel'

(b) las [las] 'forest'
les-ist-y [lɛɕistɨ] 'forested'
leś-n-y [lɛɕnɨ] 'woody'

blad-y [bladɨ] 'pale'
bledzi-uchn-y [blɛdʑuxnɨ] 'very pale'

gwiazd-a [gvʲazda] 'star'
gwieźdz-ist-y [gvʲɛʑdʑistɨ] 'starry'

miast-o [mʲastɔ] 'town'
miej-sk-i [mɛjsci] 'urban'

niewiast-a [ɲɛvʲasta] 'maiden'
niewieśc-i [ɲɛvʲɛɕtɕi] 'womanly'

rumian-y [rumʲanɨ] 'ruddy'
rumień-sz-y [rumʲɛɲʃɨ] 'more ruddy'

(c) ciasn-y [tɕasnɨ] 'tight'
ś-cieśn-i-ć [ɕtɕɛɕɲitɕ] 'squeeze up'

śmiał-y [ɕmʲawɨ] 'bold'
o-śmiel-i-ć [ɔɕmʲɛlitɕ] 'encourage'

biał-y [bʲawɨ] 'white'
biel-i-ć [bʲɛlitɕ] 'whiten'
biel-e-ć [bʲɛlɛtɕ] 'turn white'

czarn-y [tʃarnɨ] 'black'
czern-i-ć [tʃɛrɲitɕ] 'blacken'
czerni-e-ć [tʃɛrɲɛtɕ] 'turn black'

zwierciadł-o [zvʲɛrtɕadwɔ] 'mirror'
od-zwierciedl-i-ć [ɔd-zvʲɛrtɕɛdlitɕ] 'vb.'

rumian-y [rumʲanɨ] 'ruddy'
rumien-i-ć [rumʲɛɲitɕ] 'blush'

niewiast-a [ɲɛvʲasta] 'maiden'
z-niewieści-e-ć [zɲɛvʲɛɕtɕɛtɕ] 'become effeminate'

wrzask [vʒask] 'yelling'
wrzeszcz-e-ć [vʒɛʃtʃɛtɕ] 'yell'

Alternations such as these, conforming to our formula RV1, should not create the impression of full or partial phonological or even morphophonological regularity. As we stressed in the introductory part of this chapter, the same suffix can produce contradictory results with different bases, or results contrary to what our formulation of the alternation would lead us to expect. Also, in certain cases, alternative forms are acceptable. To round up the discussion of the [ɛ ~ a] exchange, consider a few cases of derivationally related forms where [ɛ] appears before a non-palatalized consonant in violation of the full form of our generalization:

(14) gwiazd-a [gvʲazda] 'nest'
gwiezd-n-y [gvʲɛzdnɨ] 'adj.'

lat-o [latɔ] 'summer'
let-nik [lɛtɲik] 'holiday maker'

sian-o [ɕanɔ] 'hay'	sien-n-y [ɕɛnnɨ] 'adj.'
prze-powiad-a-ć	prze-powied-ni-a [pʃɛpɔvʲɛdɲa] 'prophesy, n.'
[pʃɛpɔvʲadatɕ] 'foretell'	
światł-o [ɕfʲatwɔ] 'light, n.'	na-świetl-i-ć [naɕfʲɛtlitɕ] 'irradiate'

Examples such as these, as well as many of those offered in the introductory part of this section, emphasize the role of lexically encoded information. While certain subregularities can be detected in specific grammatical (morphological) contexts, the alternation at large remains a tendency which in practically every case may be overridden by the vagaries of the lexicon.[3] The vowel alternation we will now turn to will reaffirm this conclusion.

6.4 THE ALTERNATION [ε ~ ɔ]

The alternation between [ε] and [ɔ] is in many ways quite similar to the one between [ε] and [a]. Some descriptions (e.g. Kowalik 1997) present them jointly since the contexts they appear in and their morphophonological and lexical conditioning are strikingly similar. Thus, most generally, the two types of alternation are tied to the presence of palatalization alternation in the coronal consonant following the vowel in focus; the consonant alternations are predominantly evinced by specific flectional and derivational suffixes. Likewise the remarkable irregularity of alternations is shared by the two classes. But there are also differences worthy of note. Since we have discussed the [ε ~ a] alternation at length, including the theoretical issues it spawns, we can deal with the [ε ~ o] in a more succinct manner now.

The alternation at hand has very little lexical support within the nominal paradigms. There is a handful of nouns where the back vowel occurs before a non-palatalized coronal while the front one is found before a palatalized one; (15) gives some examples:

(15) popioł-y [pɔpʲɔwɨ] 'ash, nom. pl.'   popiel-e [pɔpʲɛlɛ] 'loc. sg.'
       kościoł-a [kɔɕtɕɔwa] 'church, gen. sg.'   kościel-e [kɔɕtɕɛlɛ] 'loc. sg.'
       czoł-o [tʃɔwɔ] 'front part, head'   czel-e [tʃɛlɛ] 'loc. sg.'

Derivationally related forms will later be shown further to confirm the context of the alternation as being the same as with RV1: the front vowel between palatalized coronal consonants and the back one before a non-palatalized one, with possibilities of parts of the context being suppressed. We therefore suggest the following vowel relation statement:

<RV2> (Cʲ) ε (palatalized coronal) ~ (Cʲ) ɔ (non-palatalized coronal)

---

[3] Instances of the alternation found in the modern language are detritus of a well-known Slavic phonological regularity, obscured and often undone by subsequent developments, analogy, etc. See Samilov (1964) for details of the historical background.

The first two examples in (15) provide a tight fit with the conditions of the formula, while the third one conforms to the requirement of the palatalized consonant (C^j) preceding the vowel, on the assumption that the affricate [tʃ] is treated as functionally palatalized. Otherwise the fit is partial and excludes the bracketed consonant preceding the alternating vowel.

The third example illustrates also the diacritic nature of the alternation: the polysemous lexeme czoł-o [tʃɔwɔ], on the reading 'forehead', shows no alternation and the locative singular is czol-e [tʃɔlɛ]. As before then, we expect the morphology of the language to supply the required forms while the diacritic <RV2> will relate them to other words and word forms without in any sense deriving one from the other.

There is a single instance of the alternation before the ending -i [i] representing the nominative plural of masculine personal nouns and it is also attested, with suppression of different parts of the context of RV2, in the same inflectional category of adjectives and participles. Examples:

(16) anioł [aɲɔw] 'angel'   aniel-i [aɲɛli]
      wesoł-y [vɛsɔwɨ] 'merry'   wesel-i [vɛsɛli]
      za-chęc-on-y [zaxɛntsɔnɨ] 'encouraged'   za-chęc-en-i [zaxɛntsɛɲi]
      po-ciesz-on-y [pɔtɕɛʃɔnɨ] 'comforted'   po-ciesz-en-i [pɔtɕɛʃɛɲi]
      z-męcz-on-y [zmɛntʃɔnɨ] 'tired'   z-męcz-en-i [zmɛntʃɛɲi]

The vocalic replacements take place after a non-palatalized consonant in two adjectival forms and after a functionally palatalized one in two others.

One of the differences between the two types of alternation involving the vowel [ɛ] is that alternations with [a] are quite common in the inflection of nouns while non-occurring in adjectival paradigms. The [ɛ ~ ɔ] alternation is found with very few nouns and is more general in adjectives. Further, we found just two verbal roots displaying the former alternation; the [ɛ ~ ɔ] situation is only marginally different. Consider:

(17) gnieś-ć [gɲɛɕtɕ] 'knead'   gniot-ę [gɲɔtɛ] 'I knead'
      za-mieci-e-sz [zamʲɛtɕɛʃ] 'you'll sweep'   za-miot-ę [zamʲɔtɛ] 'I'll sweep'
      niesi-e [ɲɛɕɛ] '(s)he carries'   nios-ę [ɲɔsɛ] 'I carry'
      wiezi-on-o [vʲɛʑɔnɔ] 'one carried'   wioz-ł-e-m [vʲɔzwɛm] 'I carried'
      plet-l-i [plɛtli] 'they (masc.) wove'   plot-ł-y [plɔtwɨ] 'they (fem.)
                                                  wove'

As can be seen, the vowel [ɔ] appears before a non-palatalized coronal whereas [ɛ] predominantly, but not exclusively, appears before a palatalized one. Two further verbs call for special comment:

(18) wlecz-e-sz [vlɛtʃɛʃ]   wlok-ę [vlɔkɛ]
      'you drag'   'I drag'
      bierz-e-sz [bʲɛʒɛʃ]   bior-ę [bʲɔrɛ]   br-a-ł [braw]
      'you take'   'I take'   'he took'

The first of the verbs shows the alternation before a velar alternating with a palatal, in a context that the full formula does not allow. Thus the right-hand part of its context has to be suppressed.

The second verb is even more irregular; we encounter here an alternation of the vowel [ε] which itself alternates with zero—it is a floating melody as shown by the past tense form, with [ɔ] in the context specified by RV2. This sort of complex alternation is also found in a few noun derivatives, as will be shown below. But the very existence of an alternation between what is elsewhere a floating melody seems to indicate that the verbal forms are suppletive and hence belong to idiosyncratic morphology; note that the root [ε] in *bierzesz* [bʲɛʒɛʃ] 'you take' cannot result from the principles we developed in the context of vowel∼zero alternations (see Ch. 5) since then the form should be *brzesz [bʒɛʃ]. The existence of the [ε ∼ ɔ] alternation in the present tense of the verb *brać* [bratɕ] 'take' is indicative of the presence of these two vowels in the verbal paradigm and hence their purely lexical connection to forms which have zero vocalic melody in place of the alternation. In still other words, the vowel [ε] of the present tense is not, contrary to appearances, a floating melody attached in specified conditions but rather an independent morphophonological segment which coincides melodically with the floating vowel. The forms with a floating and a lexical melody are suppletive.

Outside of inflectional paradigms the alternation [ε ∼ ɔ] is represented quite generously although hardly with any degree of rigidity. Unlike the [ε ∼ a] alternation, which favours verbal bases, it is found with particular frequency in denominal formations. As elsewhere the vowel [ε] tends to appear before a following palatalized consonant while [ɔ] occupies the complementary context; this is but a tendency, as we noted above, hence the bracketed material in our formulation of RV2. The palatalized environment may be due to the attachment of a palatalizing suffix or to the addition of palatalizing diacritics which form the so-called soft-stemmed nouns (see Ch. 4). Since the addition of suffixes creates longer forms, we place the shorter forms first although, as stressed above, the presumed morphological chain of derivation does not imply any morphophonological directionality; in fact the vowels we relate through RV2 are present as such at all levels of representation. Examples:

(19) jezior-o [jɛʑɔrɔ] 'lake'   po-jezierz-e [pɔjɛʑɛʒɛ] 'lake district'
      pszczoł-a [pʃtʃɔwa] 'bee'   pszczel-arz [pʃtʃɛlaʃ] 'bee-keeper'
      brzoz-a [bʒɔza] 'birch tree'   brzez-in-a [bʒɛʑina] 'birch copse'
      zioł-o [ʑɔwɔ] 'herb'   ziel-n-y [ʑɛlnɨ] 'herbaceous'
                                     ziel-nik [ʑɛlɲik] 'herbarium'
      popioł-y [pɔpʲɔwɨ] 'ashes'   popiel-nic-a [pɔpʲɛlɲitsa] 'ashtray'
                                     Popiel-ec [pɔpʲɛlɛts] 'Ash Wednesday'
                                     popiel-at-y [pɔpʲɛlatɨ] 'grey'
                                     popiel-e-ć [pɔpʲɛlɛtɕ] 'turn grey'
      zielon-y [ʑɛlɔnɨ] 'green'   zieleń [ʑɛlɛɲ] 'greenness'
                                     zielen-i-ć [ʑɛlɛɲitɕ] 'grow green'

wesoł-y [vɛsɔwɨ] 'merry'   wesel-e [vɛsɛlɛ] 'wedding'
wieczor-u [vʲetʃɔru]   wieczer-nik [vʲetʃɛrɲik]
'evening, gen. sg.'   'the Upper Room'
                                 wieczerz-a [vʲetʃɛʒa] 'supper'

The directionality of the morphological derivation may on occasion be non-obvious but the alternations remain related to the context in the same way as in the morphologically transparent cases:

(20) lot [lɔt] 'flight'   leci-e-ć [lɛtɕɛtɕ] 'fly'
      plot-k-a [plɔtka] 'rumour'   pleci-e [plɛtɕɛ] '(s)he talks drivel'

A particularly clear case of the relatedness between the palatal nature of the consonant following the alternation site is a class of nouns ending in a palatalized consonant to which the suffix -ek [ɛk] is attached. As shown elsewhere (see Ch. 4) the attachment of the suffix is accompanied by the loss of the palatalizing diacritic on the preceding consonant. The vowel before such a diacritic-free consonant tends to be [ɔ], as in the following examples:

(21) jeleń [jɛlɛɲ] 'deer'   jelon-ek [jɛlɔnɛk] 'dim.'
      korzeń [kɔʒɛɲ] 'root'   korzon-ek [kɔʒɔnɛk] 'dim.'
      pacierz [patɕɛʃ] 'prayer'   pacior-ek [patɕɔrɛk] 'dim.'
      jesień [jɛɕɛɲ] 'autumn'   jesion-k-a [jɛɕɔnka] 'autumn coat'
      kmieć [kmʲɛtɕ] 'peasant'   kmiot-ek [kmʲɔtɛk] 'expr.'
      pieśń [pʲɛɕn̥] 'song'   piosn-k-a [pʲɔsn̩ka] 'expr.'
      nasieni-e [naɕɛɲɛ] 'seed'   nasion-k-o [naɕɔnkɔ] 'dim.'

The same type of relation can be found in two nouns derived from roots containing a floating melody. Consider:

(22) dzień [dʑɛɲ] 'day'   dni-a [dɲa] 'gen. sg.'   dzion-ek [dʑɔnɛk] 'dim.'
      wieś [vʲɛɕ] 'village' ws-i [fɕi] 'gen. sg.'   wios-k-a [vʲɔska] 'dim.'

The alternation is similar in its irregularity to that found in the verb *br-a-ć* 'take' discussed above. Note that the floating melody [ɛ], when attached, is not involved in alternations with [ɔ], hence *pies* [pʲɛs] 'dog' (cf. *ps-a* [psa] 'gen. sg.') when combined with the diminutive suffix -*ek* yields *pies-ek* [pʲɛsɛk] and never *piosek* [pʲɔsɛk]. The words *dzion-ek, wios-k-a* will be lexically supplied with the diacritic <RV2> but the base nouns *dzień, wieś* will contain no diacritics as they are related to forms without an overt root vowel through floating melody mechanisms.

The above survey should suffice to show that the alternation under consideration to a large extent relates separate lexical items and that, despite a measure of morphological and morphophonological conditioning, it displays unpredictable properties that must be assigned to individual items in the lexicon. As a final exemplification consider the following words:

(23) czerwon-y [tʃɛrvɔnɨ] 'red'   czerwień [tʃɛrvʲɛɲ] 'redness'
                                        czerwien-i-ć [tʃɛrvʲɛɲitɕ] 'grow red'

prze-strog-a [pʃɛstrɔga] 'warning'   prze-strzeg-a [pʃɛst-ʃɛga] '(s)he warns'
za-por-a [zapɔra] 'dam'   za-pier-a-ć [zapʲɛratɕ] 'block, vb.'

There can be no doubt that the forms are semantically related and speakers identify them as such. From the point of view of the [ɛ ~ ɔ] alternation there are a few mysterious facts. The adjective *czerwon-y* [tʃɛrvɔnɨ] 'red' has the vowel [ɔ] between non-palatalized consonants; this is not fully in accordance with the formula RV2 where the preceding consonant should preferably be palatalized but the formula tolerates the existing situation as the palatalized consonant preceding the alternation site constitutes part of the bracketed material. What is puzzling, and synchronically inexplicable, is that the preceding consonant is palatalized in the related noun *czerwień* [tʃɛrvʲɛɲ] 'redness' and the verb *czerwien-i-ć* [tʃɛrvʲɛɲitɕ] 'grow red' while it is specifically the case that the [ɛ ~ ɔ] alternation does not affect the palatalized quality of the flanking consonants—recall *anioł* [aɲɔw] 'angel' ~ *anieli* [aɲɛli] 'nom. pl.', where the consonant preceding the alternation site, [ɲ], remains unaltered. The same disappearance—or emergence—of palatalization characterizes the other derivatives above, and more instances could be provided. Examples such as these require direct reference to the lexicon despite the relative frequency and partial regularity of the vocalic alternation.

Both the alternation [ɛ ~ a] and [ɛ ~ ɔ] are found in marked lexical items. The most narrowly circumscribed context includes a preceding palatalized consonant and a following coronal, palatalized after [ɛ] and non-palatalized after [a] and [ɔ]. The rich lexical support of the alternation very often entails a suppression of part or totality of the morphophonological context and thus further constrains its generality and productivity. Fundamentally, the alternations reflect lexical relations with, at best, inconsistent—morphological or morphophonological—conditioning.

6.5 THE ALTERNATION [ɔ ~ u]

The alternation of the two back vowels comes tantalizingly close to being a phonological regularity in that the context of the change looks formulable by reference to the phonological environment. The change of underlying /o/ into the surface [u] has been described as a phonological regularity within the generative tradition, even though its morphological elements were pointed out quite early (see Gussmann 1980*a*) with full-fledged morphophonological statements following suit (Herbert and Nykiel-Herbert 1991). What is particularly intriguing about the alternation is its generality both within inflectional and derivational morphology and also the fact that its context looks well-defined in phonological terms. In brief, the vowel [ɔ] is replaced by [u] before a voiced consonant followed by an empty nucleus. The voiced consonant undergoes general word-final devoicing hence we find numerous alternations like *wod-a* [vɔda] 'water' ~ *wód* [vut] 'gen. pl.'.

There are good reasons to doubt the phonological nature of the mechanism controlling the alternation. For one thing, if we take seriously the non-arbitrariness claim establishing a direct relation between a phonological process and the context in which it occurs which we have repeated several times in this book, then the regularity changing [ɔ] into [u] is a poor candidate for such a phonological process. It is difficult to see any link between raising a mid back vowel—in our terms removing the element {A}—and a following voiced consonant licensed by an empty nucleus. The change would be equally 'phonological' if it were to take place before a voiceless consonant followed by a front non-high vowel, or indeed in any context whatsoever. This theory-internal conclusion is fully borne out by additional facts: there are cases where the alternation fails to be confirmed in the required context and, conversely, it is attested in contradictory contexts. We will see examples of that below when we consider the environments in which the change is found. The additional conclusion is that we need to look at the alternation as another instance of morphophonology at work.

Our discussion of other morphophonological phenomena in Polish has produced two types of regularity: morphophonological replacements, such as PR1, and morphophonological relations, such as RV1. The former might be regarded as derivational or dynamic, the latter as lexical and static. The significance of the [ɔ ∼ u] alternation lies partly in the fact that it seems to combine properties of both types.

6.5.1 *Alternations within morphological paradigms*

One of the most striking properties of the alternation [ɔ ∼ u] is its generality within inflectional morphology. It is massively attested when the inflectional ending is represented as an empty nucleus with the preceding onset being a voiced obstruent, where the voice specification (i.e. low tone or L) is generally delinked. Within the nominal inflection this is amply found in (a) the nominative singular of masculine and feminine nouns, (b) in the nominative singular of masculine adjectives and pronouns, (c) in the genitive plural of feminine and neuter nouns, and in the second-person singular imperative (d). These categories are illustrated in (24).

(24) (a) lod-y [lɔdɨ] 'ice, nom. pl.'   lód [lut] 'nom. sg.'
          noż-e [nɔʒɛ] 'knife, nom. pl.'   nóż [nuʃ] 'nom. sg.'
          gwoździ-e [gvɔʑdʑɛ] 'nail, nom. pl.   gwóźdź [gvuɕtɕ] 'nom. sg.'
          bobr-a [bɔbra] 'beaver, gen. sg.'   bóbr [bupr̥] 'nom. sg.'
          drobi-u [drɔbʲu] 'poultry, gen. sg.'   drób [drup] 'nom. sg.'
          row-y [rɔvɨ] 'ditch, nom. pl'   rów [ruf] 'nom. sg.'
          łodz-i [wɔdʑi] 'boat, gen. sg.'   łódź [wutɕ] 'nom. sg.'
          powodz-i [pɔvɔdʑi] 'flooding, gen. sg.'   powódź [pɔvutɕ] 'nom. sg.'

      (b) zdrow-a [zdrɔva] 'healthy, fem.'   zdrów [zdruf] 'masc.'
          ow-a [ɔva] 'that one, fem.'   ów [uf] 'masc.'
          twoj-a [tfɔja] 'your, fem.'   twój [tfuj] 'masc.'

(c) sow-a [sɔva] 'owl'   sów [suf] 'gen. pl.'
     brzoz-a [bʒɔza] 'birch tree'   brzóz [bʒus] 'gen. pl.'
     mod-a [mɔda] 'fashion'   mód [mut] 'gen. pl.'
     groźb-a [grɔʑba] 'threat'   gróźb [gruɕp] 'gen. pl.'
     morz-e [mɔʒɛ] 'sea'   mórz [muʃ] 'gen. pl.'
     dobr-o [dɔbrɔ] 'possession'   dóbr [dupr̩] 'gen. pl.'

(d) wodz-i [vɔdʑi] '(s)he leads'   wódź [vutɕ] 'imper. sg.'
     rob-i-sz [rɔbʲiʃ] 'you make'   rób [rup] 'imper. sg.'
     pomoż-e [pɔmɔʒɛ] '(s)he will help'   pomóż [pɔmuʃ] 'imper. sg.'
     u-pokorz-ę [upɔkɔʒɛ] 'I'll humiliate'   u-pokórz [upɔkuʃ] 'imper. sg.'

As an initial approximation we may put forward a vowel replacement operation VR1 whereby the mid back vowel is raised before an inflectional empty
nucleus across a voiced obstruent:

<VR1> ɔ ⟹ u before C (obstruent), (voiced) and inflectional empty nucleus

The morphophonological nature of the operation can be seen in the fact that
the conditioning empty nucleus has to be a marker of an inflectional category;
furthermore, as noted above, a potential phonological regularity is ruled out by
the absence of any obvious connection between the change (vowel raising) and
the context where it occurs.

A question which arises concerns the generality of the morphophonological
replacement: does the information contained in VR1 exhaustively define the
scope of the alternation or do we need to go beyond it? The answer has to be a
resounding 'no'. There are numerous instances where no raising takes place in the
context specified; although some of the failure is typical of recent and not so very
recent loanwords, it is also found in native vocabulary, as shown clearly by the
imperatives. Consider examples of both nouns (a) and verbs (b):

(25) (a) drozd-a [drɔzda] 'thrush, gen. sg.'   drozd [drɔst] 'nom. sg.'
           węgorz-a [vɛŋgɔʒa] 'eel, gen. sg.'   węgorz [vɛŋgɔʃ] 'nom. sg.'
           perkoz-a [pɛrkɔza] 'grebe, gen. sg.'   perkoz [pɛrkɔs] 'nom. sg.'
           mimoz-a [mʲimɔza] 'mimosa'   mimoz [mʲimɔs] 'gen. pl.'
           synagog-a [sɨnagɔga] 'synagogue'   synagog [sɨnagɔk] 'gen. pl.'

      (b) chodz-i [xɔdʑi] '(s)he goes'   chodź [xɔtɕ] 'imper. sg.'
           za-orz-ę [zaɔʒɛ] 'I'll plough'   za-orz [zaɔʃ] 'imper. sg.'
           szkodz-i [ʃkɔdʑi] '(s)he harms'   szkodź [ʃkɔtɕ] 'imper. sg.'
           smrodz-i [smrɔdʑi] '(s)he stinks'   smrodź [smrɔtɕ] 'imper. sg.'
           słodz-i [swɔdʑi] '(s)he sweetens'   słodź [swɔtɕ] 'imper. sg.'
           skrobi-e [skrɔbʲɛ] '(s)he scratches'   skrob [skrɔp] 'imper. sg.'

Examples such as these show conclusively that the morphophonological and
morphological context is not enough; in brief, if we have the raising in *pomóż*
[pɔmuʃ] 'help, imper. sg.' we should also have it in *za-orz* [zaɔʃ] 'plough, imper.
sg.'. Similarly, a noun–verb pair:

(26)   pomoc [pɔmɔts] 'help, n.'   *pomóc* [pɔmuts] 'vb.'

shows that in the same context—which can be morphophonologically related to a voiced obstruent because of the verbal paradigm *pomog-ę* [pɔmɔgɛ], *pomoż-e-sz* [pɔmɔʒɛʃ] 'I, you will help', etc.—the raising may but does not have to take place. What the existing facts show is not just the insufficiency of the formulation above but fundamentally the need further to restrict the forms undergoing it by lexical marking.

The other piece of evidence which shows the inadequacy of the formulation of the regularity is the fact that there are forms, albeit not very numerous but quite unambiguous, where the raising takes place in a context precluded by VR1, namely, before a voiceless obstruent. Consider some examples:

(27)   stop-a [stɔpa] 'foot'   stóp [stup] 'gcn. pl.'
        robot-a [rɔbɔta] 'work'   robót [rɔbut] 'gen. pl.'
        sobot-a [sɔbɔta] 'Saturday'   sobót [sɔbut] 'gen. pl.'
        powrot-u [pɔvrɔtu] 'return, gen. sg.'   powrót [pɔvrut] 'nom. sg.'
        siostr-a [ɕɔstra] 'sister'   sióstr [ɕustr̥] 'gen. pl.'

Nouns which require the raising before a voiceless obstruent indicate that the voicing specification in <VR1> can be disregarded, in other words, that it is optional. However, since the raising takes place in specified lexical items, these have to be so marked by a diacritic.

Another clear instance where the raising takes place irrespective of the voicing of the consonant following the vowel is found in the masculine third-person singular past tense of verbs. Here the stem-final consonant and the marker of the past tense are followed by the empty nucleus representing the gender. Consider:

(28)   plot-ł-e-m [plɔtwɛm] 'I wove'   plót-ł [plut(w̥)] 'he wove'
        mog-ł-e-m [mɔgwɛm] 'I could'   móg-ł [muk(w̥)] 'he could'
        mok-ł-e-m [mɔkwɛm] 'I got wet'   mók-ł [muk(w̥)] 'he got wet'
        nios-ł-e-m [ɲɔswɛm] 'I carried'   niós-ł [ɲus(w̥)] 'he carried'
        za-miot-ł-e-m [zamʲɔtwɛm] 'I swept'   za-miót-ł [zamʲut(w̥)] 'he swept'
        wioz-ł-e-m [vʲɔzwɛm] 'I carted'   wióz-ł [vʲus(w̥)] 'he carted'

There are two comments the data call for. Although VR1 mentions one consonant—preferably a voiced obstruent—for the raising to take place, the presence of an additional segment before the final empty nucleus evidently is acceptable. Here we have the lateral marking the preterite in (28), but we also have had the forms *gwóźdź* [gvuɕtɕ] in (24a), *sióstr* [ɕustr̥] in (27), both with raising before two and three consonants.

The other point concerns something that might potentially be a case of inter-action between different regularities. Note that the stem vowel [ɔ] of the last three verbs in (28) has to be related to the vowel [ɛ] in, for example, their infinitives: *nieś-ć* [ɲɛɕtɕ] 'carry', *za-mieś-ć* [zamʲɛɕtɕ] 'sweep', and *wieźć* [vʲɛɕtɕ] 'cart'. This can be achieved by the regularity we formulated above as RV2, a lexical mechanism relating vowels. In other words, the preterite of the verbs in question contains lexically [ɔ] with a diacritic which relates it to [ε] in other forms of the verbal paradigm. What undergoes raising is the lexical vowel [ɔ], so there is no 'feeding relation' between the [ε ~ ɔ] and [ɔ ~ u] relations: the former is a lexical relatedness captured as RV2 while the latter is a morphophonological replacement VR1.

The restriction of the consonant in the environment of <VR1> to an obstruent obviously prompts the question of what happens if the consonant in focus happens to be a sonorant. The answer is not simple since it depends on the nature of the sonorant itself. For one thing, there is no raising, and hence no alternations, before a nasal; see (29).

(29)   dom-u [dɔmu] 'house, gen. sg.'   dom [dɔm] 'nom. sg.'
       plon-y [plɔnɨ] 'harvest, nom. pl.'   plon [plɔn] 'nom. sg.'
       koni-e [kɔɲε] 'horse, nom. pl.'   koń [kɔɲ] 'nom. sg.'

When the sonorant is a palatal semivowel, the alternation is most frequently attested (a) although there are occasional departures in loan words (b):

(30)   (a) boj-u [bɔju] 'struggle, gen. sg.'   bój [buj] 'nom. sg.'
           zwoj-e [zvɔjε] 'scroll'   zwój [zvuj] 'nom. sg.'
           moj-a [mɔja] 'my, nom. sg. fem.'   mój [muj] 'nom. sg. masc.'

       (b) goj [gɔj] 'gentile'   boj [bɔj] 'bellboy'
           kowboj [kɔvbɔj] 'cowboy'

Before liquids and the trill the situation is unstable: side by side with the raising (a), there are forms where no raising takes places (b), and also forms which admit both variants (c):

(31)   (a) sokoł-y [sɔkɔwɨ] 'falcon, nom. pl.'   sokół [sɔkuw] 'nom. sg.'
           mol-e [mɔlε] 'moth, nom. pl.'   mól [mul] 'nom. sg.'
           pozwol-i [pɔzvɔli] '(s)he allows'   pozwól [pɔzvul] 'imper. sg.'
           wieczor-y [vʲεtʃɔrɨ] 'evening, nom. pl.' wieczór [vʲεtʃur] 'nom. sg.'

       (b) żywioł-y [ʒɨvʲɔwɨ] 'element, nom. pl.'   żywioł [ʒɨvʲɔw] 'nom. sg.'
           biadol-i [bʲadɔli] '(s)he moans'   biadol [bʲadɔl] 'imper. sg.'
           jezior-o [jεʑɔrɔ] 'lake'   jezior [jεʑɔr] 'gen. pl.'

       (c) szkol-i [ʃkɔli] '(s)he educates'   szkol [ʃkɔl] or szkól [ʃkul]
                                                     'imper. sg.'
           zmor-a [zmɔra] 'nightmare'   zmor [zmɔr] or zmór [zmur]
                                                     'gen. pl.'
           doktor-a [dɔktɔra] 'doctor, gen. sg.'   doktor [dɔktɔr] or doktór
                                                     [dɔktur] 'nom. sg.'

It appears, then, that with sonorants, just like with obstruents, we cannot dispense with lexical marking. The raising regularity is found not only before obstruents, predominantly voiced, but also before sonorants as long as the following empty nucleus represents an inflectional category. This is reflected in our formulation of VR1, where both voicedness and the obstruent nature of the consonant are bracketed. It has to be admitted that the formulation misses two points: (1) there is no raising before nasals, (2) raising is predominant before the palatal semivowel. Within our analysis, stems ending in a nasal will never be marked for raising while those ending in a glide will almost always do so. Possibly this points to the need to look for more intricate morphophonological regularities than we have developed here.

6.5.2 Alternations in derivationally related forms

Within inflectional morphology the raising relation can be regarded as reasonably well-established with rampant evidence in its support. As we have seen, the contexts of the raising can be defined with a large degree of precision at least with reference to some classes of segments, and although lexical marking is still inevitable, the raising has all the trimmings of a morphophonological replacement. A very different picture emerges from an inspection of derivationally related forms: here, too, are quite numerous forms to consider but no pattern of replacement can be detected. The problem is represented in a nutshell by the following sets of words:

(32) łow-y [wɔvɨ] 'hunt, nom. pl.'   łów [wuf] 'nom. sg.'   łow-i-ć [wɔvʲitɕ] 'vb.'
      mow-a [mɔva] 'speech'   mów [muf] 'gen. pl.'   mów-i-ć [muvʲitɕ]
                                                                'speak'

Both nouns show the regular raising before a final voiced consonant followed by an empty nucleus, as formulated in VR1. The related verbs differ unpredictably in that one of them—mów-i-ć [muvʲitɕ] 'speak'—also shows the raised vowel with nothing to account for it. Note that there can be no doubt as to the semantic relatedness of the noun-verb pairs; in the morphophonologically irregular mow-a [mɔva] 'speech' – mów-i-ć [muvʲitɕ] 'speak', the same pattern is repeated in several prefixal derivatives:

(33) prze-mow-a [pʃɛmɔva]   prze-mów-i-ć [pʃɛmuvʲitɕ]
      'speech, address'   'address, vb.'
      od-mow-a [ɔdmɔva] 'refusal'   od-mów-i-ć [ɔdmuvʲitɕ] 'refuse'
      wy-mow-a [vɨmɔva] 'pronunciation' wy-mów-i-ć [vɨmuvʲitɕ] 'pronounce'
      roz-mow-a [rɔzmɔva] 'conversation' roz-mów-i-ć [rɔzmuvʲitɕ]
                                         'have a chat'

We must conclude that the verbs have lexical [u] which is related to [ɔ] by a 'relate vowels' mechanism of the sort we have seen above: vowels are related without directionality and without contextual specification:

<RV3> ɔ ~ u

As part of the lexical specification of words such as mów-i-ć it will relate the vowel [u] to [ɔ] without, however, deriving one from the other in any sense and without conditioning it by the morphological or lexical context. The existence of diacritics such as <RV3> in the lexical entries of individual words means that it is no longer a morphophonological operation but an idiosyncratic bit of information, which might as well not be there. If it is not there, the implication is that individual speakers may no longer feel the connection between words. Additionally, the presence or absence of the diacritic may accompany semantic differentiation, as we will see presently. In general terms, relating words by means of such devices reflects the gradual weakening of linkage among forms: it is strongest when the forms are related phonologically, weaker when the relation is of a morphophono-logical 'replace segments' type, and weakest when it is of a lexical 'relate segments' form. The different types appear to form a cline rather than a clearly cut hierarchy.

The gradual transition from a replace regularity to a relate one may also mean that certain classes of forms may be ambiguous as to whether they should be subsumed under one or the other rubric. Our discussion of the morphophonology of palatalization reveals a great number of affixes which predominantly effected palatalized reflexes, hence the replacement mechanism seemed most apposite. Similarly the [ɔ ~ u] alternations within inflectional morphology display system-atic replacements. Within derivational morphology we find that one and the same suffix is sometimes attached to bases with the raised vowels while elsewhere no such effects are found. Individual suffixes may occasionally give the impression of a measure of regularity, but since the number of specific derivatives is often restricted, it is difficult to be sure whether the alleged regularity is anything but a statistical coincidence. Below we provide examples of a number of derivatives where the same suffix is or is not accompanied by raising effects. In our inter-pretation, the absence of raising is due to the absence of a diacritic while its presence indicates that the lexical vowel [u] is related to the vowel [ɔ].

(34) (a) miod-u [mʲɔdu]   mióд [mʲut]   miod-ek [mʲɔdɛk]
           'honey, gen. sg.'   'nom. sg.'   'dim.'

           vs.

           ogrod-u [ɔgrɔdu]   ogród [ɔgrut]   ogród-ek [ɔgrudɛk]
           'garden, gen. sg.'   'nom. sg.'   'dim.'

      (b) row-u [rɔvu]   rów [ruf]   row-ek [rɔvɛk]
           'ditch, gen. sg.'   'nom. sg.'   'groove'

           vs.

           słow-o [swɔvɔ]   słów [swuf]   słów-ek [swuvɛk]
           'word'   'gen. pl.'   'dim. gen. pl.'

      (c) Bog-a [bɔga]   Bóg [buk]   boż-ek [bɔʒɛk]
           'God, gen. sg.'   'nom. sg.'   'idol'

           vs.

           nog-a [nɔga]   nóg [nuk]   nóż-ek [nuʒɛk]
           'leg'   'gen. pl.'   'dim. gen. pl.'

(d) zbior-y [zbʲɔrɨ]   zbiór [zbʲur]   zbior-nic-a [zbʲɔrɲitsa]
    'collection, nom. pl.'   'nom. sg.   'storage'

    vs.

    mow-a [mɔva]   mów [muf]   mów-nic-a [muvɲitsa]
    'speech'   'gen. pl.'   'rostrum'

(e) dozor-u [dɔzɔru]   dozór [dɔzur]   dozor-c-a [dɔzɔrtsa]
    'supervision, gen. sg.' 'nom. sg.'   'caretaker'

    vs.

    twor-y [tfɔrɨ]   twór [tfur]   twór-c-a [tfurtsa]
    'creation, nom. pl.'   'nom. sg.'   'creator'

(f) wybory [vɨbɔrɨ]   wybór [vɨbur]   wybor-cz-y [vɨbɔrtʃɨ]
    'choice, nom. pl.'   'nom. sg.'   election, adj.'

    vs.

    twor-y [tfɔrɨ]   twór [tfur]   twór-cz-y [tfurtʃɨ]
    'creation, nom. pl.'   'nom. sg.'   'creative'

It is superfluous to say that examples of this type could easily be multiplied; supplying them would be otiose as the point is quite clear: there is no connection between a specific suffix and its ability to effect raising. In other words, the presence of the raised vowel is not the result of the addition of the suffix and the two just happen to appear together. The vowel is [u] in specific lexical items and it is related by VR1 or RV3 to forms with [ɔ].

The non-necessary presence of diacritics relating forms leads to the formation of doublets where the selection of a variant is sometimes a matter of personal predilection, as in (35).

(35)   dziob-u [dʑɔbu] 'beak, gen. sg.'   dziób [dʑup] 'nom. sg.'
       dziob-ek [dʑɔbɛk] or dziób-ek [dʑubɛk] 'dim.'

A more interesting situation arises when the formal differentiation is accompanied by divergence of meaning, hence the emergence of distinct lexical entries. Consider a few examples:

(36)   żłob-u [ʒwɔbu]   żłób [ʒwup] 'nom. sg.'   żłób-ek [ʒwubɛk] 'crib'
       'manger, gen. sg.'
                                                     żłob-ek [ʒwɔbɛk] 'creche'
       stop-a [stɔpa] 'foot'   stóp [stup] 'gen. pl.'   stóp-k-a [stupka] 'dim.'
                                                        stop-k-a [stɔpka] 'imprint'
       sobot-a [sɔbɔta]   sobót [sɔbut] 'gen. pl.'   sobót-k-a [sɔbutka]
       'Saturday'   'Midsummer Night
                                                        festivities'
                                                        sobot-k-a [sɔbɔtka] 'dim.'

Doublets of this type indicate yet again that raising—addition of a diacritic—is not a morphophonologically necessary operation; if it does happen, it may increase the lexical stock of the language.

Finally, the morphophonological presence of the raised vowel can be supported in an interesting way by quite a productive, colloquial, process of back-formation whereby the formally diminutive suffix is chopped off (see Herbert and Nykiel-Herbert 1991: 204). The resulting augmentative formation has normally a strongly expressive meaning as in the following examples.

(37) wod-a [vɔda] 'water' wód [vut] 'gen. pl.' wód-k-a [vutka] 'vodka'
  wód-a [vuda] 'expr.'
  mrow-i-ć [mrɔvʲitɕ] mrów-k-a [mrufka] 'ant'
  'swarm'
  mrów-a [mruva] 'large (ugly) ant, expr.'
  żar-ow-y [ʒarɔvɨ] żar-ów-k-a [ʒarufka] 'electric bulb'
  'of the heat'
  żar-ów-a [ʒaruva] 'big bulb, expr.'
  pysk-owa-ć [pɨskɔvatɕ] pysk-ów-k-a [pɨskufka] 'slanging match'
  'talk back'
  pysk-ów-a [pɨskuva] 'expr.'

The expressive derivatives arise by the truncation of the diminutive morpheme, here represented as -k-. Crucially, the raised vowel of the base noun remains raised in the back-formed augmentative (expressive) derivatives; this can be achieved in the most straightforward way imaginable by recognizing that the vowel [u] is in the input to the truncation process, i.e. that it appears lexically and does not result from morphophonological replacements.

In our discussion of the [ɔ ~ u] alternation we have recognized two mechanisms at work. One of them is morphophonological replacement applying in marked lexical items. Some conditioning on the operation is included in statement of the generalization, albeit only as a frequent but not indispensable factor. This reflects the predominant tendency for the raising to be found in specific morphophonological contexts. The raising as segment replacement is most general within inflectional paradigms. A version of the replacement operation stripped of any contextual conditioning serves as a lexical-relatedness statement; as a diacritic added to words it relates its vowel [u] to the vowel [ɔ] in derivationally related forms. Lexical-relatedness statements appear to arise out of replacement operations through attrition of the environmental conditioning; their content cannot be connected with anything in the morphological and morphophonological environment, merely capturing existing intuitions about word connections.

6.6 NASAL VOWELS AND THEIR ALTERNATIONS

Polish nasal vowels are nasal in name only: as was mentioned in the preceding chapters on a few occasions, the traditional nasal vowels are complex structures with a possible nasal component. The nasal component is not necessary and, furthermore, some of the so-called nasal vowels are phonetically purely oral segments. The nasality of the vowels is phonological, morphophonological, orthographic, and historical. Of these only the orthographic issue is not contro-versial: the front mid nasal vowel is spelt ę whereas the back mid one is spelt ą. Note in particular that the back nasal is mid rather than low as might be concluded from the orthographic representation. With this remark we part with the vagaries and tribulations of the Polish nasal vowel spelling. The complex history of the nuclei is conveniently summarized in Stieber (1958, 1973); Koneczna (1965: 109–21) and Klemensiewicz et al. (1965: 102–11) provide more detailed descriptions.

Phonologically, nasal vowels constitute a separate group because of the con-textually determined distribution of their realizations, while morphophonologi-cally, we have patterns of alternations that are distinct from other vocalic alternations. Partial representations of vocalic nuclei in terms of their elemental structure were hinted at in connection with the phonology of palatalization in Chapter 3. Here we will take a closer look at the relation between the skeletal and the melodic representation of the nuclei and at ways of capturing their unity in the face of the considerable phonetic diversity. Morphophonologically, we will survey the alternations of nasal front and back vowels.

6.6.1 Phonological aspects

The phonetics of nasal vowels in Polish was subject to extensive studies within traditional and more theoretically oriented models (Wierzchowska 1960; Bied-rzycki 1963, 1978; Dukiewicz 1967; Zagórska-Brooks 1968; Rubach 1977; Bethin 1988). For our purposes it is important to note that nasality of the vowels may be detected before spirants and word-finally, and even there it tends to be realized as a nasalized bilabial semivowel following an oral vowel, in other words, as diphthongs, [ɛʷ, ɔʷ]; additionally, the diphthong [ɛʷ] tends to be realized with the palatal nasal glide, [ɛⁱ], before a palatalized consonant. The vowel preceding the nasal glide contains a negligible, if any, degree of the nasal resonance. Examples of the pre-spirantal nasal nuclei are in (a) and those in word-final position in (b):

(38) (a) mięs-o [mʲɛʷsɔ] 'meat'   więz-i-ć [vʲɛʲʑitɕ] 'imprison'
          węsz-y-ć [vɛʷʃɨtɕ] 'sniff'   ciężar [tɕɛʷʒar] 'weight'
          gąs-k-a [gɔʷska] 'gosling'   gałąz-k-a [gawɔʷska] 'branch, dim.'
          gęś [gɛⁱɕ] 'goose'   gałęz-i [gawɛʲʑi] 'branch, gen. sg.'
          wąs [vɔʷs] 'moustache'   wiąz-a-ć [vʲɔʷzatɕ] 'bind'
          miąższ [mʲɔʷʃ] 'pulp'   wiąż-e [vʲɔʷʒɛ] '(s)he binds'
          fąfel [fɔʷfɛl] 'brat'   wąwóz [vɔʷvus] 'gorge'

      (b) książę [kɕɔʷʒɛ⁽ʷ⁾] 'prince'   trochę [trɔxɛ⁽ʷ⁾] 'a bit'
          pisz-ę [pʲiʃɛ⁽ʷ⁾] 'I write'   się [ɕɛ⁽ʷ⁾] 'oneself'
          noc-ą [nɔtsɔʷ] 'at night'   zresztą [zrɛʃtɔʷ] 'after all'
          pisz-ą [pʲiʃɔʷ] 'they write'

A phonological regularity affecting the front diphthong [ɛ̃ʷ] in word-final position must be mentioned here. Word-finally the nasal part of the diphthong is optional, hence all words in (b) ending in [ɛ̃ʷ] may be pronounced with the front oral vowel [ɛ]. The tendency towards denasalization is very strong in colloquial speech to the extent that the forms with the nasal diphthong sound artificial and stilted. This happens despite the fact that morphological homophony is created, for example, between the first- and the third-person singular present tense of certain verbs or between different cases of nouns; thus *pisz-ę* 'I write' and *pisz-e* '(s)he writes' are pronounced uniformly as [pʲiʃɛ], while *rol-ę* 'role, acc. sg.' and *rol-e* 'nom. pl.' are likewise homophonous, [rɔlɛ]. Characteristically, the denasalization does not affect the back vowel so all the words in (b) ending in [ɔ̃ʷ] are pronounced with the nasal diphthong; hence, the third-person plural present tense *pisz-ą* never emerges as *[pʲiʃɔ] (even though no homophony would arise in this case!). Nasal diphthongs can be represented as single skeletal points dominating a complex melody; the denasalization of [ɛ̃ʷ] to [ɛ] would amount to a simplification of the melody with no change of the higher structure.

While nasal diphthongs appear before continuants and word-finally, before a stop we find a sequence of an oral vowel and a nasal homorganic with the stop. Again the vowel shows no traces of nasalization. Consider examples of the basic places of articulation.

(39) *Bilabial*

sęp [sɛmp] 'vulture'	tęp-y [tɛmpɨ] 'blunt'
ząb [zɔmp] 'tooth'	trąb-a [trɔmba] 'trumpet'

Dental

pęd [pɛnt] 'speed'	błęd-y [bwɛndɨ] 'mistake, nom. pl.'
nędz-y [nɛndzɨ] 'misery, gen. sg.'	trąd [trɔnt] 'leprosy'
sąd-y [sɔndɨ] 'court, nom. pl.'	tysiąc [tɨɕɔnts] 'thousand'

Palatal

pędz-i-ć [pɛɲdʑitɕ] 'rush, vb.'	chęć [xɛɲtɕ] 'willingness'
błądź [bwɔɲtɕ] 'err, imper. sg.'	sądz-i [sɔɲdʑi] '(s)he thinks'

Velar

wstęg-a [fstɛŋga] 'ribbon'	męk-a [mɛŋka] 'torture'
łąk-a [wɔŋka] 'meadow'	pstrąg-a [pstrɔŋga] 'trout, gen. sg.'

The nasal nuclei in (39) consist of two segments and as such call for two skeletal positions within the rhyme: one for the nucleus and one for the coda. The coda consonant has to be licensed by the following onset with which it shares the place element:{U} for labiality, {A} for coronality, {I} for palatality, and {_} or empty-headedness for velarity. The nasal and the stop are adjacent not only melodically but also structurally as a coda-onset contact.

Sharing place elements is referred to in derivational terms as *nasal assimilation*. Since such sharing is possible when the segments are structurally adjacent, the absence of sharing, or the presence of non-assimilated consonants, indicates that the consonants are non-adjacent or separated by a nucleus. The intervening nucleus can contain either a floating melody which will consequently emerge in specified contexts, or an empty nucleus whose existence can be justified indirectly. Consider cases of the floating melody (a) and the empty nucleus (b).

(40)   (a)   słom-k-a [swɔmka] 'straw, dim.'   słom-ek [swɔmɛk] 'gen. pl.'
             za-mk-ną-ć [zamknɔɲtɕ] 'close,   za-myk-a-ć [zamɨkatɕ] 'der. imperf.'
             vb.'
             na-dm-ę [nadmɛ] 'I will inflate'   na-dym-a-m [nadɨmam] 'der.
                                                       imperf.'
             słonk-a [swɔnka] 'woodcock'   słonek [swɔnɛk] 'gen. pl.'
             słon-k-o [swɔnkɔ] 'sun, dim.'   słon-ek [swɔnɛk] 'gen. pl.'
             garnk-a [garn̥ka] 'pot, gen. sg.'   garnek [garnɛk] 'nom. sg.'
             hańb-a [xaɲba] 'shame'   hanieb-n-y [xaɲɛbnɨ] 'shameful'
             tańcz-y-ć [taɲtʃɨtɕ] 'dance, vb.'   taniec [taɲɛts] 'n.'

       (b)   mdł-y [mdwɨ] 'bland'   mgłw-a [mgwa] 'mist'
             mdl-e-ć [mdlɛtɕ] 'faint'   cien-k-i [tɕɛnci] 'thin'
             grom-k-i [grɔmci] 'thunderous'

The left-hand column words in (a) show non-homorganic clusters, which may but need not involve morphological divisions (cf. *słonk-a* [swɔnka] 'woodcock', *hańba* [xaɲba] 'shame', *tańcz-y-ć* [taɲtʃɨtɕ] 'dance', where no morphemic boundaries can be justified within the cluster). These non-homorganic sequences can be straightforwardly interpreted as an instance of two onsets separated by a floating vowel. Since the following nucleus contains an attached melody, the floating melody remains unpronounced in accordance with Melody Association (see Ch. 5). The right-hand column's words show the melody to be no longer floating since there is an empty nucleus following. The words in (b) also contain non-homorganic sequences but no alternations with a full vowel seem to exist. We have argued in Chapter 4 that for reasons relating to the syllabic organization, the clusters have to be seen as containing an empty nucleus. The same interpretation can be extended to the words *cien-k-i* [tɕɛnci] 'thin' and *grom-k-i* [grɔmci] 'thunderous', where a suffix beginning with an empty nucleus seems a plausible representation (*cien-k-i* has the comparative degree *cieni-ej* [tɕɛɲɛj] while *grom-k-i* has a clear derivational base *grom* [grɔm] 'thunder').

It is striking that word-initially we find sequences of non-homorganic consonants only, in other words, forms like *[ndatɕ] or *[mpɔwɨ] seem impossible. A question arises whether this gap can be related to some systematic relation in the language or whether it is just an accident. Although we have no compelling answers, the area that seems worth investigating is the absence of the floating vowel between homorganic consonants. Note that alternations schematically represented as 'nasal -<e> -obstruent ~ nasal-obstruent', where the nasal is homorganic with the obstruent, do not exist—we do not find alternations like *[rɔmɛp ~ rɔmpa] or *[banɛt ~ bantɨ], with the floating vowel intervening between homorganic consonants. In other words, homorganic nasal–obstruent sequences must form a coda–onset contact; hence they are impossible word-initially.

Another striking phonological property of nasal nuclei must be mentioned here, one for which we have no insightful interpretation, namely, their exclusion before sonorants. There are no morphemes where a nasal nucleus would be followed by [m, n, ɲ, r, j, l, w]. While the absence of nasal nuclei before a following nasal onset might perhaps be viewed as implementing a form of dissimilation, the same cannot be said about the remaining sonorants. What is more, we have one very clear case where a combination of morphemes ending in a nasal nucleus with a suffix beginning with a sonorant leads to the simplification of the nasals. As an illustration consider the following two verbs of which the second represents the verbalizing suffix -ną- which appears in about a thousand verbs.

(41) za-czę-t-y [zatʃɛntɨ]   za-czę-l-i [zatʃɛli]   za-czę-ł-y [zatʃɛwɨ]
      'begun'   'they (masc.) began'   'they (fem.) began'

      krzyk-ną-ć   krzyk-ną-ł-e-m   krzyk-nę-l-i [kʃɨknɛli]
      [kʃɨknɔɲtɕ]   [kʃɨknɔwɛm]
      'shout'   'I (masc.) shouted'   'they (masc.) shouted'

As can be seen, the nasal nucleus before the past tense marker [l] or [w] loses its nasal component and is pronounced as a fully oral vowel. If we were to derive this modification with some general principle it seems that the place to look for it would be the governing relations in the coda–onset contact. It might be argued that laterals are weaker consonants than nasals and hence cannot license them; a consonant in the coda position which is not licensed by the following onset remains unpronounced (possibly floating). This reasoning might also explain why nasal vowels cannot be followed by sonorants, as observed above, and why nasal consonants followed by sonorants are generally poorly, if at all, attested.[4]

As a final note concerning the phonology of nasal vowels, we need to consider possible ways of representing the nuclei. The elemental structure of the vocalic component of the nuclei is largely uncontroversial: {A} and {I} combine to form the front mid vowel and {A} and {U} result in the back one; what remains to be determined is the nature of the nasal component. Two distinct representations are

[4] The sequence [nr] seems to be found in the name *Henryk* [hɛnrɨk], which in regional forms is transformed into *Hendryk* [hɛndrɨk] with well-formed governing relations between the consonants in the cluster [ndr]; other possible counterexamples are the word *szemr-a-ć* [ʃɛmratɕ] 'murmur', *mamrot-a-ć* [mamrɔtatɕ] 'mumble' where the [mr] sequence cannot—in view of what is claimed above—form a coda–onset contact since a weak trill would have to license a stronger nasal. Obviously we could suggest an empty nucleus between the two consonants, a solution which looks ad hoc but is not. There exists a noun *szmer* [ʃmɛr] 'murmur, rustle' where the consonants are clearly in separate onsets separated by a non-alternating vowel (cf. *szmer-u* [ʃmɛru] 'gen. sg.').

clearly called for: one in pre-spirantal and final positions, and another one in pre-stop position. In the former case the nasal component constitutes part of the nucleus, hence it forms a complex structure with the vowel and is dominated by a single skeletal point. In addition to phonetic facts this follows from the possibility of the diphthong to appear word-finally, thus the nasal component cannot occupy a separate slot as then it would need to be licensed by an onset. The pre-stop nasal nucleus on the other hand calls for a separate slot for the nasal component since it has to be licensed by the following onset. We thus need two phonological structures which are functionally identical. In phonological terms the identity amounts to the following equivalence:

(42)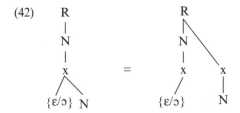

A non-branching rhyme dominating a single skeletal position is equivalent to a branching one with two slots and the melodies specified.

The two representations are phonologically distinct if only because they involve different constituent structures. Morphophonologically, however, they form a unity and Laskowski (1975a) treats them as single entities /ɛ̃/ and /ɔ̃/, which are adjusted and broken up (see also Gladney 1968). The unitary treatment has a lot to commend it since it captures restrictions in the distribution of the nasal nuclei and also, as will see directly below, their involvement in morphophonological alternations. For this reason we might assume that single morphophonological or lexical nasal vowels separate their nasal element into the rhymal complement before a following stop. Formally this amounts to a split of a single morphophonological unit into two phonological objects whose static equivalence has just been presented. This split may be charted as follows:

(43)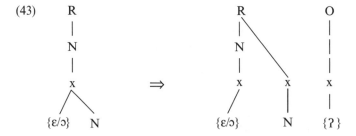

This mechanism can be regarded as a morphophonological replacement which does not differ in kind from other regularities of the same type, e.g. PR1, RV1. The morphophonological unity and the replacement of nasal nuclei ensure that their phonological properties are captured: the mid vocalic centre and the nasal glide or stop depending on the nature of the following environment plus the equivalence of the structures. The consonantal parts of the nasal nuclei are determined by general conditions on phonological representations which require the coda to be governed by the following onset; given this form of government it is not surprising that the onset plosive imposes its place property onto the governed nasal, a phenomenon familiar from numerous languages exhibiting nasal assimilation. When we discuss alternations of nasal nuclei below we will occasionally resort to the unitary morphophonological structure of the phonologically complex segments.

6.6.2 *Morphophonology of nasal nuclei*

Morphophonological nasal vowels [ɛ̃, ɔ̃] engage in alternations so that some instantiations of a given morpheme will contain the front vowel whereas others will have the back one. This happens with a degree of systematicity within nominal paradigms and far less regularly in derivationally related forms. Although the alternating segments are the same as in the case of the [ɛ ~ ɔ] alternations discussed in the second part of this chapter, there are fundamental differences between these two alternations which force us to recognize them as separate events—we shall call them nasal and non-nasal alternations for short.

The basic reasons for distinguishing the two types of alternation are connected with the nature of the context. The non-nasal alternation is, predominantly, restricted to a context of a preceding palatalized consonant, while the nasal one is found after both palatalized and non-palatalized consonants—it is insensitive to the nature of preceding consonant. This is illustrated in (44):

(44) (a) gnieś-ć [gɲɛ̃ɕtɕ] 'knead'   gniot-ę [gɲɔtɛ] 'I knead'
      (b) gęś [gɛ̃ɕ] 'goose'   gąs-k-a [gɔ̃ʷska] 'dim.'

In (a) the context preceding the alternation is the palatalized nasal [ɲ] while in (b) it is a plain velar plosive. Furthermore, the non-nasal alternation favours the front vowel before a palatalized coronal and the back one before a non-palatalized one, as in the example just given. The nasal alternation is insensitive both to the palatalized or non-palatalized nature of the following consonant and to it being a coronal or not:

(45) święt-o [ɕfʲɛntɔ] 'holiday'   świąt [ɕfʲɔnt] 'gen. pl.'
      dęb-y [dɛmbɨ] 'oak tree, nom. pl.'   dąb [dɔmp] 'nom. sg.'

In fact, the second example contradicts the non-nasal alternation on every count: it is found after a non-palatalized consonant, before a non-coronal one and the following consonant is non-palatalized before both members of the alternation. We conclude that the nasal and non-nasal alternations are separate phenomena that only fortuitously engage the same melodies.

Since nasal vowel alternations are found after both palatalized and non-palatalized consonants, the generative tradition (Laskowski 1975a; Gussmann 1980a; Rubach 1984) tried to connect the two properties—vowel alternations and consonant palatalization—in a systematic way. Specifically, it was assumed—in line with the then prevailing methods of arriving at phonological generalizations—that since front vowels 'evince' palatalization, the presence of a back vowel after a palatalized consonant involves a front-to-back shift; likewise the presence of a front vowel after a non-palatalized consonant denoted its phonological backness and a back-to-front shift. In this book we adopt the position, argued for above in Chapter 3, that consonant palatalization is not a phonological regularity apart from velar and some labial adjustments; the connection of nasal vowel frontness and consonant palatalization reflects the situation in early Slavic (see Carlton 1990: 126–30). Various phonological changes severed any link between the two phenomena over the past millennium plus, so that today there is no way of connecting them in any but an arbitrary—or highly abstract—fashion. Nasal vowels, alternating and non-alternating, can appear after all types of consonants. We will see examples of this directly below.

Nasal vowel alternations are attested in nominal paradigms. However, as with other vocalic alternations discussed in this chapter, the alternations are found with marked items only since, for the most part, vowels remain unaffected throughout the paradigm. Consider the following group of examples, where in (a) we have non-alternating back and front vowels after a palatalized consonant, while in (b) the same is found after a non-palatalized consonant.

(46) (a) ciąg [tɕɔŋk] 'sequence'   ciąg-u [tɕɔŋgu] 'gen. sg.'
         wiąz [vʲɔ̃ʷs] 'elm tree'   wiąz-y [vʲɔ̃ʷzɨ] 'nom. pl.'
         więź [vʲɛ̃ʲɕ] 'bond'   więz-i [vʲɛ̃ʲʑi] 'gen. sg.'
         pięt [pʲɛnt] 'heel, gen. pl.'   pięt-a [pʲɛnta] 'nom. sg.'

    (b) pstrąg [pstrɔŋk] 'trout'   pstrąg-a [pstrɔŋga] 'gen. sg.'
         trąd [trɔnt] 'leprosy'   trąd-u [trɔndu] 'gen. sg.'
         tęcz [tɛntʃ] 'rainbow, gen. pl.' tęcz-a [tɛntʃa] 'nom. sg.'
         gęś [gɛ̃ʲɕ] 'goose'   gęs-i [gɛ̃ʲɕi] 'nom. pl.'

Cases such as these display no striking characteristics beyond the phonological nasal equivalence—that the nasal diphthongs correspond to sequences of an oral vowel and a nasal consonant in the rhyme.

Contrasted with such cases of non-alternation we find nominal paradigms with vowel alternations, again both after a palatalized (a) and a non-palatalized (b) 1.

(47) (a) świąt [ɕfʲɔnt] 'holiday, gen. pl.'   święt-o [ɕfʲɛntɔ] 'nom. sg.'
         ksiąg [kɕɔŋk] 'book, gen. pl.'   księg-a [kɕɛŋga] 'nom. sg.'
         jagniąt [jagɲɔnt] 'lamb, gen. pl.'   jagnięci-a [jagɲɛɲtɕa] 'gen. sg.'
         jastrząb [jast-ʃɔmp] 'hawk'   jastrzębi-a [jast-ʃɛmbʲa] 'gen. sg.'

    (b) dąb [dɔmp] 'oak tree'   dęb-y [dɛmbɨ] 'nom. pl.'
         błąd [bwɔnt] 'error'   błędzi-e [bwɛɲdʑɛ] 'loc. sg.'
         wąż [vɔ̃ʷʃ] 'snake'   węż-om [vɛ̃ʷʒɔm] 'dat. pl.'
         rąk [rɔŋk] 'hand, gen. pl.'   ręk-a [rɛŋka] 'nom. sg.'

The distribution of the alternating vowels within paradigms is straightforward: the front vowel appears before some vocalic melody in the desinences, whereas the back one appears before desinential zero, that is, before an empty nucleus marking the desinences. The final say as to the shape of the forms of paradigms has to rest with morphology; here we can put forward a morphophonological interpretation in line with our analysis of similar phenomena above, namely, a segment-replacement procedure. Just like in the case of palatalization replacements we might suggest that a morphophonological operation substitutes one vowel for the other in specified contexts of lexically marked items. Two inter-related questions suggest themselves here: what is the basic or lexical segment that is replaced and in what context does the operation take place?

Since the back vowel appears before a desinential empty nucleus and the front one before a variety of vocalic melodies, the most economical model of description might be one where the back vowel emerges as a result of the replacement. This automatically supplies the answer as to the context of the change: it is found before a desinential empty nucleus. Here is a possible shape of Replace Nasal RN:

(48) Replace Nasal RN

The morphophonological replacement is subsequently subject to the phonologically conditioned split (43).

The restriction of RN to the empty nucleus implementing an inflectional category is a strong indicator of the morphophonological nature of the regularity. At the same time, however, it suggests that similar alternations should be found outside the nominal paradigms, a suggestion that is fully confirmed by aspects of verbal inflection. Consider the frequent verbalizing suffix -ną-: it appears with the back vowel in the infinitive and past singular masculine and with the front vowel in the past singular feminine and past plural.

(49)

infinitive	3 sg. past masc.	3 sg. past. fem.	3 pl. past fem.	
krzyk-ną-ć	krzyk-ną-ł	krzyk-nę-ł-a	krzyk-nę-ł-y	'shout'
[kʃɨknɔɲtɕ]	[kʃɨknɔw]	[kʃɨknɛwa]	[kʃɨknɛwɨ]	
dmuch-ną-ć	dmuch-ną-ł	dmuch-nę-ł-a	dmuch-nę-ł-y	'blow'
[dmuxnɔɲtɕ]	[dmuxnɔw]	[dmuxnɛwa]	[dmuxnɛwɨ]	
szarp-ną-ć	szarp-ną-ł	szarp-nę-ł-a	szarp-nę-ł-y	'jerk'
[ʃarpnɔɲtɕ]	[ʃarpnɔw]	[ʃarpnɛwa]	[ʃarpnɛwɨ]	

The same is true of a handful of verbs containing the nasal nucleus in the root:

(50)

pią-ć	pią-ł	pię-ł-a	pię-ł-y	'climb'
[pʲɔɲtɕ]	[pʲɔw]	[pʲɛwa]	[pʲɛwɨ]	
cią-ć	cią-ł	cię-ł-a	cię-ł-y	'cut'
[tɕɔɲtɕ]	[tɕɔw]	[tɕɛwa]	[tɕɛwɨ]	

The marker of the infinitive and of the masculine gender are empty nuclei, hence the morphophonological regularity we formulated as nasal replacement ensures that the required distribution of nasal vowel emerges. Note that phonological denasalization removes the nasal segment before the lateral, as discussed in connection with the examples in (43).

The replacement mechanism is not the only available means for capturing nasal vowel alternations. As in the case of other segment exchanges we saw above there is an alternative in the form of segment relatedness: rather than claim that the front nasal is actively transformed into the back one, it is possible to envisage a situation where both vowels are present as part of specific paradigms. Some of them, say, the more restricted forms, might additionally be specified with a diacritic indicating relatedness to the more generally occurring vowels. The relatedness statement would differ in minor parts from the replacement mechanism, and specifically it would contain no directionality indicator. Nasal Relatedness <NR> might take the following form:

(51)   Nasal Relatedness

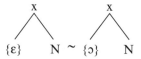

NR states simply that a specific, diacritically marked, nasal vowel is related to another nasal vowel. It would be part of lexical representations of morphemes which display alternations in combination with other morphemes. Non-alternating nasal vowels would, of course, contain no such information as they invariably appear in one shape only.

The choice between Nasal Replacement and Nasal Relatedness is sometimes not self-evident. We have seen the need for both mechanisms in connection with oral vowel alternations above and thus there is nothing new or strange about them when applied to nasal nuclei. Nasal Replacement introduces a measure of derivationality into the morphophonological system while Nasal Relatedness reflects a static connection. The selection of a specific solution depends then on assumptions about the nature of morphophonological operations. Rather than adopt a specific solution in a more or less arbitrary fashion let us consider another instance of nasal vowel alternations that appears to be a borderline case between a replacement and a relatedness regularity.

Nasal alternations are obligatorily before the suffix -ek [ɛk], which we have seen above and whose basic function is that of diminution. It starts with a floating vowel which emerges as [ɛ] in the regular fashion when the following inflectional ending is an empty nucleus, thus in the nominative singular of masculine and the genitive plural of feminine and neuter nouns. When attached to a base with a nasal nucleus, the suffix appears to enforce the emergence of the back nasal. This happens both in roots with alternating nasal vowels (a) and

those whose nasal vowel stays unmodified throughout the paradigm (b, c). Naturally, if the stable nasal vowel is itself back, no alternation is attested before the suffix
(c).

(52) (a) rąk [rɔŋk]   ręk-a [rɛŋka]   rącz-ek [rɔntʃɛk]
           'hand, gen. pl.'   'nom. sg.'   'dim. gen. pl.'
           ząb [zɔmp]   zęb-y [zɛmbɨ]   ząb-ek [zɔmbɛk]
           'tooth'   'nom. pl.'   'dim.'
           ksiąg [kɕɔŋk]   księg-a [kɕɛŋga]   książ-ek [kɕɔʷʒɛk]
           'book, gen. pl.'   'nom. sg.'   'dim. gen. pl.'
           rząd [ʒɔnt] 'row'   rzęd-y [ʒɛndɨ]   rząd-ek [ʒɔndɛk]
           'row'   'nom. pl.'   'dim.'
           gałąź [gawɔʲɕ]   gałęz-i [gawɛʲʑi]   gałąz-ek [gawɔʷzɛk]
           'branch'   'gen. sg.'   'dim. gen. pl.'

      (b) część [tʃɛʲɕtɕ]   częśc-i [tʃɛʲɕtɕi]   cząst-ek [tʃɔʷstɛk]
           'part'   'nom. pl.'   'dim. gen. pl.'
           pieczęć [pʲɛtʃɛɲtɕ]   pieczęc-i [pʲɛtʃɛɲtɕi]   pieczątek [pʲɛtʃɔntɛk]
           'seal'   'gen. sg.'   'stamp, gen. pl.'
           gęś [gɛʲɕ] 'goose'   gęs-i [gɛʲɕi]   gąs-ek [gɔʷsɛk]
           'goose'   'nom. pl'   'dim. gen. pl.'
           dziesięć [dʑɛɕɛɲtɕ]   dziesięci-u [dʑɛɕɛɲtɕu]   dziesiąt-ek [dʑɛɕɔntɛk]
           'ten'   'gen. sg.'   'a ten, gen. pl.'
           pamięć [pamʲɛɲtɕ]   pamięc-i [pamʲɛɲtɕi]   pamiąt-ek [pamʲɔntɛk]
           'memory'   'gen. sg.'   'souvenir, gen. pl.'

      (c) mąk [mɔŋk]   mąk-a [mɔŋka]   mącz-ek [mɔntʃɛk]
           'flour, gen. pl.'   'nom. sg.'   'meal, gen. pl.'
           łąk [wɔŋk]   łąk-a [wɔŋka]   łącz-ek [wɔntʃɛk]
           'meadow, gen. pl.'   'nom. sg.'   'dim. gen. pl.'
           pąk [pɔŋk]   pąk-i [pɔɲci]   pącz-ek [pɔntʃɛk]
           'bud'   'nom. pl.'   'dim.'
           trąb [trɔmp]   trąb-a [trɔmba]   trąb-ek [trɔmbɛk]
           'trumpet, gen. pl.'   'nom. sg.'   'dim. gen. pl.'

The remarkable regularity enforced by the suffix -ek is sufficiently striking to
deserve some consideration. Note that, with the exceptions listed below, the nasal
preceding the suffix is invariably back no matter whether the basic (non-suffixed)
noun alternates its nasal or not. Group (b) illustrates roots with a front nasal
which do not alternate within the paradigm but which nonetheless take the back
vowel before the diminutive suffix. In this sense the vowel in the diminutive is
more regular than the ones in basic nouns where effectively either the front or the
back nasal is admitted. In view of the generality of the back vowel before the
diminutive suffix it might be possible to obtain it through Replace Nasal: along
with the inflectional empty nucleus its context may include the diminutive suffix
-ek. Thus RN would assume the following shape:

(53) Replace Nasal <RN revised>

before ∅] infl.
before -*ek*

The formulation of RN captures the fact that the diminutive suffix is on a par with the inflectional empty nucleus. There are a few exceptions contradicting the general pattern; these we record here in view of the significance of the context of the alternation. As far as we can judge there is one exception involving an alternating nasal and a handful of non-alternating roots, which all display the front vowel before the diminutive suffix.

(54) (a) kłąb [kwɔmp]   kłęb-u [kwɛmbu]   kłęb-ek [kwɛmbɛk]
            'roll, ball'   'gen. sg.'   'bundle, skein'

      (b) kęp [kɛmp]   kęp-a [kɛmpa]   kęp-ek [kɛmpɛk]
            'cluster, gen. pl.'   'nom. sg.'   'dim. gen. pl.'
            rzęs [ʒɛ̃ʷs]   rzęs-a [ʒɛ̃ʷsa]   rzęs-ek [ʒɛ̃ʷsɛk]
            'eyelash, gen. pl.'   'nom. sg.'   'dim. gen. pl.'
            chęć [xɛɲtɕ]   chęc-i [xɛɲtɕi]   chęt-ek [xɛntɛk]
            'willingness'   'gen. sg.'   'itch, gen. pl.'
            pęk [pɛŋk]   pęk-u [pɛŋku]   pęcz-ek [pɛntʃɛk]
            'bundle'   'gen. sg.'   'dim.'
            przynęt [pʃinɛnt]   przynęt-a [pʃinɛnta]   przynęt-ek [pʃinɛntɛk]
            'bait, gen. pl.'   'nom. sg.'   'dim. gen. pl.'

On the assumption that RN regularity ensures the appearance of the back vowel before the diminutive suffix, instances like these might be handled as positive exceptions to the replacement mechanism. Alternatively, the nasal vowels of the diminutives might be supplied with a diacritic relating them to appropriate vowels in the base, in other words, we would invoke Nasal Related-ness. It is not easy to choose between the two solutions: replacing nasal vowels accounts for the cross-lexical generality of the back vowel before the suffix, while allowing for occasional exceptions. Relating the nasal nuclei does away with any exceptionality but then fails to capture the predominant pattern. On the other hand, the diminutive derivatives have to be entered in the lexicon, as we argued elsewhere on the basis of other data (see Ch. 5); the argument can be strengthened here by evoking nouns which take a competing diminutive suffix, namely -*ik* [ik], as exemplified in (55).

(55) mąż [mɔ̃ʷʃ]   męż-a [mɛ̃ʷʒa]   męż-yk [mɛ̃ʷʒɨk]
       'husband'   'gen. sg.'   'dim.'
       wąż [vɔ̃ʷʒ]   węż-a [vɛ̃ʷʒa]   węż-yk [vɛ̃ʷʒɨk]
       'snake'   'gen. sg.'   'dim.'

wz-gląd [vzglɔnt] wz-ględ-u [vzglɛndu] względz-ik [vzglɛɲdʑik]
'consideration' 'gen. sg.' 'dim'

Since the derivatives in *-ek* have to be entered in the lexicon, we might also include the information about the relatedness of their nasal vowels rather than actively derive them from some other source. On balance, then, both accounts are plausible; the one resorting to NR would probably need to be supplemented by some redundancy statement capturing the prevalent morphotactic pattern, with the back vowel appearing before the diminutive *-ek*.

A statement relating the two nasal nuclei without assigning any representational priority to one of them is massively supported by alternations found within other chunks of derivational morphology. As an illustration consider the pair of nouns:

(56) książ-ę [kcɔ\u02b7ʒɛ] 'prince' księci-a [kcɛɲtca] 'gen. sg.' książ-ąt [kcɔ\u02b7ʒɔnt] 'gen. pl.'

księż-niczk-a [kcɛ\u02b7ʒɲitʃka] 'princess'

The two words are morphologically and semantically related in an obvious way since the feminine form is derived from the masculine one by the addition of a suffix. At the same time, the vowel which is back in the nominative singular and throughout the plural is front in the oblique cases of the singular; it is also front in the feminine derivative. The derived noun belongs to a large class of feminine formations which, in ways characteristic of derivational morphology, are partly irregular and unpredictable. In fact, the noun *księżniczka* [kcɛ\u02b7ʒɲitʃka] 'princess' seems to be the only such form in Polish where we need to isolate the suffix *-niczk-*; elsewhere the feminine suffix *-k-* is attached to the masculine *-nik* with palatalization replacement, as in (57).

(57) wędrow-nik [vɛndrɔvɲik] 'wanderer' wędrown-nicz-k-a [vɛndrɔvɲitʃka] 'fem.'

Despite the morphological isolation of the derivative *księżniczka* [kcɛ\u02b7ʒɲitʃka] 'princess', no native speaker will be in any doubt as to its relatedness to the noun *książę* [kcɔ\u02b7ʒɛ] 'prince'; for this reason the morphophonological alternation of nasal vowels needs to be captured in the lexical specification of the derived noun. Following the pattern adopted in earlier discussion we regard lexical alternations of this sort to fall under the heading of lexical relatedness with little, if any, contextual conditioning. In this particular case, the function is performed by Nasal Relatedness as formulated above. In practical terms this means that the nucleus of the derivative will contain the NR diacritic which will show its connectedness with the back vowel.

The need for the relatedness approach to nasal vowel alternations is particularly conspicuous in cases where no distinct morphological pattern can be established and where nonetheless the words are clearly felt to belong together. In contradistinction to the predominantly regular suffix *-ek* [ɛk], discussed above, other derivational suffixes display erratic behaviour in that they admit both nasal vowels, even if sometimes with a clear preference of one or the other. Consider the frequent adjectival suffix *-n-y* [nɨ] attached to alternating (a) and non-alternating (b) nasal vowels in the bases:

(58) (a) błąd [bwɔnt]   błęd-y [bwɛndɨ]   błęd-n-y [bwɛndnɨ]
           'mistake'   'nom. pl.'   'erroneous'
           wz-gląd [vzglɔnt]   wz-ględ-u [vzglɛndu]   wz-ględ-n-y [vzglɛndnɨ]
           'consideration'   'gen. sg.'   'relative'
           okrąg [ɔkrɔŋk]   okręg-u [ɔkrɛŋgu]   okręż-n-y [ɔkrɛʷʒnɨ]
           'circle'   'gen. sg.'   'roundabout'
           rąk [rɔŋk]   ręk-a [rɛŋka]   ręcz-n-y [rɛntʃnɨ]
           'hand, gen. pl.'   'nom. sg.'   'adj.'
           świąt [ɕfʲɔnt]   święt-o [ɕfʲɛntɔ] o   od-święt-n-y [ɔtɕfʲɛntnɨ]
           'holiday, gen. pl.'   'nom. sg.'   'festive'

       (b) chęć [xɛɲtɕ]   chęc-i [xɛɲtɕi]   chęt-n-y [xɛntnɨ]
            'willingness'   'gen. sg.'   'willing'
            wstręt [fstrɛnt]   wstręt-u [fstrɛntu]   wstręt-n-y [fstrɛntnɨ]
            'repulsion'   'gen. sg.'   'repulsive'
            dźwięk [dʑvʲɛŋk]   dźwięk-i [dʑvʲɛnci]   dźwięcz-n-y [dʑvʲɛntʃnɨ]
            'sound'   'nom. pl.'   'voiced'
            mąk [mɔŋk]   mąk-a [mɔŋka]   mącz-n-y [mɔntʃnɨ]
            'flour, gen. pl.'   'nom. sg.'   'floury'
            żądz [ʒɔndz]   żądz-a [ʒɔndza]   żąd-n-y [ʒɔndnɨ]
            'lust, gen. pl.'   'nom. sg.'   'desireous'
            sąd [sɔnt]   sąd-u [sɔndu]   sąd-n-y [sɔndnɨ]
            'judgement'   'gen. sg.'   'adj.'
            pieniądz [pʲɛɲɔnts]   pieniądz-e [pʲɛɲɔndzɛ]   pienięż-n-y [pʲɛɲɛʷʒnɨ]
            'money'   'nom. pl.'   'monetary'
            o-gląd [ɔglɔnt]   ogląd-u [ɔglɔndu]   oględ-n-y [ɔglɛndnɨ]
            'inspection'   'gen. sg.'   'reserved'

While the alternating vowels in (a) appear to call for the front vowel before the suffix *-n-y*, those with non-alternating vowel display no clear pattern. Some maintain the root vowel in the derivatives, whereas others opt for the front one. In view of such variety it is difficult to entertain the possibility of systematic vowel replacements and vowel relatedness remains as the only option. This is additionally strengthened by the frequently non-compositional semantics of the derivative. Let us also note that the very distinction into alternating and non-alternating roots can be lexeme-specific: *wz-gląd* [vzglɔnt] 'consideration' is morphologically complex, as is *o-gląd* [ɔglɔnt] 'inspection', since both of them contain the cranberry morpheme *gląd* (found also in numerous other words, such as *po-gląd* [pɔglɔnt] 'view', *prze-gląd* [pʃɛglɔnt] 'survey', and *wy-gląd* [vɨglɔnt] 'appearance'). However, while *wz-gląd* [vzglɔnt] 'consideration' is alternating (cf.

wz-ględu [vzglɛndu] 'gen. sg.'), *og-ląd* [ɔglɔnt] 'inspection' is not (cf. *og-lądu* [ɔglɔndu] 'gen. sg.'). Any attempt to systematize such data in terms of regularities is bound to end up in artificialities and ad hoc solutions. Nasal-vowel alternations in the contemporary language are a detritus of a phonological regularity of great antiquity; despite the respect that ancient phonology is entitled to, its position in the modern language is similar to other great idols of the past in various walks of life: they should be paid respect to but prevented from meddling in current affairs. Without much exaggeration Polish nasal-vowel alternations can be compared to ablaut effects in contemporary Germanic languages: no matter how closely related *sing* and *song* may appear to the present-day language user, no phonologist is likely to attempt to relate them in any other way but through the medium of the lexicon. Since the number of related forms with alternating nasal vowels is significant in Polish, we recognize the mechanism of NR attached to vowels in the lexical representations of words. This makes the point of relating the forms without deriving one form the other, or both from some third source.

To complete this section consider a few sets of words containing the same nasal vowel root but with unpredictable and erratic alternations in derivatives:

(59) (a) błąd [bwɔnt]   błądz-i-ć [bwɔɲdʑitɕ]   błęd-n-y [bwɛndnɨ]
         'mistake'   'err'   'erroneous'
         błęd-nik [bwɛndɲik]   przy-błęd-a [pʃɨbwɛnda]
         'labyrinth of the ear' 'straggler'

     (b) mądr-y [mɔndrɨ]   mędr-sz-y [mɛntrʃɨ]   mądr-ala [mɔndrala]
         'wise'   'wiser'   'smart Aleck'
         mędr-ek [mɛndrɛk]   mędrz-ec [mɛnd-ʒɛts]   mądrz-e-ć [mɔnd-ʒɛtɕ]
         'know-all'   'sage'   'grow wiser'

     (c) sąd [sɔnt]   sądz-i-ć [sɔɲdʑitɕ]   sędzi-a [sɛɲdʑa]
         'court'   'judge, vb.'   'judge, n.'
         sędz-in-a [sɛɲdʑina] sąd-n-y [sɔndnɨ]
         'woman judge'   'of judgement, adj.'

     (d) trąd [trɔnt]   trąd-ow-y [trɔndɔvɨ]   tręd-owat-y
                                                          [trɛndɔvatɨ]
         'leprosy'   'leprous'   'leper'
         trądz-ik [trɔɲdʑik]
         'acne'

Examples could be multiplied but they all point in the same direction: in derivational morphology, alternation of nasal vowels is found in forms which cannot be systematically related either semantically or morphophonologically. The semantic irregularities are not our concern here. Morphophonologically we recognize the existence of the relatedness and encode it in the form of lexical diacritics connecting the alternating vowels.

6.7 VOWEL ALTERNATIONS IN DERIVED IMPERFECTIVES

A morphological category of the verb that has been referred to several times in the course of this book are the secondary or derived imperfectives. Most commonly they denote a repeated (iterative) activity, although with lexicalization actively involved, the meaning of some of them cannot be fully predicted (is not compositional). The imperfectives are derived from perfective verbs which themselves may be derived from some other part of speech:

(60) koniec [kɔɲɛts]   wy-kończ-y-ć [vɨkɔntʃitɕ]   wy-kańcz-a-ć [vɨkantʃatɕ]
     'end, n.'   'bring to an end'   'der. imperf.'

     dzwon [dzvɔn]   roz-dzwon-i-ć [rɔzdzvɔɲitɕ] roz-dzwani-a-ć
                                                     [rɔzdzvaɲatɕ]
     'bell'   'ring out'   'der. imperf.'
     mnog-i [mnɔɟi]   prze-mnoż-y-ć [pʃɛmnɔʒitɕ]   prze-mnaż-a-ć
                                                     [pʃɛmnaʒatɕ]
     'numerous'   'multiply'   'der. imperf.'
     śpiew [ɕpʲɛf]   do-śpiew-a-ć [dɔɕpʲɛvatɕ]   do-śpiew-ywa-ć
                                                     [dɔɕpʲɛvɨvatɕ]
     'singing'   'sing to the end'   'der. imperf.'

Imperfectives can occasionally also be derived from other imperfective verbs:

(61) mow-a [mɔva]   mów-i-ć [muvʲitɕ]   mawi-a-ć [mavʲatɕ]
     'speech'   'speak, imperf.'   'der. imperf.'

     chod-u [xɔdu]   chodz-i-ć [xɔdʑitɕ] chadz-a-ć [xadzatɕ]
     'gait, gen. sg.' 'walk, imperf.'   'der. imperf.'

The formation of derived imperfectives belongs to morphology: two suffixes, each with a few variants, are involved in the process. Their selection and distribution as well as various morphophonological modifications need to be covered by a description. Some of the modifications appear quite isolated and involve vowel alternations discussed in this chapter, such as [ɛ ~ a]; these must be captured by means of diacritics attached to lexical representation of verbs. Similarly, alternations between palatalized (including functionally palatalized) consonants and non-palatalized ones are a matter of the lexical presence of an appropriate diacritic—it is the task of the morphological and morphophonological description of derived imperfective formations to handle all such details, erratic and irregular as they might be. Here we would like to concentrate on just one type of vowel alternation which is regular and productive but restricted to the context of one of the derived imperfective suffixes, namely, -aj [aj]; the glide of the suffix is suppressed before a consonantal desinence (see n. 26 in Ch. 5). When the suffix is attached to verbs containing the vowel [ɔ], this vowel is replaced by [a]. Consider pairs of perfective verbs and imperfectives derived from them, both supplied in the third-person singular present; the nominal base of the perfective is also provided.

(62) za-robi-ą [zarɔbʲɔ̃ʷ]   za-rabi-aj-ą [zarabʲajɔ̃ʷ]   rob-ot-a [rɔbɔta]
      'earn, perf.'   'der. imperf.'   'work, n.'
      s-kłoni-ą [skwɔɲɔ̃ʷ]   s-kłani-aj-ą [skwaɲajɔ̃ʷ]   skłon [skwɔn]
      'induce, perf.'   'der. imperf.'   'bend, n.'
      o-głosz-ą [ɔgwɔʃɔ̃ʷ]   o-głasz-aj-ą [ɔgwaʃajɔ̃ʷ]   głos [gwɔs]
      'announce, perf.'   'der. imperf.'   'voice, n.'
      s-tworz-ą [stfɔʒɔ̃ʷ]   stwarz-aj-ą [stfaʒajɔ̃ʷ]   stwor-u [stfɔru]
      'create, perf.'   'der. imperf.'   'creation, gen. sg.'
      za-groż-ą [zagrɔʒɔ̃ʷ]   za-graż-aj-ą [zagraʒajɔ̃ʷ]   groz-a [grɔza]
      'threaten, perf.'   'der. imperf.'   'dread, n.'
      u-proszcz-ą [uprɔʃtʃɔ̃ʷ]   u-praszcz-aj-ą [upraʃtʃajɔ̃ʷ]   prost-y [prɔstɨ]
      'simplify, perf.'   'der. imperf.'   'simple'
      na-wod-ni-ą [navɔdɲɔ̃ʷ]   na-wad-ni-aj-ą [navadɲajɔ̃ʷ]   wod-n-y [vɔdnɨ]
      'irrigate, perf.'   'der. imperf.'   'water, adj.'
      u-wolni-ą [uvɔlɲɔ̃ʷ]   u-walni-aj-ą [uvalɲajɔ̃ʷ]   woln-y [vɔlnɨ]
      'set free, perf.'   'der. imperf.'   'free'

In view of the generality of the alternation we would like to consider the operation to be a morphophonological replacement taking place before the suffix *-aj*. This conclusion is further reinforced by the fact that when the perfective verb contains two instances of the vowel [ɔ], both of them may, but do not have to, be turned into [a]; in (63) several examples of such verbs are presented, where the two derived imperfectives are placed in the middle column.

(63) u-spokoj-ą   u-spokaj-aj-ą   s-pokoj-u [spokoju]
      [uspɔkɔjɔ̃ʷ]   [uspɔkajajɔ̃ʷ]
      'calm down'   u-spakaj-aj-ą   'peace, gen. sg.'
                                 [uspakajajɔ̃ʷ]

      u-osobi-ą   u-osabi-aj-ą   osob-a [ɔsɔba]
      [uɔsɔbʲɔ̃ʷ]   [uɔsabʲajɔ̃ʷ]
      'personify'   u-asabi-aj-ą   'person'
                                 [uasabʲajɔ̃ʷ]

      wy-narod-owi-ą   wy-narod-awi-aj-ą   narod-u [narɔdu]
      [vɨnarɔdɔvʲɔ̃ʷ]   [vɨnarɔdavʲajɔ̃ʷ]
      'deprive of national identity' wy-narad-awi-aj-ą   'nation, gen. sg.'
                                 [vɨnaradavʲajɔ̃ʷ]

      o-swobodz-ą   o-swobadz-aj-ą   swobod-a [sfɔbɔda]
      [ɔsfɔbɔdzɔ̃ʷ]   [ɔsfobadzajɔ̃ʷ]
      'liberate'   o-swabadz-aj-ą   'liberty'
                                 [ɔsfabadzajɔ̃ʷ]

      u-pokorz-ą   u-pokarz-aj-ą   pokor-a [pɔkɔra]
      [upɔkɔʒɔ̃ʷ]   [upɔkaʒajɔ̃ʷ]
      'humiliate'   u-pakarz-aj-ą   'humility'
                                 [upakaʒajɔ̃ʷ]

While individual speakers will no doubt show preferences for one or the other of the forms, the existence of the variation testifies to the reality of the regularity. We can propose a vowel replacement operation of the following shape:

<VR2> ɔ ⟹ a before (C₀ɔ) aj

The bracketed material ensures that both the nucleus directly adjacent to the suffix as well as one separated from it by another nucleus containing the same vowel will undergo the replacement. What is interesting is that the replacement does not reach the vowel of the prefix: the last of our examples in its derived imperfective form can never be *a-swabadz-aj-ą [asfabadzajɔ^{w}], with the vowel affected by VR2. The failure has nothing to do with the number of potential vowel replacement sites in the word: the verbs in (63) admit two replacements per word while the verb do-robi-ą [dɔrɔbʲɔ^{w}] 'make some more, perf.' has its derived imperfective as do-rabi-aj-ą [dɔrabʲajɔ^{w}], with just one instance of replacement and never *da-rabi-aj-ą [darabʲajɔ^{w}] with two. The culprit—or barrier—is the prefix itself which is not eligible to the replacement. Discussing the behaviour of the floating vowel at the prefix–root boundary in Chapter 5, we argued that prefixes in most cases are separated from the rest of the verb by domain boundary. This conclusion can explain the resistance of the vowel [ɔ] in prefixes to the replacement mechanism: VR2 operates within phonological domains and hence its failure to affect the vowel of the prefix is no more surprising than its failure to affect the vowel of the preceding word.

The live nature of VR2 can be further supported by the extension of the alternation to nasal vowels, a phenomenon very common in colloquial speech even if frowned upon as 'grossly ungrammatical' by normative grammarians. The verb włącz-y-ć [vwɔntʃitɕ] 'switch on' has its substandard DI as [vwantʃatɕ] (with no standard spelling) and the verb od-trąb-i-ć [ɔttrɔmbʲitɕ] 'trumpet' (cf. trąb-a [trɔmba] 'n.') can be heard in DI as [ɔttrambʲatɕ] (again with no standard spelling); the standard forms show no alternation in DI and appear as włącz-a-ć [vwɔntʃatɕ] and od-trąbi-a-ć [ɔttrɔmbʲatɕ], respectively. The colloquial or substandard forms indicate that the nasal vowel is no longer regarded as a unit and its vocalic part, the vowel [ɔ], conforms to morphophonological patterns of the language by undergoing VR2.

This brief discussion of vowel replacement in derived imperfectives has yet another intriguing implication. Discussing the [ɔ ~ u] alternation, we posited the existence of a replacement mechanism VR1 which, triggered by a diacritic attached to specific morphemes, turned the vowel [ɔ] into [u]. In a clear sense the high vowel [u] was thus derived or secondary as compared to the basic or primary [ɔ]. There are a few perfective verbs derived from nouns with the alternation where the high vowel of the alternation appears in the verbal stem. When, however, the perfective verb becomes input to derived imperfective formation, its vowel appears to display effects of VR2, in other words, it looks as if the input vowel were [ɔ].

(64) po-wróc-ą [pɔvrutsɔ̃ʷ]   po-wrac-aj-ą [pɔvratsajɔ̃ʷ]   po-wrót [pɔvrut]
      'return, perf.'   'der. imperf.'   'return, n.'
      na-mówi-ą [namuvʲɔ̃ʷ]   na-mawi-aj-ą [namavʲajɔ̃ʷ]   mów [muf]
      'persuade, perf.'   'der. imperf.'   'speech, gen. pl.'

The verbal forms themselves appear to give the impression of the existence of the
alternation [u ~ a]; the alternating nominal bases with the vowel [ɔ]—*po-wrot-y*
[pɔvrɔtɨ] 'return, nom. pl.', *mow-a* [mɔva] 'speech, nom. sg.'—may point to a
different interpretational possibility. We might regard the vowel [u] in the perfective forms as being [ɔ] with the diacritic <VR1> and derived imperfective
formation would have to take as its input just the vocalic melody without the
diacritic. In such a case it would be subject to RV2 and the forms in (64) would be
the expected ones. While plausible, this solution is not necessarily compelling:
there are verbs with the [u ~ a] alternations without an accompanying nominal or
other base form with the vowel [ɔ]:

(65) s-króc-ą [skrutsɔ̃ʷ]   s-krac-aj-ą [skratsajɔ̃ʷ]
      'shorten, perf.'   'der. imperf.'
      po-wtórz-ą [poftuʒɔ̃ʷ]   po-wtarz-aj-ą [pɔftaʒajɔ̃ʷ]
      'repeat, perf.'   'der. imperf.'

The problem here is that the nominal bases of the perfective forms *s-krót*
[skrut] 'abbreviation' (itself related to *krót-k-i* [krutci] 'short'), *wtór-y* [fturɨ]
'second' have no alternants with [ɔ]. We could suggest that the basic nominals
and the perfective verbs they motivate contain the vowel [ɔ] with a diacritic
<VR1> and it is this vowel that is subject to VR2 in the derived imperfective
formation. The difficulty which would need to be solved with the word *skrót*
[skrut] 'abbreviation' is the absence of the alernation in for instance *skrót-y*
[skrutɨ] 'nom. pl.' (where we might expect *skrot-y [skrɔtɨ]). An alternative and
patently simpler analysis would recognize the alternation [u ~ a] in the handful of
verbs in (64)–(65). When all is said and done, cases like this involve a choice
between a complicated but reasonably regular pattern and one which rests on
mechanical juxtaposition of segments. This is not a place to enter into any
extended defence of one or other of the positions; it is worth keeping in mind
that regularizing alternations into patterns complicates the description, sometimes to a point where the brute-force method of listing alternating segments may
seem preferable (and more realistic from the point of view of the learner).[5]

---

[5] In a chapter devoted to the morphophonology of vowel alternations it is somewhat otiose to add
that Polish is no different from other languages in containing regularities which are supported by large
chunks of its vocabulary and also those which are sporadic and in various ways irregular. Polish, like any
Indo-European language, contains remnants of apophonic alternations but it is doubtful whether these
should form a systematic part of its morphophonology and thus be forced into existing morphophonemic
patterns. The [ɛ ~ ɔ] alternation we discussed in this chapter should not be extended to cover cases of
such apophonic relatives as *otworz-y-ć* [ɔtfɔʒitc] 'open, perf.' ~ *otwier-a-ć* [ɔtfʲɛratc] 'der. imperf.' since
the regular alternation takes place after a palatalized consonant while here the preceding consonant is
palatalized in one form only. Subsuming all instances of a given alternation under a single heading would
make it impossible to separate synchronic regularity from chance or petrified modifications.

VOICE AND VOICE-RELATED PHENOMENA

7.1 OVERVIEW

The familiar Polish final devoicing is interpreted as the failure of the domain-final empty nucleus to license the element {L} in the preceding onset. The traditional voice assimilation domain-internally follows from a constraint which marks the last obstruent in a sequence as dominant and hence the preceding obstruents cannot differ from it in their specification for tone. The two regularities are involved in word-boundary phenomena where additionally the picture is obscured by intervening sonorants. These are shown to follow from the role that empty nuclei play in the phonological well-formedness of words. The empty nuclei and the floating melodies are crucially involved in the unexpected behaviour of prepositions (and prefixes) before word-initial sonorants. Minimal assumptions about domain structure are introduced and they complement the GP view of the restricted role of morphology in phonological patterning.

Finally, we look at the progressive voice assimilation and consider evidence forcing us to regard the two obstruents [ʒ, v] as (morpho)phonological sonorants. Once this step is taken, the progressive assimilation turns out to be yet another aspect of voice adjustment generally at work in the language.

7.2 INTRODUCTION

Phenomena relating to voicing have been discussed both within classical phonetic studies (Benni 1923; Wierzchowska 1971) and within the generative phonological tradition (Bethin 1984, 1992; Gussmann 1992*b*; Rubach 1996). Although a much-ploughed area, the voice complex is not fully understood; there are problems not only with interpreting the data but with the data themselves. The main difficulty stems from the fact that apart from relatively simple structures (consonant combinations), speakers will often differ as to the voicing or devoicing of consonant sequences, in particular where sonorants are involved. At times it is impossible to decide whether a particular variant results from the phonology of the language or from a speaker self-monitoring his/her output and trying to 'speak correctly' (i.e. in accordance with the spelling). As a case in point consider the word *jabłk-o* 'apple', which in unguarded, unmonitored, speech appears as [japkɔ], although variants such as [japu̯kɔ] with a voiceless semi-vowel or even [jabwkɔ] with a voiced one are encountered too frequently to be dismissed as marginalia. Whether the last two variants are instances of spelling pronunciation or whether they are a more or less conscious attempt to preserve the morpho-phonological structure of the word—its genitive plural form *jabłek* universally admits of one pronunciation only, [jabwɛk]—is not something that can be easily determined. In what follows we will start with the clear-cut data and move gradually towards less obvious cases. The voice complex comprises devoicing and voice assimilations.

7.3 (DE)VOICINGS OF OBSTRUENTS

The most straightforward instance of devoicing is seen with word-final obstruents in pre-pausal position. Both single obstruents and obstruent clusters are uni-formly voiceless when silence follows. This is amply evidenced through alterna-tions:

(1) chleb [xlɛp] 'bread'   chleb-a [xlɛba] 'gen. sg.'
     rad [rat] 'advice, gen. pl.'   rad-a [rada] 'nom. sg.'
     dróg [druk] 'road, gen. pl.'   drog-a [drɔga] 'nom. sg.'
     słódź [swutɕ] 'sweeten, imper.'   słodz-i [swɔdʑi] '(s)he sweetens'
     nóż [nuʃ] 'knife'   noż-em [nɔʒɛm] 'instr. sg.'
     gwóźdź [gvuɕtɕ] 'nail'   gwoździ-e [gvɔʑdʑɛ] 'nom. pl.'
     gwiżdż [gvʲiʃtʃ] 'whistle, imper.'   gwiżdż-ę [gvʲiʒdʒɛ] 'I whistle'
     drozd [drɔst] 'thrush'   drozd-ach [drɔzdax] 'loc. pl.'
     mózg [musk] 'brain'   mózg-om [muzgɔm] 'dat. pl.'

Although occasionally suppressed with foreign words (names) and for idiosyn-cratic reasons, this regularity is cross-lexical and undoubtedly phonological.[1]

In accordance with the assumptions adopted in this book, to qualify as phonological a given phenomenon must establish a direct relation with the context in which it occurs. Voicing phenomena in terms of the element theory embrace two primes, namely, High tone {H} capturing fundamental properties of voicelessness and Low tone {L} handling voicedness. Individual languages select either one or the other of the primes and occasionally adopt both of them (see Harris 1994: 133–8 for an in-depth discussion of tonal properties in the

---

[1] An idiosyncratic reason can be detected in the genitive plural of the noun *dob-a* [dɔba] 'day and night, 24 hours', where the form with the morphophonological raising of the root vowel and the phonological terminal devoicing would yield *dób* [dup], a shape homophonous with *dup* [dup], the genitive plural of *dup-a* [dupa] 'arse'. To avoid the homophony speakers will often leave the final obstruent of *dób* voiced, i.e. [dub]. Suspension also tends to be found with the pairs *kod* [kɔd] 'code' ∼ *kot* [kɔt] 'cat' and *blog* [blɔg] 'blog' ∼ *blok* [blɔk] 'block', possibly because of the foreign nature of the first members. No such suspension of the devoicing is found when other homophones arise, e.g. *dróg* [druk] 'road, gen. pl.' ∼ *druk* [druk] 'printing', *grad* [grat] 'hail' ∼ *grat* [grat] 'piece of junk' are not distinguished.

context of the cover term 'voice'). Polish settles for {L}, hence the so-called final devoicing denotes the suppression or delinking of this element. A question which suggests itself is why word-final rather than, say, word-initial position should encourage such delinking. In other words, what is the relation between the context and the change?

Recall that a consonant in word-final position is actually a consonant in the syllabic onset: it is followed by an empty nucleus which serves as a licensor for the onset. In such terms our word-final devoicing turns out to be a case of delinking of {L} before an empty nucleus. Approaching the devoicing from the point of view of the empty nucleus we can say that empty nuclei fail to license {L} on their onsets. Thus when the nucleus contains some melody, the onset licenses voicedness of the preceding consonant; when the nucleus is empty, the license is withdrawn, the effect being that an obstruent without a tone specification is pronounced as voiceless. Final devoicing turns out to be a by-product of the reduced licensing potential of empty nuclei, in fact of domain-final empty nuclei.[2] We conclude that word-final suppression of voicing in obstruents is due to the weak licensing potential of domain-final empty nuclei. It does not take place initially—or intervocalically—since the nucleus which licenses such positions is stronger as it contains a melody.

Another generalization which emerges from an inspection of the data above is the devoicing of obstruent clusters: both members of such clusters are devoiced word-finally. There are two ways of capturing this regularity. One could be effected quite simply if voicing in adjacent segments is viewed as resulting from a double attachment of {L}. If the element is not licensed, then the cluster becomes uniformly voiceless, as is indeed the case. The presence of word-final obstruent clusters differing in voicing, e.g. [ʒp, gt], is categorically ruled out. The word-final voicelessness of obstruent clusters could also be viewed as a reflection of a much broader constraint which requires that all obstruent sequences, irrespectively of their position, must be either voiced—that is, contain {L}—or voiceless, with no laryngeal element attached. Examples of word-initial and word-medial obstruent sequences, either uniformly voiced or uniformly voiceless are supplied in (2).

(2)   (a)   *Initial, voiceless*

ptak [ptak] 'bird'	skok [skɔk] 'jump, n.'
psot-a [psɔta] 'prank'	któr-y [kturɨ] 'which'
kp-i-ć [kpitɕ] 'mock, vb.'	chci-e-ć [xtɕɛtɕ] 'want, vb.'
chrzest [xʃɛst] 'baptism'	ksiądz [kɕɔnts] 'priest'
świt [ɕfʲit] 'dawn'	tchórz [txuʃ] 'coward'

---

[2] Licensing potential of different types of nuclei has been studied in Cyran (2003) where extensive discussion of a wide range of phenomena is provided. Let us note here that the behaviour of palatalized labial consonants provides another instance of a reduced licensing potential of all empty nuclei, both domain-final and domain-internal.

(b) *Initial, voiced*

brzeg [bʒɛk] 'coast'		zgon [zgɔn] 'demise'	
wdow-a [vdɔva] 'widow'		wzrok [vzrɔk] 'eyesight'	
w-gląd [vglɔnt] 'inspection'		dw-a [dva] 'two'	
zbir [zbʲir] 'thug'		żwir [ʒvʲir] 'gravel'	
gbur [gbur] 'boor'		dbać [dbatɕ] 'care, vb.'	

(c) *Medial, voiceless*

matk-a [matka] 'mother'	łask-a [waska] 'grace'
elips-a [ɛlipsa] 'ellipsis'	trakt-owa-ć [traktɔvatɕ] 'treat, vb.'
cierpk-i [tɕɛrpci] 'tart, adj.'	wartk-i [vartci] 'swift'
zbaw-cz-y [zbaftʃɨ] 'redeeming'	neptk-a [nɛptka] 'twerp, gen. sg.'

(d) *Medial, voiced*

obrzęk [ɔbʒɛŋk] 'swelling'	bazgr-a-ć [bazgratɕ] 'scribble'
gniazd-o [gɲazdɔ] 'nest'	każd-y [kaʒdɨ] 'each'
mierzw-a [mʲɛʒva] 'manure'	szmaragd-y [ʃmaragdɨ] 'emerald, nom. pl.'
wróż-b-a [vruʒba] 'prophecy'	piegż-a [pʲɛgʒa] 'whitethroat'
gżegżółk-a [gʒɛgʒuwka] 'cuckoo'	móżdż-ek [muʒdʒɛk] 'brain, dim.'

The voice-uniformity constraint is cross-lexical and carried over into loan and foreign words. This can be seen in the following examples:

(3)

futbol [fudbɔl] 'football'	anegdot-a [anɛgdɔta] 'anecdote'
Makbet [magbɛt] 'Macbeth'	Gatsby [gadzbɨ] 'Gatsby'
Nashville [nɛʒvʲil] 'Nashville'	ragtime [raktajm] 'ragtime'

The loans are instructive in addition to confirming the reality of the regularity; they indicate that it is the last obstruent in the cluster which is dominant in the sense that the preceding obstruents acquire the same, if any, tone specification as that consonant. Thus if the last obstruent is L-toned, the preceding ones acquire the same tone, hence the cluster is voiced throughout; if the last obstruent is devoid of any tonal specification, the preceding ones lose or shed their L, if they have it, and the cluster is uniformly voiceless. What in traditional terms is referred to as voice assimilation in such cases we designate as Voice Adjustment (VA) and formulate it as follows:

Voice Adjustment
The tonal specification of the last obstruent controls the laryngeal tier of the sequence.

Voice Adjustment disallows obstruent sequences differing in voicing in all positions, not only word-initially and internally but also word-finally. Since the word-final empty nucleus is not strong enough to license L on the preceding non-branching onset, VA also means that word-final obstruent clusters are invariably voiceless.

A predictable consequence of VA is the existence of alternations of voiced and voiceless obstruents when affixes with an empty nucleus or a floating melody attach. If the base ends in an obstruent toned in the same way as the obstruent starting the suffix, nothing happens; if however the two obstruents differ, it is the suffixal one that dominates and the preceding obstruent adjusts to it. Consider some illustrative examples.

(4)   (a) groz-i-ć [grɔʑitɕ] 'threaten'   groź-b-a [grɔʐba] 'threat'
           rzeźb-i-ć [ʒɛʑbʲitɕ] 'sculpture, vb.'   rzeź-b-a [ʒɛʐba] 'n.'

           vs.

           pros-i-ć [prɔɕitɕ] 'ask'   proś-b-a [prɔʐba] 'request, n.'
           licz-y-ć [litʃɨtɕ] 'count'   licz-b-a [lidʒba] 'number'

      (b) młot-a [mwɔta] 'hammer, gen. sg.'   młot-k-a [mwɔtka] 'dim. gen. sg.'
           łap-a [wapa] 'paw'   łap-k-a [wapka] 'dim.'
           ciast-o [tɕastɔ] 'dough'   ciast k o [tɕastkɔ] 'cake'

           vs.

           żab-a [ʒaba] 'frog'   żab-k-a [ʒapka] 'dim.'
           łyżek [wɨʒɛk] 'spoon, gen. pl.'   łyżk-a [wɨʃka] 'nom. sg.'
           móżdż-ek [muʒdʒɛk] 'brain. dim.'   móżdż-u [muʃtʃku] 'gen. sg.'
           gwiazd-a [gvʲazda] 'star'   gwiazd-k-a [gvʲastka] 'dim.'

Thus, no matter whether the consonants happen to have the same voice property or whether VA intervenes, the result is a cluster whose members cannot differ with respect to L.

The regularity we formulated as VA has a much wider applicability since it is also found at word boundaries as a sandhi phenomenon. As a general point we would like to observe that adjustments at word boundaries are less categorical than those found word-internally. While they certainly do take place in unmonitored, connected speech, it is possible to suppress them in ways it would not be done word-internally. Various performance factors may come into play: actual or potential pauses, conscious adherence to conventional spelling perceived as 'speaking correctly', and other considerations. In such cases we note the effects found when the words are pronounced in isolation, hence there is nothing new to add. In what follows we concentrate on the variants that display sandhi effects and which thus have a contribution to make to our discussion. The contribution of sandhi phenomena is not imposing, though. Fundamentally it confirms the conclusion arrived at by inspecting the word-internal situation, namely, the existence of VA which, as a phonological regularity, holds true in all positions, including those created by juxtaposing words. We illustrate the sandhi applicability of VA by a few types of phrases. First of all there are those whose first part ends in a voiceless (i.e. toneless) obstruent or obstruent sequence and is followed by either a toneless obstruent, in which case we expect the whole cluster to be voiceless or a voiced one when the sequence straddling the juncture is consistently voiced (a). Likewise toned final consonants appear voiceless before a toneless one in the next word and toned before a voiced one (b).

(5) (a) kosz-e [kɔʃɛ] kosz chleba [kɔʃ xlɛba] 'basket of bread'
    'basket, nom. pl.' kosz borówek [kɔʒ bɔruvɛk] 'basket of berries'
    list-y [listɨ] list polecony [list pɔlɛtsɔnɨ] 'registered letter'
    'letter, nom. pl.' list wartościowy [lizd vartɔɕtɕɔvɨ] 'value letter'
    sklep-y [sklɛpɨ] sklep spożywczy [sklɛp spɔʒɨftʃɨ] 'grocer's'
    'shop, nom. pl.' sklep warzywny [sklɛb vaʒɨvnɨ] 'greengrocer's'
    stek-u [stɛku] stek kłamstw [stɛk kwamstʃ] 'pack of lies'
    'load, gen. sg.' stek wyzwisk [stɛg vɨzvʲisk] 'shower of abuse'
    jak [jak] jak wczoraj [jak ftʃɔraj] 'as yesterday'
    'as' jak dziś [jag dʑiɕ] 'as today'
    rów [ruf] rów głęboki [ruv gwɛmbɔci] 'deep ditch'
    'ditch' rów pogłębić [ruf pɔgwɛmbʲitɕ] 'deepen the ditch'

    (b) sąd-u [sɔndu] sąd karny [sɔnt karnɨ] 'criminal court'
    'court, gen. sg.' sąd wojenny [sɔnd vɔjɛnnɨ] 'court-martial'
    zbudz-i [zbudʑi] zbudź chorego [zbutɕ xɔrɛgɔ] 'wake the patient!'
    '(s)he will wake' zbudź brata [zbudʑ brata] 'wake the brother!'
    wrog-a [vrɔga] wróg publiczny [vruk publitʃnɨ] 'public enemy'
    'enemy, gen. sg.' wróg brata [vrug brata] 'brother's enemy'
    mózg-u [muzgu] mózg pacjenta [musk patsjɛnta] 'patient's brain'
    'brain, gen. sg.' mózg doktora [muzg dɔktɔra] 'doctor's brain'
    wróżb-a [vruʒba] wróżb ponurych [vruʃp pɔnurɨx]
    'prophecy' 'sombre prophecy, gen. pl.'
        wróżb złowieszczych [vruʒb zwɔvʲɛʃtʃɨx] 'ominous
        prophecy, gen. pl.'

The examples confirm the dominant position of the last member of a consonant sequence in that the preceding consonant or consonantal cluster assumes its
tonal specification, which means either L, that is, voicing throughout or no tone
at all, hence voicelessness. The forms in (5) represent the unmonitored style of
connected speech and it is therefore not surprising that at least some of the
phrases may be found with pronunciation variants that depart from what we
have here, in particular when the emerging cluster is heavy and/or the phrase
somewhat unusual.

At this stage it might seem appropriate to pose the question of the phonological mechanism involved in the formation of the voice-sandhi phenomena:
what does it mean to say that two words may influence each other phonologically? We would like to suggest that the gist of the operation consists in the
elimination of domain boundaries separating the words. Once the internal
boundaries are removed, the final nucleus of the first member of the new formation is no longer domain-final but rather domain-internal. Thus *kosz borówek*
'basket of berries' (in (5)) is transformed from [kɔʃø₁] [bɔruvɛkø₂] into
[kɔʃøbɔruvɛkø₂]: ø₁ and ø₂ are domain-final nuclei prior to the domain modification. Once the internal domain boundaries are removed, ø₁ is no longer
domain-final and VA enforces voice uniformity, yielding [kɔʒ bɔruvɛk]. Thus

VA acts in the same way as it does word-internally across an empty nucleus. The sandhi voice adjustment amounts then to the replacement of a domain-final empty nucleus by a domain-internal one, an operation which accompanies the elimination of boundaries between words; if the boundaries are not eliminated, words are pronounced as before a pause. Thus *sąd wojenny* [sɔnd vɔjɛnnɨ] 'court martial' can also be pronounced [sɔnt vɔjɛnnɨ], just with final devoicing of the first word, even if this variant is felt to be somewhat stilted or artificial. Final devoicing is found before the domain-final empty nucleus while VA holds domain-internally, where empty nuclei may but do not have to separate the consonants in question. The two phonological regularities are separate and final devoicing is normally obligatory while Voice Adjustment is optional and serves as a clear marker of connected speech.

The abolishment of domain boundaries and the concomitant replacement of a domain-final by a domain-internal empty nucleus lead to some interesting consequences. Consider in this context the word *tekst* [tɛkst] 'text' in combination with a following noun:

(6)   tekst-y [tɛkstɨ]   tekst powieści [tɛks pɔvʲɛɕtɕi] 'text of the novel'
       'text, nom. pl.'   tekst wykładu [tɛgz vɨkwadu] 'text of the lecture'

The final consonant of the word *tekst* [tɛkst] is deleted in colloquial or unmonitored speech when the next word begins with a consonant. In *tekst powieści* [tɛks pɔvʲɛɕtɕi] 'text of the novel' the simplified consonantal cluster of the first word remains voiceless, as expected. In *tekst wykładu* [tɛgz vɨkwadu] 'text of the lecture' we find uniform voicing of the cluster which reveals the working of VA. It is striking, however, that if the final consonant of the first word were not to be deleted, the voicing of the whole cluster is most unlikely or downright impossible—*[tɛgzd vɨkwadu]—and the phrase would be pronounced as [tɛkst vɨkwadu] without VA. Can we provide a systematic account of cases like these?

The elimination of internal domain boundaries or the formation of a single new domain out of two denotes the creation of a new phonological object. The new domain, as any domain, must meet regular conditions on domainhood, e.g. the emerging consonantal sequence must be syllabifiable into (branching or non-branching) onsets and/or coda-onset contacts. We argued extensively in Chapter 5 that a sequence of two rhymes with empty nuclei is not tolerated in Polish, a condition which does not include the domain-final nucleus. The word *tekst* in isolation contains one internal and one final nucleus—[tɛkøstø]—thereby conforming to the requirements. If the domain-final nucleus were to be replaced by an internal one as a result domain formation, we would end up with a sequence of two internal empty nuclei—[tɛkøstøvɨkwadu]—a possibility we dismiss. Since an ungrammatical structure cannot be formed, what happens is that no single domain is formed and the phrase is pronounced [tɛkst vɨkwadu], without VA. Alternatively the last onset–rhyme sequence of the first word is removed and we are faced with the structure [tɛkøsvɨkwadu], with one internal empty nucleus; the sequence [sv] forms a coda–onset contact and is subject to VA resulting in [tɛgz vɨkwadu].

The constraint against sequences of empty nuclei established on other grounds in Chapter 5 turns out to play a crucial role in voice propagation. Below we will see it at work in other and more complex situations involving combinations of obstruents and intervening sonorants. It is to these cases that we turn now.

7.4 SONORANT GLITCHES

Sonorants are usually regarded as voiced since the cavity configuration in their production encourages or facilitates spontaneous voicing. Polish sonorants are voiced except for a position between voiceless consonants or after a voiceless obstruent before a pause. A handful of examples follows:

(7) krw-i [kr̥fʲi] 'blood, gen. sg.'   wiatr [vʲatr̥] 'wind'
     kadr [katr̥] 'frame'   bóbr [bupr̥] 'beaver'
     narośl [narɔcl̥] 'growth'   módl [mut(l̥)] 'pray, imp.'
     baśń [bacɲ̥] 'fairy tale'   bojaźń [bɔjacɲ̥] 'fear'
     rytm [rɨtm̥] 'rhythm'   kosmk-a [kɔsm̥ka] 'villus, gen. sg.'
     fanatyzm [fanatɨs(m̥)] 'fanaticism'   wydm [vɨtm̥] 'dune, gen. pl.'
     piosn-k-a [pʲɔsn̥ka] 'song, dim.'   mielizn [mʲɛlisn̥] 'shoal, gen. pl.'
     jabł-k-o [jap(w̥)kɔ] 'apple'   jad-ł [jat(w̥)] 'he ate'

A few comments are called for. The variants transcribed above are not the only possible ones, as noted before. Rather, they represent the unguarded standard, while individual speakers may—either regularly or on occasion—select a more careful variety with little if any sonorant devoicing. Additionally, some sonorants may be suppressed altogether interconsonantally or post-consonantally in word-final position (we enclose such segments in brackets). In general, the devoicing of sonorants in the restricted contexts is a phonetically grounded effect, not different in kind from what is found in other languages such as English. We will not be paying much attention to the devoiced sonorants themselves but rather to the inhibiting influence they may have on the propagation of voice via VA within domains formed across word boundaries.

The above variants are not the only possible ones in yet another way. Side by side with the devoiced final clusters one frequently encounters pronunciations where the toned pre-sonorant obstruent preserves its voicing. Thus a realistic description has to recognize both types:

(8) kadr [katr̥] 'frame'   or [kadr]
     bóbr [bupr̥] 'beaver'   or [bubr]
     bojaźń [bɔjacɲ̥] 'fear'   or [bɔjaʑɲ]
     fanatyzm [fanatɨs(m̥)] 'fanaticism'   or [fanatɨzm]
     wydm [vɨtm̥] 'dune, gen. pl.'   or [vɨdm]
     kadm [katm̥] 'cadmium'   or [kadm]
     marksizm [markɕis(m̥)] 'Marxism'   or [markɕizm]

In some forms the devoiced cluster sounds distinctly artificial (e.g. *wydm* [vɨtm̥] 'dune, gen. pl.', *kadm* [katm̥] 'cadmium') while in others the devoiced variant is the only possible as long as the cluster is simplified. This is particularly true about the numerous derivatives in *-izm*, *-yzm* (*marks-izm* [markçis(m̥)] 'Marxism', *fanat-yzm* [fanatɨs(m̥)]), where—despite normative admonitions—the final nasal is deleted and then the fricative must be voiceless. To conclude then, clusters of toned obstruents followed by a sonorant word-finally *tend* to become devoiced although the sonorants may prevent the devoicing from taking place. This results in the co-existence of voiced and voiceless variants controlled by factors such as word familiarity and frequency, tempo of speech, degree of speech monitoring by individual speakers and the like. Anyway, in contradistinction to the absolute word-final obstruents where the devoicing is practically categorical, sonorants intervening between the obstruent and the pause enrich the picture and introduce more variability.

Sonorants loom large also in the sandhi voice assimilation since intervening between obstruents they inhibit VA to a certain extent. Nothing remarkable happens when a word ends in an obstruent + sonorant cluster and the next word begins with an obstruent—in such cases VA holds in the usual way; the pre-sonorantal obstruent is voiced before a voiced obstruent starting the next word and voiceless before a voiceless one.

(9)   wiatr [vʲatr̥] 'wind'   wiatr zachodni [vʲadr zaxɔdɲi] 'westerly wind'
                                      wiatr wschodni [vʲatr̥ fsxɔdɲi] 'easterly wind'
       bojaźń [bɔjaçɲ̥] 'fear'   bojaźń boża [bɔjaʑɲ bɔʒa] 'fear of God'
                                        bojaźń przed [bɔjaçɲ̥ pʃɛt] 'fear of'
       pieśn [pʲɛçɲ̥] 'song'   pieśń dziecka [pʲɛʑɲ dʑɛtska] 'child's song'
                                        pieśń polska [pʲɛçɲ̥ pɔlska] 'Polish song'
       jadła [jadwa] 'she ate'   jadł zupę [jad(w) zupɛ] 'he ate soup'
                                        jadł szybko [jat ʃɨpkɔ] 'he ate quickly'

Here VA ensures that the obstruents, separated as they are by a sonorant, have the same L specification coming from the first obstruent of the second word. However, when a word ending in an obstruent is followed by one that begins with a sonorant and a voiced obstruent, the activity of VA is halted—the final obstruent of the first word remains voiceless. Examples:

(10)   widok-u [vʲidɔku]   widok mgły [vʲidɔk mgwɨ]
       'sight, gen. sg.'   'sight of mist'
       gwiazd-a [gvʲazda]   gwiazd mgławica [gvʲast mgwavʲitsa]
       'star'   'nebula of stars'
       ślad-y [çladɨ]   ślad rdzy [çlat rdzɨ]
       'trace, nom. pl.'   'trace of rust'
       kręg-u [krɛŋgu]   krąg łgarzy [krɔŋk wgaʒi]
       'circle, gen. sg.'   'circle of liars'
       obiad-u [ɔbʲadu]   obiad mdły [ɔbʲat mdwɨ]
       'dinner, gen. sg.'   'bland dinner'

krzew-u [kʃɛvu]   krzew rdestu [kʃɛf rdɛstu]
'shrub, gen. sg.'   'knotgrass shrub'

No matter whether the final consonant of the first word is toned or toneless, it is not voiced by the following sonorant+voiced obstruent sequence. Thus it seems that the positioning of the sonorant—word-final or word-initial—plays a role in the way VA is executed. The obvious question that suggests itself is how this difference translates into phonological terms.

Note first of all that there is nothing particularly surprising about the clusters in numerical terms: in the last example, *krzew rdestu* [kʃɛf rdɛstu] 'knotgrass shrub', the cluster [frd] at word junctures reaches number three, which is totally unremarkable in Polish terms. Likewise, there would be nothing unusual if VA were to hold yielding [vrd]—in fact, this very sequence easily emerges in juncture positions. Compare again the last example with three others:

(11)   krzew-u [kʃɛvu]   krzew rdestu [kʃɛf rdɛstu]
        'shrub, gen. sg.'   'knotgrass shrub'
        ślad-y [ɕladɨ]   ślad rdzy [ɕlat rdzɨ]
        'trace, nom. pl.'   'trace of rust'

        vs.

        gawr-a [gavra]   gawr dalekich [gavr dalɛcix]
        'bear's lair'   'distant lair, gen. pl.'
        manewr-y [manɛvrɨ]   manewr dywizji [manɛvr dɨvʲizʲji]
        'manoeuvre, nom. pl.'   'manoeuvre of a division'
        Piotr-a [pʲɔtra]   Piotr daje [pʲɔdr dajɛ]
        'Peter, gen.'   'Peter gives'

While *gawr* and *manewr* in isolation may be pronounced either as [gafr̥, manɛfr̥] with devoicing or as [gavr, manɛvr] with devoicing suppressed, as discussed above, no devoicing is possible when the next word begins with a voiced obstruent, so *[gafr̥ dalɛcix] or *[manɛfr̥ dɨvʲizʲji] are not possible (unless, of course, one introduces a pause separating the two words). In other words, here VA acts across an intervening sonorant. Conversely, in *ślad rdzy* [ɕlat rdzɨ], the final voiced obstruent is regularly devoiced at the end of its domain and stays so despite the presence of a voiced obstruent after the initial sonorant in the next word. The sonorant acts as a barrier here but not in *Piotr daje* [pʲɔdr dajɛ] where it ends the first word. Why does the sonorant act as a barrier to VA in *krzew rdestu* [kʃɛf rdɛstu] 'knotgrass shrub' and *ślad rdzy* [ɕlat rdzɨ] 'trace of rust' but not in *gawr dalekich* [gavr dalɛcix] 'distant lair, gen. pl.' or *Piotr daje* [pʲɔdr dajɛ] 'Peter gives'?

It seems that an answer to this question must be related to the nature of consonant sequences that arise in sandhi positions. In connection with obstruent sequences arising at word junctures we adopted a view of domain formation as consisting in the removal of domain boundaries coupled with a replacement of the domain-final nucleus ending the first word with a domain-internal one separating the two words in the new domain. As a single domain, the new structure must conform to the general constraints prevailing in the language. If the above reasoning is correct, the segment sequences arising at word boundaries must be well-formed syllabic constituents; this is unsurprising since words in isolation are made up of onsets and rhymes. Viewed from this point the phrases *krzew rdestu* and *Piotr daje* differ significantly as far as the number of nuclei is concerned. Consider their representations, where some details are irrelevant or could be different:[3]

(12) (a) *krzew rdestu* [kʃɛf rdɛstu] 'knotgrass shrub'

(b) *Piotr daje* [pʲɔdr dajɛ] 'Peter gives'

The concatenation in (a) brings about a sequence of two empty nuclei: one is the former domain-final nucleus reborn as domain-internal and another one intervening between the first two consonants of the second word. Since obviously [rd] is not a possible onset, the two consonants have to belong to separate onsets of which the first is licensed by an empty nucleus. While the words have unexceptional structure in isolation, their combination creates—or would create—a configuration of two consecutive empty nuclei, which is not tolerated within Polish. A structure which violates the prevailing constraints is simply not created, which means that the structure suggested in (a) is illicit as the two words do not form a single domain but remain separate. The rest is a mechanical consequence: domain-finally an obstruent is de-toned, hence it remains voiceless since no spreading is possible across domain boundaries. The expression in (b)—and indeed in the examples illustrating the traditional voice assimilation of obstruents above—the juxtaposition of words involves just one empty nucleus, hence a single domain can be formed and L-spreading takes place. The phrase in (b) represents a class of cases where the first word ends in a branching onset (or in a coda-onset contact), hence there is no empty nucleus separating the two

---

[3] The fricative [ʃ] could be argued to be [r] marked for palatalization (<PR1>) and thus form a branching onset with the preceding velar plosive; the palato-velar [c] results from the palatalization mechanisms discussed in Chapter 3.

consonants and the ban against two such consecutive nuclei is conformed to when words are combined.

The failure of voice spreading when the second word begins with a sonorant is then a consequence of two factors. On the one hand there is the universal constraint preventing a sonorant from being the governing member of a branching onset, hence the need to separate sequences of a sonorant and an obstruent by an empty nucleus. On the other hand there is the specifically Polish constraint disallowing sequences of two (or more) domain-internal empty nuclei, which prevents the forming of a single domain where VA could be enforced. Given these facts we could expect that similar failures of voice propagation will be found with other complex clusters arising at word junctures, where sequences of empty nuclei would have to be postulated. Although there is some vacillation in the data, by and large this prediction seems to be borne out. Below we list several examples where an empty nucleus has to be present in a heavy cluster in addition to the empty nucleus separating the words and licensing the final onset of the first member. Thus a sequence of two consecutive empty nuclei would have to emerge if the two words were to form a single domain and then the final cluster of the first member would have to be voiced. This seems not to be the case. Consider:

(13) następstw bolesnych [nastɛmpstf bɔlɛsnɨx]   *[nastɛmbzdv bɔlɛsnɨx]
      'painful consequence, gen. pl.'
      oszczerstw wyborczych [ɔʃtʃɛrstf vɨbɔrtʃɨx]   *[ɔʃtʃɛrzdv vɨbɔrtʃɨx]
      'electoral slander, gen. pl.'
      plótł bzdury [plut(w̥) bzdurɨ]   *[pludw bzdurɨ]
      'he was talking nonsense'
      wydawnictw rządowych [vɨdavɲitstf ʒɔndɔvɨx]   *[vɨdavɲidzdv ʒɔndɔvɨx]
      'government publication, gen. pl.'
      zemst wielkich [zɛmst vʲɛlcix]   *[zɛmzd vʲɛlcix]
      'great revenge, gen. pl.'
      państw wrogich [paɲstf vrɔɟix]   *[paɲzdv vrɔɟix]
      'hostile nation, gen. pl.'
      stek bzdur [stɛk bzdur]   *[stɛg bzdur]
      'load of nonsense'[4]

On the single domain assumption the last phrase would require a (somewhat simplified) representation along the following lines:

(14)
```
O   R   O   R   O   R   O   R   O   R   O   R
|   |   |   |   |   |   |   \   |   |   |   |
x   x   x   x   x   x   x   x x x   x   x   x
|       |   |   |       |       | |   |   |
s       t   ε   k       b       z d   u   r
```

---

[4] Personally I make a difference between the [k#bzd] consonantal cluster of this expression and one where the second word begins with a single consonant, i.e. *stek banialuk* [stɛg baɲaluk] 'load of baloney'.

Very clearly, we have here a sequence of two empty nuclei, a structure which we believe is not only strongly disfavoured but downright barred. To avoid violation of the constraint the domain boundary between the two words remains in its place and no sandhi assimilation can take place. The result is a cluster where neighbouring segments (obstruents) differ in voicing. It hardly needs stressing that the adjacency of the segment is melodic rather than structural since the segments in question are not only separated by an empty nucleus but in fact belong to separate domains. Our initial observations about sonorants and their inhibiting function in voice propagation have brought us to view that particular phenomenon as part of a much larger set of cases where unexpected effects are found. The basic factor behind the apparent irregularity is the ban on sequences of empty nuclei, a ban which was arrived at and defended independently elsewhere in this book. Voice Adjustment remains the sole principle responsible for voice assimilations both within words and at word junctures.

The story of the sonorant complications in juncture positions does not end here. Let us note first of all that in the standard dialect described in this book, sonorants (including vowels) beginning the second word have no influence on the obstruent ending the previous word. In other words, the obstruent regularly loses its tone and if it is toneless, it remains so. Examples:

(15) drog-a [drɔga]   dróg nowych [druk nɔvɨx]
      'road'   'new road, gen. pl.'
      druk-u [druku]   druk nowy [druk nɔvɨ]
      'print, gen. sg.'   'new print'
      głaz-y [gwazɨ]   głaz leżał [gwas lɛʒaw]
      'boulder, nom. pl.'   'a boulder lay'
      głos-y [gwɔsɨ]   głos narodu [gwɔs narɔdu]
      'voice, nom. pl.'   'voice of the people'
      gładz-i [gwadʑi]   gładź jeziora [gwatɕ jɛʑɔra]
      'surface, gen. sg.'   'surface of the lake'
      chęć-i [xɛɲtɕi]   chęć nasza [xɛɲtɕ naʃa]
      'willingness'   'our willingness'
      ślad-y [ɕladɨ]   ślad ruchu [ɕlat ruxu]
      'trace, nom. pl.'   'trace of movement'
      pot-u [pɔtu]   pot mój [pɔt muj]
      'sweat, gen. sg.'   'my sweat'
      gwóździ-e [gvɔʑdʑɛ]   gwóźdź łamał [gvuɕtɕ wamaw]
      'nail, nom. pl.'   'a nail broke'
      kośc-i [kɔɕtɕ]   kość łamała [kɔɕtɕ wamawa]
      'bone, gen. pl.'   'a bone broke'
      wrog-a [vrɔga]   wróg ojczyzny [vruk ɔjtʃɨznɨ]
      'enemy, gen. sg.'   'enemy of the land'
      wrak-u [vraku]   wrak auta [vrak awta]
      'wreck, gen. sg.'   'wreck of a car'

The situation is quite simple: sonorants as spontaneously voiced do not carry L and hence cannot spread it. As a result obstruents lose their tonal specification (if any) before the domain final nucleus and do not acquire anything from the following toneless onsets, i.e. they are realized as voiceless.[5] Against this background the behaviour of several prepositions offers an unexpected twist.

7.5 THE PREPOSITIONS

We shall discuss a group of prepositions listed in (16).

(16)   przed [pʃɛt] 'before'   pod [pɔt] 'under, by'
        nad [nat] 'over'   od [ɔt] 'away from'
        bez [bɛs] 'without'   w [f] 'in'
        z [s] 'with'

These prepositions conform to VA and appear with a voiced final consonant before a word beginning with a voiced obstruent and with a voiceless one before a voiceless obstruent. Compare:

(17)   przed zimą [pʃɛd ʑimɔ̃ʷ]   przed czasem [pʃɛt tʃasɛm]
        'before winter'   'ahead of time'
        pod bramą [pɔd bramɔ̃ʷ]   pod płotem [pɔt pwɔtɛm]
        'by the gate'   'by the fence'
        nad ziemią [nad ʑɛmʲɔ̃ʷ]   nad światem [nat ɕfʲatɛm]
        'over the earth'   'over the world'
        od wroga [ɔd vrɔga]   od przyjaciela [ɔt pʃɨjatɕɛla]
        'from the enemy'   'from a friend'
        bez granic [bɛz graɲits]   bez końca [bɛs kɔɲtsa]
        'without limits'   'without end'

---

[5] There is the often-mentioned dialectal glitch which must be recorded here. The southern and some western dialects differ from the central and northern ones described in this book in that they have sandhi voicing not only when the second word begins with a voiced obstruent but also when it begins with a sonorant (including vowels). Thus all right-hand expressions in (15) uniformly voice the final consonant or consonant cluster of the first word. The evidence is not unambiguous and considerable scope for variation must be admitted. Various interpretations of this phenomenon have been suggested in the derivational-generative literature but none of them appears very satisfactory and they all smack of gimmicky manipulations encouraged by the theoretical machinery of default filling, voice spreading from sonorants and the like (Bethin 1992; Gussmann 1992; Rubach 1996). We have nothing of great pith to add at this stage—the facts need to be thoroughly re-examined and related to other properties of the dialects rather than invoked in isolation. There is, for example, the characteristic extension of coronal nasal assimilation: in the standard language this happens only when the nasal is in the coda, in other words, when it is adjacent to the following stop of the onset. It does not happen when an empty nucleus intervenes, as in *łąk-a* [wɔŋka] 'meadow' (cf. *łąk* [wɔŋk] 'gen. pl.) vs. *rynk-u* [rɨnku] 'market place, gen. sg.' (cf. *rynek* [rɨnɛk] 'nom. sg.'). Southern dialects partially extend nasal assimilation also to contexts across an empty nucleus, hence *rynk-u* appears as [rɨŋku] (although, *rynek* is, of course, [rɨnɛk]), but the bilabial nasal remains intact, hence *słom-k-a* [swɔmka] 'straw, dim.', for instance. Whether there is a connection between voicing and nasal assimilation properties in these dialects needs to be explored in view of the frequent theoretical pronouncements to that effect (Nasukawa 1998, 2005; Ploch 1999, 2003).

w domu [v dɔmu]   w kinie [f ciɲɛ]
'at home'   'in the cinema'
z gazetą [z gazɛtɔ̃ʷ]   z książką [s kɕɔ̃ʷʃkɔ̃ʷ]
'with a newspaper'   'with a book'

These facts look unremarkable and could be accounted for in the same way as other instances of sandhi voice agreement. The evidence that the situation is different comes from the behaviour of these propositions before sonorants (including vowels). Recall that words ending in an obstruent—irrespectively of whether it is toned or toneless—are invariably voiceless when the next word begins with a sonorant. The prepositions, however, all preserve their voicedness before a sonorant:

(18) przed lasem [pʃɛd lasɛm]   przed rokiem [pʃɛd rɔcɛm]
      'in front of the wood'   'a year ago'
      pod mostem [pɔd mɔstɛm]   pod okiem [pɔd ɔcɛm]
      'under the bridge'   'under the eye'
      nad łąką [nad wɔŋkɔ̃ʷ]   nad nami [nad namʲi]
      'above the meadow'   'above us'
      od jesieni [ɔd jɛɕɛɲi]   od rynku [ɔd rɨnku]
      'since last autumn'   'from the market'
      bez nadziei [bɛz nadʑɛji]   bez nóg [bɛz nuk]
      'without hope'   'without legs'
      w mieście [v mʲɛɕtɕɛ]   w maśle [v maɕlɛ]
      'in town'   'in butter'
      z matką [z matkɔ̃ʷ]   z ojcem [z ɔjtsɛm]
      'with mother'   'with father'

A clear case of the different treatment of prepositions and content words can be seen in the following 'minimal pair' where the noun *bez* [bɛs] 'lilac' (cf. *bz-y* [bzɨ] 'nom. pl.') is homophonous with the preposition *bez* [bɛs] 'without':

(19) bez radości [bɛz radɔɕtɕi] 'without joy'
      bez miłości [bɛz mʲiwɔɕtɕi] 'without love'
      bez nadziei [bɛz nadʑɛji] 'without hope'

      vs.

      bez radości [bɛs radɔɕtɕi] 'lilac of joy'
      bez miłości [bɛs mʲiwɔɕtɕi] 'lilac of love'
      bez nadziei [bɛs nadʑɛji] 'lilac of hope'

The final spirant of *bez* stays voiced before a following sonorant when it appears in a preposition but loses its voice specification in identical contexts when it appears in a noun. In this way the preposition behaves as if it were in a single domain with the following noun or, at least, as if it did not form a domain of its own. The same is true about all remaining prepositions ending in an obstruent (since, of course, nothing happens when a preposition ends in a vowel, e.g. *na* [na] 'on', *po* [pɔ] 'after, *o* [ɔ] 'about'). The phonological behaviour tallies with the interpretation of prepositions within noun phrases which we adopted in connection with floating vowels in Chapter 5. There, for reasons relating to the problem of floating vowels, we argued that the prepositions in focus end in a floating vowel; additionally the nominal following a preposition constitutes a domain of its own. Thus *bez radości* 'without joy' may be schematically represented as [bezE [radości]]; the floating vowel (E) is not attached by morphophonological Melody Attachment since it is not followed by an unattached nucleus within its domain. Phonologically, final devoicing does not affect the preposition because it is not followed by a domain-final nucleus. When a single domain is formed, VA is inapplicable because sonorants are neutral with respect to voicing. We see then that prepositions and prefixes behave in a uniform fashion: their final consonants are voiceless before a voiceless obstruent and voiced elsewhere, that is, before another voiced obstruent and before a sonorant. Consider examples of derivatives involving prefixes; the order of prefixes follows that of the prepositions above.

(20) przed-potopowy [pʃɛtpɔtɔpɔvɨ]   przed-bieg [pʃɛdbʲɛk]
     'prediluvian'   'qualifying heat'
     przed-imek [pʃɛdʲimɛk]   przed-małżeński [pʃɛdmawʒɛɲsci]
     'article'   'premarital'
     pod-kop [pɔtkɔp]   pod-bój [pɔdbuj]
     'tunnel'   'conquest'
     pod-irytowany [pɔdʲirɨtɔvanɨ]   pod-miejski [pɔdmʲɛjsci]
     'piqued'   'suburban'
     nad-ciśnienie [nattɕiɕɲɛɲɛ]   nad-budowa [nadbudɔva]
     'hypertension'   'superstructure'
     nad-użyć [naduʒɨtɕ]   nad-miar [nadmʲar]
     'abuse, vb.'   'surplus'
     od-piąć [ɔtpʲɔɲtɕ]   od-dalony [ɔddalɔnɨ]
     'unfasten'   'remote'
     od-izolować [ɔdʲizɔlɔvatɕ]   od-mowa [ɔdmɔva]
     'isolate'   'refusal'
     bez-prawny [bɛspravnɨ]   bez-bożny [bɛzbɔʒnɨ]
     'illegal'   'godless'
     bez-imienny [bɛzʲimʲɛnnɨ]   bez-nadziejny [bɛznadʑɛjnɨ]
     'nameless'   'hopeless'
     w-pisać [fpʲisatɕ]   w-deptać [vdɛptatɕ]
     'write in'   'tread in'
     w-manewrować [vmanɛvrɔvatɕ]   s-pisać [spʲisatɕ]
     'menoeuvre into'   'write down'
     z-budować [zbudɔvatɕ]   z-integrować [zʲintɛgrɔvatɕ]
     'build'   'integrate'
     z-mierzyć [zmʲɛʒɨtɕ]   z-nieść [zɲɛɕtɕ]
     'measure, vb.'   'carry down'

The evidence of the prepositions coincides with what prefixes document, which in itself is not really surprising since the prefixes derive historically from prepositions. This is no accident since the domain structure we have developed for prepositional phrases are identical to that found in prefixed structures.

Our conclusions so far are the following:

- obstruents lose their voice specification before unambiguous domain boundaries, i.e. before a domain-final empty nucleus (e.g. *dróg* [druk] 'road, gen. pl.'—cp. *drog-a* [drɔga] 'nom. sg.');
- there is no loss of obstruent voicing before sonorants morpheme internally, i.e. in branching onsets (e.g. *grób* [grup] 'grave', *mądr-y* [mɔndrɨ] 'wise');
- there is no loss of voicing across morpheme boundaries within domains, i.e. before domain-internal empty nuclei (e.g. *groź-n-y* [grɔʑnɨ] 'severe');
- there is no loss of voicing in prepositions before a sonorant beginning the next word, i.e. before a domain-internal floating melody (e.g. *bez nadziei* [bɛz nadʑɛji] 'without hope').

These observations lead us to conclude that prepositions are not separated from the following word in a prepositional phrase by the domain boundaries that divide separate words. Thus prepositions must be viewed as not constituting single domains on their own. In other words, we can conclude that obstruent devoicing takes place before a domain-final empty nucleus only. In our terms this translates into a claim that domain-final empty nuclei fail to license {L} on the preceding onset.

A different effect of sonorants, specifically of the bilabial nasal, can be seen in the first-person plural of the imperative. The ending *-my* [mɨ] is attached to the imperative singular but the final consonant of the stem invariably devoices in this position (and obviously remains voiceless if it is toneless). Consider examples of the third-person singular present tense, the second-person singular and the first-person plural of the imperative.

(21) chodz-i [xɔdʑi] 'go'   chodź [xɔtɕ]   chodź-my [xɔtɕmɨ]
      wiąż-e [vʲɔ̃ʷʒɛ] 'bind'   wiąż [vʲɔ̃ʷʃ]   wiąż-my [vʲɔ̃ʷʃmɨ]
      rob-i [rɔbʲi] 'make'   rób [rup]   rób-my [rupmɨ]
      mów-i [muvʲi] 'say'   mów [muf]   mów-my [mufmɨ]
      gryzi-e [grɨʑɛ] 'bite'   gryź [grɨɕ]   gryź-my [grɨɕmɨ]
      gwiżdż-e [gvʲiʒdʒɛ] 'whistle'   gwiżdż [gvʲiʃtʃ]   gwiżdż-my [gvʲiʃtʃmɨ]

In the imperative plural we find the same stem-final consonant as in the imperative singular. This could mean that the plural is formed by attaching the ending *-my* to the singular form, hence the morphological operation of plural imperative formation would have to follow the regular phonology of the language, including terminal devoicing—we showed above that sequences of a voiced obstruent and a sonorant are well-attested and perfectly neutral. Since we do not adopt a model where phonology and morphology are interspersed, an alternative has to be sought. One that readily comes to mind involves domain structure: Kaye (1995) argues for, among other things, the domain structure [[A] B]. This means that the innermost material (A) is processed independently of the surrounding material (B); with reference to our imperative plurals this means that the imperative singular constitutes a separate domain, hence ends with an empty nucleus that fails to support L on the preceding onset. The addition of material B—the ending -*my*— does not affect the shape of the stem. For this reason the final consonant or consonantal cluster emerges voiceless before the sonorant-initial ending.

There is an additional argument supporting the domain solution and the crucial reliance on the final empty nucleus of the innermost domain. Palatalized labials lose their palatalization both in the imperative singular and plural; we argue elsewhere that it is the empty nucleus that appears incapable of supporting palatality on the preceding labial (see Ch. 3), so what we find in the imperative conforms to the general phonological regularity.

It is important to point out at this juncture that stress placement in Polish treats the imperative as a single domain. For purposes of penultimate stress assignment no domain structure is visible, the ending -*my* counts as the final syllable and prefixes can be stressed as well. The examples above are not instructive since all imperative plural forms happen to bisyllabic. If longer words are taken into account, the position preceding the plural imperative suffix as the focus of stress becomes obvious. Consider the same verbs as above with a prefix attached; the order is third-person singular present, imperative singular imperative first-person plural.

(22) wy-chodz-i [vɨˈxɔdʑi] wy-chodź [ˈvɨxɔtɕ] wy-chodź-my [vɨˈxɔtɕmɨ]
      'go out'
      za-wiąż-e [zaˈvʲɔ̃ʷʒɛ] za-wiąż [ˈzavʲɔ̃ʷʃ] za-wiąż-my [zaˈvʲɔ̃ʷʃmɨ]
      'tie up'
      za-rob-i [zaˈrɔbʲi] za-rób [ˈzarup] za-rób-my [zaˈrupmɨ]
      'earn'
      na-mów-i [naˈmuvʲi] na-mów [ˈnamuf] na-mów-my [naˈmufmɨ]
      'talk into'
      wy-gryzi-e [vɨˈgrɨʑɛ] wy-gryź [ˈvɨgrɨɕ] wygryź-my [vɨˈgrɨɕmɨ]
      'oust'
      od-gwiżdż-e od-gwiżdż [ˈɔdgvʲiʃtʃ] odg-wiżdż-my
      [ɔdˈgvʲiʒdʒɛ] 'whistle' [ɔdˈgvʲiʃtʃmɨ]

The middle column shows that stress can fall on the prefix if it happens to contain the penultimate filled nucleus; the third column demonstrates that the imperative plural ending is counted for stress placement purposes and thus the stress falls on the root rather than the prefix vowel.

We conclude that the devoicing of the stem-final consonant before the imperative ending is due to the general mechanism of terminal devoicing, namely, the failure of domain-final empty nucleus to license L on its onset. The sonorant of the ending cannot propagate voicing since it does not contain the element in its make-up. The domain structure of the imperative plural creates the impression that there is devoicing before a sonorant while in fact the sonorant has nothing to do with it at all. Let us note, finally, that the second-person plural of the imperative also has devoiced stem-final obstruents; the ending is -*cie* [tɕɛ] which is attached to the imperative singular:

(23) wy-chodz-i [vɨ'xɔdʑi]   wy-chodź ['vɨxɔtɕ]   wy-chodź-cie [vɨ'xɔtɕtɕɛ]
      'go out'
      za-wiąż-e [za'vʲɔ̃ʷʒɛ]   za-wiąż ['zavʲɔ̃ʷʃ]   za-wiąż-cie [za'vʲɔ̃ʷʃtɕɛ]
      'tie up'
      za-rob-i [za'rɔbʲi]   za-rób ['zarup]   za-rób-cie [za'ruptɕɛ]
      'earn'
      na-mów-i [na'muvʲi]   na-mów ['namuf]   na-mów-cie [na'muftɕɛ]
      'talk into'
      wy-gryzi-e [vɨ'grɨʑɛ]   wy-gryź ['vɨgryɕ]   wygryź-cie [vɨ'grɨɕtɕɛ]
      'oust'
      od-gwiżdż-e   od-gwiżdż ['ɔdgvʲiʃtʃ]   odg-wiżdż-cie
        [ɔd'gvʲiʒdʒɛ] 'whistle'   [ɔd'gvʲiʃtʃtɕɛ]

These forms could be interpreted as an instance of VA generally found in the language. However, since this analysis would be impossible with the first person plural we propose the same structure for the two imperative plural forms, namely, one where the stem forms its own domain and the suffix is a clitic.

Before we consider other voice-related phenomena, it might be worthwhile to re-capitulate the emerging picture of the Polish juncture phonology. It is hardly worth noting that concatenations of words bring about consonant combinations which are not necessarily found word- or domain-internally (e.g. English [ntstr] in *constant struggle* or [ŋsw] in *long swim*). A more significant question in this context is whether such combinations are indeed anything more than a mechanical splicing together of consecutive material, in other words, whether they can be regarded as clusters in the sense of potential combinations of onsets and codas which can appear within a single domain. Our evidence of voice assimilation indicates unambiguously that consonant clusters which arise when words are combined must meet the ban against two consecutive empty nuclei which we established on independent grounds. When words violating this ban are placed together, the relevant consonants will remain in their separate domains and no voice interaction will take place. This will mean that the consonant(s) of the first word will undergo regular terminal devoicing and will not be influenced by voiced consonants beginning the next word, hence *następstw bolesnych* [nastɛmpstf bɔlɛsnɨx] rather than *[nastɛmbz(dv) bɔlɛsnɨx] 'painful consequence, gen. pl.'. For exactly the same reason, words beginning with a sonorant plus a voiced obstruent cannot transmit the voicedness of the obstruent to the obstruent ending the preceding word: this, as we showed above with examples like *krzew rdestu* [kʃɛf rdɛstu] 'knotgrass shrub', would require two consecutive empty nuclei, in violation of the ban. In such cases no single domain is formed and the consonant of the first word devoices finally within its own domain, despite the fact that the initial consonants of the following word are voiced. In other words, the consonants arising as a result of word combination remain a mechanical sequence rather than a phonological cluster. Thus what we have initially called *sonorant glitch* has nothing to do with sonorants but rather with general possibilities of syllabification and, more specifically, with the fact that a sequence sonorant plus obstruent has to be broken up into two consecutive onsets with an intervening empty nucleus.

Our discussion of the voicing phenomena has covered the terminal devoicing and effects of voice uniformity (VA) both domain- and word-internally and also at word junctures. In the latter case we have argued for the dominant role of the final consonant in a cluster, which translates into the traditional regressive assimilation. There are also instances of progressive assimilation and involve, yet again, sonorants. To these we now turn.

7.6 PROGRESSIVE ASSIMILATION OR ANOTHER SONORANT GLITCH

Traditional evidence for the existence of so-called progressive voice assimilation—assimilation to the preceding obstruent—comes from both alternations and distributional restrictions. Consider some examples of alternations first.

(24) (a) gr-a [gra]   grz-e [gʒɛ]
            'game'   'dat. sg.'
            dobr-y [dɔbrɨ]   dobrz-e [dɔbʒɛ]
            'good'   'well'
            wy-dzier-a-ć [vɨdʑɛratɕ]   wy-drz-e [vɨd-ʒɛ]
            'tear out'   '(s)he will tear out'
            kr-a [kra]   krz-e [kʃɛ]
            'ice floe'   'dat. sg.'
            łotr-a [wɔtra]   łotrz-yk [wɔt-ʃɨk]
            'rascal, gen. sg.'   'dim.'
            do-cier-a-ć [dɔtɕɛratɕ]   do-trz-e [dɔt-ʃɛ]
            'reach'   '(s)he will reach'

      (b) chorągiew-ek [xɔrɔŋɟɛvɛk]   chorągw-i [xɔrɔŋʲgʲvʲi]
            'banner, dim. gen. pl.'   'gen. sg.'
            łyżew [wɨʒɛf]   łyżw-y [wɨʒvɨ]
            'skate, gen. pl.'   'nom. pl.'
            szew-ek [ʃɛvɛk]   szw-y [ʃfɨ] or [ʃvɨ]
            'seam, dim.'   'nom. pl.'
            cerkiew-n-y [tsɛrcɛvnɨ]   cerkw-i [tsɛrkfʲi] or [tsɛrkvʲi]
            'Orthodox'   'Orthodox church, gen. sg.'
            marchew-nik [marxɛvɲik]   marchw-i [marxfʲi] or [marxvʲi]
            'carrot leaves'   'gen. sg.'

A few observations need to be made about these data. The consonants that are involved in progressive voice assimilation involve the alveolar fricative and the labio-dental fricative. In this way, the scope of the assimilation is highly restricted as compared to the regressive process. One thing which the above alternations share with the regressive assimilation is the conformity to voice uniformity: as the right-hand column's examples show, the obstruent sequences there are either uniformly voiced or uniformly voiceless. This statement needs a minor correction since it oversimplifies the facts somewhat.

As shown, the last three examples of the right-hand column in (b) admit variants with the voiced labio-dental fricatives, that is, *szw-y* [ʃfɨ] can also be pronounced [ʃvɨ], *cerkw-i* [tsɛrkfʲi] can be [tsɛrkvʲi], and *marchw-i* [marxfʲi] admits [marxvʲi]. The variants which violate voice uniformity cannot be connected today with any regional variety of the language but rather they appear to be individual or idiolectal. Karaś and Madejowa (1977) treat such pairs as co-existing within the standard language.

The same type of voice uniformity in obstruent clusters is also massively supported by non-alternating or stable forms, where the second obstruent is a fricative. Here, as expected, both members will be either voiced or voiceless with the proviso that, as above, the labio-dental fricative can be either voiced or voiceless after a voiceless obstruent.

(25) (a) przód [pʃut]   brzeg [bʒɛk]
          'front'   'coast'
          trzod-a [t-ʃɔda]   drzazg-a [d-ʒazga]
          'flock'   'splinter'
          krzyw-y [kʃɨvɨ]   grzyb [gʒɨp]
          'crooked'   'mushroom'

      (b) twój [tfuj] or [tvuj]   dwa [dva]
          'your'   'two'
          swobod-a [sfɔbɔda] or   zwierzę [zvʲɛʒɛ]
          [svɔbɔda]
          'freedom'   'animal'
          Szwed [ʃfɛt] or [ʃvɛt]   żwawy [ʒvavɨ]
          'Swede'   'brisk'
          czwartek [tʃfartɛk] or   dźwig [dʑvʲik]
          [tʃvartɛk]
          'Thursday'   'crane'
          kwiat [kfʲat] or [kvʲat]   gwar [gvar]
          'flower'   'hubbub'
          chwał-a [xfawa] or [xvawa]
          'glory'

Another relevant point concerning progressive voice assimilation is the fact that it does not work in juncture position: here word-final spirants are voiced in accordance with VA (a) and likewise word-initial spirants voice the preceding voiceless obstruents the same way as other obstruents (b). Examples:

(26) (a) gotów pisać [gɔtuf pʲisatɕ] 'ready to write'
gotów drukować [gɔtuv drukɔvatɕ] 'ready to print'
mórz ciepłych [muʃ tɕɛpwɨx] 'warm sea, gen. pl.'
mórz dalekich [muʒ dalɛcix] 'distant sea, gen. pl.'

(b) smak wina [smag vʲina] 'taste of wine'
los wygrany [lɔz vɨgranɨ] 'winning number'
ptak rzeczny [ptag ʒɛtʃnɨ] 'river bird'
pas rzemienny [paz ʒɛmʲɛnnɨ] 'leather strap'

Similarly, word-internally the fricatives are voiceless before a voiceless obstruent:

(27) szafa [ʃafa] 'wardrobe'   szaf-k-a [ʃafka] 'dim.'
sow-a [sɔva] 'owl'   sów-k-a [sufka] 'dim.'
wieprz [vʲɛpʃ] 'hog'   wieprz-k-a [vʲɛpʃka] 'dim. gen. sg.'
gor-ycz [gɔrɨtʃ] 'bitterness'   gorz-k-i [gɔʃci] 'bitter'

Most of these data do not call for any additional mechanism or interpretation over and above what has been said so far: the fact that two obstruents are uniform in voicing or that they adjust their voicing to the last member of a cluster is a direct consequence of the VA regularity. At most we would have to say that the *plosive plus fricative* sequences, such as those in *przód* [pʃut] 'front' or *brzeg* [bʒɛk] 'coast' syllabically belong to two consecutive onsets separated by an empty nucleus: [pøʃut], [bøʒɛk]. This in itself would be a totally unremarkable suggestion since an empty nucleus has to be postulated in a number of cases to separate sequences of plosives, such as *ptak* [pøtak] 'bird', *db-a-ć* [døbatɕ] 'care, vb.'. What forces us to recognize an additional phenomenon are the alternations and the existence of varieties where the voiced labio-dental fricative follows a voiceless plosive, e.g. *twój* [tvuj] 'your'.

The alternations, and in particular those involving the alveolar fricative and the sonorant [r], lead us to propose an initial interpretation: the fricatives [ʃ, ʒ] are not fricatives at all but rather sonorants. The examples in (24a), above, hardly need any justification since obviously one of the alternants is undeniably a sonorant; *gr-a* [gra] 'game' is an example. In a number of contexts it undergoes morphophonological palatalization (see Ch. 4) and appears phonologically as an alveolar fricative. Thus it is a sonorant marked with the diacritic <PR1> which ensures its replacement in the required contexts.[6]

As a sonorant, [r] can appear as a dependent in branching onsets, as in *dobr-y* [dɔbrɨ] 'good', *lotr-a* [wɔtra] 'rascal, gen. sg.'. Needless to say it can also function as the only member of a non-branching onset: *gr-a* [gra] (cf. *gier* [ɟɛr] 'gen. pl.'), *do-trz-e* [dɔt-ʃɛ] '(s)he will reach' (cf. *do-cier-a-ć* [dɔtɕɛratɕ] 'reach'). If syllabification

---

[6] This is referred to as *obstruentization* in derivational frameworks.

operates on or interprets representations prior to morphophonological replacements, or if syllabification is simply an inalterable part of the representation, then
[r] will either be a dependent of a branching onset or will be an onset separated
from the preceding obstruent by an empty nucleus. Since sonorants are not
specified for voicing (tone), it can only be the preceding obstruent or the dominant segment whose tone specification, if any, controls the laryngeal tier of the
sequence. Once the sonorant is replaced by a fricative, this fricative must adjust
its tone to that of the dominant segment: if the dominant segment is unspecified
for tone, then the sonorant-turned-fricative loses the specification that the replacement operation introduced. If the dominant segment is L-toned, then a
merger of this tone with that of the fricative is effected. Viewed in this way, the
so-called progressive voice assimilation is nothing else but another instantiation
of our Voice Adjustment. Recall the crucial position of the last obstruent which
determines the voicing of the sequence; that obstruent is dominant and of course
if there happens to be only one such obstruent it still remains dominant, even if its
effects cannot be directly detected. Thus in the following sequences it is the
underlined obstruent (O) that is the dominant one in a consonantal cluster (or
sequence): OS$\underline{O}$, O$\underline{O}$, OO$\underline{S}$, $\underline{O}$SS, O$\underline{S}$, S$\underline{O}$, $\underline{O}$. Voice Adjustment ensures not only
that OS$\underline{O}$ [trz] in *wiatr zachodni* emerges as [drz] but also that O$\underline{S}$ [tr] with [ʒ]
replacing [r] by <PR1> emerges as [t-ʃ] without any additional mechanisms. The
same holds for the remaining consonant combinations.

Fundamentally the same reasoning applies to the labio-dental fricatives, on the
assumption that they are syllabified as the labial glide in branching onsets or after
empty/floating nuclei. Once it is obstruentized, it has to adjust its tonal specification to that of the dominant consonant in conformity to VA. What we assume
here without extensive justification is the nature of this obstruentization: unlike
with the sonorant [r], which is replaced into an obstruent by a morphophonological rule, the glide seems to be affected by a rule of phonetic implementation
which is responsible for the fine phonetic details. We have not explored such
regularities in this book apart from assuming their existence (there are, for
example, different possibilities of realizing [r] by individual speakers, which
would fall under the heading of such phonetic interpretation rules). Such regularities are sometimes referred to as phonetic effects (Gussmann 2002) and may
be envisaged as packaging processes whereby phonologically significant properties and structures are accoutred in a specific melody. In the case at hand this
means that the element {U} attached to a non-nuclear position appears as a
fricative, hence it coincides with a combination of {U•h•L} where the labiality
element ({U}) is the head. This latter element combination is independently
necessary in Polish since the segment [v] is not always a glide: we have seen
cases above where it behaves as a regular obstruent, hence it both undergoes and
conditions regressive voice assimilation (recall the examples in (26)). In other
words, since ours is not a paradigmatic framework we do not feel any special need
to justify the structural tenet that what sounds the same must invariably realize
the same phonological units. Quite conversely, we have seen numerous examples

where distinct elemental representations are realized by means of identical sounds. What appears as the labio-dental fricative [v] in Polish may be a sonorant, in which case it behaves differently from an obstruent: a sonorant may appear not only in a non-branching onset but also as a dependent of a branching onset. The sonorant, when obstruentized, adjusts its voicing to that of the true obstruent. In brief, then, some instances of the (morpho)phonological expression [r <PR1>] and [v] (i.e. {U}) are simultaneously sonorants and obstruents. As sonorants they occupy the dependent (governed) position in branching onsets; pronounced as obstruents they adjust their voice specification to the nearest phonological obstruent.

The need for obstruentized sonorants to adjust their voicedness may mean that the same segment within the same morpheme will adjust differently depending upon the environment. An interesting example is offered by the word *krew* [krɛf] 'blood', which will terminate our survey of voice-related phenomena. Consider the relevant examples:

(28) krew-n-y [krɛvnɨ]   krew [krɛf]
      'relative, n.'   'blood'
      krew brata [krɛv brata]   krew przyjaciela [krɛf pʃɨjatɕɛla]
      'brother's blood'   'friend's blood'
      krf-i [kr̥fʲi]   krw-o-tok [kr̥fɔtɔk]
      'blood, gen. sg.'   'haemorrhage'

The base morpheme *krew* [krɛf] 'blood'—alternating with [kr̥fʲ] in *krw-i* [kr̥fʲi] 'gen. sg.'—contains a floating vowel which emerges in accordance with regular principles. The substantivized adjective *krew-n-y* [krɛvnɨ] 'relative' maintains the attached nucleus between the initial branching onset and the next onset, where the latter is the obstruentized sonorant. Since the segment [v] does not find itself directly adjacent to a domain-final empty nucleus or another obstruent, it maintains its voicing. Word-finally in *krew* [krɛf], the context for terminal devoicing is met, hence [v] loses its {L} and is heard as [f]; similarly, at word junctures, the obstruent beginning the second word, or the last obstruent in a sequence enforces VA in the usual way and so we get the forms *krew brata* [krɛv brata] 'brother's blood' and *krew przyjaciela* [krɛf pʃɨjatɕɛla] 'friend's blood'. When the floating vowel is suppressed, the obstruentized sonorant comes to stand after the first (and only) obstruent in a sequence and likewise has to adjust which this time results in what looks like progressive devoicing—in this way the forms *krwi* [kr̥fʲi] 'blood, gen. sg.' and *krwotok* [kr̥fɔtɔk] 'haemorrhage' arise.

Viewed in this perspective, so-called progressive devoicing is a description of non-reality or, more adequately, it corresponds to no distinct reality. Rather, the traditional progressive and regressive assimilation describe voicing in consonantal sequences which is controlled by the very general principle we have called Voice Adjustment: the rightmost obstruent is the dominant segment in determining the voicing of its neighbours. The alleged progressive devoicing arises because two sonorants—[v] and [r]—are realized as obstruents; as phonetic obstruents, while remaining sonorants syllabically, they adjust their voicing to the dominant obstruent which in this case happens to precede the sonorants (either as the head of a branching onset or an onset separated by an empty nucleus). The other consideration relevant to a proper understanding of consonant voicing in Polish relates to the impossibility of two consecutive empty nuclei, an impossibility which is a general property of the language and has been established on independent grounds. Our description resorts to a single monovalent laryngeal specification, low tone, which suffices to capture all major regularities. Some voice effects appear to derive from purely phonetic adjustments which contribute little to the understanding of the working of the phonology.

REFERENCES

ANDERSEN, Henning (1969a). 'A study in diachronic morphophonemics: Ukrainian prefixes'. *Language*, 45: 807–30.

—— (1969b). 'The phonological status of the Russian "labial fricative"', *Journal of Linguistics*, 5: 121–7.

ANDERSON, John M. and Colin J. Ewen (1987). *Principles of Dependency Phonology*. Cambridge Studies in Linguistics, 47 (Cambridge: Cambridge University Press).

ANDERSON, Stephen R. (1974). *The Organization of Phonology* (New York: Academic Press).

—— (1982). 'The analysis of French shwa: or, how to get something for nothing', *Language*, 58: 534–73.

—— (1985). *Phonology in the Twentieth Century: Theories of Rules and Theories of Representations* (Chicago: University of Chicago Press).

ARONSON, Howard I. (1968). *Bulgarian Inflectional Morphophonology* (The Hague: Mouton).

BAŃKO, Mirosław, Dorota Komosińska, and Anna Stankiewicz (eds.) (2003). *Indeks a tergo do Uniwersalnego słownika języka polskiego* (Warsaw: Wydawnictwo Naukowe PWN).

BAUDOUIN DE COURTENAY, Jan N. (1898). 'Fonologja (fonetyka) polska', in *Wielka encyklopedja powszechna ilustrowana*, vol. XXII: 811–18. Repr. in Baudouin de Courtenay (1983), 15–27.

—— (1915). 'Charakterystyka psychologiczna języka polskiego', in *Encyklopedya polska*, Vol. II: 154–226. Repr. in Baudouin de Courtenay (1983), 28–98.

—— (1922). *Zarys historii języka polskiego*. (Warsaw: Nakładem Polskiej Składnicy Pomocy Szkolnych). Repr. in Baudouin de Courtenay (1983), 99–186.

—— (1983) *Dzieła wybrane*, Vol. 5 (Warsaw: Państwowe Wydawnictwo Naukowe).

BENNI, Tytus (1923). 'Fonetyka opisowa języka polskiego', in Tytus Benni, Jan Łoś, Kazimierz Nitsch, Jan Rozwadowski, and Henryk Ułaszyn (eds.), *Gramatyka języka polskiego*, 1–55 (Kraków: Nakładem Polskiej Akademji Umiejętności). Repr. in 1964 by Ossolineum, Wrocław.

BETHIN, Christina Y. (1984). 'Voicing assimilation in Polish', *International Journal of Slavic Linguistics and Poetics*, 29: 17–32.

—— (1987). 'Syllable structure and the Polish imperative desinence', *Slavic and East European Journal*, 31, 76–89.

—— (1988). 'Polish nasal vowels', *International Journal of Slavic Linguistics and Poetics*, 38: 1–39.

—— (1992). *Polish Syllables: The Role of Prosody in Phonology and Morphology* (Columbus, OH: Slavica Publishers).

—— (1998). *Slavic Prosody: Language Change and Phonological Theory* (Cambridge: Cambridge University Press).

BIEDRZYCKI, Leszek (1963). 'Fonologiczna interpretacja polskich głosek nosowych', *Biuletyn Polskiego Towarzystwa Językoznawczego* XXII, 25–45.

BIEDRZYCKI, Leszek (1974). *Abriß der polnischen Phonetik* (Warsaw: Wiedza Powszechna).
—— (1978). *Fonologia angielskich i polskich rezonantów* (Warsaw: Państwowe Wydawnictwo Naukowe).
BLEVINS, Juliette (1995). 'The syllable in phonological theory', in Goldsmith (1995), 206–44.
BLOOMFIELD, Leonard (1939). 'Menomini morphophonemics', *Travaux du Cercle linguistique de Prague*, 8. Repr. (1964) in *Études phonologiques dédiées à la mémoire de M. le Prince N. S. Trubetzkoy*, 105–15 (Alabama: University of Alabama Press).
BOGUSŁAWSKI, Andrzej (1990). 'What's in a phonological syllable?', *Wiener Slawistischer Almanach*, 25/26, 111–25.
BOOIJ, Geert E. and Jerzy Rubach (2003). 'Lexical phonology: overview', in Frawley (2003), Vol. 2: 443–7.
BROCKHAUS, Wiebke (1995a). *Final Devoicing in the Phonology of German*. Linguistische Arbeiten, 336 (Tübingen: Niemeyer).
—— (1995b). 'Skeletal and suprasegmental structure within Government Phonology', in Durand and Katamba (1995), 180–221.
—— (1999). 'Closet syllables in a syllable-denying framework: a case of déjà-vu?', in Rennison and Kühnhammer (eds.), 28–48.
BROSELOW, Ellen (1995). 'Skeletal positions and moras', in Goldsmith (1995), 175–205.
CARLTON, Terence R. (1990). *Introduction to the Phonological History of the Slavic Languages* (Columbus, OH: Slavica Publishers).
CARR, Philip, Jacques Durand, and Colin J. Ewen (eds.) (2005). *Headhood, Elements, Specification and Contrastivity: Phonological Papers in Honour of John Anderson* (Amsterdam: Benjamins).
CHAO, Yuen-Ren (1934). 'The non-uniqueness of phonemic solutions of phonetic systems', repr. in Martin Joos (ed.), *Readings in Linguistics I*, 38–54 (Chicago: University of Chicago Press).
CHARETTE, Monik 1(991). *Conditions on Phonological Government*. Cambridge Studies in Linguistics, 58 (Cambridge: Cambridge University Press).
CHOMSKY, Noam (1964). *Current Issues in Linguistic Theory* (The Hague: Mouton).
—— Morris Halle (1968). *The Sound Pattern of English* (New York: Harper and Row).
CLEMENTS, George N. and Samuel Jay Keyser (1983). *CV Phonology: A Generative Theory of the Syllable* (Cambridge, Mass.: MIT Press).
CYRAN, Eugeniusz (1994). 'Super-heavy rhymes in Modern Irish', in Edmund Gussmann and Henryk Kardela (eds.), *Focus on Language. Papers from the 2nd Conference of the Polish Association for the Study of English*, 63–81 (Lublin: Maria Curie-Skłodowska University Press).
—— (1997). *Resonance Elements in Phonology: A Study in Munster Irish*. PASE Studies and Monographs, 3 (Lublin: Wydawnictwo Folium).
—— (ed.) (1998). *Structure and Interpretation: Studies in Phonology*. PASE Studies and Monographs, 4 (Lublin: Wydawnictwo Folium).
—— (2003). *Complexity Scales and Licensing Strength in Phonology* (Lublin: Wydawnictwo KUL).
—— Edmund Gussmann (1999). 'Consonant clusters and governing relations: Polish initial consonant sequences', in van der Hulst and Ritter (1999), 219–47.
—— Morgan Nilsson (1998). 'The Slavic [w > v] shift: a case for phonological strength', in Cyran (1998), 89–100.

CZAYKOWSKA-HIGGINS, Ewa (1998). 'Verbalizing suffixes and the structure of the Polish verb', *Yearbook of Morphology 1997*, 25–58.

DARDEN, Bill J. (1989). 'The Russian palatalizations and the nature of morphophonological rules', in Caroline Wiltshire, Randolph Graczyk, and Bradley Music (eds.), *Papers from the 25th Annual Regional Meeting of the Chicago Linguistic Society*, 41–55 (Chicago: Chicago Linguistic Society).

DOWNING, Laura J., T. Alan Hall, and Renate Raffelsiefen (eds.) (2005). *Paradigms in Phonological Theory* (Oxford: Oxford University Press).

DRESSLER, Wolfgang U. (1985). *Morphonology: The Dynamics of Derivation* (Ann Arbor: Karoma Publishers).

DUKIEWICZ, Leokadia (1967). *Polskie głoski nosowe. Analiza akustyczna* (Warsaw: Państwowe Wydawnictwo Naukowe).

—— (1978). *Intonacja wypowiedzi polskich* (Wrocław: Ossolineum).

—— (1995). 'Fonetyka', in Leokadia Dukiewicz and Irena Sawicka (eds.), *Fonetyka i fonologia*, 9–103 (Kraków: Wydawnictwo Instytutu Języka Polskiego PAN).

DURAND, Jacques (ed.) (1986). *Dependency and Non-linear Phonology* (London: Croom Helm).

—— (2005). 'Tense/lax, the vowel system of English and phonological theory', in Carr, Durand, and Ewen (2005), 77–97.

—— Francis Katamba (eds.) (1995). *Frontiers of Phonology: Atoms, Structures, Derivations* (London: Longman).

—— Bernard Laks (eds.) (1996). *Current Trends in Phonology: Models and Methods* (University of Salford, Manchester: The European Studies Research Institute).

DZIUBALSKA-KOŁACZYK, Katarzyna (ed.) (2001). *Constraints and Preferences*. Trends in Linguistics Studies and Monographs 134 (Berlin: Mouton de Gruyter).

—— (2002). *Beats-and-Binding Phonology* (Frankfurt am Main: Peter Lang).

EWEN, Colin J. and Harry van der Hulst (2001). *The Phonological Structure of Words* (Cambridge: Cambridge University Press).

FÉRY, Caroline and Ruben van de Vijver (eds.) (2003). *The Syllable in Optimality Theory* (Cambridge: Cambridge University Press).

FISCHER-JØRGENSEN, Eli (1975). *Trends in Phonological Theory. A Historical Introduction* (Copenehagen: Akademisk Forlag).

FISIAK, Jacek and Stanisław Puppel (eds.) (1992). *Phonological Investigations* (Amsterdam: John Benjamins).

—— Maria Lipińska-Grzegorek, and Tadeusz Zabrocki (1978). *An Introductory English–Polish Contrastive Grammar* (Warsaw: Państwowe Wydawnictwo Naukowe).

FLIER, Michael S. (1974a). 'The v/j alternation in certain Russian verbal roots', in Demetrius J. Koubourlis (ed.), *Topics in Slavic Phonology*, 66–83 (Cambridge, Mass.: Slavica Publishers).

—— (1974b). 'The glide shift in Russian deverbal derivation', *Russian Linguistics*, 1: 15–31.

FRANKS, Steven (1985). 'Extrametricality and stress in Polish', *Linguistic Inquiry*, 16: 144–51.

FRAWLEY, William J. (ed.) (2003). *International Encyclopedia of Linguistics*, 2nd edn. (New York: Oxford University Press).

FUDGE, Erik C. (1969). 'Syllables', *Journal of Linguistics*, 5: 252–286.

GIEGERICH, Heinz J. (1992). *English Phonology. An Introduction* (Cambridge: Cambridge University Press).

GLADNEY, Frank (1968). 'Some rules for nasals in Polish', in C. Gribble (ed.), *Studies Presented to Professor Roman Jakobson by his Students*, 112–20 (Cambridge, Mass.: Slavica Publishers).

—— (1971). 'Towards economy in the description of Polish morphology', *Biuletyn Polskiego Towarzystwa Językoznawczego*, XXVIII, 29–37.

—— (2004). 'On sonorants and syllabicity in Polish', *Biuletyn Polskiego Towarzystwa Językoznawczego*, LX: 117–32.

GOLDSMITH, John A. (ed.) (1995). *The Handbook of Phonological Theory* (Oxford: Blackwell).

GÓRSKA, Elżbieta (1985). 'On the description of "phonological free variants" in word formation: Theoretical implications', in Gussmann (1985), 49–73.

GRZEGORCZYKOWA, Renata (1979). *Zarys słowotwórstwa polskiego. Słowotwórstwo opisowe* (Warsaw: Państwowe Wydawnictwo Naukowe).

—— Jadwiga Puzynina (eds.) (1973). *Indeks a tergo do Słownika języka polskiego pod redakcją W. Doroszewskiego* (Warsaw: Państwowe Wydawnictwo Naukowe).

—— —— (1979). *Słowotwórstwo współczesnego języka polskiego* (Warsaw: Państwowe Wydawnictwo Naukowe).

—— Roman Laskowski, and Henryk Wróbel (eds.) (1998). *Gramatyka współczesnego języka polskiego. Morfologia* (2nd rev. ed.) (Warsaw: Wydawnictwo Naukowe PWN).

GUSSMANN, Edmund (1977). 'Is the 2nd Velar Palatalisation a synchronic rule of Modern Polish?', *Biuletyn Polskiego Towarzystwa Językoznawczego*, XXXV: 27–41.

—— (1978). *Contrastive Polish–English Consonantal Phonology* (Warsaw: Państwowe Wydawnictwo Naukowe).

—— (1980a). *Studies in Abstract Phonology* (Cambridge, Mass.: MIT Press).

—— (1980b). 'The phonological structure of the Polish imperative', *Studia gramatyczne*, 3: 33–46.

—— (1981). 'Glide shifts in Polish', in Wolfgang U. Dressler, Oskar E. Pfeiffer, and John R. Rennison (eds.), *Phonologica 1980*, 169–78 (Innsbruck: Innsbrucker Beiträge zur Sprachwissenschaft).

—— (ed.) (1985). *Phono-Morphology: Studies in the Interaction of Phonology and Morphology* (Lublin: Redakcja Wydawnictw Katolickiego Uniwersytetu Lubelskiego).

—— (1985). Review of Rubach 1984, *Linguistics*, 1985: 609–23.

—— (1988). Review of Mohanan 1986, *Journal of Linguistics*, 1988: 232–9.

—— (1992a). 'Back to front: non-linear palatalisations and vowels in Polish', in Fisiak and Puppel (1992), 5–66.

—— (1992b). 'Resyllabification and delinking: the case of Polish voicing', *Linguistic Inquiry*, 23: 29–56.

—— (1997a). 'Polish palatalisations return to the fold', in Anders Ahlqvist and Věra Čapková (eds.), *Dán do Oide. Essays in Memory of Conn R. Ó Clérigh*, 201–11 (Dublin: Institiúid Teangeolaíochta Éireann).

—— (1997b). 'Govern or perish: sequences of empty nuclei in Polish', in Raymond Hickey and Stanisław Puppel (eds.), *Language History and Linguistic Modelling*, 1291–1300 (Berlin: Mouton de Gruyter).

—— (2001). 'Hidden identity, or the double life of segments', in Dziubalska-Kołaczyk (2001), 229–49.

—— (2002). *Phonology: Analysis and Theory* (Cambridge: Cambridge University Press).

—— (2003). 'Morphophonemics', in Frawley (2003), vol. 2: 448–51.

—— (2004*a*). 'Polish front vowels or Baudouin de Courtenay *redivivus*', *Studies in Polish Linguistics*, 1: 103–30.

—— (2004*b*). 'The irrelevance of phonetics: the Polish palatalisation of velars', in Tobias Scheer (ed.), *Corpus*, 3: 125–52. *Usage des corpus en phonologie*.

—— (2006). 'Roman Laskowski and the development of Polish morpho-phonology', in I. Bobrowski and K. Kowalik (eds.), *Od fonemu do tekstu. Prace dedykowane Profesorowi Romanowi Laskowskiemu*, 21–39 (Kraków: Wydawnictwo Lexis).

—— Jonathan Kaye (1993). 'Polish notes from a Dubrovnik café. I. The yers', *SOAS Working Papers in Linguistics and Phonetics*, 3: 427–62.

—— Eugeniusz Cyran (1998). 'Polish consonantal sequences: a phonological testing ground', in Cyran (1998), 127–38.

HALLE, Morris (1959). *The Sound Pattern of Russian* (The Hague: Mouton).

—— Jean-Roger Vergnaud (1987). *An Essay on Stress* (Cambridge, Mass.: MIT Press).

HAMMOND, Michael (1989). 'Lexical stress in Macedonian and Polish', *Phonology*, 6: 19–38.

Handbook of the International Phonetic Association (1999). (Cambridge: Cambridge University Press).

HARASOWSKA, Marta (1999). *Morphophonemic Variability, Productivity, and Change: The Case of Rusyn* (Berlin: Mouton de Gruyter).

HARAGUS, Sharon and Ellen M. Kaisse (eds.) (1993). *Studies in Lexical Phonology*, Vol. 4: *Phonetics and Phonology* (San Diego: Academic Press).

HARRIS, John (1990). 'Segmental complexity and phonological government', *Phonology*, 7: 255–300.

—— (1994). *English Sound Structure* (Oxford: Blackwell).

—— (1996). 'Phonological output is redundancy-free and fully interpretable', in Durand and Laks (1996), 305–32.

—— (1997). 'Licensing Inheritance: an integrated theory of neutralisation', *Phonology*, 14: 315–70.

—— Edmund Gussmann (1998). 'Final codas: why the west was wrong', in Cyran (1998), 139–62.

—— —— (2002). 'Word-final onsets', *University College London Working Papers in Linguistics*, 14: 53–94.

—— Geoff Lindsey (1995). 'The elements of phonological representation', in Durand and Katamba (1995), 34–79.

—— —— (2000). 'Vowel patterns in mind and sound', in Noel Burton-Roberts, Philip Carr, and Gerarld Docherty (eds.), *Phonological Knowledge. Conceptual and Empirical Issues*, 185–205 (Oxford: Oxford University Press).

HAUGEN, Einar (1956). 'The syllable in linguistic description', in M. Halle, H. G. Lunt, H. Maclean, and C. H. van Shooneveld (eds.), *For Roman Jakobson*, 213–21 (The Hague: Mouton).

HERBERT, Robert and Barbara Nykiel-Herbert (1991). 'Supletywizm fonologiczny w procesie morfologizacji: przykład polskiej alternacji *o–u*', *Biuletyn Polskiego Towarzystwa Językoznawczego* XLIII/XLIV, 197–206.

HOCKETT, Charles F. (1958). *A Course in Modern Linguistics* (New York: Macmillan).

HULST, Harry van der and Nancy A. Ritter (eds.) (1999). *The Syllable: Views and Facts* (Berlin: Mouton de Gruyter).

INGLEBY, Michael and Wiebke Brockhaus (2002). 'Phonological primes: Cues and acoustic signatures', in Jacques Durand and Bernard Laks (eds.), *Phonetics, Phonology, and Cognition*, 131–50 (Oxford: Oxford University Press).

ISAČENKO, Alexander V. (1970). 'East Slavic morphophonemics and the treatment of jers in Russian: a revision of Havlík's law', *International Journal of Slavic Linguistics and Poetics*, 13: 73–124.

ITŌ, Junko and Armin Mester (2003). *Japanese Morphophonemics: Markedness and Word Structure* (Cambridge, Mass.: MIT Press).

JAKOBSON, Roman (1948). 'Russian conjugation', *Word*, 4: 155–67.

—— (1960). 'Kazańska szkoła polskiej lingwistyki i jej miejsce w światowym rozwoju fonologii', *Biuletyn Polskiego Towarzystwa Językoznawczego* XIX, 3–34. English translation in his *Selected Writings II*, 394–428 (The Hague: Mouton).

JASSEM, Wiktor (1954). *Fonetyka języka angielskiego* (Warsaw: Państwowe Wydawnictwo Naukowe).

—— (1966). 'The distinctive features and the entropy of the Polish phoneme system', *Biuletyn Polskiego Towarzystwa Językoznawczego*, XXIV: 87–108.

—— (1983). *The Phonology of Modern English* (Warsaw: Państwowe Wydawnictwo Naukowe).

KARAŚ, Mieczysław and Maria Madejowa (1977). *Słownik wymowy polskiej. Dictionary of Polish Pronunciation* (Warsaw: Państwowe Wydawnictwo Naukowe).

KAYE, Jonathan (1990). ' "Coda" licensing', *Phonology*, 7: 301–30.

—— (1991/92). 'Do you believe in magic? The story of S+C sequences', *SOAS Working Papers in Linguistics and Phonetics*, 2: 293–313. (Also in Henryk Kardela and Bogdan Szymanek (eds.) (1996). *A Festschrift for Edmund Gussmann from His Friends and Colleagues*, 155–76 (Lublin: The University Press of the Catholic University of Lublin).

—— (1995). 'Derivations and interfaces', in Durand and Katamba (eds.), 289–332.

—— (2001). 'Working with licensing constraints', in Dziubalska-Kołaczyk (2001), 251–68.

—— Jean Lowenstamm, and Jean-Roger Vergnaud (1985). 'The internal structure of phonological segments: a theory of charm and government', *Phonology Yearbook*, 2: 305–28.

—— —— —— (1989). 'Konstituentenstruktur und Rektion in der Phonologie', *Linguistische Berichte*, 114: 31–75.

—— —— —— (1990). 'Constituent structure and government in phonology', *Phonology*, 7: 193–231.

KENSTOWICZ, Michael (1994). *Phonology in Generative Grammar* (Oxford: Blackwell).

KILBURY, James (1976). *The Development of Morphophonemic Theory* (Amsterdam: John Benjamins).

KIPARSKY, Paul (1996). 'Allomorphy or morphophonology?', in Rajendra Singh (ed.), *Trubetzkoy's Orphan*, 13–31 (Amsterdam: John Benjamins).

KLEIN, Ernest (1971). *A Comprehensive Etymological Dictionary of the English Language* (Amsterdam: Elsevier).

KLEMENSIEWICZ, Zenon, Tadeusz Lehr-Spławiński, and Stanisław Urbańczyk (1965). *Gramatyka historyczna języka polskiego* (Warsaw: Państwowe Wydawnictwo Naukowe).

KONECZNA, Halina (1965). *Charakterystyka fonetyczna języka polskiego na tle innych języków słowiańskich* (Warsaw: Państwowe Wydawnictwo Naukowe).

Kowalik, Krystyna (1997). *Struktura morfonologiczna współczesnej polszczyzny* (Kraków: Wydawnictwo Instytutu Języka Polskiego PAN).

—— (1998). 'Morfonologia', in Grzegorczykowa et al. (1998), 87–123.

Kreja, Bogusław (1989). *Z morfonologii i morfotaktyki współczesnej polszczyzny* (Wrocław: Ossolineum).

Kuryłowicz, Jerzy (1948). 'Contribution à la théorie de la syllable', *Biuletyn Polskiego Towarzystwa Językoznawczego*, VIII: 80–114.

—— (1952). 'Uwagi o polskich grupach spółgłoskowych', *Biuletyn Polskiego Towarzystwa Językoznawczego*, XI: 54–69.

Laskowski, Roman (1975a). *Studia nad morfonologią współczesnego języka polskiego* (Wrocław: Ossolineum).

—— (1975b). 'The E-O, E-A alternation in Polish verb morphology and the Slavic secondary imperfectives', *Makedonski Jazyk, XXVI:* 63–8.

—— (1998). 'Czasownik', in Renata Grzegorczykowa et al. (1998), 225–69.

—— Henryk Wróbel (1964). 'Użycie paradygmatu w funkcji formantu słowotwórczego we współczesnej polszczyźnie', *Język Polski*, 44: 214–20.

Lass, Roger (1984). *Phonology. An Introduction to Basic Concepts* (Cambridge: Cambridge University Press).

Lightner, Theodore M. (1963). 'Preliminary remarks on the morphophonemic component of Polish', *MIT Quarterly Progress Report*, 71: 220–35.

Łoś, Jan (1922). *Gramatyka polska. Głosownia historyczna* (Lwów: Ossolineum).

Lowenstamm, Jean (1996). 'CV as the only syllable type', in Durand and Laks (1996), 419–41.

—— (1999). 'The beginning of the word', in Rennison and Kühnhammer (1999), 153–66.

Maiden, M. (1991). *Interactive Morphonology: Metaphony in Italy* (London: Routledge).

Markowski, Andrzej (1999). *Nowy słownik poprawnej polszczyzny* (Warsaw: Wydawnictwo Naukowe PWN).

Matthews, Peter H. (1972). *Inflectional Morphology: A Theoretical Study Based on Aspects of Latin Verb Conjugation* (Cambridge: Cambridge University Press).

—— (1991). *Morphology.* 2nd edn. (Cambridge: Cambridge University Press).

Mohanan, K. P. (1986). *The Theory of Lexical Phonology* (Dordrecht: Reidel).

Moszyński, Leszek (1984). *Wstęp do filologii słowiańskiej* (Warsaw: Państwowe Wydawnictwo Naukowe).

Nasukawa, Kuniya (1998). 'An integrated approach to nasality and voicing', in Cyran (1998), 205–25.

—— (2005). *A Unified Approach to Nasality and Voicing* (Berlin: Mouton de Gruyter).

Nykiel-Herbert, Barbara (1985). 'The vowel–zero alternation in Polish prefixes', in Gussmann (1985), 113–30.

Palmer, Frank R. (ed.) (1970). *Prosodic Analysis* (London: Oxford University Press).

Piotrowski, Marek (1992). 'Polish yers and extrasyllabicity: an autosegmental account', in Fisiak and Puppel (1992), 67–1108.

—— Iggy Roca, and Andy Spencer (1992). 'Polish yers and lexical syllabicity', *The Linguistic Review*, 9: 27–67.

Ploch, Stefan (1999). *Nasals on my Mind: The Phonetic and the Cognitive Approach to the Phonology of Nasality*. Ph.D. dissertation, School of Oriental and Aftrican Studies.

—— (2003). 'Can "phonological" nasality be derived from phonetic nasality?', in Jeroen van de Weijer, Vincent J. van Heuven, and Harry van der Hulst (eds.), *The Phonological Spectrum. Segmental Structure*, Vol. 1, 73–116 (Amsterdam: John Benjamins).

POSTAL, Paul M. (1968). *Aspects of Phonological Theory* (New York: Harper and Row).

PRINCE, Alan S. (1984). 'Phonology with tiers', in Mark Aronoff and Richard T. Oehrle (eds.), *Language Sound Structure*, 234–44 (Cambridge, Mass.: MIT Press).

PUPPEL, Stanisław, Jadwiga Nawrocka-Fisiak, Halina Krassowska (1977). *A Handbook of Polish Pronunciation for English Learners* (Warsaw: Państwowe Wydawnictwo Naukowe).

RENNISON, John, R. and Klaus Kühnhammer (eds.) (1999). *Phonologica 1996. Syllables!? Proceedings of the 8th International Phonology Meeting* (The Hague: Holland Academic Graphics).

RITTER, Nancy A. (1997). 'Headedness as a means of encoding stricture', in Geert Booij and Jeroen van de Weijer (eds.), *Phonology in Progress—Progress in Phonology*, 333–65 (The Hague: Holland Academic Graphics).

ROWICKA, Grażyna, J. (1999). *On Ghost Vowels: A Strict CV Approach*. LOT dissertations, 16 (The Hague: Holland Academic Graphics).

—— (2001). 'How far can you go? Vowelless roots and clusters in Polish', in Gerhild Zybatow, Uwe Junghans, Grit Mehlhorn, and Luka Szucsich (eds.), *Current Issues in Formal Slavic linguistics*, 109–16 (Frankfurt am Main: Peter Lang).

RUBACH, Jerzy (1977). 'Nasalization in Polish', *Journal of Phonetics*, 5: 17–25.

—— (1984). *Cyclic and Lexical Phonology: The Structure of Polish* (Dordrecht: Foris).

—— (1985). 'Lexical Phonology: lexical and postlexical derivations', *Phonology Yearbook*, 2: 157–72.

—— (1992). 'Abstract vowels in three dimensional phonology: the yers', in Fisiak and Puppel (1992), 109–51.

—— (1996). 'Nonsyllabic analysis of voice assimilation in Polish', *Linguistic Inquiry*, 27: 69–110.

—— Geert E. Booij (1985). 'A grid theory of stress in Polish', *Lingua*, 66: 281–319.

—— —— (1990). 'Syllable structure assignment in Polish', *Phonology*, 7: 121–58.

—— —— (2001). 'Allomorphy in Optimality Theory: Iotation in Polish', *Language*, 77: 26–60.

RUSZKIEWICZ, Piotr (1992). 'Observations concerning the *beze(cny)* family of words in Polish: with morals for cyclic phonology', in Fisiak and Puppel (1992), 153–84.

SAMILOV, Michael (1964). *The Phoneme Jat' in Slavic* (The Hague: Mouton).

SAPIR, Edward (1925). 'Sound patterns in language', *Language*, 1: 37–51. Repr. in Martin Joos (ed.), *Readings in Linguistics I*, 19–25 (Chicago: University of Chicago Press).

SAWICKA, Irena (1995). 'Fonologia', in Leokadia Dukiewicz and Irena Sawicka, *Fonetyka i fonologia*, 105–98 (Kraków: Wydawnictwo Instytutu Języka Polskiego PAN).

—— Stanisław Grzybowski (1999). *Studia z palatalności w językach słowiańskich* (Toruń: Wydawnictwo Uniwersytetu M. Kopernika).

SCHANE, Sanford, A. (1995). 'Diphthongization in Particle Phonology', in Goldsmith (1995), 586–608.

—— (2005). 'The aperture |a|: its role and functions', in Carr et al. (2005), 313–38.

SCHEER, Tobias (1997). 'Vowel–zero alternations and their support for a theory of consonantal interaction', in Peir Marco Bertinetto, Livio Gaeta, Georgi Jetchev, and David Michaels (eds.), *Certamen Phonologicum III*, 67–88 (Totino: Rosenberg & Sellier).

—— (1998a). 'Governing domains are head-final', in Cyran (1998), 261–85.

—— (1998b). 'A unified model of Proper Government', *The Linguistic Review*, 15: 41–67.

—— (2004). *A Lateral Theory of Phonology: What is CVCV, and Why Should It Be?* (Berlin: Mouton de Gruyter).

—— Péter Szigetvári (2005). 'Unified representations for stress and the syllable', *Phonology*, 22: 37–75.

SCHENKER, Alexander M. (1954). 'Polish conjugation', *Word*, 10: 469–81.

—— (1964). *Polish Declension: A Descriptive Analysis* (The Hague: Mouton).

SÉGÉRAL, Philippe and Tobias Scheer (2001*a*). 'Abstractness in phonology: the case of virtual geminates', in Dziubalska-Kołaczyk (2001), 311–37.

—— —— (2001*b*). 'La coda-miroir', *Bulletin de la Societé Linguistique de Paris*, 96: 107–52.

SELKIRK, Elisabeth O. (1982) 'The syllable', in Harry van der Hulst and Norval Smith (eds.), *The Structure of Phonological Representations* (Part II), 337–83 (Dordrecht: Foris).

SHEVELOV, George Y. (1964). *A Prehistory of Slavic* (Heidelberg: C. Winter).

SPENCER, Andrew (1986). 'A non-linear analysis of vowel–zero alternations in Polish', *Journal of Linguistics*, 22: 249–80.

STANKIEWICZ, Edward (1954). 'Expressive derivation of substantives in contemporary Russian and Polish', *Word*, 10: 457–88.

—— (1955). 'Distribution of morphemic variants in the declension of Polish substantives', *Word*, 11, 554–75.

—— (1960). 'Consonantal alternations in the Slavic declension', *Word*, 16: 183–203.

—— (1966). 'Slavic morphophonemics in its typological and diachronic aspects', in Thomas Sebeok (ed.), *Current Trends in Linguistics*, Vol. 3, 495–520 (The Hague: Mouton).

—— (1967). 'Opposition and hierarchy in morphophonemic alternations', in *To Honor Roman Jakobson: Essays on the Occasion of his Seventieth Birthday*, 1895–1905 (The Hague: Mouton).

—— (1972). *A Baudouin de Courtenay Anthology: The Beginnings of Structural Linguistics* (Bloomington: Indiana University Press).

STEFFEN-BATOGOWA, Maria (1966). 'Versuch einer strukturellen Analyse der polnischen Aussagemelodie', *Zeitschrift für Phonetik und allgemeine Sprachwissenschaft*, 19: 398–440.

STERIADE, Donca (2003). 'Syllables in phonology', in Frawley (2003), Vol. 4: 190–5.

STIEBER, Zdzisław (1948). Dwa problemy polskiej fonologii. *Biuletyn Polskiego Towarzystwa Językoznawczego*, VII: 56–78.

—— (1958). *Rozwój fonologiczny języka polskiego* (Warsaw: Państwowe Wydawnictwo Naukowe).

—— (1966). *Historyczna i współczesna fonologia języka polskiego* (Warsaw: Państwowe Wydawnictwo Naukowe).

—— (1973). *A Historical Phonology of the Polish Language* (Heidelberg: C. Winter).

—— (1979). *Zarys gramatyki porównawczej języków słowiańskich* (Warsaw: Państwowe Wydawnictwo Naukowe).

SZIGETVÁRI, Péter (1999). Why CVCV? *The Even Yearbook*, 4: 117–52.

SZPYRA, Jolanta (1989). *The Phonology–Morphology Interface: Cycles, Levels and Words* (London: Routledge).

—— (1992*a*). 'Ghost segments in nonlinear phonology: Polish yers', *Language*, 68: 277–312.

SZPYRA, Jolanta (1992*b*). 'The phonology of Polish prefixation', in Fisiak and Puppel (1992), 185–218.

—— (1995). *Three Tiers in Polish and English Phonology* (Lublin: Wydawnictwo Uniwersytetu Marii Curie-Skłodowskiej).

Szpyra-Kozłowska, Jolanta (1998). 'The sonority scale and phonetic syllabification in Polish', *Biuletyn Polskiego Towarzystwa Językoznawczego*, LIV: 63–82.

Szymanek, Bogdan (1985). *English and Polish Adjectives: A Study in Lexicalist Word-Formation* (Lublin: Redakcja Wydawnictw KUL).

Trager, George (1939). 'La systématique des phonèmes du polonais', *Acta Linguistica* (Copenhagen) 1, 179–88.

Tokarski, Jan (1973). *Fleksja polska* (Warsaw: Państwowe Wydawnictwo Naukowe).

—— (1993). *Schematyczny indeks a tergo polskich form wyrazowych*. Edited by Zygmunt Saloni (Warsaw: Wydawnictwo Naukowe PWN).

Trubetzkoy, Nikolaj N. (1934) 'Das morphonologische System der russischen Sprache', *Travaux du Cercle Linguistique de Prague*, 2. Russian translation (Morfonologičeskaja sistema russkogo jazyka) in his *Izbrannyje trudy po filologii* (1987), 67–142 (Moscow: Progress).

Ułaszyn, Henryk (1931). 'Laut, Phonema, Morphonema', *Travaux du Circle linguistique du Prague*, 4: 53–61.

Vasmer, Max (1986). *Etimologičeskij slovar' russkogo jazyka* (Moscow: Progress).

Vennemann, Theo (1988). *Preference Laws for Syllable Structure and the Explanation of Sound Change* (Berlin: Mouton de Gruyter).

Waszakowa, Krystyna (1994). *Słowotwórstwo współczesnego języka polskiego. Rzeczowniki sufiksalne obce* (Warsaw: Wydawnictwa Uniwersytetu Warszawskiego).

—— (1996). *Słowotwórstwo współczesnego języka polskiego. Rzeczowniki z formantami paradygmatycznymi* (Warsaw: Wydawnictwa Uniwersytetu Warszawskiego).

Westfal, Stanisław (1955). 'Ę:Ą alternation in Modern Polish', *Slavonic and East European Review*, 34: 461–86.

—— (1956). *A Study of Polish Morphology: The Genitive Singular Masculine* (The Hague: Mouton).

Wierzchowska, Bożena (1960). 'Z badań eksperymentalnych polskich głosek nosowych', *Biuletyn fonograficzny*, 3: 67–87.

—— (1971). *Wymowa polska* (Warsaw: Państwowe Zakłady Wydawnictw Szkolnych).

Yoshida, Shohei (1993). 'Licensing of empty nuclei: the case of Palestinian vowel harmony', *The Linguistic Review*, 10: 127–59.

Zagórska Brooks, Maria (1968). *Nasal Vowels in Contemporary Standard Polish* (The Hague: Mouton).

Zwoliński, Przemysław (1958). 'Stosunek fonemu *y* do *i* w historii języków słowiańskich', *Z polskich studiów slawistycznych*, 1: 52–60.

GENERAL INDEX

The index includes terms and notions of general applicability rather than their specific use to analyze the Polish data. Although used in the context of specific interpretations they reflect general concerns. Table of contents offers a survey of areas of specifically Polish phonological interest.

INDEX OF POLISH WORDS

Listed below are all Polish words in the form they are used in the body of the book. In brackets the nominative singular of nouns, the nominative singular masculine of adjectives and pronouns, and the infinitive of verbs are supplied if these are not the forms found in the text. *n.* denotes that the form appears in a footnote. In accordance with the Polish tradition letters with a diacritic come after those without it, thus the following letter sequences are found: *a, ą; c, ć; e, ę, l, ł; n, ń; o, ó; s, ś; z, ź, ż.*

czeremch (czeremcha) 221
czerniak 256
czernić 256
czernidło 256
czernieć 256
czernina 256
czerń 256
czerwca (czerwiec) 190
czerwiec 190
czerwienić 260
czerwień 260, 261
czerwony 260, 261
cześć 174, 187, 192
często 66
częsty 69
części (część) 279
część 279
czkawka 202
człon 202
człowiecza (człowieczy) 162
człowiecze (człowiek) 119, 137 n.
człowieczy 8, 119
człowiek 8, 108, 111, 119, 134
człowieka (człowiek) 8, 162
człowiekowi (człowiek) 8, 108, 134
człowieku (człowiek) 111, 138 n.
czochrać 86
czole (czoło) 258
czołg 51
czołgi (czołg) 51
czołgista 82, 161 n.
czołgu (czołg) 82, 161 n.
czoło 257, 258
cztery 202, 204
czwartek 7, 308
czy 45
czyha (czyhać) 44
czyn 7, 37
czysta (czysty) 7
czystka 167
czystość 167
czysty 167
czyściec 166, 167
czyśćca (czyściec) 166, 167
czyta (czytać) 56
czytać 89
czytali (czytać) 9, 136

czytaliście (czytać) 9
czytaliśmy (czytać) 9
czytały (czytać) 136
czytywać 89

ćma 16, 166, 187, 202
ćmić 202
ćpun 202
ćwiartek (ćwiartka) 144
ćwierć 144
ćwok 166

da (dać) 35
dach 6, 85
daj (dać) 3, 35
daje (dawać) 3, 297, 298
daleka (daleki) 56
dalekich (daleki) 297, 309
dalekie (daleki) 56
dał (dać) 3
dała (dać) 3
dam (dać) 35
dania (danie) 95
Dania 95
danie 106
dar 104
darń 173
dasz (dać) 35
dąb 18, 275, 276
dąsać 67
dbać 204, 215, 291, 309
dech 185, 188, 191, 200, 228, 229
demokracja 95
den (dno) 56, 115, 166, 187, 201, 244
desek (deska) 185
deska 185
deszcz 62
dęby (dąb) 275, 276
diabelski 154, 155
diabeł 62, 63, 154
diabły (diabeł) 63
diwa 5, 100
dla 201
dłoń 201
dmę (dąć) 136
dmie (dąć) 171, 174
dmiesz (dąć) 136

dmij (dąć) 171
dmuchać 201
dmuchnąć 277
dmuchnął (dmuchnąć) 277
dmuchnęła (dmuchnąć) 277
dmuchnęły (dmuchnąć) 277
dna (dno) 244
dnem (dno) 166
dni (dzień) 202
dnia (dzień) 56, 195, 260
dniem (dzień) 166
dno 56, 115, 187, 201, 244
doba 289 n.
dobra (dobry) 51
dobre (dobry) 71
dobrego (dobry) 62
dobro 162, 263
dobry 17, 51, 162, 307, 309
dobrze 307, 309
docierać 307, 309
doczesny 253
dogmat 81
dogmatyzm 81
doktor 110, 265
doktora (doktor) 265, 293
doktorowie (doktor) 110
doktorze (doktor) 110
doktorzy (doktor) 110
doktór 265
dole (dół) 125
doli (dola) 29
dom 4, 47, 111, 197, 265
domek 197
domki (domek) 197
domostw (domostwo) 224, 226
domu (dom) 111, 265, 302
domy (dom) 47
dorabiają (dorabiać) 286
dorobią (dorobić) 286
dośpiewać 284
dośpiewywać 284
dotrze (dotrzeć) 307
dozorca 268
dozoru (dozór) 268
dozór 268
dób (doba) 289 n.
dóbr (dobro) 263

dół 125
draźni (draźnić) 172, 175
draźnij (draźnić) 172, 175
draźń (draźnić) 175
drągiem (drąg) 56
drągu (drąg) 56
drepcę (dreptać) 121
drepcz (dreptać) 121
drepcząc (dreptać) 121
drepczę (dreptać) 121
dreptać 121
drew (drwa) 188
drgnąć 215
drgnę (drgnąć) 213, 214
drobiu (drób) 262
droga 51, 127, 201, 289, 300, 304
drogą (droga) 238
drogi 49, 53
drogi (droga) 51
drozd 289
drozda (drozd) 263
drozdach (drozd) 289
drożdży (drożdże) 37
drożyna 127
drób 262
dróg (droga) 289 n., 300, 304
druczek 103
druga (drugi) 56
drugie (drugi) 56
druh 17
druk 103, 289 n., 300
drukarz 103
drukować 309
druku (druk) 300
drużba 133
drużbie (drużba) 133
drużyna 17
drwa 188
drwi (drwić) 172
drwij (drwić) 172
drzazga 308
drzemie (drzemać) 175
drzewo 7, 208
drzwiami (drzwi) 235, 236
drży (drżeć) 171, 175
drżyj (drżeć) 171
duch 86, 87, 111, 141

gryźmy (gryźć) 304
grzać 140
grzanka 140
grzbiecie (grzbiet) 250
grzbiet 209, 250
grze (gra) 27, 307
grzech 127, 208
grzeszyć 127
grzmot 209
grzyb 308
grzyba (grzyb) 143
grzybek 143
gwałt 221
gwar 308
gwardia 247
gwardyjski 247
gwiazd (gwiazda) 296
gwiazda 208, 253, 256, 292, 296
gwiazdka 292
gwiezdny 256
gwieździe (gwiazda) 253
gwieździsty 256
gwiżdż (gwizdać) 289, 304
gwiżdżmy (gwizdać) 304
gwiżdże (gwizdać) 7, 304
gwiżdżę (gwizdać) 289
gwoździe (gwóźdź) 47, 262, 289, 300
gwóźdź 47, 262, 264, 289, 300
gyros 101
gytia 101
gza (giez) 57
gzić 204
gzy (giez) 188
gzyms 204
gżegżółka 291

H_2O 10
haczyk 141, 148 n.
Haga 153, 157
hak 141, 148 n.
hałas 7, 86
Hamlet 157
hamletowski 157
haniebny 272
hańb (hańba) 221
hańba 272
harcerski 153

harcerza (harcerz) 153
harfa 82, 158
harfista 82, 158
haski 153, 156, 157
hazardu (hazard) 85, 141, 158
hazardzista 85, 141, 158
Helsinki 6
hełm 221
Hendryk 273 n.
Henryk 273 n.
herbata 12, 86
herszt 223
hiacynt 91
hiena 88
hierarchia 6, 88
hierarchiczny 88
hieroglif 12, 88
Hieronim 88
himalaista 160
Himalaje 160
Hindus 126, 153
Hindusi (Hindus) 126
hinduski 153, 155
hiobowy 91
histeria 6, 86
historia 88
Hitler 81
hitleryzm 81
hizop 87
hobbista 158
hobby 158
hobbysta 158
hokeista 160
hokej 160
hrabia 95
humor 83
humorysta 83
humorzysta 83
hybryda 87
hydrant 86
hydroliza 87
hymn 86, 87, 221
hyzop 87

i 6, 24, 70, 104, 105
idą (iść) 3
idea 34

kaleczka 230
kalek (kalka) 230 n.
Kalifornia 96
kalifornijski 96
kalk (kalka) 230
kalka 230
kamienie (kamień) 105, 106
kamień 105
Kanada 157
kanadyjski 157
kanalizacja 84
kanał 84
Kancie (Kant) 159
Kant 159
kantysta 159
kapelusik 129
kapelusz 129
kara 106, 150
karcić 6
karczma 31, 102
karczmarz 31, 102
kark 221
karły (karzeł) 166
karm (karmić) 174, 177
karmi (karmić) 174, 177
karmij (karmić) 177
karny 150, 293
karp 42, 47
karpia (karp) 42
karpie (karp) 47
karze (kara) 106
karzeł 166
kasa 75
Kasia 75
kasza 75
kat 157 n.
katecheza 89
katechizacja 89
kategoria 84
kategoryzacja 84
katowski 157 n.
kawaler 153
kawalerski 153
kazać 218
każ (kazać) 169
każdy 291
każe (kazać) 169

kąsać 3
kąt 72
keks 65, 69
kelner 65, 69, 70
kemping 65, 69
Kenia 65
kędy 12, 65, 69
kędzior 65, 69
kęp (kępa) 280
kępa 280
kępek 280
kęs 65, 69, 71
kicha (kichać) 44
kieca 146
kiecek (kiecka) 146
kiedy 49, 61, 205
kielich 65
kieł 12, 57, 60
kiep 187
kier (kra) 50
kier 70
kierować 68
kieszeń 68
kinie (kino) 302
kiosk 49, 91, 92, 94
kisnąć 61
kit 49, 70
kita 50, 53, 55
kiur 91
kiwa (kiwać) 175
kiwać 5
kiwnie (kiwnąć) 172, 175
kiwnij (kiwnąć) 172
klacz 48
klacze (klacz) 48
klaps 222
klasycysta 82
klasycyzm 82
klechda 85
klej (kleić) 170
kleją (kleić) 170
kleks 222
klep (klepać) 12
klimat 84
klimatyzacja 84
klinicysta 161 n.
klinika 161 n.

kotłownia 246
kotły (kocioł) 166
kowal 74 n.
kowboj 265
koza 6, 11
Kozacze (Kozak) 138 n.
kozioł 6, 246, 246 n.
koziołek 246
kozła (kozioł) 246
koźlę 8, 246
koźli 246
kółek (kółko) 197
kółko 197
kpa (kiep) 187
kpić 204, 290
kra 50, 307
kradnę (kraść) 136
kradniesz (kraść) 136
kraj 47
kraje (kraj) 47
krajobrazista 82
krajobrazu (krajobraz) 82
Krakowa (Kraków) 42
Kraków 42
kram 138
kramarz 138
krąg 296
krecia (kreci) 162, 163
kreciej (kreci) 163
krecim (kreci) 163
kres 62
kret 62, 162, 163
kreta (kret) 163
kretami (kret) 163
kretem (kret) 163
kretom (kret) 163
krew 22, 188, 194, 200, 244, 311
krewniak 138, 139
krewny 138, 311
kręgu (krąg) 296
krnąbrny 215
kroczek 128, 141
krok 128, 141
kropel (kropla) 185, 190, 192
kropla 185, 190, 192
krowa 4, 201
król 111

królu (król) 111
krótki 287
krucha (kruchy) 86
kruchą (kruchy) 72
kruchy 86, 141
kruszec 141
krwawić 194, 195
krwawy 194, 195
krwi (krew) 107, 188, 194, 200, 234, 244,
    295, 311
krwiak 194
krwią (krew) 107
krwinka 194
krwisty 194
krwotok 194, 311
krytycyzm 81
krytyk 81
krzak 208
krze (kra) 307
krzew 297, 298, 306
krzewu (krzew) 297
krzta 209
krzycz (krzyczeć) 169, 170
krzyczy (krzyczeć) 169, 170
krzyk 169
krzyknąć 273, 277
krzyknął (krzyknąć) 277
krzyknąłem (krzyknąć) 273
krzyknęli (krzyknąć) 273
krzyknęła (krzyknąć) 277
krzyknęły (krzyknąć) 277
krzywdź (krzywdzić) 221
krzywe (krzywy) 58
krzywy 58, 308
ksiądz 290
ksiąg (księga) 276, 279
książąt (książę) 281
książek (książka) 279
książę 270, 281
książką (książka) 302
ksieni 68
księcia (książę) 281
księdza (ksiądz) 146
księga 68, 204, 276, 279
księżniczka 281
księżyk 146
ksywa 204

wielbi (wielbić) 177
wielbij (wielbić) 177
wielcy (wielki) 109
wiele 10
wielka (wielki) 51
wielki 5, 51, 109
wielkich (wielki) 299
wieniec 57, 166
wieńce (wieniec) 166
wieprz 174, 222, 309
wieprzka (wieprzek) 309
wierny 251
wierz (wierzyć) 169
wierzch 221
wierze (wiara) 251
wierzy (wierzyć) 169, 171
wieś 56, 187, 195, 260
wieśniak 195
wietrzny 142, 149, 150
wieziono (wieźć) 258
wieźć 264
więcej (dużo) 68
więzi (więź) 276
więzić 270
więzień 194
więź 276
więźnia (więzień) 194
więźniarka 194
więźniarski 194
wilcza (wilczy) 51, 52
wilczy 51
wilk 52, 221
wina (wino) 309
winien (winny) 37
winna (winny) 37
wiodła (wieść) 225
wioseł (wiosło) 185
wiosen (wiosna) 202
wioska 260
wiosło 185
wiosna 202
wiozłem (wieźć) 264
wiódł (wieść) 225
wiór 5, 6
wiózł (wieźć) 264
wizja 6
wleczesz (wlec) 258

wlokę (wlec) 65, 69, 258
wlokła (wlec) 225
wlókł (wlec) 225
władny 132, 167
władza 6, 28, 107, 132, 167
władzą (władza) 72
władzy (władza) 107, 165 n., 238
własność 28
włączyć 286
Włoch 77, 109, 126, 136, 153
włosach (włos) 234
Włosi (Włoch) 77, 109, 126, 136
włoski 28, 153
Włoszech (Włochy) 238
Włoszka 77
włóczędze (włóczęga) 108
włóczęga 108
włókno 28
wmanewrować 303
wnętrze 242 n.
woda 17, 106, 140, 261, 269
wodą (woda) 237
wodny 285
wodza (wódz) 7
wodzi (wodzić) 263
wodzianka 140
wodzie (woda) 106, 235 n., 238
wojenny 293, 294
wojsk (wojsko) 223
wolny 285
WOP 82, 158
wopista 82, 158
wory (wór) 47
wozie (wóz) 110
wozu (wóz) 126
wożę (wozić) 126
wód (woda) 261, 269
wódka 17, 269
wódź (wodzić) 263
wójt 221
wór 47
wóz 110
wpisać 303
Wprost 217 n.
wprowadzić 216
wprzęgać 239
wrak 300